Introducing Japanese Popular Culture

D1063332

Specifically designed for use on a range of undergraduate and graduate courses, *Introducing Japanese Popular Culture* is a comprehensive textbook offering an up-to-date overview of a wide variety of media forms. It uses particular case studies as a way into examining the broader themes in Japanese culture and provides a thorough analysis of the historical and contemporary trends that have shaped artistic production, as well as politics, society, and economics. As a result, more than being a time capsule of influential trends, this book teaches enduring lessons about how popular culture reflects the societies that produce and consume it.

With contributions from an international team of scholars, representing a range of disciplines from history and anthropology to art history and media studies, the book's sections include:

- Television
- Videogames
- Music
- Popular Cinema
- Anime
- Manga
- Popular Literature
- Fashion
- Contemporary Art

Written in an accessible style by a stellar line-up of international contributors, this textbook will be essential reading for students of Japanese culture and society, Asian media and popular culture, and Asian Studies in general.

Alisa Freedman is an Associate Professor at the University of Oregon and Editor-in-Chief of the *U.S.–Japan Women's Journal*. Her publications include *Tokyo in Transit: Japanese Culture on the Rails and Road* (2010).

Toby Slade is an Associate Professor at the University of Tokyo. His publications include *Japanese Fashion: A Cultural History* (2009).

Introducing Japanese Popular Culture

**Edited by Alisa Freedman
and Toby Slade**

Routledge
Taylor & Francis Group

LONDON AND NEW YORK

First published 2018
by Routledge
2 Park Square, Milton Park, Abingdon, Oxon OX14 4RN

and by Routledge
711 Third Avenue, New York, NY 10017

Routledge is an imprint of the Taylor & Francis Group, an informa business

British Library Cataloguing-in-Publication Data
A catalogue record for this book is available from the British Library

Library of Congress Cataloging-in-Publication Data
A catalog record for this book has been requested

ISBN: 978-1-138-85208-2 (hbk)
ISBN: 978-1-138-85210-5 (pbk)
ISBN: 978-1-315-72376-1 (ebk)

Typeset in Bembo
by codeMantra

Visit the companion website: www.routledge.com/cw/Freedman

To our students

Contents

PART VIII
Manga

PART IX
Popular Literature

PART X
Sites and Spectacles

Figures

Contributors

Alan Cholodenko is an Honorary Associate of The University of Sydney. He is the editor of *The Illusion of Life: Essays on Animation* (1991) and *The Illusion of Life 2: More Essays on Animation* (2007).

Jayson Makoto Chun is an Associate Professor of History at the University of Hawai'i–West Oahu. His publications include *"A Nation of a Hundred Million Idiots"?: A Social History of Japanese Television 1953–1973* (Routledge, 2007).

Ian Condry is a Professor in Global Studies and Languages at MIT. He is the author of two books: *The Soul of Anime* (2013) and *Hip-Hop Japan* (2006).

Adrian Favell is the Chair in Sociology and Social Theory at the University of Leeds. His work on Japan includes the first history in English of Japanese contemporary art since 1990, *Before and After Superflat*, as well as art critic writing for *Art in America, Artforum, Bijutsu Techo, Impressions*, and *ART-iT*.

Alisa Freedman is an Associate Professor of Japanese literature and film at the University of Oregon and Editor-in-Chief of the *U.S.–Japan Women's Journal*. Her books include *Tokyo in Transit: Japanese Culture on the Rails and Road* (2010), an annotated translation of Kawabata Yasunari's *The Scarlet Gang of Asakusa* (2005), and a co-edited volume on *Modern Girls on the Go: Gender, Mobility, and Labor in Japan* (2013).

Michael Furmanovsky teaches popular culture and fashion history at Ryukoku University. His work focuses on the role of Western music and fashion on Japanese youth during the first two postwar decades.

Patrick W. Galbraith is a researcher in Tokyo. He is the author and editor of many books on Japanese popular culture and media, most recently: *The Moe Manifesto* (2014), *Debating Otaku in Contemporary Japan* (2015), and *Media Convergence in Japan* (2016).

Kendall Heitzman is an Assistant Professor of Japanese Literature and Culture at the University of Iowa. His articles include "Parallel Universes, Vertical Worlds, and the Nation as Palimpsest in Murakami Ryū's *The World Five Minutes from Now*" (*Mechademia* 10) and "The Rise of Women

Writers, the Heisei I-novel, and the Contemporary *Bundan*" (in *Routledge Handbook of Modern Japanese Literature*, 2016).

Kathryn Hemmann is an Assistant Professor in Japanese literature and popular culture at George Mason University. She runs the blog, *Contemporary Japanese Literature*, where she reviews recent translations and posts essays on gender issues in Japanese popular culture (japaneselit.net).

Kyoko Hirano has taught cinema studies at several universities worldwide, including New York University, New School University, University of Ljubljana, Keio University, and Meiji Gakuin University. She was film curator at the Japan Society of New York (1986–2004).

Rachael Hutchinson is an Associate Professor in Japanese Studies at the University of Delaware. She edited *Negotiating Censorship in Modern Japan* (Routledge, 2013) and co-edited *Representing the Other in Modern Japanese Literature* (Routledge, 2007) and *The Routledge Handbook of Modern Japanese Literature* (Routledge, 2016) and authored *Nagai Kafū's Occidentalism: Defining the Japanese Self* (2011).

James Jack, an artist and writer, was a Crown Prince Akihito Scholar and is currently an artist research fellow at the Social Art Lab, Kyushu University. He has exhibited socially engaged art works at Busan Biennale Sea Art Festival, Setouchi Triennale, Honolulu Museum of Art, TAMA Gallery, and Centre for Contemporary Art Singapore.

Eun-Young Jung served as an Assistant Director for the Center for East Asian Studies, University of Wisconsin–Madison (2008–2009) and was an Assistant Professor of Music at the University of California, San Diego (2009–2015).

Hirofumi Katsuno is an Associate Professor in the Department of Media Studies at Doshisha University, Kyoto. His recent publications include "Branding Humanoid Japan" in *Assembling Japan: Modernity, Technology and Global Culture*, edited by Griseldis Kirsch, Dolores P. Martinez, and Merry White (2015).

Izumi Kuroishi is a Professor at the School of Cultural and Creative Studies, Aoyama Gakuin University. Her publications include an edited volume on *Constructing the Colonized Land: Entwined Perspectives of East Asia around WWII* (2014). Her curated exhibits include *Kon Wajiro Retrospective* (2012).

Tong Lam, Associate Professor of History at the University of Toronto, is a historian and visual artist on science and technology, media and spectacle, ruins, and empire. He has exhibited his photographic and video works internationally. He is the author of *Abandoned Futures* (2013) and *A Passion for Facts* (2011).

Thomas Lamarre is a Professor of East Asian Studies and Communications Studies at McGill University and the author of *The Anime Ecology: A Genealogy of Television, Animation, and Game Media* (2018).

Damien Liu-Brennan holds a Ph.D. in Japanese Studies from Macquarie University, where his research made corrections to the history of fireworks in Japan and determined a rationale for the foundation of Japan's distinct *hanabi* culture.

Thomas Looser is an Associate Professor of East Asian Studies at New York University. His publications include *Visioning Eternity: Aesthetics, Politics, and History in Early Modern Noh Theater* (2008) and articles on anime, globalization, architecture, and contemporary art.

Mark McLelland is a Professor of Gender and Sexuality Studies at the University of Wollongong. He is author or editor of over ten books concerning the history of sexuality in Japan, Japanese popular culture, new media, and the Internet, including: *The End of Cool Japan: Ethical, Legal and Cultural Challenges to Japanese Popular Culture* (Routledge, 2017).

Tom Mes holds a Ph.D. from the University of Leiden and is the founder of MidnightEye.com. He is the author or co-author and translator of more than seven books on Japanese cinema, including *Re-Agitator: A Decade of Writing on Takashi Miike* (2013).

Laura Miller is the Ei'ichi Shibusawa-Seigo Arai Endowed Professor of Japanese Studies at the University of Missouri–St. Louis. She has published more than seventy articles and book chapters on topics such as slang, self-photography, divination, elevator girls, and Himiko. She is the author of a book on the beauty industry and co-editor of four other books.

Masafumi Monden holds a Ph.D. from the University of Technology, Sydney. He is the author of *Japanese Fashion Cultures: Dress and Gender in Contemporary Japan* (2015).

Hiroshi Narumi is a Professor at Kyoto Women's University teaching the sociology of culture and fashion studies. He authored *The Cultural History of 20th Century Fashion* (Kawade Shobō Shinsha, 2007) and *Doing Sociology Through Fashion* (2017) and edited *The Cosplay Society* (Serica Shobō, 2009) and *Mode and Body* (2003), among other works in Japanese. He is the co-author of *Japan Fashion Now* (2010) and *Feel and Think* (2012) in English.

Craig Norris is a Lecturer in Journalism Media and Communications at the University of Tasmania. His research interests include media tourism and fan pilgrimages, videogames, cosplay, and the cross-cultural appropriation and spread of manga and anime in Australia.

David Novak is an Associate Professor at the University of California, Santa Barbara, and Director of the Center for the Interdisciplinary Study of Music. He is the author of *Japanoise: Music at the Edge of Circulation* (2013) and co-editor of *Keywords in Sound* (2015).

Debra J. Occhi is a Professor of Anthropology at Miyazaki International College, Japan. Her recent publications include "Wobbly Aesthetics, Performance, and Message: Comparing Japanese Kyara with their

Anthropomorphic Forebears" in *Asian Ethnology* 71(1) and 2016 "Kyaraben (character bento): The Cutesification of Japanese Food in and beyond the Lunchbox," in *East Asian Journal of Popular Culture* 2(1).

Sharalyn Orbaugh is a Professor of Asian Studies at the University of British Columbia. Her publications include *Japanese Fiction of the Allied Occupation: Vision, Embodiment, Identity* (2007) and *Propaganda Performed: Kamishibai in Japan's Fifteen-Year War* (2014).

Jennifer Prough is an Associate Professor of Humanities and East Asian Studies at Valparaiso University. She is the author of *Straight from the Heart* (2011).

Renato Rivera Rusca teaches manga and anime culture at the School of Global Japanese Studies in Meiji University and comparative Japanese subculture studies at Yokohama National University. He is the coordinator of the Meiji University Cool Japan Summer Program and a member of the Board of Directors of the Astrosociology Research Institute in California.

Deborah Shamoon is an Associate Professor in the Department of Japanese Studies at the National University of Singapore. She is the author of *Passionate Friendship: The Aesthetics of Girls' Culture in Japan* (2012).

Toby Slade is an Associate Professor at the University of Tokyo. His is the author of *Japanese Fashion: A Cultural History* (2009).

Marc Steinberg is an Associate Professor of Film Studies at Concordia University, Montreal. He is the author of *Anime's Media Mix: Franchising Toys and Characters in Japan* (2012) and co-editor of *Media Theory in Japan* (2017).

Rebecca Suter is an Associate Professor in Japanese Studies at The University of Sydney. She is the author of *The Japanization of Modernity* (2008) and *Holy Ghosts: The Christian Century in Modern Japanese Fiction* (2015).

Shige (CJ) Suzuki is an Associate Professor of Modern Languages and Comparative Literature at The City University of New York (CUNY), Baruch College. He has published several articles and book chapters on manga.

William M. Tsutsui is President and Professor of History at Hendrix College in Conway, Arkansas. He is the author or editor of eight books, including *Manufacturing Ideology: Scientific Management in Twentieth-Century Japan* (1998), *Godzilla on My Mind: Fifty Years of the King of Monsters* (2004), and *Japanese Popular Culture and Globalization* (2010).

Christine R. Yano, Professor and Chair of Anthropology at the University of Hawai'i, is the author of *Tears of Longing: Nostalgia and the Nation in Japanese Popular Song* (2002), *Crowning the Nice Girl: Gender, Ethnicity, and Culture in Hawai'i's Cherry Blossom Festival* (2006), *Airborne Dreams: "Nisei" Stewardesses and Pan American World Airways* (2011), and *Pink Globalization: Hello Kitty's Trek Across the Pacific* (2013). In 2014, she curated *Hello! Exploring the Supercute World of Hello Kitty*, at the Japanese American National Museum in Los Angeles, California.

Japanese Conventions

Major Eras in Japanese History: Japanese coins, calendars, and other media are often dated both by the Japanese reign period and the Gregorian year (for example, Heisei 29 and 2017). Kamakura, Muromachi, and Edo are the names of the capital cities; subsequent time periods (after Meiji) were symbolically named by the government (for example, Meiji means "Enlightened Rule") and correspond to the reign of an Emperor.

Jōmon Period—10,000–300 B.C.E.
Yayoi Period—300 B.C.E.–250
Tomb Period—250–500
Asuka Period—500–710
Nara Period—710–794
Heian Period—794–1191 (sometimes end date given as 1185)
Kamakura Period—1191–1333
Muromachi Period—1334–1573 (Also known as the Ashikaga Period after the ruling clan.)
Edo Period—1603 (1600)–1868 (Also known as Tokugawa Period after the ruling clan.)
Meiji Period—1868–1912
Taishō Period—1912–1926
Shōwa Period—1926–1989
Heisei Period—1989–

Names: Names are given in the Japanese order of surname before given name, unless individuals refer to themselves or their eponymous brands in the English order, such as Yohji Yamamoto and Issey Miyake. In the case when celebrities use monyms or authors and artists pennames, they are referred to by these chosen titles, rather than by their last names.

Romanization: Following the Hepburn Romanization System, macrons are used to indicate long or sustained vowel sounds (for example, *bishōnen*, *furītā*, and *kaijū*), with the exception of words commonly used in English like Tokyo (not Tōkyō) and Kyoto (not Kyōtō).

1 Introducing Japanese Popular Culture

Serious Approaches to Playful Delights

Alisa Freedman and Toby Slade

Japanese characters, fashions, videogames, manga, anime, music, and more have spread worldwide, shaping Japan's international image and creating an explosion of cultural influence and hybrid creativity. Instead of choosing a person, the Ministry of Tourism made Hello Kitty, among the most recognizable logos in the world, Japan's ambassador to China and Hong Kong in 2008. In a similar gesture of mobilizing the accessibility of popular culture, the organizing committee chose nine well-known anime characters as ambassadors for the 2020 Tokyo Olympic and Paralympic Games.[1] Kumamon, featured on this book's cover, is one of Japan's approximately 1,500 local mascot characters (*yuru kyara*); marketed on a range of goods and appearing at events around Japan and internationally, Kumamon represents Kumamoto Prefecture better than any coat of arms could. The Japanese government has leveraged the global popularity of Japanese culture in attempts to improve the domestic economy, as exemplified by establishment of the Creative Industries Promotion Office in 2010 and its "Cool Japan" strategies (Iwabuchi 2010; METI 2010). Japanese popular culture has been headline news. As Christine Yano discusses in her chapter, in August 2014, the global press picked up the story that Sanrio had corrected her script for the Los Angeles Japanese American National Museum exhibit "Hello! Exploring the Supercute World of Hello Kitty" (October 2014–May 2015) to read that Hello Kitty is in fact a girl named Kitty White and not a cat; instead of being dismissed as trivia, this item became one of the most circulated stories on the Internet (Miranda 2014). The worldwide omnipresence of *Pokémon GO*, an American game that extends Japan's quintessential "media mix" marketing (extending a franchise across multiple media), and attendant concerns about safety were debated worldwide in July and August 2016. When Japan's Prime Minster Abe Shinzō visited the United States in April 2015, President Obama thanked him for karate, karaoke, anime, and emoji; Abe dressed as Super Mario at the Closing Ceremony of the 2016 Rio Olympics to accept the hand-off to Tokyo. Although these acts can be read as cultural stereotyping (e.g., Abe probably would not thank Obama for the Kardashians and Marvel Comics), they demonstrate the political role of popular culture and the expanse of transnational fandoms. The *Oxford English Dictionary* chose the "crying with joy" emoji as the top *English* "word" of 2015. Words like "otaku" and "emoji" are well known in many countries, and the suffix "–zilla" (from Godzilla) is part of American slang, illustrating Japanese popular culture's impact on communication.

The Internet has extended the reach of Japanese trends, creating new relationships between international corporations, cultural producers, and consumers. In-person fan gatherings, such as anime conventions (cons), attract tens of thousands of participants. With increased global circulation has come increased global scrutiny of the content of Japanese popular culture, as governments, including those of Japan, Australia, Canada, New Zealand, Sweden, the United Kingdom, and the United States, have regulated Japanese manga and anime (McLelland 2016). Groups that circulate fan-produced works—from Tokyo's large biannual Comics Market (Comiket) to forums on anime-streaming sites like Crunchyroll—post warnings that appropriations of commercial characters can violate copyrights and obscenity laws. While many students in the 1980s were attracted to the study of Japan out of economic interest, popular culture is among the main reasons why generations who have come of age since the 1990s have taken Japanese language and culture courses. Students use their knowledge to pursue careers in fields as diverse as business, law, psychology, computer science, art, and journalism.

What makes Japanese popular culture so fascinating, visually appealing, and hotly debated? How are cute characters like Hello Kitty transforming international relations and the ways people construct their own identities? How does popular culture both provide a means for discussing topics otherwise difficult to approach and depoliticize public issues, making them seem, instead, like personal concerns? How have people of different ethnic backgrounds, genders, sexual orientations, and age groups used Japanese popular culture to form communities and to overturn stereotypes? How do popular culture aesthetics fit the spirit of their times? How can fans encourage the creation of new content within legal confines? Are there any negative effects of regarding Japan as the "capital of cool"? Through analysis of forty historical and contemporary trends that have strongly influenced artistic production, politics, and economics, *Introducing Japanese Popular Culture* seeks to answer these questions and investigates how popular culture reveals the values of the societies that produce and consume it.

More than serving as a "time capsule" of influential objects, our book imparts enduring lessons that popular culture teaches about history, international relations, business, class, gender, sexuality, art, novelty, nostalgia, humanism, nationalism, multiculturalism, cosmopolitanism, urbanization, and notions of "home." We examine how Japanese popular culture is constructed and circulated within a nexus of discourses—those occurring in the mass media, those shaped by social practices, and those advanced through the dissemination of objects and texts. We discuss how artists and corporations have spearheaded major trends, often with support from the Japanese government and through the efforts of fans. We analyze how Japanese popular culture both "belongs" to Japan and has become "international," linking consumers around the world. More than surveying aspects that have come to characterize Japan's "gross national cool," to borrow a term from Douglas McGray (2002), we corral and make sense of the diverse meanings that arise from cultural texts. Offering enough material to satisfy the needs of an entire undergraduate course, this book helps students become aware of how they themselves engage with Japanese popular culture in order that they may fully understand its globalization.

Accessibly written with ample description but not at the expense of discursive analysis, *Introducing Japanese Popular Culture* aspires to be a university textbook, go-to handbook for interested readers, and compendium for scholars. Most chapters are new, or substantially updated, work by established professors; others are cutting-edge pieces by young researchers. Acknowledging that Japanese popular culture studies is a field in formation and drawing from disciplines often at odds in their approaches, we promote synergies among academics and provide students with examples of methodologies to use as models. We promote internationalism, with contributors from Asia, North America, Australia, and Europe, reflecting the globalization of the trends described. Most authors teach Japanese popular culture and share their pedagogical strategies in addition to their research.

Our book is an answer to our students' complaint that much contemporary literature on Japanese popular culture articulates theories that do not match the trends as they experience them. After all, our students are the ones surrounded by and involved in popular culture. At times, we find ourselves assigning readings that engaged students immediately identify as vague, orientalist, outdated, or simply wrong. Part of the problem is the tendency to fit cultural objects to current theories. Our method is the opposite. We begin with specific products and then explicate their greater meanings—what we call the "Jane Austen Approach" of writing about the particular and implying the universal, not the other way around. Our chapters do not address themselves to the abstract categories often used to explain Japanese popular culture, such as "*kawaii*," "otaku," or "Lolita," although these will be discussed. Naturally, larger abstractions, histories, and theories are explained, but to make this book approachable and convincing and to avoid the trap of developing a cultural category and then fitting evidence to it, each chapter focuses on a tangible object or phenomenon from which a whole body of work or a genre can be illuminated. We believe that this approach of building theory from data, and not attaching data to theory, makes for a useful teaching tool for beginners, encourages discussion among specialists familiar with major debates and controversies, and destabilizes some of the more orientalist or fanciful theories. By basing essays on single case studies as starting points to larger readings, we create a pedagogy that makes theory accessible, without doing away with theory or limiting the discipline to a few handpicked examples. In doing so, we also urge readers to consider what defines Japanese popular culture.

What Is "Japanese Popular Culture"?

At the heart of any definition of Japanese popular culture are a number of contradictions. First, we believe that the use of a nation-state, such as Japan, as an organizing principle for the categorization of culture, especially contemporary popular culture, is ultimately untenable. We see Japanese popular culture as a study of information flows associated with Japan rather than anything "essentially" or "authentically" Japanese. In the case of Japan, this is sometimes less arbitrary because of the barriers of geography and language. Thus we demonstrate that the designation "Japanese" in Japanese popular culture is more an associative starting point than a marker of exclusivity or locus of origin for what are indeed a globalized set of phenomena. We strive to help readers understand the positive and negative, fanciful and realistic images of Japan that popular culture presents, thereby promoting cultural literacy and avoiding cultural misunderstanding. It is true that Japanese national identity has historically partitioned foreign influence and so-called indigenous culture, a recurring idea of a "double life" [theorized by Edward Seidensticker (1983) and other scholars], but this, too, is a nationalist narrative that disintegrates with close examination, as our chapters demonstrate.

The designation "popular culture" was originally intended to relegate things to a status inferior to "high culture," thereby positing an opposition between the enduring, elite culture of museums and the ephemeral, quotidian culture of the streets. Serious academic attention has shown the culture of the streets to be as fascinating, valuable, and telling as the traditional contents of museums (e.g., Jenkins 1992, 2006; McKee 2006). Notably, the high culture of one era or place becomes another's popular culture, and vice versa. For example, Japanese art masterpieces were displayed in industrial and applied arts pavilions at late nineteenth-century world expositions, where high culture was defined according to the European history of painting. At the same time, world expositions gave masses of people the chance to interact with objects once reserved for the elite. Popular culture scholars have challenged the division of things into a simply commercial, disposable youth culture and the classical, stable, lasting objects of a cultural essence as a falsehood borne in the confusion of modernity and stubbornly remaining in contemporary nationalism. They refuse to let culture be simply a tool of social distinction, used to demonstrate social class or maturity or academic connoisseurship. The obsession with creating a unified hierarchy of cultural values is no longer a priority of scholarship. The impact of Edward Said's *Orientalism* (1978) as the most serious critique to the way academic study serves political power structures and creates cultural hierarchies has been great and has questioned and corrected many scholarly methods and presuppositions. Yet this process is far from complete, and the scope of what deserves to be studied as culture is still contested. Our book intends to make a wide and inclusive claim about what cultural forms are representative and worthy of academic attention, as the table of contents attests.

We include examples of what we deem "unpopular culture," especially in our sections on music, fashion, and art, to further explore what the avant-garde, rebellious, recycled, reclaimed, cathartic, and violent reveals about the inner workings of "popular culture" and its modes of communication. This broad category encompasses movements, like noise music, that veer toward "subculture" and things common to groups, like rural communities, not often associated with commercialized popular culture. Even if "unpopular culture" is not consumed by large swaths of the population, it represents the spirit of popular culture as something that resists control by the tastes of the elite.

The final designation of "culture" is perhaps less contested and problematic than the other two terms. In the earlier twentieth century, the study of a mass or popular culture was a project of Marxism; it was considered a potential tool for raising class consciousness. With the rise of poststructural and post-modern thought in the later twentieth century, culture was reconsidered as no longer simply a manifestation of economics, and this, in turn, allowed for new ways of approaching the understanding of culture through disciplines such as sociology and media studies.

We build on this trajectory to argue that popular culture is a key, crea-tive node of cultural production. Culture is not politics or economics. For example, in the 2010s, tourists from China and South Korea have come to Japan in droves to buy popular-culture goods, even though the political and economic relationship between the three nations has remained tense. Our chapters show that, while culture certainly has economic and political ram-ifications, the ambition of using it as a reliable tool of political influence is flawed (as evident in the top-down promotion of "Cool Japan"). In addition to the difficulties of turning culture into political currency, abetted by the fact that popular culture tends to depoliticize issues, the brand of "Japan" contin-ues to face the law of unintended consequences, as popular culture circulates and is put to originally unintended uses by global fans (Freedman 2016). We analyze how the consumption of culture has challenged Japanese business strategies, including the prevalence of the gender binary in the marketing of commodities. As Sharalyn Orbaugh notes in her chapter on *kamishibai* (street theater using paper signboards), a survey conducted in 1934 in Tokyo found that, contrary to gender expectations, almost all boys liked the melodramas and almost all girls liked the adventure stories—that is, the gender division in terms of narratives was more in the minds of the creators and marketers than in the audience's reception.

Our book provides insight into why certain texts more easily "translate" across nations and time periods than others. Anime were among the first television programs to be exported, in part because they were easy to dub into local languages. Much of the popular culture we examine has globalized because it emits the right "cultural odor," a term coined by Iwabuchi Kōichi (2002) to explain the amount of cultural context a product carries. One model is for a text to be grounded in Japan but understandable across nations.

A prime example is the growing repertoire of emoji that, on one hand, exemplify conventions particular to Japanese cellphone and Internet use, including access patterns, visual languages, gender conceptions, and corporate tie-ins. On the other hand, emoji, now preprogrammed into most smartphones, exemplify how Japanese popular culture is transforming global communication. Another model is the removal and recalibration of cultural context. As analyzed by William Tsutsui, Godzilla is a franchise that takes on new meanings when it is localized, by erasing or inventing political subtexts, adding layers of interpretation through dubbing, and becoming available in different formats. However, television dramas, some manga and anime, and Japanese idol bands demand more familiarity with Japanese society in order to be enjoyed. Technology is accelerating the ability to experience global products, with the Internet, smartphones, and instant translations continuously mixing Japanese popular culture with the culture of the world. Students who watch a Godzilla film today might do so (legally or not) on their smartphones, in their native languages, and then follow a link to a fan-produced manga about Godzilla posted on the Internet, and instantly grant it their approval with an emoji in the comments, all without realizing how much more difficult this access would have been even a decade ago and how their actions might violate marketing conventions. We strive to make our readers more mindful of the speed of cultural translation and its implications.

Twelve Popular Culture Categories

Despite our goal to be an overarching survey of Japanese popular culture, we realize the impossibility of including everything. Our twelve section themes follow our object-centered approach and adhere to a "satisficing" (satisfactory while sufficient) principle rather than a "maximizing" or "encyclopedic" principle. Some sections (e.g., manga and music) are longer than others to acknowledge the student and scholarly interest in them. We include objects, like fashion and art, not often found in popular culture volumes in order to expand the canon of popular culture and challenge its assumptions. While we aim to provide a broad and detailed overview, there remain uncharted areas for future scholars to explore.

We resist the standard ordering of categories, which tends to mirror chronologies of cultural production (e.g., placing manga before anime). Instead, we arrange categories roughly according to their economic success in Japan, furthering our book's emphasis on patterns of consumption. Within categories, we position chapters to complement and challenge each other and elucidate the breadth of popular culture. For example, included are both narrative and non-narrative trends (i.e., those with backstories and those that can be enjoyed without any prior knowledge), those that rely on technologies of their times, those bound to Japan's geography and those that are more portable, and those, which as "unpopular culture," subvert the norms of their genres to make cultural statements or express the coolness of niche.

We demonstrate that popular culture, while often considered to be new, instead has deep historical roots.

We start with characters, one of the most profitable Japanese culture industries, and analyze Kumamon and Hello Kitty: two ubiquitous non-narrative characters with very different sets of educational, commercial, and institutional meanings. Kumamon teaches people about Kumamoto Prefecture; but consumers do not need to know that Hello Kitty has a twin sister named Mimmy and is married to Dear Daniel (also not a cat) to use her goods (although this information adds interest). In these and other respects, they differ from the *tokusatsu* live-action superheroes, magical girls, robots, and other characters originating from narratives, discussed elsewhere in this book. Most characters we research have human traits (from Kumamon to Kikaider, Astro Boy to *Tokyo Jungle*'s Pomeranian), as another way popular culture reinforces our sense of our humanity.

We then explore three dominant television genres—*tokusatsu* programs, serialized dramas, and travel shows—that have shaped the historical peculiarities of Japanese broadcasting and, although originally intended only for domestic audiences, have attracted global fans. These chapters show how television tends to represent and reinforce, rather than overturn dominant social discourses, such as notions of justice, Japan's relationship to the rest of the world, and the course of a woman's life. They demonstrate how popular culture, as primarily a form of entertainment, tends to comfort and amuse, rather than offer solutions to pressing social concerns. As a contrast, our two chapters on videogames articulate how players (whether they realize it or not) engage with the imagination of disaster prevalent in Japanese popular culture.

We move from commercial production to fan media to investigate how photographic and music-making platforms and the Internet have inspired self-expression and cemented communities. Our chapters investigate key issues in the rising academic field of "fan studies": gender vocabularies of trends, media tourism, joint amateur and commercial creations, "supernormal stimuli" and the preference of the unreal to the human (e.g., Hatsune Miku), and legal and ethical issues inherent in the spread of popular culture.

Four case studies in popular music—"idols" (*aidoru*), guitar rock, Japanoise (an example of the abovementioned "unpopular culture"), and K-pop—showcase the diversity, national and transnational influences, image makers, and marketing models of the Japanese music industry, and the significance of performance events and fan interaction. Three cases in popular cinema—Godzilla and monster (*kaijū*) movies, *Yotsuya Ghost Story* (*Yotsuya kaidan*), and V-Cinema made for video distribution—demonstrate how business has shaped genres, mobilizing film traditions and the commercial power of adaptation, and, with the rise of cheaper modes of production such as video, enabling more diverse stories and directors.

We take a historical approach to anime, covering the main themes, genre conventions, producers, and "media mix" through close reading of well-known texts. We explore how merchandising and sponsors have influenced content and aesthetics and how anime is a means to understand postmodernism. Our section on manga extends our analysis of genres and modes of production as well as consumption. We study how manga producers have used narrowcasting, have sampled their audiences, and have incorporated readers' feedback to shape the industry. Manga like *gekiga* exemplify popular culture's political uses, while manga magazines demonstrate the endurance of gender stereotypes. These four essays also represent some of the different disciplines and approaches in our book: cultural studies, close reading based on literary analysis, anthropology, and philosophy. Two case studies of best-selling literature that came from outside of the establishment—(1) Murakami Haruki's fiction and the international market for his translations, and (2) amateur-authored cellphone novels (*keitai shōsetsu*) that used technology to prove the endurance of the written word in the age of visual narratives—provide new possibilities for Japanese literature in the era of globalization and digitization.

We present a variety of "Sites and Spectacles" that convey how popular culture has historically constructed, disrupted, and regulated notions of place in Japan. We have chosen places that have come, through their attachment to popular culture, to represent Tokyo as the political, cultural, and economic capital of Japan. Edo-period fireworks festivals and early twentieth-century *kamishibai* made streets into sites of popular culture. Shibuya grew into a neighborhood associated with youth fashions thanks to competition among department stores and provides insight into how urban residents have shaped the growth of the city through their use patterns. Akihabara has been a primary site for promoting and policing "otaku," avid consumers of anime, manga, and games who have become ambivalent representatives of "Cool Japan," as Patrick Galbraith argues in his chapter. Ruins, embodying the aftereffects of economic growth and decline, are cultural topoi in recessionary Japan. This and other sections explore the role of place in the historical confusion of popular culture, mass culture, and youth culture.

We end with fashion and art as two categories that perhaps most clearly comment on the historical divide between so-called "high" and "popular" culture and how ideas can flow from niche designers to the mass market and from the gallery into broad public consciousness. We explore moments and ephemerality in the relationship between fashion, popular culture, and the media through which they are disseminated, how the gender binary is taken for granted, and the prevalence of cute aesthetics (especially *kawaii*, the notion of cuteness premised on seeming vulnerable) since the 1970s. We end with artwork that, as unpopular culture by nature of its content, display, audience, and expense, among other factors, holds up a mirror to popular culture and to Japanese society at large. For example, Superflat both critiques and celebrates its superficiality, and artists' return to the rural community in various art projects on islands in the Seto Inland Sea, and to craft, can be seen as both a means to remember fading pasts and antidotes to the consumer desire for the "ever new" that characterizes much of popular culture.

Serious Study of Playful Delights

While acknowledging that appeal of popular culture lies is its escapism and easy consumption without having to think deeply, this book demonstrates that it is possible to take popular culture seriously without denying its pleasures. We challenge readers to be "aca-fans" (e.g., Jenkins 1992; Hills 2002), fans who think critically about trends they love, and to analyze how Japanese popular culture makes us think and feel and constructs our identities and worldviews. Our extensive glossary and numerous images found in the volume and the reading lists and discussion questions sourced from chapter authors, along with additional reference materials and pedagogical features, found on the companion website, assist in this effort. Some discussion questions help students process what they are learning, while others ask them to apply their knowledge to their own lives and to creatively interact with texts. The companion website provides features that help readers to experience the trends in this book so that they can better understand the serious study of playful delights.

We would like to thank Routledge editors Stephanie Rogers and Leanne Hinves and their assistants Georgina Bishop and Lucy McClune, along with project manager Rebecca Dunn, for their untiring patience and the book contributors for their unwavering enthusiasm. Felicia Gullotta assisted as copyeditor. John Moore expertly commented on several chapters and created the map of Shibuya included with Izumi Kuroishi's chapter. The book introduction benefitted from feedback by John Moore, Kendall Heitzman, and Mark McLelland. Funding was provided by the University of Oregon Center for Asian and Pacific Studies, Department of East Asian Languages and Literatures, Asian Studies Program, and Center for the Study of Women and Society.

Revised versions of six chapters appear here courtesy of their publications (full citations found with relevant chapters): *Japanese Studies* (Christine Yano), *Television Histories in Asia: Issues and Contents* (Alisa Freedman), *Baudrillard West of the Dateline* and *International Journal of Baudrillard Studies* (Alan Cholodenko), *Canadian Journal of Film Studies* (Marc Steinberg), *Routledge Companion to Global Internet Histories* (Alisa Freedman), and *K-Pop: The International Rise of the Korean Music Industry* (Eun-Young Jung). We are grateful to many individuals and organizations for permission to reproduce the images and to the people who helped us to find them. We thank Kumamoto Prefecture; Kitahara Yasuo and Taishukan shoten; Tessu and Dalfe Nai; Sega and Crypton Future Media, Inc.; Gin Satoh; Jason Nocito; Kokusai Hōei; EUKO TATSUMI; Viz Media; Danny Choo; matohu; SOU•SOU; Aida Makoto and the Mizuma Gallery; and Fukutake Foundation. We made every effort to contact copyright holders for their permission to reprint images. The editors would be grateful to hear from any copyright holder who is not acknowledged here and will undertake to assign proper credit in future editions of the book.

This book is dedicated to our students who have inspired us with their enthusiasm for and curiosity about Japanese popular culture.

Note

1 Ambassadors include Astro Boy, Sailor Moon, Crayon Shin-chan, Naruto, Luffy from *One Piece*, Goku from *Dragonball Z*, Jibanyan from *Yōkai Watch*, and Cure Miracle and Cure Magical from *Pretty Cure*.

PART I

Characters

2 Kumamon

Japan's Surprisingly Cheeky Mascot

Debra J. Occhi

The Why and How of Mascots in Japan

Contemporary Japan is famous for using mascot characters to represent brands, organizations, government agencies, and localities. This chapter discusses how Kumamon, the mascot of Kumamoto Prefecture in western Kyushu (pictured on the cover of this volume), has become a national favorite. He is part of a mascot category known as "*gotōchi kyara*" (local characters), often called "*yuru kyara*," literally, "wobbly characters." ("*Kyara*" is an abbreviated form of "*kyarakutā*," derived from the English "character.") Popular culture critic and essayist Miura Jun coined the term *yuru kyara* in 2004 to denote characters designed for public relations of local governing bodies, events, and local goods, especially when in "*kigurumi*" (full-body character suit) form. According to Miura (2004: 2–3), mascot characters derive from creature suits, likes those for sharks and squid, worn by kabuki actors and hearken back to a long tradition of anthropomorphizing natural phenomena to naturalize cultural ideals (Occhi 2009, 2012, 2014b). Japanese folktales "frequently portray the metamorphosis of animals into humans" (Ohnuki-Tierney 1990: 131).[1] When made into *kigurumi*, *yuru kyara* often seem unstable and literally to wobble, making them all the more lovable, and "one's heart feels healed" (*iyasarete*) just by looking at them (Miura 2004: 2–3). Thus local mascots represent their hometowns in hopes of sparking consumer interest, as quasi-celebrities in the national mediascape.

As one of over 1,500 contemporary *yuru kyara*, Kumamon participates in the branding of a locale and its products, not only through his public appearances, but also through his use in "*fanshii guzzu*." "*Fanshii*," derived from the English "fancy," refers to decorative designs; "*fanshii guzzu*" (fancy goods) are small, cute, decorative personal items often marketed to young women. As discussed in Chapter 3, Hello Kitty is a prime example. Sharon Kinsella (1995) analyzes the rise of *fanshii guzzu* in the context of commercialization of "*kawaii*" (cute or lovable) girls' popular culture since the 1970s. This practice demonstrates a form of cultural logic that fits with Sut Jhally's arguments about how advertising "absorbs and fuses a variety of symbolic practices and discourses" (Jhally 1990: 3). Mascot characters are given narratives and personalities and, as *fanshii guzzu*, are designed to be loveable and targeted to women in their twenties and thirties, while also appealing to men around the same age (Kondo 2006). Mascot characters compete with an astounding variety of mass-marketed *fanshii guzzu* depicting licensed characters produced by such corporations as Sanrio and San-X and those that appear in manga and anime.

Stories about *yuru kyara* are published daily in local and national Japanese news outlets as part of ongoing feel-good promotional campaigns. At live events, *yuru kyara* represent their locales and entertain audiences with spectacles and merriment (Occhi 2012). *Yuru kyara* also gather to compete for popularity rankings; the largest of these competitions is the *Yuru Kyara* Grand Prix (*Yuru kyara gurando purii*). One feels almost as if *Pokémon* characters have come to life, and, rather than fighting each other, have undertaken the care of humans, offering hugs and posing for photos. *Yuru kyara*'s "healing power" (*iyashi*) was evident after the March 11, 2011 earthquake and subsequent tsunami and nuclear disaster, for it was after then that their numbers dramatically increased.

As I will explain, popular English language news media have dismissed *yuru kyara* by reporting on these live events as one manifestation of the stereotype of an immature "wacky Japan." This reflects the notion of "cultural odor" that Iwabuchi Kōichi (2002) uses to discuss foreignness in globalized contexts, particularly in the case of media consumption beyond its culture of production. The amount of "cultural odor" a product or idea carries determines how easily it can be fit into local markets. For example, some things sell because the "cultural odor" can be easily diffused and they can blend more seamlessly into different national contexts; other products are promoted because their strong foreign "smells" distinguish them from local products. For example, the English-dubbed version of Tezuka Osamu's *Astro Boy* (*Tetsuwan Atomu*) was popular on early 1960s American television because it had plotlines familiar in the Cold War era and aesthetics that somewhat resembled those of Walt Disney, while in the mid-1990s *Pokémon* became a large global fad, in part, because it seemed somehow "Japanese." For example, *The Wall Street Journal* (Landers 2015) reported that Japan has been infected by a craze for *yuru kyara* and calls them a unique "mix of the cute and the bizarre." The online site Buzzfeed calls them "quirky ... weird and adorable" (Burton 2015). *The Japan Times* titled an article "The Obsession Over These Dumbed Down Cute Mascots" (Brasor 2008a). CNN has widely reported the Japanese Finance Ministry's 2014 call to reduce the number of tax-funded mascots (e.g., McKirdy 2014). British comedian John Oliver in his American news parody television show *Last Week Tonight with John Oliver* (HBO network) on May 10, 2015 called for a similar creation of mascots for U.S. government agencies. However, the rationale for *yuru kyara* and their impact on Japanese everyday life remains underreported.

Another misconception of Kumamon is that he is a bear, the animal he most resembles. The truth is that he is not. When I sought permission from

Kumamoto Prefecture to use his image in my chapter, I was told that any statements to that effect were not factual and should be removed. Actually, most Japanese people see Kumamon as a bear and are surprised to learn otherwise. As of July 2015, the Japanese National Tourism Organization website on *yuru kyara* labels Kumamon a bear,[2] as do *The Wall Street Journal*, *The Guardian*, and other news agencies. Perhaps this surprising aspect of his character is reminiscent of the wildly popular Internet story of August 2014, in which Sanrio insisted that Hello Kitty is not a cat (see Chapter 3). And not only is Kumamon not a bear, he is not a human in a fuzzy suit. As I was told by Kumamon's brand promotion division, "The Kumamon you see in the real world is not a *kigurumi*, the thing [you see] is his flesh and blood" (*genzai sekai no Kumamon wa kigurumi de wa naku, namami no Kumamon sono mono desu*) (Kumamoto Brand Office 2015).

This chapter will tease apart Kumamon's symbolic practices and discourses in order to show how he came to dominate the field of *yuru kyara*. Not only has he been successful for Kumamoto, but also he has become a source of pride for Japan as a whole. He has attempted to gain wider fame outside Japan, although this has not been unproblematic. Issues emerging from his Japanese "cultural odor" and sentiments lost in translation have affected his reception abroad. In addition, as his image circulates widely online, Kumamon has gained unintended meanings and alternative identities that the Kumamoto government has been unable to control, further showing how characters represent an important pattern of cultural globalization in the digital age.

Kumamon's Origin Myth

A 2013 *mook* (publication more substantial than a magazine and with more images and an A4-sized, larger format than most books) titled *Chi'iki burando no tsukurikata: How to Make a Local Brand*, tells Kumamon's origin story (Kinoshita et al. 2014). The image of this stocky, black, two-legged, red-cheeked *yuru kyara* is the largest and most prominent in the *mook*. It is followed by details usually written on a Japanese job resume (*rirekishō*). We learn that Kumamon's birthday is March 12, the day of the opening of the completed Kyushu *shinkansen* bullet train line, and that he is rumored to be five years old. As a public official, albeit a young one, he is the head of the prefectural business division, tasked with raising public awareness for the "Kumamoto Surprise" (Kumamoto Sapuraizu) advertising campaign. He is male, although emphatically in the human, not animal, sense (*osu janakute otoko no ko!*), and, like most male *yuru kyara*, is mischievous and full of curiosity (Kinoshita et al. 2014: 5). His stated mission is to make an impassioned appeal across Japan for the "delicious food and beautiful nature of Kumamoto with the intention of making everyone happy" (Kinoshita et al. 2014: 5). That sort of mission is typical of *yuru kyara*, which provide advertising representation for their sponsors along with cuddly comfort.

Kumamon occupies a sought-after position. His identity as a public official working in promotion provides an ideal argument for his activities. This kind of job bears an aura of stability sought by jobseekers, as well as by marriage-minded Japanese in this post–Lehman shock and post-3/11 era, and it echoes the overall desire to have faith in public officials. And as his popularity and that of his prefecture grow, Kumamon is the ideal advertisement for Kumamoto's government as well, which already boasts about its Governor Kabashima Ikuo's Harvard education.

The use of *yuru kyara* in favor of human spokespeople as a ready means for symbolic representation is understandable given the largely non-Christian and non-Cartesian context of Japanese worldview (Occhi 2014b). That is, humans, animals, and gods are not placed in the same kinds of hierarchies. Therefore, it is not blasphemous to say that *yuru kyara* are similar to local gods in terms of structure and function (Occhi 2012). They are cuddly deities, unlike hard Buddhist statues or seldom seen Shinto gods. *Yuru kyara* can provide an ongoing festival atmosphere in that they are mobile and on display, unlike Shinto gods that are usually hidden in shrines except when brought out on special *matsuri* (festival) days. *Yuru kyara* are also less likely to create scandals than human spokespeople, especially when they do not speak (Occhi 2010, 2014a). Kumamon is only spoken for by handlers or quoted in print, so his utterances are monitored.

Kumamon was created in 2009 as part of the larger "Kumamoto Surprise" campaign. The 2011 start date of the bullet train connecting Kagoshima and Fukuoka had created a sense of urgency for Kumamoto, which is situated at the midpoint, to share in the projected benefits of increased mobility along the western side of Kyushu. Moreover, it was considered crucial for residents to feel enjoyment and happiness about their locale. Therefore, the "Kumamoto Surprise" was intended to both "reset the locals' mentality" and "surprise" visitors with natural beauty and delicious, yet unpretentious cuisine. The words "Kumamoto Surprise," written in black, were embellished by a melted looking, stylized red explanation point, forming a logo intended to symbolize the passion of the prefecture conveyed in Kumamoto's nickname "land of fire" (*hi no kuni*) (Kinoshita et al. 2014: 7). The *yuru kyara* "boom" (*būmu*, or large-scale fad that bursts on the scene) was already underway by the time of March 11, 2011 triple disaster; decorative, licensed characters from around Japan were mobilized as comforting images in the aftermath (Occhi 2012). Kumamon's emergence one year prior, along with his PR appearances distributing business cards in the target market of Osaka, allowed him to garner some fame before these traumatic events; over one hundred people sent him New Year's greeting postcards (Kinoshita et al. 2014: 8). And although his (and the bullet train's) nationwide launch on March 12 came just on the heels of the tragedy, he won the top place in the 2011 *Yuru Kyara* Grand Prix . Amidst ongoing news of destruction, trauma, and nuclear meltdown, *yuru kyara* have provided a welcome distraction with their frolicsome antics and economic benefits.

Kumamon's success stories often pay homage to his creator. Although only the "Kumamoto Surprise" logo design was requested from the Kumamoto-born designer Koyama Kundō, his art director Mizuno Manabu included a rendering of Kumamon in two poses, as a surprise. This was no hasty sketch, however; the design of Kumamon went through 3,000 variations before Mizuno decided on the final version, which for Koyama combines appealing elements of other larger-than-life personages (Kinoshita et al. 2014: 13). One of these is Santa Claus, whose annual Santa Claus festival in Oyama's hometown of Amakusa draws outside visitors. The other is Hideki Matsui, the former New York Yankees baseball player who has enjoyed worldwide fame despite his origins in largely rural Ishikawa. The physical form of Kumamon also contains several meaningful elements. He is black, like the walls of Kumamoto Castle and the bodies of actual Japanese bears (recall that Kumamon is not a bear, nor is Kumamoto actually home to wild bears). His solid body is reminiscent of a stocky Kyushu man, a stereotyped fellow said to be tough and tempestuous (Kinoshita et al. 2014: 9). This amount of detail is just a fraction of the knowledge about Kumamon and his activities noted by the prefecture on his website, in publications (Kumamoto Ken 2012), and to obliging Japanese news agencies for whom *yuru kyara* have become a fertile topic. In a market full of *fanshii guzzu*, the ability to distinguish oneself with unique and appealing traits is essential for *yuru kyara* success. Kumamon usually wears a look of surprise, echoing the campaign theme as it evokes curiosity in its viewers, and his expression is sometimes amplified by making his mouth into a circle for emphasis. He is occasionally shown smiling by softening his eyes into two smiling arcs that resemble his eyebrows and emphasizing the rounded red cheeks that stick out of the sides of his face (Figure 2.1).

Despite (or thanks to) these oddly protruding cheeks, Kumamon won the Good Design Award from the Japan Chamber of Commerce and Industry in 2013 (Japan Institute of Design Promotion 2013). These red circles are said to symbolize the "land of fire," as well as the mark of Katō Kiyomasa (1561–1611), who became the first feudal lord (*daimyō*) of the Kumamoto region during the early years of the Tokugawa Shōgunate (Kinoshita et al. 2014: 13). Notably, they are also reminiscent of the *"hi no maru"* ("sun circle," or rising sun) of the Japanese flag, as are the cheeks of two other widely known characters, *Pokémon*'s Pikachu and the eponymous hero of the long-running children's anime series *An-Pan Man*. Kumamon's red cheeks even disappeared in a publicity stunt that cost 600 million yen (roughly US$6 million) held in Tokyo's posh Ginza neighborhood, where the Kumamoto products store is located, as well as on television and on social media and video-sharing sites like YouTube in late October and early November 2013. This promotion intended to whip up interest in Kumamon, Kumamoto produce, and the Santa Claus festival in Amakusa. Along with Kumamon, Governor Kabashima and several other human celebrities from Kumamoto, including the *enka* (Japanese folksong) singer Aki Yashiro and the impersonator known popularly as *korokke* (Croket, from French *croquette*), joined the search for Kumamon's

Figure 2.1 Kumamon in his original pose.
Source: © 2010 kumamoto pref.kumamon.

cheeks while wearing replicas. The cheeks were eventually found through a ruse in which Kumamon held two tomatoes to his face, celebrating them and by extension, other red products of Kumamoto.

This hide-and-seek tactic has been part of Kumamon's successful strategy, starting from his first public visit outside the prefecture. At a promotion for Kumamoto held in Osaka in October 2010, he handed out ten thousand business cards to spectators and then disappeared; spectators were invited to search for him (*Yomiuri Shinbun* 2012a). The tactic was the theme of a free game for cellphones and tablets released in late 2012. This practice reiterates the theme of surprise to which Kumamon is associated, and it fondly reminds us of the earliest pastimes of childhood.

Another game that spectators play with Kumamon centers on his imagined problem of *metabo* (metabolic syndrome) indicated by his blocky body and indexed by his career as a busy public official. The prefecture tells us he is as tall as six to seven large watermelons (another red product of Kumamoto). These would typically be roughly 25 centimeters (9.8 inches) in diameter, yielding a height of 150–175 centimeters (59–69 inches). His waist circumference is 270 centimeters (106 inches) (Kumamoto Ken 2012: 15). The combination of this information renders a BMI (body mass index) of 67.5, far over the suggested upper limit of twenty-five in the normal range, indicating that he might be at risk of heart disease, stroke, and diabetes. If measured at the annual health check customary for most adults in Japan, this would result in a request for him to exercise. This problem evokes sympathy among many people worried about receiving a similar diagnosis given Japan's increased concern with obesity prevention. While the Kumamon *taisō* (exercise) song appeals to children, it invokes memories of performing *rajio taisō* (radio exercises) and other group exercises in a comical way. In the accompanying video for the "Kumamoto Surprise" tune, as Kumamon and a female assistant dance, the song lyrics praise the prefecture by describing its location as the "belly button of Kyushu over which the bullet train runs" (Fujii 2013). In another song called "Kumamon mon" (KAN 2013), we are reminded of his obesity as well as his capacity to make people happy. A performance of this exercise dance welcomed the Japanese Emperor and Empress on their October 28, 2013, visit to the prefectural office.

Kumamon also invites us to replicate and promulgate him, creating our own simulacra. Producers of goods wishing to use his image need only gain prefectural permission; 57,610 goods spanning thirty categories were available in July 2015 on amazon.co.jp. (Japan's local Amazon.com) website, including toys, car seat cushions, cookie cutters, *sake* cups and coffee mugs, and USB memory sticks. These goods and categories proliferate across Japan, creating a national souvenir shop of sorts, even finding a home in one-hundred-yen (or "dollar") shops alongside Hello Kitty goods. The manager of a spa hotel in rural Toyama Prefecture I stayed at in February 2014, complained of a caller soliciting to place Kumamon goods for sale there, despite the distance (1,000 kilometers [621 miles] by car) and an utter lack of connection between the two places. One can easily make one's own Kumamon goods. For example, books about Kumamon include directions for constructing his likenesses out of paper, clay, and felt, and even for food as part of *kyara bentō* (character lunchboxes, abbreviated as "*kyaraben*") (Buteikkusha 2013). In spring 2015, out of the 584 *yuru kyara bentō* recipes on the Japanese recipe website cookpad.com, 115 (roughly 20 percent) were for Kumamon. The popularity of Kumamon in *kyaraben* no doubt owes in part to its ease of preparation, for it simply requires black *nori* (seaweed) either cut into shape or embellished with facial features made of sliced cheese, laid atop rice, with his two cheeks easily made from circular slices of carrot or processed meat, or a halved cherry tomato. An especially speedy option involves only *nori* with cheese eyes and mouth placed on the side of *nori*-wrapped roll sushi, whose outer plastic wrap is then embellished with black marker and red stickers (Tanabe 2013).

Although Not a Bear, Kumamon Bears Comparison

Kumamon is not a bear, but if he were, he would not be the only bear in town. The number of competitors renders his success all the more surprising—or does it? The variety of bear characters available in Japan range from children's stories both imported (Winnie the Pooh and Paddington Bear) and local (the bear's school, Gloomy, and Rilakkuma), to name a few. However, Kumamon's identity contrasts with the first three. His simple black-white-red motif is clean looking; in character design black lends strength, white adds purity, and red gives passion (Pukumuku 2013). This combination also makes him more likely for adult consumption, particularly by men, who according to survey research (as well as my personal observation) have typically been less likely than women or children to consume *kyara* goods (Aihara 2007). This strategy of juxtaposing the normative public servant image with the persona of a mischievous five-year-old also contrasts strongly with the identities of local *fanshii guzzu* bears. Chief among these is the laid-back Rilakkuma, whose mysterious rear neck zipper suggests to me that he may be symbolic of a lazy boyfriend. He sponges off the unfortunate office lady Kaoru in whose apartment he appears (Kondo 2003). Gloomy, the "naughty grizzly" designed by Mori Chack, appears in a variety of bright colors, including hot pink, that belie a vicious bloodthirstiness depicted on his bloody mouth and exposed, reddened claws. Although the name Gloomy may be a word play on *gurumi*, (covering) as in *kigurumi* or *nuigurumi* (stuffed toy), Gloomy is much more like an actual bear, as he is liable to attack his owner, who in this case is a boy named Pitty.

These bears also compete with other local mascot bears—the frightening, fanged Melon Kuma (a bear with a melon head) and cute but gross Zombear (a zombie bear), both from Hokkaido and both of which, like Gloomy, are appealing more to the *kimo kawaii* (gross-cute) sensibility than the typical *yuru kyara* realm. As character producer Kondo Keisuke (2006: 52–54) points out, it is important to create the world in which a character lives, and the other *yuru* and *fanshii guzzu* bears clearly require particularized worlds that limit their popularity. "the bear's school" is a school-based world, and those goods are aimed at small children and their parents. Gloomy's world is dangerous for us, hence his popularity among the disaffected teenaged set. Rilakkuma embodies a dreamlike world of procrastination that requires someone else's financial support, which, as anthropologist Carolyn Stevens argues, may explain his appeal with college students (Stevens 2014).

Kumamon, Be Ambitious

When *yuru kyara* have gone abroad, as Kumamon has, they have often had to divest of the reliance on ready identification with known locales that they enjoy domestically, and which forms the very source of their identity. This loss of "cultural odor," in Iwabuchi Kōichi's terms—which domestically lends a pleasing fragrance—potentially includes the loss of symbolic identity tied in with their very names. *Yuru kyara* naming typically relies on the layering of meanings that resonate both with words for or about their sponsors and also includes sound symbolism that is itself emotionally evocative. This sound symbolic word class in Japanese is extensive and useful not only in onomatopoeic "*giseigo/giongo*" (animal sounds/sound effects) but also in explaining actions and reactions. These mimetic terms, known collectively as "*gitaigo*," play an important role in modifying verbs. For example, they are often used with the verb "*suru*" to do (e.g., "*waku waku suru*," "to be excited") (Hamano 1998). This word class is felt by native speakers to be naturalistic and concomitantly difficult to translate (Occhi 1999). These fantastic, humorous resonances of word and image make *yuru kyara* memorable and contribute to their success. In my database of just over 1,000 *yuru kyara* dating up to and including Kumamon, only his name ends in *–mon*.

There is an obvious symbolism in Japanese that Kumamon represents Kumamoto. One part of his name that mistakenly led me to believe that he was a bear is the word for "bear" that appears in the name Kumamoto (*kuma*). The ending *–mon* is also a dialectal morpheme in Kumamoto dialect usually rendered "*mono*" (thing or person). So Kumamon is a "Kuma(moto) person" as well as an emblem of Kumamoto. When Kumamon's speech is rendered in print (because he does not speak audibly), the use of *–mon* at the end of his utterances functions as "*yakuwarigo*," or "role language" (Kinsui 2003) identifies him uniquely among *yuru kyara* and as someone from Kumamoto. He has also taken a part in internationalization efforts in Kumamoto through his appearance in English language middle schools' ethics texts. In these texts, local human heroes are presented in simple English stories with Kumamon appearing in the margins to introduce them or to provide commentary. Whenever feasible, his utterances end in *–mon*. On his resumé described above, he lists additional greetings that employ this playful kind of role language: "*yoroshi-kuma*," a play on "*yoroshiku*," meaning to "look on me with favor" and often used as a form of "please" in requests; "*monjūru*," a play on French "*bon jour*" (good day); and even "*kumantarebū*" for "*comment allez-vous*" (How are you?).

These phrases play on both Japanese and global languages, revealing Kumamon's aspirations to represent Kumamoto on the world stage, a goal that has been further attained by his involvement in Japan EXPOs held in various locations in France and Belgium, accompanied by two unofficial *yuru kyara*: Funassyi (Funasshii) the crazy, genderless pear from Funabashi City and Hyogo Prefecture's Chichai Ossan, or "little old man." Kumamon's other forays abroad include visits to China and France, where he both participated in official promotion events and just wandered around with his camera operator and other handlers near famous landmarks to garner attention (toshiokun77). Kumamon has also visited Boston along with Governor Kabashima, who gave a lecture at his alma mater Harvard titled "The Political Economy of Kumamon: A New Frontier in Japan's Public Administration" (Boston.com 2013).

Notably, Kumamon has been globalized in ways unintended by the Kumamoto government through the Internet, where his image has circulated widely since 2011 (Boston.com 2013). A prime example is the meme begun around December 2011 on the aggregator website FunnyJunk in which his official photos were embellished with the English language phrase "For the glory of Satan"; the meme quickly spread through social media sites like Reddit, Tumblr, and Facebook (forsatan91 et al. 2014). Perhaps this parody is a spinoff of the "Hell Kitty" meme that Sanrio's *fanshii guzzu* character Hello Kitty underwent, as described in Yano (2013b: 186–187). Or could it have been done in anger when the name Kumamon supplanted the English name for a character in the *Digimon* anime franchise originally called Chakkumon in Japan. A Japanese news report suggests that while this meme was probably just a joke, it might have stemmed from the similarity between the word Kumamon and the English term "demon," or specifically, Ammon or Mammon, and the mismatch between Kumamon's cuteness and the idea of Satan (Livedoor 2014). This suggestion reflects the Japanese tendency to incorporate multiple meanings into character naming. Another permeation of this gag has also appeared in Russia where Kumamon's image has been used on a road sign to mark a "Hell Road" that is full of potholes. That news report stressed that Kumamon's image was used without prefectural consent and that the government did not take the devilish connotations too seriously (*Nichi Nichi Shinbun* 2014). The Russian response indicated that they interpreted Kumamon as a "funny wild beast resembling a beaver" (Livedoor 2014).

Is Any Fame Better than None?

When I discussed memes and other creative responses to the globalization *yuru kyara* and potential misinterpretations of their local meanings at an international conference, I was reminded that, for most Japanese, Satan is just one of countless numinous figures of record, good or evil, and therefore that this problem may not be as grave as it might seem. However jovial or sarcastic this international treatment of Kumamon may be, it does point to some deep differences in treatment and/or acceptance of mascots between, broadly speaking, Japanese-speaking and non-Japanese speaking cultural groups that potentially impact the success of *yuru kyara* abroad.

In Japan, local responses to the misuse of mascot characters further indicate that parodic treatment is taken less seriously than copyrights infringement. Kumamon reacted benevolently to his parodic depiction in a gag manga published in the April 22, 2014, issue of the popular manga magazine *Weekly Shōnen Jump*. The comic depicted a boy whose spirit was displaced into his toy bear after a car accident. The "toy" grew up to resemble a human wearing an undersized bear suit. Notably, the bear-boy made critical comments against the use of *yuru kyara* as promotion, claiming that "Japan had gone rotten." The gag specifically about Kumamon involved a reimagination of his origins as an actual bear that had undergone plastic surgery. Yet the only part of this manga that caused official offense was the unapproved depiction of Kumamon. The *Weekly Shōnen Jump* office was visited by Kumamon who received an apology with "*dogeza*" (prostration) by the artist Usuta Kyōsuke, and photos of this apology along with the revised version of the manga were made available online. This escapade also seems to indicate that the

English language "Glory to Satan" meme may not damage Kumamon too deeply after all. We can only watch and see whether this ambitious *yuru kyara* may enjoy the global domination he seeks.

Currently, as the most popular *yuru kyara*, Kumamon provides a case study for the success within this genre. Although he is not a bear, his position in comparison to similarly shaped characters that are described as bears is one that has yielded maximum appeal. His design and presentation contain a wealth of detail typical of the genre; these strategies for Japanese character creation include wordplay, colors, shapes, and a backstory intended to have a distinctive and memorable impact. However, Kumamon's treatment in popular international media shows how these elements of "cultural odor"—in its fragrant sense that has led to domestic popularity—become bleached out with exportation and may even be overlaid with a "stench" that reflects foreign interpretations and different attitudes toward mascots in general. The resulting interpretation of these newly attributed traits (e.g., that Kumamon could be seen as demonic) points back at the Japanese tendency to imbue layers of meaning in the naming of *yuru kyara*. Eventually, it appears that for Kumamon any publicity could be considered good publicity, so long as permission is received for the use of his image.

Notes

1 A poignant example is "Oshidori" included in *Kwaidan: Stories and Studies of Strange Things*, a 1904 book of ghost stories translated from old Japanese texts by Lafcadio Hearn. Here, the female of a pair of mandarin ducks appears as a beautiful, grieving woman in the dream of a hunter who has killed her husband (Hearn 1971 [1904]).
2 See the Japan National Tourism Organization website at http://us.jnto.go.jp/popculture/yuru.php?y=1.

3   Hello Kitty Is Not a Cat?!?

Tracking Japanese Cute Culture at Home and Abroad[1]

Christine R. Yano

On October 11, 2014, the Japanese American National Museum in Little Tokyo (historical Japanese enclave of Los Angeles) opened its doors to the global world of Japan's cute *kyarakutā* (character) industry with a first-of-its-kind exhibition, "Hello! Exploring the Supercute World of Hello Kitty," which I curated. Over the course of its nearly eight-month run (and extended through a traveling version for three to five years), the exhibition drew crowds of all ages and ethnicities by the thousands. They came as part of the legions of fans in the United States and elsewhere who have made Japanese Sanrio's Hello Kitty a household name and symbol of cute, not only in Tokyo, Fukuoka, and Sapporo, but also in New York, London, Paris, and São Paulo. The now ubiquitous name "Hello Kitty" may have different sets of meanings within different cultural contexts, but the point here is the degree to which Sanrio's iconic *kyarakutā* has become embedded as everyday life in many parts of the world.

Attendees of the exhibition also came intrigued by the media buzz that preceded its opening. The buzz began with an August 26, 2014 post by Carolina A. Miranda in the online blog of the *Los Angeles Times* with the headline, "Hello Kitty is Not a Cat, Plus More Reveals Before Her L.A. Tour." The post was based upon an hour-long interview Carolina did with me about the upcoming exhibition. In closing the conversation, Carolina asked, "So was there anything you learned in curating the exhibit?" to which I quickly answered, "Hello Kitty is not a cat!" In answering Carolina's question, I was referring to the feedback that I received from Sanrio to the script I wrote for the exhibition. Whereas I referred to Hello Kitty as "Sanrio's cat" or "a feline icon," the company gently but firmly pushed back, saying, "We prefer to refer to Hello Kitty as a girl or a friend." However, that quick headline went viral worldwide, traveling at lightning speed and shock-wave impact. And what was mentioned lightly, cryptically, and somewhat in jest, had Hello Kitty fans and others a-twitter.

Two months later, the world's first Hello Kitty convention was held in Los Angeles at the Geffen Contemporary at MOCA (Museum of Contemporary Art), adjacent to the Japanese American National Museum. Over the course of three days, from October 30 through November 2, 26,000 fans converged upon Hello Kitty Con 2014 celebrating forty years of Hello Kitty's existence (Marchi 2015). The sold-out event included Hello Kitty fashion, themed food, live performances, workshops, panel discussions, and even a tattoo parlor with exclusive Hello Kitty inkings. With doors open from 10:00 a.m. to 7:00 p.m., fans began lining up at 3:45 a.m. To Hello Kitty's motto, "You can never have too many friends," this event demonstrated ways in which the enthusiasm of these fan-friends runneth over in manifold ways.

How do we understand the phenomenon of Hello Kitty as a Japanese *kyarakutā* with such global impact? This chapter considers some of the corporate strategies behind Hello Kitty's worldwide success and takes her popularity as a starting point for explaining the larger social functions of *kyarakutā* in Japan and beyond. Sanrio's icon exemplifies what I have called "pink globalization"—"the spread of goods and images labeled cute (*kawaii*) from Japan to other parts of the industrial world" (Yano 2013b: 6). Indeed, this is a business success story exceeding the wildest dreams of Sanrio's founder Tsuji Shintarō; but even more so, it has become a success story of girl culture stretching far beyond the girl herself and into the terrain of society that embraces an aesthetic and affective presence.

"Small Gift, Big Smile"

Sanrio labels its marketing strategy and the emotions it wants its good to induce as "social communication" (Sanrio's coinage), which relies on an emotional affect, as well as the aesthetics of *kawaii*, a kind of cute premised on seeming lovable or vulnerable (see Chapter 35). This social communication becomes a commodity: bought, sold, and traded as part of the multivalent affective labor of *kawaii* (Allison 2004). These qualities of sociality, affect, and cuteness circumscribe a genre of products known as *kyarakutā guzzu* (literally, "character goods," commodities of anthropomorphized figures), of which Sanrio has been a chief purveyor. *Kyarakutā guzzu* transform the mundane material world, depersonalized by mass production, into one occupied everywhere by the sensate and the sociable. It repersonalizes the depersonalized goods of modern industrial society. The power of animism lies in this very intimacy, here made ineffably cute by infantilized figures.

Sanrio trades in social communication through its various *kyarakutā*, among which Hello Kitty reigns supreme. But why Kitty? Among Sanrio's pantheon of *kyarakutā*, not only was she one of the first, but she was and is the company's most enduringly popular one through the simplicity and genius of her design. Some say it is the blankness of Hello Kitty's mouthless figure that sustains her chameleon-like ability to become multiple things to many people in varied contexts. The notion of "Hello Kitty everywhere" (not coincidentally, the title of a picture book issued by Sanrio) represents nothing less than "everywhere" as Hello Kitty-ed. Visually, Sanrio's iconic *kyarakutā* represents the sparseness of childhood figuration, invoking early primers through clean lines, primary colors (at least in the early years of her existence), and conceptually simple shapes (the circle of her head, the triangle of her squat, seated body). Indeed, the Hello Kitty figure may be simple, but she is not symmetrical: her constant hint of off-kilter asymmetry is assured by the tilted red bow above one ear. Here, less is clearly more, each element of her sparse design contributing to an overall appeal that piques the imagination in subtle ways.

Sanrio understands gifting as foundational to social communication and, as part of a larger industry, specifically targets females from 'tweens to young adults. By calling itself a promoter of "social communication," Sanrio adopts the unassailable position of enabling and even enhancing Japan's interpersonal ties. Sanrio made "social communication" a genre and a central part of its brand. Through "social communication," the company claims to uphold the very fabric of social life in Japan. This "communication" takes place through gifts.

Indeed, gift exchange carries great historical depth in Japan, playing an important sociocultural role from premodern times to the present (Rupp 2003). Yet Sanrio's clever branding of itself as a gifting center focuses attention not so much on economics as on emotion. In celebration of the company's fifty years in 2010, the Sanrio website locates the foundations of the business of gift exchange in long-standing Japanese social practice: "Sanrio began in Japan where customary greetings are accompanied by an exchange of small gifts. Sanrio turned this gift-giving tradition into the company's 'small gift, big smile' mission to 'help people express their heartfelt feelings'" (Sanrio n.d.c.). Those "heartfelt feelings" are not always a part of gift-giving in Japan, which is typically laden with obligation and careful calculation (Rupp 2003: 50). Purchasing a cute Hello Kitty product as a gift for a friend becomes not only an individual act but addresses a national need to assert and sustain social and emotional ties between people. These ties go beyond the social, with its obligations and responsibilities, and into the realm of affect. Following company logic, inasmuch as Japan needs a strong interpersonal network of citizens sustained through practices of gift exchange, and inasmuch as that network comes under threat from modernity and the stresses of daily life, Sanrio plays its part by addressing a national need. By promoting "social communication," Sanrio handles that need not through rigid, formal ties that bind, but through informal, flexible bonds of *kawaii*. This is not business so much as old-fashioned social and emotional healing—physical and psychological.

Sanrio's company slogan—"Small gift, big smile"—encapsulates its claim to be not only a center but a catalyst of social communication. The slogan creates a modest calculus of affect: for the price and ease of a small gift, one may receive a big smile in return. The message suggests that Sanrio makes this exchange possible by providing gifts for all people, budgets, and occasions. The inherent strength of the company lies exactly in this flexibility. If one has a large budget, one may purchase expensive items, such as Hello Kitty diamond-encrusted watches (US$2,900 at Neiman Marcus). However, more commonly, if one has a limited budget or even when money is not an issue, Sanrio can offer gifts that may be modestly priced *and* pleasing, from gum to erasers (less than a few dollars).

Sanrio's attraction for consumers revolves around *kawaii* goods, whose production does not necessarily entail large sizes or prices. Here is the hallmark of the "social communication" industry: the "big" gift does not necessarily count. On the contrary, one might say that the smaller and, to an extent, the cheaper the gift—not only in actual price, but in its seeming trivialness— the closer to the spirit of *kawaii*. This is reflected in the colloquialism that a price (*nedan*) may be considered "*kawaii*," that is, not only inexpensive, but attractively and artlessly so. This results in expressions such as *kawaii nedan* ("cute" price) or *nedan mo kawaii* (even the price is "cute"). By these criteria, what could be more *kawaii* than a Hello Kitty eraser, cellphone strap, or coin purse? Here, size matters: smallness carries significant cultural weight as a direct link to *kawaii*, goods, and *kyarakutā*. These elements form the affective cornerstone of the large-scale empire of gift-giving called Sanrio.

The notion of a small gift eliciting a big smile suggests various overlapping implications. First, it may be a gift for a child (or a childlike adult), the size of the gift befitting the actual or symbolic size of the receiver. Second, it may be a relatively inexpensive gift, but one that still elicits a warm reaction, especially through its cuteness. This is the warm-and-fuzzy emotional quotient that, in effect, may be enabled through *kawaii nedan*. Third, it may be a gift particularly appreciated because of its miniaturization; in this case, the smaller the gift, the bigger the smile. Fourth, it may be a gift whose low price generates the impulse to give—that is, the goods themselves, including their *kawaii* appeal and accessible pricing, may prompt gift-giving. It is this generative gifting—informal, voluntary exchange prompted by the *kawaii nedan* of the object in conjunction with affect—that becomes Sanrio's social key.

In these ways, gifting by way of Sanrio may occur not as a means to balance the ledger of social obligation so much as a spontaneous act of affection— or "heartfelt feelings," as the Sanrio website explains. This is as the company would like to position itself: outside the structures of obligation, inside the structures of feeling. With the availability of small gifts (generating big smiles), then one may regard gifting—whether as giver or receiver— as a constantly unexpected possibility. One may gift another casually and intermittently, which alters the social calculus. The possibility of gifting ever present, presentation can be built upon a whim—whether of sincere emotion or impulse shopping—rather than as codified practice. It is exactly the element of surprise that Sanrio enables, leading to "heartfelt communication." The surprise gift is embedded in Sanrio's structure, taken as the name of some of its corporate boutique stores globally—Sanrio Surprises.

Kyarakutā: Cute Animism as Intimacy

As developed from the 1970s up to the 2000s, *kyarakutā* function by steps: (1) emotionalizing and humanizing the everyday material world through embodied *kawaii*, and (2) commercializing that same world. Although not all *kyarakutā* are commodified, those that are bought and sold allow the consumer to take a part of that figure home in what Anne Allison calls "pocket intimacy" or portable companionship (Allison 2004: 45). Surrounding oneself with *kyarakutā* creates a nest of comfortable familiarity. The convenience of their miniaturization means that that nest is as portable as the cellphone strap in one's purse. In fact, the cellphone strap offers the convenient opportunity of customizing one's surroundings with *kyarakutā*, turning an everyday appliance into an expression of *kyarakutā* identity. Ownership of *kyarakutā guzzu* holds forth the possibilities of buying into and creating an intimate relationship with some part of what the figure represents.

The genius of *kyarakutā* lies in the fact that they are not only objects but, more commonly, transferable logos—that is, branded, recognizable symbols that identify goods. And as logos, they can "mark" their territory endlessly, increasing the number and variety of goods for sale. This is exactly the process of Sanrio, as it extends the range of Hello Kitty products through licensing agreements in the 2000s. Sanrio, of course, is not alone in this. The character licensing business in Japan continues to grow, reaching new markets, cultivating new strategies, and developing new means to extend itself. In effect, Hello Kitty as logo is perfectly encapsulated by one of Sanrio's smaller, cheaper items. This is a pair of cardboard-framed lenses through which any concentrated light source magically transforms into an outlined image of Hello Kitty. The Hello Kitty glasses are nothing short of marketing genius. Look through them in the evening and every streetlight becomes an illuminated Hello Kitty face creating a mind-boggling Sanrio world. Through the logo principle, any surface or object can be decorated with a *kyarakutā* such as Hello Kitty and thereby stamped indelibly as *kawaii* and linked to a company or institution.[2] In fact, the work of logo goes both ways, especially as two recognizable commodities enter into a mutual licensing agreement: Hello Kitty on a Fender guitar suggests that the hard-rock world of the guitar is made more accessible to the *kawaii* world, at the same time as Hello Kitty and *kawaii* are given a new tongue-in-cheek wink of meaning.

The proliferation of these logos means more than the "cutification" of the everyday world; it suggests the corporatization of *kawaii* and its brand of *asobi* (play) through *kyarakutā*. As Allison argues, "No longer confined to particular objects ... spaces ... or times... 'play' [through *kyarakutā*] becomes insinuated into far more domains of everyday life. The border between play and nonplay, commodity and not, increasingly blurs" (Allison 2004: 47). The resulting *kyarakutā* overload potentially turns the everyday world visually into an elaborate, excessive playground whose every detail is planned, executed, and coordinated around cartoon figures. This is the work of the Hello Kitty glasses. Call this a "theme park" for the logo-driven visual scape of *kyarakutā*, as well as for its foundationally commercial impulse. Certainly, Sanrio's Hello Kitty theme park Puroland is an overt manifestation of the principle. But I argue that the logo-driven proliferation of *kyarakutā* makes urban Japan a kind of visual theme park of *kawaii* as an embodied, commodified, and feminized world.

Kyarakutā as Past in the Present

It is easy enough to dismiss *kyarakutā* as the "cutification" of the material world, as many might in response to the constant barrage of cartoonish figures dotting the cityscape of contemporary Japan. While not denying the critique, it is equally productive to assess the cultural and socioeconomic resources that might generate the widespread use of *kyarakutā*, such as Hello Kitty, as well as suggest some implications wrought by their ubiquity. The question here is not only why *kyarakutā*, but why *kyarakutā* now? What do Hello Kitty and other cartoon-like figures say about contemporary Japan? I suggest that we look not only to current issues of *kawaii* but also to past practices in seeking answers. It is this combination of the past in the present that gives the *kyarakutā* phenomenon—including Hello Kitty—particular significance.

The proliferation of *kyarakutā* suggests cultural processes at work that define particular, ongoing relationships to material objects. The work of Ellen Schattschneider on spirituality and human-made resemblances—first in the mountain asceticism of northern Honshu and subsequently in bride dolls at Tokyo's Yasukuni Shrine—transform our discussion of *kyarakutā* in contemporary Japan from mere commercialism to culture, past and present, in its most profound sense (Schattschneider 2003, 2009). Schattschneider draws specifically on two Japanese concepts to interpret objects: *mitate* (referentiality) and *migawari* (substitute, surrogate). She utilizes the principle of *mitate* (a compound made of the verbs "to see" and "to arrange")—the bestowing of objects with often oblique meaning—to understand processes of intertextual reference. Dubbed by anthropologist Yamaguchi Masao (1991) the "art of citation," *mitate* rests in the human act of juxtaposition in order to create semantic linkages (58). Yamaguchi (1991) explains:

> When an object is displayed on ceremonial occasions … a classical reference [in history or literature] … is assigned … so that the … object merges with … [that which] is being referred to … *Mitate*, then, is the technique used to associate objects of ordinary life with mythological or classical images.
>
> (Yamaguchi 1991: 58)

Mitate, in effect, operates within a continual, highly referential mode of citation, the circulation of meaning extending backward and forward in time. Although *kyarakutā* like Hello Kitty may not reference mythological or classical images, cute icons work on a symbolic level to "cite" particular places, times, or objects, especially those associated with childhood. *Mitate* is useful in thinking through *kyarakutā* because it assumes the power of objects and figures as loci of referential meaning. One sees, then, not simply a mouthless catlike image, but a highly codified figure that calls up nostalgia, childhood, or the multivalent *shōjo* (young unmarried female, ranging in age from eight to eighteen).

Indeed, the meaning system of *mitate* can connect objects with the spirit world. Schattschneider (2003) emphasizes the fluid relationship between the mortal and the divine, the one becoming, representing, and quoting the other at any given moment, so that the potential for both is omnipresent (55). That potential is actualized through human acts of imitation and representation, including that of *migawari*. Dolls and other anthropomorphic figures act as "prophylactic guardians" that "ease people through personal and cosmological transitions" (Schattschneider 2009: 302). Seen in light of Schattschneider's analysis, *kyarakutā*—as dolls, as surrogates, as guardians—may be interpreted as not mere decorations but as buffering protectors, easing the stresses and strains of daily life.

The buffering presence of *migawari* acts in two ways. First, *kyarakutā* can act as surrogates for specific persons or institutions. In other words, *kyarakutā* render potential elements of fear and anxiety *kawaii*, and thus more approachable. Second, *kyarakutā* can act as a more generally comforting presence in daily life. Here it may be one particular *kyarakutā*, as well as the overall proliferation of these figures that provide comfort. This is akin to what childhood psychologists call a "transitional object"—something that helps the child shift from the dependence of the home to a more independent state. The classical "transitional object" in EuroAmerica is the much beloved blanket or teddy bear carried around by toddlers everywhere. The omnipresence of *kyarakutā* frames daily life as always accompanied, constantly swaddled in public and private by cute anthropomorphized talismans. Guardianship by way of *kyarakutā* runs parallel with Japanese ideals of infant mothering, which are characterized not so much by verbal interaction (e.g., American style), but by physical co-presence (Lebra 1976: 139–140). *Kyarakutā*, like mothers, provide comfort and nurturance by simply being there. It is the constancy that counts. We can thus reinterpret Hello Kitty's oversaturation as part of the very constancy that makes of her a comforting presence. By this cultural logic, familiarity does not breed contempt so much as intimacy.

These miniature mascots suggest a life always accompanied, sharing intimacies with the support group of pocket pals like Hello Kitty. Her mouthless countenance provides a sounding board to synchronize with the mood of her viewer. She is the "blank" mirror that never fails, providing the right touch at the right moment. In fact, Hello Kitty needs her fans to sustain her commercial viability, as much as her fans may need her to sustain their lives. Her inveterate cuteness speaks to the helplessness that is part of her appeal. She draws people to her through her vulnerability. Indeed, it is the mutuality—Hello Kitty and consumer, each dependent upon the other—that locks the relationship. She can thus become the one-cat *kyarakutā* support group upon which one may continually and unabashedly inter-depend.

"Hello Kitty Is (Not) a Cat"

Hello Kitty has a backstory that gives her an identity that goes far beyond cat-dom. Since her inception in 1974, Sanrio has provided a complete biography of Hello Kitty, which I contend was never crucial for Hello Kitty consumption. Instead, Hello Kitty has existed first and foremost as pure product, not tied to narrative. For example, in their publicity for Hello Kitty's thirty-fifth anniversary, Sanrio reiterated Kitty's story in a three-part, detailed data sheet: (1) Kitty's Profile, (2) Kitty's Family, and (3) Kitty's Friends (Sanrio 2009a: 6–7). We find out that she is British, having been born on November 1, just outside of London. We learn details of her physical self, including weight (three apples), height (five stacked apples), blood type (A; the most typical among Japanese, as noted in Sanrio's profile of Kitty), and exact anthropometric dimensions (in mock centimeters, height, face width, length of head, distance between eyes, length of nose, width and length of torso, length of feet). These details help make Kitty real. We learn her full name, Kitty White, along with members of her family: father George (a salaryman with a sense of humor), mother Mary (a housewife who likes to bake apple pies), identical twin sister Mimmy (who wears her bow over her right ear, while Kitty wears hers over her left), grandfather Anthony (who paints as a hobby), and grandmother Margaret (who makes puddings). (It seems more than coincidence that the names of her parents and grandparents echo those of British royalty.) We learn that Hello Kitty's hobbies include tennis, piano (with ambitions to become a classical pianist like her mother, supported by her parents who purchased a grand piano for the family in 1981),[3] eating cookies her sister Mimmy bakes, tending to her goldfish, and playing with her childhood "boyfriend" (*hatsukoi*, first romance) Dear Daniel. Among other things, we learn that the country Hello Kitty most likes to travel to is Japan, where she can wear a kimono. Why does Kitty have no mouth? Sanrio's answer: Kitty has no mouth, so that she may better reflect the feelings of those who look upon her. Sanrio points out that in earlier cartoons, Kitty did have a mouth, but now she does not (Sanrio 2009a: 42).

The first thing to note is that Sanrio creates and uses these biographical details in a process of constant "real-making." Information acts as a narrative force, providing details that make Hello Kitty (and her family and friends) not simply a plush logo but a being with agency. Through these fictionalized details, *kyarakutā* become true, individuated characters with whom one may form relationships, a logic used by other companies such as Mattel (U.S.) for Barbie.

Secondly, in all of these myriad details, Sanrio presents Hello Kitty as a middle-class British girl living the quintessential, comfortable life in a white family, coincidentally named White. The only elements that tie her to Japan are her blood type and an appreciation for certain things Japanese, such as wearing kimono. The inherent ironies of such a fictive possibility do not faze her Japanese consumers in the least. Hello Kitty speaks to their own cosmopolitan possibilities in a Japanese version of the global world, enhanced by the horizon of both Sanrio's and consumers' imagination. Thus Hello Kitty is neither Japanese nor a cat; she is a *kyarakutā*.

The details of Hello Kitty's biography position her exactly where she was always intended, as a global figure. In short, an important component of Hello Kitty's middle-aged achievement lies in her popularity outside Japan. She has received affirmation from American female celebrities—Lady Gaga, Mariah Carey, Paris and Nicky Hilton, Britney Spears, and Cameron Diaz, all caught sporting Hello Kitty. Sanrio stores are found on every continent: New York, Paris, Bogota, Seoul, Shanghai, Moscow, Dubai, and Oman, to name a few. Several foreign locations warrant their own special goods (*meibutsu*), including Hawai'i (Hello Kitty as hula girl, pineapple, and more) and San Francisco (Hello Kitty as the Golden Gate Bridge). Hello Kitty's strong connection to Asia proves a critical stronghold, as exemplified in the opening of a Hello Kitty theme park in China (Zhejiang Province) in 2014.

Reaching Back: Nostalgia as Social Communication

Through images, one can chart Kitty's transition from the original 1974 seated Kitty in red, white, and blue, to the suddenly trendy 1987 "mono-tone Kitty" with Kitty in white outline against a solid black background, to the predominantly pink Kitty of the 1990s, to the thematic black, white, and pink Kitty of the late 2000s. The retrospective display of products includes key moments in product development, inevitably including the first coin purse, and quickly moving to the plethora of goods through the years. Just as 1987 produced the black and white Kitty image, so, too, did products from that year onward include more and more goods for young adults; these include black bikini underwear (1987), neckties for men (1996; to give as a present), a pink cellphone holder (1997), a pink sake set (1999), a bottle opener for wine (2002), and a Fender guitar (2007).

There are more than objects at stake here. Rather, by sketching the historic arc of products and design, Sanrio traces the development of a Hello Kitty lifestyle. The book *Hello Kitty Memories* (Sanrio 2009b) displays the developing array of Hello Kitty objects for use by adults (primarily women) in home decor, tableware, cooking, cleaning, entertaining, and relaxing (e.g., aromatherapy). The *Hello Kitty 35th Anniversary Book* (2009a) illustrates "Yoga Kitty," with both Hello Kitty and a human model assuming poses. In short, these books present Hello Kitty as a lifestyle brand. Hello Kitty touches each aspect of her consumers' lives, from day to night. And if one began as a consumer of Hello Kitty in one's childhood, one's opportunities to cultivate the Hello Kitty lifestyle may extend well into adulthood.

Thus Kitty's history becomes one's own. This is why the Sanrio retrospective may speak with such poignancy to longtime fans. One may chart one's own life through Kitty products: each object serves as, in Marita Sturken's (1997: 9) words, a "technology of memory," each design a visual, Proustian madeleine. Because Hello Kitty does not get older, she can represent eternal, blissful childhood, the perpetual *shōjo*—in other words, one of the most powerful sources of nostalgia in Japan. This kind of nostalgia-making becomes nothing short of nostalgia-marketing, as Hello Kitty slips effortlessly into yet another basket of consumer desire. The beauty of Hello Kitty is that she never changes, yet never stays the same. Trading on the familiar, Sanrio's genius rests in always providing the consumer with something new to buy. This may be postmodern kitsch to some or ironic overload to others. But for the true believers (devotees, including many who have become Sanrio employees), nothing could be more blissful than to be surrounded by Hello Kitty images invoking one's *shōjo* past.

In fact, Sanrio takes memory seriously as a central part of its business and a key element in the affective labor of "social communication." Sanrio informally refers to what it does as "memory work" (*omoide no oshigoto*)—that is, the production of memories. "Memory work" involves more than a sense of the past; it includes deliberate manipulation of affect, resulting in a positive imaging of that past. Furthermore, "memory work" need not be restricted to a person's particular past, but may be fictionalized as a general sense of the past that Hello Kitty's consumers may or may not know firsthand. Sturken's (1997: 3) notion of cultural memory—that is, "memory that is shared outside the avenues of formal historical discourse yet is entangled with cultural products and imbued with cultural meaning"—informs our discussion. Here, the cultural product of Hello Kitty imbues a faux European storybook past with Japanese cultural meaning. This is memory as reworked image, marking someone else's past (more to the point, an imagined version of someone else's past) as one's own. The constructed past, then, becomes a resource for nostalgia, packaged and commodified, fairy-tale style. For example, one of Hello Kitty's 1985 product lines detailed as "memory work" in the anniversary book is named "Country Series." Here the "country" is the United States, and the memory is of cherry pies baked as part of life in San Francisco (dubbed "American lifestyle"). Sanrio physicalizes this "memory" in deep "cherry" reds, sepia-tone backgrounds with checkerboard patterning, and the English words, "Down Home; Kitty's best home cooking" (Sanrio 2009b: 86–87). This form of "memory work" creates and commodifies a fictive "American" past as nothing more than a style resource. Nostalgia thus works in two ways here—first, to pull the consumer back to her own childhood filled with Hello Kitty objects, and second, to remind us that those objects typically reference a storybook past set in England, with mothers who bake pies and fathers who tell jokes while smoking a pipe.

Hello Kitty's Continued Success

Nostalgia as a style resource situates Hello-Kitty-the-product as ever-the-same, ever-changing. The shifting retro feel of Hello Kitty deliberately places her outside of time and within the highly marketable realm of memory. This appeal—far more to adults, far less to children—demonstrates Hello Kitty's many reconfigurations from her original coin purse image. Indeed, she is all grown up, even as she remains a child. Through the disarming quality of *kawaii*, Hello Kitty embodies social communication itself, whether through gifts or stationery. That she does so with a global reach only adds to the luster and achievements of her more than forty years. What becomes this icon most? I argue that it is exactly Hello Kitty as enabler of social communication— bridging people through "heartfelt communication," providing the affective labor of *kawaii kyarakutā*, appealing simultaneously to female children and to adult women in their shared girlhood, spanning generations of consumers, leaping oceans to transnational fame, transcending years through nostalgia— that drives Sanrio's marketing claims of gendered iconicity. At the very least, Hello Kitty proves the potency of this repersonalization of everyday objects via the aesthetic of *kawaii* as this commodified form of social communication sweeps through Japan and elsewhere. Through Hello Kitty and other cute *kyarakutā*, *kawaii* has come to rock the world.

Notes

1 Much of this chapter was originally published as "Reach Out and Touch Someone: Thinking Through Sanrio's Social Communication Empire," *Japanese Studies* 30,1, pp. 23–36. www.tandfonline.com. I would like to thank the journal editors for permitting the republication.

2 An inversion of the Hello Kitty glasses are Hello Kitty contact lenses, which turn the wearer's pupils into small images of Hello Kitty's head.

3 Many of these hobbies and personality traits reflect those of Yamaguchi Yuko, Hello Kitty's third designer (since 1980).

PART II
Television

4 The Grotesque Hero

Depictions of Justice in *Tokusatsu* Superhero Television Programs

Hirofumi Katsuno

Introduction

In the beginning of the 1970s, the *tokusatsu* (live-action) superhero genre dominated children's television programming. Although this genre had been part of children's television culture in Japan since the mid-1950s, the first half of the 1970s was its golden age. Japanese television companies produced at least forty-five distinct *tokusatsu* programs between 1970 and 1975, some of which competed for viewers during the same time slots on different television channels. But the "*tokusatsu* boom" (*būmu*, or large-scale fad that bursts on the scene) of this period could not simply be characterized as a mere programming trend. Rather, two distinctive elements of early 1970s *tokusatsu* hooked children: (1) these superheroes underwent *henshin* (metamorphosis) and (2) their post-*henshin* figures were marked by *igyō* (grotesque and monstrous) characteristics that turned them into anthropomorphic animals, insects, and machines, whose ontological ambiguity deviated from the conventional image of superheroes and called into question earlier absolutist depictions of justice.

This chapter explores the golden age of *tokusatsu* superhero programs in the socio-political context of the early 1970s, a time of momentous change for Japanese society. In the economic realm, the 1973 oil crisis ended the period of high economic growth that raised living standards for most of the country since the late 1950s, begetting the ideological myth of Japan as "a nation of middle-class people." More broadly, this entailed the demise of the legacy of the wartime regime, as the high-growth economy was fundamentally a continuation of wartime political and legal systems (Yoshimi 2009). In the political realm, the 1972 Aasama-Sansō Incident, a ten-day hostage standoff between police and the United Red Army, is typically considered to mark an end to the "age of politics" whose heyday in the 1960s saw a series of ideological struggles, from student riots to institutional conflicts over the U.S.-Japan Security Treaty and the anti-Vietnam War movement (see Chapter 24). Viewing this turbulent period, researchers and critics state that 1970 was the approximate year in which Japanese society experienced a major socio-cultural change from modern to postmodern; this shift is characterized by the declining credibility of modern grand narratives that united the postwar Japanese nation (Mita 1996; Miyadai 2011; Ōsawa 1996; Ōtsuka 1996).

This chapter addresses how the early 1970s *tokusatsu* superhero genre reacted to this paradigm shift, particularly in its depiction of justice. Since the debut of the prototypical *tokusatsu* superhero franchise *Moonlight Mask* (*Gekkō Kamen*) in 1958, the genre had centered on invincible superheroes and had portrayed justice in absolutist terms.[1] As these superheroes were immensely popular with children, profiting corporations through viewership and merchandizing, this trend served both ideological and commercial ends. However, the state of socio-political flux from the 1960s to early 1970s upset the superheroes' identity as the embodiment of justice. An early sign of this emerged in the *Ultraman* series in 1966 and reached a critical point with the rise of the 1970s grotesque superheroes. In this chapter, I first provide a historical overview of the pre-golden age *tokusatsu* superheroes, beginning in the mid-1950s. I then discuss the 1970s "*tokusatsu* boom," specifically focusing on *Kikaider*, also known in English as *Android Kikaider* (*Jinzō Ningen Kikaidā*, broadcast 1972–1973) as a paradigmatic series. This show pivots on themes of relativized justice and self-uncertainty, which continue to recur in Japanese popular culture. In other words, my analysis suggests this transitional period of the 1970s is an origin of critical concerns in Japan's superhero genre that continue to the present day.

Tokusatsu **Superheroes Before the 1970s**

Although *tokusatsu* is an abbreviation of "*tokushu satsuei*" (special effects), it more generally refers to live-action movies and television programs that rely on such effects to portray imaginary worlds. While special effects have been in use since the early days of film history, they were a prominent aspect of the Japanese cinema industry during the 1950s and the early 1960s. The field's leading expert was Tsuburaya Eiji, co-creator of the *Godzilla* series and producer of *Ultraman*, known as the "God of *tokusatsu*" for his special effects in over 150 films. Among the techniques he developed from the 1930s to the 1960s, "suitmation," the use of human actors playing monstrous nonhuman characters in costumes surrounded by scale model scenery, brought a distinctive flavor to Japanese popular culture (Allison 2006). Tsuburaya originally introduced suitmation in Tōhō's *Godzilla* series to simulate *kaijū* (giant monsters), and it became an essential element of superhero television programs when Tsuburaya used it in *Ultraman* in 1966. This effect helped establish *tokusatsu* shows' dramatic form, in which each thirty-minute episode contains two distinctive types of scenes: (1) the main dramatic storyline with non-suited actors and (2) the superhero's post-*henshin* action scenes with fully costumed "suit actors."

The live-action superhero genre in Japan can be traced back beyond *Ultraman* to the 1957 film *Starman* (a.k.a. *Super Giant*, *Kōtetsu no kyojin*), directed by Iishii Teruo and produced by Shin-Tōhō (for more on Shin-Tōhō, see Chapter 19). *Starman* was produced in light of the popularity of the 1956 premiere of *Adventures of Superman*, the first Japanese television series featuring the comic book superhero Superman, in terms of its hero's name, costume (tights and a cape), and storyline—an alien superhero fighting evil organizations to maintain peace on Earth. The film's success spawned a popular series with nine individual films between 1957 and 1959 by Iishii and other directors. A year after *Starman*—and just five years after Japan's first television broadcast on KRT (now TBS) in 1953—the first *tokusatsu* superhero program appeared: Senkosha's *Moonlight Mask (Gekkō Kamen)*. In this smash hit show, the pistol-wielding hero in a white turban and sunglasses performed a characteristic jump from great heights onto a moving motorcycle. Although the show established a model for the Japanese *tokusatsu* superhero as a "masked-biker superhero," it was cancelled in 1959 after a child attempting to emulate Moonlight Mask's stunt fell to his death (Abel 2014: 199).

To produce a Japanese superhero that could compete with Superman, *Moonlight Mask*'s creator and scriptwriter Kawauchi Kōhan got inspiration from the image of Moonlight Bodhisattva (Gekkō Bosatsu) that serves Yakushi Nyōrai (Medicine Buddha). Kawauchi's basic idea is that the superhero is not the embodiment of justice but instead an "ally of justice." These words appear in the show's theme song, also written by Kawauchi: "That guy, Moonlight Mask is an ally of justice, a good guy" (Abel 2014: 190). This "ally" status is illustrated in "Chapter Mammoth Kong" (third season, fifth episode) when Moonlight Mask tells members of an evil organization: "Killer gangs, I know you are trying to drive the people in Japan to the depths of despair by murdering one national leader after another. But … however you intend to plunge Japan into chaos, you will wind up with nothing… You would never understand why … it is because Japanese people love and cherish their native land" (Funatoko 2008). Here, Moonlight Mask suggests the common people, who identify justice with patriotism, are society's true protectors, and that he appears only when villains threaten the people's justice. In this sense, depictions of the superhero-as-ally potentially make audiences realize that justice is their responsibility.

At the same time, Moonlight Mask's standpoint as an ally of justice shows the difficulty of depicting a Japanese brand of justice, as embodied by a new superhero, on 1950s Japanese television. As Jonathan Abel indicates, the hero's origins and true identity remain unknown, symbolizing 1950s Japanese uncertainty about justice:

> The mask does not hide an inner face or truth of postwar justice, but rather it is itself the truth. The mask represents the contemporary perception of postwar justice—a masked justice that cannot be easily located, identified, or named.
>
> (Abel 2014: 191–192)

Thus the first *tokusatsu* superhero program left the location of justice ambiguous. In the context of 1950s Japan—undergoing national reconstruction as an

American-influenced capitalist democracy in a new bipolar world order, in which several of its neighbors became communist—the ambiguous location of justice reflected the sense that "postwar justice originated from abroad and ... concomitant doubts about the possibility of a truly native Japanese justice" (Abel 2014: 188).

This primary stage of *tokusatsu* history overlaps with the heyday of "the era of ideals," a division of socio-political periodization of Japan's postwar history originally proposed by sociologist Mita Munesuke (1996) and later developed by sociologist Ōsawa Masachi (1996). According to Ōsawa, the era of ideals was from 1945 to 1970, when people throughout Japan shared the goal of rebuilding their devastated country by realizing the American way of life.[2] In this socio-cultural environment marked by growing American power, justice, too, was considered to come from an external, idealized America. The masked superhero as an "ally of justice" represented ambivalence between the lament for Japan's postwar powerlessness and the preparation to reinvent justice under the American-influenced ideals of human rights, democracy, and peace.

The challenge of depicting justice in *tokusatsu* superhero programs reached a critical point in 1966 with the creation of *Ultraman* (*Urutoraman*) by Tsuburaya Eiji. As the film industry declined, the "God of *tokusatsu*" first brought his distinctive, revolutionary techniques to television programs earlier that year with the TBS series *Ultra Q* (*Urutora kyū*). Bringing movie-quality production values to a weekly television schedule, this smash hit sparked the first television-based *kaijū* boom. Influenced by American science fiction television programs such as *The Twilight Zone* and *The Outer Limits*, the series follows the stories of three human characters investigating supernatural phenomena caused by *kaijū*. Building on this dramatic structure, Tsuburaya created the sequel series *Ultraman*, introducing the idea of a giant superhero that fights against *kaijū* and aliens to protect Earth. This character became so popular that the series continued intermittently from 1966 to 2006, during which fifty different Ultramen appeared, and the franchise still inspires new productions.

Ultraman is a forty-meters-tall space ranger from the "Land of Light" in Nebula M78. He usually disguises himself as an ordinary-sized human, Hayata Shin, who works to defend Earth as a member of the "Science Search Special Team." Once confronted with a crisis, Hayata transforms into a red-and-silver giant being and fights giant monsters to protect Earth. Sculptor Narita Tōru designed Ultraman to embody justice, modeling Ultraman's face upon the "archaic smile" of Miroku Bosatsu (Maitreya Bodhisattva) and his streamlined silver body on spaceships (Kashiwara 2013: 87). While the spaceship symbolized the latest technology, Ultraman's red part evokes a feeling of vitality.

Despite the destruction they wreak, *kaijū* in the *Ultraman* series are not simply cast as evil. As with Godzilla,[3] these giant monsters appear as natural phenomena, raising questions about their interrelationship with the issues causing their appearance (Tsutsui 2004). In many cases, *kaijū* are mysterious giant creatures living in unpeopled, remote areas of Earth since ancient times, but the modern logic of anthropocentric development and exploitation leads to their disturbance by and conflict with humans.

Ultraman's narrative structure shapes justice in conjunction with the exercise of public authority. Critic Uno Tsunehiro (2011: 166) argues that Ultraman, a titan that helps human beings to expel giant city-destroying *kaijū*, functions as an analogy of state-sponsored violence, similar to Orwell's personification of state power as "Big Brother" in *1984*. Such totalizing and moralizing symbolizations of states as giant superheroes and *kaijū* became more explicit in the series *Ultraseven* (TBS, 1967–1968). Ultraseven, a giant extraterrestrial from the same planet as Ultraman, works with the Ultra Guard of the Territorial Defense Force to combat highly intelligent alien invaders. From Uno's viewpoint, this schema in which a giant superhero fights against giant foreign invaders represents a total warfare scenario in which the transcendental Big Brother stands up against invasion by foreign nations. As other critics have also indicated, it allegorizes the U.S-Japan Security Treaty in the Cold War's bipolar world order: The Science Search Special Team and the Ultra Guard represent Japan's Self-Defense Force, while Ultraman and Ultraseven represent U.S. forces in Japan, and the invasive *kaijū* are Communist powers including the Soviet Union and China (Kiridōshi 1993; Satō 1992).

However, the American-centered socio-political system represented in the structure of the early *Ultraman* and *Ultraseven* series became anachronistic and dysfunctional during the strained social conditions of the 1960s. Throughout the 1960s, Japanese society grew increasingly skeptical of the United States because of the struggle over the U.S.-Japan Security Treaty, the Vietnam War, and environmental problems. Particularly, the prolonged Vietnam War increased the inconsistency between views of the United States as the bestower of the normative model of peace, democracy, and abundance and as an executor of self-approving justice through war. In this liminal social condition, it became difficult to depict Ultraman as the embodiment of absolutist justice, given his allegorical meaning as U.S. troops. The gap between the two visions of the United States led *Ultraman* scriptwriters to write self-critical episodes about Ultraman's absolutist justice and the society that he protects (Uno 2011).[4] This trend became more explicit in *Ultraseven*, which included various episodes focused on the dark side of postwar modernization under the strong influence of the United States, such as nuclear development, territorial dispute, and problems with ethnic minorities and pollution. For instance, at a crucial moment in the twenty-sixth episode, "The 8,000 Megaton Mistake," Ultraseven's human alter ego, Moroboshi Dan, criticizes the Terrestrial Defense Force's stance, "Weapons breed peace," implicitly criticizing the United States' nuclear arms race with the Soviet Union.

Kikaider and the Golden Age of *Tokusatsu* Superheroes

The internal contradictions that emerged in the *Ultra* series cooled the 1960s fervor for giant *tokusatsu* superheroes, but a different type of superhero soon emerged. Starting with the smash hit *Masked Rider* (*Kamen Raidā*), broadcast from 1971 to 1973, Toei produced strings of titles in collaboration with the legendary manga creator Ishinomori Shōtarō. The superheroes in these works are not giant but life sized. They transform into *igyō* (grotesque) figures, often hybrids of human and nonhuman creatures, including insects, animals, and machines. The idea of the superhero's transformation had been a cliché from the beginning of this genre, but the 1970s phenomenon later called the "*henshin* (metamorphosis) boom" distinctively emphasized the visual sequence of metamorphosis with a distinctive pose that signaled the moment of transformation. This pose drew on the kabuki theater tradition of *mie* and was mimicked by Japanese youngsters on playgrounds.

Kikaider was paradigmatic of Ishinomori's work in the 1970s *henshin* boom, during which he was director, author, and/or scriptwriter for over twenty *tokusatsu* superhero series. Following the huge success of *Masked Rider*, Toei produced forty-three episodes of *Kikaider*. Toei planned it as an original series with Ishinomori as the writer and character designer. At the same time as the television show aired, Ishinomori drew a manga version for the magazine *Weekly Shōnen Sunday* (published by Shogakukan since 1959 as a competitor to *Weekly Shōnen Jump*), which then influenced the program's directors and scriptwriters. Thus the production of *Kikaider* took place at the confluence of various creativities and intentions in conjunction with the "media mix" (*media mikkusu*) marketing strategy pervasive in the post-1960s Japanese entertainment industry, in which a text or character simultaneously appears in multiple media outlets such as television, comics, music, and toys[5] (see Chapters 22 and 23).

Kikaider plotlines center on an ongoing epic battle between Kikaider and DARK, a villainous organization attempting to conquer the world with robotic monsters and android soldiers. At the beginning of the series, DARK captures Dr. Kōmyōji, a robotics expert, and his assistant and daughter Mitsuko, to force them to build robotic warriors. While imprisoned by DARK, Kōmyōji secretly creates a conscience circuit in Jirō, a motorcycle-riding, guitar-playing, denim-clad android who transforms into the red-and-blue superhero Kikaider. Professor Gill, the head of DARK, discovers what Kōmyōji is up to and stops him before he can install the final piece of the conscience circuit, so Kikaider's conscience remains incomplete. Kikaider rescues Mitsuko, and they escape from DARK. Kōmyōji also manages to escape from Gill but suffers amnesia and wanders from town to town in a mental fog, taking jobs including gardening, driving a cab, and bartending. *Kikaider* follows Jirō's journey with Mitsuko and her younger brother Masaru as they track down their father.

The core element of *Kikaider* is the conscience circuit: the robot's heart. DARK robots created by Dr. Kōmyōji are in the condition of *tabula rasa*, simply following Professor Gill's orders without reflection. Jirō's conscience circuit is a retrofit that turns him into Kikaider: a robotic hero of justice that acts on his own moral judgment, rather than at human command. However, because the circuit is incomplete, Professor Gill can use his evil, mind-control flute to bring Jirō back to DARK, causing Jirō excruciating pain as he is torn between good and evil. Jirō's ambivalent identity is represented by his grotesque, post-*henshin* asymmetrical appearance as Kikaider: his blue-colored right side symbolizes good whereas his red-colored left side reveals evil. The exposed panels on the right side of his head emphasize his incompleteness.

Kikaider episodes follow a conventional format: (1) Professor Gill introduces a robotic monster to perpetrate a criminal plot. (2) Mitsuko and Masaru get involved in the sinister plan when searching for Dr. Kōmyōji. (3) The robotic monster and android soldiers attack and try to capture them but are interrupted by Jirō, who appears in a high place, playing familiar guitar music. (4) Jirō drives off the destructive monster and androids and rides off on his yellow motorcycle. (5) Mitsuko and Masaru continue to search for their father but get attacked again and Jirō reappears to save them. (6) Professor Gill in the distance targets Jirō's incomplete conscience circuit with his evil flute. Jirō suffers but manages to find a way to block the sound and performs the *henshin* sequence: "Change! Switch on! 1-2-3!!" When the transformation is complete, the lively Kikaider theme song begins playing. (7) Kikaider smashes the foe with his signature final move. (8) After saving the day, Jirō once again rides off on his motorcycle, leaving Mitsuko and Masaru behind.

In this predictable formula, the faulty conscience circuit constitutes a cliché that puts the superhero in crisis and forces him to regain himself to win, exciting viewers, especially children. The sorts of serious political issues treated by the late 1960s *Ultra* series never carry weight on *Kikaider*; rather, like other 1970s Toei superhero shows, it is pure action entertainment. As Uno (2011) suggests in his analysis of *Kamen Rider*, this contrast partially derives from the different backgrounds of their production teams: Tsuburaya developed his *tokusatsu* techniques while making propaganda films for the war under Tōhō,[6] whereas Toei members had made samurai movies. Toei *tokusatsu*'s most distinctive features are martial arts combat scenes by costumed "suit actors." Their theatrical combat techniques originate in kabuki's *tate* stage fighting, later incorporated into the swordfight choreography of samurai action films.

Nevertheless, *Kikaider* is not a simple, didactic show. Rather, over the course of the series, it provokes open-ended, reflexive questions regarding the location of justice, which are attributable to its protagonist being an *igyō* superhero with an incomplete conscience circuit. The grotesque characteristics central to the 1970s *tokusatsu* superhero reverse the conventional relationship between superhero and villain. In pre-1970 superhero narratives, villains brought the drama. Superheroes have civilian personas, but when evil powers threaten society's peace and stability, they become superheroes and restore social order. In these worlds where right and wrong are clear-cut, villains are basically external menaces, such as invasive alien species and international groups of assassins or spies.

In the case of Ishinomori's superheroes, however, the drama arises from the superheroes' *igyō* backgrounds, as robots, cyborgs, and mutants inhabiting an ambiguous space between human and nonhuman, good and evil. Jirō/ Kikaider's *igyō* background is strengthened by the fact that he is a creation of an evil organization, compelled to rebel against his intended purpose. While Ultraman's heroism is transcendental intervention by an external "Other" from the "Land of Light," Kikaider's inter-clan conflict setting blurs dualistic boundaries between good and evil.[7] In other words, *Kikaider* redefines the raison d'etre of the superhero and the location of justice by depicting a hero who suffers from internal conflict.

It is through this betwixt and between-ness that Kikaider—and the 1970s *igyō* superheroes—evokes a new type of thinking similar to the sociocultural role of the monster. Jeffrey Jerome Cohen argues the monster embodies:

> a certain cultural moment—of a time, a feeling, and a place... A construct and a projection, the monster exists only to be read ... the monster signifies something other than itself: it is always displacement, always inhabits the gap between the time of upheaval that created it and the moment into which it is received, to be born again.
>
> Cohen (1996: 4)

In other words, cultures produce monsters when changes force them to reevaluate their internal values. Following this logic, the early 1970s *igyō* superheroes do not embody justice. Rather, their post-*henshin* ambiguous bodies reflect the social confusion about justice at that transitional time. The "age of politics" ended with the 1972 Asama-Sansō incident, and the myth of Japan's endless economic growth ended with the first oil shock in 1973. In Ōsawa's periodization, these events were linked to the transition from the era of ideals to the era of fiction, in which individual values and identities are diversified as society becomes defined as consumer markets. As the grand narratives of modern nation state became less effective, grotesque heroes appeared, asking people to reevaluate their cultural assumptions about justice.

Robots with hearts appear in a long list of Japanese media texts, starting with Tezuka Osamu's *Astro Boy* (*Tetsuwan Atomu*), a serialized manga from 1951 to 1968 and an animated television series on Radio Tokyo (now TBS) from 1963 to 1966. One of the best-recognized robotic fantasy heroes in the history of Japanese popular culture, Astro Boy fights monsters and bandits in the name of peace with his 100,000 horsepower strength powered by a nuclear reactor (Shimotsuki and Shida 2003: 58). Yet he became popular not only because of his physical strength but also because he is highly intelligent and emotive, able to see into people and recognize whether their hearts are good or evil. He is a moral agent with a strong sense of justice that continually spurs him to leap to the defense of both humans and robots in quandaries that often involve high technology.

Astro Boy's heroic image in the televised anime version as an android with feelings that helps mankind was shaped by and linked with the high growth era's techno-nationalist uncritical celebration of science and technology. He became a symbol etched into the national consciousness as the embodiment of expectations and dreams in the era of ideals. In contrast, Jirō's heroic stature was not formulated in relation to national symbols. His story takes place in relatively closed situations surrounding the Kōmyōji family and DARK. Also, while Astro Boy is undisputedly a "child of science," as it says in the lyrics of the animated series (Mushi Production 2008), Jirō struggles with his identity as a product of science and technology.

Jirō's distress will not be resolved by becoming "complete." He has several chances to get his conscience circuit fixed by Mitsuko, but he refuses, instead coming to terms with himself. For example, in Episode Three, Mitsuko tries to fix Jirō:

JIRŌ: I'm happy just as I am. It's unnecessary.

MITSUKO: Don't stop me! This was Father's wish.

JIRŌ: Dr. Kōmyōji's conscience circuit may be incomplete. But I can compensate with my will. I will be fine.

(Kitamura et al. 2004)

In this conversation, Jirō positions his "will" in opposition to his conscience circuit. Here, the will works metaphorically to sharply distinguish Jirō/Kikaider from pre-1970s superheroes. By emphasizing that his will is the foundation of his actions, Jirō implies that to be equipped with a complete conscience circuit would ironically reduce him to an ideological puppet, for it is merely a replaceable program of social norms and morals. On the contrary, Jirō expresses his intention to choose good independently, which implies the potential to commit evil. In short, this decision leads to his battle against himself—specifically against his vulnerability to Gill's flute—as well as against DARK's robots. Paradoxically, Jirō attains heroic stature by refusing to become an absolute superhero—an ideological puppet. Thus by focusing on Jirō's internal struggle, *Kikaider* is revolutionary, uncovering the illusory nature of the modern justice that was unquestioningly embodied by pre-1970s superheroes.

This respect is most evident in his relationship with the rival robot Hakaider. Hakaider was made in order to destroy (*hakai*) Kikaider. He only appears in the last five episodes but is recognized as one of the most popular villains in the history of *tokusatsu* because of his strong antihero characteristics (Katsuno 2006: 175–176). Hakaider's cultic status resulted in the production of the original *tokusatsu* film *Mechanical Violator Hakaider* (*Jinzō ningen Hakaidā*), directed by Amemiya Keita in 1995. Hakaider is a cyborg equipped with an evil circuit, countering Jirō's conscience circuit. He is black from head to toe, is an expert gunslinger, and rides a 750cc Kawasaki motorcycle. His living part is Dr. Kōmyōji's brain, revealed within Hakaider's transparent head. Hakaider was programmed to be the ultimate Kikaider killer and considers this to be his personal agenda, regardless of the wayward tactics assigned by his master. Hakaida can be read as Kikaider's younger brother, because he, too, was created by Kōmyōji. However, he is also in a sense Kikaider's father, as he is technically a form of Kōmyōji himself. Kikaider cannot kill Hakaider or Kōmyōji will die, but if he does not fight back, he will fall victim to his enemy's tenacity.

In Episode Forty-Two, when Kikaider is destroyed by another DARK android (although Mitsuko later fixes him), Hakaider loses control, saying, "What am I? What purpose was I created for? .... What is left for me to live for?! What is my purpose? How will I live from now on? .... I despise Professor Gill for creating me!" (Kitamura et al. 2004). Hakaider's desperation demonstrates that he ironically fulfills the conditions of the conventional superhero: he fights the presupposed opponent without reflecting on the justice of his actions. In this sense, this scene of Hakaider losing his purpose shows the fate of conventional superheroes that inevitably self-destruct with the decline of their puppeteers: politically-shaped grand narratives of absolutist justice.

Concluding Thoughts

The early 1970s boom of *henshin tokusatsu* superhero programs cooled with the end of Ishinomori's *Kamen Rider Stronger* (*Kamen Raidā sutorongā*) series in 1975, but the *tokusatsu* superhero genre continued even as the focus of children's media moved to anime. Toei revived the *Masked Rider* series for NET in 2000, after a decade of inactivity, with *Kamen Rider Kuuga* (*Masked Rider Kūga*), which has been followed by fifteen other series (as of 2015). Among these, some series intentionally tackled *Kikaider*'s main theme: self-uncertainty in the face of relativized justice. For example, in *Kamen Rider Ryuki* (*Masked Rider Ryūki*, broadcast in 2002), thirteen different Masked Riders battle each other to fulfill their own wishes. Here, there is neither absolute evil nor transcendental justice but only individual desire. A similar trend is recognizable in Hollywood's "superhero decade" of the 2000s (Gray II and Kaklamanidou 2011: 1). Unlike the traditional superhero genre, lines between good and evil are blurred in the new millennium. Ostensibly villains have their own reasons and justices. The global tendency toward the relativization of justice seems to be triggered directly by the ever-increasing moral panic since the attacks of 9/11 (Gray II and Kaklamanidou 2011: 1). And yet, on a larger level, this relativization is grounded in the diversification of contact zones that accompanies the globalized social condition. In the light of this social fragmentation, the single master narrative of the modern nation state undergoes liquefaction (Bauman 2000), disrupting absolutist justice. In this postmodern, liquid society, superheroes lack a unified, self-evident justice, but must navigate multiple conceptions of justice. In this sense, the philosophical underpinnings of the *igyō* superhero in the transformative period were by no means just a temporary phenomenon. Rather, as embodiments of relativized justice, these grotesque heroes were the seeds for what have become enduring trends in Japanese popular culture.

Notes

1 The trajectory of superhero stories can be further traced back to *Golden Bat* (*Ōgon Batto*), which originally debuted as a *kamishibai* (picture-story show) in 1931. (See Chapter 31.)
2 Based on the idea that the order of reality is always constituted in relation to its counter-reality, Mita (1996) periodizes Japan's postwar history into the following three divisions according to the dominant mode of counter-reality of each era: (1) the era of ideals from 1945 to 1960; (2) the era of dreams from 1960 to 1970; and (3) the era of fiction from 1970 to 1995. In reaction to Mita's periodization, Ōsawa (1996) regarded the era of ideals and that of dreams as a continuum—more specifically, taking the era of dreams as a transitional period to the following era of fiction—and redefined the period between 1945 and 1970 as the era of ideals.
3 There is a "direct" connection between Godzilla and Ultraman, as the suit of Jirass, a *kaijū* that appears in the *Ultraman* episode "The Mysterious Dinosaur Base," is actually a modified 1964 Godzilla suit.
4 The main scriptwriter Kinjo Tetsuo was a native of Okinawa, a key staging area for U.S. air power during the Vietnam War.
5 In response to the success of the *tokusatsu* version, Toei produced the subsequent series *Kikaider 01* (1973–1974), which was followed by *Android Kikaider: The Animation* (2000–2001) and *Kikaider 01: The Animation* (2001). Most recently, the original *Kikaider* series was remade into a movie called *Kikaider Reboot* (*Kikaidā Reboot*) by Shimoyama Ten in 2014.
6 His best-known work as special effects director is *The War at Sea from Hawai'i to Malay* (*Hawai Mare oki kaisen*) (1942).
7 The basic storyline of the *Kamen Rider* series is also an inter-clan conflict (Uno 2011).

5 Tokyo Love Story

Romance of the Working Woman in Japanese Television Dramas[1]

Alisa Freedman

Japanese Television Dramas and Working Women

Since their development in their current format in the early 1990s as a means to attract female viewers in their twenties, Japanese primetime television dramas—known commonly as "*dorama*" (the Japanese pronunciation of "drama")[2]—have featured working women. While most plots involve the pursuit of love, scenes of work are integral to narrative structures and character development. Even police procedurals, medical dramas, and serials based on *shōjo* manga (comics for girls) portray women employed outside the home. The *dorama* most watched by Japanese audiences older than age twenty-five and those that continue to attract global fans present daily lives of independent women working in Tokyo. These fictional protagonists enact fantasies about female professionals while depicting real issues facing the generations they represent. Viewers may not want to be these characters, but perhaps they can see aspects of themselves in them or aspire to their confidence and coolness.

While various television categories of working women have emerged, the narratives through which they have been portrayed support the family as the nation's backbone and work as a rewarding, necessary part of life. *Dorama* cannot take controversial stances as easily as novels, fine arts, and other media due to the need for mass audiences, advertisers, and state support of commercial networks. Yet *dorama* express women's choices empathetically and thereby are a barometer of the emotional impact of historical change.

My approach, which combines cultural history and genre studies and focuses on narratives, is twofold: I overview working women on Japanese dramas and survey commonalities in their potrayals, especially from 1990 to 2017. What has not changed is as illuminating as what has: both reveal how *dorama* negotiate social norms. I then analyze *Tokyo Love Story* (*Tokyo rabu sutōrī*, Fuji Television, January-March 1991), a seminal series that both marks a turning point in television history and propagates patriarchal views toward women's life choices. *Tokyo Love Story* had many television firsts: it was one of the first *dorama* to be based on manga, to attract global fans, and to have an unhappy ending in terms of love. The series was popular because of its exuberant protagonist Akana Rika (played by Suzuki Honami)—one of the first television heroines to aggressively pursue romance and take the initiative at work, actions intertwined in the story. Rika's love interest Nagao Kanji (played by Oda Yūji) is her coworker; a subtheme is how she fosters Kanji's career, helping him to become a capable "salaryman" (*sarariiman*), or middle-class businessman. Rika's inability to have all she desired, along with her positive attitude and exciting lifestyle, captivated audiences, thus encouraging empathy for a character type scorned in earlier programs. By watching *Tokyo Love Story* with hindsight, we can see the genesis of career women characters and television's unwavering promotion of the family. While packed with titles of *dorama* to serve as evidence and provide context, this chapter does not claim an exhaustive history of women on television but instead seeks to expose how television has used employment to assess women's successes in other aspects of their lives.

Working Women on Early Japanese Television

Since the beginning of television broadcasting, Japanese dramas have idealized the stability of the home and have positively presented characters who maintain the family. Japan's first television drama *Before Dinner* (*Yūgemae*, NHK) aired on April 13, 1940, thirteen years before NHK public television started regular programming in 1953 and fifteen years before the current five commercial networks—Nippon Television (NTV), Fuji Television, TBS, Asahi TV, and TV Tokyo—began in 1955. This twelve-minute family drama was shown on a television set in an electronics exhibit at Tokyo's Mitsukoshi department store. Although seen by few people, *Before Dinner* established two tropes of later drama series: the dominant mother figure and depiction of meals to show a family's social status and emotional health. In part because they demanded a regular viewing commitment unlike the earliest programming of one-shot concerts and other events where cameras could easily be present, serialized dramas did not develop until television became more affordable in the 1960s. By 1965, 90 percent of Japanese households had purchased televisions, and serialized programs had become a primary form of entertainment (Schilling 1997: 35).

Three kinds of serials that developed in the late 1950s and early 1960s, "home dramas" (*hōmu dorama*), "morning television novels" (*renzoku terebi shōsetsu*), and "historical dramas" (*taiga dorama*)—the latter two still thriving today—presented the notion that women, even as they work, should prioritize roles of wife and mother. Most prevalent between the 1960s and 1980s, home dramas, with a name derived from English, were American-inspired situation comedies (e.g., *I Love Lucy*, aired on NHK, 1957, and *The Donna Reed Show*, TBS, 1959), and Japanese films about middle- and working-class families (e.g., by directors Ozu Yasujirō and Naruse Mikio).[3] Home dramas often depicted the domestic lives of seemingly ordinary multi-generational families but did not mirror lived reality; for example, series about large families aired during the construction boom leading up to the 1964 Tokyo Olympics, when the numbers of youth moving alone to cities for employment and nuclear families living in apartments increased (Jonathan Clements and Motoko Tamamuro 2003: xxi). The broadcasting period was lengthened from thirty minutes to an hour, and extended families provided more plotlines (Sata and Hirahara 1991: 113). Female characters, especially mothers, ran small family businesses. Examples include the beauty shop owner in *Off the Bus Route* (*Basu dōri ura*, 1958–1963), NHK's first primetime serialized drama. Their work outside the home marks a difference with the women on American programs broadcast in Japan, who are happy being housewives and mothers, as evident in Donna Reed's glamorous housekeeping and Lucy's slapstick humor through repeated failed attempts at a range of jobs.

Since they first began in 1961 with *Daughter and Me* (*Musume to watashi*), NHK morning dramas, nicknamed "*asadora*" ("morning" [*asa*] plus "*dora*" from "*dorama*"), have focused on young women from undistinguished backgrounds who come of age by overcoming hardships, including those caused by poverty, war, and urbanization. In 1966, NHK made centering around a female protagonist a convention; TBS's *Pola Television Novels* (*Pola terebi shōsetsu*), airing from 1968 to 1986, followed suit. Set in either the historical past or the present moment, the heroine's struggles often parallel those of the nation. These dramas exemplify the ethic that hard work and perseverance will be rewarded that has propelled Japanese society. The most famous is *Oshin* (1983–1984), which followed the life of a poor woman who moves to the city, set before and immediately after World War II. Several *asadora* heroines train for traditional service professions (e.g., *ryokan okami* [inn manager] in *Perfect Blue Sky* [*Dondo hare*, 2007]) or to master classical Japanese male-dominated arts (e.g., *rakugo* comedic storytelling in *Chiritotechin*, 2007–2008). Others have been based on historical women who set modern trends and raised children alone after their husbands died. For example, *Carnation* (*Kānēshon*, 2011–2012) about Koshino Ayako and her three daughters, Hiroko, Junko, and Michiko, all of whom were fashion designers. To date, no *asadora* has depicted a university-educated career woman in contemporary Japan. Two of the most popular *asadora* have featured female doctors, but both were set in the past: *Ohanahan* (1966–1967) in the early twentieth century and *Dr. Ume-chan* (*Umechan sensei*, 2012) in the 1940s through 1960s (Harada 1983: 140–141). *Massan* (2014–2015) was the first NHK drama with a non-Japanese heroine (played by American Charlotte Kate Fox); yet the series was named after the male protagonist, based on the founder of the Nikka Whiskey Distilling Company, rooting the story in a Japanese man's success.

Yearlong *taiga* historical dramas, airing since 1964, are fictionalized biographies of people instrumental in Japanese national growth before the twentieth century. *Taiga dorama* present an array of jobs performed by elite women, which can be contrasted to the labor of lower- and middle-class women in home dramas and *asadora*. For example, women worked by supporting men in power, as exemplified by *Princess Atsu* (*Atsuhime*), one of the most popular television series of 2008, about wives and mistresses of the Tokugawa Shōgunate.

Working Women for the 1980s and 1990s

Home dramas, *asadora*, and *taiga dorama* turned women's employment into a television trope; primetime series of the 1980s and 1990s made jobs for young, unmarried women look fashionable. To boost ratings, commercial networks developed so-called "trendy dramas" (*torendi dorama*) in the mid-1980s, based on a series about characters in their early twenties living in the city. The emphasis was fashionable lifestyles ("trends") believed possible in Tokyo and on romance and friendship, as reflected in such titles as *I Want to Hold You!* (*Dakishimetai!*, Fuji Television, 1988) and *You're in Love!* (*Aishiatteru kai!*, Fuji Television, 1989); the female protagonists in both series are teachers. After a few flops, producers, including Fuji Television's Ōta Tōru who created *Tokyo Love Story*, revised the genre in the early 1990s, further emphasizing and diversifying romance. The resulting formula, outlined below, remains largely unchanged.

Dorama, which are divided into four seasons, air weekly for around eleven episodes (shorter than the older thirteen-week season) on nighttime slots that carry certain connotations. *Tokyo Love Story* helped associate Monday 9:00 on Fuji Television ("*getsuku*" or "*gekku*") with love stories (Matsumoto et al. 1999: 30–33). In part due to television's ties with singers (see Chapter 14), *dorama* have theme songs that climb the pop charts. Most are set in Tokyo, and characters have a favorite restaurant where they meet for heart-to-heart talks. Tokyo's impact upon the characters' mindsets is evident in the titles and the establishing shots. *Dorama* are successful because of the star power of their casts, who are often hired before scripts are finalized. Originally intended for domestic audiences, they have attracted worldwide attention, thanks more to efforts by fans than television networks, and have shaped global images of Japanese women (Iwabuchi 2004b). They have inspired and have been influenced by similar programs in Taiwan and Korea, a topic outside this chapter. *Tokyo Love Story* was arguably the first *dorama* to achieve an audience outside Japan.

Akana Rika: A New Kind of Working Woman

Tokyo Love Story aired from January to March 1991,[4] and its fame in Japan increased after it became popular in other parts of Asia. On Valentine's Day 1993, a special—a *dorama* convention that reviews the plot through flashbacks and shows what has happened to the characters—demonstrated how influential *Tokyo Love Story* had become.

Tokyo Love Story set trends for television. Following *Classmates* (*Dōkyūsei*, 1989), it was the second of several manga by Saimon Fumi to be adapted by Fuji Television when the global fad for Japanese manga was beginning.

Tokyo Love Story was serialized from 1988 in *Big Comic Spirits* (*Biggu komikku supirittsu*), a weekly magazine targeting men in their early twenties, and published as a bestselling four-volume set in 1990. *Tokyo Love Story* was one of the first dramas to portray characters who came to Tokyo and were not raised there. In *dorama* after *Tokyo Love Story*, women moved to Tokyo seeking love and work, the latter a means to the former, as evident in *Tokyo Elevator Girl* (*Tokyo erebētā gāru*, TBS, 1992). *Tokyo Love Story*'s series tagline was "In Tokyo, everyone becomes the star of a love story" (*Tokyo de wa dare mo rabu sutōrī no shujinkō ni naru*). This notion was reinforced by Oda Kazumasa's theme song "A Sudden Love Story" (*Rabu sutōrī wa totsuzen ni*), which sold more than 2.58 million copies (Oricon Style 2004). The theme song sequence, a *dorama* convention to introduce characters and convey their thoughts, presents Tokyo at work and play and shows fashionable technologies, including cars by series' sponsor Toyota. Several scenes display Tokyo under construction at a time when the real estate bubble was bursting. Rika gazes at the city when she needs to think, and her important conversations with Kanji occur on rooftops or in parks.

The plot follows one year in the romantic relationships of three women and two men, a character ensemble used in later series like *Long Vacation* (*Rongu bakēshon*, Fuji Television, 1996) and *Love Generation* (*Rabu jenerēshon*, Fuji Television, 1997) (Itō 2004: 29). Through camerawork, especially close-ups of her face, Rika is made the focus of viewers' empathy. Rika, who grew up in Los Angeles, is an important employee of the First Sales Division of Heart Sports. The story begins as she greets her new junior colleague, Nagao Kanji, at Haneda Airport. "Kanchi," as Rika nicknames him, has moved from Ehime on the island of Shikoku and feels unsure of his Tokyo future. From the start, Rika advises him in matters of love and work. Although she is having an affair with her married section head Waga, Rika soon falls for Kanji, who still has feelings for his former classmate Sekiguchi Satomi (played by Arimori Narimi), now a nursery school teacher. Satomi first chooses Kanji's classmate and rival Mikami Ken'ichi (played by Eguchi Yosuke), a womanizing medical student. Ken'ichi soon becomes enamored with his classmate Nagasaki Naoko (played by Sendo Akiho), who is engaged to a man chosen by her parents. Through coincidences possible only on *dorama*, the characters become friends and seek each other's love advice. Kanji and his classmates turn from twenty-three to twenty-four; Rika's age is undisclosed, but it is implied that she is older. Career women of later series were also older than their love interests, as seen in *Around 40: Demanding Women* (*Araundo 40 ~ chūmon no ooi onnatachi*, TBS, 2008). Much of the story revolves around Kanji's decision of whom to love and marry—Rika or Satomi. There are many differences with the manga, which is told from Kanji's perspective. Rika, mostly drawn angry at or trying to seduce Kanji, is a less sympathetic character. Having grown up in "African wilds," she cannot adjust to Tokyo manners (Saimon vol. 1 1990: 223). She and Kanji work at a small advertising firm owned by Waga.

Previous romantic leads were like Satomi. Their rivals were like Rika. Producer Ōta did the reverse and made the two a pair of opposites (as is true of Kanji and Ken'ichi), a notion reinforced through parallel scenes. Rika becomes more independent, as Satomi hesitates to make her own decisions. Both women initiate relationships with Kanji, who was cast in the role often given to female characters of having to choose between suitors. Rika successfully seduces Kanji after he sees Satomi kissing Ken'ichi. Her scandalous proposition—"Let's have sex." (*Ne, Kanchi, SEX shiyo*)—was reported in the real mass media. (Tokyo News Mook 1994: 580).

Tokyo Love Story launched a fad for "*junai*," or "pure love," stories in which all characters seek true love, a goal unobtainable to at least one of them. Ōta remarked that many dramas between 1991 and 1996, such as *Long Vacation*, included characters like "Kanji, the indecisive guy, Satomi, the hateful woman, and Rika, the poor adorable woman" (Ōta 2004: 74; Itō 2004: 29–30). The concept also appeared in bestselling novels like Murakami Haruki's 1987 *Norwegian Wood* (*Noruwei no mori*).

Rika and Kanji's romantic relationship develops while they work together, thus tying career and romance and promoting the popular notion that women can find spouses through their jobs. Rika balanced viewer expectations for female characters consumed with love but depicted them in a new light—as more competent at work than men. Rika is the one everyone at Heart Sports turns to in crises, and no men challenge her authority. She works overtime alone and fixes Kanji's mistakes. She goes on business trips, while Kanji remains in the Tokyo office. Yet the story focuses on how a man becomes a high-level salaryman in a prospering company. As I will explain, Rika quits the company, but Kanji becomes an integral member.

The key to understanding working women is in ending, which went against precedent in terms of love and work (Ishida 1999: 42). In the manga, Rika becomes pregnant with Waga's baby. Kanji urges her to choose Waga, who might leave his family for her. Kanji chooses Satomi but feels regrets; the story ends by Kanji asking readers if they see Rika somewhere in Tokyo to give her his regards, for she is the women he loved (Saimon vol. 4 1990: 226). In the drama, Rika, sensing that Kanji has chosen Satomi, accepts a transfer to the Los Angeles branch, making it easier for him to marry a woman whom it is implied will be a fulltime wife and mother. Rika feels she belongs more in the United States, where she believes people are as cheerful and as frank as she is. Women who chose work over love in 1990s *dorama* were often transferred to the United States. The ability to speak English has been a shorthand way to indicate sophistication on Japanese television since around the 1980s, but this plot device shows that the kind of women they represent was not an accepted norm. Rika wavers in her decision and asks Kanji to convince her not to go. He refuses, telling her that he does not want to impede her career, and, ultimately, Satomi prevents Kanji from meeting Rika to discuss their future.

Living in Tokyo provides opportunities for freedom in love and marriage on most *dorama*, but couples usually leave the city during turning points that determine the fate of their relationships. Rika takes an emergency vacation from work and goes to Ehime to carve her name next to Kanji's at his elementary school. Kanji joins her, and the two enjoy a nostalgic tour of places from his youth. Rika intentionally returns to Tokyo on a train earlier than the one she told Kanji she would take with him. She writes goodbye on a handkerchief and ties it to the Baishinji Station fence, a gesture later mimicked by fans. Rika cries (for the first time in the series) on the train, the sunset over the Inland Sea framed by the window behind her.

In a coda to the last episode, a common *dorama* convention, three years have passed. Kanji is confident at work. Waga compliments him, saying he is finally ready to bear the weight of Rika's love. Through their conversation, viewers learn that Rika quit the Los Angeles office after only six months for an undisclosed reason and has not been in touch with the company. Later that evening, Kanji and Satomi meet Rika after Ken'ichi and Naoko's wedding ceremony. As Satomi squats on the sidewalk to tie Kanji's shoelaces for him, he spots Rika in the crowd. Rika's pants suit and briefcase are signs that she is employed at a corporation. Rika calls him "Nagao-kun," showing their relationship has grown distant. Satomi allows Kanji and Rika a private reunion. As they talk on a rooftop, Rika states, with a reassuring smile, that she is accustomed to being on her own and refuses to give her contact information to Kanji, who is more reluctant to part. She merely suggests that someday they will meet again by chance, for Tokyo brings everyone together. Rika affectionately calls him "Kanchi" one last time and then confidently strides through Tokyo, swinging her briefcase, as the theme song plays. In the end, she gazes down at the city from the roof of Shinjuku's Nihon Seinenkan hotel. After an extreme close-up of her content face, the camera cuts to a panorama of the West Shinjuku financial and government district under construction, indicating that Rika realizes the possibilities for her in the city. In the special, Rika, still single, takes a business trip to Ehime with a junior male colleague (played by Tsutsui Michitaka) and revisits Kanji's elementary school. Memories of her relationship with Kanji flood back to her, but she voices no regrets. The drama, popular for bringing viewers to tears, ended on a hopeful note in terms of Rika's independence and career aspirations. Before returning to the broader implications of this point for Japanese television history, it is necessary to gain a more composite view of the influence of *Tokyo Love Story* on a generation that came of age with *dorama*.

Working Women for the *Dorama* Generation

The development of *dorama* has paralleled the growth of a generation born in the 1960s (Freedman and Iwata-Weickgenannt 2011). *Tokyo Love Story*'s target audience of female viewers in their twenties had entered the workforce shortly after the 1985 Equal Opportunity Law was being implemented to reduce the protective legislation restricting women's working hours and thus preventing them from high-level positions. Because of legal, educational, and economic developments, and thanks to activist movements, women of this generation, in theory, have had more choices in employment, marriage, and childbearing than women before. In general, policies enabling women to have careers and to be mothers have not been instituted to establish a gender-equal society but to augment the labor force and increase the number of children as Japanese society ages, as evidenced in early twenty-first-century strategies promoting "work-life balance" (Itō 2008). While praised for setting standards in work, this generation has been scorned for having fewer babies. Their marriage patterns became a topic of political interest in 2005, when, for the first time in Japanese history, population decline was not due to disasters but to falling below replacement level fertility. That year, birthrates reached an all-time low of 1.26, prompting then Prime Minister Koizumi Jun'ichirō to declare the fertility crisis a national problem (Kitazumi 2006). For most of their lives, women of this generation have been in the media spotlight and targeted as a consumer market, and television producers and advertising sponsors have continued to create characters with whom they can empathize.

The evolution of *dorama* since the early 1990s has reflected media discourses on working women of this generation in particular. Characters working in businesses comment on women's adverse treatment and reveal unexpected positive ways women have supported corporate structures underpinning the Japanese economy. For example, "OL," or "office lady secretaries," characters of such series as *Shomuni* (Fuji Television, 1998, 2000, 2002, and 2013), based on a manga by Yasuda Gumi), enacted plots of revenge to satirize workplace hierarchies and to lightheartedly expose darker sides of companies during real economic recession. The spate of *dorama* that pit established anchorwomen against younger rivals portray regrets of prioritizing careers over family and friendship. This is evident in *Newswoman* (*Nuusu no onna*, Fuji Television, 1998, one of a few 1998 *dorama* about single mothers), *Top Anchor* (*Toppo kyasutā*, Fuji Television, 2006), and *Fake Bride* (*Hanayome wa yakudoshi*, TBS, 2006). Especially since the 1950s, flight attendants have been promoted as model workers and ideal marriage partners. In *dorama*, they gain self-worth through helping others and by maintaining attractive appearances. This notion is romanticized in *Stewardess Story* (*Stewardess monogatari*, TBS, 1983) and parodied in *Perfect Woman* (*Yamato nadeshiko*, Fuji Television, 2000). Renegade female detectives working on their own or leading a force of misfits, as exemplified in *Unfair* (*Anfea*, Fuji Television, 2006, followed by a 2006 special and feature films in 2007 and 2011) and *BOSS 1* and *BOSS 2* (Fuji Television, 2009 and 2011), have a powerful role outside the company but are less respected than their male colleagues. In many cases, these women choose their jobs because of failures in love.

Especially after 2005, female romantic leads pursuing success in both high-level careers and personal lives proliferated. Examples include *The Man Who Cannot Marry* (*Kekkon dekinai otoko*, Fuji Television, 2007), *Woman Workaholic*

(*Hatarakiman*, TBS, 2007), *Around 40: Demanding Women*, and *Last Cinderella* (*Rasuto shinderera*, Fuji Television, 2013). Before, most female professionals were cast in supporting roles or as main characters forced to choose between careers and romance. Although these heroines embody progressive transformations in corporate structures, educational institutions, and attitudes toward working women, their appearance during national concern over low fertility rates does not subvert the belief that women should prioritize becoming wives and mothers. In 1990s *dorama* like *Tokyo Love Story*, the question was if the protagonist would marry or not. Now that the characters are older, the more pressing question is if she will have children. Characters react to media discourses that make single women turning forty, an age seen as the social, if not medical, cutoff for giving birth, seem a social problem (Freedman and Iwata-Weickgenannt 2011). Work compensates for missing parts of life.

Dorama have reacted to changes in Japan's employment system by showing new kinds of workers, such as "*haken*" dispatch staff. More women have been able to enter corporations as *haken*, while men have been forced into part-time tracks once reserved for women. An example is *Dignity of the Temp* (*Haken no hinkaku*, NTV, 2007) about a *haken* with superpowers, created in response to a 2006 government report that Japan's ratio of temporary to fulltime employees had doubled in eight years. While the fictional series presents real problems, it does not offer solutions but advocates coping with the status quo. It teaches that workers of all genders must unite to ensure corporate Japan's survival. Female temps gain acceptance, but they are still seen as fungible.

Female characters who prioritize their careers share other similarities. For example, they are paired with younger female characters who are less devoted to work and seek their advice. Their love interests are younger men whose careers they foster. Marriage remains one these women's goals, but it is not often reached. These aspects are all true in *Tokyo Love Story*.

Conclusion: *Woman Workaholic*

Woman Workaholic (*Hatarakiman*) seems like an updated version of *Tokyo Love Story* and a measure of women's acceptance into the company in the ten years since the former drama was broadcast. *Woman Workaholic* is not the newest career woman drama, but it is a milestone of drama history. Based on Anno Moyoco's manga (2004) and also adapted into television anime (2004), the story depicts the busy life of the twenty-eight-year-old Matsukata Hiroko, who tries to balance her journalism career at Gōtansha (a play on Kōdansha, publisher of the manga) and relationship with her boyfriend Shinji, a disillusioned engineer at a construction firm. Hiroko is able focus single-mindedly on work, even for days without bathing. Her colleagues call these moments her switch into "male mode" (*otoko suicchi irimasu*). Hiroko eats *natto*, fermented beans supposedly rich in female hormones, to offset these so-called masculine work habits. Most action takes place in the office, and the viewer has an intimate look at a family of coworkers. On one hand, the female lead is a positive role model, promoting a progressive lifestyle to viewers through the use of voiceovers. On the other hand, she needs male colleagues to help her through emotional crises. It is implied that she cannot marry or have children if she continues to pursue a high-powered career.

These notions are reinforced in the last episode, which takes place on Hiroko's twenty-ninth birthday. Hiroko has a few choices: she is being recruited to be chief editor of a new magazine for working women. She could follow Shinji, who finally begins to enjoy his job when he is transferred to the southern island of Kyushu. (Men rarely get transferred abroad on Japanese dramas.) Hiroko instead decides to remain at the tabloid magazine, where she has worked since her early twenties. Hiroko dashes to Haneda Airport to say goodbye to Shinji, who has broken up with her. Their goodbye is cut short when Hiroko receives a text message. Shinji gives her an encouraging push and laughs as she runs, as usual, back to work. In a final voiceover, Hiroko tells the viewer that being a workaholic is lonely and may damage her and Japan's future, but she is not ready to change her lifestyle. Both characters acknowledge—Rika to Kanji and Hiroko to the audience—that they will remain single as long as they keep their current priorities. Both are shown content with not having it all, feelings expressed while the viewer is shown the expanse of Tokyo.

From the earliest series until now, *dorama* show that, because women can never achieve all they desire, they should be happy with their current situations. Viewers more poignantly reacted to Rika's unrequited love than to her job troubles, but, significantly, the hopeful message of *Tokyo Love Story* was about work not about love. Whether intentionally or not, Rika furthered beliefs that women who prioritize their careers are sexually liberal and cannot be wives and mothers. The series' ending, similar to that of *Woman Workaholic*, is telling in this regard and demonstrates that *dorama* are also coming of age stories for men, depicting how women can help them fit their roles in the family and workplace. Unlike the working mothers on home dramas, young workers on NHK morning dramas, and historical women in *taiga* dramas, women on primetime *dorama* need to choose between having careers and families of their own. They cannot have both, whether to remain empathetic characters or to comment on women's realities. Although often pictured as more competent than their male colleagues, female employees cannot be seen as more successful. The most positive change has been the diversification in the work fictional women do. Women are portrayed as integral to Japanese companies, especially as lifetime employment breaks down and hiring patterns become more differentiated. *Dorama* convey the message that women, like men, need to ensure the future of corporate Japan. *Dorama* exemplify television's continued influence in classifying gender roles and giving an emotional face to discussions about women occurring in the mass media.

Notes

1 A version of this chapter appeared in *Television Histories in Asia: Issues and Contexts*, edited by Jinna Fay and Graeme Turner, 112–126 (Routledge 2015). I would like to thank the editors for their feedback and for allowing the republication.

2 Other terms include "idol dramas" (*aidoru dorama*, coined by Taiwan Star TV), "pure-love dramas" (*junai dorama*), and "J-drama." I am using "*dorama*" because it is the most common term among global fans and the one that covers the largest swath of television history.

3 There were Japanese dramas not categorized as "home dramas," including geisha stories and police procedurals.

4 The most popular drama that year was *101st Proposal* (*101 kaime no puropozu*) (Matsumoto et al. 1999: 33).

6   The World Too Much with Us in Japanese Travel Television[1]

Kendall Heitzman

From the beginning, travel television in Japan has represented an impossibility. When NHK (Japan's public broadcasting network) aired the first Japanese travel television series produced abroad, *African Journey* (*Afurika tairiku o yuku*, December 1959–March 1960), with less than a month from recording to broadcast (Toyohara et al. 1960: 253), it brought to Japanese viewers a world that was still off-limits to most of the population. NHK Archives suggests that no more than 50,000 Japanese had traveled abroad when the program first aired (NHK Archives). By the end of the 1970s, over four million Japanese citizens were traveling abroad each year (Carlisle 1996: 12, cited in Yano 2013a: 88). Today, when millions of Japanese travel domestically and abroad for business and pleasure, Japanese television networks are littered with travel television shows, to the extent that the viewer is overwhelmed by options, unable to find a corner of Japan or the globe that has not been documented and broadcast. There is a new impossibility at the heart of contemporary Japanese travel television, however: in an era in which viewers can go anywhere they please, Japanese travel television continues to keep the world at a distance.

Here, we look at three of the most popular travel programs in contemporary Japan. On all these shows, alienation from the very world such programming promises to make available reveals itself via a variety of distancing subject positions. On the domestic front, NHK's celebrity-driven *Tsurube's Salute to Families* (*Tsurube no kazoku ni kanpai*, 1995–present) spotlights regional Japan but emphasizes the host and his celebrity guests. Fuji Television's long-running *Ainori* (1999–2009) demonstrated how it was possible for the entire world to play second banana to even anonymous, "regular" Japanese young people. NHK's ubiquitous *Walk the Town, Encounter the World* (*Sekai fureai machiaruki*, 2005–present) would seem to solve the problem by removing the travelers altogether and having the camera itself stand in for them, but it proves not to be so simple.

It is worth asking how Japanese travel television shows reflect and resist a contradictory era in which the world has never been closer and yet is still kept at a respectable distance. Without denying the great pleasures of these clever iterations of one of the most banal of genres—and while recognizing Japan's complex television culture—it is possible to perform a counter-reading that connects Japanese travel television to a mainstream unwillingness to confront a national past.

Tsurube's Salute to Families: **Wandering Star**

On *Tsurube's Salute to Families*, actor and traditional *rakugo* storyteller Shōfu-kutei Tsurube II, known across Japan simply as Tsurube, is accompanied each episode by a celebrity guest to a different small town in Japan. There, they travel first together, then separately, making their way around the town and supposedly letting serendipity guide them to "terrific families" (*suteki na ka-zoku*). The show delights in using the power of television to force its way into households that are media-shy and hardly prepared for the small onslaught of NHK crew members appearing at the front door already recording. Stock figures appearing in nearly any town Tsurube visits include the older woman covering her mouth to hide her embarrassment and complaining that she hasn't cleaned the house for visitors and her slow-to-appear husband finally wandering out to the front of the house and treating Tsurube like an old drinking friend. The celebrity guests range from the famous to the C-list. They demonstrate modesty about their fame by politely introducing them-selves to the townspeople, who reply with a panoply of variations on "I know who you are," ranging from adoring to (occasionally) near hostility, with a fair number of "I *think* I know you"-type responses for good measure. Guests are charged with the task of insinuating themselves into the tight networks of local communities, hinting that they would like to see the household's prized collection of such-and-such or be invited to dinner with the family. In one episode from 2014, the actor Nishikawa Takanori, who sings under the name T. M. Revolution, decided to milk his fame by brazenly walking up to a high school and instigating a near-riot when students screamed from the windows and poured out of the building to swarm him, earning him a scolding from the faculty. Most guests pretend to try a little harder to fly under the radar, but they are pleased to be recognized whenever possible.

While *Tsurube's Salute to Families* would seem to suggest that this is a kind of tourism that anyone could do, without even leaving Japan—just get out there and meet people!—it proves to be a show more about terrific celebrities than terrific families, even without Mr. Revolution's hijinks. On a two-part episode broadcast on October 28 and November 4, 2013, Tsurube meets Agawa Sawako, daughter of the famous postwar writer Agawa Hiroyuki and a prominent author in her own right, at—appropriately enough—Agawa Station in Shimonoseki City, Yamaguchi Prefecture. Agawa-san was allowed to choose the location, and she explains to Tsurube in the opening scene that she chose Agawa based on her last name, for good reason: she had come here with her father long ago. Her father once went to a place named Agawa in Canada and found a number of families there with the name Agawa. He found that they were all Aboriginal people and that their name meant the same thing as his own ("winding river"). He developed a theory that the Agawas of Canada and the Agawas of Yamaguchi are two branches of the same family. "I'm not sure they had family names back then," Agawa Sawako muses, but she is off in search of Agawas of her own. Over the course of their travels, she finds no fewer than three people who know of her father's theory: the chief priest of Agawa Hachimangū shrine, a local tatami maker, and the relative of a woman she has met along the road and who brings her home to cook dinner together.[2] As much as Agawa tries to turn the focus toward the people of the town, she is made the center of attention everywhere she goes, even by people who only partially recognize her.

For his part, Tsurube is not only quickly identified by any and all across Japan, he is also identified as this show's host. People tend to know immediately why he is there, and the most ambitious of them attempt to steer him toward their own families; word travels quickly through the town that Tsurube has arrived, and in some episodes strivers descend from all sides. Tsurube must make a decision to go with them or fend them off, often with a cheery insult. This, too, adds to his aura; he bears a passing resemblance to the portly traditional god of good luck and abundance Hotei, and it is clear that some families see a visit from Tsurube to be just as auspicious as prayers at the local temple. In the Agawa episode, Tsurube meets a young woman carrying a baby who is walking from her own parents' home to her husband's parents' home just down the street. Tsurube says it must be wonderful for both sets of grandparents that their children stayed in town, but he learns that the husband's family has only recently moved here from Osaka after his brother was killed in a car accident near their home there, making it too painful to stay. Tsurube prays at the deceased man's shrine in the house, and offers advice to his still-grieving mother: "You need to carry within you the life that he didn't get to live." It is a near-religious experience for the family.

One problem that is effaced in Tsurube's television program is perhaps the very reason for its existence: small-town life in Japan is dying, as young people move to large cities and the birthrate dwindles. Regional Japan has become part of the "discourse of the vanishing," as Marilyn Ivy (1995) has termed it, and this show not only argues for the relevance of rural Japan at the moment it is disappearing, it puts a cheerful face on an undeniable social problem. Reality occasionally slips through the cracks: the priest at a temple that used to host a nursery school (*hoikuen*) tells Agawa that, when the nursery school opened in 1950, it had 160 students, and now there are only twenty-seven students at the local elementary school in total. When Tsurube meets a young fish wholesaler more interested in fish than people, the program offers his parents the opportunity to shame him in front of millions for not getting married and giving them grandchildren, but without any suggestion of how difficult that is for men whose work ties them to rural areas. One gets the sense that just about any rural problem can be made better by the optimistic presence of Tsurube, except for the ones that really matter: Tsurube doesn't do depopulation, he doesn't do base towns, and he doesn't do nuclear power facilities, to give a short list.

For his national audience, it is a format that situates them not as travelers but as travelees; one watches Tsurube not to live vicariously through Tsurube, but to live vicariously through the families he visits. We may want to visit that town; the townspeople hope that we do and are given the chance to plug their "famous products." But there is also a part of us that says, "I wonder when Tsurube will come to *our* town." Considering his more than two decades of wandering, it is easy to feel that the odds are in our favor that we, too, will be traveled upon by Tsurube someday.

Ainori: A Movable East

The long-running Fuji Television series *Ainori* offers up what would seem at first glance to be a solution to the problem of celebrity: anonymous, "representative" Japanese young people. The title is an untranslatable pun, a homonym for the Japanese word meaning "to ride together" but here with the character for love (*ai*) to mean, loosely, "loving and traveling." A rotating cast of seven young Japanese travelers is driven around the world in a pink van, called the "Love Wagon," to see the sights and fall in love, but not necessarily in that order. Along the way they eat local food, see things both famous and not-so-famous, and interact with the locals—in particular, the locally-hired Love Wagon driver, always a national of the given country they are in—but always with one goal in mind: to fall in love with one of the other six passengers and return to Japan with that person. Once a participant confesses, there is no turning back; he or she will go back to Japan, either alone or with the confessee. The next episode, the Love Wagon will stop to pick up as many new participants as are needed to bring the number back up to seven, and the journey continues on.

A show in which participants vie to leave an open-ended free trip around the world and return to their anonymous lives would seem to break the unwritten rules of contemporary reality television. The desperate gamification of "real life" on display in the panoply of elimination contests that the (originally UK-Swedish) show *Survivor* helped to spawn around the world in the 2000s has conditioned viewers to expect that people appearing on reality television will act outrageously and stay on the program as long as possible in hopes of becoming celebrities. The rules of celebritydom in Japan are complicated, however, and the routes to semi-stardom are largely controlled by agencies and resist individual opportunism and accidental celebrity.[3] On *Ainori*, most participants minded their manners and willingly left in a timely fashion. Many a participant went back to Japan alone but claiming to feel satisfied just at having made a public confession of love to a fellow traveler.

Most participants were normatively attractive, fashion-conscious people. Given the time they needed to take off to participate, they tended to be *freeters* (*furītā*), part-time workers who could not or did not want to join companies as fulltime, salaried employees and often had vague creative aspirations: artists, hairstylists, and perpetual travelers abounded. Even while purportedly portraying a new generation of cosmopolitan, emotionally open Japanese youth, *Ainori* was in some aspects deeply conservative. Among its many sins of omission, *Ainori* was predictably heteronormative; all participants were exclusively heterosexual, or at least played so on television. The practice of having contestants participate under nicknames, meant to be a cute touch, often served to calcify their personalities and restrict their narrative freedom. Because there were usually four men and three women in the Love Wagon at any given time, perhaps to generate more scenarios that catered to the traditional expectation that men should compete for the attention of women, it was easier for the producers to make one of the male selections a comic relief. Shrek was a slow-moving, slow-talking, lovable lump, who failed to find his princess. Painfully shy San-chan[4] was a pet of the women on the show—it was clear that they would never consider him as a viable partner. At the same time, other men who tried to trade on their professional qualifications ("Dentist," "Doc") tended to lose to their more ordinary rivals. One painfully earnest participant, Yokokume Katsuhiko, was given the nickname Sōri (Prime Minister) after he expressed interest during his audition in becoming Prime Minister of Japan (*sōri daijin*). Sōri was a nervous, somewhat officious object of ridicule—qualities that may well make him a perfect fit for high political office but which disqualified him from finding love on *Ainori*. "I could picture her making tea for my supporters at election headquarters," he later said of the woman who sent him packing (*Ainori 9* 2007: 52).[5] The women tended to fall mostly in the normative camp and had nicknames that steered toward cute: Ringo (Apple), Neko (Cat), and Bambi all made appearances. The square-peg women who did make it through the casting process largely went back to Japan alone, unless the producers engaged in some deus-ex-machina matchmaking; irrepressible "bombshell hip-hop girl" Ōse (participating under her actual name) seemed doomed until the arrival of equally wild Bukurō, the self-proclaimed "wolf of Ikebukuro" (*Ainori 7* 2005: 94).

The primary goal of the show was to reinforce among its audience the received wisdom that conventionally attractive and socially comfortable men and women go home (to Japan) together. This was reinforced by the aggressive participation of the trio of well-known hosts, who watched the episode in front of a mostly female, mostly young studio audience: Hisamoto Masami, Imada Kōji, and Katō Haruhiko, the last later replaced by Wentz Eiji. Hisamoto and Imada, in particular, could be lacerating in their judgments of anyone who deviated from social norms. Their comments could be heard over the videotape of the proceedings, along with the laughter or cries of the studio audience, as they attempted to score comedic points on anything the participants did that stepped outside the supposedly established rules of courtship. From the makeup of the studio audience and the fact that the commercials for the duration of its run were dominated by Sophie feminine products and a variety of hair-care brands for women, *Ainori* was clearly aimed at young women. Yet the fates of its couples and the ongoing activities of its alumnae in particular were of interest to men's weekly magazines and occasionally lascivious online bulletin boards throughout the 2000s. The August 2005 issue of *Flash Exciting* magazine, for example, tracks down returnees and updates us on recent developments: Ōse is working at a hostess bar, Itchii is a bartender, and so on (*Flash Exciting* 2005: 16–22).

On *Ainori*, one stays at the social center by participating in the world, but never too much. In effect, the urge to see the world and step outside of the comfort zone of the traveling pink embassy is overwhelmed by the domestic drama occurring among the seven Japanese participants in the hotel, over dinner, and, yes, inside the van; what one critic called "ethnocentrism in the name of unity" on Japanese television shows about foreign lands appears to have been alive and well on *Ainori* (Painter 1996: 203). Often, the succession of images shown over the opening theme music—a different sequence of shots every week that updates viewers on what participants have been up to since the last episode—portrays the group interacting with the locals in a country more in the span of a minute than does the remainder of the half-hour.

The opening sequence served as proof that these relationships were being formed off-screen and in-country, and, to be fair, *Ainori* paid more than lip service to the notion of travel as edifying. Over its run, *Ainori* brought its viewers reportage about the dangers of nuclear power at Chernobyl in Ukraine and the hazards of global warming in low-lying Tuvalu, and viewers were encouraged to send donations for the construction of *Ainori*-branded pink schools in various impoverished places. And yet, national insularity enveloped the show in design and practice. There was never a real question of dating outside of the Love Wagon. One participant was allowed to confess her love to the driver in South Africa, a spur-of-the-moment addition to the rules by the producer, who appeared briefly to say he thought it would be good for a lark. In Tanzania, a young Tanzanian woman was allowed to confess her love to Hide; it is treated as an outlandish joke, even though Hide refuses as gently as possible. Even multicultural Japan was outside looking in: at least one biracial Japanese man participated as a regular, as did a Filipina exchange student, but neither succeeded in finding love on the show.

Ainori is thus a contested space, in which the closed circle of entertainment value and the educational imperative of the wider world vie for screen time. The world's victories are fleeting, however. The episode broadcast on September 11, 2006, contains what is perhaps the most extreme test case for *Ainori*'s tensions. In Poland, the Love Wagon arrives at a museum consisting of a series of red-brick buildings. It is Auschwitz. The participants know the name but they are all caught off guard. ("I thought Auschwitz was in Germany," one participant whispers.) A Japanese guide brings them through a tour that leaves them shaken: they visit the gas chambers, see the massive display case of human hair, and hear that prisoners took part in killing their fellow inmates in order to survive. "If you were put into this kind of concentration camp, you would probably do the same thing," the guide tells them.

"The will to survive overrides reason. It's a powerful force." They meet with a pair of young German docents and ask how they feel about Auschwitz. "There is a responsibility for us" to do this, one of the Germans responds. "What did we learn about this in junior high?" one participant tries to recall in her superimposed diary. "Now I regret not studying in junior high or high school. As soon as I get back to Japan, I want to go to the A-bomb dome in Hiroshima and visit the peace museum." When the show returns to the hosts in the studio, they dwell on the horrors of Auschwitz for the grand sum of exactly thirty seconds before one says, "We've forgotten all about San-chan," to which Wentz replies, "I was thinking of him the whole time," pointing out that he shared his umbrella with one of the female participants on the Auschwitz tour. The episode returns to its regularly scheduled hijinks: landscaper Uekki is aroused when he rides a horse with Chaki, the object of his affection; the women take an eyelash curler to poor San-chan; and man of passion Tachi and Junko shop for pendants together in Krakow. While Tachi is visibly smitten with Junko, the episode ends with a glimpse of Junko's diary in which she writes that she is convinced Tachi is in love with one of the other female participants. The audience and hosts gasp.

The failures to look the world in the eye are numerous at this point. The participants have learned how to see Auschwitz through the eyes of the victims, but they have missed what the guide and young Germans try to tell them about identifying with the *perpetrators*, about what it means to be complicit as an ordinary citizen. Their Japanese guide is clearly not talking in hypotheticals; he is encouraging his Japanese visitors to consider their own place in the world as citizens of a country that continues to hedge on the issue of war responsibility. But the show and its participants hedge as well. The horror of Auschwitz has been replaced by the disproportionate horror of having one's crush misunderstand one's intentions. A meaningful encounter with the world lasts only until the last participant climbs back into the Love Wagon and slams the door shut, sealing them in their insular ecosystem, an island country on wheels.

Walk the Town, Encounter the World: The Mechanical I

The NHK BS Premium travel program *Walk the Town, Encounter the World*[6] ostensibly offers an unmediated virtual-reality travel experience. The camera itself is the traveler—is *us*—bobbing down the street past a sea of mildly curious faces. We see exactly what it sees and identify with it as we drift along both well-traveled main streets and back alleys: we belong here, we are passing for locals! The narrating voice is cheerful and speaks from a position of power. It comes as a consumer of information and experiences but never of physical commodities. Because it is our avatar, speaking on our behalf, the illusion would be ruined if a pair of hands unlike our own were to appear on the screen to receive an empanada in San Juan or a döner kebab in Berlin. In an episode broadcast November 6, 2012, when a woman drops a load of oranges at the top of a steep cobblestone street in Lisbon, our avatar shrieks but does nothing to help as the oranges bobble past us like pachinko balls down into the city below. We are physically and morally invisible.

The narrator (usually a female voice, but not always) has been gifted with universal translation. The locals she encounters speak to her in their own languages, with Japanese subtitles appearing on the screen, and she responds in Japanese. She can occasionally be relentless, trying to get her interlocutors to show her the back garden, or an artisanal process most visitors don't get to see, but a lot of the time the locals fall over themselves trying to offer us—through her—a variety of experiences without our needing to ask.

An episode from June 17, 2014, shows our avatar in complete control on our behalf. "Tokyo?" a garrulous Frenchman asks when the avatar turns her gaze toward his group, sunning themselves in front of a café in Paris' Saint-Germain-des-Prés neighborhood, and his companions cheer our arrival: "Bravo!" They have been meeting here every day for forty years, the man says, adding that his friends come because they want to see him. "Aren't you here because you heard a rumor I was here?" he asks us.

"Are you somebody worthy of rumors?" we ask, playing along. The man and his friends enjoy this very much.

"We get nothing out of coming here," one of his companions says, good-naturedly digging at the man, "but we come because we like the sun."

When we announce that we are moving on, the facetious men have been tamed by our confident, literally unblinking demeanor. "Have a wonderful day," the braggadocio tells us.

Is it real?, one feels compelled to ask. Some people appear genuinely surprised and charmed, others scowl and dart away, but even this is an illusion; they are pleased or annoyed not by the sight of a single intrepid traveler, of course, but by what is clearly a small team of documentarians. Only one major tic gives the game away: often on *Walk the Town, Encounter the World*, our interlocutors look not directly at the camera but slightly to the side of it, where the interviewer was, of course, standing beside the camera operator. There are other times on the street when reality creeps in despite the best efforts of the production editors to cull children and locals who insist on treating the camera as a camera, waving at it. For the most part, however, viewers are not reminded of their Japaneseness or of the sutured narrative. If anything, our avatar is a cultural chameleon. There is no doubt the program attempts to be a force for mutual understanding. In San Diego (broadcast June 24, 2014), a woman in a mansion with a view catches us rambling around her rather large garden. Rather than call the police, she beckons us in and out onto the patio, where she is hosting a brunch with friends together with her wife. "Did you say wife?" we ask, curiously but not incredulously, and our extremely genial hosts provide us with a brief explanation of American marriage laws and an introduction to their life together. Not all that shocking, our avatar decides for us, and viewers have been able to have a conversation about a still-foreign-to-Japan societal shift in a low-stress way.

As a demonstration of the aspirational possibilities of foreign travel, it is likely more depressing than inspirational to some viewers. NHK provides an online FAQ for the program that pulls back some of the curtains, and one of the questions is, "Would *I* be able to travel in this way? Even on a package tour?" The response is a nearly unqualified yes: the people making this program "walk around the streets just like regular travelers, are called out to from all directions, and have wonderful encounters. This program portrays the everyday life of these locales. The vast majority of the people who appear on the show live in these areas or have some other sort of connection to the places. [...] Of course, language ability is crucial, and there are dangerous parts of town even in the cities we choose, so it is important to take ample precautions" (NHK Online). So, sure you can do it, as long as you are fluent in the local language and know the city well. When are caveats so large that they are no longer caveats but disqualifiers?

In the same FAQ, NHK admits what should be obvious, that *Walk the Town, Encounter the World* sutures narrative fragments together to create a seemingly seamless whole; the person having the conversation with the local informants is a "coordinator fluent in the local language," and that person is edited out, leaving only the ambient sounds, so that a Japanese voice track can be added in the studio (NHK Online). But what is also deleted, of course, is everything that makes travel, travel: the misunderstandings, ruined shots, confrontations, wrong turns, romantic encounters, missed connections, undercurrent of danger, and even potential for crime and violence. It is not simply that we the viewers cannot have that experience; it is that *no one had the experience in the first place.* The experience is akin to the last phase of the image of Jean Baudrillard's (1994b: 6) famous "precession of simulacra," in which "it has no relation to any reality whatsoever: it is its own pure simulacrum." It attempts to duplicate for broadcast a journey for which there is no original.

It is probably safe to say that travel television around the globe operates as a hedge against reality to one extent or another, but it seems particularly true in long-postwar, long-conservative Japan, which has substituted monetary aid for actual progress or reform both domestically and abroad, which allows only a statistically insignificant number of immigrants to enter each year, and which has a fangless broadcast news tradition and a generally conservative-leaning television landscape. These shows involve a pact between all parties involved to sublimate the subject itself for the sake of the narrative. We want to believe that the absence we feel at the center of these narratives leaves room for us to travel vicariously through them in imitation of the cosmopolitan Japanese traveler they posit, but in the absence of the original, our efforts to be a reflection of it can be nothing more than a self-delusion designed to divert us from that very absence. Viewers have no standing to consider why we are where we are, and what history has brought us here. The simulacrum, the copy with no original, flickers all the more brightly in a long-post-bubble, post-disaster Japan, in which the lights have been dimmed and only the TV has been left on: in a Japanese town full of wonderful families but missing its children, in Auschwitz as a romantic destination, and in warm memories of a wonderful stroll that never happened.

Notes

1 This research was enabled by a grant from the Japan Society for the Promotion of Science (JSPS), with additional support from the Center for Asian and Pacific Studies and International Programs at the University of Iowa. I am grateful to Kitahara Makoto for his research assistance.
2 Agawa Hiroyuki's memoir of his visit to the Agawa Canyon can be found in Agawa 2006: 117–138.
3 The most notable alumni is film director Horie Kei, one of the original group of *Ainori* participants.
4 The suffix –*chan*, generally used as a diminutive for babies and females, when applied to men can be a way of domesticating a physically imposing man (cf. Shuwa-chan, popularly known outside of Japan as Arnold Schwarzenegger), or of further diminishing an already weak figure, as in San-chan's case.
5 After Yokokume's run on the show was over, he briefly parlayed his fame (and University of Tokyo degree) to a seat in the Japanese Diet.
6 An English-dubbed version appears on NHK World (NHK's international broadcasting service) as *Somewhere Street*.

PART III

Videogames

7 Nuclear Discourse in *Final Fantasy VII*

Embodied Experience and Social Critique

Rachael Hutchinson

Introduction

The videogame is now one of the major narrative forms through which so-cial and political issues are critiqued and problematized by Japanese artists. Like film, literature, popular music, and other contemporary narrative forms, videogames express ideas of national identity as well as social and political critique, such as resistance to nuclear power. While this issue has been studied in terms of Japanese literature, film, and fine arts, I hope to demonstrate that videogames also contribute. This chapter examines the issue of nuclear power in one of the bestselling videogame franchises of all time, Square's *Final Fantasy* series (*Finaru fantajii*, first released in 1987). Square is the Tokyo-based videogame development company founded by Miyamoto Masafumi in 1986. Square merged with the development company Enix in April 2003 to form Square Enix, one of the foremost RPG development companies in the world. *Final Fantasy* is a transmedia phenomenon, encompassing anime, manga, light novels, and films (most notably *Final Fantasy: The Spirits Within*, 2001). Titles are usually abbreviated to *FF* with a Roman numeral. As of 2015, there are fourteen titles in the main series, with two direct sequels (*FFX-2* and *FFXIII-2*). *FFXI* and *FFXIV* are massively multiplayer online role-playing games (MMORPGs). The franchise has also experimented with non-RPG game formats, such as the fighting game *Dissidia Final Fantasy* (2008).

This series of role-playing games is vast in theme and scope, with each dis-crete title examining different ideas of life, death, and a world in danger. *Final Fantasy X* (2001) has been analyzed for its commentary on organized religion (Hahn 2009) and retelling of national memory (Washburn 2009), while *Final Fantasy VII* (1997) has been analyzed in terms of environmentalism and the Gaia theory (Foster 2009). Throughout the series, the fear of nuclear war and ambivalence toward nuclear power appears in different allegorical forms—most notably in *FFIV, FFVI, FFVII* and *FFX*.[1] The ethics and safety of using nuclear power as an energy source comes under intense scrutiny in *Final Fantasy VII* (*FFVII*), released as the flagship title for the original PlayStation console in 1997. The anti-nuclear message is conveyed through scripted dia-logue, visual cues, cinematic sequences, and overarching narrative themes.

The Japanese role-playing game, or JRPG, is known for its linear plot structure, deep psychological characterization, and sheer length of the text, with games taking anywhere from fifty to one-hundred hours to complete. The JRPG may be readily analyzed as a narrative genre that engages with contemporary social issues from a certain ideological standpoint. But what makes a game different from other texts in terms of how the message is conveyed to the audience? Literature, film, manga, and anime are specific kinds of narrative that produce different effects on the audience through the use of words, illustrations, placement of panels on the page, camera angles, drawn movement, editing techniques, and so forth. Theories of consumers' readership or spectatorship abound. While on one level it seems reasonable to assume that the consumer "gets the message" of the text by reading or viewing it, the dynamic processes of message-interpretation are also tied to media-specific methods of message creation and conveyance. This is equally true for the game text, which involves the player in specific ways to immerse them in the gameworld and experience the narrative firsthand. Game Studies scholar Ian Bogost argues that videogames have unique capabilities to persuade players of embedded ideology through "procedural rhetoric"—conveying ideas through the coded regulations of gameplay dynamics rather than written or verbal text (2007: 28–9). Gameplay dynamics, such as decision making, item use, and character identification, create a sense of immersion in the gameworld and engagement with its ideology.

FFVII is a good example through which to analyze this process. The game is highly immersive, "known for leaving the first-time gamer with an experience that is nothing short of profound" (Wood 2009: 167). Player agency and character identification are manipulated and disrupted by the designers, creating a self-reflexive environment where players are forced to draw connections between the gameworld and the real world. This necessitates engagement with the ideological message—in this case, anti-nuclear critique. While my basic approach comes from cultural studies and literary analysis, gameplay dynamics will also be taken into account. I will first situate *FFVII* in historical context and then detail several scenes from the game's narrative to show how nuclear power is represented—as raw material for energy and weapons, and as a radioactive element that can affect the human body. The third section looks more closely at player agency and embodiment, concluding with some considerations of embodiment as a learning experience.

Nuclear Discourse in Japan

Since the atomic bombing of Hiroshima and Nagasaki in 1945, the Japanese have problematized and critiqued the use of nuclear power in a range of art forms, from literature, film, and manga to anime and videogames.[2] I will refer to the continuing focus on nuclear power in Japanese media as Japan's "nuclear discourse," a set of artistic and political utterances on the use of nuclear power for both military and peaceful purposes. Examining the nuclear discourse in Japanese narrative texts allows us to understand Japanese attitudes towards war, technology, and power. In most twentieth-century texts concerned with these issues "nuclear power" implies atomic weaponry, Japanese victimhood at foreign hands, the importance of preserving world peace, respecting rather than abusing the formidable power of nuclear energy, and avoiding the past mistakes of others—most notably the United States (Hutchinson 2014). The unleashing of incredible power and the instant destruction of life and cityscapes is a recurrent image in the Japanese arts, seen in Ibuse Masuji's novel *Black Rain* (*Kuroi ame*, 1969, and 1989 film version directed by Imamura Shōhei), Nakazawa Keiji's autobiographical manga *Barefoot Gen* (*Hadashi no Gen*, 1973–1974), and Kurosawa Akira's film *I Live in Fear* (*Ikimono no kiroku*, 1955). It also appears indirectly through allegory, as in Honda Ishirō's film *Godzilla* (*Gojira*, 1954) and Ōtomo Katsuhiro's anime *Akira* (1988) (see Chapters 18 and 21).

The reaction to nuclear weapons in Japanese art has attracted much academic attention, and the fear of nuclear attack is a universal human concern. However, Japanese nuclear discourse focuses not only on weaponry, like atomic bombs and missiles, but also on nuclear power as an energy source. Nuclear power is consistently represented in dual terms, as the source of both (negative) destruction and (neutral or positive) energy. The key to the narrative is often the liminal nature of that duality, since at any time the neutral energy may turn to destructive force, whether due to human failings or the material's inherent instability. Conversations between characters in texts within the nuclear discourse tend to focus on issues of responsibility and control—how can nuclear power be contained, and how can we humans use this extraordinary power in a responsible, ethical way?

In March 2011, Japan experienced the triple disaster of earthquake, tsunami, and nuclear reactor meltdown, centered on the northern city of Fukushima (Fukushima Prefecture). Since then, the nuclear duality has dominated Japanese discourse, as artists struggle to come to terms with an energy source that contaminated vast areas, with little trustworthy information supplied by the government. Rachel DiNitto (2014) analyzes Fukushima-related literature and film as voicing a collective identity coping with national trauma. The 2013 academic conference "Between 'Cool' and 3.11" held at Elizabethtown College asked how teachers of Japanese popular culture should take account of Fukushima in their classes. In short, Fukushima looms large in any current analysis of nuclear discourse in Japan, overshadowing the fact that nuclear duality was a strong theme in the Japanese arts before 2011.

Writing before the Fukushima disaster, sociologist Utsumi Hirofumi demonstrated that the dual image of nuclear power as both negative and positive was consistent in Japan from the 1960s to 2010, with the majority of the population holding both views simultaneously (2012: 175). Utsumi argues that what connects the two views of nuclear power is Japan's self-image as a nation—at once the victim of A-bomb weapons and also the champion of peaceful scientific advancement in the nuclear age, driven to keep pace with the global utilization of nuclear energy despite fears of radiation. Even after the Chernobyl disaster of 1986, Utsumi contends:

> The infatuation of Japan with itself as a cyborg nation may well be too deep to consider any risk.... It may not be easy to change this 'scientific-technological' self-image, even if whole areas are contaminated by nuclear power plants accidents.
>
> (Utsumi 2012: 196)

The fear of radiation from nuclear reactors has been studied in terms of political protest (Hasegawa 2004: 128–73; Aldrich 2010: 119–51), but less in terms of artistic expression. Little attention has been paid to the idea of nuclear duality in the postwar Japanese arts, nor the image of nuclear reactors themselves. *FFVII* takes the issue of nuclear reactors and the instability of nuclear materials as the basis of its narrative, providing a good opportunity for study.

Reactors, Radiation, and the Planet

In *FFVII*, nuclear power is thinly disguised as "Mako" energy, an extremely efficient energy source.[3] The Shinra Electric Power Company uses Mako reactors to extract energy from the Lifestream of the Planet, the fictional world in which the game is set. Mako energy is non-renewable, and Shinra's actions are bleeding the Planet dry. Because the extraction process causes vegetation and animals around the reactor sites to die, the capital city Midgar appears as a dark blot on the world map. No plants grow in Midgar, except in the beautiful gardens of the flower-seller Aeris, one of the "Ancients," a race that has lived in harmony with the Planet for thousands of years. Shinra's monopoly on Mako energy affords the corporation great political power—the president of Shinra is effectively the ruler of the Planet, as the mayor of Midgar admits. The importance of energy production and the corrupt nature of those who control it are established very early in the game. The player's first task is to blow up Midgar's Mako Reactor 7 to help the guerilla resistance movement AVALANCHE, positioning the player against Shinra from the very beginning.[4]

The player-controlled main character is a young man named Cloud Strife (*Kuraudo Sutoraifu*), a mercenary dressed in the uniform of SOLDIER, the military arm of Shinra. Cloud's second mission is to help AVALANCHE destroy Mako Reactor 5. Escaping the reactor core, they meet President Shinra, who recognizes Cloud from the glow in his eyes. This glow characterizes all members of SOLDIER, exposed to Mako radiation as part of their training to gain superhuman strength. However, we later discover that Cloud never joined SOLDIER but was exposed to "Mako Radiation Therapy" in a scientific experiment. Indeed, Cloud is exposed to so much Mako that he suffers severe "Mako poisoning" twice in the game—once as a result of the experiment and once when he falls into the Lifestream and becomes saturated with the material. The immediate symptom of Mako poisoning is an inability to move or speak. The fact that Mako leaves a "glow" as an aftereffect of exposure, is described in terms of "radiation," and causes poisoning resulting in deathly immobility, makes the player think of Mako as the equivalent of nuclear energy.

FFVII explores conventional questions of nuclear discourse through allegory. Mako is never expressly described as nuclear energy, but this is implied throughout the narrative. The non-renewable nature of Mako has led some to see it as a fossil fuel equivalent (Foster 2009: 48), but it is clear from the narrative that Mako has replaced coal and fossil fuels as a more efficient and supposedly clean power source. Mako is also found in its natural state throughout the gameworld, in the form of "materia," a rock-like solid which may be gathered by characters and used to fuel magical attacks in battle. Materia grows and mutates into different forms depending on frequency of use, so the unstable nature of the element can be seen as a benefit to the player. The gameplay dynamic of item usage in the battle system thus ties into the narrative to show how a natural element may be innocuous or helpful to the righteous, but harmful in the hands of the corrupt. It is the forced extraction of materia by Mako reactors, rather than the substance itself, which causes harm.

Halfway through Disc One we discover that a Mako reactor supplanted coalmines in the mountain town of Corel. When Shinra first suggested building a Mako reactor outside the town, a citizen named Dyne protested: "Our coal's been protected for generations. Our fathers, and theirs before them, risked their lives for it. We have no right to throw it away so easily!"[5] Dyne's friend Barret Wallace replied: "No one uses coal nowadays. It's the sign of the times." Shinra promises to guarantee the town's livelihood after the reactor is complete, but this is a lie, and citizens later complain about their poverty and misery to Cloud. When the reactor inevitably explodes, the town is burned by Shinra soldiers, who blame the accident on the villagers. As an advocate for the reactor, Barret is held responsible for the destruction of his hometown. Barret's wife Myrna dies in the attack, and Dyne commits suicide four years later, consumed with anger against Shinra and the world. Corel's destruction provides motivation for Barret to form the resistance movement AVALANCHE.

The Corel reactor explosion reveals the unstable nature of Mako energy, as well as Shinra's duplicity. Later on Disc One, Cloud visits the town of Gongaga, where another reactor exploded three years ago. Entering the village, the first thing Cloud sees is a graveyard with two mourners. The man is silent. The woman kneels at her husband's grave, asking, "Do people really need reactors to live? Aren't there more important things in life…?" The Item Seller, Innkeeper, Mayor and Weapons Seller in Gongaga elaborate on the reactor explosion:

Shinra built the reactor, without even thinking about the town's safety. And this is the result.

One day, there was a huge explosion. Many townspeople died in it...

The Shinra people told us that everyone would be happy once the Reactor was built. But, all it brought us was sadness...

We voted to outlaw the use of Mako energy and live with nature, ever since the explosion.[6]

The scene in Gongaga repeats and reinforces the sense of Mako reactors being volatile and dangerous, causing destruction in the wake of false promises by those in power. When the Head of Shinra's Weapons Development Program arrives in the village and searches the reactor ruins for "Huge Materia" to make an ultimate weapon, the destructive potential of Mako is revealed.

An alternative way of life is put into practice in Cosmo Canyon, where a community of people and lion-like beings dedicate themselves to the study of the Planet, living in harmony with nature. The village elder Bugenhagen explains that the Lifestream that generates Mako is made up of the spirit energy of all living things, which returns to the Planet after one's death. Mako extraction therefore hastens the death of the Planet. Bugenhagen professes love for technology but wonders whether humans are inherently good or evil in their use of Mako energy. *FFVII* joins other texts of Japanese nuclear discourse in questioning the nature of humanity and whether we are responsible or ethical beings.

Although scenario writer Nojima Kazushige and his Event Planning team called *FFVII* "dark" in nature, as so many characters deceive themselves in some way (Noda 2000: 183), it ends with a hopeful scene. As a Meteor summoned by the villain Sephiroth crashes into the Planet, Aeris's magical materia "Holy" is released to intercept it. Holy is unequal to the task, burning in the red-hot impact. Just as all hope seems lost, pale green tendrils of the Lifestream emerge from the depths of the Planet and embrace Meteor, Midgar, and Holy alike in a bright green light. Meteor dissolves, and we see the face of Aeris for a moment. After the credits, the title "Five hundred years later" heralds a final cinematic sequence showing Red XIII and two cubs overlooking the city of Midgar, overgrown with greenery in the midst of a lush forest. The Planet has healed itself. This ending prompted character designer Nomura Tetsuya to see the healed Midgar as the "Promised Land" of the game narrative, although he admits that scenario writer Nojima may have had a completely different idea (Noda 2000: 33). The dual message of environmentalism and anti-nuclear discourse intertwine in *FFVII*, serving as a commentary on and warning against the use of nuclear power for weapons and energy.[7]

Player Agency and Embodiment

In the simplest terms, the player's goal in playing an RPG is to experience a role and reach the end of the adventure, "beating" the game by completing the narrative and defeating the final boss (an enemy character controlled by the computer). Depending on skill and game literacy, a player may or may not be able to finish the game. In this case, playing the role becomes the aim in itself. When players are immersed in gameplay, they feel as if they are living the narrative, identifying strongly with the main character. *FFVII* is widely recognized as a game that created an unprecedented sense of immersion and emotional involvement in the narrative (Wood 2009: 167; Games[tm] staff 2014). This partly came from the lush visuals and 3D environment that were newly available with the hardware capabilities of the PlayStation console but also stemmed from the sense of power and control that was given to and stripped away from the player in the course of the game (Games[tm] staff 2014: 142). This manipulation of player agency was significant for the legacy of *FFVII*, which had a great impact on the games industry in Japan and abroad.

In all role-playing games, whether the tabletop classic *Dungeons and Dragons* or PC games like *Baldur's Gate*, player choices and decisions influence the story and sometimes the outcome of the game, giving the player a feeling of control, involvement, and immersion in the gameworld. Dialogue trees, for example, allow players to choose what their character should say in certain situations, which may affect later events. (Dialogue trees are scripted dialogue with many options, branching into different outcomes depending on choices made by the player.) The JRPG as a genre is often criticized for allowing very little leeway in the script, with fewer choices available to the player than commonly found in a Western RPG. Examining the script of *FFVII*, it is clear that many dialogue choices have no bearing on the narrative development. Instead, a high degree of agency is given to the player in the fully explorable game environment. The World Map is accessible first by foot, then by riding a Chocobo (a bird-like creature), followed by a series of vehicles with increasingly greater power and range of movement, culminating with an airship. The player can revisit areas to buy more items from shops, talk to new characters, discover hidden materials, and so forth. However, some areas are completely inaccessible unless the player obtains a certain breed of Chocobo that can traverse mountains and other obstacles. These Chocobos must be bred specially from other Chocobos lured from the wild, secured in a ranch, and fed special food. The Chocobo strategies of *FFVII* are complex and challenging, targeted at serious players and completionists who would gladly spend hours of gameplay on side missions.

Similarly, much of Cloud's backstory is hidden in cut-scenes (cinematic sequences separate from the field of play), only triggered by exploring obscure places. The Shinra mansion's basement in Nibelheim holds a key cut-scene and hidden documents revealing the truth of Cloud's exposure to Mako Radiation Therapy. The Shinra basement also holds the character Vincent Valentine, but acquiring Vincent is optional, even though his backstory explains Shinra's experiments in genetic manipulation. The backstory of another optional character, Yuffie Kisaragi, explains the history of Shinra's colonial-industrial expansion over islands in the Western seas. Players who explore the whole world and take the trouble to add Vincent and Yuffie to their party gain much insight into the evil nature of Shinra Corporation. Further, certain cut-scenes can only be triggered in certain areas with the right characters in Cloud's party. In other words, the amount of narrative backstory experienced by the player is directly tied to the time and effort that the player invests in exploring the Planet and revisiting areas with different party members. This amount of player agency and control is crucial to the player's emotional involvement in the narrative.

At the same time, *FFVII* also strips away player agency to an unprecedented degree. The sudden death of Aeris at an advanced point in the narrative is often cited as the one event that most changed game plot development from the 1990s onward.[8] The shock experienced by the player is intense, not only encompassing a feeling of loss and mourning for a loved character in the story but also the shock of losing a valuable party member in the game. Aeris's death represents the loss of time and effort that the player invested in leveling-up a character; assigning materia, weapons, armor, and other equipment; and strategizing the best and most well-balanced membership of the questing party. If the player has always included Aeris in the party for her healing powers, an enormous sense of frustration is felt at the realization that it is now necessary to level-up another character to perform the same healing function. Aeris's death is a brilliant combination of narrative surprise and player frustration. This event makes the player grasp the strategic nature of any character in the game, in a self-conscious realization that the player is only a person in the non-diegetic space, playing the game called *Final Fantasy*. A high degree of self-awareness is engendered in the player, who feels manipulated by the developers, realizing afresh that the game is a product, constructed and created by a development team.

At the same time, the identity crisis experienced by the main character Cloud disrupts player-character identification. Cloud's memory loss and self-delusions make him an unreliable hero, a questionable "self" that makes the player question their own role in the game narrative. At one point, we must determine which of three possible Cloud-selves is real, while Cloud himself hovers spectrally above the scene, clutching his head in pain. The jarring disruptions in character identification make the player focus more closely on the intricate narrative twists, greatly increasing player immersion. Player agency is therefore manipulated in *FFVII* in ways that had not previously been experienced by gamers. By establishing direct and visible links between diegetic and non-diegetic space, *FFVII* makes the player consider the relationship between the gameworld and reality in new and thoughtful ways. The player must engage actively with the issues, not just sit back and watch passively as events unfold. The player is complicit in the nuclear enterprise and feels more motivated to fight against Shinra for the good of the dying Planet. The anti-nuclear message of *FFVII* is not just "read" by the player but also fully experienced, carried in the guilt of Cloud and Barret and also in Cloud's continuing battle to define his own identity. This kind of player experience is known as "embodiment" (Grodal 2003; Gregersen and

Grodal 2009), providing deep engagement with the ideology of the game text. Living through the narrative as the person controlling the main character, strategizing and making choices that inform details of narrative development, makes the message of the game more likely to "stick" with the player as the result of active rather than passive learning (Gee 2003).

Conclusions

It is little wonder that this game resonated so strongly with the Japanese imagination in 1997, a time of national introspection following the economic recession, the Great Hanshin Earthquake (January 1995), and Aum Shinrikyō attacks on the Tokyo subway system (March 1995). A number of power plant accidents in the 1990s also heightened concern over the safe use of nuclear energy: the Mihama (Fukui Prefecture) steam explosion of September 1991 released radiation into the atmosphere due to a broken tube in the steam generator; the Monju nuclear power plant (also in Fukui Prefecture) was shut down in December 1995 when a sodium leak caused a significant fire; and a minor explosion in the nuclear reprocessing plant at Tōkaimura in Ibaraki Prefecture occurred in March 1997. A more serious accident occurred in the Tōkaimura uranium reprocessing facility in September 1999. High-profile protests resulted in the cancellation of two nuclear power plants in the towns of Hōhoku, Yamaguchi Prefecture, in 1994 and Kushima, Miyazaki Prefecture, in 1997. *FFVII* was a text of its time, commenting on and reflecting the historical reality of anti-nuclear feeling in Japan.

Ideological messages in game narratives cannot be treated like literature or film due to player involvement and the nature of authorship in the medium.[9] "Authorship" of the text is diffused, since different teams work on each aspect of the game. Although more than one hundred people may work on a *Final Fantasy* game, that team is a small unit in the development company Square, whose management oversees the series and considers aspects such as market appeal and target audience. The critique of *FFVII* is not an expression of one person's ideas, values, and attitudes, but an amalgam of the ideas, values, and attitudes of a group. Where a "text" in cultural studies is seen as a single utterance of a broader discourse, I would argue that one game text manifests broader social discourse in and of itself.

The JRPG is highly linear in plot, while gameplay dynamics such as player-character identification, battle strategy, and character level-ups are strictly regulated by computer code dictating what the player can and cannot do. This linearity affords the developer more power to present their desired ideology, aided by a liberal use of cut-scenes, which can act on the audience more like films as they put down the controller and watch for a moment.[10] The JRPG player is aware of the genre's limitations, experiencing frustration when their movement is restricted or when there are few dialogue options. Conversely, this makes the player more aware of the game as a constructed space and authored product. The ideology of the game is not taken as "natural" but as a message that the developers want to convey. This is especially true for games like *FFVII* which incorporate self-reflexivity into the text in creative ways. The embodied experience of gameplay combines with the linear plot of the JRPG to force the player into decision-making practices with which they might not always agree, giving a self-conscious quality to the gameplay. If this does not always result in internalization of the developer's ideology, it certainly necessitates engagement with it. *FFVII* may be read as a site of convergence between the historical reality of anti-nuclear discourse and the increasing self-reflexivity of a maturing narrative form. The two processes work on each other, and inevitably on the player, to create an ideological impact through the lived experience of the game text.

Notes

1 I thank Andrew DiMola and Kevin West for their insights into *FFIV* and *FFVI*. On nuclear discourse in *FFX* (see Hutchinson 2014).
2 On atomic bomb literature see Treat (1995); on atomic bomb cinema see Shapiro (2002). Contributors to Robert Jacobs' (2010) volume examine a range of art forms with respect to nuclear metaphors and messages.
3 The kanji characters are "magic" and "clarity," while "clarity" comprises the characters for "sun" and "light/radiance." While the transliteration Makō is more accurate, I follow conventions of the localized game, using terms and character names that appear onscreen in the English language version
4 AVALANCHE and SOLDIER are capitalized in the English language version, occasioning discussion on fan forums (GameFAQs 2011). The capitalization probably reflects the fact that in Japanese, the words appear as *katakana* and thereby stand out from the surrounding text.
5 All quoted dialogue comes from the localized U.S. version of the game. The dialogue appears in text boxes when characters speak (RPGAMER 1998).
6 These lines are spoken randomly each time the player encounters one of these characters.
7 Hasegawa (2004: 82) sees anti-nuclear protest as one part of the anti-pollution movement advocating green energy, one of many grassroots environmental movements in Japan.
8 *Retro Gamer* (2011: 25, 28) describes the death as a "defining moment" in "the RPG that changed the genre," a "shocking, sad, and brilliant" move that made *FFVII* "enormously influential," for many players "the first videogame narrative to leave a mark on them."
9 Some argue that player actions change the game to such an extent that we should think of them as co-authors (Tavares et al. 2005).
10 James Newman (2013: 88) argues for player engagement rather than passivity during the cut-scene, as a "critical, reflective space."

8 The Cute Shall Inherit the Earth

Post-Apocalyptic Posthumanity in *Tokyo Jungle*

Kathryn Hemmann

Alan Weisman's 2007 thought experiment *The World without Us* imagines a world in which humankind has suddenly disappeared from the face of the earth. The roofs of houses and apartment buildings collapse as weeds and trees push their way up through concrete and asphalt. Native flora and fauna proliferate as they intermix with exotic imported species used for decoration and kept as pets, and new ecosystems emerge. Shells of automobiles rust silently away while the steel frames of bridges and skyscrapers remain, even as they are grown over with flowering vines and kudzu. "Central Park's grass is gone," he writes:

> A maturing forest is in its place, radiating down former streets and invading empty foundations. Coyotes, red foxes, and bobcats have brought squirrels back into the balance with oak trees tough enough to outlast the lead we deposited, and after 500 years, even in a warming climate the oaks, beeches, and moisture-loving species such as ash dominate.
>
> (Weisman 2007: 44)

This is how Weisman pictures New York City after the departure of humankind, but it could just as easily be a description of *Tokyo Jungle* (*Tōkyō janguru*), an open-world urban survival game published for the PlayStation 3 game console (and digitally released over the PlayStation Network in Region 1 territories) in 2012. In this game, the player takes on the role of a solitary animal or pack of animals fighting to stay alive on the mean streets of Shibuya after humanity has mysteriously vanished (see Chapter 32 for more information on Shibuya). The railway bridges are intact, but there are no trains. The lettering on the signs hanging beside the unbroken windows is legible, but everything is covered with dust and grime. The game's fully interactive environments provide a striking visual contrast between the cold gray concrete and metal structures human beings have left behind and the lush greenery that has begun to overtake them. As in Weisman's visualization of a depopulated Manhattan, there is a thrilling juxtaposition between the player's understanding of Shibuya as a thriving metropolis and the game's invitation to view familiar landmarks through the eyes of a nonhuman animal focused not on the acquisition of consumer goods but rather on the means of survival.

Japanese videogames have featured a multitude of apocalyptic and post-apocalyptic scenarios. Well-known examples include Nintendo's 2002 open-world adventure game *The Legend of Zelda: The Wind Waker* and Square Enix's 2009 role-playing game *Final Fantasy XIII*, in which the player's goal is not to prevent an apocalypse from occurring but rather to come to terms with an apocalypse that has already occurred (see Chapter 7). What's especially interesting about *Tokyo Jungle* is that it was released in Japan in the June of 2012, a little more than a year after the triple disaster earthquake, tsunami, and nuclear meltdown on March 11, 2011. Furthermore, the game eschews stylishly rendered graphics and instead encourages its player to enter an environment saturated with gritty realism, with area maps closely modeled on the urban scenery and layout of the Shibuya Station vicinity and the surrounding district. *Tokyo Jungle*'s producer and distributor, Studio Japan, is a well-known and well-respected team with direct ties to no less than Sony Computer Entertainment, which published the game. Why would such a major media development studio release a high-profile title featuring a fantasy disaster so shortly after a real disaster whose real effects were still being felt and analyzed across Japan and across the ocean? Why does the game seem to celebrate the absolute disappearance of humanity from the urban landscape of Tokyo? Furthermore, *Tokyo Jungle* received generally favorable critical reviews, with North American and European reviewers praising its originality and Japanese reviewers praising its setting and accessibility (Eisenbeis 2012; Gibson 2012; Moriarty 2012). What is the appeal of such a dark post-apocalyptic environment in not only *Tokyo Jungle* but in other titles in contemporary Japanese popular media as well?

When examined in the context of other depictions of disaster in contemporary Japanese fiction, cinema, and television, the ideology of *Tokyo Jungle* demonstrates an emerging awareness and acceptance of philosophical posthumanism and a literally posthuman world. Fears concerning disaster and the resulting annihilation of humanity are ameliorated by the game's representation of the nonhuman harbingers of the post-apocalyptic world as being primarily small, furry, and adorable. I argue that this link between cuteness and the nonhuman is tied to a broader connection between apocalypse and the feminine in contemporary Japanese media, in which adolescent female sexuality is often imbued with anxiety over the possible extinction of the human species mixed with an affective longing for healing and regeneration. Far from being merely escapist or nihilistic, the narrative attraction to the nonhuman and the posthuman, especially as represented by the animal and the feminine, can be understood as a speculative alternative to the irrational rationalism of the masculinist grand narrative involving the equation of scientific progress with economic growth that has shaped Japan's postwar history yet come increasingly under fire in the wake of the nuclear disaster at the Fukushima Daiichi power plant (Aldrich 2013; Miyamoto 2013).

Cuteness as a Catalyst for Affective Gameplay

The mascot for *Tokyo Jungle* is a tiny, fluffy Pomeranian dog, one of the first animals the player is able to control and a lone spot of cuteness against a dreary urban backdrop. The cute, or *kawaii*, aesthetic and related subcultures of contemporary Japan are well known (see Chapter 35); yet it may be difficult to associate the survival-of-the-fittest struggle for life in post-apocalyptic Tokyo with the image of "a haven of play and nostalgized childhood" associated with mascot characters such as Hello Kitty and Rilakkuma (Yano 2013b: 11). The cuteness factor comes into play with the fifty species of animals that the player can choose to control, which range from pet dogs and horses to lions and elephants. Even the largest of these animals appears tiny against the Shibuya skyscrapers, and each has endearing characteristics, such as the whining noises it makes when hungry and the happy yips and chirps it makes when satisfied. Each of these animals has a set of strengths and weaknesses that affect gameplay in a rock-paper-scissors configuration (e.g., an animal with low stealth and attack power, such as the sheep, might have high stamina and an increased resistance to environmental toxicity). The game's Japanese language and English language promotional video trailers promise players that they will be able to hunt for food, flee from danger, and generate offspring. Watching a cast of fluidly rendered animals undertake and succeed in these life-or-death scenarios has a clearly affective appeal; players may find excitement and humor in using a chicken to attack a wolf in the face in order to protect a nest full of fluffy yellow chicks, for example. By sharing the trials and triumphs of her onscreen avatars, the player is able to establish an emotional bond with these animals and their offspring.

The affective appeal of *Tokyo Jungle* is underscored by the game's roleplaying aspects. Each of the playable animals has its own storyline, one of which will take a typical gamer approximately five to ten minutes to complete. The majority of these storylines are simple and follow a similar narrative pattern: a lone and hungry animal, formerly under the care of humans, must leave its familiar surroundings and venture into the world in order to grow stronger and achieve territorial dominance. The Pomeranian dog, which is one of the first animals the player can control, serves as an example of this narrative pattern. In the suburbs of Shibuya, the Pomeranian lives in its owner's apartment even though the whereabouts of its owner are unknown. Having run out of food, the Pomeranian can no longer live as a pampered pet. As the onscreen text tells the player, "The time to rise from toy dog to noble beast is at hand" (Kataoka 2012). The scene then shifts to the street outside the apartment building, and the player is prompted to begin hunting. Bars representing the dog's life, hunger level, and stamina appear in the corner of the screen, and the game is afoot. After sneaking under abandoned vehicles and leaping over crevasses that have appeared in the pavement, the Pomeranian finds itself in the territory of a hostile cat, which promptly attacks. Upon defeating the cat and claiming its territory, the player is rewarded with the message, "You're a bona fide hunter now!" Thus encouraged to share the animal's sense of achievement, the player becomes invested in the survival of each animal and is, through the game's story mode, strongly encouraged to identify with the animal itself.

After having beaten an animal's story mode, the player is free to play as the animal in a more open-ended survival mode while exploring the abandoned streets, alleyways, and buildings of a post-apocalyptic Shibuya, a digital playground that partially mirrors the architecture and topography of the area surrounding the real-world Shibuya Station. By playing in survival mode, the player can find at least one USB stick as each animal, and the data stored on these drives provides clues concerning the fate of the human race.

To abbreviate a complicated story involving the more speculative aspects of quantum physics, the human population of the year 2215 exhausted its resources and attempted to send itself back in time, which backfired and resulted in a world with no humans at all. Towards the end of the game, the player must take on the role of one of the advance scouts of the human species, a robotic dog clearly modeled on Sony's dog-like robot companion AIBO. As ERC-003, a cyborg that supposedly contains organic canine DNA, the player must choose whether to restore humanity to the present time. If the player chooses to do so, the screen goes black, and no further gameplay or narrative fragments are accessible. If the player chooses not to do so, then the player is rewarded with beautiful music accompanying the ending credits and images of a gorgeously overgrown Shibuya that is teeming with wildlife. The return of humanity is thus configured as the "bad ending," while the banishment of humankind is the "good ending." From the beginning to the end of *Tokyo Jungle*, the player is thus encouraged to sympathize with animals instead of humans, especially since the empowerment of animals is characterized as being directly tied to the absence of humans. After hours of playing through the stories of the various species that have come to inhabit Shibuya, the player has presumably been influenced to experience the extinction of the human race as a crowning achievement for animals as the end credits roll.

Digital Animals as Stewards of Posthuman Philosophy

The story and gameplay features of *Tokyo Jungle* encourage the player to develop an antagonistic attitude towards humanity and its failed stewardship of the environment. This view reflects theories of such environmental philosophers as Nick Bostrom, founder of Oxford University's Future of Humanity Institute and proponent of human enhancement, and John A. Leslie, member of the advisory board of the Lifeboat Foundation and strong critic of the anthropic bias, or the seductive and persistent ideological fallacy that the universe was created for the benefit of humankind. Both Bostrom and Leslie champion astrophysicist Brandon Carter's Doomsday Argument, which holds that there is no cause to believe that we are not more than halfway through the lifespan of the human species, as it is statistically unlikely that more than a trillion human beings will ever live (Leslie 1996: 2). Therefore, the greater the birthrates and lifespans of the members of our species are, the more likely that we will self-inflict a doomsday scenario. In *The End of the World: The Science and Ethics of Human Extinction*, Leslie details many such scenarios, from nuclear threats to unforeseen consequences of nanotechnology to Schopenhauerian pessimism (namely, the troubling notion that it is a small step between deciding that all life should be annihilated to making it so) (Leslie 1996: 172). Leslie dispassionately skips through dozens of global catastrophic risks, making no overt value judgments but rendering the consequences of human irresponsibility abundantly apparent.

At the end of the book, in a chapter titled "Why Prolong Human History," Leslie makes the utilitarian argument that perhaps we should not. Perhaps the happiness of a small population is preferable to the misery of a large population. How ethical is it, however, to demand unconscionable sacrifices of individuals in order to ensure the survival of the human species? Leslie writes:

> Obligations to keep the human race in existence may sometimes be recognized in theory, but are then eroded by a thousand considerations: uncertainty about what future people would be like; loving concern for those already in existence; the reflection that things like pollution control might have to be imposed undemocratically or in defiance of 'rights' which manage to be 'genuine' or 'taken seriously' only because they must never be overruled, and so forth.
>
> (Leslie 1996: 184)

The action we as a supposedly civil society may be forced to undertake in order to guarantee our survival may not justify the means. If the global population is to be reduced, how do we decide who must die? Furthermore, do our obligations concerning the happiness of the people of the future truly outweigh our obligations concerning the happiness of the human beings presently on the earth? Indeed, how are we to measure a concept such as "the quality of life" if a high quality of life for some is presupposed by a low quality of life for others? As Leslie is careful to point out, he is not suggesting that we should strive toward human extinction or to discourage efforts to oppose risks against its continued existence. Rather, he advocates an almost Buddhist disavowal of the attachment to the notion of the cosmic importance of human existence. In other words, we will almost certainly perish as a species, but this eventuality is not something over which we should be unduly concerned.

Philosophers such as Nick Bostrom have pursued this line of thinking in a different direction, arguing that there is no need for future sentient life to be human at all. We can instead become "transhuman," a term that designates *Homo sapiens* in a transitional period as a species, a state into which we have already made tentative progress though mechanical and medical advances ranging from eyeglasses to organ transplants. Far from being somehow "un-natural," or "better than evolution," selective human enhancement may instead be understood as an intervention into many of the problems we have created for ourselves by allowing processes such as global population growth, climate change, and reliance on nuclear energy to progress unchecked (Bostrom and Sandburg 2009: 408). Moreover, as evolutionary theorists such as Christopher Willis have argued, the only way to circumvent the existential risks facing the human race is to either alter our physical selves or our behavior as a species so profoundly that we, as a group of sentient organisms, might even become unrecognizable to contemporary humans (Willis 2008: 68).

Although such ideas may seem lifted directly from the pages of a science-fiction story, certain policy makers take them quite seriously. In a short essay on transhumanism published as part of the "World's Most Dangerous Ideas" series run by *Foreign Policy* magazine, political scientist and former U.S. policymaker Francis Fukuyama describes transhumanist ideals as hubristic "Promethean desires" that will ultimately lead us to "deface humanity with [...] genetic bulldozers and psychotropic shopping malls" (Fukuyama 2004: 43). These strong words succinctly encapsulate the neoconservative argument Fukuyama sets forth in his 2002 monograph *Our Posthuman Future: Consequences of the Biotechnology Revolution*, which essentially states that the loss of human dignity and affronts against "human nature" implicit in speculative scientific practices such as genetic modification will result in the swift downfall of liberal democracies across the world. Posthumanists themselves disagree on the means and benefits of transhumanism and human extinction, with some scientists and philosophers favoring gradual yet complete human extinction over evolution. Les Knight, one of the leaders of the Voluntary Human Extinction Movement, sees the vast majority of human impacts on the natural environment as negative, meaning that the story of our time on earth can have only one possible conclusion. If *Homo sapiens* is indeed doomed to drag itself and countless numbers of other species into oblivion, voluntary extinction is "so much nicer than involuntary extinction, don't you think?", Knight quips (Southan 2012).

Nonhuman "Life" as a Theme of Apocalyptic Popular Media

Tokyo Jungle falls on the extreme end of the posthuman philosophical spectrum, leaving the fate of the human race in the hands of robotic canines that become more attached to the Shibuya wildlife than they ever were to their former human masters. Just as the player vicariously feels the triumph of the Pomeranian who leaves its owner's apartment and claims a small section of the abandoned Shibuya suburbs for its own, so too is the player guided to understand the game's "good" ending, in which the robotic dog ERC-003 (its design a play on Shibuya's iconic "loyal dog" Hachikō) consigns humanity to oblivion so that all other animals might prosper, as a positive and even welcomed scenario. Should the player achieve this ending, the final reward after the credits finish is a warmly lit image of ERC-003 overgrown with moss and flowers overlaid by peaceful music. Although this is a fair and fitting conclusion to the game, as the theme of social collapse and human extinction has been foreshadowed, explored, and reiterated in each animal's individual story, we cannot fail to note the emotional discrepancy created by the game's proximity to the March 2011 triple disaster, especially as some of the game's environmental settings, from collapsed highway bridges to irradiated water, could have been drawn directly from the news and footage that flooded the media in the wake of these events.

Crispy's, the studio responsible for *Tokyo Jungle*, is the brainchild of director Kataoka Yōhei, who founded the collective of game designers with no previous industry experience in 2006. Crispy's received funding through a Sony Computer Entertainment project called Playstation C.A.M.P. (Creator Audition Mash Up Project), which has provided young industry hopefuls the chance to pitch game ideas to Sony. When Kataoka first proposed the idea for *Tokyo Jungle* in 2009, Sony Worldwide Studio president Yoshida Shuhei's response was not positive. One of the primary objections to the project was that North American and European gamers would not be able to appreciate the game's Japanese setting or lack of human protagonists (Kumar 2013), but the positive reception to a short advance demo of the game at overseas videogame trade shows resulted in a substantial budget increase (Dutton 2012). The advance demo was a hit at the 2010 Tokyo Game Show as well, which allowed Crispy's to retain the privilege of designing promotional materials for *Tokyo Jungle* according to Kataoka's vision for the project (Klepek 2012). The game's development period continued through the aftermath of the March 2011 disasters for its scheduled release in the summer of 2012. If the project had not found widespread appreciation and acceptance with such a large audience, it may well have been canceled. Its Tokyo setting was not altered, however, nor was the creative vision of its developers unduly affected, as they saw their work as a positive celebration of life.

"Life" (*seimei*) emerges as a frequent thematic keyword in Kataoka's descriptions of *Tokyo Jungle* in his interviews with the Japanese gaming press. The director's insistence on a gritty and muted color palette and a visual emphasis on emptiness instead of busyness was strongly influenced by the photography collection *Tokyo Nobody* released in 2000 by Nakano Masaaki. The photographs in *Tokyo Nobody*, mostly taken in the early hours of the morning, depict the streets of Tokyo, both large and small, completely devoid of human beings. Far from being disturbed by such images, Kataoka, who was searching for "a setting that would be conducive for life to thrive," admits that, "The moment I saw [these pictures], I thought, 'What a gentle (*yasashii*) perspective on the world; this is exactly what I was looking for'" (Ōji 2012). The game's music producer TaQ (Sakakibara Taku), who was specifically assigned to the project by Sony, recounts a similar search for an appropriate atmosphere. In an interview with *Famitsū*, Japan's foremost videogame magazine, TaQ explains:

Since animals are the stars of the game, music too strongly reminiscent of a human presence (*ningen aji*) wouldn't be a good fit. For example, I thought, 'if we're talking about a jungle, then the first thing that comes to mind is drums,' so I tried it out. But really, since drums are made from the hide humans skin from animals, and since humans are the ones who beat drums, the music ended up feeling way too human.

(*Famitsū* 2012)

In order to portray a world devoid of human influence yet alive with possibilities, TaQ finally settled on electronically produced techno music, a decision that Kataoka enthusiastically embraced. *Tokyo Jungle*'s staff and producers were thus intensely committed to creating a window into a post-apocalyptic world that was not frightening or upsetting like the aftermaths of real-world disasters, not to mention many fictional and religious depictions of the apocalypse, but rather exciting and vivacious. Of course, the game's adorable mascot animals do not detract from this intended impression, instead enhancing the international marketability of the game by bypassing the need to code human characters with racial and ethnic markers.

Although the appeal of apocalyptic and dystopian themes is universal, there is evidence that North American and European gamers enjoyed *Tokyo Jungle* not in spite of its Japanese origin but rather because of it. In an interview with the online gaming magazine *Gamasutra*, producer Yamagiwa Masaaki recounted that "he is often told by *Tokyo Jungle*'s Western fans that they love the game for being so Japanese, rather than attempting to please Western culture" (Rose 2012). The widespread familiarity with contemporary Japanese media among gamers, bolstered by the successful localization of bestselling Japanese videogame franchises such as *Pokémon* and *Final Fantasy*, has resulted in an international audience of gamers eager to experience the newest titles from Japan. Japanese videogame production companies have offices in multiple overseas territories and pay close attention to international markets during the production phases of not only high-profile titles but often more niche-market projects as well. These companies also typically use different marketing strategies for different territorial markets based on perceived and demonstrated differences in these markets, which may include emphasizing or de-emphasizing the product's "Japanese cultural odor" (Consalvo 2009: 140; Iwabuchi 2004a: 48).

Tokyo Jungle is not a flash in the pan of popular culture or a lone radical voice in a crowd of stories vociferously advocating human survival. As scholars of Japanese religion have argued in various contexts, Japanese eschatologies on both a personal and a societal scale are more cyclical than teleological (Glassman 2012; LaFleur 1986). This broad perception of the end of the world as something inevitable yet not final manifests itself in anime, manga, and videogames through the common scenario of characters living in a world that is slowly fading away after the apocalypse has already occurred. Some of these scenarios, such as those of the 2006 animated series

Ergo Proxy and the 2009 videogame *Final Fantasy XIII*, feature a dystopia that is largely a result of humanity artificially clinging to life through an authoritarian application of advanced technology. In other scenarios, such as those of the 2013 animated series *From the New World* (*Shinsekai yori*) and *Humanity Has Declined* (*Jinrui wa suitai shimashita*), extremely low birthrates and sparse population densities have resulted in relatively peaceful agrarian societies in which most humans lead rich and satisfying lives. As opposed to the narrative tendency in many popular media titles in which a lone male hero or small (and mostly male) band of heroes attempt to avert an apocalypse, the apocalypse has already happened in many recent anime and manga, and the heroes left to pick up the pieces afterwards tend to be attractive young women, or *bishōjo*.

Many of the most iconic characters of anime and manga are *bishōjo* directly associated with apocalyptic and transhuman themes. The gynoid Chi from *Chobits* (2002) and the clone Ayanami Rei from *Neon Genesis Evangelion* (1995–1996, *Shin seiki Evangerion*) spring immediately to mind, as does the genetically posthuman Nausicaä, who makes a choice at the climax of the manga *Nausicaä of the Valley of the Wind* (*Kaze no tani no Nausicaä*, 1982–1984) quite similar to the "good ending" choice made by the player at the end of *Tokyo Jungle*. Cultural critics such as Susan Napier (2005), Saitō Tamaki (2011a), and Thomas Lamarre (2009) have highlighted the parallels between attractive young *bishōjo* characters and themes of freedom, flight, hope, healing, and regeneration, so it is interesting that so many of these characters are so closely related to the apocalypse and the resulting end of humanity. Perhaps, through the regenerative reproductive capacity of these characters, whose nascent sexuality is not yet tainted by male bodies and masculinist ideologies such as nationalism, militarism, and scientific rationalism, the end of the world may indeed be coded as a positive event whose promise of ecological balance and emotional serenity extends beyond Susan Sontag's (1965) conceptualization of the "delight in disaster" inspired by visually stimulating spectacle and an almost anarchist glee in the collapse of the established order. As Raffaella Baccolini (2004) writes concerning dystopic fiction, the apocalypse is capable of overturning artificial boundaries, erasing political borders, and providing "a subversive and oppositional strategy against hegemonic ideology." The post-apocalyptic world is thus fertile ground for the seeds of new and different ideas to spread roots and thrive, and what better symbols of a potential new order than those marginalized by the old order, such as young women and animals? In their co-authored monograph *Ecofeminism*, Maria Miles and Vandana Shiva make a case for ecological feminism, which "creates the possibility of viewing the world as an active subject, not merely as a resource to be manipulated and appropriated" (1993: 34). Miles and Shiva argue that the capitalistic and patriarchal ideologies underlying many scientific discourses construct the environment as something to be consumed, commodified, or preserved as a site of future production. Fictional young women and animals thereby serve as potent symbols for the possibility of an existence that is not limited by masculinist and anthropocentric views of the natural world.

In *Tokyo Jungle*, the affective response of hope and delight hidden in a post-human, post-apocalyptic world is facilitated by player identification with cute animals adorably engaging in life-or-death struggles against the backdrop of a ruined Tokyo that has started to bloom. Just as the Pomeranian must leave behind its owner's apartment in order to fulfill its potential, the player must leave behind the social and political baggage of the human species in order to fully enjoy the game and its lush environment and to achieve the "good ending" in which humanity vanishes forever from the face of the earth. Like the animated and illustrated *bishōjo*-centered narratives that mediate fears concerning the collapse of society, *Tokyo Jungle* serves as a means of addressing anxiety relating to disaster. If social and environmental catastrophe and the eventual extinction of humanity are just as unavoidable and unpredictable as earthquakes and tsunamis, then perhaps it is comforting to take a more posthuman view of a post-apocalyptic world instead of continuing to struggle against the inevitable. Cute animals fighting for survival and dominance in a jungle growing out of the ruins of Tokyo are therefore an expression of a positive posthuman hope for the survival of life in all its forms.

PART IV

Fan Media and Technology

9 Managing Manga Studies in the Convergent Classroom

Mark McLelland

Introduction

When I first began to study Japanese language, history, and culture while residing in the United Kingdom in the late 1980s, "Japan" to most people meant cars and compact electronic devices such as the Sony Walkman portable cassette player, first marketed in 1979. For most people at this time, Japan was known as the world's second largest economy, a major business hub, and a leader in innovative manufacturing practices. It was a common assumption that those learning Japanese were doing so for career purposes. Of course, this is distant history for today's undergraduate students who were not born at the time. For young people encountering Japan now, the image is not of economic or business prowess but one of popular culture: manga, anime, computer games, fashion, and music.

Although it seems strange to recall this now, this shift in consumer interest from Japanese technology to Japanese cultural products was not discernable a quarter of a century ago. Indeed, in 1983, manga scholar and translator Frederick Schodt anticipated that it would be difficult for Japanese cultural content to find a foothold in the United States. He asked:

> Will Japanese comics now follow Toyotas and Sony overseas? The obstacles they face are formidable. The same cultural isolation that has helped Japan develop such a rich comic culture is also a factor limiting the ability of people in other nations to understand—and enjoy—them.
>
> (Schodt 1983: 153)

Indeed, early attempts to introduce manga to a U.S. readership in the late 1980s involved a localization process whereby manga's distinctive Japanese features—the right-to-left organization of content, avoidance of color, use of gray-scale shading, and heavy reliance on onomatopoeia and other sound effects to indicate movement or mood—were modified to cater to perceived local tastes (Matsui 2009: 13). However, as I will discuss, by the early 2000s, the fandom for Japanese anime, manga, and games had grown to the extent that there was a new enthusiasm to consume *authentic* Japanese content—unmodified by U.S. distributors—as a new generation of fans was attracted to the study of Japanese language as a means to access a greater range of material than that made available through official licensing and distribution systems.

Accordingly, by the late 1990s, the Japanese government had become aware that young people's interest could be an effective means of promoting a positive image of Japan abroad, especially across Asia where memories of Japan's wartime aggression were still very much alive. From the early 2000s, emphasizing "Cool Japan" (McGray 2002) became a common marketing strategy on the part of Japanese businesses, government agencies, and both domestic and overseas universities offering Japanese language and culture courses.

However, this strategy required widespread changes to the way that cultural content is distributed and made available in today's convergent media environment. When I was first studying Japanese, it was difficult to get hold of Japanese books or manga and almost impossible to find Japanese videos or other spoken-word media like radio shows or cassette tapes. It was not until I first arrived in Japan in 1987 that the full range and dynamism of Japanese popular culture became apparent—manga everywhere, J-pop the soundtrack in every store, anime on television all day, and Harajuku street fashion on parade every weekend.

These days, of course, all these different cultural products are accessible via convergent media devices, such as smartphones, tablets, and computers, making them available for viewing and purchase via the Internet any time, any place. In addition, the digital technology that enables content distribution via the Internet also allows the easy manipulation and "remix" of that content allowing users to reproduce, modify, and distribute their own versions of content, for example by themselves translating or dubbing original Japanese manga and anime. Hence, students and fans now live in a convergent media environment where they occupy multiple roles as fans, students and "produsers" (producers + users; Bruns 2008) of Japanese cultural content—a scenario not anticipated by educators in the 1980s. One result is that, today, no young person visiting Japan for the first time will be surprised by what they find there—the food, fashion, culture, and language will be familiar from years of online immersion in Japanese anime, manga, and games. In many ways, this makes teaching and learning about Japan much easier. Many students bring a wealth of knowledge of Japanese popular culture genres to the classroom and are no longer the blank slates of yesteryear. However, this new situation also brings challenges and difficulties concerning some aspects of Japanese popular culture, particularly the different cultural codes governing sexual content.

Using manga as my primary example, first I offer a brief history of the shift in production and consumption patterns of manga in the United States—from the perceived need for localization strategies toward an increasing demand for an "authentic" product. This requires an analysis of how "comic books" were received as a cultural product in the 1980s. I then look at how fans' Japanese language literacy that developed alongside increasing ease of access to original Japanese material via the Internet led to new, fan-based modes of manga distribution and consumption. Unlike the old days when it was necessary to request Japanese materials in "hard copy" from a library or bookstore, today almost anything can be found and downloaded in a few minutes. Much of this material has not been licensed for overseas distribution and hence raises issues about copyright violations and the circumvention of official product ratings. These moral and legal issues have implications for classroom practice that is often unforeseen by students but which cannot be ignored by educators in the increasingly bureaucratized "corporate university." This chapter will explore some of these issues.

The Development of a Comics' Culture in the United States

There is a long history of young people's engagement with comic book art in the United States, going back to the development of serialized comic strips in broadsheet newspapers of the 1920s. First published in book form as reprints of these earlier serials (Pustz 1999: 26), comics were seen as a lowbrow form of popular entertainment and were often criticized for promoting sex and violence. Comic books gained popularity during World War II as they were a cheap form of entertainment for U.S. troops. This new market led to an increase in depictions of "scantily clad women in classic pinup poses or compromising positions, sometimes involving bondage" (Pustz 1999: 31). Sales of comic books increased rapidly after the war, especially to male youth.

However, by the 1950s, the "pervasive conflation of sex and violence in comics" (Strub 2010: 15) had emerged as a target for social reformers, disturbed by rising levels of juvenile delinquency. These concerns were fueled by a rising class of "experts" trained in psychology, who claimed to be able to diagnose the source of social instability in the deleterious effects of exposure to popular culture, particularly comic books. In the developing Cold War climate, the dangers of drugs, homosexuality, and delinquency on the nation's youth were rehearsed in the media, and popular pundits pushed for an inquiry into comic books and their effects. Typical of this trend was psychiatrist Frederic Wertham's 1954 book *Seduction of the Innocent* that devoted hundreds of pages to "the various depravities of comics" (Strub 2010: 18).

The media furor surrounding the book's release led to a Senate committee hearing into the relationship between comic books and "juvenile delinquency." Although when the committee handed down its findings in 1955 it was ambivalent about any clear cause-and-effect role played by comics, instead understanding delinquency to be the effect of multiple causes, this did not dampen the media's interest in pushing Wertham's agenda. As a result, a number of state legislatures passed laws regulating or banning altogether certain comic genres and titles (Strub 2010: 20). The Comics Magazine Association of America (founded in October 1954) responded by establishing a voluntary code that reined in displays of violence and sex, ensuring that depictions of crime underlined that crime does not pay and images of sex and romance emphasized the sanctity of marriage (Strub 2010: 21).

Some artists did, however, continue to explore controversial themes in underground comics, often known as "comix," which satirized the "conformist middle-class values of America in the early 1960s" (Pustz 1999: 61). The references to drug use, graphic violence, and sexual scenarios meant they were aimed squarely at an adult audience and only available from specialist comic stores or via mail order. Since comix were not governed by the conformist Comics Code, artists "had no qualms about including depictions of all manner of sexual acts in their stories" and "did not hesitate to depict a variety of bodily functions" (Pustz 1999: 63). Hence, the Japanese manga that today are often criticized in the English language press for their preoccupation with sex and other bodily functions actually have a lot in common with the underground U.S. comix genre (see Chapter 24).

The Comics Code also sanitized the content of mainstream comic art and played a role in "the redefinition of the comic book audience toward younger readers," as publishers chose to focus on safe issues more appealing to children (Pustz 1999: 43). Hence, the moral panic surrounding Wertham's book and subsequent establishment of the Code not only put a dampener on the development of comic book art in the United States but also reinforced the stigma that there was something dangerous and anti-social behind reading comics.

However, despite the continuing stigma attached to comic books and the limited reading ability of their presumed audience, since the early 2000s there has been increased interest by booksellers, librarians, and educators in the use of "graphic novels" as a means of encouraging literacy among the school-age population. The term graphic novel, first used in the 1960s, was actively promoted as a category in bookstores and libraries in the early 2000s (MacDonald 2013). There has been an acknowledgement that, rather than appealing to the functionally illiterate, comics have their own specialized mode of communicating content and "[u]nderstanding the transitions between panels is ... an important part of developing comics literacy" (Pustz 1999: 118). Hence, these days "[c]omics, once the bane of librarians, now populate the shelves of most school and public libraries" (Nyeberg 2010: 37).

Graphic novels, like manga, "are a medium in which many genres are represented" (Holston 2010: 11), and a number of classics in the field broke down the once fast distinction between popular culture and literature. During the 1980s, there was a renewed interest in the narrative potentialities of the comic book format. Reframed as "sequential art," the combination of words and pictures was seen as a direct and powerful means of communicating a wide variety of storylines to readers. However, it was precisely this impact factor that caused concern among some that exposure to graphic novels might have a negative effect on young readers. Although there is no one industry standard, publishers in the United States have been cautious to provide ratings information. This makes American-produced comics different from manga published in Japan, where only extreme adult content is labeled with an adult (*seinen*) rating but "adult themes" can be found in a range of manga targeting youth audiences.

Introducing Manga to the United States

In the 1980s, there was skepticism whether Japanese manga, with its radically different style, format, content, history, and cultural assumptions from American-style comics, would attract readers. Accordingly, Viz Comics, American-based subsidiary of the Japanese publishing company Shogakukan, initially pursued a policy of localization. The manga that were licensed, translated, and distributed in the United States in the late 1980s were "flipped" so that they could be read from left-to-right in the more conventional American fashion. Yet other localization techniques, such as the inclusion of thought bubbles and increased use of color, proved unpopular with the Japanese artists who resisted attempts to make their work seem "more American" (Matsui 2009: 14).

Another serious issue impeding the localization of manga was thematic—the extent to which Japanese comics depicted sex and violence that were judged inappropriate for a youth audience in an American context. This is a particular problem for sexual content since in most U.S. jurisdictions' standards applying to sexuality are more rigorously enforced than those applying to violence (Sahlfeld 2010: 225). Hence, it has not been unusual for manga artists to be asked to "retouch sexual or other explicit scenes by hiding them behind sound effects and/or speech balloons" (Matsui 2009: 15).

The movement toward the production and distribution of more "authentic" manga in the United States took off in the late 1990s with the founding of a new publisher, TokyoPop, in 1997, which did not flip its translated titles. In addition, TokyoPop retained more original features; for instance, it did not translate onomatopoeic sound effects and released its translated volumes in a format and size closer to the Japanese originals (Matsui 2009: 18). This strategy of stressing the authenticity of the manga proved successful thanks to the Japan-literate audience for manga engendered by Viz's pioneering efforts. Additionally, by the early 2000s, Internet technology had been widely taken up in U.S. homes, schools, and universities, and it was much easier for fans to network, share information, and access material directly from Japanese sites.

By the mid-2000s there was such a degree of manga-literacy among readers that attempts by U.S. publishers to alter original manga by deleting scenes to fit in with local ratings was met by fierce resistance by fans, many of whom had accessed original versions online. For instance, although TokyoPop did pioneer translations from the "Boys Love" (BL for short) genre popular with girl readers that features boy/boy couples, the publisher tended to prefer safer titles with less emphasis on sexual scenarios and often changed the cover or deleted scenes and even "aged-up" characters from high school to college in order to make the stories less controversial for the U.S. market (Pagliassotti 2008). Fans, however, were frustrated by publishers' timidity in not licensing titles considered too edgy, giving readers no option other than to seek the originals online.

This means that today it is not possible to study manga reception overseas simply by looking at officially licensed products and sales figures since new communications technologies have given audiences much more control over the content they wish to view, often circumventing conventional licensing and distribution networks entirely. It is necessary to take note of the fan communities own circuits of distribution and reception.

From Manga Consumers to Manga "Produsers"

Although certain franchises—such as the *Super Mario Bros.*, *Pokémon*, or Studio Ghibli anime—appeal to an international market, only a tiny, and in many ways unrepresentative, number of Japanese titles make it onto the English language market through official licensing. Even with licensed products, the time lag between the publication in Japan of new installments and the distribution of English language versions tests the patience of fans and encourages other more direct means of accessing this material via the Internet (Lee 2009: 1016).

Fan engagement with Japanese cultural content precedes the Internet and took place at fan clubs and fan conventions. American television viewers had been introduced to Japanese animation via Tezuka Osamu's *Astro Boy* (*Tetsuwan Atomu*) series, first aired in 1963. However, it was unlikely that viewers at the time noticed that the series was from Japan as "an emphasis on the cartoon's stylistic and cultural differences would probably have held the show back from mainstream success" (Ruh 2009: 218). This began to change in the 1970s when small groups of fans began to actively seek out Japanese anime. In 1975 a program of Japanese science fiction anime was screened as part of an event hosted by the Los Angeles Science Fantasy Society, and by the late-1970s there were groups of fans in Los Angeles who visited the city's Japan town and subscribed to Japanese anime magazines (Patten 2004: 16, 19). By the early 1980s groups of manga and anime fans were organizing anime screenings at science fiction, comics, and other popular-culture events around the United States (Patten 2004: 16–18). The development of VHS technology during the 1970s had already facilitated the import of original material from Japan, aided by the fact that both the United States and Japan employed the same NTSC formatting system (Patten 2004: 60). Although a niche interest for much of the 1980s, the international success of the 1988 anime movie *Akira* (Ōtomo 1988) introduced anime to a wider audience. By 1994 the volume of anime titles on the U.S. video market was reported as outnumbering domestic titles (Patten 2004: 19, 104).

What were probably the first computer networks of anime fans were the Cal Animage club at the University of California, Berkeley campus, and the rec.arts.anime newsgroup, both founded in 1987 (Patten 2004: 38, 122). By the early 1990s fan groups began to emerge on USENET (established in the late 1980s) and other dial-up bulletin board systems where fans could store, share, and comment on their favorite manga and anime. This period also saw the birth of "scanlation" (scan + translation) where a fan with a source text or "raw" manga would upload the raws and other fans would collaborate, using software to blank out the Japanese text and provide English translations. For example, in 1996 a fan group impatient with the speed at which Viz was able to release new episodes of the popular series *Ranma ½* began to offer scanlations online (Inside Scanlation n.d.). This was one of the first operations to come to the attention of the publishers and be shut down after complaints received from the licensee. Subsequently, with free hosting offered by providers such as GeoCities (founded in 1994), numerous scanlation groups were set up online and linked together in a series of web rings, making it much easier for fans to network and organize around favored titles and genres. The amount of fan activity online has only increased, and, as media scholars Cheng-Wen Huang and Arlene Archer note, "For Western audiences, scanlations are far more accessible and feasible than manga in the traditional book form" and "are therefore likely to attract more readers than manga in book form" (2012: 53).

There are serious issues with these kinds of fan activities in regard to copyright violations that have been discussed elsewhere (e.g., Inside Scanlation n.d.; Lee 2009). However, I want to highlight something that has not yet received much discussion—the manner in which fans access to scanlations circumvents publishers' manga ratings system in the United States and thus exposes students and fans to material that can violate local regulations, especially in regard to sexual content.

Regulating Sexual Content in Manga in the United States and Japan

There is growing awareness in the media of the cultural clash between the highly violent and sexualized nature of some Japanese manga and anime and local ratings systems aimed at segregating this material and keeping it out of the reach of those under eighteen. As Frederik Schodt has noted:

> Feeding suspicion about manga among certain sectors of the public are several high-profile arrests in the United States and Canada of fans who possess manga and anime images or works commonly seen in Japan but are deemed to be child pornography overseas.
>
> (Schodt 2013: 24)

These anxieties have only been amplified with the passage in Japan in June 2014 of legislation criminalizing the possession of child pornography (production and distribution had already been criminalized in 1999). Inaccurate reporting in the English language press made much of the fact that manga and animation had been explicitly excluded from this legislation, suggesting that in Japan there is no oversight of content in this area. This is of course not the case, and it is worth comparing the development of sexual content in manga in Japan with our earlier discussion of the impact of the Comics Code on U.S. comics.

In Japan, the introduction of sexual themes in manga began somewhat later than in U.S. comics, taking off in the late 1960s when such content had been largely removed. In Japan, the increasing sexualization of mainstream media saw even content directed at young people begin to deal with sexuality in a new, less restrained manner. In 1968, the popular monthly boys' manga magazine *Weekly Shōnen Jump*, pushed the envelope with Nagai Gō's serialized comic story, *School of Shame* (*Harenchi gakuen*), about the sexual antics and frustrations of life at a co-educational high school. Although very popular with young male readers, this series, which alluded to such things as the male teaching staff's sexual obsession with female students, caused considerable outrage among teachers and Parent Teacher Associations (PTA) throughout Japan (Shimokawa 2009: 201).

The sexualization of media directed at young people, particularly boys, continued apace throughout the 1970s and 1980s. One genre, in particular, "*lolicon*," or "Lolita complex," manga (highly sexualized representations of school-age girls) was often singled out by parents as a bad influence on young people's sexual values. By the end of the 1970s, however, girls' manga, too, had increasingly begun to deal with sexual themes, although on the whole it does not contain the same level of violence that characterizes some boys' manga.

Female artists have proven to be just as interested as male artists in exploring sexual issues even in manga aimed at a youth audience. For example, the all-female manga collective CLAMP are authors of the highly successful *Chobits* manga series, which Thomas Lamarre describes as "overtly *ecchi*— that is risqué, naughty or dirty—and pornography plays a major role" (2009: 240). One of the most sexualized genres within girls' manga is BL that contains representations of sexual acts and complex sexual scenarios including incest, rape, and inter-generational seduction between two males. Such was the concern over the volume of BL materials available in public libraries that in 2008 there were unsuccessful attempts in Osaka prefecture and elsewhere to have BL titles designated "harmful to youth" and removed from the shelves (McLelland 2011).

The sexualization of youth media has of course long been controversial in Japan. One of the most sustained calls for reform of manga content followed the tragic murder of four young girls between 1988 and 1989 by serial killer Miyazaki Tsutomu. An investigation of Miyazaki's background and lifestyle revealed that he was an isolated youth who had been an avid collector of *lolicon* manga and animation, as well as adult pornography (see Chapter 33 on Akihabara). Following the Miyazaki scare, a coalition of PTA committees, feminist groups, and women's organizations lobbied local and national politicians for increased surveillance and regulation of violent and sexualized imagery in manga and animation, particularly those marketed to young people. One result of this increased vigilance was a spike in 1990 in the number of manga designated "harmful to youth" (Kinsella 2000: 149).

The industry's response to this popular movement calling for increased vigilance concerning manga content was to set up or reinforce existing systems of self-monitoring. However, unlike the similar industry-administered Comics Code in the United States, rather than tone down the level of fantasy sex and violence across all manga genres, the major publishers began to designate manga that might be considered harmful to youth as "adult manga" (*seinen* manga). These manga were clearly labeled and were sold shrink-wrapped to stop young people reading them in stores since "*tachiyomi*," or "standing reading," is a common practice in Japanese bookshops.

Japan's obscenity legislation has been applied very specifically to rule out representations of genitalia and pubic hair, but overall sexual scenarios that can include violence, group sex, and even rape are not captured by the legislation, so long as the offending organs are blurred or blanked out and an appropriate age rating is published on the cover. Of growing concern to some international agencies are sexual and violent representations of characters who are or may "appear to be" underage. The manga aesthetic tends to exaggerate youthful appearance, and many representations do seem to be of young or childlike characters. This means many manga and anime that deal in sexual themes fall foul of "child-abuse publications" legislation in some countries including Canada, the United Kingdom, and Australia, which have all seen successful prosecutions for possession of such material (McLelland 2012). Japan does not include purely fictional representations in its definition of child pornography, although the production and distribution of actual child pornography was outlawed in 1999 and "simple possession" of these materials followed suit in 2014. This point has been misrepresented in the English language press that has portrayed Japan as deviant in this regard (e.g., Fackler 2014). Legislation in Japan covering purely fictional images is similar to that in the United States. The prohibition of actual child pornography in the United States was first addressed in a 1977 federal statute, the *Protection of Children against Sexual Exploitation*. Subsequent legislation saw the kinds of material that fell under the statute both clarified and broadened.

The 1996 *Child Pornography Prevention Act* sought to prohibit child pornography even if the characters appearing in the pornographic item were not actual children; this included young-looking adults or computer-generated images. However, in 1999 The Ninth Circuit U.S. Court of Appeals found that phrases included in the Act such as, "appears to be a minor" and "conveys the impression that the depiction portrays a minor," were too vague and thereby placed limits on free expression. In response, the 2003 PROTECT (Prosecutorial Remedies and Other Tools to End the Exploitation of Children Today) Act replaced the words "appear to be a minor," instead with prohibiting imagery "that is, or is indistinguishable from, that of a minor," making clear that obviously fictional representations were not included.

However, the Act emphasized that "*obscene* visual representations of the sexual abuse of children" (my emphasis) were still prohibited and that this could include purely fictional representations, since obscenity is not protected speech (Russell 2008: 1486).

The implications are that "virtual" (that is unreal) depictions of children in sexual scenarios are, in fact, protected free speech in the United States so long as the depictions are not judged obscene. The U.S. legislation in this regard is close to that of Japan where Article 21 of the Constitution declares that "no censorship shall be maintained" (Constitution of Japan 1947), but, as in the United States, this freedom does not apply to obscenity that is legislated separately in Article 175 of the Penal Code (Penal Code 1907). Hence, when Iowa resident Christopher Handley was given a six-month jail sentence in 2010 for importing manga from Japan that depicted obscene images of child-like characters, he was prosecuted on grounds of the obscenity, not the age, of the images in question (Zenor 2014: 577–78). Handley came to the attention of the authorities because he was importing hard copy materials from Japan via the postal service. Ironically, once details of some of the banned titles were leaked, scanned copies were made available on the Internet, actually increasing their availability.

The potential for young fans who access and consume problematic Japanese popular culture content of being charged and prosecuted for these activities is slim in the United States so long as their activities fall below the radar of parents and school authorities. However, students and academics travel with their entertainment media and study-related materials on devices such as laptops and iPads. People are increasingly reliant on an Internet environment that enables "multi-tasking and mobility" (Han 2011: 73), and the archiving of personal material on convergent devices exposes them to increased surveillance. While U.S. authorities have been more interested in issues of copyright, the Canadian Customs and Border Control have demonstrated an enhanced scrutiny of manga and anime in pursuit of obscene content, to the extent that the American-based Comic Book Legal Defense Fund has issued advice for comics' fans traveling to Canada (CBLDF n.d.).

Conclusion

Changes in the media environment have radically altered the dynamics and conditions for the study of Japanese language and culture. Those enrolling in Japanese language and culture classes today are likely to be well versed in a range of popular-culture genres and are likely to have a more detailed knowledge of specific genres and titles than the professors teaching them, the majority of whom were educated when successful gatekeeping of class-room materials was ensured by the general lack of availability of original Japanese language materials. Thus the power dynamic between teacher and student has been reversed in terms of access to popular-culture materials, with students being more likely to be on trend with developments in Japan and able to source materials easily, albeit illegally. Although this kind of student-generated knowledge can be a positive factor in the learning environment, it is also necessary to address the ethics of the kind of consumption practices that underlie this knowledge acquisition.

Given the legal and ethical issues raised by certain fan practices, this is a necessary inquiry, and one that needs to engage students. One way to do this would be to start a conversation about students' fannish activities and how their consumption practices might be in tension with local laws, university regulations, and even the expectations of their fellow students. To adopt this kind of pedagogical approach is not to try to censor student activities but to make them objects of research and academic inquiry. This approach would be one example of what Huang and Archer refer to as "literacy education," noting that "[p]opular culture texts are reflective of ideologies and meaning-making mechanisms of our current society" (2012: 58) and, hence, deserve a place in the curriculum. I am suggesting that we need to move our attention away from the texts themselves and look at the broader picture of how cultural content is produced and (re)circulated in today's hyper-mediated world. I have suggested some ways to do this in this chapter: firstly, by historicizing fan engagement with manga and comic book culture more generally, and, secondly, by highlighting how different cultural understandings about acceptable levels of sexual content has informed the reception of manga in the United States.

10 *Purikura*

Expressive Energy in Female Self-Photography

Laura Miller

Self-photography among Japanese schoolgirls developed into a major preoccupation by late 1999. Girls love taking photos with friends and exchanging copies that can be pasted into cute albums. During the 1990s, cheap, lightweight cameras, disposable cameras, and mini-Polaroid cameras (girls called them "*mini pora*") were heavily targeted to young women and girls by manufacturers eager to take advantage of this trend. Fujifilm's Instax Mini Instant Cameras, affectionately called "*cheki*," were especially popular. The photography craze among girls, who had been taking photos of friends for sharing and for pasting into cute albums for years, was reflected in the sensational recognition given to Toshikawa Hiromi, known as Hiromix. In 1995, when she graduated from high school, she received recognition from Canon for her photo diary album entitled "Seventeen Girl Days." Her assemblage of everyday photos of pets, adored things, and self-posing seemed unusual to adults, but it was representative of a normal activity among schoolgirls (*Yomiuri Shinbun* 1997). The album included a pioneering "selfie," a shot taken while holding the camera in front of herself (Ono 1996).

In addition to archiving everyday life with photographs, another fad among schoolgirls was the collection and exchange of colorful stickers that filled up pages of adorable mini-albums and key-chain albums. In the summer of 1995, young women were offered a new technology that perfectly suited both of these interests. It was the "*purikura*" booth, a name derived from the clipped form of "*purinto kurabu*" (print club) and pictured in Figure 10.1. The term *purikura* is used for both the machine and its product, the photo sicker. Use of the *purikura* machine is relatively inexpensive, costing between 300 and 400 yen for a sheet of four to sixteen small, self-adhesive photos. The stickers are placed on the pages of albums as well as in letters, diaries, greeting cards, and other communications. Makers of *purikura* machines compete in a saturated market that has experienced a drop in consumption after a peak in 1999. Nevertheless, *purikura* is now a venerable institution in Japanese culture and is most likely something everyone under the age of thirty has done at least once.

Figure 10.1 Girls cram into a *purikura* booth. Harajuku, Tokyo. June 2007.
Source: Courtesy of the author.

Inspired Photo Sticker Technology

The *purikura* booth was originally intended for young female consumers (*Yomiuri Shinbun* 1996a). As they matured, their boyfriends and family members were brought into its fantasy space. *Purikura* are not only fun and interactive, they have evolved into a type of creative art that encodes many interesting linguistic and cultural features (Miller 2003). It is mainly pairs or groups of girls and women who pile into the *purikura* booth, closing the curtain as they sit or crowd around a bench that faces a video camera. They are presented with a series of choices, selecting desired backdrops, borders, insertable decorations, icons, and text writing options. For example, the Shinderera Supesharu (Cinderella Special, I.M.S., 2005) machine allows the customer to add hair extensions or twinkling diamond tiaras to her image.

The success of the *purikura* is largely due to how skillfully the technology has evolved to address more than one social function. In 2010, Bandai Namco introduced a *purikura* machine that had the capability to upload the photo stickers to cellphones and to social media sites. This was soon followed by several cellphone applications that enabled the addition of *purikura*-type annotations to cellphone photos, such as the Puri Memory for Android. Perhaps we may call *purikura* a type of "selfie," but unlike many selfies, *purikura* is not something one ever does alone. To go solo into a print club booth would be seen as aberrant or pathetic behavior. *Purikura* is primarily called on to memorialize and construct friendship networks. Additionally, *purikura* have carved out a shared format where women and girls are able to play with and occasionally resist gender codes and cultural norms. Unsurprisingly, the *kawaii* (cute) aesthetic is strong in many *purikura*, calling on colors, embellishments, and icons to index cuteness. Yet some *purikura* reflect deliberately grotesque or creepy aesthetics as well, and self-defacement and writing of rebellious or mischievous sentiments is common. These small stickers therefore provide visual-linguistic insight into the ideas and attitudes circulating in girl's culture.

The idea for creating a photo sticker booth came from Sasaki Miho, who worked for the videogame and software company Atlus (a subsidiary of Sega). Aware of both the sticker craze and girls' love of photography, Sasaki suspected that being able to print self-photographs onto small stickers would be very appealing to girls and young women. Men and boys also had a long history of interest in taking photographs yet theirs were normally tied to the domains of art or tourism photography. The cameras they used were often expensive. In contrast, women and girls used cheaper cameras, such as pre-loaded disposable cameras or mini Polaroid cameras, to document friendship events. It was this type of girl's photography that Sasaki had in mind when she envisioned *purikura*. Initially, her male coworkers at Atlus were not convinced that this was a viable product and openly voiced doubts about developing such a machine (*Yomiuri Shinbun* 1996b). But by 1995, they gave Sasaki's concept a chance and green-lighted the manufacture of the first *purikura* machine. It was unveiled in July 1995, and within a few years had become a sensational success. The *purikura* booths that appeared in shopping centers and game arcades generated 70 percent of the company's 36.5 billion yen in sales by the following year (Saitō 2003). The machine got a huge boost in popularity due to a tie-up with the weekly variety television program SMAP x SMAP, featuring the J-pop band SMAP (For more on SMAP, see Chapter 14). Members of the group presented *purikura* of themselves as gifts, and afterwards fans began to get their own *purikura* taken as well (*Yomiuri Shinbun* 1996b).

By the late 1990s, the majority of high-school girls were fervent *purikura* enthusiasts (*Yomiuri Shinbun* 1996c). But something unexpected happened as girls used the earliest *purikura* machines. They did not feel that a self-photograph was truly finished until it had been embroidered with colorful stars, hearts, flowers, and other decorative elements. The machine engineers had been fixated on the photograph. Instead, it was the way one's photograph could be idiosyncratically annotated and decorated that was the true selling point for *purikura*. As the craze escalated, a handful of videogame companies entered the market with more than fifty different machines touting new and more sophisticated editing features. After the success of the Atlus/Sega Purinto Kurabu (Print Club) in 1995, the first wave of machines included Neo Purinto (Neo Print, SNK, 1996), Puri Puri Kyanpasu (Print Print Campus, Konami 1997), and Sutoriito Sunappu (Street Snap, Towa Japan, 1998) (Ippan Shadanhōjin Nihon Amyūzumentomashin Kyōkai n.d.). Having many different types of machines available together in print club arcades contributed to the *purikura* boom, because once they were in the arcade girls would experiment with more than one machine.

Textual and Linguistic Innovations in *Purikura* Culture

The evolution of *purikura* technology is the result of the machine designer's close attention to the use patterns found among schoolgirls. The first Atlus/Sega Print Club machine, which gave us the name for the subject, added pretty borders and a few cute icons to images, but developers noticed that girls also wrote exclamations and humorous captions on the stickers after they were printed. These early "graffiti photos" (*rakugaki shashin*) not only circulated among friends, they were mailed to girls' magazines, such as *egg*, *Popteen*, and *Cawaii!*, and printed in special sections. Permanent ink pens were used to write names, dates, and messages on the photos shared with friends and collected into albums. *Purikura* companies in competition with each other soon included formulaic expressions and words as another option that could be added to the photo. Eventually, they developed new editing features that let users write their own words and phrases onto the photo prior to printing it out as a sticker. This in turn led to the development of numerous script possibilities, such as outline-style text and "*kira moji*" (sparkling characters) made of tiny twinkling diamonds. A few of the common words inserted onto *purikura* were "*chū*" (kiss), "*gē*" (yuck), "*hengao*" (weird face), and "*nakayoshi*" (good friends).

Occasionally, annotations written on *purikura* are in a special script innovation called "*gyaru moji*" (girl characters). Coinciding with the use of both *purikura* and cellphone text messaging, *gyaru moji* are a set of elements—parts of graphs, mathematical symbols, and Cyrillic letters, used as substitutes for Japanese syllabic characters. In addition, some Chinese characters and Japanese syllabic characters are disarticulated, and, while the resulting writing is a straightforward substitution system, to those who do not know the principles involved, it is impenetrable (Miller 2011a). For example, the word "*ganbare*" (do your best), would normally be written in the *hiragana* syllabary as がんば れ, but in *gyaru moji* it can be カ\ "w レ よ" Я ё. The diacritic mark becomes a backwards slash, the character for the nasal becomes a small "w," the character for "*ba*" is disarticulated into two separate characters ("*re*" and "*yo*"), and the Cyrillic letters for "*ya*" (Я) and "*yo*" (ё) are used to represent the final syllable "*re*."

Other examples are:

kirai	≠ЯaT	hate it
tanoshii	ナニЙoU()	enjoyable
maji kimoi	マジ≠毛T	seriously gross

Understanding the conventions and customs that surround the making and sharing of self-photography has resulted in the development of a unique *purikura* lexicon, reflecting just how deeply entrenched it has become in girl culture. The *purikura* lexicon below tell us that *purikura* is more than a mindless pastime or wasteful form of consumption:

purichō	print club album
purikome	print club commentary
hatsupuri	first print club
hisashipuri	print club after a long time
pinpuri	print club done by oneself
rabupuri	print club with boyfriend
kapuri	print club for couples
suppinpuri	no makeup print club
sagipuri	fraudulent print club
eropuri	erotic print club
kosupuri	costume play print club
yabapuri	gross print club
kimopuri	creepy print club

Once girls and young women began collecting sticker photos into albums and examining others' albums, a unique term for this vehicle of the art arose, the "*purichō*" (print club album). The albums are sold as uniquely suited for this and are generally small ring binders with decorative covers and pages for writing and drawing alongside the stickers. Blogs and magazines often carry information about how to best organize the layout and decoration of the *purichō*, similar to the affiliated scrapbooking craze. Magazine articles offered tips for taking the best shots, as well as album display and posing (*Cawaii!* 2003a, 2003b; *egg* 2003). Books and websites also appeared with advice on how to use the different features of the various machines in order to produce the most exciting *purikura* (Purikura Kōjō Iinkai 1996; Puri Kenkyūbu). Articles provided information on ratings of machines, their level of enjoyment, how long they take, and the types of fonts, icons, and other features they offer (*Popteen* 2004).

Magazines for teenagers such as *Cawaii!*, *Seventeen*, and *Popteen* usually include special sections with appraisals and analysis of *purikura* machines and photo creations. The booths are evaluated on ease or difficulty of use and on any unique qualities. In addition to the technology, young female editors were invited to write about camera techniques and editing suggestions and to give their honest assessments of the photo stickers that readers mail in (*Cawaii!* 2003b, 2003c). They have been severe in their appraisals of *purikura* art, skewering the poses, written text, and aims of the creators. The critiquing of the different machine capabilities, as well as the merit of photos that one might be able to produce, reflects a high level of cultural knowledge, as well as the important role the photo stickers have assumed. This genre of writing is sometimes called *"purikome"* (print club commentary). For example, magazines rushed in to offer critiques of Namco Bandai's first Jewella machine in 2007. It was named Hikaru Meiku (Bright Makeup) and could extend the eyelashes, add eyeliner, and allow cellphone uploading (*Popteen* 2008). Eventfully it evolved into the Jewella Eye, a machine that supposedly increases eye size by 120 percent. Reception has been ambivalent, as some users describe the results as *"kimo kawaii"* (creepy cute). The Jewella machines were part of a line of *purikura* introduced in 2003 called Kachō Fūgetsu (literally Flower, Bird, Wind, Moon but referring to the "beauties of nature"). The name is from a famous four-character idiom that means that one should experience nature as part of self-understanding. Another machine that used a four-character name was Yamato Nadeshiko (Atlus), a retro concept suggesting the pure essence of traditional Japanese femininity. In addition to Kachō Fūgetsu and Yamato Nadeshiko, more than ten other machines have been subjected to girls' critical assessments, including Netsuretsu Bibi (Ardent Beauty, Omoron), Tensai Kameraman Tanjō (Birth of the Genius Cameraman, Omoron), Biteki Kakumei (Aesthetic Revolution, Namco), Shinderera Supesharu (Cinderella Special, I.M.S.), and Bihada Wakusei (Planet of Beautiful Skin) (*Popteen* 2004). Critiques of each new machine are found in many girls' magazines not long after they debut (*Cawaii!* 2003a; *Popteen* 2008; *Rabuberi* 2006).

Making a record of one's circle of friends and acquisition of new acquaintances is one of the primary reasons for the popularly of *purikura* (Chalfen and Marui 2001). The text on *purikura* stickers often describe the occasions that brought about the gathering, such as Seijin no hi (Coming of Age Day), Hinamatsuri (Doll's Festival), or someone's birthday. The memorialization of friends getting together in the pages of a *purichō* thus supplants the role that the traditional diary once played in Japanese culture. If the taking of the *purikura* is an inaugural event for a particular group of friends, it is called "*hatsupuri*" (first print club).

If two of more friends who have not seen each other in a long time get together and have a *purikura* taken, they might call this "*hisashipuri*" (print club after a long time). Because doing *purikura* is at its core a social activity, entering a booth alone to make a self-photo sticker is marked as deviant, and thus we find the term "*pinpuri*" (print club done by oneself). As the users and creators of *purikura* grew older, they dragged their boyfriends into arcades in order to document their special relationship. The *purikura* taken with a special fellow is called "*rabupuri*" (print club with the boyfriend, derived from the English loanword "love"). There is also "*kapuri*" (from *kapuru*, couples print club) that document a long-standing relationship. In addition to terminology that tracks social relationships, special activities, and events, many genres of *purikura* refer to the appearance of those being photographed. Virtually all women and girls after a certain age wear makeup, therefore not wearing makeup is manifestly unusual behavior. The term for allowing oneself to have a self-photograph taken in such a vulnerable state is "*suppinpuri*" (no makeup print club).

A comic (Figure 10.2) utilizes named *purikura* genres to document the trajectory of a boyfriend relationship. In the first frame, the mutually happy couple celebrates their new relationship with *hatsupuri*. In the second frame, after they have been together for a bit, it is *hisashipuri*. In the third frame, the woman allows a *suppinpuri* because she thinks he has a forgiving heart. But the last frame shows how wrong she was: she ends up with a *pinpuri*.

There are many other *purikura* types that indicate the photo-taker's appearance. Some of the newest machines, such as the Jewella Eye mentioned above, automatically alter the subject's eyes. Other machines smooth out the skin to make one look more photogenic or make the face look thinner. If the machine user miscalculates, however, the resulting photo will be labeled as a patently "*sagipuri*" (fraudulent print club).

Females in Japan have grown up in a society in which eroticized and sexualized photographs of schoolgirls and other young women are plastered everywhere. One way they process ambivalent or conflicted feelings about the societal expectations about normative femininity is to reenact the scripted porn-poses that surround them. Thus there is a genre of *purikura* in which they try to show cleavage, or pull up their skirts to reveal underwear (Miller 2005). In some cases, they might perform different types of racy gender vamping that serves to spoof these very poses. This genre of intentional or, more often parodic, sexy *purikura* is called "*eropuri*" (erotic print club).

Figure 10.2 The relationship path through *purikura*. Kitahara Yasuo, ed. 2006. *Minna de kokugo jiten—kore mo, Nihongo* (Dictionary of Japanese for Everyone: This, Too, Is Japanese). Tokyo: Taishukan, p. 45.

Source: Courtesy of Taishukan.

Within the *purikura* arcade, machine developers continually try to come up with novel ways to entice customers. Enterprising companies noticed the popularity of costume play among young people, so came up with the idea of providing a selection of costumes to put on before getting into the booth to have their photo taken. This type of *purikura* became known as *"kosupuri"* (costume play print club). Among the favorite costumes used for *kosupuri* are Stewardess, Nurse, Chinese Girl, and Mini-skirted Policewoman. The costumes are often uniforms or stereotypical dress associated with female roles but recast in sexier or cuter forms. The Chinese Girl costume is a short qipao, while the Stewardess, Nurse, and Policewoman costumes use mini-skirts. The importance of identifiable uniforms, particularly ones that denote modern female occupations, is a notable feature of modern Japan (Freedman et al. 2013; McVeigh 2000). However, the way costumes in *purikura* are used often reflects ambivalence about the cute femininity and gendered norms encoded in such scripted attire. For example, five girls wearing the Nurse outfit wrote "What about those huge boobs?" on their *kosupuri*. They used the crass term *"oppai"* for breasts together with ultra-feminine linguistic forms, a juxtaposition that together with their poses and facial expressions made the intent of the gender parody clear. The *purikura* arcades that offer costume play service will post signs prohibiting the entry of men who are not accompanied by a chaperoning girl or woman.

Beyond Cinderella Technology

Purikura manufacturers assume that all machine users are narrowly interested in enhancing their appearance and presenting themselves in the cutest and most feminine ways possible. Engineers and media experts, for example, have coined the term "Cinderella technology" to describe the various methods now available to aid in the creation of new identities through transformation in appearance. In an article that tracks the engineering technology behind some of the *purikura* machines that lengthen eyelashes, make the face thinner, and do other enhancements, a technology researcher considers these as merely aspects of Cinderella technology (Kubo 2013). Yet, along with the production of cute, glamorous, and pretend-erotic *purikura*, many young women also produce a variety of complex self-photographs that engage with contrary aesthetic modes.

Minor forms of resistance might surface briefly in the miniature realm of the sticker. Uncertainty, dissatisfaction, or rejection of normative cute femininity is seen in *purikura* that display deliberately defaced or marred images. This rival aesthetic might be produced in any number of ways: distorted facial expressions or sticking out the tongue, pulling the eyes down or pushing the nostrils up or inserting objects into the nostrils. Jarring camera angles and unsightly objects inserted into the photo (such as skulls or icons of a coil of feces) are common. The written text is also used to contribute to these inelegant *purikura*. Purposely unattractive artifacts are called *"yabapuri"* (gross print club). A similar type that might entail elements of cuteness yet be un-nerving or disturbing is called "*kimopuri*" (creepy print club). From the 1990s on, the aesthetics of "grotesque cute" (*guro kawaii*) and "creepy cute" (*kimo kawaii*) became part of general girls' culture, although the mainstream rarely paid attention to this thread (Miller 2011b).

Along with many other types of Japanese popular culture, *purikura* offers us insight into culturally-specific concerns and constraints. Self-photography is unregulated cultural production, created and shared away from the scrutinizing gaze of parents, teachers, and other authority figures. They reflect an incredible spectrum of imaginative thinking and playful creativity. The photo-textual representations we find in the world of *purikura* display fine-tuned conscious-ness of gender norms, at the same time that those very norms are tested or spoofed. Through the tiny sticker square we gain visual-linguistic access to the realms of female adolescence and young adulthood.

11 Studio Ghibli Media Tourism

Craig Norris

Introduction

Miyazaki Hayao has built an extensive and elaborate world through his animated feature films and broader media work done through Studio Ghibli, the commercially and critically acclaimed animation studio he co-founded in 1985. Studio Ghibli has produced many of Japan's highest-grossing films: *Kiki's Delivery Service* (*Majo no takkyūbin*, 1989), *Only Yesterday* (*Omoide poro poro*, 1991), *Porco Rosso* (1992), and *Pom Poko* (*Heisei tanuki gassen pon poko*, 1994), and *Spirited Away* (*Sen to Chihiro no kamikakushi*, 2001, its biggest commercial successes to date). The studio has won international honors, including the American Academy Award for Best Animated Feature in 2003 for *Spirited Away*. In 2014 Miyazaki became the second Japanese film director after Akira Kurosawa to be awarded an Honorary Academy Award in recognition of his contribution to motion pictures. Thematically, Studio Ghibli films, and in particular those of Miyazaki, have been praised for their engagement with environmentalism and depictions of the destructiveness of war, as exemplified in *Nausicaä of the Valley of the Wind* (*Kaze no tani no Naushika*, 1984). They have also been admired for sensitively conveying complex emotions of nostalgia and coming of age, often by focusing on strong female protagonists, to an audience of children and adults.

In addition to anime feature films, Studio Ghibli has produced short anime films, music videos, videogames, and books. Within this extensive fictional universe, there is a network of real locations worldwide that have inspired settings and cultural details; some of which have become popular tourist attractions. For the purpose of my research, I divide these places into two categories: official and unofficial sites linked to Miyazaki's films. The first type involves tourism of locations that Miyazaki and Studio Ghibli have incorporated into promotional materials and other information surrounding their films. For example, the documentary *Ghibli's Scenery: Japan Depicted in Miyazaki Hayao's Works/European Travel Encountered through Miyazaki Hayao's Works* (*Ghibli no fūkei: Miyazaki sakuhin ga kaita Nihon/Miyazaki sakuhin to deau Europa no tabi*, Studio Ghibli 2009) offers a travelogue of the real-life locations in Europe and Japan used for Ghibli's films, including *Nausicaä of the Valley of the Wind, My Neighbor Totoro (Tonari no Totoro,* 1988), *Spirited Away, Kiki's Delivery Service,* and *Howl's Moving Castle (Hauru no ugoku shiro,* 2004). Other examples include the Japanese island of Yakushima that inspired the forest in *Princess Mononoke (Mononoke hime,* 1997) and features a sign proclaiming that it is "*Mononoke Hime no mori*" (Princess Mononoke's Forest).

Within the category of officially sanctioned sites is the Studio Ghibli Museum in Mitaka (opened in 2001). The museum offers information about the production of animation, as well as an immersion into the sights and sounds of the Ghibli world, in a theme-park-type setting. As the Ghibli Museum English language website proclaims: "Open the door and welcome to wonderland!" (Museo d'Arte Ghibli 2015). According to Rayna Denison (2010), this hybrid museum/theme park should be regarded as an example of "*popular* cultural tourism," (549, emphasis in the original), as the museum combines an interest in popular culture with instruction about the craft of animation. Denison (2010: 549) argues "anime tourism in Japan brings together high culture legitimizations of anime as art, with entertaining and commercially motivated museum experiences."

The second category includes locations not officially endorsed by Miyazaki or Studio Ghibli. This is where our case study of tourism to Australia resides. Travel to these destinations is promoted by a steady stream of rumors circulating by word-of-mouth and online. In the case of Australia, these sites include buildings and native flora and fauna that have been appropriated into the world of Ghibli by fans who share their hypotheses primarily on blogs and social network sites. That Studio Ghibli has denied using Australia in any of its works makes the resilient fan attention to these sites remarkable. As Studio Ghibli representatives remarked: "Ghibli does use some real places

Figure 11.1 Cosplayer Nadia dressed as Kiki with Jiji the cat from *Kiki's Delivery Service* at the Ross Bakery, Tasmania, 2013.
Source: Courtesy of Tessu and Dalfe Nai.

around the world as references, but there are no places in Australia that Ghibli have used, so it is very funny and strange that this rumor has spread" (Studio Ghibli 2002). The official Ghibli website includes information about real-world locations used in its films. For example, the locations that inspired the idealized European village in *Kiki's Delivery Service*, a film often linked to the Ross Bakery in Tasmania pictured in Figure 11.1, were listed as "Stockholm (Sweden), Wisley (UK), and Gotland (Sweden) in the Baltic Sea" (Studio Ghibli), but not Australia.

Yet reports of fans immersing themselves in "Ghibli's Australia" continue to spread. For example, in 2007 Japanese actor and celebrity Hidehiko Ishizuka visited Tasmania's Ross Bakery dressed as the cat Jiji from *Kiki's Delivery Service* for the Japanese television travel special *Ishi-chan's Comic Travelogue of the Animal Kingdom: Journeying 1000 km to the Southern Paradise of Tasmania* (*Ishi-chan no dōbutsu oukoku dajare kikō. Minami no rakuen Tasumania 1000km jyūtan SP*, Nakane Takuya and Shōtarō Tsuji 2007). An advertisement for a tour company offering Ghibli-themed trips in Australia reads, "Landscapes from those scenes are found in Australia! To travel the world of Miyazaki's anime" (Hirano Miki).

This raises the question of how has Australia—a location never used by Studio Ghibli—become a portal into Miyazaki's fictional world? To answer this question, from July 2014 to February 2015, I explored the forum posts of the Mixi social network community, *Hayao Miyazaki's World in Australia* (*Miyazaki Hayao no sekai in Ōsutoraria*), established in April 2006 to discover links between Australia and Miyazaki's films. In January 2015, there were a total of 12,426 group members, discussing forty-two topics. The two most commented upon topics were the connections between Ross Bakery in Tasmania to *Kiki's Delivery Service* and Queensland's Paronella Park's to *Laputa: Castle in the Sky* (*Tenkū no shiro Rapyuta*, 1986). There was an average of twenty-eight comments per topic, suggesting a reasonably active and involved community for such a niche topic.

Mixi was founded in 2004 as a social network specific to Japan and quickly became a market leader. Some commentators (Barker and Ota 2011; Karnas 2014; Takahashi 2010) have considered the key appeal of Mixi to be its early adoption of mobile access, integration of music and news sharing, its ease of reviewing products, anonymity, its open-sourced software community, and group discussions about both broad and specific topics. Mixi reached its peak in popularity between 2010 and 2011, with around twenty million users (Leplan 2010). In 2012 the site began a downward spiral in use, revenue, and membership because of the increasing popularity of competitors, particularly Facebook (Corbin 2014; Ghedin 2013). It also suffered because of its restrictive sign-up process that effectively excluded potential users outside of Japan.

However, the success of its *Monster Strike* (*Monsutā sutoraiku*) mobile game, released in 2013, shows that Mixi was still alive (Corbin 2014). Additionally, many niche groups seem to have maintained their core members, even if they are posting less. As of 2015, there is no equally visible Ghibli tourism community on Facebook or other social media. While Mixi is certainly no longer the vibrant social network it once was, it presents a useful archive of content produced across a reasonable duration of time. My research of the *Hayao Miyazaki's World in Australia* group was inspired by my interest in grassroots practices that contributed to Studio Ghibli media tourism. In this chapter, I closely analyze selected posts to understand how this community has used the Ghibli brand as raw material and a cultural resource (Fiske 2010; Jenkins et al. 2008) for their ongoing discussions and creativity and their journeys to actual locations.

Participating in Popular Culture Tourism

Miyazaki-related tourism to Australia is part of a larger global phenomenon in which various locations have become popular tourist destinations based on their links to films and television shows. There has been a growing body of research focused on tourism to locations in Japanese films, television, books, manga, and anime, or as it is referred to in the Japanese literature, "*kontentsu tsūrisumu*" (contents tourism) (Beeton et al. 2013; Seaton and Yamamura 2015). Imai Nobuharu (2010), for example, explored three of Japan's largest fan culture locations—Tokyo's Comic Market (Comiket), the *Lucky Star* (*Raki☆suta*) anime fan pilgrimage to Kasukabe and Washimiya in Saitama Prefecture, and the proliferation of otaku interests in Akihabara. As Yamamura Takayoshi (2009) found, *Lucky Star* tourism exemplifies how fan pilgrimages can revitalize actual towns. Thematically related is Brian Bergstrom's (2014) exploration of Japanese *Anne of Green Gables* fans, in particular the experience of Okuda Miki who traveled to Canada in the early 1990s to immerse herself in the "real" location of the story. Bergstrom examines how the "embodied experience and cross-cultural practice" of Japanese *Anne of Green Gables* fans reveals a complex interplay between experience, identity, and space, as fans' experience of an actual place is both "an extension of their engagement with a fictional world" (233) and "portable landscape" (243) through which to explore their personal relationship to the world around them.

I argue that media tourism around Miyazaki has been a grassroots phenomenon, in which fans have, to a large degree, defined their experiences outside the management or influence of a media studio or other commercial industry. I apply the scholarly notion of "participatory culture," which explores the rise of user-generated content in online spaces as a means to engage with texts and build communities (Benkler 2006; Jenkins 2006). Henry Jenkins et al. (2009: 3) defines a participatory culture as having "relatively low barriers to artistic expression and civic engagement, strong support for creating and sharing one's creations, and some type of information mentorship whereby what is known by the most experienced is passed along to novices" and where "members believe that their contributions matter, and feel some degree of social connectedness with one another." Jenkins (2006: 257) further claims that the "power of participation comes not from destroying commercial culture but from writing over it, molding it, amending it, expanding it, adding greater diversity of perspective, and then recirculating it, feeding it back into the mainstream media." Like Joshua Green and Jenkins' (2011) focus on participation and the circulation of content online, my use of the term does not assume that all fans will be involved in creating labor-intensive content and that even the most basic, low-level efforts of clicking "like" on a forum post has implications for the spread and impact of cultural material. It is within the practices and processes of media users as tourists that we can best understand the *Hayao Miyazaki's World in Australia* Mixi community.

Being a Miyazaki Fan-Tourist

In discussing their trips to Australia, being a Miyazaki or Ghibli fan was contextualized most commonly as an engagement with nature and the environment. This is not surprising given the significance of environmentalism and related theme of spiritualism in Miyazaki's films. *My Neighbor Totoro* provides a particularly vivid example in which objects and places are imbued with life and power, from the dust-creatures named *susuwatari* to the forest creatures like Totoro and fantastical animal forms like the *nekobasu* (cat-bus). Some scholars (Smith and Parsons 2012; Wright 2004, 2005) have shown the connection between notions of Shinto and Miyazaki's interrelatedness of nature, objects, and humanity, while other scholars have argued Miyazaki uses these themes to convey environmental concerns (Lim 2013; Mayumi, Solomon, and Chang 2005; Niskanen 2007, 2010). To members of the Mixi community, traveling to Australia is an opportunity to visit spectacular locations and experience Miyazaki's theme of the awe and wonder that nature inspires. For many fans, discovering connections between Australia's environment and Miyazaki's settings comes as an epiphany. For example, one member wrote:

> Even though I have been staying in Australia for over six months, I didn't know that so many Australian locations have been used for Ghibli movies. I have been to many places in Australia, and I have found that the scenery is great. I think Miyazaki is very intuitive. I'm going to the *Nausicaä: Valley of the Wind* location Kata Tjuta in Australia next week. I'm very surprised that Uluru is also called 'Valley of the Wind'.
>
> (September 22, 2006)

Here, there is a clear emphasis on Australia's natural beauty and how well it overlaps with the image of nature in Miyazaki's films. This assertion is underpinned by the belief that Miyazaki himself must have traveled to Australia and been inspired by these locations. The discovery that "so many Australian locations have been used for Ghibli movies" is also presented as a means of participating in the collaborative mapping of Miyazaki's locations.

The traveler has drawn upon the locations discussed by the Mixi community to create an itinerary and is posting an update. The member announces that the next location will be the famous group of large rock formations in Australia's Northern Territory—Kata Tjuta and Uluru—which many fans link to the desolate yet beautiful landscape of the post-apocalyptic anime *Nausicaä of the Valley of the Wind*. As the post reveals, there is a popular bushwalk in the Uluru-Kata Tjuta National Park known as the "Valley of the Wind" walk due to the strong winds and winding valley which the trail covers.

The collective act of locating, documenting, and sharing sites on Mixi is one of the guiding principles of this community. As explained in the group guidelines: "The purpose of this community is to upload photos of scenery that is similar to the scenery in Ghibli movies." The emotional importance of collaboratively collecting information is articulated in one of the earliest posts:

> Ghibli movies are great. Ghibli movies are one of the best parts of Japanese popular culture, and they can remind us about things we tend to forget today. When I found this community, I felt really inspired. Mixi is incredible.
>
> (May 17, 2006)

A number of posts expressed the sense of community created through sharing information:

> I used to live in Sydney about three years ago, however I didn't have a chance to visit any Ghibli locations. I am going to Australia again next year, and I will definitely go to these places. However, does somebody know about the bakery in Tasmania that is believed the model of Kiki?
>
> (April 6, 2006)

Another member wrote about how the community's hunting and gathering of information has benefitted their work as a tour guide:

> I live in Adelaide. I am a freelance tour guide, driver, interpreter, Japanese language teacher, and writer. I decided to join this community because I would like to know information about Ghibli places that I have been as a tour guide. If you would like to know more, check this link.
>
> (October 18, 2006)

The member presents the rumors around Ghibli being inspired by Australia as information to use with Japanese visitors. Instead of claiming that tour guides have knowledge of locations, the post presents the discovery of Ghibli's film locations as an ongoing improvisation and exploration through digital media.

Regular exchange of information and photos, and inquiries about the authenticity of the rumors establishes the collective vision of Miyazaki tourism as imaginative, participatory, and inquisitive. For example, the following two posts present the surprise of discovering Australia's connection to Miyazaki's films within broader global Ghibli tourism:

> I didn't know that there are places in Australia that were the models for Ghibli movies. Is this true? I lived in Germany until this year, and I found many places that were identical to the scenery used in Ghibli films. I particularly felt that *Laputa* fitted these places well. Actually, I know some Ghibli locations in Japan, too.
>
> (September 4, 2006)

> My most favorite Miyazaki movie is *Kiki's Delivery Service*, so my dream is to visit the places that were used as models for this movie. I am so surprised that the model was in Australia, because I used to think the model should be somewhere in Europe. However, I have heard that many places around the world are used as models. Could somebody who knows about this reply?
>
> (September 17, 2006)

The uncertainties around the film's connection to Australia are presented as needing further investigation. Instead of privileging "authentic" locations, media tourists are free to explore any possibility of discovering Ghibli in the real world. By allowing the uncertainty to exist around locations, the writer of the second post establishes an open-minded position in respect to the Australian locations, one that is broadened by their own travel experiences and discoveries.

The emphasis on discovery through travel, taking "leaps of faith" to follow one's curiosity down the metaphorical rabbit-hole of Ghibli's real-world locations, is analogous to the sense of adventure of many of Miyazaki's protagonists, such Kiki in *Kiki's Delivery Service* and Chihiro in *Spirited Away*, and child-like wonder, as seen in *My Neighbor Totoro* and *Ponyo* (*Gake no ue no Ponyo*, 2008). In his research into fans' media pilgrimages, Matt Hills (2002) defines "creative transpositions" as acts of identifying with the key tropes and character traits of a television show or film and performing them in a real location. Examples include acting out key scenes for a photograph, dressing like a character, or projecting a main character's story arc onto a fan's own experience. Visitors to Tasmania's Ross Bakery have dressed like Kiki (see Figure 11.1) and enacted parts of her coming-of-age story (Norris 2013). As the rumor of the shop's ties to *Kiki's Delivery Service* spread, the owners set up a small room above their bakery designated as "Kiki's Room." As one member wrote:

> I am a big fan of *Kiki's Delivery Service*. After watching the movie, I pretended I was flying in the sky with a broom (smile). I would like to visit the bakery one day.
>
> (May 2, 2006)

However, such identifications and performances do not go unchallenged. While some members framed their experiences around the belief that Miyazaki himself must have visited these locations, others admit not knowing if Miyazaki or anyone from Studio Ghibli has used Australia as a reference source for these films.

The Framing of the Truth

To further understand the emotional significance of Miyazaki media tourism and the relationship between global popular culture and national places, I will now consider how community members frame the authenticity of their experiences. Their posts reveal the central paradox of media tourism: fans' identification with and performances in these places involve a suspension of disbelief that gives actual cultural meaning to these sites. The locations in Australia are doubly "not real" in terms of the films themselves being fictional and the fact that these locations were not used by Miyazaki or Ghibli; yet they take on a sense of reality through Mixi discussions. An undated post on the FAQ section by the group administrator shows how this paradox is negotiated:

> Actually, in the Ghibli films never used any Australian locations. However, because many Japanese visitors may think, "this looks like Ghibli," this community is a way to collect these rumored locations. We can just enjoy these rumors and share in the atmosphere when we visit there.

As well as defining the purpose of this Miyazaki community, this post tries to be inclusive of the community's acts and practices. In doing so, while acknowledging the lack of authenticity in these Australian locations, members are encouraged to continue circulating their experiences and discoveries of finding Ghibli's "atmosphere" within Australia.

Conclusion

This chapter has focused on the appropriation of Miyazaki's films into real-world locations by Japanese fans on the Mixi forum *Hayao Miyazaki's World in Australia*. This community reveals creative and imaginative ways in which fans have negotiated Miyazaki's key themes, motifs, and narratives through identification and performance grounded in such places as Ross Bakery in Tasmania. These posts also show how fans playfully and paradoxically blur the real and fictional, the authentic and inauthentic. Although there is no truth connecting Australia to Miyazaki's films, the resilience of rumors and fan-travelogues is remarkable. As Jenkins (2006) has suggested, fans and audiences are increasingly able to participate in the production and circulation of content online in a way that is more visible and public than it has ever been before.

In the context of the continued spread of Australia's virtual links to Miyazaki's world, the truth that Miyazaki never visited or used Australia for his locations is bittersweet. While the persistence of these links within fan communities reveals the power of Japanese fans to repurpose popular culture for their own needs, the inauthenticity of these locations is problematic. However, if there is an authenticity, it is a highly personal and subjective one based on a convergence of travel, life experience, and an ironic transposition of the fictional onto the real. The process of experiencing the world through Miyazaki's films and their themes of environmentalism, nostalgia, and transformation can potentially provide an entry point into a deeper, emotional engagement of the world rather than a distortion of reality.

12 Hatsune Miku

Virtual Idol, Media Platform, and Crowd-Sourced Celebrity[1]

Ian Condry

In a video of a concert in Japan, we see around a thousand fans packed into a Tokyo music club, many with glow sticks in the shape of green leeks, eagerly anticipating the arrival of the star of the show. The music starts, a mid-tempo hi-hat counting off the beat, and suddenly Miku appears, as if rising through the stage (Figure 12.1). There is a live band behind her, but all the focus is on Miku, a life-size animated cartoon of a teenage girl with long blue ponytails and enormous eyes, singing and dancing on stage.

Miku's first live concert was in a club called Zepp on the manmade island of Odaiba in Tokyo Bay, a short train ride from downtown Tokyo. The Miku show was held in 2010 on March 9, an auspicious date because "3/9" can be read in Japanese as "*mi ku*." I saw Miku perform at a similar concert in New York City in October 2014, and at Anime Expo in Los Angeles in July 2011. The approximately 6,000 tickets for the Los Angeles show sold out within days (Saenz 2011). In the concert hall before the show began, the air was festive and electric. I overheard a fan sitting next to me, speaking to her friend, both in costume. "We're making history," she said, and her friend nodded solemnly. I agree. But what kind of history is being made? What does this phenomenon mean?

Hatsune Miku ("hot-sue-nay mee-koo") is Japan's leading virtual idol. She began life as voice synthesizer software released in 2007 by Crypton Future Media, Inc. (hereafter, Crypton), a company based in Sapporo in northern Japan. Crypton sells the software but takes a more open-source approach to the use of Miku's image, generally allowing fans to use the image for free. An enormous fan community has emerged around Miku, primarily in Japan but extending worldwide. A variety of businesses and professional artists have arisen from grassroots productivity. What makes Miku remarkable is the course of her emergence as a star. She demonstrates that, in some cases at least, communities of shared interest form a foundation on which new businesses can be built. At a time when there is growing frustration at the failures of our current political economy, it is worth reminding ourselves that capitalism is a mixed system, with different flavors and varieties competing with one another.

Miku's world is recognizable as part of a *dōjin* (pronounced "dough gene") culture populated by fans who create derivative works, such as manga, figurines, illustrations, based on their favorite "2D" characters. The term *dōjin* uses the characters "same" and "person," implying a peer but also an amateur, generally more than a consumer, someone who makes things, usually in a group. Fan "circles" (*saakuru*) are the groups that make *dōjinshi* (fan comics), *dōjin* music, *dōjin* games, and so on. A successful *dōjin* franchise is Touhou Project (*Tōhō purojekuto*), which began as a "bullet hell" videogame but includes a range of music and other "derivative works" (*niji sōsaku*). Analogous examples can be seen in many places. All kinds of amateur activities—hobbies, sports, cultural enrichment, and more—are similar in the sense of being driven by personal commitments and group camaraderie. Rather than judging *dōjin* franchises' success in terms of economic value, it is worth considering how democratic, supportive, and competitive they are. Miku is a prime example of a social and economic assemblage that emerges from fan activities as much as from business activities. In this, the Miku phenomenon offers lessons for rethinking music industries, and perhaps industries more generally, in a more balanced way, that is, highlighting the importance of considering both social and economic factors together.

Creative Communities and the Emergence of New Economies

In 2007, the Miku voice synthesizer software gave desktop musicians a new instrument: a woman's singing voice. This was Crypton's business, namely, selling digital sounds and software to be used in audio production. But as music creators began sharing their songs online, others in the online (and offline) world participated in other ways, such as making accompanying illustrations or videos, in part because Crypton was not in the character licensing business. An audience also emerged through commenting—positively, negatively, sometimes seriously, often irreverently—and in the process lent moral support, engaged in aesthetic criticism, or just had fun. In the first couple of years, the business of Miku was Crypton selling the software, and the other fan production was largely non-commercial (fans pay but do not get paid). Tara Knight's *Mikumentary* short films present a nice portrait of this activity.

Creative communities are spaces where social value takes precedence over economic exchange, and, arguably, it was there that Miku changed from a singing voice instrument into a "vocal character." Amateur creators and active audiences formed the foundation upon which economic activity would later develop. And businesses did develop, with a popular videogame for arcades and handheld devices, songs popular for karaoke, CDs that have become bona-fide hits, and DVDs of music videos. Importantly, an expansive collective of people generating interest around Miku, and other characters have developed from voice synthesizer software, known collectively as "Vocaloids" ("vocal androids").

The larger significance is that new areas of the music world are developing new audiences and, in the process, new models of support at a time when the market for recordings is in steep decline, although spending for other aspects of music is increasing, such as for live shows and musical instruments. In contrast to record companies, might Miku offer a more equitable, democratic realm of popular culture? It is too soon to tell, but there are some promising signs. Miku illuminates how creative communities, often energized by non-economic motivations, can form the basis for the emergence of new businesses and industries. The significance of those industries depends not only on their capitalization but also on the social dynamics that underpin the economies. This is not to say this "foundation" is devoid of exploitation and excess, but, as we will see, what is interesting is how the maker of Miku software, Crypton, has dealt with the challenges of mediating between the social communication through Miku and the businesses emerging around her.

Who is Miku?

To describe what the screen image of the Vocaloid 3 version of the Hatsune Miku software: the keyboard image along the left side allows you to choose the notes, and words are added in the middle. You can shape the vocals with other controls. At the level of software interface, this is what Miku looks like. But for most people, the image of Miku derives from an official cartoon produced by the illustrator KEI and commissioned by Crypton (Figure 12.1).

Figure 12.1 Miku performing in New York City, 2014.
Source: © Sega / © Crypton Future Media, Inc. www.piapro.net
Graphics © Sega / Marza Animation Planet Inc., production by Crypton Future Media, Inc.

Crypton offers a few details about Miku in her profile:

- Age: 16
- Height: 158 cm (5′ 2″)
- Weight: 42 kg (92 lbs.)
- Favorite genre: J-Pop, Dance Pop
- Favorite Tempo: 70–150 beats per minute
- Best Voice Range: A3–E5

Her fashion and waifish appearance align with a distinctive "idol" style in Japan, epitomized by the expansive girl group AKB48 (see Chapters 15 and 33). The short skirt and tight-fitting top are in line with other idol costumes, walking a line between youthful eroticism and innocence.

Hello Kitty is sometimes criticized as an icon of cute because she has no mouth (see Chapter 3), a trait that allows fan-consumers to inscribe their emotions upon her. Similarly, because Miku is all voice, fan-producers can have her sing whatever they want. The relative absence of backstory means that creators can develop their own interpretations of Miku. When the CEO of Crypton, Itoh Hiroyuki, visited MIT to discuss the phenomenon in 2010, he said, "Miku is a blank page. That's one reason people like her" (Itoh 2011). Crypton did not go further in determining who Miku should be, creating no books, films, anime, or manga to define her.

I have been asked by American journalists how could the Japanese fall for a virtual idol? The implication is "That would never happen in America." But how different is Miku from "real" celebrities like Lady Gaga, who featured Miku as her opening act for her 2014 tour? Even "real" celebrities adopt different roles, and their movies and albums achieve success, in part, by building on a foundation of people who are already fans. Yet it is not Miku herself that becomes the platform, but Miku plus the people who care about her. This helps us see how communication and creativity flow through Miku, and this may be more important than her "content." Or put another way, Miku shows us how celebrities can be platforms as much as they are people. Even so, as Tarleton Gillespie (2010) argues, the idea of a "platform" is always embedded in distinct politics. Note, for example, that the politics of Miku communities are generally more democratic than, say, fans' roles in regular idol groups, whose fashions and lyrics are decided by professional producers. But what else does Miku show?

Changing the World by Challenging Copyright's Primacy

Music journalist Shiba Tomonori describes the effect of Miku as nothing less than "changing the world" (*sekai o kaeta*). He notes, for example, that everyone can be a creator (*kurieetā*) and, more importantly perhaps, can connect with like-minded creators:

With the Internet of the twenty-first century, anyone can make a name for his or herself by becoming a creator. Nowadays, it's become normal for amateur creators, not only professionals, to make various kinds of content and have it consumed. Moreover, the Net is giving rise to creators making relationships among themselves. A new culture is blossoming, nurturing collaborations across fields. Put simply, this is entrance to an era of "100 million creators."

(Shiba 2014: 4)

The phrase "100 million creators" is perhaps an ironic reference to a prediction by a 1950s social critic that television would create in Japan a nation of "100 million idiots" (Chun 2007).

There is something remarkable happening in the world of media where amateurs and independent professionals can create works reaching enormous audiences without requiring access to television or radio, an antithesis to the industry Jayson Makoto Chun analyzes in his chapter in this volume (Chapter 14). One example comes from my own experiences studying Japanese hip-hop. Since 1994, when I began my research, I have heard American colleagues express skepticism: "There is no way some Asian rapper, whose lyrics we cannot even understand, is ever going to be popular in the United States." Of course, PSY, the Korean rapper, in the 2012 global hit song "Gangnam Style," was no amateur creator, and the video features numerous television celebrities, so its popularity cannot be viewed as a bottom-up phenomenon. Still, he is an example of how mass popularity can come from unexpected places, especially in this era of peer-to-peer promotion. This opens up possibilities for "end-around strategies" of cultural action that work best by ignoring or changing the rules of the game (Condry 2011). According to Crypton's website in 2016, over 100,000 songs have been produced by "Miku-P" (i.e., Miku producers), and over 170,000 videos have been posted on YouTube (Crypton Future Media, Inc. n.d.b.). By far the largest participation involves the over one million fan-made artworks in circulation on Crypton's sharing site PiaPro, Japan's image-sharing site Pixiv, and American sites like Deviant Art and Tumblr. (PiaPro is short for "peer production.") Some musicians, such as Supercell and Senbon Sakura, achieved greater fame as the makers of noteworthy Vocaloid songs (Bekkiini 2015). Toyota and Google have both used Miku for television commercials. How did Crypton negotiate with big corporations while allowing fans to create as they please?

For countries other than Japan, fans and creators can make original illustrations of Miku under a Creative Commons license (non-commercial, with attribution). In Japan's legal and cultural context that allows for some *dōjin* works, as of 2015, Crypton maintains a three-tier system of copyright control, called the PiaPro Character License (PCL). To summarize (Crypton Future Media, Inc. n.d.a.):

1   If you are making images but not selling them in any way, you may do so without getting permission from Crypton.

2   If you are making goods and selling them, but only to support the activities of your club or group (i.e., "non-profit" enforced through an
honor system rather than legal designation), then you are asked to
send a merchandise sample to Crypton. In return, Crypton will send
a 2D barcode (QR code) that you affix to your goods to show official
approval.
3   If your Miku goods sell profitably, Crypton expects to be part of the
process, resulting in discussions on a case-by-case basis.

This approach creates multiple tiers of copyright depending on the users
and their profitability, rather than on the type of work (i.e., original or
derivative). These rules depend on the broader community's acceptance.
In some ways, this is similar to the informal operation of music sampling
for DJs. If you are an indie-level DJ, you can often get away with sampling
famous artists and sometimes even selling the works. But if you are famous
or backed by a major recording company, then the artists being sampled can
expect (and/or demand) payment. What's different about Crypton is that
they make this informal treatment of copyright official and central to their
business.

Miku songs cross genres and subjects with wild abandon, from the self-
assured braggadocio (e.g., "World Is Mine" (*Wārudo izu main*) to more heartfelt expressions (e.g., "Cremation Song," *Kasō kyoku*). Moreover, mixtures
of fan-created works and collaborations with professional producers have
generated interesting outcomes. For example, tangentially related to Miku,
the transmedia project "Kagerō Daze" (Kagerō purojekuto, or "Heat Haze
Daze") spun out of a hallucinatory song about a violent day that constantly
repeats. At Anime Boston 2014, the anime screenwriter Satō Dai noted that
this was possibly the first time that an official studio relied on this process to
create a new series (Satō 2014).

Some aspects of Miku's original vocal design had profound consequences.
Why did Crypton, a company that made music software, use established
voice actress Fujita Saki for the original sampling for Miku's voice? Crypton
answers that this is more a desire to create a new kind of value than an appeal
to otaku culture:

> Personally, I don't really watch anime, and I don't know much about
> otaku culture. Even so, when I ask myself—why did we decide to go
> with a voice actress? It's because we wanted to suggest to the world a
> new kind of value. We've always been a company devoted to sound,
> making new kinds of sounds and instruments. Vocaloids are one style
> of this. In order to propose a new way of using software to synthesize a
> singing voice, we thought that even better than a singer or a television
> announcer's voice, more appropriate would be voice actors because they
> have more distinctive voices with wider variations.
>
> (Quoted in Shiba 2014: 103)

After listening to hundreds of voice actresses, Crypton settled on Fujita. When the Miku software was released in 2007, the consumer demand surprised even Crypton. It sold around 4,000 copies in the first two weeks, and over 15,000 copies in the first month (Shiba 2014: 114). One reason was that the software, unlike earlier Vocaloid attempts, was finally good enough for professional musicians.

The video sharing site Nico Nico Douga (launched in 2006) also played a key role. The site, renamed Niconico in 2012, is similar to YouTube (launched in 2005) in that you can upload your own videos and comment on uploads of others. Niconico is distinctive in that user comments scroll across the screen as videos play. This layering of content and comments is emblematic of participatory media today, whereby what we watch may be as much the commentary as the video itself. In 2015, the parent company Dwango (which became part of multimedia giant Kadokawa) announced Niconico boasts 50 million users and over 2.5 million premium users (Dwango 2015).

Niconico's logic of emphasizing comments grew out of the company's history. Before video sharing, the company sold ringtones, which one founder explains were not viewed as "music content" for personal listening:

> Rather, the point is, in the instant your ringtone goes off, it can spark a friend's reaction in the middle of everyday conversation. In other words, we viewed ringtones less as "content" (*kontentsu*) and more as a vehicle for sparking communication.
>
> (Quoted in Shiba 2014: 120)

Similarly, the videos streamed on Niconico are a means of sparking communication, rather than content to be consumed. Unlike on YouTube, on Niconico, user comments are associated with particular timing, something also seen on the audio distribution platform SoundCloud, founded in 2007. Miku's release in August 2007 was fortuitous for Niconico, which was facing objections from record companies about infringing material on the site. This left a great hunger for original content, and Miku producers filled this need.

What surprised Itoh and his Crypton coworkers was the enormous number of fan-made illustrations also posted online. This phenomenon can be explained by the idea of "media ecology," developed by Marshall McLuhan (1964), Neil Postman (1970), and later scholars (e.g., Mizukoshi et. al. 2014) to draw attention to the interconnected nature of diverse media. For example, amateur illustrators and manga artists have been making alternate versions of their favorite characters for years. At Japan's largest annual convention, Comic Market (Comiket), held twice a year in Tokyo, fans buy and sell *dōjin* materials often based on copyrighted characters. Many manga publishers have taken efforts to regulate the dissemination of fan-produced works, such as creating Doujin Mark (*Dōjin maaku*) in August 2013 to place on the cover of manga that they have approved for use for *dōjin* works. The implication is that fans cannot appropriate manga without the mark. The Doujin Mark and similar efforts have been met with limited success and much online debate. Comiket exists in a gray zone, technically illegal under copyright law but tentatively permitted (see Chapter 9).

Crypton stepped into this space of fan-made creativity with an unusual position on copyright and, as a result, has benefitted from the widespread practice of creating new art with licensed characters. Cosima Oka-Doerge, who works in U.S. and European marketing for Crypton, explained the development of Crypton's position on copyright:

> There was no distinct "change" or "start" of the licensing business, but rather Miku grew in popularity and fans, and, at the same time, companies demanded official collaborations and merchandise. It was not Crypton's intention to begin with licensing business in this sense. It was a "soft" shift, but first collaborations/merchandise took place within three months after the initial software release in 2007.
>
> (Oka-Doerge 2015)

By allowing relatively free uses of Miku, Crypton opened up a space for a participatory culture to emerge around Miku producers' content. Henry Jenkins (e.g., 2010) helped coin the term "participatory culture" to characterize such communities of collaboration, driven by the norms and values of the group, which may or may not entail commercial interactions. Miku's release in 2007 was fortuitous timing for the video platform Nico Nico too, providing lots of content just as the threats of copyright take-downs were afflicting other music postings. This not only helps explain Miku's success, but it also draws attention to a shift underway in our understanding of what media is, how it works, and how we study it.

Media as Platform Versus Media as Content

The digital era is challenging us to see media less in terms of *content* (e.g., the messages that media convey) and more in terms of *platforms* (e.g., the ways media can operate as tools for collective participation, and, of course, for marketing and surveillance). In general, media studies developed out of an interest in mass media—newspapers, advertising, photography, radio, film, and television—such that we could study each media form in terms of its own material possibilities for representation and interaction with audiences ("affordances") as well as in terms of their respective industrial configurations (political economy of media). If we think in terms of historical mass media, such as newspapers and television, we can easily grasp the paradigm of media as content. From this perspective, we analyze "texts," such as newspaper articles and television programs. There is a boundary between professional producers, whether as journalists or show runners, and the audience. From this perspective, the politics of media can revolve around questions of bias and propaganda in the production and distribution of media messages. In turn, with media as content, the politics for audiences tends to revolve around media literacy, that is, how audiences can interpret media more sensitively (Napier 2005; Ruh 2004).

Other scholars emphasize the materiality of media in terms of the social dynamics that emerge through media use (Jenkins 2006; Novak 2013). As people become more accustomed to encountering media through non-traditional channels, such as Facebook or Twitter, it starts to make sense to think of media in terms of platforms. From this perspective, we see how the division between producers and audiences is breaking down with user-generated content, some of which, of course, is reposting of professionally made content. Anyone can post our videos to YouTube, and, sometimes, have them removed as "infringing content." We often encounter media through friends' or acquaintances' recommendations, which is maybe not so different from the pre-digital era. But when we view media as a platform, we can pay more attention to communities of participation, crowd-sourced production, and styles of collaboration and networking. Politics do not disappear but rather take on a different cast as we consider whether we are living in echo chambers, hearing only opinions that we already agree with or are presented with information that exists only in our "filter bubble" (Pariser 2011), that is, pre-selected information that conforms to the social networking platforms algorithms and, hence, ideologies. Of course, even when we consider media as "platform," there are still messages and content being conveyed so these are not completely separate realms of analysis. Rather, each perspective offers a different view of what is important and why.

Yet if "participation" is a keyword for understanding the uses of platforms, how should we analyze it? Some scholars fear that participation in these on-line realms can constitute a new form of exploitation, both in terms of getting "free labor" (Terranova 2004) and in terms of unseen, yet monetized, surveillance of online activities. Trebor Scholz (2013: 1) writes, "Social life on the Internet has become the 'standing reserve,' the site for the creation of value through ever more inscrutable channels of commercial surveillance" which has important ramifications for "struggles around privacy, intellectual property rights, youth culture, and media literacy." This is certainly a fruitful area for critical perspective. At the same time, we should not conflate "getting paid" with "an end to exploitation." The broader question that accompanies the rise of participation in media platforms is, as Henry Jenkins and Nick Couldry (2014) ask, "Participation in what?"

A forum in the *International Journal of Communication* discusses some of the complexities of thinking about exploitation and participation as well. Couldry notes, "Some see spaces of positive social and political potential, whereas others see new forms of labor exploitation" (Couldry and Jenkins 2014: 1110). Anthropologist Chris Kelty goes further in highlighting the stakes:

> Participating in Facebook is not the same thing as participating in a Free Software project, to say nothing of participating in the democratic governance of a state. If there are indeed different "participatory cultures," the work of explaining their differences must be done by thinking

concretely about the practices, tools, ideologies, and technologies that make them up. Participation is about power, and, no matter how "open" a platform is, participation will reach a limit circumscribing power and its distribution.

(Quoted in Couldry and Jenkins 2014: 1108)

So, how does the Miku phenomenon measure up in terms of the power associated with participation? In my opinion, history is still being made in this regard.

When Crypton CEO Itoh visited MIT, we held a brainstorming session with students interested in Miku. Itoh mentioned the conundrum that the company faces: how to manage the relationship between the participatory and businesses that came along after. He gave this example: many people share their works on Crypton's community site PiaPro. An app developer made it easier for people to search PiaPro via mobile devices. This allows users to access, free of charge, images and songs that other users have posted, but the app developer charges money for the app. The only reason the app is useful is because people contribute work for free; yet those contributors do not make any money on the app. Itoh asked what should we do in this situation. What's fair? We had a lively discussion, but we could not come to a consensus on the issue.

This raises larger questions about exploitation. One thing is clear: exploitation of the labor of fan production is not solely related to who gets paid and how much. There are forms of participation that would not be improved by getting paid for them. Sometimes the reward of community accolades, or even just a few positive comments, can be enough to encourage creators. But does that mean all content creators should just come to terms with working for free? No. We need to develop terminology, ethics, practices, and technologies that help us manage this uncertain and ambiguous world where businesses are built on top of community-motivated labor. As a starting point, it seems to me that questions of exploitation must consider factors beyond the form of reward that users receive. Also important are other issues:

- "Opt in, opt out": do we have control over what the uses of our work will be?
- "Transparency": how are our works, data, profile, and interactions being used?
- "Credit where credit is due": are the right people getting credit for the work they've done?

Certainly, this list can be expanded, but at least it illustrates that the questions of exploitation are not only about payment for labor. Fairness depends on designing systems of participation that achieve balance in building on community standards while managing transitions from non-commercial to commercial exchange.

Conclusion

So what does the Miku phenomenon mean? What kind of history is being made? Since around 2000, the global recording industry has seen sharp declines in the sales of recorded music. At the time, some people predicted the end of music (Witt 2015). The argument sometimes went, "Why would anyone make music if it can always simply be downloaded for free?" Such dire warnings have proved to be misplaced. Instead, new music businesses are emerging in ways that reveal the importance of recognizing the social value of music, which is related to economic value, but only indirectly. The Miku phenomenon demonstrates that creative communities can be the foundation on which economic value is built. Miku's emergence as a crowd-sourced celebrity reveals how participation in media platforms can develop in unexpected ways and that this participation is not driven primarily by economic motivations. Ideally, such systems can develop in ways that avoid the worst forms of exploitation by being transparent, reflecting community values (opt in/out and giving credit, for example).

There are many reasons to be concerned about the directions of society globally today. From climate catastrophes to worsening economic inequality and expansive regimes of debt and control, we face challenges on many fronts. So, too, in Japan, "precarity" seems the order of the day. Anne Allison (2013) portrays a "precarious Japan" in the aftermath of the March 11, 2011 earthquake, tsunami, and Fukushima nuclear meltdown, amid continuing anxiety about the country's economic future. In a chapter on the cleanup in the tsunami devastated area of northeastern Japan, she writes of a pattern she saw repeatedly "in these early stages of post-3/11 Japan: the hydraulics of life pinched in various directions, attempts to (re)claim order by structures and rituals already in place and new alliances—and dangers— in the efforts to survive" (Allison 2013: 181). It is precisely in the arena of "new alliances—and dangers" that Miku's example of musical success creates for musicians and fans. Precarity refers in part to vulnerability, arising from participating in worlds where our chances for success seem to hinge on actions beyond our control. By throwing energy into communities that respond to their needs, Miku fans and producers carve out a space of legitimacy and value amidst a precarious world. Deeper understandings of how such fan-made spaces work will offer new ways to conceive of the mutually constitutive nature of such continually evolving economic and social relations.

Note

1 Thanks go to Crypton CEO Itoh Hiroyuki for visiting MIT and sharing his insights into the Vocaloid phenomenon and to the Japan Foundation New York for helping to facilitate his visit. Thanks also to Crypton representative Cosima Oka-Doerge for her thoughtful comments on the chapter and for arranging for the image clearance.

PART V

Music

13 Electrifying the Japanese Teenager Across Generations

The Role of the Electric Guitar in Japan's Popular Culture[1]

Michael Furmanovsky

In 1990 novelist Ashihara Sunao won the Bungei Literature Prize for *Jangling Strings of Youth* (*Seishun den deke deke deke*), the story of a group of electric guitar fans in Kagawa, Shikoku (a southern island of Japan) who form a Ventures cover band in their high school. Two years later the book was made into a successful movie, directed by Ōbayashi Nobuhiko; and an American remake with the working title *The Rocking Horsemen* is slated for future release. Seven years after the book's publication, the Fukuoka area division of NHK (Japan's national broadcaster) launched the television program *Hot Blood! Battle of the Middle-Aged Men* (*Nekketsu! Oyaji batoru*), a competition between middle-aged musicians with a minimum average age of forty. Not surprisingly, the majority of these "*oyaji*" (old men) bands played pop and rock songs from their youth, with most songs featuring one or more electric guitars. Many of those entering the competition came of age musically during the years of the so-called "*ereki būmu,*" or "electric boom," between 1964 and 1967 (Maruyama and Hosokawa 2006: 155–56). (*Būmu* is a fad that explodes on the scene.) This four-year period saw an electric guitar craze fueled primarily by teenage boys forming their own bands, a trend boosted by Fuji Television's weekly *Battle of the Electric Guitar Bands* (*Kachinuki ereki gassen*, 1965–1966), which was avidly watched by a significant segment of adolescent Japan. The so-called *ereki būmu*, one unparalleled elsewhere in the world, resulted in sales of an estimated 550,000 electric guitars (Maruyama and Hosokawa 2006, 155; Cope 2007: 88). In the same period, the United States, with its 2.5 times larger population and four times greater per capita income, experienced electric guitar sales of around 400,000 (Millard 2004: 3). Although several Japanese companies, most notably Teisco and Guyatone, were able to bring retail prices below the average American price of US$150, even the most inexpensive instrument would have cost the equivalent of a month or more of the typical worker's salary in the mid-1960s, thus making the outlay greater than that of an acoustic piano today (Billboard Online 1966; Koyama 2007; Tanaka 2013: 78; Demont 2014; Matsumoto Guitars 2014). This means that around 10 percent of the five million men between fifteen and twenty-four in Japan might have owned an electric guitar.

Given these statistics, the *ereki būmu* and the intense interest in the electric guitar that it triggered among young Japanese males deserves attention as a cultural phenomenon shaping life for high school and university age boys, and one which continues to resonate within the nation's popular culture. In the decades after the *ereki būmu* and the obsession with American and British rock that came in its wake, learning and performing mostly foreign covers, and later domestic rock hits, for their peers became a rite of passage for many Japanese boys. Indeed, even today, despite the prevalence of programming and keyboard-based electronic dance music, the electric guitar, with all of its equipment and paraphernalia retains a unique status among young Japanese youth, including since the 1990s many high-school and university-age women.

Much has been written about how the modern solid-body electric guitar emerged out of the American jazz and blues world of the late 1950s to become the instrument of choice for the mostly male, working-class musicians who remade jazz, blues, and country into first rockabilly and then rock 'n' roll (e.g., Waksman 1999). Outside of the mid-1960s *ereki būmu* narrative itself, however, the story of how the instrument became ubiquitous within Japanese everyday life from the mid-1970s onwards has not yet received full analysis. Part of the reason for the focus on the mid-1960s is the attractive and visually beguiling nature of the *ereki būmu* subculture, as well as its real and perceived connection to the pop revolution led by the Beatles and British bands. The phenomenon has received particular attention from both rock music journalists (Kurosawa 1994; Cope 2007; Halterman 2009) and Japan studies scholars (Stevens 2009; Furmanovsky 2010; Bourdaghs 2012). These studies have helped us understand the pivotal role of two Japanese musicians, Terauchi Takeshi and Kayama Yuzo, who, inspired by the live performances of the visiting Ventures instrumental combo in 1962 and 1965, went on to create their own bands and spark what would become the Group Sounds (GS) movement. The latter, generally regarded as the Japanese equivalent of the British Merseybeat phenomenon (1963–1965), short-lived though it was, visibly changed the image of the teenager. As will be seen, by virtue of its close connection with the aspirations of the massive *"dankai* generation" (baby boomers born between 1947 and 1949), the GS boom would fashion a musical and cultural template that pervades the world of electric guitar ownership and performance in Japan to this day.

Terauchi Takeshi and the Origins of the Ereki Būmu, 1961–1964

The *dankai* generation's desire for a new cultural expression, combining with their ingenuity and drive, helped Japan become one of the leading consumers and producers of British and American inspired rock and pop music in the final third of the twentieth century (Fukuhara 1979). Born in 1939, Terauchi (Terry) Takeshi grew up in an affluent family in Ibaraki. While still in his mid-teens, he formed his own jazz band and began a lifelong obsession with sound and experimentation that resembles that of American solid-body electric guitar pioneer Les Paul. While a student at Meiji University in Tokyo, Terauchi was swept along by the rockabilly boom (1957–1959), and, by his early twenties, he already earned a good living playing at American military bases and dance halls. It was at one of these concerts that the teenage prodigy bought a Fender Telecaster—possibly the only one in Japan at the time.

In 1962, Terauchi launched a new rockabilly-styled group, The Blue Jeans, and signed with Nabe Puro (a shortening of Watanabe Productions), then Japan's leading music production company. Enormously impressed with the power and dexterity of the Ventures' records, he worked assiduously to create his own version of the so-called "*deke-deke-deke*" sound as the American group's powerful sonic rhythms were dubbed in Japan. Always willing to experiment, the pioneering guitarist also added stylistic elements from American country blues guitarist Chet Atkins and choreography borrowed from *West Side Story*. This blend of sounds and on-stage moves defined the musical and visual persona of The Blue Jeans, and their 1964 album *Korezo Surfing*, arguably Japan's first rock LP, became the model for "*ereki*" bands in Japan, an influence still evident at the prevalence of GS revival nights at "live houses." The instrumental album, not only showcased Terauchi's frenzied picking style but was also a technological breakthrough featuring individual microphones for the drums and an early version of electric piano custom-made by Yamaha (Halterman 2009: 117; Furmanovsky 2010: 2–3).

Terauchi's innovations were a clear hint that Japan's own electric guitar pioneer was more than just an imitator. In January 1965, The Blue Jeans leader was among many other musicians mesmerized by the powerful white Mosrite Mark 1 guitars and customized amps that the Ventures brought with them on their first tour of Japan. Unavailable in Japan, the Mosrite's narrow necks and light-gauge strings, when allied with the long dexterous fingers of the Ventures guitarist Nokie Edwards, achieved a range of effects that stunned Japanese fans. Japanese rock music legend has it that Terauchi bought tickets for the same trains the Ventures rode their gigs in order to learn their techniques from the accommodating lead guitarist (Brasor 2008b). Bemused and impressed by the intense interest in their guitars and equipment, as well as by the personal adulation they received, Edwards and the other members were persuaded by some fans to sell their Mosrite guitars, a transaction that may have helped trigger the *ereki būmu* because the tour was immediately followed by the release of semi-legal and illegal imitations of the guitar by Japanese manufacturers like Guyatone and Teisco, including the now much admired Mosrite Avenger. One of these, Narumo Shigeru, would (will be seen below) go on to form his own group and play a role in popularizing Mosrite guitars in particular and high-end guitar equipment in general (Halterman 2009: 118, 121). The "scientific and focused" image of the Ventures carefully choreographed on-stage persona, with its precise timing and self-evident total mastery of the electric guitar, reached a mass audience on the group's return to Japan in July (Cope 2007: 75). The impact of this now legendary fifty-plus venue sold-out tour was greatly enhanced by the debut in June 1965 of the *Battle of the Electric Guitar Bands* television program, featuring competitors mostly in their late teens. Every leg of this tour was recorded for the concert movie *Beloved Invaders* (1966), shot in a manner that tended to emphasize the technical prowess and error-free performance rather than the musical creativity of the band (Halterman 2009: 129–31).

Kayama Yuzu and the Co-Option of the Electric Guitar, 1965–1966

Given the high cost of the electric guitar, it is perhaps not surprising that many of the bands participating in the Fuji Television program were from Japan's elite universities. These included the 1967 winners, Keio University's the Fingers, whose leader Narumo Shigeru became a guitar designer for Greco (History of Greco Guitars 2007; Bourdaghs 2012: 122). In addition to Terauchi, the judges included Keio graduate Kayama Yuzo. Kayama, an actor, singer, songwriter, and musician from a pedigreed family, emerged in 1965 as one of the leading figures in the *ereki būmu*. His stardom was amplified in early 1966 with the release of a new movie in his popular teen-oriented "Young Guy" (*Wakadaisho*) film series (1961–1971), *Guitar-Playing Young Man* (*Ereki no wakadaisho*). The plot of this movie included a battle of the bands competition, several displays of expensive guitars, and numerous excited female fans. Featuring several songs written by Kayama that became pop standards, the film showed a deft and hip sense of humor that perfectly captured the optimism felt by many in the *dankai* generation growing up in the years immediately after Tokyo's successful 1964 Olympic Games. The release of the movie, just months after the Ventures tour, catapulted Kayama's new LP *Exciting Sounds of Yuzo Kayama and the Launchers* to the top of the charts and helped expand the *ereki būmu* well beyond the major urban centers (Schilling 1997: 202; Cope 2007: 81–83; Furmanovsky 2010: 4–5).

The image of the electric guitar in Japan differed significantly from that in the United Kingdom and United States in large part because Japan's two leading electric guitar exponents and innovators were from affluent backgrounds and the instrument and its accessories were considerably more expensive in Japan. For Terauchi and Kayama, the immaculate suits and self-confident collegiate image of the tall and decidedly Caucasian Ventures with their white Mosrites, seemed the epitome of American middle-class masculinity. In addition, the two Japanese guitar aficionados, already almost thirty years old, were by this time either uninterested in vocals (Terauchi) or were focused on achieving success in the domestic market through ballads with Japanese lyrics (Kayama). By contrast, the men who underpinned the British-led pop music revolution—George Harrison (Beatles), Keith Richards (Rolling Stones), Pete Townsend (the Who), and Jeff Beck and Jimmy Page (Yardbirds and Led Zeppelin)—came almost entirely from middle- and lower middle-class backgrounds. Where Terauchi and Kayama took the highly technical styles of Nokie Edwards of the Ventures and Hank Marvin of the Shadows as their template, their British counterparts took most of their guitar licks and attitude from African-American blues and rock guitarists such as Muddy Waters and Chuck Berry or white Southern guitar pioneers James Burton and Chet Atkins (Waksman 1999: 245; Perone 2009: 43). The result of this divergent socio-cultural narrative would be a different cultural trajectory for the electric guitar in Japan, even after the spread of American and British rock among the next generation of Japanese musicians.

Firmly tied to Japan's hierarchically structured and conservative popular music industry, neither Terauchi nor Kayama proved willing or able to go much beyond his comfort zone, although Terauchi has been widely respected for his ability to adapt other musical genres, including Japanese folk songs and classical melodies, to the basic Ventures-GS template. The guitar pioneer also produced numerous guitar books and popularized his style among tens of thousands of young men, playing in countless high schools in the 1970s, in part to prove to school authorities, some of whom had disciplined students who attended GS concerts, that the guitar was an instrument that deserved respectability (Schilling 1997: 204). As Michael Bourdaghs has pointed out, however, Terauchi's card was "pop novelty and spectacular virtuosity" for the masses, and the man who called himself a "living fossil" and embraced the "*ereki kamisama*" (Electric God) label bestowed on him by his fans, never seemed interested in making the transition to the new more intellectual late-1960s rock culture (Bourdaghs 2012: 136–37). The same was even more the case for Kayama who, in 1966, chose to take advantage of the success of his *kayokyoku*-style ballads (a style of Japanese sentimental pop developed in the early 1950s) and remake himself into a mainstream national entertainer along the lines of late 1970s Elvis Presley. At the same time, however, one cannot help being impressed by the sheer longevity and consistency of these two living icons. Equally important, their very success and virtuosity on the electric guitar is a reminder of their ability to master a cultural import and achieve a level of proficiency that demands respect.

From Group Sounds to the Second British Invasion, 1967–1975

The late 1960s saw the rise and rapid decline of the *ereki* and vocals formula that Kayama famously dubbed Group Sounds. The GS movement, much of it shaped by such talent agencies as Nabe Puro and full of carefully manufactured American and British affectation, was encapsulated in the careers of superficially Beatlesque groups, such as the Spiders, Tigers, Wild Ones, and Blue Comets, all of whom enjoyed considerable commercial success. Three other GS groups, however, would partially break from management strictures in the late 1960s and produce a handful of tracks that emulated, and at times expanded, the rock guitar sounds coming from the United Kingdom.

The most notable of these were Eddie Ban of the Golden Cups who introduced the sound-distorting fuzz box; Matsuzaki Yoshiharu of the Tempters whose dedication to the sounds of the Animals and Rolling Stones was built around his skill on a white Mosrite; and Hiroshi Koshikawa of the Carnabeats whose Eric-Burdon-influenced fuzztone lines are highly regarded by garage band aficionados (Cope 2007: 90, 95; Bourdaghs 2012: 126–30).

While none of the Western rock-oriented tracks released by these bands achieved significant sales, they did pave the way for the post-GS generation of guitarists. These "underground" artists would take their musical and style cues from the mid-1970s blues and heavy-rock style guitarists mentioned earlier and self-consciously shun the mainstream music business. The most notable among this cohort were ex-Spiders member Hiroshi (Monsieur) Kamayatsu, Mizuhashi Haruo of the short-lived but influential Jacks, and Katō Kazuhiko of the legendary Folk Crusaders. Influenced by such politically-oriented hippy rock artists as the Grateful Dead and King Crimson, they nevertheless failed to achieve the kind of guitar "*kamisama*" status that might have expanded or broadened the instruments' aura in mainstream Japanese popular culture. Indeed, the work of these artists was largely dismissed in mainstream society as self-indulgent noise designed to appeal largely to university students, and in 1969 electric guitar sales plummeted to around 23,000, a fraction of their mid-1960s level (Maruyama and Hosokawa 2006: 155; Demont 2014).

The inability of the Japanese pop music business to produce a commercially and artistically potent post-GS rock group in the early 1970s would be mitigated in terms of guitar sales by a series of seminal tours by the British rock bands Led Zeppelin, Deep Purple, Pink Floyd, and Beck–Bogert–Appice, as well as Eric Clapton between 1972 and 1974. Performing for a primarily university audience during the peak years of the student movement in large venues, these visits, especially the 1972 Led Zeppelin and Deep Purple tours, featured loud and lengthy guitar solos delivered to rapturous applause. Taken together, performances by Jimmy Page, Richie Blackmore, David Gilmour, Jeff Beck, and Eric Clapton defined the sexualized and aggressive British male "guitar god" image. With their low-slung "axes" taking on an overt phallic symbolism that owed much to the performance style of recently deceased Jimi Hendrix, these five rock stylists defined a new template for Japanese teenage boys, many of whom aspired to a more rebellious or edgy image than that afforded by Kayama and Terauchi. As discussed below, one of these rapturous fans, Matsumoto Takehiro, would become the top-selling musician in Japanese pop music history.

The heavy-rock template set by the visiting British rock legends and the availability of cheaper and better guitars manufactured by Greco would provide the foundation for Japan's own psychedelic rock movement (History of Greco Guitars 2007). While none of the Japanese bands or musicians attained much commercial success, they demonstrated high levels of technique. Perhaps the most striking was the tall half-Chinese, Yokohama-born Shinki

Chen, whose 1971 album *Speed, Glue, and Shinki* was much influenced by British super group Cream (Cope 2007: 128–33, 181–85; Grunebaum 2011). Dubbed the Japanese Jimi Hendrix, the long frizzy-haired, uber-hippy disappeared from the scene almost as quickly as he arose. His onstage performances, however, attracted wide admiration and imitation. Equally adept and considerably more influential in terms of both image and creativity was Ishima Hideki of the legendary Flower Travellin' Band, a super-group that achieved some success in the United States and whose 1971 *Satori* album is regarded as among the best Led Zeppelin-influenced "progressive" rock albums of the era. Three years later, former Folk Crusader guitarist Katō Kazuhiko attained considerable critical acclaim for his guitar playing on the Sadistic Mika Band album *Kurofune* (Black Ship), recorded in the United Kingdom. By the mid-1970s, however, these innovative artists had been pushed aside by the soft rock and singer-songwriter pop epitomized by Yōsui Inoue, Ōtaki Eiichi, and multi-million-selling female artist Matsutōya Yuming, and it was these non-rock styles that would dominate the decade between 1975 and 1985 (Bourdaghs 2012: 161–62, 180–86).

Hide, Tak, and the Revival of the Guitar Hero, 1985–1995

The late 1970s saw the emergence of arguably Japan's two most successful bands of the late twentieth century: the pop-oriented Southern All Stars (1978–2008, 2013–present) and the electronic music pioneers Yellow Magic Orchestra (YMO). While nominally "rock" bands, neither of these two groups featured the electric guitar or connected themselves with the kinds of rebellious or progressive rock attitude that had been standard a few years earlier. With a dearth of new domestic rock, the decade from 1975 to 1985 saw most high-school or university band male guitarists settling into a safe routine of carefully rehearsed covers of the "classic" rock canon. In retrospect, the widespread societal image of the electric guitar and its extensive paraphernalia as a middle-class teenager's expensive toy as well as the marginal cultural role of what remained of Japan's working-class movement by this time, are the most likely reasons why British punk music—with its self-consciously proletarian indifference to technique, dismissal of high end equipment, and DIY approach to recording—failed to attract a mass audience outside Tokyo clubs during this decade (Gordon 1994: 3). Indeed, while the neo-punk Blue Hearts, who exhibited a sound and persona that was equal parts Ramones and Sex Pistols, did have several national hits a few years after the punk era (most notably "Linda Linda," 1987), they were not a guitar band and had little long-term impact. With the emergence of the keyboard and synthesizer-driven music by YMO and the relative disinterest in punk's simple but raw "garage band" guitar sound, the electric guitar seemed in the early 1980s to be in danger of becoming a tool for Japanese hobbyists to play their favorite 1960s and 1970s oldies at local weekend events or on television variety programs.

The unexpected savior of the electric guitar's status as an aggressive weapon for the articulation of alienation and youthful angst was X-Japan, a mid-1980s heavy metal group helmed by charismatic drummer Toshiki. The band's somewhat bloated progressive rock image was reshaped in 1987 by twenty-three-year-old Matsumoto Hideto, a talented guitarist, nicknamed "Gibson" by his school mates for his devotion to his hobby. Adopting the moniker "Hide" (pronounced "he day"), the talented guitarist had an unlikely background as a cosmetologist and hairdresser, experiences that would help his role in the band's popularization of so-called "Visual Kei," a Japanese version of the glitter rock style pioneered by David Bowie and KISS, both of whom were major influences on the band. Hide's androgynous persona, heavily made-up face, and tall bright pink pompadour mohawk attracted a large and loyal female following, as did his sexual lyrics and sarcastic but playfully boyish demeanor. However, it was his high-speed wailing guitar sound on his signature "Fernandes MG" series, that may have appealed most to teenagers. With the 1993 release of the band's *Art of Life* a twenty-seven-minute track featuring twenty minutes of guitar solos, the X-Japan guitarist was elevated to a "guitar god" status unequaled since the era of Terauchi and Kayama. Meanwhile his unpredictable stage demeanor, offensive lyrics, and frequent drunken episodes ensured that his appeal stayed firmly in the fifteen- to twenty-five-year-old cohort (Strauss 1998). In the decade before his suicide and the extraordinary outpouring of grief by 50,000 fans at his funeral in 1997, Hide defined the template of the guitar playing Japanese rock star (Stevens 2005: 149). Both as X-Japan's guitarist and as a solo artist, his impact on Japanese youth can be compared only with that of fellow fallen rock guitar gods Jimi Hendrix and Kurt Cobain, both of whom also inspired thousands of aspiring guitarists. Among his fans were the future members of three Visual Kei bands: Glay, L'Arc-en-Ciel, and Luna Sea, all of which built on his persona and went on to sell millions of CDs with a strikingly similar sound (Strauss 1998; X-Japan, n.d.).

While less important as a cultural icon, Hide's namesake Matsumoto Takahiro ("Tak") can lay claim to being one half of the most popular musical act in Japanese pop music history, selling an estimated eighty million albums overall (B'z Wiki, n.d.). In 2010, he became Japan's sole U.S. Grammy winning guitarist and only the fifth artist ever to have his own Gibson signature model guitar. Fronting the two-member B'z, formed in 1988 with vocalist Inaba Koshi, Matsumoto bought his first guitar, a Japanese Les Paul knock-off at the age of fifteen after hearing Deep Purple's Richie Blackmore's play "Smoke on the Water" on the band's legendary *Made in Japan* album. Four years later, he bought an authentic Gibson Les Paul and earned his reputation as an aggressive soloist playing with female rocker Hamada Mari. Much influenced by heavy rockers Van Halen and Aerosmith, Matsumoto's appeal differed markedly from that of the three-years younger Hide and is more akin to that of his generational predecessor Terauchi in that he was primarily a role model for musicians interested in technique, technology, and equipment. An additional comparison can be made when looking at the group's live performances. Just as Terauchi drew on the sporting atmosphere of actual high-school gyms in the 1970s to make rock guitar concerts both respectable and fun, so Matsumoto took B'z's ultra-commercial blend of hard rock, blues, and synthesizer pop on lengthy so-called "LIVE GYM" (capitals used in the original name) tours of the nation's stadiums and arenas. These concerts, with the duo usually clad in the leather and jeans uniform of the then archetypal rock band, were designed to convey the duo's desire to generate the high energy of a live sports game. Featuring a carefully choreographed twenty-song set, the concert culminated in the audience's shout of *"otsukaresama"* (well done) and sales of the group's vast array of merchandise. Whatever labels can be given to Hide and Matsumoto, their role in the resurrection and reinvention of the Japanese guitar hero is beyond question; they facilitated the instrument's entrance into new modes of mass media cultural products (Patterson 2012; B'z Wiki, n.d.).

Girls and Guitars: The Role of the Runaways in Re-Gendering the Electric Guitar

Given that the electric guitar attracted little mainstream female interest in the United States and United Kingdom until the mid- to late 1970s, it is hardly surprising that this was also the case in Japan. Despite this, however, the late 1970s saw a surprisingly strong interest in relatively minor guitar-based female artists like British guitar rocker Suzi Quatro and the all-female Runaways. While the former played mostly small venues in 1975, her aggressive glam rock helped pave the way for the much greater success of the latter two years later. Fronted by the Quatro-like Joan Jett on rhythm guitar and featuring Lita Ford on blisteringly aggressive lead guitar, the Runaways were a group of teenage girls from Detroit whose pop anthem "Cherry Bomb" was an unexpected hit in Japan, outselling worldwide best-sellers by ABBA and Boney M (Bukszpan 2012: 211). The song's success led to an invitation by Tats Nagashima, the promoter who had brought the Beatles to Tokyo eleven years earlier, to play in four cities in Japan in the summer of 1977. This tour attracted a large audience for the band's flamboyant, dynamic performances, and the group's popularity was further boosted by their appearance on several Japanese magazine covers. The June 1977 tour footage shows thousands of female fans outside the Tokyo Kōsei Nenkin Kaikan, reminiscent of the scene of the Beatles' arrival (McDonnell 2013: 193–94).

Not surprisingly, Japanese media coverage of the group emphasized its "bad teen" sexuality: on-stage use of porn-like spandex, lingerie, and platform boots, along with cheaply dyed hairstyles. While many Japanese fans were no doubt enthralled by the band's daring reinvention of the male glam-rock persona, it also seems likely that a segment were attracted to the powerful, gender-busting rock guitar playing of both Jett and Ford. The latter in particular, with her natural blonde hair, powerful physique, and accomplished heavy rock style, was perhaps the closest that any female guitarist came in this era to the British male guitar idols. As such, it seems likely that Ford's playing on the band's classic *Live in Japan* album, issued shortly after the tour, may well have inspired some of those who saw and heard her to form bands of their own. These young women in turn would help make the electric guitar an instrument that could be more readily adopted by high-school girls who sought to create a more rebellious feminine identity for themselves at a time when teen idols were dominating mainstream music.

While the Runaways success did not see a major movement toward female guitar-based rock bands, the late 1980s band Princess Princess (nicknamed Puri Puri) modeled much of their persona on the American group. Although the group was created and groomed by TDK Records, the members wrote most of their own lyrics and music and in Nakayama Kanako possessed a round-faced, big-haired Japanese version of a female rocker who combined genuine talent with wide appeal. Although the band's increasingly pop orientation and mainstream commercial success between 1989 and 1991 may have lost them credibility as "rockers," they deserve attention for their role in creating a template for the Japanese girls' rock band and in helping demasculinize the image of the electric guitar. In more recent years, the all-girl glam rock group, Scandal, led by Sasazaki Mami, has followed in the footsteps of Puri Puri to become the best-selling female rock group of the past twenty-five years, with all five of their albums placing high in the Oricon charts and several songs being used in anime series such as *Bleach* and *Fullmetal Alchemist*. The group has also played at the Nippon Budokan stadium and made several tours of Asia and the United States (Baseel 2014b; Scandal Band Wiki, n.d.).

Understanding the Electric Guitar within Postwar Japan's Popular Culture Revolution

The late 1990s saw the beginning of the *oyaji* band phenomenon described earlier and the return of many baby-boomers to their guitars and the music of their generation. It also marked the beginning of a fundamental shift in the larger J-Pop world towards a new kind of dance-oriented idol pop represented by female acts Hamasaki Ayumi and Utada Hikaru, boy bands from production company Johnny & Associates, synthesizer pop from Komuro Tetsuya's AVEX Group, and hip-hop-inspired dance acts such as EXILE (See Jayson Makoto Chun). Surprisingly, however, this musical sea change has not affected the ubiquity of the electric guitar in music shops or among high school and university bands. The now half-century Japanese love affair with the electric guitar shows few signs of any significant slowdown. Beginning as a U.S. cultural product, the continued popularity of the instrument is best understood as part of Japan's postwar reinvention of itself as a nation. The *dankai* generation of the immediate postwar period, in particular, exhibited an extremely strong cultural orientation towards and a high degree of both deference and yearning for the lifestyles, status, and indulgent pleasures embedded in American and later British popular culture. For many boys of that era, the electric guitar, with its combination of artisanal and technological appeal, its enduring attraction as a collector's toy, its ability to transform an ordinary or introverted teenager into a powerful or even sexually potent figure, and its capacity to express strong emotions without a human voice, allowed it to reach an extraordinarily pervasive presence. Reaching its peak appeal during the years 1965–1975 when the *dankai* generation came of age and then again in the mid-1990s when this generation's children reached adulthood, the electric guitar, despite its still rebellious image, has achieved a status unmatched by any instrument except its cultural antithesis, the acoustic piano. While electronic instruments of all kinds have already displaced it as the primary instrument of pop music creation, its iconic status within the entire range of rock and pop music production and its ability to electrify the new generations of Japanese teenagers remains unchallenged.

Note

1 Research for this chapter was funded by a grant from the Faculty of International Culture, Ryukoku University.

14 The "Pop Pacific"

Japanese-American Sojourners and the Development of Japanese Popular Music

Jayson Makoto Chun

The year 2013 proved a record-setting year in Japanese popular music. The male idol group Arashi occupied the spot for the top-selling album for the fourth year in a row, matching the record set by female singer Utada Hikaru. Arashi, managed by Johnny & Associates, a talent management agency specializing in male idol groups, also occupied the top spot for artist total sales, while seven of the top twenty-five singles (and twenty of the top fifty) that year also came from Johnny & Associates groups (Oricon 2013b).[1] With Japan as the world's second largest music market at US$3.01 billion in sales in 2013, trailing only the United States (RIAJ 2014), this talent management agency has been one of the most profitable in the world. Across several decades, Johnny Hiromu Kitagawa (born 1931), the brains behind this agency, produced more than 232 chart-topping singles from forty acts and 8,419 concerts (between 2010 and 2012), the most by any individual in history, according to Guinness World Records, which presented two awards to Kitagawa in 2010 (Schwartz 2013), and a third award for the most number-one acts (thirty-five) produced by an individual (Guinness World Record News 2012). Beginning with the debut album of his first group, Johnnys in 1964, Kitagawa has presided over a hit-making factory.

One should also look at R&B (Rhythm and Blues) singer Utada Hikaru (born 1983), whose record of four number one albums of the year Arashi matched. Starting from her debut in 1999 until her hiatus in 2011, she was, as Phil Brasor (2009) of the *Japan Times* proclaimed, the most influential Japanese artist of the 2000s. Her album *First Love* (1999) was the best-selling album in Japanese music history, with over 9.5 million units in sales (Farley and Sekiguchi 2001). Utada also sold more than 52 million records worldwide (Liu 2010).

But the successes of Kitagawa and Utada conceal a key aspect of Japanese popular music. Guinness World Records, in its announcement of Kitagawa's world records, referred to him as a Los Angeles native (Guinness World Record News 2012). And Utada was also a Japanese-American, having been born and raised in New York City. Fluent in English and Japanese, she released albums in both languages. Thus some of the most influential musicians in Japanese music history were Americans who sojourned across the

Pacific, seeking fame in Japan. What does this tell us about the Japanese music scene when two of its most influential players are Americans?

In a manner similar to how Paul Gilroy (1993) looked at the "Black Atlantic," where Africans and Americans interacted to create a hybrid culture we often identify as "African-American" culture, so has emerged what I dub "Pop Pacific" as a space of transnational cultural construction of "Japanese popular music." This involved a process of exchange across the Pacific mediated through the physical presence of Japantowns in the United States, American military bases in Japan, television, and the Internet. These are what Jan Nederveen Pieterse (1995) has called "hybrid sites," where hybrid formations like Japanese popular music are created and manifested. This hybridized popular music culture largely took root from the mid-1920s with Japanese-American jazz musicians performing in Japan; in the postwar period, the presence of music on American military bases in Japan and the growing interplay between television and Japanese music corporations accelerated and mediated this transnational flow. By the turn of the new millennium, the Internet allowed for near instantaneous access to information and provided easier means for fan interactions, helping to expand the global market.

A study of the "Pop Pacific" reveals the hidden transnational and hybrid aspects of Japanese popular music, or J-pop, as recent Japanese music since the 1990s is known today.

Given the primacy of the United States as the key source of postwar Japanese popular music, I focus on the transnational links between Japan and the United States. A study of the U.S.-Japan music connection discloses that, because much Japanese popular music was part of a larger global web of world music, labels of national origin like "Japanese" or "American" hide the true transnational nature of popular music.

Postwar Japan, the Pop Pacific, and Military Bases

In 1952, Kitagawa arrived in Japan during the Korean War (1950–1953) as an interpreter for the U.S. Embassy, the beginning of his sojourns across the Pacific. Born and raised in Los Angeles as the son of a Buddhist priest from Japan, he was sent to Japan at the outbreak of the war as part of a group of Japanese in exchange for U.S. officials. After the war, he returned to Los Angeles where he finished high school and entered the U.S. military during the Korean War, before becoming part of the administrative staff at the U.S. Embassy in Tokyo (Fukue 2009; Ōtani 2012: 218–219).

American influences have flowed into Japan since Commodore Perry's official opening of Japan in 1853, but this process accelerated during the 1920s and 1930s. Jazz, which was popularized by Filipino musicians working on cruise ships, took hold in port cities (Yoshida 1997: 42–116). Listeners associated jazz with the United States and with middle-class urban lifestyles. The most famous jazz vocalists of the 1930s were Nisei (second generation) Japanese-Americans singers, such as Fumiko Kawahata, Rickey Miyagawa, and Betty Inada, who were frustrated by racial barriers in the American entertainment industry. In Japan, their American nationality bestowed an aura of authenticity that contributed to their popularity, while their Japanese faces made audiences feel more familiar or comfortable with these entertainers (Atkins 2001: 81–82). These singers benefited from what Iwabuchi Kōichi (2002) has called "cultural odor"—the amount of cultural features of its country of origin (or the imagined way of life there) that a commodity carries. According to Iwabuchi, cultural odor is closely associated with racial and bodily images. In this case, these Japanese-American jazz singers erased the racial and ethnic characteristics of American jazz singers.

Much U.S. cultural influence came via Japantowns, and, in Kitagawa's case, Little Tokyo in Los Angeles, where he learned stage management techniques while working as an assistant at a local theater (Kosuga 2007: 14–15). In 1950, he served as an interpreter for Misora Hibari when she performed on a stage at his father's temple during her California tour. These experiences provided him with valuable contacts in Japan (Furmanovsky 2012; Ōtani 2012: 8–9; Schwartz 2013).

Kitagawa's sojourn to Japan as a U.S. official shows the role of the American military in postwar Japanese popular music. During the Allied Occupation, American bases opened up new avenues for cultural flows, as jazz from the U.S. military radio network became for many Japanese people the soundtrack of the Allied Occupation (Bourdaghs 2012: 29–35; Mitsui 1997: 166). As encounters with American military personnel ceased to be a part of people's everyday lives starting from the late 1950s, the United States was generally seen as less of an occupier and more of a model of consumer lifestyles (Yoshimi 2003: 443–444).

Kitagawa's first music act, Johnnys (1962–1967), was a revolutionary development in Japanese music: good-looking male singers who could dance, sing, and act. This group also exemplified the "Pop Pacific" intersection of U.S. bases, U.S. popular culture, and U.S. television. Kitagawa came into contact with the future members of his band when he lived at an apartment in Washington Heights, a U.S. Armed Forces housing complex in Tokyo. Kitagawa coached a local youth baseball team which he named "Johnnys" after himself (Ōtani 2012: 16–18, 219). Therefore, the site of interaction occurred at a U.S. government installation, with a game that originated in the United States.

The deluge of American cultural influences was mediated through movies. Kitagawa came up with the idea for the band after taking four members of the baseball team to see *West Side Story*. In an interview with *Newsweek*, Kitagawa noted, "I had started in an era when boys, male stars, did not sing and dance in Japan. That was a challenge, and it became a unique spot in the entertainment world, something unprecedented" (Poole 2012: 51). The idea for a singing and dancing boy group also had transnational roots with Kitagawa's teenage years in Los Angeles, during his involvement in theater and with Hibari's tours. Thus American-style musicals and Kitagawa's groups were linked from the beginning. Johnnys performed on stage as back dancers and later performed in musicals, like Ishihara Shintarō's *Curb of Flame* (*Honno no kābu*), and Kitagawa's *Whenever and Until Somewhere* (*Itsuka doko made*), which was inspired by *West Side Story* (Ōtani 2012: 224–225). Kitagawa wanted to be acknowledged while remaining in the shadows.

But Kitagawa needed to repackage his American concept as a Japanese concept—in other words, localize it for Japanese audiences, as this was also a time of growing domestic self-confidence. For example, by 1966, sales of domestic Japanese records exceeded those of non-Japanese imports (de Launey 1995: 206; Kawabata 1991: 336), and although Western pop music had an 80 percent share of the Japanese market immediately after World War II, when the influence of the Allied Occupation was keenly felt, the younger generation, which grew up in this affluent Japan, did not idolize the United States in the same way as their elders (de Launey 1995: 204–207). While the Johnnys manifested the American practice of dancing while singing, their song lyrics were in Japanese. The sound of their debut single "Young tears" (*Wakai namida*, 1964), miles removed from the pop sound of Johnny's groups today, was likened by a critic in 2012 to Mitch Miller style young men's chorus with childlike voices, helping to project the potential of youth of the time (Ōtani 2012: 17). Mitch Miller's television program *Sing Along with Mitch* (NBC, 1961–1962) aired on Japanese television in the early 1960s (Ōtani 2012: 17).

Thus Johnnys would become a uniquely "Made in Japan" group, aimed at young teenage Japanese girls. Prominent 1950s author about rebellious youth and later Governor of Tokyo Ishihara Shintarō, watching them perform in his play *Curve of Flame* (*Honoo no kābu*), noticed this potential: "They exactly fit the image of the 'noisy biker gang' [*kaminari-zoku*, or "Thunder Tribe"] that I had written about. What was unexpected was how the mood of the Nissay Theater, which until now was stuffy, was transformed by Johnnys and their fans into something completely different" (quoted in *Yomiuri Shinbun* 1965: 6).

Kitagawa turned to television to spread news of his idols nationwide. Introduced to Japan in 1953, television had become a universal household appliance by the mid-1960s. Popular music programs helped promote Japanized pop and forge a national popular media culture (Chun 2007). Kitagawa, grasping the power of this medium, had Johnnys appear on television shows targeting young teenage girls. It did not matter that their broadcast debut as back singers in NHK's program *Let's Meet in Our Dreams* (*Yume de aimasho*, 1962) was widely panned, for his formula involved good-looking boys who could sing, dance, and act, so exceptional singing talent was not particularly important. To appeal to families gathered around the television set, networks needed non-threatening entertainment stripped of political protest or ideology. One talent agency executive noted, "The era of vocal groups who can only sing has passed. From now, singing, dancing, and acting—like a concert of three instruments—it's no good if they don't become good at all of them" (*Yomiuri Shinbun* 1965: 6).

But training and promoting this new type of celebrity would take time and money; the stream of idols from Johnny & Associates (formed by Kitagawa in 1962) showed the power of the "*jimusho*" (talent agency). A development of the 1960s, the *jimusho* reflected the corporatization of Japanese daily life, with the top *jimusho* heading loose hierarchical organizations of smaller affiliated *jimusho* (Marx 2012: 39–42). Johnny & Associates thus represented a hybridized system of the American-inspired dance unit married to the hierarchical Japanese corporation. Kitagawa built his "Johnny's Jr." system, which probably represented every evil that young Japanese radicals in the late 1960s perceived about corporate Japan. Johnny & Associates was organized around seniority and hierarchy, just like Japanese corporations were. Young boys, like young "salarymen" (Japanese businessmen), were recruited and housed in a dormitory and trained over a period of years. Just like in Japanese companies, the young trainees have to obey their older "*senpai*" (senior colleagues) who had joined earlier. Trainees had to practice their singing, dancing, and acting before debuting as backup dancers for older established stars. Kitagawa also made good use of his ties with television networks. He placed popular members of his groups into television dramas and comedies, and any network that dared feature rival boy groups faced a boycott by Johnny & Associates stars (Furmanovsky 2012).

Kitagawa made a breakthrough with his boy band the Four Leaves (1967–1978, reunited 2002–2009), which also targeted the teenage female demographic. He presented them as five *shōnen* (adolescents), who would still retain their boyish appeal even as they became adults. Although beyond the scope of this article, the homoerotic styling of this and subsequent groups allowed female fans to interpret the male closeness as male friendship or sexual attraction. This also prevented heterosexual scandals (like sexual misconduct) from sullying the idols theoretical romantic availability (Darling-Wolf 2004; Nagaike 2012; Glasspool 2014: 120–123).

By the early 1990s, Kitagawa's model of promotion through television began to rule Japan. Kitagawa cultivated his band members as television personalities who could host programs and serve as celebrity spokespersons for advertisers, generating income from non-music sources (Brasor 2014). The rise of SMAP (Sports Media Assemble People, 1988–2016, a five-man group (six members until Mori Katsuyuki left in 1996), signaled the domination of Japanese popular music by Kitagawa's talent agency. SMAP, along with other Johnny's idols, became a ubiquitous part of Japanese mass media through appearances on television dramas, commercials, and variety, and talk shows (Stevens 2009: 54). Given the intertexuality of Japanese media, with television programs making references to radio, and audiences knowing the band members' roles in other dramas, "idols" (*aidoru*, celebrities the perform multiple functions) like SMAP became more than just musicians but rather hyper-familiar television personalities (Galbraith and Karlin 2012b: 10–12) (see Chapter 15). The *jimusho* strictly controlled idols' images and sounds.

Above all, the *jimusho* practiced information control through media. The *jimusho* provided artists; media provided favorable coverage. This bears some coincidence to the information control practiced by the Allied Occupation government, for which Kitagawa worked, which censored news critical of the Occupation. By pulling his stars from any television program that used talent from a rival *jimusho*, Kitagawa caused networks to cater to his agency's demands, for example by booking other Johnny's musical acts on their music programs or by blacklisting other boy bands (Marx 2014: 49). And the press made sure to minimize unfavorable news coverage of any Johnny & Associates groups. Calvin Sims of the *New York Times* noted in 2000 that the Japanese media made only scant coverage of accusations of Kitagawa's improper sexual relationships with his young singers, lest they lose access to his entertainers (Sims 2000). Even today, it is rare to see rival pretty boy idol bands on television, and videos of Johnny & Associates groups are strictly regulated for the public.

Utada Hikaru: New York City Cool in a Japanese Package

Utada Hikaru represents another case of the "Pop Pacific" at work, hybridizing and domesticating American influences, and shows how popular music reflects general changes in Japan's worldviews. Her success, like that of Kitagawa, also shows the process of hybridization and cultural concealment. By 1991, Japan's system of high-speed growth went into stagnation, unable to generate sufficient growth for a post-industrial age. After the bursting of the Japanese stock market and real estate bubble, the nation entered into what has been called the "Lost Decade" (*ushinawareta jūnen,* or "Lost Decades" because of its continuance past ten years), characterized by a deflationary spiral and the seeming inability of the government to enact effective measures to reform the economy. A degree from a good university was no longer a guarantee of economic security. This also meant that many Japanese youths started to aspire for jobs outside large corporations. This openness to outside influences in ways perhaps more directly than earlier generations was reflected in the music industry. One of the most successful singers was Utada Hikaru, a Japanese-American from New York City who sparked the Japanese R&B boom of the early 2000s. Part of her appeal was her New York City upbringing, which gave her an air of authenticity. Her new sound counterbalanced that of Kitagawa's American-influenced but Japanese-localized idols, who continued to dominate the charts.

Utada's parents did not move to America out of economic necessity. Her father was a music producer while her mother, Fuji Keiko, was a famous *enka* (Japanese folk song) singer. Utada was born in New York City, a melting pot of different cultures and the home to thousands of Japanese nationals. Like Japanese-American jazz singers over half a century earlier, Utada debuted in the United States with limited success. She first appeared as the

artist Cubic U, releasing *Precious* (1998) in both the United States and Japan,
an album of R&B songs sung in English. Either because American audiences
were not ready for an Asian-American R&B singer or because it was a bad
album, sales in the United States were poor. Utada's American nationality
and fluent English imparted authenticity to Japanese audiences, and she sang
in an R&B style sound characteristic of the late 1990s. And when first introduced to Japanese press as Cubic U on NHK's *New Midnight Kingdom* (*Shin
manaka no oukoku*, 1998) television program, a tanned Utada demonstrated her
English abilities and stressed the African-American influences in her music.
But perhaps she came across as too American, and the album failed to chart
when first released in Japan.

Like Kitagawa, Utada in her next album downplayed her Americanness
while playing up her ethnic similarity to Japanese audiences. She re-debuted
using her given name and a lighter R&B sound perhaps less jarring to Japanese
audiences, with Japanese lyrics and English-style phrasing and American
words. Brasor writes about Utada's use of her American musical training:

> [S]he sang what she heard, from the diaphragm and with her own take
> on the kind of melisma that became de rigueur in American pop after
> the ascendance of Mariah Carey. Previous Japanese pop artists, who were
> bred not born—and certainly not self-invented—couldn't handle this
> style for the simple reason that they weren't trained for it. Boy bands like
> the ubiquitous SMAP couldn't even sing harmony.
>
> (Brasor 2009)

Interestingly, *Precious*, her Cubic U album was reissued in Japan after the success of *First Love* and made the top ten in the Oricon ranking charts, selling
702,060 copies and becoming the thirty-fifth bestselling album of the year
(*Cubic You*; Kazuhaya and Hosokawa 2004).

What made Utada popular was her hybridity that combined aspects of Japan
and New York City. According to popular discourse, she was influenced
by the urban sounds she heard while growing up in New York City, but
Takemura Mitsuhige (1999: 206), in a book-length analysis of Utada Hikaru,
disagreed, noting that "implying that one developed a black sense of rhythm
[by living in New York] was like saying that being born and raised in Japan
means that one could do karate and judo." Takemura wrote, "No matter
how much I listen to her, she doesn't sound like a black woman singing,"
and that her songs were "more like a good song with the feel of an R&B essence, and the melody itself is nothing more than Japanese pops" (Takemura
1999: 8). Utada's New York City background made it seem "natural" for her
to sing this way, with an R&B flavor but not trying to be black. Takemura
felt that other Japanese R&B, artists such as UA (debut in 1995) and Misia
(debut in 1998), from their black-inspired singing, hairstyles, and tanned
skin, made it clear that they wanted to be black. He believed that since Utada
had white skin and straight black hair like other Japanese singers and only

differed in her sense of rhythm (Takemura 1999: 9) and one could argue that Utada reflected a multicultural and internationalized ideal: a Japanese person comfortable with multicultural New York City who could sing on equal footing alongside African-American singers with no sense of inferiority about speaking English (Takemura 1999: 11–13, 209). These comments may be more reflective of Takemura's views on race than Utada's listeners, but he does bring up an interesting take on stereotyped racial views of hybridity. Utada alluded to her hybridity when asked whether she was Japanese or American. In an interview with *Time* magazine, she remarked, "When people ask me exactly how much time I spend in each country, I always tell them I have no idea.... [This is] because my parents have taken me back and forth ever since I was a baby" (quoted in Farley 2001). Arguably, Utada's success paved the way for mixed race Japanese artists such as Crystal Kay (debuted in 1999) or AI (debuted in 2000) or for Japanese artists who sang in an R&B style, like Kuraki Mai (Brasor 2009).

Media changes were also responsible for these singers' popularity, just as the growth of television had enabled Kitagawa. These singers' debuts coincided with the rise of satellite television and the Internet, among other technological developments that affected the globalization of popular culture and mediated the "Pop Pacific" for non-Japanese audiences. The ban on Japanese music in South Korea was lifted in 1998, and Japanese performers were popular in places like Taiwan and Singapore, despite the older generation's memories of Japanese wartime atrocities. *First Love* sold one million copies in Asia (despite rampant piracy), demonstrating Utada's role as part of a larger wave of Japanese artists breaking into the Asian market thanks in part to the popularity of Japanese television dramas in Asia during the 1990s (Chung and McClure 2000: 53). Yet Utada's overseas appeal faced limits. Her English language album, *Exodus*, experienced lackluster sales in the United States, with only 55,000 copies sold, reaching only 169th place on the U.S. Billboard chart (Benson 2013: 26; Harrison 2014). Perhaps the United States was not ready for an Asian American pop star, or perhaps it was poor marketing, or just a bad album. We cannot know, but it is notable that the flow of the "Pop Pacific" was mainly one way, from America to Japan. On the other hand, *Exodus* sold well in Japan, as it broke the record for largest one-day shipment of an English language album by doubling Mariah Carey's previous record of 500,000 (Harrison 2014).

By the late 1990s, a transnational Asian popular culture spread over the Internet, which allowed fans to easily access overseas music (if the record company did not remove these illegal copies) and to with other fans. Utada had fans from all walks of life, but special mention must be made of her Asian American subculture fan base. If the U.S. mainstream media marginalized Asian American youth (by the lack of Asian American characters on television or movies, or lack of Asian American singers who made it on the mainstream charts), then these youths turned to their own online-based popular culture. Although Utada's English language albums disappointed in overall sales, she was a star to Asian American youth. For example, *Exodus* hit number one on the album sales charts in October 2004 in Hawai'i, with its large Asian American population (*Honolulu Star Advertiser* 2004). A 2009 study by Philip Benson (2013: 29) of her English language song "Easy Breezy" showed it was the third most viewed Utada Hikaru video, with 1,320,402 views, mostly from Japan and Thailand, followed by the United States. Judging from fan comments on the YouTube clips, Benson noted that some fans liked it better when she sang in both Japanese and English, showing that many English-speaking fans saw Utada primarily as an Asian or Japanese performer, not an American performer (Benson 2013: 23–33). It is interesting to note that Utada's popularity outside of Japan coincided with the changing international consumption of Japanese popular culture; by the early 2000s, Japanese videogames, anime, and manga were popular overseas, signaling the rise of Japan as a global cultural exporter. Utada's hybridity meant that she was able to traverse the "Pop Pacific" via the Internet to fans interested in Japanese culture. However, overseas viewers had trouble accepting her English language songs and American identity. Thus Benson argued, her Japanese identity was problematized when she chose to sing in full English.

Conclusion: "Pop Pacific" in the 2010s

Utada went on hiatus in 2011 (according to her blog on August 9, 2010, she wanted to take a break from "flashy artist activities" and focus on "human activities" [Utada 2010]), and with no superstar to replace her, changing tastes worldwide, and the Japanese music industry secluding into formula music aimed at the domestic market, the R&B boom in Japan seemed to end by the first decade of the 2000s. And surprisingly, the overseas appeal of Japanese artists like Utada was replaced by those from South Korea, where in contrast to the Japanese government and industries, the South Korean government and music industries made use of digital media to promote their own brand of K-pop (Korean pop) (Russell 2012) (See Chapter 17). At the turn of the millennium, Japanese singers like Utada or Hamasaki Ayumi (debuted 1998) had earned substantial Asian followings; it was predicted that J-pop would have a 10 percent market share in South Korea (McClure 2000a: 49). Yet the predicted dominance of Japanese popular music in Asia never materialized.

One of the reasons was the Japanese music industry withdrawal into a digital seclusion from the "Pop Pacific" by the 2010s. With the economic "Lost Decade" stretching past two decades, the industry focused on easier profits from the domestic market through price fixing and marketing strategies aimed at encouraging fans to buy multiple commemorative CDs (see Chapter 15). Also, strict Japanese laws on copyrights and illegal downloading maximized profits at home but made it increasingly more difficult for overseas fans to obtain Japanese music. Thus Japanese music's overseas presence declined as companies deprioritized overseas marketing and focused on their large domestic market, and Korean companies, dependent on exports due to their smaller music market, filled in the vacuum by marketing acts created for global consumption.

While Utada may have represented a multicultural Japan appealing to international audiences, the dominance of Johnny & Associates and idol groups like AKB48 represented "Galapagos Japan": an insular nation cut off from world currents. The term "Galapagos Syndrome" (*garapagosu-ka*) was first used to describe Japanese cellphones so advanced they had little in common with devices in the rest of the world, similar to Darwin's animals on the Galapagos Islands that had evolved separately in isolation (Stewart 2010; Wakabayashi 2012) (see Chapter 29). Because of the large size of the domestic market, companies considered foreign fans an afterthought and lacked urgency to reach overseas consumers. In the case of Arashi, who debuted in 1999, although they dominated Japanese record sales, it was expensive to watch authorized copies of their music videos overseas, and except for fan groups, they were largely unknown overseas. In fact, local media coverage of Arashi's first American tour in Hawai'i focused mainly on the economic impact of the concert (Blangiardi 2014).

Yet the "Pop Pacific" lives on. The Internet has helped to strengthen the global flows of music by making it difficult for *jimusho* to control information. While Johnny & Associates may have cowed Japanese media into favorable coverage, an online search will reveal pages devoted to allegations against Kitagawa, and rumors of cover-ups about the activities of his idols members, such as underage drinking and sexual misconduct. Although it is hard to determine the accuracy of these rumors, it is important to note that this information can be accessed outside of the control of mainstream Japanese news sources. Also, the Internet has allowed for instantaneous sharing of music and information, helping to break the monopoly of the talent management agencies. While online videos and songs of Johnny & Associates groups are quickly removed, there are numerous back alley avenues for illegal downloads of the songs, music videos, and concerts on pirate sharing sites. As quick as these pages are shut down, others will take their place. One cannot predict the future of Japanese music overseas, as the music market is too precarious. In 2000, no one could have predicted the rise of K-pop and the decline of J-pop's appeal overseas. And no one will be able to predict what will happen ten years from the publication of this chapter. For all we know, Taiwanese or Vietnamese pop could become popular. The Internet, along with devoted fan communities, and an increasingly globalized and multicultural world has ensured that the "Pop Pacific," forged out of the aftermath of war, will live on for decades to come.

Note

1 Note that the Oricon charts only measure physical releases, not downloads, but their sales numbers are used in magazines and news reports (Nak 2012).

15 AKB Business

Idols and Affective Economics in Contemporary Japan

Patrick W. Galbraith

Introduction

When examining contemporary Japan, one cannot help but be struck by the prevalence of "idols" (*aidoru*) on television, on magazine covers, and in advertisements (Galbraith and Karlin 2012a). Idols are young men and women not necessarily blessed with exceptional looks or talents but nonetheless somehow attractive. Rather than being one thing in particular, idols perform multiple functions from singing and dancing to modeling, acting, and more. Appearing regularly and simultaneously across media platforms, one gets to know, if not care, about idols through constant exposure. First noted in Japan in the 1970s in relation to media darlings such as Minami Saori, Yamaguchi Momoe, and Pink Lady, idols are a product of information–consumer society. They act as a connective technology that brings together corporations and audiences, who organize around idols. In a simple example, an agency produces an idol and makes a deal with television producers, who put the idol on a show; corporations have been brought together by the idol. The television producers cast the idol because they know that the idol will attract an audience; the audience and corporation have been brought together by the idol. The television producers sell advertisers time slots on the show, which has an audience attracted to the idol; again, corporations come together. The advertiser may hire the idol to appear in commercials for their products; the audience, tuned into the show to see the idol, will watch the commercials more intensively for images of and information about the idol. The idol is connected to the product, connecting the audience to the product.[1]

In this way, Japan excels at what Henry Jenkins calls "affective economics" (Jenkins 2006: 59–92), specifically the (re)production of "fan audiences" (Karlin 2012) (For more discussion of affective economics, see Chapter 12). Japan, one of the largest music markets in the world, is dominated by domestic performers (de Launey 1995), and the bestselling among them are idols. Even as old mass media, such as television and magazines, decline in Japan (albeit less dramatically than elsewhere in the world), idols not only persist but thrive. The economic recession and global competition of the 1990s did not lead to the disintegration of the Japanese media system but rather to the strengthening of fan audiences, or "affective alliances," around domestically produced content featuring idols (Lukács 2010: 4, 23–24). Today, there are thousands of idols active in Japan—"the greatest number in the history of Japanese entertainment" (*Yomiuri Shinbun* 2012b). The 2010s have been dubbed the "idol warring states period" (*aidoru sengoku jidai*) (Okajima and Okada 2011), which brings to mind the bloody battles between warlords that ravaged Japan from the mid-1400s until 1603, when the nation was unified. "Idol warring states" is a provocative turn of phrase that not only suggests many groups in competition but also a struggle for control of Japan.

In the "idol warring states period," a massive group called AKB48 occupies a nearly unassailable position at the top of the charts. In May 2013, AKB48 held the honor of most CD singles sold by a female artist or group in Japan—a whopping 21.852 million copies (*Asahi Shinbun* 2013). The following month, their single "Sayonara Crawl" sold 1.872 million copies, the most ever for a female artist or group in Japan (Tokyo Hive 2013a). By October 2013, they had fourteen consecutive million-selling singles, another record in Japan, which they proceeded to break in December 2013 (Tokyo Hive 2013b and c). Given these numbers, it may seem natural that the members of AKB48 are referred to as "national idols" (*kokumin-teki aidoru*). They certainly contribute the most to Japan's economy, or to what one critic has called Japan's "idol national wealth" (*aidoru kokufu*) (Sakai 2014). We must note, however, that the title of "national idol" is more prescriptive than descriptive. In numerous publications (Tanaka 2010; Kobayashi et al. 2012; Kitagawa 2013; Sayawaka 2013), the success of AKB48 is tied to its very devoted fans. AKB48 is supported by fans, not all of Japan, as made clear when the media personality Matsuko Deluxe expressed embarrassment at the proposition of AKB48 performing at the opening ceremonies of the 2020 Tokyo Summer Olympics (*Japan Today* 2015). AKB48's success depends on capitalizing on relations between idols and fans, techniques that are collectively referred to as "AKB business" (*AKB shōhō*). This chapter focuses on AKB business, specifically how relationships with idols are managed and fans are mobilized to increase CD sales. It concludes with a brief discussion of affective economics.

The Business of Intimacy

Every day, somewhere in Japan, numerous idols are performing. Of these, only a minority appears in the mass media, while the rest operate as "underground" (*chika*) or "indies" (*indīzu*) idols with perhaps only a handful of fans. While an analysis of production logics does much to explain idols in the context of an integrated system of mass media and commodities in Japan, it cannot account for the success of these other idols; herein lies an important point: more than a type of media performer, idols are fundamentally performers who appeal directly to fans for support. Intimate interaction with fans is characteristic of idols, whose existence depends on cultivating and maintaining relationships with fans. This is why Kyary

Pamyu Pamyu, a cutesy female artist who may appear to be an idol denies that designation: "In my opinion, the job of an idol is more or less to suck up to men, like thinking about what they can do to catch male fans' attention" (quoted in Kono 2013). The dynamic is not necessarily limited to capturing male fans' attention, as male idols such as Arashi and others from Johnny Kitagawa's production agency appeal directly to female fans (see Chapter 14). Regardless of gender, idols are meant to be objects of affection. The relationship between idols and fans can be experienced as "love"—some might say "pseudo love" (*giji renai*)—and cultivating that relationship is key to an idol's success.

Rather than a media phenomenon, AKB48 started out as idols who performed live for small audiences and appealed directly to fans. AKB48, an abbreviation of Akihabara 48, produced by Akimoto Yasushi, began its activities in 2005. The concept is forty-eight young women (mostly teens to twenties) who perform regularly on a dedicated stage in Akihabara, a district in Tokyo known as a hotspot for fan cultures (see Chapter 33). Given their current dominant status in terms of media appearances and CD sales, some might be surprised to hear that AKB48 was not an immediate success. Those who witnessed the group's formation recall receiving fliers printed on simple copy paper, which was for them nothing if not "suspicious" (*ayashii*).[2] Others recall that AKB48 used to perform "guerilla lives" (*gerira raibu*), where they would announce a time that they would appear at a public place, but it was unclear if they actually had permission to do so. Whether or not these accounts are accurate, they speak to a shared memory that AKB48 started out small. Indeed, when Akimoto held auditions for the group, he did not have enough talented applicants to sign forty-eight members and instead settled on twenty-four. According to Akimoto, the debut performance of AKB48 attracted an audience of only seven people (Coren 2012). Nevertheless, AKB48 did eventually reach forty-eight members, who were divided into three teams and rotated on a schedule so that one team performed live at the AKB48 Theater in Akihabara almost every day year-round. AKB48's slogan—"idols that you can meet" (*ai ni ikeru aidoru*)—speaks to the core dynamic of appealing to an audience that sees idols in person on stage regularly.

The place where fans came to meet their idols, the AKB48 Theater, is a peculiar one. Situated on the eighth floor of a building above a Don Quijote discount store, its defining characteristic is that it is "very small" (*kiwamete semai*) (Hamano 2012: 90): the stage and seating occupying approximately half of the total 926.4 square meters. The building was not designed to house a theater, and forcing one in resulted in a unique layout. The AKB48 Theater has at its center, in the middle of audience seating, two massive support pillars, which block some of the audience's view of the stage. The AKB48 Theater seats only 145 people and can accommodate a maximum of 250 people (Wikipedia 2015). A ticket costs only 3,100 yen (2,100 yen for minors and women), and estimated revenue does not cover the operational costs (Hamano 2015). Despite this seeming failure to turn a profit, above the entrance to the AKB48 Theater is a sign that reads, in English, "Japan's Most Sophisticated Show, Presented by the AKB48 and 48 Girls."

While hyperbolic and awkward, the sign announces the innovative approach to idols emblazoned by the AKB48 Theater. Specifically, the architecture of the AKB48 Theater has contributed to the formation of fan audiences, in that only a small number of people can see a live show; when one does get in, he or she is close to the stage, a mere two meters from it in the front row; performances and interactions are intimate. As Hamano Satoshi, a researcher of information society who became interested in the phenomenon of AKB48 and conducted auto-ethnographic fieldwork on his journey into fandom, points out, the two supporting pillars encourage audience members to focus on the idols appearing in their limited lines of sight (Hamano 2012: 124–132). Although originally skeptical about the appeal of AKB48 and finding the group's fans to be somewhat pathetic, Hamano recounts an experience of being powerfully affected by recognizing an idol on stage and seeing her recognize him back (Hamano 2015). This feeling of "recognition" (*shōnin*), of eyes meeting, is something akin to "love at first sight" (*hitomebore*). As Hamano sees it, the AKB48 Theater is "a platform for face-to-face communication" where fans can "savor an illusory experience that is close to 'the unexpected moment when our eyes met'" (Hamano 2012: 89, 132). Hamano could not deny the powerfully moving experience of interacting with an idol, which was for him not unlike a religious experience, and he became a devoted fan of AKB48 (Hamano 2015). If we resist the urge to dismiss fans and instead take them seriously, then an experience such as Hamano's is neither self-delusion nor the suspension of disbelief but rather an interaction with a known fiction—the idol performance as "something made" (Yano 2002: 16), not false—that moves in real ways. If we abandon appeals to authenticity, then we can see that one falls in love with AKB48 by design but that this is still love nonetheless.

In 2006, AKB48 released its third single, "I Wanted to See You" (*Aitakatta*), which became a signature number performed at the start of live shows at the AKB48 Theater. The song begins with the phrase "I wanted to see you," repeated three times with enthusiasm, punctuated by a "yes" shouted by the performers and audience members in unison; these four lines are repeated and then followed by "You..." When saying these lines, the idols look at members of the audience and seem to be speaking to them, and the audience returns the words and gaze. When the members of AKB48 sing "You...," which in the Japanese is a second-person pronoun (*kimi*) followed by a particle indicating direction (*ni*), they draw out the sound of the particle and double the indication of direction by pointing directly at members of the audience, who often reciprocate the gesture. Given their close proximity, members of AKB48 and the audience often recognize who is pointing at whom. After the show, when the idols used to give members of the audience "high fives" (a charged moment of physical contact), one might mention to her fan, "We made eye contact back there." It is hard not to see this as flirtation, which the idol does to earn support (i.e., to encourage fans to fall and stay in love).

Indeed, fans recognize themselves as supporters of idols. The member of AKB48 that a fan points to, the one that he wants to see and be seen by, is known as "the member I support" (*oshimen*). The fan not only buys merchandise featuring his idol and photographic prints of her but also makes a point of shouting her name when she appears on stage. In fact, the music written for AKB48, as is common for idols, ensures that popular members get to sing parts on their own or as duets, which provides an opportunity for fans to shout the idol's name and show support. "Talk" (*tōku*), which refers to times where idols banter on stage instead of singing, are important chances for the audience to get to know them better and shout out responses—Hamano's "face-to-face communication"—that are both private and public, personal and shared, constructed and real.

AKB Business

AKB48's massive sales are linked to idols appealing directly to fans and fans consuming in order to support their idols and/or to gain access to them. For example, CDs are packaged with premiums, which might be posters or photograph prints, perhaps signed, or tickets to events where fans can interact with idols more intimately. Early on, AKB48 began to include tickets for "handshake events" (*akushukai*) with the purchase of designated CDs. Given that seeing the idols and being seen by them is so important to AKB48 fans, it should come as no surprise that these handshake events were extremely popular. Not only does the fan get to meet his idol but also gets to touch her hand and exchange a personal greeting, imagining that she recognizes him from multiple previous encounters (Hamano 2012: 79–88). Even after buying a CD and getting a ticket to a handshake event, fans, who show up en masse, have to wait in line (sometimes for hours) to reach their idol, with whom they only have a few precious moments. This leads to AKB48 fans owning physical copies of CDs, even of the same CD, all purchased at full price, which is anachronistic in an age of digital downloads and free music (Figure 15.1).

The place of the premium in AKB business is even more obvious in the General Election (*sōsenkyō*), instigated in 2009 in response to fans' criticism of Akimoto for not promoting the members of AKB48 that they felt he ought to promote. Building on earlier experience as the producer of Onyanko Club (Furuhashi 1989), Akimoto seized on the concept of "the member I support" and told fans to step up and decide for themselves AKB48's "center" (*sentā*), or the most popular member who enjoys the most exposure, as well as the "select members" (*senbatsu membā*) around her. Fans vote in the General Election to determine these positions, or simply to vote for the member they support, regardless of rank. The members voted into the select group then sing in the next single and appear in the promotional video. This enfranchisement encourages fans to participate in the General Election and to have

Figure 15.1 AKB48 General Election, June 2015.
Source: Screenshot courtesy of Kendall Heitzman.

an impact on the career of the member they support, as well as the overall composition of AKB48 (compare this to *American Idol* in Jenkins 2006: 64). While a General Election sounds democratic, the caveat is that fans need to buy new copies of a designated CD in order to get ballots. That is, the right to vote, the ballot, is the premium. And there is no limit to how many votes an individual can cast; to get more votes, one simply buys more CDs. Even more so than tickets to handshake events, this use of the premium spurs AKB48 fans to buy multiple copies of the same CD, leading to record-breaking sales.

Consider that in 2009, when the General Election was first held, AKB48 was not in the top ten of the Oricon Yearly Singles Chart (Oricon 2009). Instead, the chart was dominated by male idols such as Arashi, KAT-TUN, and Kanjani 8. However, in 2010, with the General Election established and AKB48 gaining more media exposure, they had the top two spots with "Beginner" (954,283 copies sold) and "Heavy Rotation" (713,275 copies sold) (Oricon 2010). The increase in sales correlates with greater participation in the General Election, when a rivalry between AKB48 members Maeda Atsuko and Ōshima Yūko mobilized fans to buy CDs and vote. Indeed, in addition to more people buying more CDs to cast more votes for more members (a distributed increase), a major factor in AKB48's increased sales was Ōshima's fans (a focused increase), who voted her into the center position over Maeda, winner of the first election in 2009 and the accepted center of AKB48. In 2009, Maeda earned 4,630 votes (Stage48 2009), but in 2010, Ōshima earned 31,448 (Stage48 2010). In 2011, when Maeda's fans mobilized to support her comeback, she earned 139,892 out of a total 1,081,392 votes cast for the top forty spots (Stage48 2011). By this time, the General Election had become a media event, with results announced during a ceremony at the Nippon Budokan stadium and streamed live to eighty-six theaters in Japan, and to theaters in Hong Kong, Taiwan, and South Korea (Barks Global Media 2011); an estimated 150 media outlets reported on the event (Morita 2011). AKB business, which mobilized fans to buy CDs, proved to be extremely effective. In 2011, AKB48 had *all top five spots* on the Oricon Yearly Singles Chart (Oricon 2011), a record achievement that they repeated in 2012 (Oricon 2012). That year, each of their top five singles sold over a million copies. Further, AKB48's sister group SKE48 (from Nagoya) held spots eight through ten, leaving only six and seven open for the male idol group Arashi.

What is significant about the General Election is not only that Akimoto Yasushi places idols in front of fans and profits from allowing them to "freely" choose, but also that it recognizes fans' affection, attachments, and activities as a source of value.[3] Faced with public scrutiny over AKB business' apparent manipulation of fans and encouragement of wasteful consumption, Ōshima explained to her critics, "Votes are love" (*tōhyō wa mina-san no ai*) (*Daily Sports* 2011). While in the center position, Ōshima led AKB48 in singing their smash single "Heavy Rotation" (2010), which begins with the words "I want you! (I want you!) I need you! (I need you!) I love you! (I love you!)" In the context of the General Election, it almost seemed like Ōshima was saying the words to her supporters, who repeated them back to her. The performance seems a statement on the idol-fan relationship.

While acknowledging that one buys votes in the General Election, note that it is the electorate, not candidates, who do the buying, motivated by love. Idols inspire their fans to act as supporters, or, put another way, to act on their love. What might you think if you discovered hundreds of AKB48 CD singles emptied of their ballots and discarded in the trash (Rocket News 2011a)? Perhaps that it is waste of money and resources. But what might the fan who bought those CDs think? Perhaps that it was a meaningful and fulfilling way to support his idol and express his love by participating in the General Election. Fans who buy dozens of copies of the same CD are not ashamed of their actions—quite the opposite, actually. AKB48 fans sometimes pile their CD purchases up, take photographs, and post them to social media for other fans, and possibly the idols themselves, to see and comment on. The expectation is that the fan's actions, his labor of love, will be assessed based on social rather than economic understandings of value.

Consider the following scenarios. Angered by a scandal that banished Sashihara Rino from Tokyo to a sister group (HKT48) in Fukuoka in 2012, fans rallied to right the wrong and elect her to AKB48's center position in the 2013 General Election. Famous for her rapport with fans and her use of social media to interact with them, Sashihara received a record 150,570 votes (Stage48 2013), with one of her fans claiming to have spent approximately 14 million yen to buy 9,108 votes for her (Artefact 2013). The incredible result was that Sashihara bounced back from a scandal (not common for idols, especially young women) and reached the pinnacle of AKB48—the first time someone from a sister group held the coveted center position. Fans were also happy because they achieved their goal and kept Sashihara in the spotlight. Needless to say, Akimoto Yasushi, who had banished Sashihara and angered the fans, smiled all the way to the bank. But it did not end there. In the 2014 General Election, a forty-two-year-old strawberry farmer, who claims to spend between eight and nine million yen a year to support his idol, bought 4,600 CDs to vote for Sashihara in the General Election, only to see her come in second place (Anahori 2014). While in some ways the strawberry farmer failed, he succeeded in expressing his love for Sashihara and having it recognized by others. The election results also provided a reason for fans to rally behind Sashihara in 2015. Also remarkable, in the 2014 General Election, was the story of Takahashi Juri, who for two years had failed to break into the top forty-eight selected spots (by this point, there were 140 members in the four main units of AKB48, in addition to more members in sister groups in three Japanese cities, Jakarta, and Shanghai). Deciding it was time to vote her up in rank, one of Takahashi's fans spent 31,502,400 yen on CDs for votes for her; although the supporter chose to remain anonymous, he posted photos to prove the enormity of his achievement (Baseel 2014a).

Concluding Remarks: Affective Economics

In 2010, Japan led the world in sales of recorded music, followed by the United States, which had more than double the population (RIAJ 2012: 24). That year, AKB48 was Japan's top idol group and accounted for a significant percentage of overall CD sales (Oricon 2010). As we have seen, many of those CDs were purchased by fans, and not necessarily a broad cross-section of Japanese society. Indeed, AKB48's story is not about the nation embracing what fans do, but rather the successful capture of the value of fans' affection, attachments, and activities. Rather than a single group, AKB48 is multiple groups comprised of multiple members, each with her own small number of fans, and all the members and fans are in competition with one another. Ultimately, it is the proximity to idols and their direct appeal, the intensity of fan response, and competition between idols and fans against others that drives AKB business.

In many ways, AKB business can be understood in terms of affective economics, for example, the phenomenon of "inspirational consumers" or "brand advocates" (Jenkins 2006: 73), who are only a small percentage of the audience but make up a disproportionate amount of purchases. Even before the formation of AKB48 in 2005, researchers in Japan recognized how fan activities could be harnessed as a productive force, and Akihabara was used as a prime example (Kitabayashi 2004: 6–7). Researchers have also shown that idol fans support performers before they become extremely popular because they can at this time establish a relatively close relationship (Furuhashi 1989: 31). Given the presence of such fans in Akihabara, it is perhaps not surprising the neighborhood is home to numerous venues where virtually unknown idols perform and attempt to win support. In fact, there were so many idols coming to Akihabara to perform in the mid-2000s that they spilled out onto the street (see Chapter 33). Akimoto Yasushi has stated that, "Idols are born from the place with the most energy," and he chose Akihabara as the base of operations for AKB48 in 2005 for precisely this reason (Wikipedia 2015).

If the "affect" in affective economics can be understood as the "power to act" and "value from below" (Negri 1999: 78–79), then a critic might suggest that AKB business demonstrates how it is captured in, for example, the General Election. Struck by the sight of young men purchasing multiple copies of the same CD single to obtain ballots, comedian Okamura Takashi criticized AKB48 for its exploitative business practices (Rocket News 2011b). Drawing a comparison to host clubs, where professional male entertainers sell female clients the fantasy of a romantic relationship and encourage them to order overpriced food and drink to boost their monthly sales and rank in the club (Takeyama 2005: 207–208), Okamura described AKB48 as a "reverse host club" (*gyaku hosuto kurabu*). In this statement, Okamura plays on the widespread perception that women are manipulated and taken advantage of in host clubs. In calling the dynamic a reverse host club, Okamura suggests that AKB48 idols are like hosts selling the fantasy of a romantic relationship, which they abuse to take advantage of male fans, who are in the same position as hosts' female clients.

While Okamura is right to point out the striking similarities between hosts and idols engaged in intimate relations with clients and fans and encouraging them to make purchases in order to boost their rank, he falls into a familiar trap by reducing this to a narrative of exploitation. A critique of affective economics requires a more nuanced approach, which comes from closer examination. For example, Takeyama Akiko, who conducted field-work in Tokyo host clubs, does not see clients as purely victims or hosts as victimizers—or the other way around, hosts as purely victims of a system where employers and clients (ab)use them for their own needs. Instead, Takeyama suggests that host clubs, like affective economics more generally, "satisfies multiple players and institutions in mutual yet asymmetrical ways" (Takeyama 2010: 238). Takeyama points out that Japan's affect economy is "nested in the service and entertainment industry" (Takeyama 2010: 238), which invites an application of her analysis of hosts (service) to the case of idols (entertainment industry). As Takeyama suggests of hosts, an asymmetrical relationship is also characteristic of relations between idols and fans (Yano 2004a: 47), but this is not to say that these relationships are not real or meaningful for those involved (Ho 2012: 177–179). Further, insofar as affective labor can be extremely rewarding (Lukács 2013: 48), neither idols nor fans—all engaged in forms of affective labor, laboring for love in relation to one another—are purely victims.

Relationships between idols and fans satisfy in asymmetrical ways, and are evaluated in different ways by the multiple players and institutions involved.

Focusing only on the institutions would be to ignore the agency of idols and fans, while focusing only on the players would be to ignore the structure that allows and limits (inter)action. In future discussions of idols, we need to consider the various ways in which multiple players and institutions come together, raising questions about how relations are asymmetrical, who is satisfied and how, and what are the costs and benefits for those involved. However, the simple economic model suggested by costs and benefits will not do; instead, we must also account for individual and social dimensions of value (Condry 2013). In the affect economy, it is possible for the divergent values and interests of corporations to converge with those of idols and fans. A critique of AKB business can only come from working through these complex relations and entanglements.

Notes

1　Accordingly, idols are used excessively in advertisements in Japan. Some critics have gone so far as to call this a structural "dependency on celebrity" (Kaji 2001: 106). Around 70 percent of commercials in Japan feature celebrities, many of them idols, whose production logic is geared toward earning lucrative contracts with advertisers (Marx 2012: 49–51). Successful idols have become ubiquitous in (and as) advertisements. On a single day in February 2012, AKB48 appeared in ninety different commercials for Wonda Coffee, which earned them a Guinness World Record for "Broadcasting the Most Same-Product Television Endorsements within 24 Hours" (Tokyo Hive 2012).

2　These statements come from group interviews with Japanese male fans of AKB48 convened by the author on August 14, 2010 and September 16, 2014.

3　Akimoto Yasushi's position recalls a statement attributed to the famously corrupt American politician Boss Tweed: "I don't care who does the electing, so long as I get to do the nominating." In the General Election, fans choose from among AKB48 members, who Akimoto has placed in front of them; whoever wins, he wins. Francesco Alberoni notes something similar in the Hollywood star system, which "never creates the star, but [...] proposes the candidate for 'election,' and helps to retain the favor of the 'electors'" (quoted in Dyer 1979: 19). Speaking of the reality television program *American Idol*, Henry Jenkins explains that elections are a "fantasy of empowerment—'America' gets to 'decide' upon the next Idol. This promise of participation helps build fan investments" (Jenkins 2006: 64). While Jenkins notes that some fans of *American Idol* critique elections as unfair, such debates are muted in the General Election for AKB48, which is known to be dominated by those who care more and spend more money.

16 In Search of Japanoise

Globalizing Underground Music

David Novak

In 1990, I had just returned from a year of teaching English in Japan, so I was surprised when I came back to college in Ohio and started to hear about "Japanese Noise Music." Some cut out the "music" idea altogether and called it all "Japanese Noise," and others just compressed it to "Japanoise." The name was supposed to identify a specific Japanese type of "Noise," which was already a pretty vague genre name. Some friends added that its top artists mostly came from the Kansai region and the cities Osaka and Kyoto where I'd been living. I'd run into some noisy punk rock and experimental music in little underground record stores and small clubs around Japan ... but *Japanoise*? I had never heard of it until I was back in the United States, when the Boredoms' LP *Soul Discharge* found its way to the college radio station where I was a DJ, and tapped into the emerging independent music scene.

At the time, the flow of underground cassettes, CDs, and vinyl into the station was increasing on a daily level. But dropping the needle on *Soul Discharge* released the most spectacularly dissonant racket I'd ever heard, toggling through a spectrum of styles and sounds. Sometimes Boredoms sounded like a hardcore band, sometimes a random Dada cutup of popular culture: it was desperately heavy but also funny as hell. You couldn't possibly take it seriously, but, at the same time, it demanded your full attention. The two women on the cover had their faces obscured by ski masks, earmuffs, and 7" records, and the title was scrawled in a kind of Graffiti Rock dayglo script. The names of the performers listed on the record jacket were equally bizarre: the drummer was called "Yoshimi P-we," the guitar player was "Yama-motor," one performer went by "God Mama," and the lead singer was simply called "Eye." Was this really from Japan? And was this noise really a new form of Japanese pop music?

The first track, "Bubblebop Shot," starts with someone squealing like a donkey. Then different voices explode into a chaotic mix of operatic singing; screams and moans in a reverb chamber; a gunshot; burble and blabble; a mockery of a Southern drawl. What language was this? Except for one repeated shout that was either "Fuck You" or "Thank You," it was unintelligible syllables and shouts, a stream of nonsensical, guttural scat. Although it may have been a small thing to hold onto, at least I knew it was gibberish and not Japanese … but no translation was going to make sense of this.

I finally got to see Boredoms perform at the Kennel Club in San Francisco in 1993. Although the group had visited once before, a year earlier, this was their first tour since the U.S. release of *Soul Discharge*, and the hall was buzzing in anticipation. Walking calmly onto the stage, they seemed positively normal, setting up their gear, busily adjusting mic stands and drum equipment—just like a regular rock band, I thought—as the audience howled and cheered at them. Eye waved to the crowd and nodded distractedly; he climbed up on top of a speaker cabinet and surveyed the crowd. Drummer Yoshimi P-we adjusted her headset mic, and in a strange growling voice announced, "Hello! We are Boredoms! It's not a fucking joke! We come over the sea! And now … we rock you motherfucker!" Then she turned to the band: "*Iku yo.*" (Let's go). Eye leapt into the air, wielding what looked like an electric field hockey stick, while Yoshimi leaned back from her drums and pierced the air with a scream like a riot whistle. The band smashed into a burst of cymbals and grinding chords, and from there it was pure chaos. Eye jammed the microphone into his mouth and staggered around the stage, head lolling; Yoshimi stood up on her drum throne, bleating and blasting on a trumpet; Yoshikawa was chanting alongside Eye and playing what appeared to be a pizza box; bassist Hila was a mass of hair and distortion on the left side of the stage. All of this made guitarist Yama-motor seem even stranger, as he stood to the side calmly picking out his solos with precision, dressed in a check shirt and baseball cap while everyone else stripped off their shirts and bounced between the amps, the ceiling, and the frenzied crowd. It was the best hardcore and the most psychedelic drum circle and the weirdest art rock I'd ever heard. It was a mass of transformative energy; Boredoms could take any music and turn it into ecstatic Noise.

If Boredoms can be considered as a representation of Japanese popular culture, they also exemplify the noisiness of that category. It is difficult to say what exactly is Japanese about them, and it is even more difficult to describe their music as "popular." Most Japanese would find it absurd if something like *Soul Discharge* should attain the emblematic global status of Japanese cultural forms like sushi, *ukiyo-e* woodblock prints, or Zen meditation. At the same time, the overseas reception of Boredoms exhibits several core values associated with modern Japan in the global imagination throughout the twentieth century, ranging from its apparent incommensurability with so-called Western aesthetic values, to its postmodern mix of media influences and styles, to the cathartic expressions of violence and radical subjectivity associated with its postwar avant-garde (Miyoshi 1991; Ivy 1995; Iida 2001; Iwabuchi 2002; Allison 2006; Yoda and Harootunian 2006; Sakai 2008; Marotti 2013). Despite hewing uncomfortably close to an underground version of these historical Orientalisms—in which "Japan" appears equally unique and inscrutable—the cultural force of Boredoms is also a productive outcome of the contemporary distortions of transnational circulation.

Their "Japaneseness" was formed at the edges of North American reception in the 1990s, at a moment when notions of "Cool Japan" flowed into global consciousness through the spread of Japanese animation, comics, toys, games, and videogames, which together seemed to constitute much of Japan's contemporary cultural milieu. These foreign receptions of Japanese culture exhibit their own form of agency, which feeds back into Japan's contemporary society, influencing social identities, aesthetic projects, and even national cultural and economic policies as a form of "soft power" generated through the global reception of popular media.[1]

All of these productive miscommunications reinforced the unstable cultural identification of Japanoise, which constantly obscured its own tracks even as its networks grew to represent a new transnational scene. Boredoms were certainly a very noisy band. Their cacophonous sounds seemed to fit perfectly into the empty space under "Noise" in the categories of my existing knowledge; I knew that there were other Japanese artists who did name their work as *Noizu* (using the English language loanword for Noise), and I presumed that Boredoms must be the archetype of the genre. I was surprised, then, to learn that Boredoms themselves didn't accept the name, but instead pointed to a number of other groups, such as Hijokaidan and Merzbow, which they identified as true Noise. I would eventually follow this trail back to Japan and into years of multi-sited ethnographic research, discovering a trans-Pacific world of "harsh" Noise that represented a fragmented hardcore listenership at the edges of a deeply marginalized media circulation (Novak 2013).[2]

Japanoise, then, did not emerge fully formed as a local "scene" with a specific narrative of stylistic origins and cultural styles and identities. Rather, the very notion of the genre was constructed outside of Japan; it then looped back to Japanese performers like Boredoms, who were typically more oriented towards overseas reception than local audiences. Rather than being an identifiable form or style of Japanese popular culture, Japanoise is part of a process of "cultural feedback" that generates its social and aesthetic force through a transnational exchange of media, which redefines Japanese culture in the context of its noisy global circulation.

Big in America

Boredoms quickly came to represent the sound of the Japanese underground in the 1990s, as "alternative music" became the catchphrase of a rapidly consolidating global music industry. The group was signed to Reprise, a U.S. division of Warner Brothers, for the release of *Pop Tatari*, and their older Japanese releases were reissued overseas on Warner Japan (WEA). Boredoms opened for Nirvana at the height of their major label exposure, playing the influential 1994 Lollapalooza tour for huge crowds of young concertgoers across the United States. Eye collaborated with Sonic Youth, Ween, and NYC "downtown" composer John Zorn, while Yoshimi P-we joined members of Pussy Galore and Pavement to form Free Kitten. Meanwhile, other Japanese bands such as Ruins, Melt Banana, and Zeni Geva began to tour North America, inspiring even more attention to the idea of an emerging new musical style from Japan.

The concept of Japanoise might never have taken hold without the North American media flow that Boredoms achieved in the 1990s, via the retail boom in "alternative music" that made independent CDs available in national distribution networks. A sprawl of Boredoms side projects (e.g., Puzzle Punks, Grind Orchestra, Hanadensha, OOIOO, AOA, UFO or Die) popped up in record stores and radio stations, sometimes appearing to create a cross section of the Japanese underground in and of themselves.[3] Meanwhile, audiences struggled to keep up with Eye's rapid-fire name changes from Yamatsuka to Yamantaka to Yamataka to eYe and then EYƎ and the group itself from Boredoms to Vꝏredoms to Boadrum. All of this inspired further attention to the elusive character of Japanoise, which was so richly productive of brilliantly confusing images and sounds.

Before Boredoms appeared as if out of nowhere in the early 1990s, recordings by Merzbow, Hijokaidan, Incapacitants, C.C.C.C, Solmania, Masonna, Aube, MSBR, and The Geriogerigegege had already filtered into North American reception, beginning with mail exchange of cassettes and then with independent labels through mail order catalogues. College radio stations and independent record stores circulated releases from Osaka's Alchemy, Public Bath, and Japan Overseas, while fanzines like Mason Jones' *Ongaku Otaku* (Music Nerd, 1995–1998) or Matt Kaufman's *Exile Osaka* (1993–1998) informed fans of archetypal examples of Noise and helped them assemble a rudimentary map of its generic boundaries in Japan. North American tours, especially by Merzbow and Masonna in the mid-1990s, allowed select fans to experience Japanese Noise live and related legendary stories for those who had missed their chance. Within this sub-subculture of purified style, Boredoms were simultaneously the best known and least representative example of the emerging genre of "Japanoise," which itself became the central cultural archetype of a larger transnational network of "Noise."

In the 1980s, "Noise" was already widely in use as a general term in punk and hardcore music circles, but new confusions between the overlapping terms of "Noise," "Noise Music," and "noisy music" helped create a space for imagining Japanese participation in a global underground network. "Noise" had been a loose but inclusive metageneric term for "experimental," "industrial," "hardcore," or otherwise non-musical sounds that were too noisy to be absorbed into a commercial mainstream or to be recognized as a distinct genre. It was a name for everything on the margins of musical product: recordings with no consumer market, sounds that could never be confused with any kind of normal music, performances that pushed the boundaries of entertainment or art. But the sudden appearance of Japanoise seemed to represent a more particular and discrete form of Noise from even further beyond the fringe. Japanese recordings were differentiated from local "Noise Music" by the term "Japanese Noise Music" and finally the neologism "Japanoise." In the independent media networks of the 1990s, Noise was now something that "came from Japan." The invention of the term "Japanoise" also helped support the belief that the distant "Japanese Noise scene" was bigger, more popular, and more definitive of this extreme style.

Ironically, the deep strangeness that made Boredoms so appealing to overseas listeners also made it practically impossible for their music to be circulated within Japan. For one, the group was located in Osaka, outside of the hyper-centralized Japanese media industry in Tokyo. Without any significant independent media network to circulate their recordings to retail locations, distribution was limited to mail order and direct face-to-face sales. Without a major label contract and professional management, it was practically impossible for an artist or group to get recordings into stores or to be covered by televisual or print media. Another factor was the radically confrontational performance style adopted by some underground groups. Eye's duo Hanatarashi ("Snotnose," also spelled Hanatarash) only managed to play a handful of shows in the mid-1980s before they were banned from most clubs (Figure 16.1). During one performance, Eye cut his leg open with a chainsaw and terrorized the audience with flying chunks of metal. In the most infamous episode, Eye destroyed a Tokyo club by driving an abandoned backhoe though the space, smashing the stage, running into walls, and chasing the crowd out of the room.

Stories of these shows quickly became canonical in illustrating the extreme character of Japanoise for those in the know, and photos were circulated in underground magazines in Japan and in the United States for years (and decades later on the Internet). But at the time, the destructive nature of these events effectively eliminated all future performance opportunities for these bands in Japan—at least for a few years, until American bands came to Japan and invited Hanatarashi and Boredoms to open for their concerts. Yet while these conditions made it difficult to establish a local fan base, they also motivated Japanese groups to establish a foreign audience by sending recordings overseas, essentially forcing them further underground until they broke into America as a new wave of Japanoise.

Japanoise appeared to be a unique local style of music from a particular place and time, with representative musicians, sounds, and a body of recordings that could be collected under the name. But the genre could really only have been formed in this disconnected history of circulation between Japan and the United States, in the distant exchanges of a pre-Internet mediascape at the end of the twentieth century. The features of this particular distribution of global popular media in the 1990s—at a moment in which Japanese recordings were newly available to U.S. audiences, while information about the musicians and their social context was much less accessible—resulted in a trans-Pacific network of musicians and listeners who were joined by aesthetic sensibilities but fragmented by lack of knowledge and intercultural dialogue.

Figure 16.1 Hanatarashi's first performance, Shibuya La Mama, Tokyo, March 20, 1985.
Source: Courtesy of Gin Satoh.

Through the flow of extreme recordings from different Japanese groups (many of which, as I've mentioned, were primarily offshoots of Boredoms), it was easy for North American fans to imagine Boredoms as springing forth from a cohesive, politically transgressive, and locally resistant community in Osaka—essentially, the Japanese version of a familiar punk or hardcore DIY scene in the United States. But it was more accurate that groups like Boredoms had few opportunities to perform live and did not necessarily know the other representatives of Japanoise with whom they were associated. Instead, they poured their sounds into cassettes and CDs like messages in bottles and sent them across the Pacific, where they were received as unintelligible, but fascinating, objects of a distant Japanese scene.

The Alchemy of Cultural Feedback

This is not to say that a local underground history of Noise cannot be found in Kansai; on the contrary, Kyoto and Osaka both housed a large number of influential performers through the 1980s and 1990s. The infamous group Hijokaidan, for example, formed around 1978 in a small hangout space called Drugstore near Doshisha University in Kyoto. Students and experimental music fans would gather to listen to rare imported records of strange electronic, psychedelic, and punk music—European and American recordings of underground rock, punk, and free jazz by groups like Can, the Los Angeles

Free Music Society, Albert Ayler, The Velvet Underground, Butthole Surfers, and so forth—all of which they called "Noise" (*Noizu*) to mark its perverse character and distance from "normal" music. Their choice of the English language loanword *Noizu* for the emerging style reflected their assignation of its origins to an international context, rather than a particular local Japanese setting.

Eventually, Hiroshige Jojo and some other Drugstore fans decided to make Noise for themselves as Hijokaidan, beginning with improvised sounds and collaborations with poets and dancers at Drugstore, and moving on to radically confrontational performances that featured acts like urinating on stage and throwing fish guts and *natto* (fermented soybeans) at the audience; like Hanatarashi, they were quickly banned from most local clubs. In order to continue producing Noise, guitarist Hiroshige Jojo started an independent label called Alchemy Records in 1983. "I decided to release all of the strange music from Kansai," Hiroshige said, "and distribute it everywhere. I was into the idea of alchemy [*renkinjutsu*]: that you could make money from junk. Our sound is junk, but we can record it, release CDs, and make money" (quoted in Novak 2013: 112).

Even if the label barely broke even over the next three decades, Alchemy put out hundreds of Noise recordings that defined Japanoise for overseas listeners, including the first two Hanatarashi LPs and other projects by Boredoms members. While a handful of Alchemy issues were passed around the Kansai scene, the majority sold via mail order to North American and European listeners, who discovered the label through experimental music magazines and independent distribution companies like Public Bath and Japan Overseas. While Alchemy Records were sold as expensive and rare imports in the United States, this only increased their appeal as "hard-to-get" underground music, and solidified the reputation of the distant Japanoise scene.

In important ways, then, the cultural object of Japanoise did not just "come from" Japan, but was created and perpetuated in the feedback of transnational circulation. And even as these channels enabled the increasing flow of Noise to other places in the world, they amplified the miscommunications, distortions, and delays that have become structural conditions in the global representation of Japanese popular culture. If objects of foreign culture must be translated in order to become meaningful elsewhere, Japanoise was instead subjected to a process of "untranslation" that generated new meanings outside of any original context. In these formative channels of circulation, the imagined differences of Japanese culture were projected onto Japanoise, sustained in North American receptions, and expanded in secondary Japanese identifications with this new cultural object.

Despite the fact that Japan possesses a robust popular culture industry and boasts one of the most powerful export economies in the world, its media exchange with the United States has been surprisingly unbalanced. Most popular music in Japan sounds very much like Western pop music and some artists (e.g., Matsuda Seiko, Utada Hikaru) have even gone as far as to record albums entirely in English to court overseas fans. But while American popular culture is deeply integrated into everyday knowledge in Japan, the sounds of "J-pop" have not done the same in the United States; Americans can rarely identify more than a handful of Japanese musicians of any genre. As scholars such as Taylor Atkins (2001), Ian Condry (2006), Jennifer Matsue (2009), and Marvin Sterling (2010) have described, Japan boasts jazz, hip-hop, hardcore punk, and dancehall reggae scenes that are among the largest in the world, but Japanese artists in these genres have rarely been received as authentic producers, and are sometimes disregarded outright. Beyond considering Japanese popular music as inauthentic and unoriginal, Americans sometimes disparage Japanese audiences as clueless and out-of-touch for their unorthodox preferences. When an American musician or band becomes "big in Japan"—for example, surf group The Ventures has remained enduringly popular for many decades—this Japanese reception often implies that their value has diminished at home; their popularity, it seems, must result from some sort of distortion, springing from the lopsided feedback of an unreciprocated media circulation.

In connecting with an American audience as a new and unique creative object of Japanese popular culture, Boredoms represented an anomaly in the historical course of transnational flows between modern Japan and the U.S. media market. This is not to say that Boredoms makes any particular sense as a "crossover" success from one culture to another; far from it, the group was never fully rooted in Japan in the first place. Rather, their overseas reception was generated in part by the misalignments of their transnational distribution, making them appear central to a Japanese cultural zeitgeist when their development was actually much slower and more fragmented. Foreign audiences historicized the group through their recordings, which appeared out of order and out of context, as U.S. reissues typically trailed behind Japanese releases, often by years. For example, Boredoms' earlier albums *Anal by Anal* and *The Stooges Craze in Osorezan* (*Osorezan no Stooges kyo*) were released in 1986 and 1988 in Japan on Trans and Selfish Records, but not issued in the United States until 1994 on Reprise, and then with a redesigned cover and under the new major label title *Onanie Bomb Meets the Sex Pistols*, which effectively reordered the group's catalogue for overseas listeners. For the U.S. release of *Soul Discharge*, some tracks were removed and replaced with Eye's unreleased solo recordings; later albums were released in special Japan-only editions, which became rare collectors' items in the overseas market. But despite—or even, perhaps, due to—these gaps and disjunctures, Boredoms *did* eventually become generative of a long-term transnational audience, as each side reached out to the other to discover "the real Noise scene."

Japanese media receptions are often characterized by the phenomenon of *"gyaku-yunyu,"* or "reverse importation," through which Japanese artists become validated at home after gaining status on a foreign stage (exemplified by, for example, nightly broadcast news segments dedicated to Japanese baseball players in the American Major League). For example, Boredoms were almost completely unknown in Japan until they were asked to open for American indie stars like Sonic Youth and Caroliner Rainbow on their Japan tours in the early 1990s. As Japanese audiences heard the American groups praise the band and had a chance to see them appear live in large venues, Boredoms finally became local heroes. Over the next few years, a mini-media flurry buzzed around the group as emblems of the growing "alternative music" scene in Japan, with Eye and Yoshimi appearing in fashion magazines and briefly as television hosts, and watched hordes of college students at Boredoms shows storm the merchandise booth to clean out the entire stock of t-shirts in minutes. Eye became a popular club DJ, spinning cut-up samples and beats as DJ光光光 (*Pika Pika Pika*, meaning "flash" or "bling"); guitarist Yamamoto Seiichi toured with Rashinban and Omoide Hatoba and opened the now-iconic hardcore and punk club Bears in downtown Osaka; Yoshimi started the all-female group OOIOO, and bassist Hila created psychedelic sounds as Hanadensha (Flower Train), both of which had releases on WEA Japan; the band scored Miike Takashi's controversial 2001 film *Ichi the Killer* (*Koroshiya 1*); and American experimental rock stars The Flaming Lips narrated an imaginary tale of Yoshimi saving the world on their breakthrough album *Yoshimi Battles the Pink Robots* (Flaming Lips, 2002). All of these projects reinforced Boredoms as the symbolic center of the Japanese underground and the heart of Japanoise, even as their circulation came to represent a scene unto itself.

Spiraling In and Out of Circulation

Naturally—or at least in the tidal nature of media cycles—this sudden flow of recognition ebbed. By the early 2000s, Boredoms had lost their major label connections, changed their names and their lineup many times, broke up, reformed, and shifted back into indie publishing. But over the years, the group firmly established a hardcore international fan base that continued to discover their recordings, tell their stories, and book them at mega-festivals (such as the Fuji Rock Festival and All Tomorrow's Parties) well into the 2000s and 2010s. As one of the most enduring underground acts in the world and a central node in a global network of musicians and listeners, Boredoms can still suddenly draw together new circulations in their rare overseas appearances.

In 2007, Boredoms traveled to Brooklyn, New York, to perform *77 Boadrum* (Figure 16.2), a free outdoor concert in Empire-Fulton Ferry State Park, beginning precisely at 7:07 PM on July 7, 2007, and ending 77 minutes later. Spread across the lawn at the bank of the East River beneath the Manhattan Bridge were 77 drum sets, arranged in a large spiral pattern; at the center was a raised stage where Yoshimi and newer Boredoms members Tatekawa Yojiro and Muneomi Senju sat behind drums facing Eye, who stood before a 7-necked guitar-like structure called "The Sevener." Within the enormous spiral of drum sets spinning out from the stage were the other 74 performers, drawn from underground bands across North America, including members of Gang Gang Dance, Lightning Bolt, Dymaxion, Oneida, No Neck Blues

Figure 16.2 77 Boadrum.
Source: Courtesy of Jason Nocito.

Band, and many others. Hundreds of listeners crowded around the spiral, while many more watched above from atop the Brooklyn Bridge. This was less a concert than a cosmic event, a gathering of the tribes, a conference of drummers playing out the noise of a transnational network to become, as Eye wrote in the program notes (2007), "a giant instrument, one living creature. The *77 Boadrum* will coil like a snake and transform to become a great dragon!"

The collective roar of *77 Boadrum* was almost nothing like the stylistic free-for-all of *Soul Discharge*. It reflected the group's slow shift over two decades, transforming their early abrasive, jagged hardcore attacks into a psychedelic sonic ritual. Standing at the center, Eye conducted the sounds around the spiral, the noise traveling around the circuit of drummers and eventually building into a visceral, primal beat. In the words of Unwound's Sara Lund (Drummer #67):

[T]he cymbal washes gradually rolled out from the center, the WHUSH-HHHHH getting louder and louder. Then, the single hit on the toms started as the cymbal wash reached the tail of the spiral. As the tom hits made their way through the drummers, the WHUSHHHH got quieter as the whoomp WHOOMP WHOOMP of the toms grew louder and louder until finally all 77 of us were hitting our toms in unison. The ground shook and tears sprang to my eyes as I was completely overcome with emotion. My breath was caught in my throat and the corners of my mouth were grabbing at my ears.

(Lund 2007)

Part of what made this moment so powerful was its materialization—if only for a particular group of people in a singular point in space and time—of a long-dreamed and hard-won community, built and maintained through the confusions of distance and separation. That, and the recognition that this scene was only temporary, and necessarily so: this world of sound could only continue to exist by feeding back into circulation, dissipating into stories, recordings, and images.

77 Boadrum became a legendary event almost overnight, as photos and YouTube clips of the performance circulated to fans around the world; eventually two different films, (both directed by Kawaguchi Jun) were released on DVD, on Thrill Jockey in the United States (2010) and Commons in Japan (2008). Following *77 Boadrum*, Boredoms did four more numerological performances on 08/08/08, 09/09/09, 10/10/10, and 11/11/11, each in a different location. *88 Boadrum* was held at the La Brea Tar Pits at 8:08 in Los Angeles, while a satellite performance featuring 88 different drummers took place at 8:08 in Brooklyn; Boadrums 9 and 10 stripped down to a core group of 9 and 10 drummers in Manhattan and Melbourne, respectively, and *111 Boadrum* gathered another huge spiral of 111 drummers in Byron Bay, Australia.

Over three decades, Boredoms emerged, submerged, and re-emerged, each time taking a different shape and reflecting a different angle in the obscure narratives of Japanoise. Whether or not they were ever really representative of Japanoise—or whether there ever really could (or should) be a definitive archetype of its elusive form—is another question. In its essence, Japanoise is less a genre of music than a process of global imagination that conjoins different actors separated by space, time, language, and culture. But this feedback also questioned the meaning of cultural origins, undermining the nature of things that might be called "Japanese popular culture," and what it might mean for a globally circulating form to "come from" a particular cultural location. Even as Japanoise loosened the links between musical genres and local scenes, its networks began to create a new transcultural project of radical sonic aesthetics. If "Noise" can become "Music," what do we mean by "Culture," or for that matter, "Japan?"

Japanoise moves in this way, as a force of circulation, materializing through distortions and delays over time. It spiraled into being through alternating cycles of realization and confusion, appearing and then disappearing again. It was something that could easily be named, and yet remained hard to define; that never ceased to move and change; that continued to transform, even to the point of losing its own form. The elusive movements of Boredoms across the transnational mediascape of the 1990s left a breadcrumb trail into an underground imaginary. Japanoise disappears and reemerges in different forms in different places; it is perpetuated across online networks and momentarily flashes into being in spectacular once-in-a-lifetime events. The listener backs into its presence, stumbling across thresholds of recognition that suddenly flip into consciousness, like a microphone slowly approaches a speaker, and a feedback loop springs into being. It was the emergence of this feedback—and the possibility of an incomprehensible, incommensurable world of sound—that became so compelling in the global, and ongoing, search for Japanoise.

Notes

1 One exemplary model is the notion of "gross national cool" proposed by American reporter Douglas McGray (2002) and subsequently adopted by Japanese governmental and trade organizations as a way to describe the instrumentalization of Japan's popular media to influence global perceptions of its culture industry.

2 For more information, see *Japanoise: Music at the Edge of Circulation* book website at www.japanoise.com.

3 The short list of Boredoms-related side projects includes Audio Sports, Dendoba, Destroy 2, Concrete Octopus, Free Kitten, Noise Ramones, and many others. A complete discography would take up several pages, as Dave Watson has demonstrated on his exhaustive Boredoms website *Sore Diamonds*. Available at http://eyevocal.ottawa-anime.org/boredoms/boreside.htm.

17 Korean Pop Music in Japan

Understanding the Complex
Relationship Between Japan and Korea
in the Popular Culture Realm[1]

Eun-Young Jung

Introduction

Despite intensified cultural flows between Japan and Korea since the late 1990s, the two countries' national relationship has continued to be strained and problematic. Along with dramatic increases in cultural consumption and tourism between the two, political disputes and cultural competition in the transnational media marketplace have revived antagonism. To understand political-cultural relationships between Japan and Korea in the realm of pop music, it is necessary to examine both Japanese responses to the Korean pop music presence in Japan and Korean responses to Japanese pop music in Korea,[2] which are neither parallel nor even. However, given limited space, this chapter narrows its focus to the rise of K-pop in Japan and Japan's ambivalent responses to K-pop, reaffirming the longstanding "close-but-distant" relationship between the two countries.

What is K-pop? The term is as problematic to define as its origin and usages are ambiguous. Around the mid-2000s, as some of the Korean idol bands began to gain popularity outside Korea, the term K-pop emerged among international fans and in various English websites and blogs. However, it was rarely recognized by Koreans in Korea until recently, when Korean media began to use the term (e.g., since 2011 in SBS's *Survival Audition K-pop Star*). Instead, most Koreans use the term "*kayo*" (or *gayo*) to refer to Korean pop music as a whole. Among international fans and media circles, some use K-pop to refer not only to all kinds of Korean pop music genres but also to other kinds of Korean popular culture products, such as television dramas and fashion styles. Also, while it is easy to suppose the term K-pop to be comparable in scope to J-pop, their connotations and references are different and contingent (Stevens 2009; Mōri 2009). Furthermore, some Korean pop musicians have become singers of J-pop or crossover performers of both K-pop and J-pop music, often produced by or with American or European writers and producers. Internationally, the term K-pop has centered on idol bands and their music ("idol pop") from Korea. Based on the typical Japanese idol/*aidoru* pop style and its business practices, highly formulaic Korean idol pop is exclusively manufactured by all-in-one idol-making companies, such as S.M. Entertainment, YG Entertainment, and JYP Entertainment, with transnational exports in mind. For these reasons and following the Japanese media practice, in reference to Korean popular music in Japan, I prefer to use the term K-pop only for the cases in Japan after 2011, when the Japanese media began to label Korean idol bands' success in Japan as the "K-pop Boom," with Korean bands performing a combination of songs originally released as K-pop (usually mixing Korean and English, and no Japanese) but with lyrics translated into Japanese, along with original J-pop songs.

This chapter is divided into four sections, ordered chronologically. The first covers the 1980s and 1990s, when a few Korean singers gained popularity in the Japanese *enka* market.[3] The second introduces four trends of the early and mid-2000s, the first-round of the Korean Wave (*Hallyu*, the spread of Korean popular culture overseas since the late 1990s) in Japan. The third covers the late 2000s, as TVXQ/Tohoshinki became the most successful K-pop band in Japan. The fourth discusses the second-round of the Korean Wave, also known as the "K-pop boom" in Japan, begun in 2011. With this approach, we can learn the unique patterns of Japanese consumption of and reactionary responses to the presence of Korea in Japan that are shaped by Korea and Japan's political, economic, and cultural relationships.

Pre-Korean Wave, 1980s and 1990s

Prior to the initial penetration by Korean pop music in Japan in the late 1990s, a few Korean pop singers did gain popularity in Japan. One of the most famous singers in Korean pop music history, Cho Yong-pil, was popular in Japan in the 1980s and 1990s, giving numerous concerts and receiving multiple awards. The Japanese version of his 1980 hit *trot*[4] song "Come Back to the Pusan Harbor" (Korean: Dorawayo Busanhang-e; Japanese: Pusan kō e kaere) was especially popular. Appealing primarily to the Japanese *enka* market due to *trot*'s similarities to *enka*'s vocal style, he was invited multiple times to perform his Korean hit songs in Japanese at NHK *Kōhaku uta gassen* (the most prestigious annual music show in Japan, airing every New Year's Eve). Two female *trot* singers in the 1980s—Kye Eun-Sook and Kim Yeon-Ja—also became successful in Japan as *enka* singers after relocating there in the late 1980s. Known for the emotionality of their singing (Yano 2004b), both were invited to *Kōhaku* multiple times.

The legendary male hip-hop trio Seo Taiji and Boys also had an active following in Japan without major promotion and released original Korean language albums in Japan in 1994 and 1995. One of the most popular female singers in the early 1990s, Kang Suji, had a relatively long career in Japan as a *tarento* (multi-entertainer) during her residency there from 1995 to 2000. Kang released a few Japanese singles, produced photo albums, and appeared on variety shows—typical activities of Japanese pop idols and *tarento*. As noted by Aoyagi (2000) and Iwabuchi (2002), Kang's career in Japan is relevant to Japan's "popular Asianism" in the 1990s, which led many Asian pop singers to debut in Japan.

Japanese reception of Korean pop music and musicians in the 1980s and the 1990s was limited to *enka* and other genres outside the mainstream Japanese pop music scene. Given the rarity of collaboration and transaction between the two countries' music industries, the success of these Korean singers in Japan was rather anomalous.

As I have discussed elsewhere (2007), the first important instance of Japan's acceptance of Korean singers within its mainstream media and pop music industry was S.E.S.—Korea's most popular girl group in the late 1990s and early 2000s. Modeled after typical Japanese female idol groups, such as Speed (debuted in 1996), and carefully formed to be marketable internationally by its management company S.M. Entertainment (SME), the trio included Korean American and *zainichi* (Korean resident in Japan) members, along with a Korean member. S.E.S. gained moderate popularity with their J-pop songs and released J-pop singles and albums during their activities in Japan from 1998 to 2001. *Zainichi* member Shoo's native Japanese language skills facilitated the group's smooth entrance into Japanese television shows. Korean and other Asian singers are expected to have sufficient Japanese language skills, as they integrate into the Japanese media industry as J-pop singers, not as international pop singers. Since the 1970s, such accommodation for local Japanese audiences has been an integral to the localization process for pop singers from elsewhere in Asia.

Another key factor was S.E.S's adoption of idol performance familiar to Japanese fans. However, because S.E.S. was not promoted by a major Japanese multimedia company, it was unable to attain superstar status in Japan or to compete with Japanese idol groups. Music industry control in Japan rests almost entirely in the hands of a few giant multimedia companies, such as AVEX[5] and SONY, and Korean pop musicians had yet to gain the promotional attention of these companies.

The First Round of the Korean Wave in Japan

BoA—a Korean female who debuted in 2002 as a J-pop singer in Japan—heralded a new phase of Japan's engagement with Korean singers. Trained, groomed, and marketed with greater care by SME, BoA registered remarkable success in Japan during the first half of the 2000s. Under AVEX's management, she was produced and promoted as a typical J-pop singer. The timing coincided with important political and cultural developments. First was Korea's Open-Door policy—a four-stage process (1998–2004) whereby the Korean government relinquished its decades-long ban on the importation of Japanese cultural products, including popular music (Jung 2007). Second, in 2002 Korea and Japan cohosted the 2002 FIFA World Cup, which required intensive collaborative planning and spawned various goodwill cultural activities. The following year, the Korean Wave came to Japan with the spectacularly popular television drama *Winter Sonata* (*Gyeoul yeonga; Fuyu no sonata*). With all the right components aligned, including her fluent Japanese language skills, BoA became one of the leading female J-pop singers in Japan and was invited to perform at *Kōhaku* six times consecutively from 2002 through 2007, making her the most frequently invited foreign singer of J-pop in *Kōhaku* history. It is important to stress that BoA's success as a mainstream J-pop singer in Japan contrasts with Japan's reception of other Korean musicians during this period.

The Korean Wave's exploding popularity in Japan from 2003 was predominantly based on television melodramas, especially the male actors who played ideal men. Yet as the boom expanded to other kinds of Korean cultural products, including pop music, four trends emerged in Japanese engagement with Korea within the mainstream pop music industry: (1) collaboration between the two countries' major music companies; (2) Korean television actors becoming pop singers; (3) new Korean singers debuting as J-pop singers in Japan before being introduced professionally in Korea; and (4) Korea producing superstars with huge followings in Asia and beyond (Jung 2007).

The first trend was set by BoA's career path in Japan as a J-pop singer, her localization—de-Koreanization and Japanization through systematic repackaging strategies—via SME and AVEX collaboration. Following BoA's success, SME's popular boy band TVXQ/Tohoshinki, adopting Japanese male idol band expectations, smoothly entered the mainstream J-pop industry under AVEX's management in 2005, confirming the effectiveness of this collaboration.

The second trend was created in response to Japanese female fans' desire to consume all things relating to *Winter Sonata* and its leading male actors, Bae Yong-Joon and Park Yong-ha, with the following results: (1) drama theme song singer Ryu—all-but-unknown in Korea—was frequently televised in Japan and held concerts there in 2004; and (2) actor Park Yong-ha, little known in Korea then, became popular as a singer in Japan and regularly appeared on major Japanese music television programs, such as *Hey!Hey!Hey! Music Champ*, and *Utaban*. With a series of J-pop singles, albums, and concerts well received by his dedicated female fans in Japan, Park enjoyed much greater popularity in Japan than in Korea, even after his suicide in 2010.

The third trend signaled growing interest in the Korean Wave from the mainstream Japanese media and music industries as the new Korean singers—including Younha and K, who had not even debuted in Korea—were introduced through the conventional Japanese media "tie-up" strategy.[6] In contrast to the others, these singers' promotional focus was on their singing skills rather than visual (often dance-oriented) performance. The male singer K debuted in Japan as a J-pop singer after being scouted by SONY Music personnel, who heard him playing in a bar in Seoul in early 2005. K's debut songs "Over…" and "Only Human" were tied-up with popular Japanese television dramas. With the successful debut album *Beyond the Sea* (2006), and his near-perfect Japanese language skills, K had a notable career in Japan as a J-pop singer during these years.

The fourth trend in Japanese reception of Korean pop music was the focus on the two male superstars Se7en and Rain, who had already established extensive popularity throughout Asia. With their Asia-wide star status, they did not need to adopt the strategies that the other Korean singers had but simply released their hit Korean songs in Japanese.[7] The Japanese fans' embrace of these two pop stars exemplified the expansion of the Korean Wave in Japan in the mid-2000s.

During the first round of the Korean Wave, then, led by television dramas, Japan's consumption of Korea within the music industry was not so much about the music as such but about the musicians, who mostly delivered typical Japanese pop songs and were produced and promoted by Japanese companies. While their being Korean was certainly a part of the picture during the boom, most of their deliberate Japanization complicated the nature of the overall Korean Wave phenomenon in Japan in the mid-2000s by the simple but glaring fact of their suppressing their Korean-ness.

Even so, some Japanese found the very presence of Koreans within their domestic media consumption to be unacceptable, challenging previous Japan-Korea power dynamics. The infamous anti-Korean Wave manga *Hating the Korean Wave* (*Kenkanryu*, 2005) by a manga artist using the penname Yamano Sharin caught international media attention (Onishi 2005) as it became an instant bestseller in Japan. As Iwabuchi argues (2002), postcolonial Japan's superior position over the rest of Asia—"similar but superior" and "in but above Asia"—was greatly challenged by Japan's own voluntary embrace of cultural products from Korea, its "inferior and backward" neighbor and former colony. Although the Korean Wave was not an overpowering force for Japan's culture industry, as the patterns of consumptive desire unexpectedly expanded to include many things Korean and created surprising social phenomena—such as the sudden rise of Japanese women's interest in Korean men through international dating and marriage services (Onishi 2004)—the mainstream Japanese media began to criticize the main consumer groups, ridiculing middle-aged housewives' fascination with the Korean Wave as unsophisticated, unrealistic, and even embarrassing. As the first-round of the wave began to lose strength in Japan with the steep decline in Korean television drama hits in the late 2000s, the continued importation of and desire for Korean singers (e.g., TVXQ/Tohoshinki) by a still sizeable number of Japanese women did not trigger massive media coverage or further controversy since they were doing J-pop.

TVXQ/Tohoshinki in the Late 2000s

Between the end of the first-round and the beginning in 2010 of the second-round of the Korean Wave, TVXQ (Dongbangsin'gi in Korean) played an important role by establishing platforms for the future K-pop idol bands in

Japan. Known as Tohoshinki in Japan, the band became the first foreign male group to reach the number-one position on the Oricon single chart (in January 2008[8]) and released singles and albums that continuously topped the Oricon charts. In contrast to BoA and the other Korean singers active in Japan, Tohoshinki debuted in Japan after gaining popularity in Asia and subsequently remained there, focusing on their career in Japan. Tohoshinki built a strong base with mostly young female fans. What catalyzed their supremacy was their unrivaled versatility in addition to familiar musical and visual styles. All five members boast great linguistic talent, high-quality musical and dancing skills, not to mention attractive appearance coupled with fun personalities suited to variety shows.

Tohoshinki achieved huge success, rivaling Japanese groups such as Arashi (see Chapter 14). Tohoshinki's basic format is almost identical to typical idol pop practice in Japan. Yet their musical and visual styles include some elements recognized as "different" and have fed into what is known as "K-pop style." The songs were written by or in collaboration with SME's in-house producer Yoo Young-Jin, known for his eclectic mix of electro-pop, dance-pop, rap, and R&B and heavy use of Auto-Tune (e.g., "Purple Line" [2008] and "Jumon: Mirotic/Magic Spell" [2008]). Also, with their much faster tempos and variety in song structure, Tohoshinki's musical style is different from that of conventional Japanese idol pop, which tends to employ lighter, bubblegum-pop styles, and simpler song structures. Other obvious differences are Tohoshinki's more muscular body features, intentionally emphasized in powerful dance moves and revealing clothing. Yet such physical masculinity is toned down by their feminized facial features, enhanced by makeup. This feminizing is engineered so as not to overwhelm the Japanese fans, who are accustomed to Japanese male idols' "life-sized" young boy qualities (Aoyagi 2000).

The Second Round of the Korean Wave in Japan: The K-Pop Boom

The sharp rise in the popularity of K-pop in Japan in 2011, the "K-pop Boom," is no less complex than the earlier Korean Wave in 2004. Tohoshinki, returning as a duo after the breakup in 2010, began to be perceived by some as a J-pop idol band rather than a K-pop idol band, as the duo's main activities were in Japan, not Korea. The new five-girl group KARA (formed in Korea in 2007) rose to popularity in Japan as a K-pop idol band starting in 2010. Despite their mediocre status within the K-pop idol industry in Korea, their K-pop songs met with success in Japanese. Signed by Universal Sigma (Universal Music Japan), KARA topped Oricon charts, selling over one million singles between 2010 and 2011, and became the first Korean act to perform at Tokyo Dome in January 2013.

Following the standardized K-pop musical trends of the late 2000s, KARA also exhibits near-constant use of Auto-Tune, short, catchy, and highly repetitive refrains, minimalist lyrics, and synchronized dance movements specific to each song. Their dance moves, including the popular "*oshiri*-dance" (butt-dance) from "Mister" (2010), were seen as much sexier than those of typical Japanese female idol groups. Any potential offensiveness is mitigated by their cute, lively, fun, happy, and silly sides evident in their variety program appearances, triggering favorable responses by the Japanese media industry (e.g., multiple commercial endorsements) and Japanese fans. Even their imperfect command of the Japanese language seems to have worked in their favor, contributing to their public image by sounding cute and childish.

With the successful penetrations by Tohoshinki and KARA into the Japanese idol pop market, other leading male and female K-pop idol bands, such as BigBang, 2PM, SHINee, After School, 2NE1, and Girls' Generation, all soon released singles and albums in Japan. These consisted mostly of Japanese versions of their K-pop songs. They held concerts, showcases, and fan meetings, and were invited to various television programs. Among them, SME's nine-girl group Girls' Generation (Sonyeosidae in Korean, Shōjo Jidai in Japanese) became SME's third act to achieve major success in Japan.

Some scholars argue that Girls' Generation's success in Japan was achieved by "rejecting the localization processes," as most of the members do not speak Japanese (Jung and Hirata 2012). However, the band's success is still due, at least in part, to their following the basics of the standardized localization process. Several members are fluent enough to communicate in Japanese without a translator. More importantly, Girls' Generation released a series of original J-pop songs (e.g., "Mr. Taxi" [2011] and "Paparazzi" [2012]), specifically for Japanese fans, in addition to releasing their K-pop hits in Japanese. While their foray into variety programs has been less frequent than Tohoshinki's and KARA's, they regularly appear on major music programs and television commercials.

The commonly perceived difference is that their visual images are considered to be sexier and more mature than the typical Japanese female idols. However, female sexuality is certainly one component in conventional Japanese female idol performance. The most popular Japanese female idol band AKB48's 2010 video release of their song "Heavy Rotation" contains racy adult images (see Chapter 15). Also, while their costumes may look girlish and their dance movements not particularly suggestive, song lyrics tend to be blunt (e.g., their 2007 song "My School Uniform is Getting in the Way" [Seifuku ga jama o suru] and its remake of the Onyanko Club's (Pussycat Club, 1985–1987) 1985 song "Don't Make Me Take Off My Sailor Uniform" [Sērāfuku o nugasanai de]). Furthermore, Girls' Generation has consistently played the familiar cutesy, girly, and all-pink young girls' images in their songs and music videos, including "Flower Power" (original Japanese single, 2012). Famous for their beautiful legs, Girls' Generation's popularity is centered on their extremely manicured, feminine, stylish beauty that has attracted many fashion-conscious young Japanese female fans. Meticulously manufactured by SME's so-called "system of cultural technology" (Seabrook 2012), Girls' Generation is readily available to accommodate local aesthetics and tastes.

Like Tohoshinki and KARA, Girls' Generation's perceived identity in Japan is complex, as their songs, styles, and images often crossover between J-pop idol specifics and K-pop idol specifics. In other words, Japan's K-pop boom is closely related to its domestic idol industry and readily available idol fans. K-pop idol music is not perceived as a completely new and *different* genre of pop music but is consumed within the larger frame of J-pop idol performance practices.

K-pop idols in their physical appearance and demeanor are just-familiar-enough and just-foreign-enough to attract Japanese fans.

The expanding K-pop boom in Japan and friendly cultural collaborations and consumption took a dramatic turn in 2012 as the Japanese public's anti-Korea/Korean/Korean Wave sentiments began to grow again, aggravated by political disputes, including the resurgence of the Dokdo/Takeshima islets sovereignty issue following former Korean president Lee Myung-Bak's visit to the islets in August 2012. Japan's reactionary responses to have gone beyond nationalistic cultural conservatism or economic protectionism to reference broader national conflicts. As the multimedia presence of Korean pop culture became pervasive and undeniable, Japan's resistance to and rejection of this K-pop boom became increasingly and alarmingly evident. Protests were staged in public places against all things Korean, fed by Japan's national anxiety over questions of its superiority within Asia. More than the first-round Korean Wave, the K-pop boom was difficult to ignore as the popular K-pop idols took typical idol-*tarento* roles in multimedia. Furthermore, many K-pop idol groups' broader international popularity was abundantly evident on the Internet, thanks to the K-pop industry's successful adaptations and clever marketing strategies through new social media spaces such as YouTube, which gave unprecedented strength to K-pop's global exposure.

The revived anti-Korean Wave movements were sparked by male actor Takaoka Sousuke's xenophobic anti-Korean Wave tweets that initiated a series of protests against Fuji Television from 2011. Although some protesters claimed that the protests were not against Korea or Koreans but against the network and Japanese media, they singled out the Korean Wave and shouted loudly, "Get out of Japan," indicating quite clearly their animosity toward Korea and towards Korean immigrants (*zainichi*). Their particular claim concerning Fuji Television being unfairly pro-Korean/Korean Wave may well have been due at least in part to their perception of Fuji Television being partially owned by *zainichi*. Other controversial tweets were posted by popular entertainer Tamura Atsushi who asked *Kōhaku* to invite Japanese singers only. Despite these sentiments, the three most popular K-pop idol bands—Tohoshinki, KARA, and Girls' Generation—were invited to *Kōhaku* in 2011. However, as the wider Japanese public's anti-Korea fervor rose, no K-pop act was invited to *Kōhaku* in 2012. This anti-Korean stance predominated despite the continued record-breaking sales figures of these leading K-pop idol bands (Sophie 2012).

The Korean Wave became the site of Japan's conflicting desires, stimulating both consumption of and rejection of Korea's pop cultural products. It also exacerbated Japan's national anxiety as its status as a world superpower has been challenged by China's overpowering economic and political rise and Korea's advance as a transnational cultural powerhouse. In a *Korea Times* newspaper interview, a Japanese public servant said:

> In times of sagging economy, the Japanese have solaced themselves with the belief that Japan is still superior to any other Asian countries in terms of culture content and related business. But the steep rise of K-pop and Korean dramas in Japan shattered that belief. I think the broken self-confidence played a crucial role in prompting anti-Korean Wave sentiment.
>
> (Park 2014)

The ultranationalist group Zaitokukai (full name, Zainichi Tokken o Yurusanai Shimin no Kai, meaning Citizens Group That Will Not Forgive Privileges for Koreans in Japan) organized a series of anti-Korea public protests in Shin-Okubo, Tokyo's popular Korea town. Since 2011, members of Zaitokukai have waved the war flags of the imperial Japanese army in their street protests, shouted slogans like "Kill Koreans" and "Kill Zainichi," and carried signs saying "Cockroaches," "Criminals and Rapists," "Racist," "Like Hyenas Stealing from Us," "Go Back to Korea," and "Plastic Surgery Addicted K-pop Singers" (Osaki 2013). Zaitokukai's racist attack on *zainichi* reveals their desire to maintain the postcolonial power relationship—superior Japan, inferior Korea—by continuously marginalizing *zainichi*. By constantly confronting *zainichi* and Japanese consumers who come to Shin-Okubo for Korean merchandise, Zaitokukai have tried to prevent *zainichi* from gaining economic and cultural power within Japan.

From the standpoint of the Japanese music industry, the popularity of K-pop internationally has been bittersweet. Japanese media and music companies have certainly profited from the K-pop boom through their exclusive partnership deals. However, their failure to make J-pop singers internationally popular from the 1990s, especially in the United States, may have hurt their national pride. There is no need for Japan's music industry to assume a protectionist stance, considering its self-sufficiency and its sheer size as the world's second largest music industry. However, seeing Korea's success despite its small size and its heavy dependency on foreign markets (especially Japanese) has been hard to comprehend for a substantial number of Japanese. That the music itself and the very notion of "idol" are so clearly indebted to Japanese popular culture only exacerbates the situation.

As Japan's anti-Korea/Korean Wave protests have grown in size and frequency, Shin-Okubo's businesses have suffered sharp drops in sales. Since 2013, the presence of K-pop in Japan has diminished dramatically, though not entirely because of Japanese hostility. Some of the established idol bands have become inactive for various reasons. (For example, after losing two members between 2013 and 2014, KARA's return with a new member in 2014 was not well received.) Yet some K-pop idols and stars are still well received by their loyal fans in Japan and continue their promotion in Japan (e.g., Tohoshinki, BigBang, JYJ, New: U-KISS, F.T. Island, Boyfriend, EXO, Crayon Pop, and A-Pink). Even though Japan is still an important marketplace, K-pop's growing exposure beyond Asian markets via social media marketing has led the K-pop industry to expand its main target to a global marketplace rather than a single region.

Concluding Remarks

The past decade has been eventful for both Japan and Korea in terms of their already-strained relations. The flow of cultural products has created conflicting dynamics, evident in recent patterns of consumption and rejection. The focus of this chapter has been on Japan's consumption and rejection of Korean pop music. By tracing both sides of Japan's two-pronged responses to the Korean Wave and the subsequent K-pop boom, we have seen how Japan's contested national pride is played out in the realm of pop music.

The recent international spotlight on Korea through the Korean Wave, and particularly the K-pop boom, has rekindled the fire of Japan's anti-Korea sentiments to an astonishing level. The surprising allure of Korean popular culture in Japan has resulted in ultranationalist Japanese groups such as Zaitokukai displaying hatred against Korea in their public protests. The growth of K-pop's presence globally and the Japanese fandom that is playing a major part in this rise have simultaneously taken away the Japanese industry's international supremacy and diminished their local market share. The K-pop boom in Japan, just like any kind of cultural boom, has begun to decline, which seems only natural, although many new and old K-pop acts continue their Japan promotion as part of their typical overseas market activities.

Due to the intensified resistance to K-pop in certain circles in Japan since 2012, the current status of Japan-Korea relations seems to be even more strained than during the long period between the end of Japanese colonization and the beginning of the Korean Wave in Japan in early 2004. As the dynamics of their diplomatic ties can shift at any time, we can only expect that their cultural flows can also make dramatic turns in the future, adding still newer layers of complexity to the ongoing saga of Japanese-Korean relations. Popular culture and diplomatic relations often are unpredictable. Although neither is resultant or subordinate to the other, they can interact. How the popular culture and diplomatic terrain will look in a decade or even a few years from now is difficult to predict, but the Korean Wave phenomenon has already inscribed itself into twenty-first-century Japanese history—a development that will continue to invite interpretation and inspire debate at many levels in the years to come.

Notes

1 A version of this chapter was published *K-Pop: The International Rise of the Korean Music Industry*, edited by JungBong Choi and Roald Maliangkay, 116–132 (Routledge 2014). Thanks to the editors for allowing the republication.
2 While casual observers may apply the terms K-pop and J-pop to the broad array of popular music practices in Korea and Japan, respectively, each of these two terms has several narrower meanings to those who follow popular culture closely as consumers, performers, or scholars. The term J-pop emerged in the 1990s and K-pop in the 2000s, neither of them referring to earlier pop music of their respective countries and both applied to mainstream, youth-oriented popular music.
3 *Enka* is a genre of Japanese popular music incorporating Western popular music instruments and harmony along with Japanese scales and vocal styles since the 1920s. The repertory consists mostly of sentimental ballads, predominantly consumed by older generations.
4 *Trot* (or *ppongtchak*) is considered to be derived from Japanese *enka* as it shares many stylistic similarities (Lee Pak 2006).
5 S.E.S. joined AVEX when its Korean management company SME realized its importance, but soon after, the trio disbanded and released only one compilation album under AVEX.
6 "Tie-up" (or "tied-in") is a typical marketing strategy of the Japanese pop music industry from the early 1990s that involves the packaging ("tying-up") of a newly released song with a new television drama, movie, commercial, or videogame in order to maximize promotion. Rarely available to new or unknown singers, the "tie-up" strategy indicates a strict structure of Japanese pop music and media industry practice (Asai 2008: 477–478).
7 Se7en's adequate Japanese language skills were welcomed by the Japanese media although they were not critical to his initial entrance to the Japanese market.
8 Japan's Oricon provides the most important weekly music charts. Tohoshinki's sixteenth Japanese single "Purple Line" became their first number-one song.

PART VI
Popular Cinema

18 The Prehistory of Soft Power

Godzilla, Cheese, and the American Consumption of Japan

William M. Tsutsui

The very possibility of Japan wielding "soft power" from the global circulation of media exports like films and animation is a relatively recent phenomenon, a development of the past quarter century, at most. Yet Japanese popular culture products have been widely available in the United States (and through much of the rest of the world as well) since the mid-1950s. Speaking of Japanese soft power in the United States in the early postwar decades is nearly inconceivable, however, as what Douglas McGray (2002: 46) so cleverly tags "the whiff of Japanese cool," most emphatically did not swirl around Japan's earliest pop exports, monster movies (*kaijū eiga*), *Astro Boy*, *Ultraman*, *Speed Racer*, and the like. Understanding this "prehistory" of Japan's soft-power potential will not only help us makes sense of the later rise of Asia's "mighty engine of national cool" (McGray 2002: 52) but will also help us appreciate the complexity of the global embrace of Japanese popular culture and the limitations of new-found international appeal in altering longstanding patterns of consuming (and constructing) "Japan."

This chapter focuses on the reception of Japanese popular cinema, especially the Godzilla film series, in the United States after World War II. In the postwar advance of Japanese popular culture into international markets and the global consciousness, Godzilla was a pioneer. Although highbrow films (like *Rashōmon*) and exotic symbols (the geisha, the samurai) preceded Godzilla abroad, the cinematic monster introduced by Tōhō Studios in 1954 was the first creation of Japan's burgeoning mass entertainment industry to gain large international audiences. *Gojira*, the somber story of an irradiated saurian mutant that ravages Tokyo, was a box office hit in Japan and, as the heavily edited *Godzilla, King of the Monsters*, a version made palatable both linguistically and politically for the American market, filled movie theaters around the world in the mid-1950s. A franchise soon followed and, over the next five decades, twenty-eight Godzilla movies were produced by Tōhō (and one, in 1998, by TriStar in Hollywood and another, in 2014, by Legendary Pictures), making the series the oldest and longest running in world cinema. Longtime staples of movie palaces, drive-in theaters, and late night television, the Godzilla films—which evolved over time from sober adult fare to playful children's entertainment to high-tech action thrillers—developed an international cult following and their giant, radioactive star became a global icon (Tsutsui 2004, 2006).

Even by the early 1960s, Japanese creature features, with their less-than-state-of-the-art special effects, formulaic plots, and exaggerated dialogue and acting, had gained the reputation in the United States as the ultimate "B movies," unintentionally humorous works so bad that they were good, frequently described as "campy" and "cheesy." This chapter will explore how it was that Japan came to be perceived in postwar America as the home of the world's finest cinematic cheese (rivaled only perhaps by Italy's "spaghetti Westerns" and Hong Kong's martial arts films) and what it was about *kaijū eiga* that made them so appealingly deplorable to Western audiences. Specifically, I will consider how extensive editing and voice dubbing by Hollywood distributors, eager to "improve" Godzilla films for American release, accentuated (and even fabricated) their cheesiness, creating politically sanitized self-parodies that affirmed America's global superiority and underlined Japanese cultural and racial difference.

At the heart of my analysis is the American taste for cinematic cheese which, at least through the medium of monster movies, structured Japan as a distant, frequently incomprehensible, and thoroughly, indeed laughably inferior place. Over the years, scholars have given surprisingly little attention to cheesiness, and only slightly more to the related concept of camp. Cheese, camp, and Godzilla films were, however, intertwined in postwar U.S. culture, to the extent that Susan Sontag (2001 [1964], 2001 [1965]), the first literary arbiter of American camp, was also the first Western writer to take the solemn subtexts of Japanese science-fiction movies seriously. Annalee Newitz (2000: 59) later wrote a spirited exegesis of cheesiness, although she saw America's cheesy sensibility as being contemporary, mainstreamed only with Generation X, and largely retrospective—"a kind of snide nostalgia for serious cultures of the past which now seem so alien and bizarre as to be funny"—rather than as a central feature of the postwar American popular culture experience. Following on Newitz's typology (2000: 59), I suggest that "*cheese* describes both a parodic practice and a parodic form of textual consumption" and that cheesiness is associated with cheapness, with media products where one can "see the strings" and the cinematic illusion is not complete. Cheesiness, Newitz (2000: 61) observes, pivots on "an idea of cheapness, usually a literal description of the low-budget production values or a B-movie, but also a condemnation of certain genres (like 'space movies' or 'movies-of-the-week') as being beneath us." This affirmation of the superiority of the spectator-consumer—which spans economic, aesthetic, and cultural categories—is, I would argue, a fundamental feature of America's cheesy sensibility as well as of the postwar appeal of Japanese monster movies. In the case of the Godzilla series (as with Hong Kong martial arts films), racial difference and foreign origin also contribute substantially to the marking of the "cultures and multicultures of the Pacific Rim" (Newitz 2000: 60) as cheesy, derivative, ridiculous, and inherently subordinate. Not surprisingly, then, with a vision of Japanese popular culture (and indeed Japan) as being definitively cheesy, as was embedded in the American collective imagination for most of the postwar period, the potential for Japanese soft power in the United States was elusive for decades, and may just prove illusive today.

Editing: Censorship and Superiority

Needless to say, the monster movies produced in Japan from the 1950s to the 1970s underwent significant changes in their trans-Pacific journeys to American theaters. Not only was there translation—the rendering of the Japanese dialogue into English—but also elaborate editing of the films to make them more appealing narratively, visually, and ideologically to American viewers. According to Henry Saperstein, the B-movie impresario who distributed many Tōhō features, American moviegoers simply did not have the patience to watch the laboriously plotted Japanese originals:

> Every Japanese monster film starts with a conference. Either the press or government officials or scientists.... This goes on for five minutes, by which time every American viewer tunes it out.... We would edit the films and make such additions or deletions as we felt would make better progression.... We edited almost every film we distributed here so it would play better.
>
> (Quoted in Galbraith IV 1998: 102)

The editing of Godzilla films by distributors ran the gamut from well-planned cinematic surgery to capricious butchery: extensive cuts were made, new segments, characters, and plotlines spliced in, stock footage added, musical scores substituted, scenes shuffled, and stories changed. The effect of these alterations was to scrub the films politically (stripping away any social satire and any potential criticism of the United States), to objectify both the original films and the image of Japan they conveyed, and to render the movies exaggeratedly self-parodic, often making them "play better" by making them worse and thus presumably more cheesily humorous. Indeed, as the history of the Godzilla series reveals, much of the cheesy goodness of postwar Japanese popular culture was actually manufactured in Hollywood.

The most famous case of Americanizing a Godzilla film was the treatment given to the original *Gojira*, which gained Raymond Burr but lost twenty minutes of footage and most of its political message in being reworked into the 1956 U.S. release *Godzilla, King of the Monsters*. The dark, anti-war, and understatedly anti-American *Gojira* was not thought bankable by Hollywood distributors, who wanted an action-packed, thrill-a-minute feature in the "monster on the loose" tradition for (presumably) easily offended, easily bored American audiences. Thus new material featuring Burr as a U.S. reporter voyeuristically observing the monster's rampages through Tokyo was spliced in and "better progression" ensured by stripping out much of the substance (what Donald Richie [2001: 267] termed "all of the good stuff") from the Japanese original. The result was a clever job of cinematic surgery, revealing much more sophistication than later attempts to edit Godzilla films for American distribution. But, compared to *Gojira*, *Godzilla, King of the Monsters* emerged from the cutting room a far less ambitious, challenging, and substantive work, dumbed down and politically neutralized for stateside consumers (Tsutsui 2004: 38–42).

Although producer Richard Kay would later vigorously deny censoring *Gojira*, innocently arguing that the editing "just gave it an American point of view" (quoted in Ryfle 1998: 57–58), the fact was that all scenes which could conceivably be considered critical of the United States or the atomic bombings of Japan were trimmed out of *Godzilla, King of the Monsters*. A discussion on a commuter train explicitly linking the creature to wartime bombing was excised; the miserable cry of a woman, about to be crushed by Godzilla, to a husband killed in the war is left untranslated; the ethical anguish of Dr. Serizawa over the creation of a super-weapon is abbreviated and trivialized. Significantly, the ending of the American version completely rewrote the ambiguous, chilling close of the Japanese original, with its solemn warnings of the dangers of future nuclear testing and the possibility of other destructive mutations. *Godzilla, King of the Monsters* instead fades out on a contrived note of sunny Hollywood closure: "The monster was gone," Raymond Burr declares. "The whole world could wake up and live again." In the end, Americanization "rendered *Gojira* a standard monster-on-the-loose action film, radiation became a gimmick rather than a moral crisis, and Godzilla was firmly recast in the inoffensive tradition of American atomic-age science-fiction cinema" (Tsutsui 2004: 41). Reviews at the time (as well as *Godzilla, King of the Monsters*' strong American box office) reveal that the political scrubbing of *Gojira* was thorough and, from the distributors' perspective, completely successful. As a *New York Times* reviewer (1956) observed:

> We might note that the film was produced in Japan and Godzilla is explained as a freak offspring of nature, dislodged and reactivated by H-Bombs. One might remotely regard him as a symbol of Japanese hate for the destruction that came out of nowhere and descended upon Hiroshima one pleasant August morn. But we assure you that the quality of the picture and childishness of the whole idea do not indicate such calculation. Godzilla was simply meant to scare people.
>
> (Crowther 1956b: 129)

Thus, even in his American debut, Godzilla was established as low quality and childish, recast by Hollywood as a politically insipid, mass-market slice of imported cheese.

The model set with the Americanization of *Godzilla, King of the Monsters* became standard treatment for Japanese monster films over the next two decades. Political messages continued to be excised for American consumption and the Godzilla movies, which became increasingly lighthearted even in their Japanese incarnations over the 1960s and 1970s, were made even goofier and more self-parodic in the name of "improvements" for the U.S. market. Thus the sharp satirical edge of *King Kong vs. Godzilla* (1962), a humorous but barbed take on the American-style commercialization of postwar Japan, was blunted by Hollywood editing. Instead of social commentary, the film was reduced to vapid slapstick in its Americanization, with far-from-faithful translations ("My corns always hurt when they are near a monster!") and selective edits changing satirical wit to madcap inanity. Mistranslations, both conscious and unconscious on the part of U.S. distributors, were a readily apparent feature of all the American adaptations. In *Gigantis the Fire Monster*, the American release of *Godzilla Raids Again* (1955), lines like "Ah, banana oil!" and "Ha, ha, ha. Trying to please a woman is like swimming the ocean!" were most likely intended to be tongue-in-cheek. But frequently ungrammatical and incoherent dialogue (which was humorous in its own way and went on to become a hallmark of the genre) may often have been the simple result of over-literal, inexpert, and inexpensive translation. Whether from ham-fisted editing or imperfect translation, Japanese creature features were almost always left stilted, degraded, or just plain incomprehensible from the exertions of Hollywood editors.

The American version of *King Kong vs. Godzilla*, as with several films in the series, also had numerous scenes added in order to create a "documentary" feel to the proceedings. Thus new sequences from the "United Nations News Center" featuring American reporters and experts were interspersed throughout the movie, the faux solemnity and authoritativeness of the newscasters creating a (perhaps unintentionally) humorous dissonance with the farcical tone of the Japanese footage. Moreover, this addition of all-knowing (and all Caucasian American) commentators served to add a kind of ethnographic distance to the edited film: not only did this approach highlight the exoticism of the Japanese original, but it also served to objectify both the Japanese film and the action which took place within it. As with the classic anthropological documentary (featuring Olympian voice-over and curious footage of "primitive" peoples) (Longfellow 2004), the Americanized *King Kong vs. Godzilla* placed its viewers on an elevated, culturally superior plane, rendering the Japanese characters from the original film virtual specimens, strange, distant, and unquestionably inferior. Raymond Burr's insertion in *Godzilla, King of the Monsters* had much the same effect, as did the fact that the edited movie was structured as one long flashback sequence (Tucker 1996: 72). Condescending narration in *Gigantis*—"This, then, is the story of the price of progress to a little nation of people"—was particularly unsubtle. In short, after the ministrations of Hollywood distributors, American audiences were frequently presented with Godzilla features at a remove, lifted above the Japanese original as spectator-consumers, and invited to look down on and laugh at the impenetrable, alien, and ridiculous antics of Godzilla and his Japanese co-stars.

Although Newitz (2000: 78) warns us that "[c]alling something cheap, or 'for children' is a form of condescension," we should acknowledge that the Godzilla films were, at least by the mid-1960s, in fact both cheap and for children. By a Hollywood yardstick, even the priciest of *kaijū eiga* were virtually Z-grade in terms of production costs, a fact betrayed by the simple (yet genuinely clever) special effects in the Japanese creature features. The films were not even particularly expensive by Japanese industry standards and were made as quickly (and with the same slapdash energy) as was the norm in Japan's major studios at the time. Furthermore, reflecting changes in the Japanese movie audience (above all the impact of television), the target age of Godzilla viewers in Japan dropped precipitously, from the adults for whom *Gojira* was made to elementary schoolers by what is generally judged to be the artistic nadir of the series in the 1970s. Juvenile audiences demanded humor and constant action more than intellectual substance, aesthetic niceties, or polished production values (Tsutsui 2004: 51–63). This was, as it turns out, exactly what Hollywood distributors were looking for as well.

It is not surprising, then, that Japanese filmmakers were often complicit in the cheesing up of their exported products. As U.S. sales could translate into significant profits, studios like Tōhō eagerly cooperated with distributors in making films suitable for American audiences. If Henry Saperstein and the moviegoers of middle America demanded another crowd-pleasing "hoho from Tōhō" (Doherty 1988: 170), then Japanese producers readily obliged, whether that meant inserting washed-up Hollywood talent (like Nick Adams) for "star appeal" or putting more characters in uniforms (which one distributor claimed was necessary so American viewers could distinguish one Japanese actor from another) (Tucker 1996: 204). Thus we might well conclude that the Godzilla films, including some of the more sophisticated works in the series, were already quite cheesy by American standards even before they were subjected to extensive editing and redoubled cheesing by Hollywood distributors. And, indeed, such global "circuitries of cheesiness" reflected the complex international hybridity and intertextuality of Japanese monster films: the Godzilla features that ended up in U.S. drive-ins were Japanese-made movies, initially inspired by Hollywood monster-on-the-loose flicks, made with the input of American distributors, and often intended themselves as parodies of American cinematic genres (notably espionage, science fiction, and superhero movies), which were then, in turn, suitably "Americanized" through translation and editing (Gallagher 2004: 176).

All this being said, the overall effect of the "improvement" of Japanese monster movies for American consumers was to inscribe Japan and the Japanese in a familiar position of laughable inferiority. The Japanese were portrayed as wacky and inscrutable, irrational and incomprehensible, small and victimized, helpless and hapless; Japanese filmmakers inevitably came off as unskilled, old-fashioned, derivative, and indisputably low budget. In the making (and remaking) of Godzilla films for the American market, we see the creation of a "Japanese" cinema which, through its technical and creative deficiencies, became a theater of U.S. superiority, very much reflecting the asymmetric power relations of the Cold War international order (Rich 2004). American moviegoers could hoot at the cheesiness of Japanese creature features—the unsophisticated special effects, the craziness of narratives, the obtuseness of the dialogue—and feel confident of their own innate superiority, distanced from the Japanese films and the culture from which they emerged, secure in the knowledge of America's preeminence aesthetically, culturally, politically, and economically. Popular cinema from Japan, "Americanized," objectified, and politically sanitized in the workshops of Hollywood distributors, thus affirmed as well as amused, substantiating American dominance through the spectacle of Japanese lacking.

Dubbing: Domestication and Difference

Dubbing—the re-voicing of a movie with translated dialogue—has been the subject of an extensive critical literature. A few commentators have praised the practice as a powerful means of making films available to foreign audiences and even as a "creative act," "one way in which a film can be re-written, re-structured, re-invented" (La Trecchia 1998: 113). Yet most observers have damned dubbing as "a kind of monstrosity," an act of "cultural violence and dislocation" perpetrated on innocent, "authentic" films and performances (Ascheid 1997: 33; Shochat and Stam 1985: 52). Dubbed films are seen as "bastardized versions" with an "inartistic, sham quality" that upsets "the feeling of unity, of plenitude, of the character, and thus the spectator position" (Fodor 1976: 14; Shochat and Stam 1985: 50; Vicendeau 1988: 33). According to the French filmmaker Jacques Becker, dubbing "is an act against nature, an assault on decency, ... a monster" (quoted in Piette 1998: 191; Borges 2004: 118; Nornes 1999: 17–34).

Dubbing has often been castigated, in particular, for its efficacy in domesticating the foreign and erasing cultural and linguistic difference. As Martine Danan has argued:

> Dubbing is an attempt to hide the foreign nature of a film by creating the illusion that actors are speaking the viewer's language. Dubbed movies become, in a way, local productions.... Foreign utterances are *forced* to conform to the domestic norms and frame of reference.... Dubbing, in short, is an assertion of the supremacy of the national language and its unchallenged political, economic and cultural power within the nation's boundaries.
>
> Martine Danan (1991: 612)

As others have stressed, "dubbing is a domesticating strategy which neutralizes foreign elements of the source text and thus privileges the target culture" (Szarkowska 2005: 8); it is "the best method for repressing alterity in the cinema" (Fawcett 1996: 84). Moreover, the nature of the deception created through dubbing, which allows for a kind of invisible ventriloquism impossible in subtitling, not only creates "a false sense of cultural affinity" (MacDougall 1998: 175), but also, "[g]iven our desire to believe that the heard voices actually emanate from the actors/characters on the screen, [represses] all awareness of the possibility of an incorrect translation; in fact, we forget that there has been any translation at all" (Shochat and Stam 1985: 49). Scholars have also observed that authoritarian governments have historically favored dubbing; the regimes of Franco in Spain and Mussolini in Italy encouraged the re-voicing of imported films not just to promote a standardized national language, but also because dubbing (at least compared to subtitling) allowed for the almost undetectable censorship of cinematic content (Danan 1991: 611ff; Whitman-Linsen 1992: 158ff).

It is tempting to read such interpretations of dubbing—as violence, as domestication, as political suppression—onto Japanese monster movies, all of which were routinely dubbed for American release until the 1990s. Dubbing, of course, has come to define the Godzilla series in the American imagination and cement its reputation as the ne plus ultra of cinematic cheesiness. Critics ever since the 1950s have commented frequently on the films' hilariously awful translations and re-voicings. As one noted in 1970, beautifully summarizing the artistic impact of the genre, "Japanese monster films have all the signs of catchpenny productions—faded American stars in featured roles, abysmal dubbing, uneven special effects" (John Baxter quoted in Ryfle 1998: 77). The journalist Steve Ryfle further observed:

> It has become a cliché as old as Godzilla himself: Japanese monster movies are known for the cartoonish voices, out-of-sync lip movements, and sub-thespian dialogue that result when foreign films are re-dubbed into English. Ever since he first appeared ... Godzilla has been synonymous with "bad dubbing."
>
> (Ryfle 1998: 149)

As even the advertising for a vinyl Godzilla toy distributed in the United States in 2005 archly proclaimed, "Bad dubbing not included."

The reasons for dubbing the Godzilla films for American release were primarily economic. Although "art house" fare from Japan like *Rashōmon* was regularly subtitled into English, the American audiences most likely to buy tickets for offerings like *Godzilla vs. the Thing* were notoriously hostile to reading their movies. What's more, as monster movies in the United States were aimed largely at a pre-literate kiddie demographic, the accessible, affordable expedient of dubbing was a natural choice for Hollywood distributors. The crews hired to undertake this work were an odd and varied lot of professional dubbers, inexperienced dilettantes, and out-of-work actors, spread over small operations in New York, Los Angeles, Tokyo, and Hong Kong. Some took the job seriously, laboring to marry translated dialogue to on-screen lip motions, provide credible English-speaking voices to Japanese actors, and maintain fidelity to the original script, although many emphasized speed and economy over quality and accuracy. In the early days, Asian American actors (including Keye Luke, James Hong, and George Takei) were used to give the films "an 'authentic' sound," but distributors were later satisfied to have Western actors adopt fake "Japanese" accents that were stereotyped, exaggerated, and humorous at the time (if remarkably distasteful to our ears today) (Ryfle 1998: 150–151). The cartoonish tone of the dubbing of Godzilla films was perhaps unavoidable, as many of the English language voices were provided by actors better known for their work on television animation: Daws Butler (the man behind Yogi Bear), Peter Fernandez (who spoke as Speed Racer), and Paul Frees (the voice of Boris Badenov), to name but a few. And the dubbers even further accentuated the cheesiness of the final product by improvising, adding jokes, and generally "improving" the translated dialogue. According to one re-voicer, "We practically had to create the entire translation in the dubbing process. We tried to be faithful to the original dialogue, to preserve the original story and whatever nuances we could. Of course, we Americanized it...." (Peter Fernandez quoted in Ryfle 1998: 151).

But despite all the ways (intentional and more haphazard) that Japanese monster movies were Americanized and aligned with cheesy taste in the dubbing process, it would be an oversimplification to conclude that dubbing was simply a means of domestication in the case of the Godzilla series. The objective of professional dubbing, and the height of domesticating domination, is the creation of a seamless deception:

> The most important goal of making a dubbed version is that it should be absolutely convincing to the audience. Dubbing should create the perfect illusion of allowing the audience to experience the production in their own language without diminishing any of the characteristics of the original.... The work is well done when no one is aware of it.
>
> (Dries 1995: 9)

Assertions of the possibility of such completely inconspicuous re-voicing (and thus imperceptible domestication) almost invariably come from Europe, where linguistic and racial similarities make the "chameleonism of dubbing" a real possibility (Shochat and Stam 1985: 49). Such a "perfect illusion" may never be attainable, however, when dubbing Asian films for American audiences. As Mark Gallagher notes:

> Japanese and Hong Kong films dubbed into English often provoke laughter among Western audiences not only because of simplified, literal, or erroneous translations but also because of the visual incongruity of Asian actors seemingly speaking in unaccented English... ill-matched to their facial expressions and mouth movements.
>
> (Gallagher 2004: 178–179)

In other words, what was "bad" (and, of course, funny) about the dubbing in Godzilla movies were not just low-budget re-voicing and inaccurate translations, but also the obvious mismatches of race and language, the visual/aural disconnect between Asian faces and English speech. Rather than erasing difference, then, dubbing emphasized the gap—economic, cultural, linguistic, and (perhaps above all) racial—between American spectators and Japanese cinematic characters.

The Godzilla films might thus have been Americanized in dubbing, yet were never truly domesticated; in order for Japanese monster movies to retain their distinctively cheesy appeal, they could not entirely cease to be foreign. Dubbing created accessibility for American audiences (as well as a heightening of cheesy pleasure) but not intimacy or identification. Like editing, then, the dubbing of imported creature features affirmed American superiority, reinforced the cultural distance between U.S. consumers and Japanese producers, and enhanced the laughable spectacle of Japanese racial difference and national inferiority (see also Kushner 2006).

Making American Cheese

Antje Ascheid has argued that

> the employment of dubbing as a translation technique must be seen as transforming the original into a blueprint, which shifts its status from that of a finished and culturally specific text to that of a transcultural denationalized raw material, which is to be reinscribed into a new cultural context via the dubbing process.
>
> (Ascheid 1997: 33)

This may be conceivable in the context of intra-European or European-American cinematic exchange, but (as the history of the Godzilla series suggests) racial difference would seem to preclude the possibility of Asian films becoming truly "transcultural denationalized raw materials" in many world markets. And yet, at the start of the new millennium, the global popularity of Japanese popular culture—from anime to Hello Kitty—has regularly been attributed to just this sort of cultural anonymity. Scholars and critics have written frequently of the "*mukokuseki*" (stateless) quality of contemporary Japan pop, a rootless, unaccented essence that allows consumers around the world to inscribe (one might even say dub) their own meanings and desires onto Japanese products. But the first postwar generations of Japanese popular culture exports—the Godzilla movies and the other cinematic, television, and animated creatures in their slipstream—were not "stateless," in spite of (or, one could well conclude, thanks to) Hollywood editing, dubbing, translation, and general Americanization. Godzilla may not have had "the whiff of Japanese cool," or even a hint of the alluring cultural "fragrance" of which Iwabuchi Kōichi (2002) has written, but Japanese monster movies did have an odor, the distinctive smell of cheese.

The very appeal of the Godzilla films to American audiences was their difference, a blend of non-quite-Hollywood production values, culturally inflected genre conventions, and ethnographic (as well as ethnic) exoticism. Denatured politically, dubbed for easy consumption, and given an extra shot of cheesiness by obliging U.S. distributors, Japanese monster movies offered American viewers not only a humorous distraction, but also a blush of sophistication and a buzz of cultural (and racial) superiority. The American taste for cheese was, it seems, the lowbrow orientalism of the postwar drive-in, the Saturday double feature, and the midnight rerun (compare Klein 2004).

In the 1970s and 1980s, as the Japanese economy surged, the circulation of "cheesy" Japanese popular culture in the United States seemed to decline, and the market expectations of Japan's media products traced the same trajectory as Japanese automobiles, from cheap and laughable to technically sophisticated and desirable. But at the start of the twenty-first century, the Japanese image in the American popular imagination would seem to have bifurcated: while Japanese fashion and videogames may still (like Hondas and Toyotas) have had a lingering fragrance about them, the vision of Japan as cheesy and inferior returned, as did the time-honored strategies of editing and dubbing for exaggerated impact on American consumers. U.S. cable subscribers had access to Japanese game shows (*MXC, Most Extreme Elimination Challenge*), food programs (*Iron Chef*), and "human interest" news programming (*Sushi TV*), edited, dubbed, often re-scripted, and "Americanized" as cheesy spectacle (Klein 2004). Classic Japanese monster movies were ridiculed and satirized in the voiced-over cult hit *Mystery Science Theater 3000*. And Hong Kong martial arts pictures, which, along with *kaijū eiga*, are the traditional avatars of American cheesy taste, were revived as laughingstocks with the cinematic spoofs *Kung Pow!* and *Kung Faux*.

Japan, with its economic star now eclipsed, has apparently been reinscribed in the American popular imagination as an unthreatening place: wacky, childlike, alien, and hilariously inferior, the stereotyped land of cultural cheese. Portraying Japan as "a nation of lovable kooks" (Gallagher 2004: 181), media products like *MXC* and *Iron Chef* returned Japan to a familiar spot in a marginalized, orientalized, comically foreign corner of the American mental map of the world. Even the 2014 Hollywood reboot of the Godzilla series relegated Japan to the role of scenic backdrop, a cartoonish stage-set through which the story fleetingly passed on the way to the real action in the United States. In the twenty-first-century world of Legendary Pictures, Godzilla's Japan is depicted as a fanciful, storybook locale, caricatured in almost Gilbert and Sullivan fashion, with Mount Fuji towering over every shot and suburbs dressed up in ersatz Asian architecture like Shinto shrines (Tsutsui 2014). One must wonder just how much things have changed since the days of Raymond Burr in monster-ravaged Tokyo, dubbing with fake Japanese accents, and "Ah, banana oil!" Has the historical moment of Japan's potential soft power already passed, if indeed it ever existed at all?

19 The Rise of Japanese Horror Films

Yotsuya Ghost Story (Yotsuya Kaidan), Demonic Men, and Victimized Women

Kyoko Hirano

Background

Yotsuya Ghost Story (*Yotsuya kaidan*) has been one of the most popular kabuki plays since Tsuruya Namboku IV's (1755–1829) version was first performed in 1825. Namboku adapted folklore, added references to then current issues, and fictionalized his play by adding Tōkaidō, the main route between Edo (name for Tokyo before 1868) and Kyoto, to the title. This popular tale of haunting and revenge has been adapted into film since the 1910s (Yokoyama 2008), along with television dramas, *rakugo* comedic storytelling, manga, anime, and commercial theater, thus entertaining generations of audiences and showing the enduring appeal of ghost stories.

The plot of *Yotsuya Ghost Story* is simple: *Rōnin* (masterless samurai) Iemon marries Oiwa, after murdering her father who had opposed their marriage. After Oiwa gives birth to their son, her health declines, and Iemon, frustrated by the lack of a prospective employer, continues to drink and gamble. When Iemon meets Oume, a young lady from a wealthy family, he poisons Oiwa, who dies in agony. After Iemon marries Oume, he sees Oiwa's ghost (Figure 19.1). Deranged, Iemon kills his bride and her father and then takes his own life at the behest of Oiwa's ghost.

Movie audiences have enjoyed watching how different filmmakers visualize this well-known story and how different stars interpret the main roles. In Kinoshita Keisuke's *New Interpretation of Yotsuya Ghost Story* (*Shinshaku Yotsuya kaidan*, 1949), Oiwa is played by Shochiku studio's then top star Tanaka Kinuyo and Iemon by matinee idol Uehara Ken. Daiei Studio's immensely popular Hasegawa Kazuo plays Iemon in Misumi Kenji's 1959 version; Nakadai Tatsuya and Okada Mariko are featured by Toyoda Shirō in his 1965 version for Tokyo Eiga Studio. Other highly respected film directors, including Katō Tai (1961, *Ghost Story: Oiwa's Ghost* [*Kaidan Oiwa no bōrei*]), Mori Kazuo (1969, *Yotsuya Ghost Story: Oiwa's Ghost* [*Yotsuya Kaidan Oiwa no bōrei*]), and theater director Ninagawa Yukio (1981, *Summer of Devils: From Yotsuya Ghost Story* [*Mashō no natsu: Yotsuya kaidan yori*]), have made cinematic versions.

In addition, *Yotsuya Ghost Story* and its variations have inspired creative adaptations that take even greater liberties with the characters and story. For

Figure 19.1 Iemon confronted by Oiwa's ghost in *Tōkaidō Yotsuya Ghost Story* (*Yotsuya kaidan*), directed by Nakagawa Nobuo, 1959.

Source: Courtesy of Kokusai Hōei.

example, director Fukasaku Kinji, known for his energetic and subversive gangster films, made *Crest of Betrayal* (*Chūshingura gaiden Yotsuya kaidan*, 1994) by combining *Yotsuya Ghost Story* with the samurai revenge story *Forty-Seven Rōnin* (*Chūshingura*). Some of the same characters appear in both stories, and, in Namboku's time, the two kabuki plays were performed back to back over two days. Nakata Hideo, who initiated the international popularity of J-horror, directed *Ghost Story* (*Kaidan*, 2007) based on a few popular Edo-period ghost stories and featuring young kabuki star Onoe Kikunosuke surrounded by several appealing film and television actresses.[1] In 2014, prolific director Miike Takashi, known for his raw energy and quirky sense of humor, made *Over Your Dead Body* (*Kuime*), produced by another young kabuki actor, Ichikawa Ebizō who starred in the film. In this adaptation, events in a stage production of *Yotsuya Ghost Story* parallel the real-life love interests and adulteries of its actors. Ninagawa's second film adaptation *Laughing Iemon* (*Warau Iemon*, 2004) is based on Kyōgoku Natsuhiiko's 1997 novel of the same name and portrays Oiwa as emotionally strong despite her physical ugliness (Yokoyama 2008). In the 2013 stage play by Betsuyaku Minoru, known for existentialist works, Oiwa has extramarital affairs and some members of the Forty–Seven Rōnin are, in fact, reluctant to participate in the revenge plot against the regional lord who had instigated the death of their master, contrary to the conventional story that emphasizes their unwavering loyalty to the cause (*Nihon Keizai Shinbun* 2013). These adaptations star popular theater, television, and film actors, utilize computer graphics, and include explicit sexual scenes.

This chapter analyzes how director Nakagawa Nobuo (1905–1984) turned this classic ghost story into a sympathetic tale of a woman's suffering in patriarchal Edo-period (1603–1868) society in his 1959 *Tōkaidō Yotsuya Ghost Story* (*Tōkaidō Yotsuya kaidan*). Nakagawa satisfied his cult followers by pursuing his own audacious artistic scheme in color, composition, camera movement, editing, music, and sound design, while perpetuating historical customs for adapting *Yotsuya Ghost Story*. He used tropes of kabuki, showing the continued influence of Edo-period mass culture in the twentieth century, while at the same time pioneering conventions for the developing genre of J-horror. My close reading of *Tōkaidō Yotsuya Ghost Story* is intended to serve as a model of how to analyze Japanese film and understand its artistic and historical significance.

Nakagawa's *Tōkaidō Yotsuya Ghost Story*

Nakagawa Nobuo directed a total of ninety-seven films between 1934 and 1982 for various studios and production companies. He worked in diverse genres, including period films (*jidai geki*), love stories, and literary adaptations. However, he is best known for his horror films, characterized by the creative techniques I analyze below. His stars were not as established as their counterparts at other studios with bigger budgets. Therefore, Nakagawa relied on cinematic style and deft craftsmanship to achieve artistic and commercial success.

Nakagawa's *Tōkaidō Yotsuya Ghost Story* was released by Shin-Tōhō Studio on July 1, 1959, the same day as Misumi's version. It was not uncommon for competing studios to simultaneously release different versions from the same source text. However, when Shin-Tōhō executives heard that Daiei was making another version, they became nervous. Shin-Tōhō (meaning new Tōhō) was created during a 1947 labor union strike as Tōhō's second studio. Although Shin-Tōhō occasionally produced highly acclaimed masterpieces like Mizoguchi Kenji's *The Life of Oharu* (*Saikaku ichidai onna*, 1952), it specialized in low budget B-pictures with tendencies toward kitsch and the exploitation style. When Shin-Tōhō went bankrupt in 1964, the company name was changed to Kokusai Hōei, which remains in business today mainly producing television programs, renting out studio space, and managing Shin-Tōhō film copyrights.

One of Shin-Tōhō's most important stars, Arashi Kanjurō (1902–1980), was originally cast as Iemon for Nakagawa's film. However, studio executives were afraid of hurting Arashi's reputation and his feelings if he were beaten by Daiei's enormously popular star Hasegawa. The executives persuaded Arashi to resign from the role, and a younger, lesser-known actor, Amachi Shigeru (1931–1985), was cast. Amachi, who had originally been turned down for the part, was twenty-nine years younger than Arashi and full of ambition and passion, as apparent in his unique interpretation of Iemon (Amachi 2000; Ōsawa 2008).

Shot in twenty-three days with only twelve million yen, *Yotsuya Ghost Story* reflects Shin-Tōhō's low-budget policy at a time when the average production required forty to forty-five days and production costs were sixteen to twenty million yen (Ōsawa 2008). Shin-Tōhō's president Ōkura Mitsugu glibly proclaimed that company policy was "first comes speed; second comes speed; and third comes the fact that time is money" (Amachi 2000). Ōkura's directive ordered that films be made quickly and economically and be fast moving to keep audiences' attention; Nakagawa satisfied both demands in *Tōkaidō Yotsuya Ghost Story.*

Yotsuya Ghost Story Tradition and Rituals

Historically, in Japan ghost stories have been performed during the summer when the weather is hot and humid, cooling audiences by giving them cold chills. The Japanese film industry has observed this practice by releasing ghost story films during the summer. This timing also coincides with the August Buddhist Obon festival, when the spirits of the dead are believed to return to their families. Traditionally, the most important opportunities for ticket sales in the Japanese entertainment business are twice a year: in the middle of summer and at the beginning of the year during workers' holidays.

Another popular practice calls for actors and key members of the crew to pay their respects to the spirit of Oiwa by praying at Myōkōji Temple where Oiwa's tomb has been preserved and at Oiwa related shrines in Tokyo in order to prevent bad omens from visiting the production. According to legend, if they ignore this ritual, misfortune will befall them; part of the set or a prop might fall onto an actor or a crewmember might be injured by broken equipment. A photograph of the actors praying at the shrine is usually circulated in mass media as part of the film's promotional campaign. This was true of a photograph of Nakagawa and his main actors praying at the Oiwa shrine in 1959 (Nakagawa 1969).

Even in the summer of 2013, when young kabuki star Onoe Kikunosuke was interviewed about his new production of *Yotsuya Ghost Story*, he mentioned that he had prayed at Oiwa shrines and lit candles in front of a talisman placed backstage. He remarked, "I am not particularly superstitious, but I do not want anything bad to happen" (Onoe 2013). The press note to Miike's *Over Your Dead Body* stated that the film's producers went as far as to organize a tour for the main cast and crewmembers to two Oiwa-related shrines and Oiwa's tomb (Kuime Press Note 2014).

Edo Theater in Film

Ōkura requested that the film incorporate *gidayū*, the kabuki convention of musicians playing *shamisen* and singing along with the play, sitting visibly to the left side of the stage. Nakagawa begins his film with a shot of a theater stage, showing two *gidayū* musicians, thus immediately establishing the film's close relationship with kabuki. In addition, Nakagawa followed his art director Kurosawa Haruyasu's idea of showing *kuroko* (a stagehand dressed in black) holding a candle and walking across the stage as the credits roll (Nakagawa 1969).

After the credits end, the title of the location "Bizen" (currently Okayama) appears. The opening scene begins with a close up shot of frozen rice paddles, continuing to an unusually long traveling shot, showing Iemon following Oiwa's father and asking his permission to marry his daughter. The father flatly refuses because of Iemon's low social status and bad reputation. Infuriated, Iemon draws his sword and, demonstrating his short temper and masterful swordsmanship, kills Oiwa's father and his friend, the father of Yomoshichi, who is engaged to Oiwa's sister Osode. The servant Naosuke, who accompanies them and is in love with Osode, blackmails Iemon. This scene was originally intended to be shot in nineteen cuts, but, during the rehearsal, Nakagawa decided to shoot it in one take, over four minutes using two rails for the tracking shot (Nakagawa 1969). This long take accompanied by *gidayū* provides the audience with the feeling that they are watching a kabuki performance. At the same time, Nakagawa reminds his audience that they are watching a film by making them conscious of camera movements.

Nakagawa faithfully depicts highlights of *Yotsuya Ghost Story* familiar to audiences, such as the scene of Oiwa's poisoning. Iemon gives poison to Oiwa, telling her it is medicine. After he leaves, the masseur Takuetsu, sent by Iemon, visits Oiwa. She begins to feel the physical effects of the medicine on her face. When she combs her hair, it falls out. Oiwa then sees her face in the mirror and is startled by her own grotesque image. In the kabuki performance, the exaggerated movements and voices of the actors, eerie lighting design, and sound effects of drums and wooden percussion instruments heighten the mood.

Nakagawa entertains his viewers not only by fulfilling their appetite for horror but also by surprising them. Nakagawa shows poison first in a close up of white powder on red paper. The striking colors catch the viewer's eye. A shot of brightly colored fireworks in the dark sky is then inserted. While further alerting the viewer, this image also functions as a point-of-view shot of someone—possibly of Iemon anxious to get rid of Oiwa—outside looking at an actual firework. The firework is thus metaphorically employed to show Iemon's state of mind, exploding with the realization of the seriousness of his crime and his expectation of a glorious future life.

After Iemon leaves, Oiwa pleads with Takuetsu that her face is burning, but Nakagawa does not reveal Oiwa's face right away. Only after he shows her stumbling around the room and Takuetsu terrified, does the audience see Oiwa look at the mirror and become horrified by her own image. After the close up of the mirror, her shriek is heard, followed by a reaction shot of Takuetsu shivering. Suspending the visual revelation of her face heightens the viewer's sense of urgency and anxiety. Although the audience knows what to expect, they are shocked when actually seeing Oiwa's face. On the stage, this suspense is realized by seating Oiwa with her back to the audience so that they are unable to see her face, and the *kuroko* helping to put makeup on the actor's face. In film, this manipulation can be rendered more effectively by editing strategies and camera positions, and Nakagawa utilizes these cinematic privileges to their full extent. At the same time, he uses music reminiscent of kabuki to pay respects to theater traditions.

Color Scheme and Horror

Nakagawa's color scheme is also remarkable. Red symbolizes both poison and blood. Iemon receives the poison from Naosuke in an outdoor scene in which red is prominently revealed as the characters move across the screen, in the narrow pieces of cloth hung to be dried, flapping in the wind against the blue sky. First, the background shows white cloth, then, as the two men walk, they pass those with red and white plaid, and finally those that are completely red.

In the scene in which Iemon discusses Oiwa's murder with Naosuke near the pond, art director Kurosawa used red because Nakagawa wanted the sunset to be reflected on the pond (Kurosawa 2000). Towards the end of the film, the scene of Osode and Yomoshichi attacking Iemon is tinted in red (Nakagawa 2000). Red is also seen in the cloth draping the chairs of the roadside café, and in the *noren* (curtain marking an entrance) of the brothel where Naosuke and Takuetsu spend their time. Kurosawa, however, was not totally content with the color effect. He instead felt that the domestic color film stock was imperfect and that the red in the film looks misty and worn out, almost like orange (Kurosawa 2000).

In the scene when Iemon sees Oume in a room at an inn, the sunset light coming from the window is an unusual array of orange, brown, and yellow, and their silence and gradual physical intimacy give an impression of uneasiness rather than happiness. This sense of unease is furthered by the unmatched eye-line shots between Iemon and Oume, atypical of the shots of two lovers, as seen in other such scenes in the film (Ōsawa 2008).

Yellow is also used to symbolize the characters' uneasiness. Early in the film, while Iemon, Oiwa, Naosuke, and Osode are traveling together, they see a wedding procession beyond the yellow of a rice field. Instead of encouraging celebratory feelings, this sight foretells the approach of something sinister. For the scene when Naosuke and Iemon carry a board to which the bodies of Oiwa and Takuetsu are nailed into a field, Nakagawa wanted the eerie color of yellow, and Kurosawa labored to cause this effect by planting many evening primrose (*tsukimisō*), a yellow autumn flower, on the set (Kurosawa 2000).

Sound and Symbolism

When Iemon and Naosuke meet by a pond, accentuated by the artificial red lighting design, the sounds of cicadas chirping, frogs singing, and birds shouting fill the scene. The chirp of cicadas symbolizes both the energetic height of summer and the characters' short lives. Various other noises, including those that cannot be specifically identified, combine to create a mysterious atmosphere.

Other sounds evoke both summer and ephemerality. The sounds of wind chimes (*fūrin*) usually evoke summer when people want to feel air coming in as an auditory effect. They also symbolize pilgrims traveling with bells, referring to Buddhist dead spirits. The sounds of wind chimes are used occasionally in the film, suggesting both of these associations, along with the ephemerality of life. Sounds of insects, birds, and chimes are all carefully designed, inserted between the actor's lines. When an actor stops speaking, the silence and uneasiness are emphasized by the use of these sounds.

Images and sounds of fireworks are also used symbolically, such as in the scene of Oiwa's poisoning I have described above. Fireworks are used frequently in subsequent scenes; in some, only their sounds are heard. For example, they are used in the murder scenes of Oiwa and Takuetsu and that of Naosuke killing the man he told Osode was her father's murderer. The sound of fireworks sometimes scares Iemon, with their light revealing the face of Oiwa in the darkness.

Watanabe Michiaki, Nakagawa's composer, used Japanese traditional musical instruments like *kokyū* (a string instrument played with a bow), *tsuzumi* (drums) and *hyōshigi* (handheld wooden clappers) throughout the film following Ōkura's request for *gidayū*. Watanabe also used Japanese traditional folksongs to create the sense of sadness (Watanabe 2000). Music resembling traditional lullabies accompanies the image of Oiwa's baby.

Nakagawa laboriously recreated the authentic sounds from the Edo period. For example, Emi Shuntarō who played Naosuke, stated that Nakagawa consulted a specialist on Edo-period street vendors for the scene of Naosuke and Takuetsu peddling medicine (Emi 2000). Miyagawa Ichirō, Nakagawa's producer and screenplay writer, and film critic Katsura Chiho, both praised Nakagawa's pursuit of authenticity, which they said is also thanks to his literary erudition (Miyagawa 2000). While Nakagawa audaciously used surreal visual imagery and auditory designs, he also knew the importance of achieving authenticity.

Certain visual symbols are used throughout the film. For example, snakes, commonly perceived as sly and sinister, appear often. At a roadside café on the way to Edo, Iemon kills a snake despite Oiwa's protests that she was born in the year of the snake and snakes are messengers from the gods. In the original kabuki play, Oiwa was born in the year of the rat, and rats appear occasionally as her spiritual embodiments; the reason for Nakagawa's change from the rat to the snake is unknown. After Iemon and Oume's wedding, a snake is seen on the ceiling just before Oiwa's ghost appears, as if signaling Oiwa's appearance. Naosuke sees an illusion of multiple snakes in a bucket after he was fishing for eels and starts washing his feet at home. Iemon hides at a temple in Hebiyama, literally "snake mountain." In the temple, he stumbles over a large string of beads like a snake placed on the floor, as if Oiwa is hindering his movement.

Revenge and Coincidences

Promising Oiwa that he would avenge her father, Iemon convinces her to move with him to the city of Edo, where he says the murderer resides. Osode and Yomoshichi join their trip, accompanied by Naosuke. On the way, Naosuke and Iemon attack Yomoshichi and push him off a cliff. Naosuke promises Osode that he will seek revenge. Oiwa falls ill, and Osode and Naosuke keep traveling, leaving Oiwa and Iemon behind. Reluctantly, Osode has to depend on Naosuke, and they hurry to Edo but cannot find Iemon and Oiwa.

The theme of revenge is prominent because it was part of the samurai code (*bushidō*)—if a family member is killed, the remaining relatives must seek revenge in order to preserve the family name. Oiwa, Osode, and Yomoshichi are therefore obliged to avenge their fathers. Osode's case is more complex because, as she tells Naosuke in the film, she would not depend on a servant unless he promised to avenge her father. When Naosuke urges

Osode to marry him, she insists that he should perform his duty first. Oiwa is obsessed by her duty of revenge, to Iemon's annoyance. After Iemon murders Oiwa, she devotes herself to killing Iemon for his betrayal, and, after victimized, she transforms from an obedient and dutiful wife to a fierce aggressor (Hirosue 2000).

Thus, in *Yotsuya Ghost Story*, the principle of cause and effect underlies the theme of revenge—one character wrongs another, the former is doomed as a consequence, and the latter is devoted to bringing about this result. This kind of story may have taught a didactic lesson to Edo-period masses, encouraging them to get along with each other. In many revenge tales, chance meetings enable the main character to achieve his or her goal. In kabuki plays, coincidences and twists of fate take place frequently, as they did in Greek tragedies and Shakespearean plays. Nakagawa's version of *Yotsuya Ghost Story* includes some original plot devices: for example, Oume's evil nurse happens to be Naosuke's mother, and Yomoshichi did not die after all. Moreover, Nakagawa's film, like other versions, omits certain coincidences, such as Yomoshichi becoming a customer at the brothel where Osode works. Nakagawa may have believed that too many coincidences would spoil the sense of reality.

Sacrificed Women

According to Nakagawa, ghosts result from human obsessions, and period films should portray the various tragic contradictions of the feudal system (Nakagawa 1987). In fact, the theme of the victimized woman's revenge is a common trope of traditional Japanese ghost stories. For example, in one version of the ghost story *Plates of the Banchō Mansion* (*Banchō sara yashiki*), an ill-fated maid accidently breaks one expensive plate from a set of ten. Infuriated, her lord executes her. To her employer, a perfect set of plates is more important than her life. Then, a female ghost appears at the mansion at night, counting "one plate, two plates...," stopping before reaching ten plates, and then weeps. The lord's family is doomed, and misfortunes befall them. *Peony Lantern* (*Botan dōrō*), based on a Chinese ghost story, tells the tragic fate of two young lovers. Japanese variations pair a samurai's daughter and a *rōnin*, or a prostitute and *rōnin*. In each case, the woman kills herself out of overzealous passion, and she keeps meeting her lover, who does not realize that she is a ghost. Once he learns the truth, he is horrified and tries to avoid her and protect himself by acquiring a Buddhist charm, inciting her anger. The female ghost is pure hearted, but the man she loves does not reciprocate her passion.

Kasanegafuchi Ghost Story (*Kaidan Kasanegafuchi*), is another example adapted into kabuki, *rakugo*, film, and television drama. The story involves a husband who kills his ugly wife. Thereafter, whenever he starts a new relationship, his lover or wife keeps dying, haunted by the murdered wife's ghost. This pattern repeats itself for two generations. Finally, a priest pacifies the murdered wife's angry spirit and rescues the man and his family.

In traditional Japan and elsewhere worldwide, women were considered dirty and taboo, associated with blood through menstruation and childbirth. This notion applies to Oiwa and exemplifies how women were stigmatized by male-centered society and the class system during the Edo period (Matrai 2014). Wives who committed adultery could be executed along with their lovers by their husbands, but not vice versa, in the feudal Japan. Iemon entices Takuetsu to seduce Oiwa, and then kills him for committing adultery. Victimized women's vengeful spirits become ghosts haunting the men and their accomplices who had wronged them.

In contrast, today's horror films usually portray random attacks. One does not have to be a victimizer to be haunted by a ghost but instead simply has to be in the wrong place at the wrong time (Jones and Yoshimoto 2003). Nakata's *Ring* (*Ringu*, 1998), based on Suzuki Kōji's 1991 novel, is one of the most popular J-horror films of the late 1990s. The story features the spirit of Sadako, whose supernatural power was not recognized by her society and who was raped and murdered. Being wronged, her spirit attacks the people who watch a video of her performance, but her victims have done nothing wrong to her. With no particular reason, they happen to watch the video, thus get haunted by her spirit. In the movie version, Sadako comes out from a well and then from a television monitor, wearing a white, loose, knee-length dress, her long black hair hiding her face. This image is based on Edo-period female ghosts, who had long black hair and loosely worn white kimono. It is not clear whether Sadako's ghost lacks legs, a visual convention of Edo period ghosts, because she comes out by crawling on the ground. Her unusual movements add to the sense of abnormality.

In Nakata's *Dark Water* (*Honogurai mizu no soko kara*, 2002), based on a short story by Suzuki, the only reason why the female protagonist Yoshimi is attacked by a dead spirit is because she happens to choose the wrong apartment. Yoshimi, a book editor, is embroiled in divorce proceedings with her husband and is fighting for the custody of their daughter Ikuko. Lacking finances, Yoshimi has no other recourse but to rent a cheap, dilapidated apartment for herself and Ikuko. She soon sees water leaking from the ceiling, but nobody lives in the upstairs apartment. After realizing that a dead spirit is haunting their apartment, Yoshimi sacrifices herself to save her daughter. Yoshimi is a victim of society, class difference, and her mean husband. Yoshimi does not become a ghost but instead becomes a victim of a ghost. The image of a lone female warrior confronting an overwhelming evil spirit reflects the contemporary feminist sensibility, but the theme of self-sacrifice is old-fashioned. Suzuki's sympathy for working women is obvious. While a young aspiring writer, he took care of his household and two young daughters, and his wife worked as a schoolteacher. From this experience, he understands the difficulty of women's situation in society and the value of women's work inside and outside of home (Suzuki 2000).

American film critic Kent Jones has pointed out that contemporary American horror films have no cause and effect relationships or subtexts.

Victims have done nothing wrong so as to infuriate the dead spirits. By comparison, American horror films of the 1950s and 1960s used to have subtexts, such as critiques of the Red Scare or the Vietnam War (Jones and Yoshimoto 2003). Random killings by malevolent spirits have become more prevalent in both Japanese and American horror films.

Redemption

It is interesting to note how the wronged spirit is placated in each ghost story. When the victimizer dies, justice has been done, and the story ends in most cases. Oiwa declared that she will eliminate Iemon's family bloodline and is not satisfied by killing only Iemon. Through this theme of family, Nakagawa also added salvation to Oiwa's spirit. After Oiwa makes Iemon kill himself, she changes her appearance from a horrifying and disfigured woman portrayed in dark light to a peaceful and beautiful woman shown in soft and bright light, holding her baby as if Buddhist salvation has been given to her. It looks like Oiwa was invited to go to heaven, rather than hell. Wakasugi Katsuko who played Oiwa remarked that Nakagawa told her that he rewarded her in the end by making her look pretty after many scenes in which the actress looked ugly and grotesque (Wakasugi 2000).

Iemon may be considered to be a victim, too, of the failure of Edo-period economic policies, losing his job and unable to find another. However, he lacks moral integrity. He is weak-willed and opportunistic, opting for the easy solution of marrying a rich woman and obtaining a respectful position by her father's financial power and social connections. Oiwa is a victim of a weak and selfish man. Amachi has argued that *Yotsuya Ghost Story* is similar to Theodore Dreiser's *American Tragedy* (1925). Amachi wanted to reflect human weakness in his characterization of Iemon, and he believed that Iemon committed suicide murmuring "Oiwa, forgive me," while thrusting Osode's sword into his body (Amachi 2000).

American Tragedy was translated to Japanese in 1930, and one of its film versions—*A Place in the Sun* (*Hi no ataru basho*, 1951) released in Japan in 1952—seemed to have had a strong impact on many viewers (Ōsawa 2008). In the novel and its film version, an ambitious but poor man kills his equally poor lover in order to marry a rich woman. Similar stories have appeared in Japanese literature and film, such as Ishikawa Tatsuzō's *The Bitterness of Youth* (*Seishun no satetsu*, 1968) and adapted to film by Kumashiro Tatsumi in 1974, featuring popular stars Hagiwara Kenichi and Momoi Kaori. Although described as similar to *American Tragedy*, Ishikawa's novel is based on a real-life incident in Japan in 1966.

In many stories worldwide, a young man's ambition for a better life invites the destruction of the happiness of the women near him and eventually himself. The man who resorts to immoral options often has to pay for his dishonorable deeds in the end. In many other versions of *Yotsuya Ghost Story*, this characterization of Iemon's is the central focus, and, as a result, Oiwa becomes a secondary character. Yet Nakagawa portrays Iemon ambiguously because he often hesitates to act and reveals no clear feelings (Ōsawa 2008). This makes Iemon inscrutable but more nuanced. Furthermore, Nakagawa fully portrays Oiwa's roles as a daughter, wife, and mother, making her the main character (Yokoyama 2008). Nakagawa's Oiwa thus becomes a powerful heroine and stands out among many versions of *Yotsuya Ghost Story*.

Thus Nakagawa, well aware of commercial demand, stimulated the popular imagination by visually demonizing the female ghost, but, at the same time, he garnered his viewer's sympathy for a victimized woman in patriarchal Edo-period society. He adapted this popular classic ghost story into an allegorical tale of an abandoned wife's revenge. His 1959 film has had a lasting impact on Japanese cinema, stylizing subsequent horror movies, and on popular culture representations of ghosts. This and other cinematic adaptations of *Yotsuya Ghost Story* demonstrate how Edo-period entertainments have transcended generations and media forms and continue to influence popular culture.

Note

1 J-horror is a genre that emerged in the late 1990s in Japan primarily based on popular horror stories or ideas featuring contemporary characters facing random supernatural attacks, normally made in low budget with no stars.

20 V-Cinema

How Home Video Revitalized Japanese Film and Mystified Film Historians

Tom Mes

The growth of home video as a consumer product in the 1980s helped revitalize the Japanese film industry, which had been crippled by competition from television since the early 1960s, and became a radical new way to create, distribute, and promote film. The success of home videos as a business scheme attracted outside investors and people looking to increase profits, dodge taxes, and launder money. New production outfits arose to channel this money stream into the production of films expressly for the video market. Bypassing cinemas entirely, this formed a parallel film industry commonly referred to as "V-Cinema." By the early 1990s, over a hundred new feature films were released directly onto video every year (Tanioka 1999: 345). The video arm of the Toei film studio alone released between fifteen and twenty direct-to-video features a year between 1991 and 1995 and reached a peak of thirty-two new releases in 1997 (Mitsumoto et al. 2014: 148–158). The large production quantity offered unprecedented opportunities for filmmakers, technicians, and creative talent. Some of these workers were experienced hands, but many were newcomers, among them people who are now well-known names, such as director Miike Takashi and actor Kagawa Teruyuki.

As I will analyze, V-Cinema has at least three outstanding features that, in combination, were a radical departure from what came before: (1) production costs were extremely low, (2) there were no theatrical releases, and (3) it provided a breeding ground for new artistic talents. These factors encourage us to redefine and rewrite the history of national cinema, as the role of home video has remained largely overlooked by scholars.

The monumental status of Donald Richie and Joseph L. Anderson's pioneering 1959 study *The Japanese Film: Art and Industry*[1] makes it all the more peculiar that subsequent Japanese film histories have leaned heavily toward film art, all but ignoring the structure and workings of the industry that generated it. The result has been the formation of a canon of consecrated auteur filmmakers based largely on films shown and awards won *outside* Japan, rather than on a profound knowledge of the industrial environment that enabled these filmmakers and informed their films. Kurosawa Akira is a case in point: much has been written about the twenty-nine features he directed, but our grasp of the workaday routine at the Tōhō studios, where he made the majority of these works, remains tenuous. What were the popular genre releases like the *puroguramu pikuchā* (program pictures) and *B-kyū eiga* (B-movies) whose week-to-week success functioned as Tōhō's bottom line and provided Kurosawa with relatively generous production budgets? Who made these once popular but now overlooked films? How were they screened? Who watched them?

Recent years have seen an increasing awareness of such omissions in the history of Japanese cinema, both within and outside academia. Daisuke Miyao's *The Aesthetics of Shadow: Lighting and Japanese Cinema* (2013) analyzes how lighting and cinematography shaped industry practices in the early days of commercial filmmaking and admirably steers the reader along unbeaten paths away from the commonly (or rigidly) practiced auteurist approach. Similarly, Jasper Sharp's *Behind the Pink Curtain: The Complete History of Japanese Sex Cinema* (2008) is a history of more than just cinematic erotica, while Mark Schilling's *No Borders, No Limits: Nikkatsu Action Cinema* (2007) convincingly demonstrates that the canonized Suzuki Seijun was far from alone in directing the kind of stylish action films the Nikkatsu studio churned out on a weekly basis during the 1960s.

The recent era in Japanese film offers a more diverse and vibrant film scene, in terms of industry as well as art, than the then record low in audience attendance conveys—122.9 million in 1996, compared to a record high of over 1.1 billion in 1958 (Motion Picture Producers Association of Japan, Inc.). The largely ignored home video market not only challenges prevalent perceptions of a gradual industrial and creative decline that supposedly coincides with dwindling audience numbers. Instead, it sheds light on the process by which certain filmmakers have risen from humble beginnings to the status of internationally recognized auteurs. This chapter demonstrates that industry insiders, commentators, and consumers all regarded the production of feature films for video release as a legitimate form of filmmaking. This understanding allows us to convincingly argue the merits of certain filmmakers' oeuvres, thus challenging the existing canon of Japanese film.

Shaping an Industry in Crisis

A relatively recent industry development, video has had an extremely large economic and creative impact. In particular, the strategy of releasing feature films directly onto home video created an additional step in the conventional sequential phases of film release, which had customarily begun with theatrical distribution and "ended" with free television screenings.

The distribution model bypassing theaters and pay television in favor of releasing new productions directly onto home video had been in use for animation since the early 1980s. The first title distributed in this manner in Japan was *Dallos* (Oshii Mamoru, dir. 1983) (for discussion of Oshii Mamoru's anime, see Chapter 27). Alexander Zahlten, whose doctoral dissertation *The Role of Genre in Film from Japan* is currently one of the few and most detailed studies on V-Cinema in any language, notes that between 1982 and 1984, the large Kadokawa film company "created a multimedia platform that attempted to do away with temporal sequence: videos, films, and books were released simultaneously" (Zahlten 2007: 286). Zahlten (2007: 483) adds, "As the importance of the video market increased, Kadokawa discontinued the practice and stopped selling the video rights, preferring to distribute the films via Kadokawa Video," implying that the change in the company's strategy and the subsequent creation of new corporate divisions were due to the increasing economic viability of the home video market in its own right (for more on Kadokawa's business model, see Chapter 23).

This viability attracted other film distributors. In 1987 and 1988, the home video branch of Toei, one of the six major studios that dominated filmmaking in Japan through the 1950s and 1960s, released the first six installments of the eight-part yakuza film series *Battles Without Honor and Humanity* (*Jingi naki tatakai*, 1973–1976) on VHS. Film critic Yamane Sadao (1993) notes that the success of this series encouraged Toei Video to consider releasing films directly onto video cassette.

Yamane quotes a 1990 interview with Toei Video producer Yoshida Tatsu from *Gekkan Shinario* (*Monthly Scenario*) magazine, in which Yoshida recounts that he had noticed young customers of a video store renting up to five tapes at a time. Asked how they could watch so many movies in a short time, they replied, "By fast-forwarding" (Yamane 1993: 63). Yoshida then decided to produce a screenplay titled *Crime Hunter* (*Kuraimuhantā ikari no jūdan*) that he had received from television writer Okawa Toshimichi for the video market as "a film that would not be fast-forwarded" (Yamane 1993: 63).

In March 1989 Toei Video released *Crime Hunter* into Japan's estimated 16,000 video stores (Zahlten 2007: 313). Its storyline follows Joe, a cop with the "Little Tokyo" police department, and his hunt for the gang responsible for his partner's death. Along the way, he joins forces with a feisty young nun named Lily and a fugitive named Bruce, his former nemesis who has his own bone to pick with the gang.

The one-hour running time that resulted from Toei Video's chosen strategy (although soon abandoned in favor of the more common feature length of around ninety minutes) inevitably resulted in narrative condensation. In *Crime Hunter*, the focus is on action and the build-up toward it. Many action scenes are further condensed into montage sequences. Dialogue scenes exist only to deliver essential exposition, while character development is limited to mood swings that are usually expressed not through acting but formally, as expressionistic visual mood pieces. This makes *Crime Hunter*, in a sense, pure action cinema, kinetic spectacle for its own sake—a procession of shoot-outs, car chases, and explosions, situated in archetypal settings: harbor docks, nighttime streets, nightclubs, and warehouses. Its bandana-sporting, alpha-male protagonist and its lack of irony place the series under the influence of Sylvester Stallone and Arnold Schwarzenegger. Yoshida had felt that Japanese films were "too explanatory, so they have no speed" when compared to

American films like those starring Stallone (Zahlten 2007: 315). Toei Video consciously positioned *Crime Hunter* as the first entry in its new "V-Cinema" product line. The video box packaging included the tagline "V-Cinema First Shot" (*V shinema daiichidan*), suggesting the excitement awaiting within.

Toei Video sold around 16,000 tapes of *Crime Hunter*, meaning one cassette per rental store of a film with a reported production cost of roughly sixty million yen (at the time around US$550,000). The official wholesale price of a single cassette of *Crime Hunter* was 12,800 yen (US$118) (Zahlten 2007: 317). Before the end of the year, the company released *The Shootist* (*Sogeki*, Ichikura Haruo, dir.), as well as *Crime Hunter 2* (*Kuraimuhantā 2 uragiri no jūdan*, again directed by Okawa Toshimichi).

After the commercial success of Toei's first few V-Cinema releases, other film companies followed suit. By the end of 1991, when Toei Video was releasing at least one new V-Cinema title every month, all the major players in film distribution, as well as a good number of minor ones, had their own line-up of made-for-video products under imprints like "V-Feature" (Nikkatsu), "V-Movie" (Japan Home Video) and "V-Picture" (VIP). None of these derivative trademarks stuck. In spite of all the blatant imitations, the original Toei brand name quickly came to refer to the entire straight-to-video phenomenon. The other oft-used generic term "original video" (*orijinaru bideo*) is almost exclusively used to refer to individual products and not the industry as a whole and also encompasses such audio-visual content as instruction videos and music releases. Yet this did not stop distributor VAP from christening its straight-to-video label "Za Orijinaru Bideo" (The Original Video).

The Many Forms of a Strictly Limited Medium

With as much as 70 percent of video rental store memberships around the late 1980s and into the early 1990s held by men (Kinema Junpōsha 1993: 360), the target audience for V-Cinema was distinctly male, although not uniquely. Although Daiei chose to make its first foray into V-Cinema with the romantic tragicomedy *Asatte Dance* (Isomura Itsumichi, dir. 1991) aimed at women. The largest proportion of V-Cinema was popular genres, such as action films, gangster films, and sex romps (although not hardcore pornography, which is produced and distributed by specialist outfits that exist outside of V-Cinema's confines).

A company such as KSS could be considered a distributor in commonly used film industry terms but had an in-house *kikakubu*, or planning division, that would come up with a basic story idea, couple it with a star to take the lead role, and raise funds on the basis of the combination of these two elements. It would then delegate the actual making of the film to a production company like Twins Japan. Working according to this model, KSS launched its first straight-to-video title in November 1990, *Tuff/Tafu*, (Harada Masato, dir.). The following year it released twelve titles, steadily increasing its output to forty films in 1993 (Zahlten 2007: 345).

Such an industrial, and industrious, approach to film production and distribution could only be achieved by imposing strict limitations on budgets and time schedules. The resources Toei Video made available to its early V-Cinema productions were more generous than the means at the disposal of filmmakers for other companies.

However, this prolific output resulted in an increasing demand for labor: new talent arose both in front of and behind the camera. With the in-house training of the studio era long a thing of the past, V-Cinema producers had to look for experienced hands on the margins of filmmaking. *Crime Hunter* director Okawa Toshimichi came from television. Miike Takashi, who made his directorial debut in 1991 with two V-Cinema productions, *Eyecatch Junction* (*Toppū minipato tai*) and *Lady Hunter* (*Ledī hantā koroshi no pureryūdo*), had been an assistant director working for such veteran filmmakers as Imamura Shōhei and Kuroki Kazuo. Mochizuki Rokurō made hardcore pornography before attracting critical attention with the independently made feature *Skinless Night* (*Sukinresu naito*) in 1991 and subsequently finding a home in V-Cinema for much of the decade. Zeze Takahisa had made his directorial debut in 1989 in "*pinku eiga*" (softcore pornography), which was also one of the realms in which Kurosawa Kiyoshi had been active.

Hands-on filmmaking experience was not a prerequisite for those wishing to ascend the director's chair in V-Cinema. The opportunities were so plentiful that even a complete novice with the right connections could become a director, as was the case with Muroga Atsushi and Tsuruta Norio, both employees of Japan Home Video assigned to helm projects that they proposed to their superiors. As I will discuss, Tsuruta's directorial debut, *Scary True Stories* (*Honto ni atta kowai hanashi*, 1991), became one of V-Cinema's most influential works.

Actors were found in music (like *Crime Hunter* star Sera Masanori), sports (such as boxer Yamato Takeshi who starred in the Miike-directed *Bodyguard Kiba* series), and among the ranks of swimsuit and topless models (who formed the main sales point of Toei's *XX* [*Daburu ekkusu*, beginning in 1993] series that stars a different actress in each installment). Professional actors who had mostly appeared in supporting roles in theatrical features could find themselves launched to V-Cinema stardom, as was the case for Nakamura Tōru, Takeuchi Riki, and Shimizu Kentarō.

V-Cinema was not, as this sudden appearance of new talent might suggest, an industry hermetically sealed from the film world at large. The new sector afforded directing opportunities to such established filmmakers as Ishii Teruo, Hasebe Yasuharu, Konuma Masaru, and Jissōji Akio. Most of these men, not coincidentally, had their roots in previous models of production-line filmmaking: Ishii hailed from Shin-Tōhō, Hasebe started out directing Nikkatsu action pictures, and Konuma rose from the ranks of Nikkatsu Roman Porno (which is comparable to Toei V-Cinema as an effort to ensure a company's survival by relying on low-budget genre fare, thereby offering opportunities for fledgling talent on both sides of the camera). Jissōji came from television, where he provided many of the most interesting features of the *Ultraman* series.

There were also veterans in front of the camera. Harada Yoshio, an immediately recognizable actor in everything from early 1970s Nikkatsu youth movies to Terayama Shūji's countercultural experimental cinema works, had a supporting role in *Crime Hunter*, although he was not given guest star billing in the credits or on the packaging. This also suggests that V-Cinema, at least as produced by established major Toei, from the beginning was seen as "legitimate" filmmaking, not as disreputable, low-budget fare.

In spite of the key role of the *kikakubu*, the supervising producer credited with providing the basic creative concept of a film, Japan's straight-to-video industry was not strictly a director-for-hire medium. Nagasaki Shunichi's Toei V-Cinema production, *Stranger* (*Yoru no sutorenjā kyōfu*, 1991), for example, was made from an original script and starred established actress Natori Yūko. Nagasaki had emerged in the late 1970s from a background of amateur filmmaking and was, by this time, a well-established writer-director of both independent productions, such as *Heart, Beating in the Dark* (*Yamiutsu shinzō*, 1982), and larger-scale releases like *The Enchantment* (*Yūwakusha*, 1989).

At first, film critics noted the possibilities of V-Cinema. For example, in his 1993 essay "The potential of Toei V-Cinema" (*Tōei V shinema no kanōsei*), film critic Yamane Sadao was the first to draw parallels between these made-for-video features and the program pictures of the 1950s and early 1960s, like Shochiku's Sister Pictures (*sisutā pikuchā* or SP) or those made at Second Toei (Daini Toei, also "New Toei"): genre movies of around sixty minutes in length meant as supporting halves of theatrical double bills and as a stepping-stone toward feature filmmaking for fledgling filmmakers and stars, including such then-novice directors as Kudō Eiichi and Fukasaku Kinji. However, as its image declined, V-Cinema received little critical attention, with one exception, film critic Tanioka Masaki (e.g. 1999, 2005) doggedly observed and chronicled the development of V-Cinema. V-Cinema's invisibility in the critical (and academic) discourse has, as Zahlten suggests, "more to do with the inability of omnipresent auteur theory to cope with [V-Cinema] than with a deficit in overall relevance... Rarely is V-Cinema as vulgar, mind-numbingly simplistic or uncompromisingly sensational as it advertises itself" (Zahlten 2007: 326).

Theatrical and Foreign Exposure

The aforementioned example of Nagasaki's *Stranger* shows V-Cinema made room for auteur-driven projects and offered potentials for underrepresented roles. As Nagasaki stated in a personal interview:

> It was a project that I brought to Toei. While I was writing it, I felt it could work as V-Cinema. Toei V-Cinema had momentum at the time.

If a project had a certain degree of action and suspense, then a film with a female protagonist could get made even if it didn't contain any sexual scenes.

(Nagasaki 2013)

This artistic talent helped attract international attention for V-Cinema.

Already during the 1990s, the influence of V-Cinema was felt outside of the domestic market at which it was originally targeted. Programmers for events like the Rotterdam and Vancouver International Film Festivals and the Brussels International Fantastic Film Festival noticed the industry's more outstanding progeny in the latter half of the decade—not coincidentally, the moment when some V-Cinema productions began to outgrow the self-imposed confines of home viewing by giving certain films token domestic theatrical releases in 35 mm prints.

As the reputation of made-for-video films declined into "a vulgar, artistically underwhelming product, churned out for quantity rather than quality" (Zahlten 2007: 325), releasing a film theatrically (usually a mere one week on a single screen in Tokyo or Osaka with the actual profits made on the video release) allowed the distributor to proudly mention this feat on the video packaging to help it stand out from the glut of supposedly cheaply-made fare. Since this move to the big screen was often accompanied by a slightly more comfortable production budget, it created a profitable middle tier of commercial filmmaking that became important for the progression of talent both behind and in front of the camera. An example of this phenomenon that predates the increased international availability of V-Cinema made possible by DVD, is Kudō Eiichi's 1998 yakuza film *A Tale of Scarfaces* (*Andō gumi gaiden gunrō no keifu*). It is a characteristic V-Cinema-derived, middle-tier production that stars video-store mainstay Nakajo Kiyoshi. It went on to receive theatrical and VHS release in France after a selection at the Vienna International Film Festival.

Aoyama's first two films as director were released directly on video: the sex comedy *Not in the Textbook!* (*Kyōkasho ni nai!*, 1995) and the action film *A Cop, a Bitch, and a Killer* (*Waga mune ni kyōki ari*, 1996). After his international festival breakthrough with the independent theatrical production *Helpless* (1995), he delivered a string of middle-tier genre productions. He remarked:

My films *An Obsession* [*Tsumetai chi*, 1997], *Wild Life* [1997], *Shady Grove* [*Sheidī gurōbu*, 1998] and *Embalming* [*EM Enbāmingu*, 1999] had budgets that weren't very different from V-Cinema productions, so they could be counted as V-Cinema…. What I think happened was that their producers had the ambition to make 'films' and not V-Cinema. They had a desire to make films, so they turned those projects into Aoyama Shinji films in order to release them in theaters.

(Aoyama 2013)

In other words, not only the directors but also the producers of V-Cinema had artistic ambitions, even amid the everyday reality of modest budget levels, with the exception of Bitter's End, the production outfit behind *Shady Grove*, all the examples Aoyama mentions were producers active in the field of V-Cinema.

Daiei had launched this strategy as early as 1991. *Asatte Dance*, the first title under its V-Cinema imprint "Shin Eiga Tengoku" (New Film Heaven) received a limited theatrical release, with video as the main source for recouping costs and making a profit. Like Toei, Daiei had been one of the former major studios and therefore had a long history in producing and re-leasing films theatrically. Note the lack of any reference to the word "video" in the Shin Eiga Tengoku trademark.

A prime example of how theatrical prints helped V-Cinema productions gain a wider, international audience is Miike Takashi's *Fudoh: The New Generation* (*Gokudō sengokushi fudō*, 1996). This film was intended for the video shelves but was blessed with an intrepid, idiosyncratic producer in the form of Gaga Communications employee Chiba Yoshinori, whose earlier V-Cinema production *Zeiram* (Amemiya Keita 1991), a science fiction film with action and comedy, had been sold for video release to the United States and several European countries as early as 1994. Chiba saw the potential of *Fudoh* and its director. He revealed in an interview:

> Back then, all straight-to-video films were still shot on film, but they rarely made 35 mm prints because there was no need for them. They went directly to video, so all they made was a video master tape. But *Fudoh* was coming out so well, good enough to play on the big screen, that I decided to have a print made. There was no room for it in the budget Gaga had given me, so I tricked them into giving me more money. The Tokyo Film Festival had a fantasy film sub-festival. I told my bosses that *Fudoh* had been selected for the festival and that we needed to make a 35 mm print. I was lying, of course.
>
> (Mes 2006)

Fudoh become Miike's first film to play to overseas audiences, as the 35 mm print made at Chiba's behest was screened at both the Brussels International Fantastic Film Festival and Toronto International Film Festival in 1997.

Among the most influential early adopters was Tony Rayns, program-mer for the Vancouver and London international film festivals and regular guest curator and advisor for Rotterdam. Rayns' appreciation for the genre films growing out of V-Cinema was rooted in the "termite art" tradition coined by American film critic Manny Farber (Farber 1998: 134), who held aloft American B-movie makers of the 1940s and 1950s like Don Siegel and Joseph H. Lewis. Rayns emphasized early on that the directors who worked in V-Cinema were "not frustrated aesthetes forced to slum it in 'disrepu-table' genres," as he wrote about Mochizuki Rokurō (Rayns 1998: 230).

Instead, he viewed them as "supreme pragmatists," whose work consisted of "genre movies, made on a for-hire basis, with the generic elements left on auto-pilot while the director busies himself with form, rhythm, texture, and the implications of the characters' sexual pathologies" (Rayns 2000: 30). Gatekeepers such as Rayns and Toronto International Film Festival programmer Colin Geddes helped reshape the canon, presenting V-Cinema works by Miike, Mochizuki, Kurosawa, Nagasaki, and Aoyama, as auteurs with individual signature styles.

The filmmakers themselves did not deny that they possessed a signature or that the industrial nature of producing V-Cinema was at odds with their artistic desires. The example of Kurosawa Kiyoshi demonstrates that the breakneck pace of production required for making the films could actually shape a filmmaker's style and methods. "It's been very valuable for me to have the experience of making program pictures," said Kurosawa in 2001. He continued:

> Generally, in that type of production environment, the subject and the story are already fixed. Also, you recreate the same type of film several times with only a slight difference. When the studio system still existed, many directors went through that experience. Today there is only V-Cinema that can give you a similar experience. For me, compared to before the time I started working in V-Cinema, I came to handle the subjects as well as the technical aspects of my films better and with more flexibility.
>
> (Mes and Sharp 2004: 95–96)

From V-Cinema to J-Horror

The international proliferation of V-Cinema and its offshoots was not purely the result of auteurist appreciation of individual film directors, however. *Scary True Stories*, mentioned earlier, is arguably the single most influential film to emerge from V-Cinema, but its director Tsuruta Norio never achieved individual acclaim.

Released in 1991 by Japan Home Video, *Scary True Stories* is an omnibus of three short segments involving supernatural phenomena. Its influence lies in the fact that, as Zahlten noted, the film's themes, style, and structure have been incorporated into what is now marketed under the term "J-Horror," or Japanese horror (for more on the roots of J-Horror, see Chapter 19). In his formal approach, Tsuruta chose to focus on "[a]tmospheric tension and an aesthetics of concealment" (Zahlten 2007: 334) rather than on explicit splatter effects as had been the norm in Japanese horror productions.

This switch in formal approach to a well-established genre was partly motivated by the murders of four young girls by Miyazaki Tsutomu in 1988 and 1989 (see Chapter 33). According to director Tsuruta Norio:

> The police found thousands of porn and horror videos and manga in his apartment, and that gave horror videos a bad name. They even found

several films in the *Guinea Pig* [Za Ginīpiggu, 1985–1988] series, which Japan Home Video had distributed, and Japan Home Video had gotten a lot of heat over it.

(Zahlten and Kimata 2005)

In addition to a "restraint" (Martin 2009: 31) that resulted from a desire to avoid controversy by shunning explicit portrayal of violence, the change in formal approach was also inspired by factors inherent to the mechanics of V-Cinema itself: a low budget and a tight shooting schedule. According to its director, *Scary True Stories* was made for a total of 7 million yen (at the time roughly US$65,000, or one tenth of a Toei V-Cinema budget) and shot in seven days (Zahlten and Kimata 2005). There was not enough time or money to create more than "an aesthetics of concealment."

The focus on atmosphere over explicit violence helped the film appeal to younger audiences than most V-Cinema productions, and "it was placed in the same corner as animation and Disney films" (Zahlten and Kimata 2005). The long-term impact of the various tropes and visual touches introduced in *Scary True Stories* was immense; many of the Japanese horror films that found international exposure in the late 1990s and early 2000s drew on the aesthetics founded by this cheap three-part series, which in turn inspired Hollywood remakes.

Scary True Stories also influenced the auteurs who surfaced through V-Cinema, most notably Kurosawa Kiyoshi, who views it as a turning point from his pre-V-Cinema theatrically released horror film *Sweet Home* (*Suīto hōmu*, 1989). Kurosawa states:

This was a different type of horror movie, a very different expression of horror than *Sweet Home*. This series had a great impact on me, in how they showed a new way of creating fear in the audience.... For me it was a change in the way I worked.

(Kurosawa 2013)

Kurosawa honed his own style of horror films mainly on television productions during the mid-1990s, such as the *Haunted School* series (*Gakkō no kaidan*, beginning 1994), while simultaneously directing yakuza and action films for the V-Cinema market, including the *Suit Yourself or Shoot Yourself* series (*Katte ni shiyagare!!*, 1995–1996). His 1997 horror film *Cure* (*Kyua*), made as a middle-tier V-Cinema derived release for Daiei, became Kurosawa's breakthrough film. It displayed many stylistic elements associated with J-Horror and *Scary True Stories*.

Conclusion

V-Cinema, the production of feature films destined primarily for the video market, gave the ailing Japanese film industry a new source of revenue.

Countering the decades-long decline in production, it allowed for the mass production of low-budget films in popular genres. Comparable to the "program pictures" of several decades earlier, V-Cinema's industriousness became a breeding ground for new talent. A number of directors, including Miike Takashi and Kurosawa Kiyoshi, have developed into internationally lauded filmmakers, appreciated for their creativity and originality. These filmmakers challenge the accepted, limited canon of auteur filmmakers from Japan as established abroad. V-Cinema's unique set of production circumstances directly impacted filmmakers' formal choices, which had a strong creative influence beyond the confines of the V-Cinema industry and led, for example, to the international genre film phenomenon later dubbed "J-Horror."

Note

1 The first English language study of Japanese cinema, Anderson and Richie's tome set many of the parameters through which Japanese cinema has been studied, explained, and screened—in short, canonized—for the following decades.

PART VII
Anime

21 Apocalyptic Animation

In the Wake of Hiroshima, Nagasaki, *Godzilla*, and Baudrillard[1]

Alan Cholodenko

Jean Baudrillard (1929–2007) is not only a thinker of animation—of the at once life and motion of people and things, subjects and objects, the mass and the media (including film), thought and the world—and of the *animatic* processes—processes of Seduction, Illusion, Evil, radical irreconcilability, reversibility—in which they are caught, but an *animatic* thinker of them, which means his work not only fictions but performs, not only reanimates but seduces. Of course, this means that all that I say about and after Baudrillard is likewise fictional and performative.

This essay, like my "'OBJECTS IN MIRROR ARE CLOSER THAN THEY APPEAR': The Virtual Reality of *Jurassic Park* and Jean Baudrillard" (Cholodenko 1997), takes up a place in my ongoing project of theorizing film and animation, indeed film as a form of animation, after Baudrillard, and vice versa. It focuses on one of the major modes of animation—apocalyptic anime, the post-World War II animation of Japan. Apocalyptic anime is in the wake of The Bomb, in the wake of Hiroshima, Nagasaki, and, as well for us, *Godzilla*. I will consider anime's most astonishing example to date—*Akira* (Ōtomo Katsuhiro, 1988), which not only put anime on the map in the West but exploded onto the West, in the process "devastating" not only the West but that map. And I shall elucidate its extreme nature and processes, in the wake of, Baudrillard.

Here a further reason surfaces for interrogating anime and *Akira* through the work of Baudrillard, and vice versa. Baudrillard has addressed not only the subjects of the Apocalypse and The Bomb but also that of post-World War II Japan, including in terms of the global, universal, and singular. For us, Baudrillard's work offers a singular take on and performance of the *animatic* processes at play not only *in* film animation but *of* film animation, not only *in* the world but *of* the world, and at play between and across them—in this context, the extreme processes at play—the hypertelic, viral, paroxystic—not only within post-World War II Japanese film animation and American film animation but between them, at play not only within post-World War II Japan and America but between them, and at play across them. The radical, inextricable co-implication, short-circuit and implosion of film and reality for Baudrillard—for us, film and world, too—results in an increasingly definitive lack of differentiation between film animation and nation animation—this, too, the play of the *animatic*.

It is a classic humanist and media cliché to say that the war—World War II—ended in 1945. This is just too easy. In *On War*, Carl von Clausewitz says, "War is merely the continuation of policy [politics] by other means" (Clausewitz 1984 [1976]: 87). I would say that politics, economics, science, and technology can be the continuation of war by other means. The Japanese "economic miracle" can be, and obviously has been, so thought by many in Japan and abroad. For example, Frederik L. Schodt writes how Professor Takemochi Ishii claimed that the roots of Japanese postwar progress lay

> not only in political changes but in the fact that Japan was overwhelmed by being a guinea pig for Western military technology. "World War II was technological competition between nations," he [Professor Ishii] writes, "like that between corporations today. Japan, which had not even fully mastered the mass production of automobiles, never had a chance." The result was a bloody lesson, pounded into the brains of every man, woman, and child.
>
> (Schodt 1988: 77)

Ishii here acknowledges Japan, Inc.'s connection to and continuation of war in its global campaign for technological supremacy.

My point here is a corollary. Japanese cinema and anime can also be thought as the continuation of war by other means.

In *The Evil Demon of Images*, Jean Baudrillard writes of Francis Ford Coppola's *Apocalypse Now*, "War becomes film, film becomes war, the two united by their mutual overflow of technology" (Baudrillard 1987: 17). Baudrillard states that cinema, television, media images are the continuation of war by other means. This would, of course, include the cartoon, include animation. I propose that anime, as a form of hypercinema, of hyperanimation, is also a continuation of (that) war by other means, or rather, given the hyperreal pure and empty form of both anime and war today, is precisely the continuation of the absence of (that) war by other means—what might be called a war game in virtual form, a virtual war game, a game of virtual war, even as such hyperwar is a continuation of hypercinema, of hyperanimation. But not solely. As we shall see, after Baudrillard, the game is not over.

It is arguable that apocalyptic anime—anime in the wake of The Bomb—in general and *Akira* in particular have a major precursor in *Godzilla* (*Gojira*, 1954), the first Japanese monster film (see Chapter 18). *Godzilla* is about a prehistoric creature reanimated and irradiated by American nuclear bomb testing who in turn irradiates and otherwise lays waste to Tokyo until "destroyed." Stuart Galbraith (1998: 23) quotes *Godzilla* director Ishirō Honda on what inspired his work: "when I returned from the war and passed through Hiroshima, there was a heavy atmosphere—a fear the earth was already coming to an end. That became the basis for the film."

I agree with Susan Napier (1993) and Freda Freiberg (1996), who consider that *Godzilla* is a precedent for *Akira*—for Freiberg not only because *Akira* also inscribes the war, Hiroshima, The Bomb, the U.S. Occupation, but because *Akira* was only the second Japanese film to break into the Western mass entertainment market, the first being *Godzilla*. This latter reason can also be read as an aspect of war.

Of *Godzilla*, Galbraith states: "Through the character [of Godzilla], Honda sought to, in his words, 'make radiation visual'" (Galbraith 1998: 23). He made Godzilla a symbol of the Atomic Bomb (see also Freiberg 1996 and Noriega 1996). And for Chon Noriega, Godzilla is more. It is a hybrid creature, representing not only the United States but Japan, a Japan, writes Noriega, "as transitional monster caught between the imperial past and the postwar industrial future" (62), in other words, a hybrid within a hybrid, a monstrous doubling. And in my view, it is more again, as we shall see.

What of the "place" of *Akira* and anime in film animation "history"? Philip Brophy (1991) contrasts the symphonic character of Disney with the cacophonic nature of Warner Bros., describing how, as opposed to Disney animation, Warner Bros. animation is about speed, technology, violence, and war. He especially cites the Road Runner movies of Chuck Jones as examples.

What for Brophy is classical Disney animation and modernist Warner Bros. animation is superseded by "postmodernist" animation—anime. The cute of Disney animation is exceeded/superseded by the hypercute of anime, even as the speed, violence, and war of Warner Bros. cartoons is exceeded/superceded by the hyperspeed, hyperviolence, and hyperwar of anime. In this regard, it is highly significant that Brophy, in his paper "Sonic—Atomic—Neumonic: Apocalyptic Echoes in Anime" (1995), focuses on *Akira* more than any other anime.

Both Napier and Freiberg describe *Akira* as postmodernist. For Napier (1993: 329, 344), *Akira*'s image "of social, material, and… spiritual collapse"—of the corruption of all forms of authority and authenticity—is *unrelentingly* dark, "nihilistic," postmodernist, offering, rather than a moral center, a "dystopian center," for me, a black hole.

But here let me pause to describe the plot of *Akira*. *Akira* begins on July 16, 1988, as World War III begins, with the unleashing of The Bomb on Tokyo. After flashing its title, the film jumps from the crater—the black hole—of what was Tokyo to Neo-Tokyo 2019—2019 is the same year in which *Blade Runner* is set—a Neo-Tokyo very reminiscent of the dystopian Los Angeles of *Blade Runner*. Here, we find a *mise-en-obscène* of civil and millennial chaos, with delinquents in biker gangs warring with each other, with revolutionary terrorists and religious sects also running riot, with civil government, run by corrupt and stupid politicians, collapsed, with the military going to war against the police. All the while, an enigmatic army Colonel charged with state security is inexplicably involved with scientists who are continuing their secret medical experiments with esper mutants—espers are those possessed of telekinetic powers—in the quest, it seems, to acquire the power over and of pure energy, to unlock the memory of, and harness, the life force animating the universe "even before the beginning of time," says Kyoko, an esper mutant, through Kai, a revolutionary, a force animistically resident in "all things in existence," even in an esper's aura.

In this setting appears Tetsuo, a young, short, small biker delinquent plagued with feelings of insecurity and hostility, and his friend Kaneda, who plays the role of big brother to him, but at the same time, like the other bikies, tends to patronize him. It is when Tetsuo encounters the mutant Takashi, who is trying to escape the experimental hospital with the help of a terrorist, that the plot kicks into hyperaction, for Tetsuo is taken back to the hospital with Takashi; and there Tetsuo is tested, the results suggesting that he has powers that resemble those of Akira, who reached the limit stage of their experiments and was in some way responsible, with his psychic powers, for triggering World War III. Given Tetsuo's sociopathic nature—the association with Dr. Frankenstein's creature from the 1931 film, as well as Dr. Strangelove, will be made—and the experiments upon him, the increasing psychic powers he acquires push him to an extreme, unstable, chain-reactive, runaway state, a delirous, psychopathic condition, against which Takashi and his two mutant allies—Kyoko and Masaru—rally to try to control him, to get him to try to control himself.

But Tetsuo is at once increasingly in control, controlling, and at the same time increasingly out of control, uncontrollable, experiencing more and more paroxysms of mind and body, sending him in search of Akira—to challenge him to a duel to see who has superior power—and sending him to a face-off with the army, Tetsuo even ascending to the Sol satellite weapon being directed against him from its orbit above Japan and destroying it. And then, inside the Olympic Stadium, he undergoes a sequence of mutations, from one where his blown-off right arm is replaced with a prosthetic, cyborg one, recalling that of *Terminator*'s T-101, which then turns organic, to one where his entire body becomes a mass of uncontrollably proliferating tissue that reaches gigantic size and swallows up not only Tetsuo's girlfriend Kaori but Tetsuo himself, that is, until Akira now reanimated—"called back" and "released" by the mutants to take Tetsuo away—returns as pure energy Bomb and, in turn, swallows up and metamorphoses Tetsuo, as well as the mutants. The mutant Kyoko declared this Tetsuo becoming the latest member of the family! In what the head scientist pronounces as "like a cosmic rebirth," the Akira Bomb (A Bomb!) again lays waste to much of the city; but Kaneda, the female revolutionary Kai, and the Colonel somehow escape to see another day. As the film "ends," another ambivalent, indeterminate, radically uncertain cycle in the life of Japan—of *Neo* Neo-Tokyo—is begun.

One could say, after Brophy, that *Akira* is perhaps the strongest, most extreme example of how anime is *itself* an extreme form/"event"/phenomenon, the unleashing, liberating, of extreme energy, of explosive and implosive atomic, nuclear (and psychic) energy, animation that explodes and implodes, including exploding and imploding animation itself, exploding and imploding American animation, including Disney animation, as well as itself. In its "constant bombardment and battering of the senses, [its] barrage of high intensity experiences...its stunning spectacles of violence and destruction"— Freiberg's characterizations (1996: 95), full of terms of war—*Akira* is literally a visceral (or should I say evisceral), gut-wrenching, mind-blowing, mind-boggling experience, *and technological weapon* of hyperspeed, hyperviolence, and hyperwar.

So anime can be thought to be at war, continuing Japan's World War— at war with American animation, at war with America. If one thinks of the nucleus of the atom as a figure of cohesion, coherence, and unity, its fission-explosion—and/or fusion-implosion—equate to a loss or absence of cohesion, coherence, unity, and interiority, which is played out in anime in all its various modes of narrative, characterization, *mise-en-scène*, simulated camera work, editing relations, light, sound, line, etc. That loss or absence of nucleus can be thought of as that postmodernist "dystopian center"—that black hole, that void, empty nucleus (*noyau*) of the nuclear, around which everything happens, everything turns—that Napier finds at the "core" of *Akira*, figured topographically in the black crater that was Tokyo.

One could call *Akira* an irradiated, irradiating, atomized, enucleated animation, one not only participating in and conducting a war but exhibiting the effects of one, a war not only of but on image and sound. A war at once "external" and "internal." Also, one could say that the organic metabolism of anime is irradiated, and its operations are irradiating, cancerous, viral, "out of control," running riot, like Tetsuo's hyperproliferating body at the end of the film. Anime at once materializes the immaterial energies and immaterializes the material forms, including itself, exhibiting, and performing, a nuclear and biological war, a war of and on the nucleus of both the atom and the cell.

After Baudrillard, it might be said that Hiroshima and Nagasaki are the apocalypse of the Apocalypse, the end of the End, and that they will never come because they already have and do so repeatedly, endlessly, in our daily lives, not as actual Apocalypse, actual End, but as virtual ones, and that *Akira*, like Japan "itself," is a limit case of it. Such would be our "Apocalypse Now," our holocaust, a virtual, simulacral one.

Such an apocalypse is associated for Baudrillard with the hyperreal, the advent of which he perennially describes with reference to Elias Canetti's words:

A tormenting thought: as of a certain point, history was no longer *real*. Without noticing it, all mankind suddenly left reality; everything happening since then was supposedly not true; but we supposedly didn't notice. Our task would now be to find that point, and as long as we didn't have it, we would be forced to abide in our present destruction.

(Canetti 1985: 69)

These words appear in the tellingly entitled "August 1945" subsection of Canetti's chapter "1945" in *The Human Province*. Soon after, he states: "the atomic bomb has become the measure of all things" (67). Without being explicit on the point (!), Canetti seems thereby to associate the point of (and) passage beyond reality with The Bomb. Its dropping on ground zero at Hiroshima, irradiating and enucleating not only Japan but the world, instituted that dead point, blind spot, vanishing point, black hole as void nucleus (*noyau*), a point for Baudrillard thereafter impossible "as such" to locate.

In *The Evil Demon of Images* (1987), Baudrillard characterizes World War II by two events—The Bomb and the Holocaust (the extermination of six million European Jews by the Nazis)—through which the world passed beyond the horizon of the real into hyperreality. *Webster's Dictionary's* definition of holocaust is from the Greek *holokaustos*, burnt whole, from *kaiein*, to burn: (1) an offering the whole of which is burned; burnt offering; (2) complete destruction of people or animals by fire [fire as agency of genocide, etc.]; (3) great or widespread destruction. By the concatenation of these definitions, Hiroshima and Nagasaki are holocausts, too. The Bomb is symbol also of holocaust. Godzilla and Akira—films and characters—are, too.

Significantly, after treating of *Apocalypse Now*, including characterizing it as "a holocaust of means" (Baudrillard 1987: 17)—which means a film can be a holocaust—Baudrillard immediately contrasts *The China Syndrome* and The Bomb with *Holocaust* the televised event and Holocaust the historical event. For Baudrillard, The Bomb is the last great event of hot, explosive systems. The Holocaust is the first great event of cold, implosive systems. And the media, including film but especially television, are for him part and parcel of the apocalypse, The Bomb and the Holocaust, sites of both modes of nuclear destruction—explosion (fission) and implosion (fusion)—but especially and increasingly post-World War II of the latter, sites of the implosion, the denegation, of meaning, truth, reality through their hyperrealizing, their virtualizing. The "telefission of the real" (19).

In anime—animation of the apocalypse and apocalypse of animation—animation becomes hyperanimation—the pure and empty, virtual apocalyptic and holocaustal form of animation, for which *Akira* is exemplary. As hyperanimation, animation at once more and less animation than animation, *Akira* metamorphoses/reanimates American cartoon animation, including metamorphosing/reanimating Disney cute into hypercute (*kawaii*), most notably in what is arguably the most horrifying sequence in the film, when Tetsuo is attacked by the cute toys. Insofar as the theme of the film is metamorphosis/reanimation, insofar as it presents itself as between two apocalypses, thereby suggesting it *itself* is never not in a process of apocalyptic metamorphosis/reanimation, insofar as it is never not allegorizing, dramatizing and performing the cyclical, spiraling, spherical processes of at once *re*death and rebirth from its "beginning" apocalypse to its "ending" apocalypse, from The Bomb at its "beginning" to The Bomb at its "ending," *Akira* presents us with an anime whose theme, content, plot, characterizations, and narrative of reanimation are conjoined with a style, structure, and form marked by reanimation in a mode which is itself that of reanimation—anime. Here, we find the same extreme processes of the explosive and the implosive at work that I spoke of after Baudrillard earlier, processes associated with the chain-reactive life of postnuclear atomic image/sound energies of micro-cosmic and macro-cosmic character that pervade all that Brophy highlights in anime, most of all in *Akira*.

Even as its theme and form are fractalized as reanimation, *Akira* is an event, a performing, of reanimation. Insofar as the day the film performs the apocalypse on Japan—its epicenter Tokyo—was the very day it premiered there—July 16, 1988, the date of the beginning of World War III (Napier 1993: 336, n. 17) and crucially the forty-third anniversary of the U.S. test explosion of the first nuclear bomb at Trinity Site in New Mexico that inaugurated "the nuclear age" and spelled the defeat of Japan in World War II by its avatars "Little Boy" (!) and "Fat Man" that were dropped on Hiroshima and Nagasaki, respectively—and did so within seconds of its "beginning," *Akira* sees itself not only as an allegory of the apocalypse but as an agency of it. As a weapon of war! As a bomb! As The Bomb!—Trinity Site bomb included. The Bomb not only whose target sur-vives (*survivre*)—lives on—in its wake, through the target's "own" metamorphosis/reanimation, but that sur-vives—lives on—in the wake of itself, through its "own" metamorphosis/reanimation. And not only is the viewer the witness to these processes, it itself "re-dies" and is "reborn," to live on in the wake of itself, through its "own" metamorphosis/reanimation, like the film, like Tetsuo. With *Akira*—the convulsive, paroxystic, seismic events imaged within it as well as on and of it—we are witness to the process of the ecstatic—the pushing of things, including animation, to their limit, to their pure and empty form—even as we are witness therein to the postnuclear, post-apocalyptic, postmodern, metastatic form of the life and motion—the "animation"—of energies, exemplified best in the Sergei Eisenstein (1988: 21) protean *plasmatic, animatic* character that in its metastatic form Tetsuo comes to assume in the climactic sequence at the stadium (Cholodenko 2000b: 10). "Deprived" of its "essence" as of its "cause," "animation" functions all the better in its hyperreal, hyperproliferative, hyperviolent, hypersaturated, hypertrophic, atrophic, enucleated, irradiated, irradiating, cancerous, viral, paroxystic form of "the life, moving of itself, of that which is dead" (Baudrillard quoting Hegel, in Baudrillard 1993: 108), of lifedeath—that obese, obscene, terrorist form that is anime. That is *Akira*. That is Tetsuo.

As hyperreal hypercartoon, the pure and empty form of the cartoon, *Akira* takes cartoon animation to its limits, annihilating it. But it does more than that. It takes live action there, too, for it issues a challenge to live action, saying it is more live action than live action. In this sense, it could be said that *Akira* is more *Godzilla* than *Godzilla*.

In fact, at several points I could not tell if I was watching cartoon animation or live action, such are the powers of its animation to simulate live action, to hyperconform to it, seducing it, making it enter the realm of metamorphosis despite itself, even as it simulates and seduces American cartoon animation. Such are the powers of apocalyptic anime in general and *Akira* in particular.

Here we arrive at a crucial turning point, exemplary of many in and of (the) film, for such powers accord not only with the hypertelic, ecstatic process but with the turn—the reversion—of Seduction, for Baudrillard game of challenge (agonistics) and outbidding, of duel, defiance and leading astray, of reversibility—the hallmark of a world of metamorphosis and myth, illusion and the immaterial, the rule and the dual, magic, dance and theater—that power that is not only animating but of the order of the *animatic*.

Moreover, such an ironical, paradoxical, strange turn accords with the simulative and seductive powers of "post-historical" "snobbish" Japan, as Alexandre Kojève called it (1980 [1969])—a "snobbishness" that would be a strategy of artifice, of affectation, of exacerbation, of pure formalism, of pure and empty form—Japan seducing America through challenge, defiance, and outbidding, through simulating, hyperconforming to and ecstasizing America, imitating America better than America imitates itself, at the same time preserving, by means of this game, this play, its own distance, its own radical foreignness, "Radical Exoticism"—as Baudrillard conceptualizes such exoticism after Victor Segalen in the nineteenth century.

Drawing his image of Japan from Kojève, Segalen and as well Roland Barthes (1982 [1966])—who filmically visioned Japan as the graphic empire of pure and empty forms and signs and Tokyo (notably for *Akira*) as a place without a center—Baudrillard offers his own evil demonesque filmic vision, his own *animatic* vision, which models and mirrors what for him is the "model other" (Baudrillard 1994a: 136) that is Japan, which we see in and with anime in general and *Akira* in particular.

For Baudrillard, Japan offers what I propose Akira offers Tetsuo and anime and *Akira* offer the viewer—a "lethal hospitality" (Baudrillard 1993: 143)—at once a hostile hospitality and a hospitable hostility. At once host and terrorist, Japan—what Baudrillard might call the evil demon of nations—takes hostage, miming, absorbing, devouring, assimilating, integrating, incorporating—I'm reminded here of the highly loaded (!) term "Japan, Inc."! —its guest/enemy and its powers, while at the same time neutralizing—"defusing" (!)—them, doing so, I suggest, even to The Bomb, Japan becoming at once more The Bomb than The Bomb and less The Bomb than The Bomb. Japan turns its hostage to its own logics, strategies, advantage, even as it has turned that catastrophe to non-catastrophe, that apocalypse to nothing.

And in terms of the global, the universal and the singular, for Baudrillard, Japan is a singular example of the singular, not only "as such" but insofar as it has "succeeded in globalizing (technologically, economically, financially) better than the whole world *without passing through the universal* (the succession of bourgeois ideologies and of forms of political economy) and without losing anything of its singularity, whatever one might say of it" (Baudrillard 1997: 177).

Diverting and evading Western universality, Japan for Baudrillard offers its cannibalistic, murderous hospitality to globalization, absorbing, incorporating, ecstasizing, and seducing American capital, technology, and modernism, thereby paradoxically, strangely returning (*un retour étrange*) (175) "itself"—"post-historical" Japan—to "itself"—Japan "as such"—thus preserving "its" radical foreignness, "its" singularity, the virtual of the third and fourth orders absorbed by, strangely turning into, the ritual, the ceremonial, of the first order, and what enables it—the unconditional simulacrum, pure Illusion, Seduction, Evil—the cruel, savage power of the sign—the pure sign—to erupt.

For us, *Akira* allegorizes, stages and performs Baudrillard's visions of "hospitable" and singular Japan, turning Tetsuo's straight line to the virtual into a *détour* that is a *retour* to the singular, a *turning away from* that is at the same time *a turning toward* what it always was, an ironic turning toward Seduction, Illusion, Evil, Radical Exoticism. Which is what Japan, anime, *Akira* do for America, virtual reality, globalization, capital. The point—dead point, blind spot, vanishing point—of the turn turns (on) itself. And Seduction is the turn.

Such seductive processes operate decisively in *Akira*'s narrative, where Akira, as more and less The Bomb than The Bomb, is reanimated not only by the mutants but arguably by Tetsuo, by his actions as form of destiny, and ironically returns to swell and swallow the swelling and swallowing Tetsuo, incorporating, metamorphosing, and reanimating him in his void nucleus (*noyau*), his nothing, even in his "nuclear family" (!)—a cannibalistic allegory and performance of Japan swallowing, incorporating, and reanimating America in "itself," its void, its nothing. Japan, as Baudrillard speaks of it, as phagocyte (1994a: 72). As Pac Man.

The double game of Japan, apocalyptic anime and *Akira* is akin to the fatal strategy of conformity, of seduction, of Leonard Zelig and the film *Zelig* (Woody Allen, dir., 1983) as Baudrillard (1987: 15) treats of them in *The Evil Demon of Images*: "To begin to resemble the other, to take on their appearance, is to seduce them, since it is to make them enter the realm of metamorphosis despite themselves." Zelig is "launched on an adventure of…global seduction"—making it—the global—enter the realm of metamorphosis despite itself—in that process hyperconforming to and leading astray all interpretations, by means of which the Radical Otherness—the singularity—of Zelig—and of Japan, apocalyptic anime and *Akira*—its/their "eternal incomprehensibility" (Segalen quoted in Baudrillard 1994a: 95)—are safeguarded. I would add, such a seduction characterizes the seduction of film animation and the world by the snobbish *animatic* apparatus of film animation "itself"— apparatus of not only the illusion of life (simulation) but the life of illusion (Seduction).

Avatar of Godzilla—character and film—Akira—character and film—is (figure of) The Bomb, at once more and less The Bomb than The Bomb, that explodes/implodes both America and Japan, even as it revivifies/reanimates them, even as Tetsuo, the monster-on-the-loose avatar of Godzilla and

Akira, takes up his nuclear-powered, chain-reactive, absorbing place within that lineage, donning a red cape to complete the highly loaded tricolor—red, white, and blue—in that process metamorphosing not only "himself" but the returned/reanimated/absorbing Akira become "savior" into something "eternally incomprehensible," enigmatic, Radically Other, around which everything turns—that inexchangeable nothing that, like Eisenstein's *plasmaticness*, at once enables and disenables all exchange, while itself being beyond value—that void, empty nucleus (*noyau*)—dead point, blind spot, black hole—not only (at the "center") of *Akira*, not only of the nuclear Bomb, not only of the nuclear "as such," not only of the/its/their animating of the point of (and) passage beyond reality for Canetti but of Japan "itself."

For us, analogous to Tetsuo, and to Akira vis-à-vis Tetsuo, Japan swallows, incorporates, gives its lethal hospitality to, makes a new "member of the family" of, the *noyau* (nucleus) of The Bomb (that war technology made by America and first tested at Trinity Site, July 16, 1945)—The Bomb itself for Canetti having become the measure of all things—the *noyau* of the/its animating of the point of (and) passage beyond reality for Canetti and the *noyau* of "post-historical" Japan in its "own" *noyau*, as it incorporates as well America, globalization and the West in "itself." Indeed, Japan is for us also "avatar" of the nuclear "in itself," as well as of the Big Bang and the Big Crunch.

Baudrillard writes of this *zone vide* at the "core" of Japanese civilization, around which things finally organize themselves:

> For Japan, one does not draw a conclusion; but one can see in spite of everything that, even at the summit of a technological, contemporary civilization, there remains nevertheless a sort of nucleus [*noyau*] absolutely blind or void, which corresponds to that which Barthes described as the "void of the signifier."
>
> (Baudrillard, 1994a: 95)

For us, Japan "itself" is dead point, blind spot, black hole—empire of the void, we would call "it"—subsuming all into "it," fatal even to "itself." Insofar as for Baudrillard Japan directly associates the point of (and) passage to hyperreality, virtuality, and globalization with its singularity, with its power of ritual (Baudrillard 1997: 177)—and agonistics and the duel are features of the first order—I propose that that could not but include the associating of Japan, Inc. with The Way of the Samurai (*Bushidō*)—what Inazo Nitobe, in 1905, called "the animating spirit, the motor force of our country" (Nitobe 1969: 171).

For Baudrillard (1996: 2), not only is Japan eternally incomprehensible void, empty, blind nucleus (*noyau*), so, too, is America, of which Zelig, and Andy Warhol, are exemplary. For America as well is singular. And so, too, is that passage between, where the radical significance of Japan rejoins the radical insignificance of America (Baudrillard 1994a: 101)—two absences in "communication," in impossible exchange, we would say, with each other, each offering the other a viral hospitality, each at once completely symbiotic and completely incompatible with the other, forming a Moebius strip, a radical inextricable co-implication, a complicity, a knot that cannot be disentangled—each at once friend and foe, model and mirror—to paraphrase Schodt's book *America and The Four Japans: Friend, Foe, Model, Mirror* (1994)—but after Baudrillard equally *Japan and The Four Americas*...(!)—but where these nations and terms are not only inextricably entangled, exchanging with, reversing/returning on, each other—a friendly foe and foeish friend, a model mirror and mirror model—but where each nation and term is at the same time potentializing on its own, so that at the same time as there is hyperexchanging, there is hypernonexchanging, the virtual conditional form of ritual unconditional impossible exchange—defeating Schodt's hopes for a yin/yang reconciliation of Japan and America. And making of Canetti's "the atomic bomb has become the measure of all things" a measure beyond measure. Japan and America—marvelous indistinguishability!

Insofar as for Baudrillard singularities lie beyond measure, cannot be deciphered, understood or reconciled—to themselves or to each other—so Japan, anime, *Akira*, America, Zelig, Warhol, *plasmaticness*, the *animatic*, the objective irony of science and technology cannot be.

Such are the reanimating processes for us not only at work *in* animation, in anime, for which *Akira* is exemplary, but the work *of* animation, of anime, including reanimating nations and their relations. As Tetsuo/America reanimate/metamorphose/seduce Akira/Japan, Akira/Japan at the same time reanimate/metamorphose/seduce Tetsuo/America, absorbing them into its/their game.

Akira and Tetsuo, like Japan and America, are the destiny of the other. Together, Akira—character and film—and Tetsuo *demon*strate, through anime, that irresolvable, irreconcilable, fatal, singular monster that is what I call jap*anime*rica—a hyperhybrid, protean *plasmatic*, *animatic* monster arguably cryptically incorporated "in" (at the void nucleus of) each and every film animation, country, culture, and institution ("nuclear family" as much as national film animation industry)—even Disneyworld Company—"in" (at the void nucleus of) each and every individual—even the hero of cryogenics, of suspended animation, Walt Disney "himself"—and "in" (at the void nucleus of) the passage between each and every element of this constellation.

Which is to say, not only is it the case that "OBJECTS IN MIRROR ARE CLOSER THAN THEY APPEAR," peoples, nations, institutions, and individuals—in their relation to themselves and to each other—are, too, exacting their revenge—the revenge of the mirror people—for which *animatic* Japan and America offer singular example. To paraphrase: "PEOPLE IN MIRROR ARE CLOSER THAN THEY APPEAR."

And the fatal/object theorist is, too. As with (his challenge to and impossible exchange with) Japan and America, Baudrillard issues a singular challenge to world, to thought, to be more, in that very seduction provoking radical uncertainty as to whether he lies in their wake or they in his. Is

Japan hyperconforming to him or he to Japan? And what of me? Marvelous indistinguishability!

In the seductive, fatal, snobbish, *animatic*, singular world of Jean Baudrillard, strange returns spiral around a point, a spot, a void, a sphere, like spiral nebulae around a black hole, appearing to disappear in a singularity.

"FATAL/OBJECT THEORIST IN MIRROR IS CLOSER THAN HE APPEARS."

Note

1 A longer version of this chapter appeared in *Baudrillard West of the Dateline*, edited by Victoria Grace, Heather Worth, and Laurence Simmons, 228–244 (Dunmore Press 2003), and *International Journal of Baudrillard Studies* 11(2): n.p.

22 Toy Stories

Robots and Magical Girls in Anime Marketing

Renato Rivera Rusca

Introduction

Since the 1960s, Japanese television animation has been governed by paradigms formed through relationships in the anime industry. Two genres that best represent the existence of pervasive paradigms have relied on the sale of toys: the "robot" genre (*robotto anime*), featuring giant humanoid fighting machines usually controlled by young male pilots, and the "magical girl" genre (*mahō shōjo anime*), depicting the adventures of pre-pubescent girls with magical powers. The simple, remote-controlled robot from the first robot series, *Tetsujin 28-gou* (*Tetsujin nijūhachi-gō*, 1963–1966, hereafter referred to as *Gigantor*, its U.S. title), became the prototype for complex super-machines in series like *Voltes V* (*Chōdenji mashiin Borutesu Faibu*, 1977–1978) and *Super Dimension Fortress Macross* (*Chōjikū yōsai Makurosu*, 1982–1983, hereafter referred to as *Macross*, which aired in the United States as part of *Robotech*). The magical mirror from *The Secret of Akko-chan* (*Himitsu no Akko-chan*, 1969–1970) evolved into the Minky Stick from *Fairy Princess Minky Momo* (*Mahō no purinsesu Minkī Momo*, 1982–1983, hereafter referred to as *Minky Momo*). However, by the mid-1980s, these accouterments were no longer necessary, although their legacy remained apparent.

I argue that the continued existence of the magical girl and robot genres has been possible because of the reliance on industry frameworks established through the evolving relationship among anime creators, commercial sponsors, and television networks. I will explain how this relationship imposed "opportunistic restrictions" on creators during the "golden age" of television anime, from the 1970s through early 1980s, until paradigm shifts initiated by Original Video Animation (OVA) in the mid-1980s. The dynamics of robot and magical girl genres provided for intellectual property to be reproduced across the "media mix," the marketing of franchises through various commercial formats that characterizes the anime industry (see Chapter 23).

Sponsorship Frameworks in Early Television Anime

Tezuka Osamu's *Astro Boy* (*Tetsuwan Atomu*, 1963–1966) established conventions of weekly television animation series; it was based on a popular manga begun in 1952 and the first Japanese anime to be broadcast abroad. *Astro Boy* involved a tight working relationship between Tezuka's Mushi Productions, broadcaster Fuji Television, and sponsor Meiji Seika confectionery and pharmaceutical company, often with an advertising agency managing this arrangement. The advertising agency bought broadcast time from the network and organized sponsorship deals. That dynamic was in its early stages and sponsors did not exert much creative control, as was apparent from the content of the episodes. Meiji Seika products sometimes appeared in *Astro Boy* as a form of tongue-in-cheek product placement but did not affect the narrative (Steinberg 2012: 37–39). In fact, most early television anime were sponsored by food companies. To name a few other examples, *Ken the Wolf Boy* (*Ōkami Shōnen Ken*, 1963), the first made-for-television anime series not based on a previously existing work, was sponsored by the Morinaga confectionery company and *8-Man* (*Eitoman*, 1963–1964) by Marumiya Foods. The opening theme song of *Tetsujin No. 28* repeated the name of its sponsor Glico.

From the mid-1970s to the 1980s, toy companies became the main sponsors, and narratives shifted to those that required accoutrements. The once numerous anime series based on classic children's literature, like *A Dog of Flanders* (*Furandaazu no inu*, 1975) and *Heidi, Girl of the Alps* (*Arupusu no shōjo Haiji*, 1974), both sponsored by Calpis beverages, became the minority. They were replaced with series that could sell robots, dolls, and accessories, thus constructing a rigid template for age and gender targeted audience anime.

Itano Ichirō, the action animator who revolutionized high-speed sequences in robot anime, contrasts the relationship between content and merchandising of the 1970s with that of the 1990s. He argues that, in the past, sponsors like Calpis were primarily concerned about promoting a positive corporate image, but toy companies wanted designs that would sell:

> During the 1970s anime boom, *Heidi, Girl of the Alps* was running against *Space Battleship Yamato*. But you would never hear Heidi say, "Calpis tastes better than milk," right? I think Heidi's sponsor was proud just to have invested in such a good show. Their philosophy was to invest in a show that is positive for children and then hope that when the children grow up, they will look back at the show and somehow reciprocate to the company. Now it's more like, they invest to 'avoid going into the red this season,' and they don't think twice about copying whatever other show is currently successful.
>
> (Futabasha 2008: 94–97)

To illustrate the major change in attitudes towards anime sponsorship that occurred in the early 1980s it is helpful to compare the 1963 and 1980 incarnations of *Gigantor*. Often credited as the first "giant robot" in Japanese manga and anime, the original anime series' tie-in merchandising strategy was mostly comprised of collectable ink stamps, felt badges, and simple fixed-pose mini figures, all included as bonuses in packets of chocolate and gum. Other bonuses included "sono-sheets" (vinyl records for children) that featured songs on Side A and audio drama on Side B. As anime viewers increased in age, sono-sheets were replaced by soundtracks. This can be seen as a precursor of the "anime song" ("*anison*") industry, an integral to Japan's music market and anime merchandising.

Starting with *Mazinger Z* (*Majingā Zetto*, 1972–1974), the giant robot craze kicked into high gear, and sponsorship shifted from confectionery companies to toy companies. Looking at the evolution of the robot genre from *Mazinger Z* through *Combattler V* (*Chōdenji robo Konbatorā V*, 1976–1977), *Voltes V*, *Mobile Suit Gundam* (*Kidō senshi Gandamu*, 1979–1980, hereafter referred to as *Gundam*), and *Macross*, it is clear that the robots become increasingly complex, with more pieces combining and transforming, or splitting into smaller vehicles, thus potentially making a toy that was more fun than a simple one-mode action figure. This also helped to ease the transition from "super robots" to the more realistic, military weapon-styled "real robots" with dramatic storylines for older buyers of toys and model kits explained later in the chapter.

When presented with the plan to remake *Gigantor* in 1980, Murakami Katsushi, then an in-house toy designer at Popy (Bandai subsidiary founded in 1971 and merged back into its parent company in 1983), struggled with how to make a classic character appealing to viewers who had grown up with complicated robot designs and toys. *Gigantor* originally had no weapons, no alternate transformation modes, no vehicles to combine with, and was instead remote-controlled. Murakami created a sleek design that was approved by Yokoyama Mitsuteru, *Gigantor*'s original creator, and marketed as a high-end toy for Popy that helped the company become known for robot toys with ample die-metal content (known as "*chōkinzoku*"). The *Gigantor* model was an enormous figure of sheet steel with complex features, such as hatches to open and close, and a number of other gimmicks unheard of at the time. Its size and features put it in a different league from the "*chōgōkin*" (medium-size die-cast robot figures), "Jumbo Machinder" (large, hollow plastic figures with spring-loaded firing missiles), and other toy lines. Essentially, unlike the 1960s series, the 1980 show became a vehicle to sell this one toy. Subsequent robot series would likewise be formulated according to the desires of sponsors. Sponsors would first design the robots and then determine the storylines for them. The gradual shift toward more "realistic" robot stories, such as *Gundam*, is where we begin to see a struggle between the desires of the creators and the sponsors.

Growing Pains

Today we think of *Gundam* as a continual force in the creation of Japanese popular culture. A gigantic *Gundam* robot towered over the Diver City shopping mall in Odaiba in Tokyo Bay from 2012 until 2017, and a feature exhibit on the series was held in Tokyo's Mori Art Museum in 2015. Thus it is hard to believe that in 1979 the decision to cancel the show came from the sponsor, toy manufacturer Clover (in business from 1973 to 1983).[1]

The decision was partly due to co-creator Tomino Yoshiyuki's (b. 1941) insistence on realism and his refusal to use the gimmicks of the earlier 1970s like combining robot shows like *Voltes V* and *Combattler V*, which featured lengthy transforming and combination sequences before the all-powerful robot would deliver the final blow to the enemy. These sequences were banked and reused in several episodes. This trope was also prevalent in the *tokusatsu* "Super *Sentai*" (superhero team genre) television programs marketed squarely at children with toys being at the center of merchandising campaigns. *Gundam* was ahead of its time in that its creators wanted it to be taken seriously as a science fiction war drama, although sponsors and broadcasters insisted on marketing it to children. To this end, the settings were realistic and based on the designs for space habitats by Gerard O'Neill (1927–1992), NASA engineer and author of the bestselling 1976 book *The High Frontier: Human Colonies in Space.* Tomino took O'Neill's concepts of a near-future society one step further by acknowledging that conflicts would arise. In *Gundam*, the struggle between the Federation forces and the Principality of Zeon seems reminiscent of both World War II and George Lucas' *Star Wars* (opened in 1978 in Japan), thus creating a complex backstory that Clover felt was too difficult for children to follow. The *Gundam* robot design and its combination sequence were therefore somewhat incongruent with the otherwise realistic O'Neill settings.

Due to low ratings, the series was cancelled in 1980, but it was revived as a feature-length animated film thanks to the takeover of the license by Bandai, which profited from producing *Gundam* model kits. The model kits were targeted to an older audience and matched the show's content, thus propelling the *Gundam* franchise into the level of a cultural institution. In a 2013 interview, anime writer Hirota Keisuke revealed that, as a young viewer of *Gundam* in 1979, he and his friends were smart enough to know that low product sales meant that the series could be cancelled. He then tried to buy as many *Gundam* toys as he could to support the series, even though he found the first batch of products to be subpar.

This realistic trend of the late 1970s and early 1980s—a reflection of the gradual coming-of-age of the anime viewership—also meant a change of focus from "heroic" robots to robots as "weapons of war." This was a boon for toy companies thanks to the ease with which they could sell multiple variations of essentially the same toy. *Macross* is a good example, for the main robot, a transformable robot-plane known as the VF-1 Valkyrie, is the mainstay fighter of the futuristic military; this means that the same design could be used for all the main characters' robots, which were thus differentiated only by small differences such as livery colors. At the initial stage of the project, the goal of mechanical designers Kawamori Shōji (b. 1960) and Miyatake Kazutaka (b. 1949) was to bring their Studio Nue's design aesthetic and science fiction realism to a wider audience through the medium of animation.

Humanoid robots were not part of their original vision, which instead featured an ostrich-like machine with inverted knee joints. However, none of their potential sponsors was interested in a realistic space-age machine. It was humanoid robots or nothing—robot toys sell. Accordingly, Kawamori and Miyatake revised their plan and changed their proposal from a serious science fiction tale to something more lighthearted and parodic of *Space Battleship Yamato* and *Gundam*. Even then, their eventual sponsor, Takatoku Toys, was not pleased that the Valkyrie could transform into a fighter jet, for they were convinced that toy planes did not sell well. There was a generational rift between the younger employees at Takatoku who "understood" the show and the older management who banked on the main spaceship (the titular "Macross" space fortress) as the product to push (World Photo Press 2009: 35).

This "generation gap" reflects an important shift. As we have seen, the anime industry's dependence on marketable commodities was in a state of flux as the first generation of viewers was reaching adulthood and expecting anime stories to mature with them. This desire for more mature plots and characters was at odds with sponsors' target market of elementary school children. The sponsorship system and the framework requisites of anime series were starting to seem antiquated.

Marketing Magical Girls

Magical girl anime evolved in a similar way to robot anime. The U.S. sitcom *Bewitched* (1964–1972, broadcast in Japan 1966–1968) brought about a craze for magical witch-like female characters in Japan, as evident in such anime series as *Sally the Witch* (*Mahō-tsukai Sally*, 1966–1968) and *The Secret of Akko-chan*. Although simplistic, these anime, both produced by Toei Animation,[2] were extremely popular and established tropes that are still in effect. Toy companies helped propel the trend by producing replicas of the magical items that the characters used just as they did giant robots and their accouterments. For example, they sold toy replicas of the compact mirror Akko-chan uses to cast a spell and transform into anything she wishes. Later variations on this theme included magical wands and pendants; the basic template continues, as exemplified by the 2011 hit *Puella Magi Madoka Magica* (*Mahō shōjo Madoka Magika*).

A key turning point in the magical girl genre came with *Fairy Princess Minky Momo*, which premiered in 1982 at the peak of the "anime boom." *Minky Momo* producer Ōno Minoru explained that it was extraordinary for Ashi Productions to undertake a "magical girl" series, and they did so because the toy manufacturer Popy wanted to venture into this realm (Yōsensha 2011: 89).[3] *Minky Momo* director Yuyama Kunihiko stated that, rather than borrowing elements from the original Toei magical girl series, he set out to make something that the staff would enjoy working on. This was in spite of the fact that, according to main writer Shudō Takeshi, the sponsor told the production staff explicitly at a planning meeting that "*Sally the Witch* sold well, so just make it [*Minky Momo*] like one of those Toei magical girl shows" (Minori Shobō 1983: 65). In fact, Yuyama had seen only a few episodes from those older shows and was more influenced by U.S. programs like *Bewitched* (Yōsensha 2011: 70). The rest of the staff shared his attitude and wrote in motifs from their favorite movies, including *Dr. Strangelove*, the James Bond series, and *2001: A Space Odyssey*. As a result, the series seemed to feature a different genre each week, and almost anything in the plot seemed acceptable. The general theme was that Momo transformed into an adult version of herself, performing different occupations depending on the storyline.

Yuyama states that the first episodes were not as over-the-top as the later ones, and that the irreverent humor began after the eighth episode. At first, Momo used her powers to help other people. (The more people Momo, a princess from Fenarinarsa, helps, the more gems that appear on the magic crown of Fenarinarsa. When the crown is complete, the floating land of Fenarinarsa would return to Earth where it belongs.) In Episode 8, she instead used her powers for her own purposes, turning into a policewoman so that she could move through traffic quickly and meet a boy who left a love letter for her. Yuyama explains that the first episodes were more orthodox to give the sponsor a sense of security, and after that the staff was left to its own devices (Yōsensha 2011: 71). Ashi Productions founder Satō Toshihiko claims that "Bandai [then "Popy"] didn't touch the series itself" and that the staff was "allowed to create original work within the frame set up by the sponsor" (Galbraith 2014: 47). This was an unprecedented situation for Ashi Productions. While Ōno's claim that the staff had polled kindergarteners to ask what kinds of jobs they would like to hold in the future was corroborated by Satō (Galbraith 2014: 48), Ōno points out that the first episode involved Momo turning into a jockey and winning a horserace—something kindergarteners would neither know nor care much about. This instead reflects the interests of the staff members, in particular Yuyama and Shudō (Yōsensha 2011: 89).

There is also the concept of the Gourmet Poppo: a little car pulling a large white trailer, which combine and fly like a helicopter to other continents, thus allowing episodes to be set anywhere on Earth. Popy had requested that this vehicle appear in the show because it would be one of its most marketable toy items. Ōno recalls that Popy came to him first, giving him the chance to pitch the demand as an opportunity for the production staff. He "interpreted" this business strategy as a source of creative inspiration, and the three-way relationship between the staff, producer, and sponsor resulted in a product that satisfied everyone involved (Yōsensha 2011: 89).

Killing Magical Girls

Yet *Minky Momo*, like *Gundam*, fell prey to its sponsor's change of heart. Originally planned as a 52-episode, yearlong series, it was canceled at Episode 46, despite moderately successful toy sales. Ōno claims that Popy wanted to reduce the number of anime series it sponsored (Yōsensha 2011: 90). The series did not spawn a large variety of toys; only the Minky Stick, Gourmet Poppo, and Momo's three animal companions (dog, bird, and monkey) had any merchandising potential. Ironically, this was one of the factors that gave the animators the freedom from sponsors' mandates. Nevertheless, Popy had made its decision, and Yuyama explains that there was not enough time to put together an ending that would satisfactorily bring Fenarinarsa back to Earth (Yōsensha 2011: 72). It takes four episodes of "good deeds" by Momo for a single gem to appear on the crown, and, because several episodes had resulted in her failures, such as the aforementioned policewoman episode, there were not enough episodes left to place the final gem and complete the task.

It was Shudō's idea to kill off Momo in a car accident in Episode 46. This dark turn was foreshadowed in the previous episode by the vanishing of the Gourmet Poppo (because "the magic ran out") and the destruction of the Minky Stick, thus effectively eliminating the toys from the show altogether. In the latter half of Episode 46, Momo chooses to be reincarnated as a real girl instead of a Fairy Princess. She can now have her own dreams and desires, and once she realizes them, Fenarinarsa will return to Earth.

A rumor surrounding the "car accident" ending developed among viewers, who symbolically interpreted the death scene of Momo being hit by a truck carrying toys that then spilled onto the road. Shudō was known to have been vocally against toy sponsors' demands to "make 30-minute commercials, not masterpieces" (Minori Shobō 1983: 64). This fateful scene was assumed to be a message to the viewers that "it was the toy company that killed Momo." Yuyama denied this rumor, stating that the decision to make the truck carry toys was a different kind of symbolism. Fallen toys substituted for Momo's body or her being carried to hospital, which would have been too graphic to show viewers (Yōsensha 2011: 72). The final shot in the sequence is a small toy ambulance rolling along the road.

Ironically, the toy company ended up saving the show by not having a replacement series ready as a vehicle for a new toy—a cute dragon-crocodile character called "Kajira." According to Shudō, Popy agreed to extend *Minky Momo*'s funding if Kajira were added (Web Anime Style 2006). This decision was controversial because many in the staff felt the story had been told, but declining an offer to extend the work was unheard of. Yuyama managed to negotiate the survival of the three animal companions, who appeared along with Kajira. The series was expanded until Episode 63, using a mix of reworked, previously discarded, episode scripts to tell an overarching story of Momo defending dreams from nightmares. While Satō differentiated Momo, who used her powers to help others, from the heroines of later magical girls, such as the *Sailor Moon* and *Pretty Cure* that focused on fighting evil with magic (Galbraith 2014: 49, 50), these final episodes of *Minky Momo* undeniably portray a fantasy good-versus-evil showdown, removed from the earlier part of the series that had advocated using hard work and effort to solve problems. Despite its tribulations, *Minky Momo* established a template for subsequent series, and Ōno later produced *Magical Angel Creamy Mami* (*Mahō no tenshi Kuriimii Mami*, 1983–1984), the final episode of which boasted a phenomenal 20 percent viewer rating (Anime Anime 2014), for Studio Pierrot, which took over the production of almost all magical girl genre series, as Sunrise (producer of *Gundam* and several other series) did for the robot genre.

Transforming Robot Anime

The truncation and then extension of a series at the whim of the sponsors and broadcasters, while extremely rare, was also the case in robot anime. A prime example is, again, *Macross*. Here, too, the original plan was for a 52-episode run, which was reduced to twenty-six episodes, and then extended at the last minute, placing the production staff in a predicament. The story about an alien invasion and subsequent space war reaches its climax by Episode 27. The humans, at war with an alien race called the Zentradi that knows nothing of culture, use the power of music to "educate" the aliens and make them understand that there is more to life than endless fighting. This climax results in the destruction of the surface of the Earth, with the inhabitants aboard the space fortress Macross (in which there is a full-size city with civilian citizens) being the sole remaining humans. The show's extension takes the story two years into the future and depicts the aftermath of the war and the conflicts that arise as humans and aliens coexist.

Much like the case of *Minky Momo*, *Macross* completed the development arc of its characters in the "first" climax. Thus it seems odd to see their continuing adventures depicted almost as if the previous events were irrelevant. In *Macross*, the narrative uses the war as a backdrop to the protagonist Ichijō Hikaru and his growing turmoil over whom he loves more, the singing superstar Lynn Minmay or his superior officer Hayase Misa. Episode 27 shows him bidding farewell to Lynn, who is tasked with the all-important song for the aliens, and rescuing Misa from a base on Earth under bombardment. The image of Hikaru and Misa alone on the surface of the now-desolate Earth, riding off into the sunset (or, in this case, sunrise) closes the show on a poignant note, with no ambiguity as to whom Hikaru chose. The remaining nine episodes then undo all that development and reset the love triangle.

Despite the fact that the series' structure was thrown off balance, *Macross* as a *franchise* thrived largely *because* of the story elements introduced forcefully in the final arc. These elements—much like the Gourmet Poppo's role in *Minky Momo*—gave the series an infinite range of settings for future stories, capitalized upon in a plethora of sequels and mixed-media offshoots.

In a sense, both *Minky Momo* and *Macross* were testbeds in a transitional period at the crossroads of post-*Astro Boy*-style sponsorship, the rise of savvy anime fans, and the onset of home video, which proved to be a game-changer in terms of anime production and storylines and evolved the robot and magical girl genres into something unprecedented. The two shows are products of a marketing tradition that, in the twenty years since *Astro Boy*, was becoming outdated as audiences shifted. This tradition was not phased out but instead was adapted into the framework requisites of robot and magical girl anime. The expected media literacy of the viewership meant that these tropes could be underplayed, subverted, or exaggerated in later works.

The End of Toys and Beginning of Anime as "Product"

While some series were extended in unexpected ways, others were cancelled before the end of their runs due to poor toy sales. This situation continued until the advent of OVA, made to be viewed at home on VCRs, which were then becoming common household equipment. OVA content could be as violent and sexual as the producers (and end-users) wished because they were no longer subject to strict television regulations (see Chapter 20). OVA also revolutionized the production method by completely cutting the broadcast station and toy sponsor out of the equation. Instead, the distributor, such as a record company—Victor, for example, in the case of the bestselling *Megazone 23 (Megazōn 23*, 1985) OVA—became the main marketer of the project. In short, instead of anime being a commercial for certain products, it *became* the product. This was an enormous turnaround. Laserdisc and VHS formats were still new and commanded a high price, but hardcore fans were willing to invest in the latest, no-holds-barred animation.

This meant that, although mechanical design continued to evolve, they were not merely intended to serve the toy market, and, as a result, robot anime split into two types: children-oriented shows such as the *Brave* series (*Yūsha shiriizu*, 1990–2005, produced by Sunrise), planned by toy-maker Takara (today known as Takara-Tomy) to market simplistic robot toys, and more serious, science fiction OVA fare appreciated by avid fans with broad knowledge of the genre, like *Hades Project Zeorymer (Meiō keikaku Zeoraimā*, 1988). The clearest example of this division is the 1994 revival of *Macross*, when the OVA series *Macross Plus (Makurosu purasu)* and television series *Macross 7 (Makurosu sebun)* were simultaneously produced and marketed to these two audiences; they maintained common threads so fans could enjoy both. Both sequels to the 1982 series, the former was a mature science fiction story with almost no tie-in merchandise other than soundtrack albums. The latter featured similar yet simplified designs and was marketed with a variety of toys by Bandai. *Macross Plus* was directed by Kawamori Shōji, who, as discussed above, had tried unsuccessfully for twelve years to convince sponsors to allow the series to feature "realistic" nonhumanoid designs but had to concede to their demands. Now that there were no toy sponsors to convince, why continue humanoid robots? It is because this genre in its OVA incarnation had grown to be accepted as "mature" and "real" by anime fans.

The simultaneous 1994 release of the *Macross* OVA and television series distinguishes "superhero" (marketable and child-friendly) and "real" (militaristic, mechanical, and gritty) robots. The VF-19 from *Macross 7* is a bright red, simplistic yet iconic design with clean lines and a face. The YF-19 from the *Macross Plus* OVA, on the other hand, shares the transformation pattern and basic silhouette with the VF-19 (and is, in-universe, its original prototype). Yet its outward appearance is strikingly different with detailed vents, thrusters, and intakes. Its face is replaced with a mechanical sensor head unit. A 2009 article in *Animage Original* points out that this practice of altering the same design for different fanbases could only have happened during the 1990s (Tokuma shoten 2009: 34).

In addition, the shift to OVA introduced the "production committee" (*seisaku iinkai*) system. Serving to green-light animation projects which may otherwise get turned down by toy-company sponsors, the production committee comprises smaller companies (from record labels to toy manufacturers) and distributors, all "chipping-in" to the production budget. Most anime not centered on toys are shown on late night television slots because they are cheaper than primetime ones, and ratings mean little since the aim is to regain the production costs through DVD sales.

Nunokawa Yūji (b. 1947), the founder of Studio Pierrot, writes that the method of "selling" shows began to change around the time of *Magical Angel Creamy Mami*. Originally Bandai sponsored about half of the anime on television, but, as times changed, they targeted a new type of fan and established a home video business, Bandai Visual, and later produced tie-in videogames (Nunokawa 2013: 114–115). Bandai partnered with Namco to form Bandai-Namco Games in 2005, further illustrating shifts in merchandising intellectual property.

Thus we arrive at a time when merchandising has transcended toys and is truly part of a "media mix," with intellectual property, by necessity, a cross-platform entity, requiring facets suited for every interpretation. As a result of the production committee system, anime series have generally become shorter, with just two-arc (twenty-six episodes) or even one-arc (thirteen episodes) runs. This mode of production relies on the tropes and standards set decades ago by robot and magical girl anime, with subversive twists on their themes and concepts. Formulaic deconstruction and reconstruction, and subsequent variation thereof, are key features of anime today. Yet these are only possible through an adherence to the frameworks established over fifty years due to the evolving relationship between the creators, producers, and marketers of televised animation.

Notes

1 Earlier sponsors had controlled content. For example, Meiji Seika retained the copyright on the *Astro Boy* character when Mushi Production declared bankruptcy in 1973. In 1977 Tezuka wanted to produce a color version of the series due to broadcasters' reluctance to rerun black-and-white shows and the unavailability of the original episodes before the home video market (Schodt 2007: 159). It proved difficult for him to obtain rights to his own protagonist. Tezuka's new company Tezuka Productions teamed up with Toei Animation to produce *Jetter Mars* (*Jettā Māzu*, 1977), which was basically *Astro Boy* in a different guise. Once

the rights were cleared, Tezuka could bring *Astro Boy* back to the small screen, with the original voice actress (Shimizu Mari), and a more modern look.

2 During Toei's command of the magical girl genre, these series were collectively known as "*majokko anime.*" Toei later produced the influential, team-based battling magical girl franchises, *Sailor Moon* (*Bishōjo senshi Seeraa Mūn*, 1992–1997) and *Pretty Cure* (*Futari wa Puriti Kyua*, 2004–present).

3 Ashi Productions, today known as Production Reed, was synonymous with toy-oriented robot shows in the early to mid-1980s, such as *Space Warrior Baldios* (*Uchū senshi Barudiosu*, 1980-1981) and *Dancougar* (1985).

23 Condensing the Media Mix

The Tatami Galaxy's Multiple Possible Worlds[1]

Marc Steinberg

Is it a coincidence that stories of multiple possible worlds proliferate in a world of proliferating media forms? Is it a coincidence that multiple possible world narratives are on the rise in an era of the intensified migration of works across media? It would seem not. Yet here is the rub: contemporary discussions of transmedia storytelling tend to presume a necessary unity and consistency across media. In part, this presumption is informed by a focus on Hollywood media productions; in part, it is informed by the absence of a more nuanced understanding of transmedia narratives and the worlds they presuppose. Hence, we need to rethink what a world is and what it means to discuss the consistency of a world in order to develop a more adequate theoretical model for the multiple possible media worlds at present. A start is to look at a particularly poignant, metacritical reflection on multiple possible media worlds in the Japanese context, undertaken by the television anime series *The Tatami Galaxy* (*Yojōhan shinwa taikei*, literally, *The Mythical System of the 4.5-Tatami-Mat Room*, 2010), offered up by the *enfant terrible* of Japanese commercial animation Yuasa Masaaki. Yuasa had his directorial debut with the feature-length anime *Mind Game* (2004). He went on to direct the most visually experimental (and sometimes narratively unhinged) television anime series of the early twenty-first century, giving him a reputation of an animator's director but also one whose commercial bankability was questionable. The combination of the two led him to some of the most visually and conceptually exciting projects of the last decade, first and foremost being *The Tatami Galaxy*. The uniqueness of *The Tatami Galaxy* is that it condenses the logic of the transmedia movement of the Japanese media mix into a single series. As such it presents attentive viewers with a visual theorization or parable of the function of the "media mix" (*mejia mikkusu*).

The media mix, broadly defined, is the popular and industry term used in Japan to denote the multiple media formation developed across a single franchise. In its most typical form, a given property begins as a comic or novel, is adapted to a film or animation series, spawns soundtracks, toys or figurines (for children or adults), videogames, and production notes, along with the requisite newspaper articles, magazine features, and advertising. The term media mix originates in marketing discourse of the 1960s, but in the 1980s it came to designate the anime and film franchising with which it is currently associated. It names the entire phenomenon of transmedia storytelling that Henry Jenkins (2006, 2014) and others have, in the North American context, alternatively called "convergence culture," or transmedia.

Important questions of a comparative nature arise here. Are there significant differences between the terms "media mix" and "transmedia," as well as the practices they designate, that prevents them from being collapsed into a single phenomenon? Are there notable differences between the Japanese media mix and North American media convergence such that we should make efforts to distinguish them? The position I adopt here is that there are significant differences between the practices these two terms designate, and that these differences should be noted. In this chapter, I sketch a somewhat speculative, and inevitably generalizing, account of these differences through a reading of *The Tatami Galaxy*, and focus on the distinct relations between totality and world found within Japanese versus North American media-industrial formations.[2] I should acknowledge that there are dangers in reifying the differences between industrial practices along national or territorial lines. There is a porosity in these media practices that allows them to easily seep past national boundaries. Consequently, we can find media mix-style practices in North America, just as we can find convergence-style practices in Japan. Nonetheless, the differences between media mix and convergence are marked enough that they deserve to be foregrounded. Moreover, an analysis of the Japanese media mix such as I will undertake it here also allows us to question some assumptions underpinning the North American model of media convergence.

Seeing as the specificity of a phenomenon is often signaled in the analytical work that describes it, I begin with a comparison of the uses of the two terms by two representative figures: the convergence culture advocate Henry Jenkins and the media mix developer Ōtsuka Eiji. I then move to a consideration of the possible worlds theory of the seventeenth-century philosopher Gottfried Wilhelm Leibniz (1646–1716), whose theory of multiple possible worlds may well be the critical tool we need to grapple with the media mix. Following on my discussion of Leibniz, I suggest that we read *The Tatami Galaxy* as a metacritical presentation of the phenomenon of the media mix that would seem to embrace divergence more than convergence. This, in turn, points to differences in industrial practice: Japanese media industries have tended, since the late 1980s, to embrace a model of media divergence, while Hollywood has tended to stay closer to a model of media convergence.

Media Convergence Versus Media Mix

As one of the key figures within studies of convergence, Henry Jenkins, likely needs no introduction. A passionate advocate for considering fandom as a positive force within media studies since the 1990s, he has continued this work into the 2000s, using the concept of "convergence culture" to make the case for the significance of fans and fan activity in contemporary media culture. In what is perhaps his most widely read work on the subject, *Convergence Culture: Where Old and New Media Collide*, Jenkins (2006) suggests that media franchises are not made by companies alone but also depend on the participation of fans in the consumption of their products. Moreover, as digital media have become a constitutive part of media franchises, fans have taken increasingly active roles in the development and survival of franchises. Media operate not through one-off acquisitions, but through the perpetual consumption, whether through in-store purchase, online blogging, web searches, or offline discussion. Collective intelligence is the name of the game, and the model of the passive consumer has been replaced by the active *produser*—a subject who is as much a producer of their media experience as a consumer of it (Bruns 2010) (see Chapter 9).

What I would like to hone in on here is Jenkins' discussion of the part-to-whole relationship of transmedia franchises. It is here that we begin to see the contours and limits of Jenkins' image of convergence. Put more directly: in Jenkins' account, while hardware diverges media converge, narratives converge, and fans converge. Take *The Matrix* series, one of Jenkins' primary objects of analysis. Within *The Matrix* franchise each "piece" of the work—whether film, videogame, *Animatrix* animated segment, or comic book—gives a clearer picture of the whole. The principle underlying this is "additive comprehension" (Jenkins 2006: 123). "The animated films, the game, and the comics function in a similar way in *The Matrix*, adding information and fleshing out parts of the world so that the whole becomes more convincing and more comprehensible" (Jenkins 2006: 116). The invocation of the term "world" is by no means arbitrary; as Jenkins notes, "More and more, storytelling has become the art of *world building*, as artists create compelling environments that cannot be fully explored or exhausted within a single work or even a single medium" (Jenkins 2006: 114). As he writes elsewhere, "World building is part of the structuring logic of the new transmedia franchises" (Ford and Jenkins 2009: 34). If the "whole is worth more than the sum of the parts"—and here the "whole" should be understood to be roughly analogous to the concept of the world—it is also because the whole is never exhausted by any of the parts; it must be built, sought after, consumed, and imagined from part to part (Jenkins 2006: 102).

Synergy—the principle that the whole is greater than the sum of the parts—is at the core of the model of transmedia storytelling Jenkins elaborates in his chapter on *The Matrix* franchise, and this "transmedia impulse" is, Jenkins concludes, "at the heart of what I am calling convergence culture" (Jenkins 2006: 129). "A transmedia story unfolds across multiple media platforms, with each text making a distinctive and valuable contribution to the whole" (Jenkins 2006: 95–6). Key here is the presupposition that the whole is singular and consistent. Within this convergence culture, consumers are hunters and gatherers of information, assembling their informational catches to form a total picture of the transmedia world in question. The emphasis here, and in convergence as a media practice, is on the (re)constitution of the whole based on the assembly of distinct parts.

This consumption and compilation of fragments in order to gain a greater picture of the whole or the world of the work in question rings familiar to those familiar with analyses of the Japanese media mix developed in the late 1980s by critic and media producer Ōtsuka Eiji. Ōtsuka was central to the formulation of the contemporary model of the Japanese media mix, working in the 1980s for Kadokawa Media Office, a subsidiary of the publisher Kadokawa Books and a company on the frontlines of media mix practice headed by Kadokawa Tsuguhiko (for Kadokawa's role in cinema, see Chapter 20). While I offer a fuller analysis of Kadokawa's work in my book *Anime's Media Mix* (2012), it bears repeating here that the model of the media mix developed around Kadokawa Tsuguhiko in the late 1980s itself marked a shift from a film-soundtrack-novel *bounded* model of the media mix (pioneered by Tsuguhiko's older brother, Kadokawa Haruki), to a relatively *unbounded* model of the media mix that saw a multiplication of transmedia products. It was within this context that Ōtsuka developed his theory of narrative consumption, articulated in *A Theory of Narrative Consumption* (*Monogatari shōhiron*, 1989), expanded and republished as *A Theory of Narrative Consumption: Standard Edition* (*Teihon Monogatari shōhiron*, 2001).

In an analysis of the Bikkuriman Chocolates freebie campaign from the late 1980s, Ōtsuka isolates the mechanism behind narrative consumption. Ōtsuka suggests that each commodity—whether an anime episode, a weekly manga installment, or the sticker from a chocolate candy that bears a fragment of a narrative—should be seen as a "small narrative" (Ōtsuka 2010). Consumers use these small narratives to access the "grand narrative" that lies partially concealed behind them. Each small narrative gives the consumer a greater sense of what this grand narrative is, fueling consumption. Finally, once the consumer has attained a sufficiently broad understanding of the grand narrative, they are empowered to produce their own small narrative. Each consumer then becomes a producer in their own right.

How does Ōtsuka's account of the media mix differ from Jenkins' account of convergence? The key difference lies in their respective conceptions of the relation of parts to whole. Everything hinges on the concept of convergence. Jenkins' model, as we have seen, is one of additive synergy. From part to part, we slowly approach the vision of the whole. At first, Ōtsuka would seem to be offering us the same model of additive consumption when he writes that, within a given animation series, the "accumulation of settings into a single totality is what people in the animation field are accustomed to calling the 'worldview'" (Ōtsuka 2010: 107). And yet there is a fundamental point of ambivalence: fan production. Fans, Ōtsuka notes, take an existing narrative and reconfigure it, for example, by spinning narratives of a sexual relationship between two lead male characters where in the "official" version no such relationship exists. How far away from the central narrative world can a program stray before the worldview is irrevocably transformed? Does each variation in turn presuppose a *different world*? The multiplication of narratives and the corresponding *multiplication of worlds* is indeed how the contemporary Japanese media mix operates. Contrary to Ōtsuka's suggestion of a single world, his conception of fan production and his own media practice presumes the coexistence of multiple worlds.

What we have here, and what we should ultimately understand Ōtsuka to be developing in theory and practice, is not merely an *additive* logic, but a *transformative* one, where each drama or medium offers a potentially divergent world. Returning to the logic evoked by Jenkins, is it really possible to assimilate the narratives of boy-boy love into the otherwise heterosexual worldview presumed by the so-called "original" work? Does this open model of production suggest the potential for narrative world divergence rather than convergence? And if this is the case, how should we understand the difference between convergence and divergence?

Multiple Possible Worlds

Here we may turn to the remarkably useful theory of "simple substances" or "monads," developed by Gottfried Leibniz. Leibniz was a philosopher who, in order to explain the existence of evil in the world, developed a highly original theory of multiple possible worlds, which was taken up by literary scholars to explain the coexistence of multiple worlds within fiction (Ryan 1992; Doležel 2009), as well as by analytic philosophers exploring, in sometimes radical ways, the theory of multiple coexisting worlds of which ours is only one (Lewis 1986). What makes this work so useful is its articulation of the relationship between individual monad and world and the typology of relationships it offers (convergent or divergent, *compossible* or *incompossible*). If convergence culture and media mix practices are organized around the creation of narrative worlds, what we require is a clearer understanding of the relationship between the individual or monad and its world, and a more concrete distinction between convergent and divergent worlds. The work of Leibniz, particularly as it is extended by French philosopher Gilles Deleuze (1925–1995) and when reread in light of *The Tatami Galaxy*, offers us the necessary tools to develop a nuanced understanding of the part-whole and character-world relations in the potential proliferation of worlds within transmedia narratives.

As noted above, Leibniz posits the co-existence of multiple possible worlds, of which our actual world is only one (albeit the *best* one). According to Leibniz, God creates the world before he creates the monads that exist therein (Deleuze 1993: 60). Conversely, each monad contains within itself the entirety of the world in which it exists. Two monads can be said to exist in the same world insofar as they reflect the same series of events or circumstances that make up this world, each from its own perspective (Leibniz and Rescher 1991: 19). Each monad contains the world in its entirety; since monads "have no windows through which something can enter into or depart from them," they cannot be causally affected by any other monad, except insofar as they are pre-programmed to be so affected from the beginning of time (Leibniz and Rescher 1991: 17). While the monad cannot be causally affected directly, it is in fact a reflection of the entire universe; each monad is a "perpetual living mirror of the universe," such that any change in one part of the world would require a change in all the reflecting monads that inhabit it (Leibniz and Rescher 1991: 24). The consequence of this double presupposition of closure and reflection is that a monad—or individual—is assumed to have an essential, in-built connection to its world.

It is around this essential, predetermined relation between a monad and its world that Leibniz develops the key concepts of "compossibility" and "incompossibility." Two persons are said to exist in a compossible, or convergent, world insofar as a series of events in one person's world matches the other's. Two persons are said to exist in incompossible worlds if within one person's world events exist that do not exist in the other's. For Leibniz, God is the guarantor of compossibility and the harmony of all within each world and is the divine knowledge that chooses the best of all possible worlds.

Leibniz scholars tend to follow the philosopher in emphasizing the compossible. Deleuze, following the lead of theoretical fiction writer Jorge Luis Borges (1899–1986) instead, takes a more productive position for understanding the media mix, putting a good deal of thought into incompossibility. The incompossible, as Deleuze formulates it, does not mean impossible or incompatible, it merely involves a different conception of the world—one that includes divergences instead of excluding them (Deleuze 1994: 48). To be sure, this involves a different worldview than that offered by Leibniz and his God-selector, but this is precisely the point.

Let us return to the question: what is a world, and what are its contours? A world, much like the narrative worlds of contemporary media, is defined by the series of events that inflect it and the individuals that inhabit it. A possible world is defined as "the maximum set of compossible individuals"; once that maximum number has been reached, new worlds must be conceived (Jolley 2005: 171). A world is hence defined by the series of singularities it brings together (Deleuze 1994: 60), rather than, say, geographical territory. The world is convergent insofar as each monad reflects the same world, with the same series of singularities. The world would begin to diverge considerably should we add subsequent singularities that contradict existing ones.

The addition of a new term, then, offers up two possibilities. The first is that the term will add to the definition of the existing world, prolonging a given series. As such, it does not differ much from the additive logic of transmedia storytelling that Jenkins identifies. The second is the possibility that the addition of a new term will force a branching of the series, introducing a divergence that will ultimately lead to the generation of a new world. Terms, or singularities, do not merely add to an existing narrative, nor do they necessarily instigate a "breaking point," as Jenkins (2006: 127) suggests, "beyond which franchises cannot be stretched." New terms may also create a branching effect whereby a single narrative bifurcates into multiple incompossible worlds, developed, in the case of some media mix works, simultaneously in different media (or in some cases, within different incarnations of the same medium).

The specificity of the media mix in Japan can be said to lie in the general interest in the generation of bifurcating series, and a tendency, at least in the more experimental works, to deploy multiple incompossible worlds. This tendency is found in fan practices of reimagining narrative worlds (with fans creating the narrative world equivalent of counterfactual histories); it has been a trend since the late 1980s within the media industries, as they responded to and incorporated fan practice into official media productions. Hence, incompossibility is not only a radical and creative narrative possibility; it also makes economic sense.

The Tatami Galaxy's Divergent Worlds

The Tatami Galaxy deals explicitly with multiple possible worlds but suggests that divergence, not convergence, is what lies at the heart of the media mix. *The Tatami Galaxy*, it should be said, is relatively tame as media mixes go, at least when considering the basic level of its transmedia incarnations. It has the requisite media platform crossover, starting as a 2004 novel by Morimi Tomihiko. In typical Kadokawa media mix style, the novel and other works by Morimi were bought up by Kadokawa Books, which re-released them with cover art by Nakamura Yūsuke, the artist brought in to create the original character designs for the anime series. The television anime series is faithful to the novel more in spirit than in form; it takes some of the text, narrative, and formal devices (repetition first and foremost) and runs with them. It runs quite far, in fact. Directed by Yuasa and produced by Madhouse, the series is one of the most conceptually rigorous and artistically experimental anime in recent years. Blending media forms (photographs, live-action film, cel-style and digital animation, and even odes to cut-out paper animation), drawing styles (heavily processed, color-saturated photographic images, exaggerated or curved perspective within drawn images, characters that are at times three-dimensional and at other times completely flat), and rhythms of movement (from fluid and flowing to relatively still limited animation, slide show sequences, and live-action digital video), it is a series that pulls all stops to visually depict a world that is at once geographically anchored and realistic (most events take place in recognizable sites around Kyoto) and fantastical.

The series of eleven episodes is rigorously divided into two segments. The first nine episodes generally begin and end with the same plot device. The narrator-protagonist (nameless and known as "I"), a third-year university student, recounts his expectations upon entering university that he would be met with a "rose-colored campus life," wherein he would encounter many people, have trysts with numerous women, and fall deeply in love with one "raven-haired maiden" in particular. To start this life off on the right foot it is essential that he choose an appropriate club to join. Each episode, after a brief prologue, begins with this narration, a repeated animation sequence and the choice of a club, and ends with the complete failure of his rose-colored dreams of university life. Each episode ends in the present time, in despondent failure, and with the protagonist burning with the desire to restart his university life. We see an image of a clock rewinding, and the particular episode's events stream by as if rewound on a videotape. The next episode starts from the beginning, only this time the protagonist chooses a different club and lives a different version of his world, albeit one in which he again makes the wrong choices and wants to start his university life anew.

Unlike most anime, this one is not a serial in the sense of having a narrative arc that spans multiple episodes, each episode building on the last. Nor is it a simple loop narrative—a form of narrative particularly prevalent, as critic Azuma Hiroki notes, in anime-related works of the 2000s (Azuma 2007: 159–60). Differing from both the serial (which presumes a single world whose events unfold over time) and the loop (which similarly presumes a single world, whose events are repeated over and over again), *The Tatami Galaxy* operates on the principle of multiple possible worlds. Each episode traces another path the protagonist could have taken, and each one—until the final episode—fails to take him towards his desired goal: the blissful union with the raven-haired maiden. We have, then, images of multiple possible worlds, every one of which (save one) leads to failure. Moreover, in each world, regardless of his choice of club, the protagonist goes through a roughly parallel configuration of events.

The final installments, Episodes Ten and Eleven, constitute the second segment of the series. Unlike earlier episodes, university life seems neither enticing nor rose-colored, and the protagonist refuses to join a club. Instead, he becomes a "Tatami Ideologue," preferring to remain in his room away from the cold, grey-toned outside world. The 4.5-tatami-mat room is the perfect size for a person, he tells us, and he spends more and more time there until one day he wakes up to find that the door to his hallway no longer leads to his hallway, but to another, seemingly identical, tatami room. It is his very own room, replicated. This room leads to another room, and that to another, each one almost the same as the last. After the initial shock of his discovery, the protagonist begins a voyage traversing tatami rooms, increasingly desperate to find an outside that he, until then, had little interest in. Here the meaning of the opening sequence of each episode becomes clear: the photographic traversal of one identical tatami room after another is a preview of the experience of the protagonist in the closing episodes of the series. As our protagonist traverses the rooms, though, he realizes that they are not identical; small differences characterize each one, markers of his different possible lives. And so, dawns the realization: the protagonist is in fact in a world that traverses all his possible worlds. He is in a veritable vertical and horizontal complex of 4.5-tatami-mat rooms that he traverses in a trans-world journey.

The first segment of the series, we realize, offered us a red herring: an image of a single world rewound at the end and restarted at the beginning of every episode. Yet by the second segment of the series, it is clear that the parallel worlds remain fundamentally distinct and divergent. This parallel world interpretation is the one privileged by the tenth and eleventh episodes—the key episodes of the entire series—as well as by the opening and closing credit sequences, both of which visually suggest multiple parallel, if contiguous, 4.5-tatami-mat worlds. But these last two episodes also suggest something further: that these worlds may intersect, resulting in the creation of a divergent yet coexisting incompossible worlds scenario.

So here, in the two sections of *The Tatami Galaxy* series, we have two models of Leibnizian philosophy. First, we have multiple mutually exclusive, discrete worlds, each of which is compossible within itself and which are to be understood as being parallel (if incompossible) worlds. And second, we have the coexistence of multiple actual, incompossible worlds. Indeed, the protagonist meets himself—or rather, *another* himself—over the course of his journeys through the infinitely extending and contiguous tatami rooms. These are not, then, unpopulated worlds, but multiple worlds that are populated by different, incompossible yet coexisting versions of the protagonist himself.

As the hyper-planar animation of the end credit sequence of each episode of *The Tatami Galaxy* visualizes clearly, with this series we are no longer in a world governed by the distinction between actual and possible, regulated by God and the theological necessity to have the best of all possible worlds. The series of rooms is not arrayed in the shape of a pyramid. Rather the end credit animation gives us a nonhierarchical, completely planar world of multiple possible contiguous worlds. Mimicking the birds-eye-view floor-plan maps (*madori*) used by real estate agents to diagram the spatial arrangement of an apartment, the end credit sequence of *The Tatami Galaxy* visually expresses the narrative thrust of the series: one room connects to the next in an endless series of growing, shrinking, modulating, and proliferating rooms. Moreover, taking us even farther away from Leibniz's model, these worlds are not hermetically sealed universes. Rather, they are intersecting and, as we see in the last two episodes, crossed by a protagonist who is able to exist in incompossible fashion, across multiple worlds. In this last section, the protagonist is "astraddle over several worlds" and "is kept half open as if by a pair of pliers" (Deleuze 1993: 137).

Divergent Worlds: Media Convergence and the Media Mix Reconsidered

Let us return here to the distinction between media convergence and the media mix to draw some conclusions from our reading of *The Tatami Galaxy*. The series, when read as a parable of the media mix, presents two distinct models of transmedia storytelling. The first is a model of convergence: the elimination of incompossible elements from a particular media franchise, with each element adding a piece to the whole or the world. This is the model we can find within individual episodes of the first segment of the series; each develops a different possible world, which is internally compossible. Each episode presents what is potentially the basis for an internally consistent media franchise. Events in one medium cannot be contradicted by events in another medium. The totality and consistency of the world must be consistently maintained. Bibles, concordances or timelines may be created for particular worlds, and each piece is supposed to fit together like a puzzle. Additive comprehension is key to this model, and each element adds up to a whole, coherent picture. While exceptions abound, this model of convergence could be said to generally characterize the Hollywood media industries.

The second is a model of divergence. Moreover, divergence itself can be subdivided into two types: first, a multiplication of individually compossible but mutually incompossible worlds, hermetically sealed like the first nine episodes of *The Tatami Galaxy*; or second, as in the last two episodes of these series, an encounter of divergent worlds within a single incompossible world. The second type presents the possibility of a world reconceived; one whose boundaries are no longer the Leibnizian limits of compossibility but rather encompass mutually incompossible but nonetheless coexisting events; a media mix that "works" with its mutual contradictions or incompossibles rather than avoiding them. Such a world does not function merely through the progressive logic of additive comprehension, but *addition conjoined with bifurcation*. Every moment of addition potentially leads to divergence.

In this second type of divergence, addition is conjoined with bifurcation insofar as the addition of one piece of information undermines the consistency of the whole. As *The Tatami Galaxy* beautifully demonstrates, the media mix may work as much through divergence and bifurcation as addition. Each new strand may add to the contours of a given world or place us in a coexisting yet divergent one. Hence, we find that spectators pursue worlds for the pleasures of divergence that they offer—and not simply, as in the convergence model, for the joys of totalization. Media mixes work best, we conclude from *The Tatami Galaxy*, when they imagine worlds differently, deploying divergence as a creative practice, and embracing bifurcation on both narrative and visual levels.

In sum, *The Tatami Galaxy* is instructive because it condenses the logics of convergence and divergence into a single media form—the television anime. In so doing, the series evokes in a metacritical fashion the productive coexistence of compossibility and incompossibility within the media mix as a post-1980s Japanese industrial practice. While this style of transmedia practice is not exclusive to Japan, nor necessarily found in all forms of the media mix, *The Tatami Galaxy* highlights a tendency towards additive bifurcation and the creative proliferation of worlds that underpins much of media mix practice. It thereby shifts our understanding of convergence, suggesting the complexity of media mix worlds and providing a more nuanced conception of transmedia practice.

Notes

1 This chapter is a shorter version of an article published in the *Canadian Journal of Film Studies* 21(2): 71–92. My thanks go to the editors of the journal for permitting its republication.
2 This chapter compliments my book *Anime's Media Mix: Franchising Toys and Characters in Japan* (2012).

PART VIII
Manga

24 *Gekiga,* or Japanese Alternative Comics

The Mediascape of Japanese Counterculture

Shige (CJ) Suzuki

Introduction: What Is *Gekiga*?

In today's Japan, the term *gekiga* is loosely applied to manga with a long narrative (story manga), typically with little or no comical effect, oriented toward young adult or adult male readers. In manga criticism, *gekiga* has been defined in contrast to mainstream manga in terms of visual style and content, whereas postwar mainstream manga was formed around the style of Tezuka Osamu (1928–1989)[1]—Disneyesque doe-eyed characters drawn in curvy, clear lines appearing in his earlier manga—*gekiga* is commonly associated with a more (photo-)"realistic" character design with serious or darker themes (Natsume and Takeuchi 2009: 28; Norris 2009: 242). Although fully integrated into contemporary Japanese manga culture, *gekiga*, from its nascent state in the 1950s and its subsequent thriving period in the 1960s, assumed a distinct characteristic of being *alternative* to mainstream manga.

This chapter discusses the socio-historical context of the development of *gekiga* as alternative comics, examining the shifting media ecology, its formal innovations and readership, and its impact on other artistic and cultural practices. I focus on two key players in the development of *gekiga*: Tatsumi Yoshihiro (1935–2015) and Shirato Sanpei (b. 1932). Tatsumi is known as a pioneer of *gekiga*, the term he coined in 1957. Under this term, he began producing more youth-oriented genres, such as suspense, mystery, and thriller, while diverging from the more child-oriented story manga of that time. In North America, Tatsumi is perhaps best known for the stories he created around the late 1960s and early 1970s, as anthologized in *The Push Man and Other Stories* (2005), *Abandon the Old in Tokyo* (2006), and *Good-Bye* (2008), many of which focus on the struggling lives of working-class people.[2] On the other hand, Shirato is celebrated for his works about classic tales of ninja and the revolt of the peasants set in feudal Japan, such as *Scroll of Ninja Martial Arts: The Legend of Kagemaru* (*Ninja bugei-chō: Kagemaru-den,* 1959–1962) and *The Legend of Kamui* (*Kamui-den,* 1964–1971), both of which exemplified the use of comic medium for philosophical exploration and social critique. These two artists contributed to the development of *gekiga* as a distinct form, expanding the horizon of Japanese manga expression. *Gekiga* grew in tandem with Japanese counterculture in the 1960s, when Japan witnessed student uprisings, civic and intellectual participation in politics, and artistic radical experimentalism. During this time, many people raised voices of dissident against the disparity of economic classes, environmental pollution, the renewal of the U.S.-Japan Security Treaty (Anpo), and the Vietnam War. It was one of the thrilling moments in Japanese cultural history when the popular closely intersected with the political, synchronically corresponding to radical cultural praxes and movements in other parts of the globe. Tracing these two *gekiga* artists' innovations and contributions in Japanese manga history, this chapter argues that *gekiga*, as Japanese alternative comics, played a significant role in shaping Japanese counterculture.

The Emergence of *Gekiga* in the 1950s

As well-documented in his 2008 semi-autobiographical work, *A Drifting Life (Gekiga hyōryū)*, Tatsumi's invention of the term *"gekiga"* was motivated by his intent to differentiate his works and target audience from Japanese mainstream story manga. In those days, story manga were produced primarily for children, although other kinds of comics, such as political cartoons and comics strips for the general public, continued to appear in newspapers and magazines from prewar Japan. Aware of the gradual maturing of the first generation of the postwar story manga readers, Tatsumi and other comics artists began to create works with more complex narrative structures and thematic depth that would attract young adults. In 1959, Tatsumi founded the *Gekiga* Workshop (*Gekiga kōbō*), the artist collective that spawned the first *gekiga* boom. The members of the *Gekiga* Workshop, including Tatsumi, Matsumoto Masahiko, Satō Masaaki, Ishikawa Fumiyasu, Sakurai Shōichi, Yamamori Susumu, K Motomitsu, and Saitō Takao, were interested in creating detective fiction, mystery, and psycho-suspense thriller short-story *gekiga* that required higher literacy to "decode" the protagonists' psychologies, the layered narratives, and the symbolism implied only by visual cues. Although commercially oriented, this artistic collective obtained some control over editorship, negotiation with publishers, and even financial management. This was rather unorthodox in light of the then manga industry conventions that gave company executives or editors editorial decision-making power (see Chapter 25). Also, at this time, the manga industry had not fully been systematized by larger, Tokyo-centered publishers. In the mid-1950s, small independent publishers co-existed with large publishers, and they distributed books and manga books directly to local *kashihon-ya* (pay libraries/rental bookstores). This regional publishing and distribution system granted small publishers the chance to take risks in creating unconventional genres and works, while training *gekiga* artists to be aware of the importance of balancing commercialism with artistic innovation.

Another key factor of Tatsumi's implementation of the term *gekiga* was the social pressure for censorship over manga in the mid-1950s (see Chapter 9).

Due to some graphic content, manga had become subject to criticism from conservative sectors of society, including PTAs, the mass media, and citizen groups in Japan (Nagaoka 2010: 94–144). Tezuka once wrote that even his manga was perceived as "harmful" to children and vetted and boycotted by a department store at this time (Tezuka 1999: 190). Across the Pacific, the American comics industry faced similar pressures and censorship, (in)famously spearheaded by psychologist Frederic Wertham, whose 1954 book, *Seduction of the Innocent,* warns of the negative influence of comic books, especially horror and crime genres, on children. In the general mood of conservatism, a moral panic about comic books swept the United States, which resulted in the industry's self-adopted "Comics Code," a set of regulations on comic expression in 1954. The Code banned graphic depictions of violence, gore, sexual innuendo, and obscene or sacrilegious language by which comic books were "nearly sanitized to death" (Schodt 1996: 52). In his biography, Tezuka (1999: 191) reminisces that American journalist Albert. E. Kahn's 1953 *The Game of Death: Effects of the Cold War on Our Children,* a book that makes the same criticism as Wertham's book, was introduced to Japan in 1955, giving further impetus for the censorship on manga. Given this context, Tatsumi's usage of *gekiga* can be considered, in part, an attempt to avert repeated criticism towards comics—clarifying that what he was creating was *gekiga* for adolescent and more mature readers, not "manga" for children. In other words, Tatsumi's deployment of the term was a nimble tactic to dodge direct criticism from the public, while safeguarding a space in the Japanese comics industry where he and other *gekiga* artists could maintain relative creative freedom.[3] Whereas the Comics Code confined the status of American comics within a sterilized domain of children's entertainment, Tatsumi ingeniously allowed manga to grow out of its childhood into *gekiga.*

Gekiga was also born in the shifting media environment of the 1950s, in particular, the pervasion of other forms of audiovisual media such as television and film into everyday life. Tatsumi's de facto manifesto of *gekiga* reads: "More recently, the story manga has been vitalized through the influence exerted by the supersonic development of other media, such as film, television, and radio. This vitalization has given birth to something new, which is *gekiga*" (Tatsumi 2009: 730). It is often pointed out that postwar mainstream story manga is "cinematic" in terms of narrative and aesthetics (Schodt 1996: 25; Power 2009: 38–65); the same can be said of *gekiga.* Yet *gekiga* creators turned their gaze specifically to British and American film noir and French New Wave films to innovate their narrative and visual styles. Tatsumi's *Black Blizzard (Kuroi fubuki,* 1956), for instance, appropriates formal techniques from films like Carol Reed's *The Third Man* (1949) and François Truffaut's *Shoot the Piano Player* (1960), including the low-key lightening, chiaroscuro (high contrast of light and darkness), distorted camera angles, and jarring montage, in order to convey the characters' anxiety, fear, and/or tension in a scene. In relation to this cross-media dialogue, *gekiga* creators were concerned with the (often gloomy) ambience of setting or scene.

In fact, some *gekiga* creators—representatively, war veteran Mizuki Shigeru (*NonNonBa* and *Kitarō*) and Kojima Gōseki (a graphic artist for the bestselling *Lone Wolf and Cub*)—skillfully use background or setting as important visual and narrative elements, often employing "aspect-to-aspect" transition, one of the panel transition patterns categorized by American comics artist and critic, Scott McCloud.

In his seminal book *Understanding Comics* (1994), McCloud discusses the prevalent use of "aspect-to-aspect" panel transitions in Japanese comics. While typically in comics, spatial transitions between panels indicate the passage of time, moving the narrative forward, the aspect-to-aspect panel juxtaposition is one of the irregular transitions that depicts the same scene or object from multiple perspectives without showing any actions by characters. This transition, according to McCloud, is not interested in the procession of narrative but in "establish[ing] a mood or a sense of place" where "time seems to stand still in these quiet, contemplative combinations" (1994: 79). Although McCloud ahistorically overgeneralizes it as "an integral part of Japanese mainstream comics" connected with traditional Japanese aesthetics (i.e., Japanese gardens and *ukiyo-e* woodblock prints), Deborah Shamoon, author of Chapter 26 in this volume, rightly claims that this panel transition was in fact "one of the cinematic techniques developed by *gekiga* artists of the late 1950s and 1960s" (2011: 28). Yet the appropriation of the cinematic technique in *gekiga* is different from the ones employed by Tezuka-inspired mainstream manga. While postwar mainstream manga tried to emulate the "moving image" by increasing the number of frames, as exemplified Tezuka's earlier works, *gekiga* artists dexterously manipulated backgrounds or visual images to underscore ambience by stalling the progression of the narrative.

Gekiga's relationship to other audiovisual media produced another formal innovation: diverse uses of onomatopoeia. Scholars (e.g., Schodt 1988; Natsume and Takekuma 1995; Petersen 2009) have pointed out that the use of onomatopoeia is generally more prevalent in Japanese manga than in American comics; *gekiga* is, to a great extent, responsible for this prevalence. Yomota Inuhiko (1999: 131–132) discusses the increasing diversity and abundance of onomatopoeia in post-*gekiga* work. Natsume Fusanosuke (1995: 127) also claims that *gekiga* artists invented unique kinds of onomatopoeia, especially for more dramatic sound effects. For instance, gunshots are rendered using invented sound-symbols, such as "*dokyūn*" or "*baūn*," instead of the more typical "bang" (*ban*) that had already existed in Japanese lexicon. Although neither critic discusses the reason for the inventions of new onomatopoeia, it is probable that *gekiga* artists strove to make the comics medium more alluring to compete with other audiovisual media, particularly television that was entering into the everyday mediascape in the mid-1950s.

In his short-story *gekiga* works published in the late 1960s and early 1970s, for which he is best known in North America, Tatsumi introduces social realism to foreground the struggling lives of blue-collar workers, downtrodden middle-aged men, and working students who toil away in places like underground sewers, dark factories, and junkyards. His *Abandon the Old in Tokyo*, for instance, visually narrates (without much relying on words) the alienated living conditions of the protagonist through the effective use of aspect-to-aspect transition. A panel from the work depicts the protagonist stranded in a jam-packed train, followed by an ironic juxtaposition of an advertisement that reads "spacious vacation home." The next panel (Figure 24.1) shows a crowd of countless people, giving a sense of suffocation while the protagonist's individuality is obscured into anonymous urban mass (Tatsumi 2006: 43). Later in the same work (Figure 24.2), the bullet train (*shinkansen*), constructed in 1964 as the symbol of modernized Japan (or so presented by the state in preparation for the 1964 Tokyo Olympics), psychologically torments the protagonist (Tatsumi 2006: 64). Like this, Tatsumi's works delve into the underside of Japan's economic and technological ascendency, disclosing the social inequality, repression, and contradictions underlying the nation's economic success.

The Maturation of *Gekiga* in the 1960s

Gekiga thrived as a distinctive subgenre of Japanese manga in the 1960s with the rise of youth counterculture. An important *mangaka* who contributed to the growth of *gekiga* in this period was Shirato Sanpei (b. 1932), who experimented with and expanded on the potential of the medium for socio-political and philosophical explorations. Shirato appeared in the manga industry first as a *shōjo* manga (girls' comics) artist in the late 1950s. His earlier works touched on social problems in postwar Japan, a topic not often found in *shōjo* manga at the time. *The Crow Child* (*Karasu no ko*, 1958), for instance, narrates the life of a female protagonist who is discriminated against due to her skin color. Although the protagonist's parents are not clearly mentioned, her darker skin indicates that she is one of the interracial children born to Japanese mothers and American soldiers during the Allied Occupation (1945–1952). Another example, *The Vanishing Girl* (*Kieyuku shōjo*, 1959), is one of the earliest postwar manga to address the issue of the atomic bombing, featuring a young female *hibakusha* (survivor of the atomic bombings) suffering from radiation sickness. An orphan, her life is full of maltreatment, abuse, and alienation; the only person who tries to save her is an ethnically Korean man. The man, partly based on a real person, had escaped from a wartime forced labor camp in Japan, which suggests heated discussion on the precarious status of "*zainichi*" Korean residents in the mid-1950s at the backdrop of both the postcolonial condition of the Korean Peninsula and the post-Korean War conditions (Yomota 2004: 79).[4] Although still filled with the melodrama and sentimentalism demanded by the mercenary manga industry, both works point to the social oppression and marginalization of ethnic and other minorities in postwar "democratic" Japan.

Figure 24.1 In Tatsumi Yoshihiro's *Abandon the Old in Tokyo*, the protagonist's individuality is obscured into the anonymous urban mass.

Source: Courtesy of Tatsumi Euko.

Figure 24.2 The newly-built high-speed train causes the protagonist psychological torment.
Source: Courtesy of Tatsumi Euko.

Such implied social issues in Shirato's works perhaps derive from his familial genealogy and his childhood experiences. Shirato was born Okamoto Noboru in 1932, son of well-known leftist painter Okamoto Tōki, who was active in the proletariat art movements of the 1920s and 1930s. In vibrant social and labor movements preceding wartime crackdowns, leftwing artists and Japanese *mangaka* worked together to produce politically charged works for mass-produced, popular magazines. While American comic strips such as George McManus' *Bringing Up Father*, Bud Fisher's *Mutt and Jeff*, and Pat Sullivan's *Felix the Cat* were translated into Japanese, several Japanese painters, political cartoonists, and caricaturists contributed satirical illustrations and comic strips to newspapers and pro-working class magazines (Kinsella 2000: 20–22). Okamoto was one of them, occasionally contributing political cartoons and illustrations for the satirical magazine, *Tokyo Puck*, including a George Grosz-like front cover illustration of a pig-nosed (greedy) capitalist who carries a gun in 1930. During the escalation of the repressive Japanese wartime regime, however, several leftist *mangaka* were targeted by the government, and Okamoto, an active organizer of artist/leftist political groups, repeatedly underwent interrogation, harassment, incarceration, and even torture by the wartime *tokkō* police (Mōri 2011: 19). After the proletarian literary author Kobayashi Takiji was tortured to death in 1933, Okamoto, who was among the mourners gathered around Kobayashi's corpse, created a painting of his death mask. To avoid persecution from the authorities, the family moved to different places in Japan, where Shirato experienced poverty and came in contact with ethnic minorities and a discriminated pariah group (*buraku*) (Mōri 2011: 35–36). Along with his father's leftwing political orientation, his childhood experiences are reflected in his comics, for motifs about social inequality, injustice, and oppression (and resistance to it) repeatedly surfaced throughout his career.

Shirato is renowned in Japanese manga history not only as an excellent *gekiga* artist but also the co-founder of the monthly *Garo*, one of the first alternative comics magazines. Officially, *Garo* was established by editor Nagai Katsuichi (1921–1996) and initially funded by Shirato, who served as an editor for the first couple of years (Holmberg 2010: 6). *Garo* was exceptional among commercially oriented manga magazines in that artistic aspiration was more important than sales; thus it offered a space for the work of such unorthodox *gekiga* creators as Mizuki Shigeru (b. 1922), Kojima Gōseki (1928–2000), Tsuge Yoshiharu (b. 1937) (*Screw Style* or *Screw Ceremony* [*Nejishiki*]), Hayashi Seiichi (b. 1945) (*Red Colored Elegy* [*Sekishoku erejī*]), and Sasaki Maki (b. 1946) (*Ding Dong Circus and Other Stories, 1967–1974*). These *gekiga* creators, many of whom were former *kamishibai* (storytelling performance using painting) painters, brought unconventional aesthetics, formal experimentalism, and idiosyncratic subject matters into the comics medium (see Chapter 31).

The primary objective in founding *Garo* was to feature Shirato's *The Legend of Kamui* (*Kamui-den*, 1964–1971). *The Legend of Kamui* is set in feudal Japan of the Edo period, introducing multiple protagonists, such as skilled ninjas, masterless samurai warriors (*rōnin*), a powerful merchant, discriminated minorities, and resourceful farmers, all of whom resisted, in one way or another, the Tokugawa ruling system. Unlike his earlier *gekiga* works in which minority protagonists remain victims of social oppression, the main characters in *The Legend of Kamui* actively attempt to defy the power structure in hopes of forming a fairer society. The narrative focuses on not only the main characters' individual talents and struggles but also on the importance of solidarity and alliances across social divisions. This idealistic, utopian drive appealed to student activists, intellectuals, and artists in the 1960s. In Japan, citizens and radicalized student groups raised dissident voices against the university administrators, the technocracy, and the bureaucratization of society; particularly, they raised a collective voice against the security treaty that allowed the U.S. military to be stationed in Japan and, subsequently, protested against the Vietnam War, considering it to be an expansion of American militarism into Asia under the logic of the Cold War.

It is not difficult to imagine that radicalized students and activists found their reflections in *The Legend of Kamui*'s fictional characters. In fact, a graduate student at Kyoto University sent a letter to *Garo* stating that he regarded Shirato's *The Legend of Kamui* as a "previous proposition" for the "revolutionary theory of Marxism" that he was studying (quoted in Yomota 2004: 232).[5] In the tumultuous period of the 1960s, Shirato's works, along with other *gekiga* in *Garo*, functioned as a site for symbolic resistance, in which *mangaka* and their readers explored the potential and limitations of their resistance and struggles against the power structure of society, superimposing their own efforts over the fictional feudal resistance. Such politicization began to be reflected on the pages of *Garo*.

Like other Japanese manga magazines, *Garo* featured not only serialized story manga but also single-image satirical cartoons, readers' columns, short stories, mini-essays, explanation on drawing manga, and advertisements for recruiting new talent. In the section "*Meyasubako*" (Petition Box), named after the Edo period political practice of collecting commoners' voices, contributors voiced journalistic criticism of domestic and international issues, including the censorship of school textbooks and the involvement of the Japanese government with American imperialism. They also included anti-Vietnam War messages in a form of (parodied) poetry accompanied by a sketch that depicts then Japanese Prime Minister Satō Eisaku helping to carry a bomb for the U.S. Air Force (Kurokawa 1965: 116).

Readers of *Garo*, who were not only high-teens but also university students and radicalized activists, were not passive receivers of comics and their political messages. Rather, they engaged with the artists and writers. In a published response to one of the *Meyasubako* essays, one reader complains about its use of abstruse philosophical language, accusing its writer of a didactic and elitist orientation; the contributor replied to this criticism in the next issue (January 1967). In another letter, a reader points out the narrative contradiction in Shirato's work, proclaiming this flaw as artwork (*Garo* 1967: 110). Thus *Garo* encouraged communication between readers, contributors of articles, and the authors through the non-comics content. This participatory interactivity is characteristic of Japanese comics magazines and establishes a sense of community, as Jennifer Prough discusses in Chapter 25. *Garo* established a community through both the featured *gekiga* works and the dialogical space of non-manga sections, registering a shared sense of political awareness, which, in turn, fostered the (self-) fashioning of a youth countercultural subject.

There were emblematic instances that exemplified what *gekiga* meant for radical youth. In the late 1960s, the phrase *"Journal* in the right hand and *Shōnen Magazine* in the left hand (*migi-te ni jānaru, hidari-te ni magajin)"* commonly circulated among university students, which meant that the leftist intellectual magazine *Asahi Journal* (*Asahi jānaru*) and the comics magazine *Weekly Boys' Magazine* (*Shūkan shōnen magajin*) had the same value to them. Despite its title, *Weekly Boy's Magazine* featured *gekiga* works, including a popular boxing *gekiga, Tomorrow's Joe* (*Ashita no jō*, 1968–1973), written by Takamori Asao (a.k.a Kajiwara Ikki, 1936–1987) and illustrated by Chiba Tetsuya (b. 1939). This work narrates the struggling life of a boxer named Joe, an underdog from a Tokyo slum who makes his way in an adverse environment and fights until his death. It captivated not only young comics fans but also adult readers, including cultural critics and artists. In March 1970, a media event ensued when a rival character, Rikiishi Tōru, died in the story. More than 800 comics fans attended the staged "funeral" for this fictional character planned and performed by avant-garde artist Terayama Shūji and his Tenjōsajiki theater group. In the same month, a sect of the Japanese Red Army, a communist, far-left militant group, hijacked an airplane and fled to North Korea. Upon leaving Japan, the group's leader made a declaration in which he compared the group members to the protagonist Joe. Newspaper headlines scoffed at these incidents as travesties, calling them "manga-esque" (*Asahi Shinbun* 1970). Yet what they failed to understand was the fact that manga had evolved into a medium that was no longer simply children's entertainment. This cognitive gap provided an opportunity for young adults to claim comics as a culture of their own, positing them against the older generation. To put it differently, the youth in the 1960s embraced comics culture, claiming its legitimacy and countercultural value for their generation vis-à-vis the political establishment.

Gekiga's aesthetic sophistication, along with its thematic depth and diversity, in the late 1960s further attracted artists and intellectuals, prompting cultural criticism and intellectual conversation across disciplines. In 1967, art critic Ishiko Jun founded the first manga criticism journal series, *Mangaism* (*Mangashugi*) in which he and other critics discussed and even theorized on *gekiga* within a leftist-oriented framework. Concurrently, Harvard-educated philosopher and historian Tsurumi Shunsuke devoted most of his book *Postwar Theory in Manga* (*Manga no sengo shisō*, 1973) to *gekiga*. The presence of substantial manga criticism enhanced the awareness of comics' methodology and thematic importance, which, in turn, spurred *gekiga* creators to further employ the medium for philosophical, artistic, and political explorations.

Gekiga also inspired film directors and musicians; most famously, Japanese New Wave film director Ōshima Nagisa produced an experimental film *Band of Ninja* (*Ninja bugei-chō*, 1967) based on Shirato's work with the same title. Observing the popularity of *gekiga* among university students, Tezuka Osamu, who had been creating childrens manga, hurriedly founded a new magazine named *COM* in 1967 in order to feature his manga aimed at mature audiences, including his "lifework" the *Phoenix* series (*Hi no tori*, 1967–1988). The flocking of cultural critics, intellectuals, and artists to *gekiga* helped legitimize the status of comics not merely as an important part of Japanese popular culture but also as something similar to either serious literature or modern art (or so argued by some cultural critics).

The rapid massification and commercialization of *gekiga* in the 1970s were predictable in that many *gekiga* artists had already begun to be hired in the 1960s by major publishing houses for their newly founded *seinen* (young men's) manga magazines. By the 1980s, *gekiga* was integrated into part of Japanese comics culture, diminishing its alternativeness as the manga industry became even more commercialized. Yet in retrospect, it is hard to deny the legacy of *gekiga* in the current form of Japanese comics in general. *Gekiga* not only nurtured the comics medium into something similar to serious graphic narratives, but it also enriched manga expression with its formal innovations. Some might argue that without *gekiga*, Japanese manga could not flourish as it does now. Internationally acclaimed manga works, including Nakazawa Keiji's *Barefoot Gen* (*Hadashi no gen*, 1973–1974) that includes graphic depictions of *hibakusha* and Tezuka's later works, including *The Book of Human Insects* (*Ningen konchūki*, 1970–1971) and *Ayako* (1972–1973), inherited stylistic and thematic sophistication from 1960s *gekiga*.

Conclusion: *Gekiga* as Part of Japanese Counterculture

Counterculture in Japan germinated in multiple locales and contexts, taking diverse cultural forms and media: comics being one of them. The examples discussed above—including the artist collective, a politicized alternative comics magazine, *gekiga* criticism *dōjinshi*, artistic experimentalism, and transgressions of established cultural and artistic borders—all manifested alternative aspirations through cultural productions, often against the political establishment. Japanese countercultural praxes largely responded to the nation's specific conjunctures but were in synch with radical cultural movements in other parts of the globe. Steven Ridgely (2010: ix) claims that it is "[b]etter [to] conceive counterculture as a rhizomatically structured and globally synchronic mode," not as an imitation or influence of the "West". *Gekiga* supports this view and demonstrates that Japan was on the vanguard of global countercultural movements. Tatsumi disavowed awareness of the American "underground comix" movement (small or self-published comic books appearing from the counterculture on the U.S. West Coast) because of its similar rebellious mood and the synchronicity of the 1960s (Tomine 2005: n.p.).

In North America, the rise of alternative comics in the mid-1980s—most famously Pulitzer Prize-winning Art Spiegelman's *Maus* (1986), which initiated a "paradigm shift" (Chute and DeKoven 2006: 440) in the world of American comics—has increasingly attracted scholars' interests in "serious" graphic narratives. From a Japanese perspective, this American "growth" of comics might seem like a belated "maturity," since Japan already underwent it a couple of decades earlier. Yet it is wrong to assume that manga—and for this matter, American comics too—had grown into a serious medium for adults for the first time in comics history. As Roger Sabin (1993: 1) warns, it was "just one stage in the long and complicated evolution of the form." For example, in Japan, from the late nineteenth century to the early twentieth century, several *mangaka* and painters and illustrators (including Shirato's father Okamoto Tōki) produced political cartoons and comic strips for newspapers, photo-journalism magazines (*gurafu-shi*), political in-house organ magazines (*seiji kikan-shi*), and satirical humor magazines (Lent 1989: 226–227). In this broader view of Japanese comics history, *gekiga* can be considered as a cultural moment as the popular medium of comics regained its socio-political and critical potential without losing its visual pleasure.

Notes

1 Often called the "god of manga," Tezuka Osamu is one of the most celebrated artists among manga fans, critics, and other *mangaka* due to his pioneering works, innovations on the media, and the visual style. His 1947 bestselling work *New Treasure Island* (*Shin-takarajima*), a collaboration with Sakai Shichima, was a seminal work that initiated the postwar mainstream "story manga" convention.
2 Although several *gekiga* were translated into English in the 1980s, the term became better known in North America after American comics artist Adrian Tomine (re-)introduced Tatsumi as the "grandfather of Japanese alternative comics" in 2005, when Tatsumi's short-story *gekiga* collection *The Push Man and Other Stories* was published by Canada-based publisher *Drawn & Quarterly*.
3 Yet several *gekiga*/manga works were exposed to criticism even after Tatsumi's intervention due to the unchanged perception of mainstream society that "story manga" was meant as entertainment for children.
4 Yomota Inuhiko claims that Shirato was responding to a real-life incident in which a Chinese person hid in a cave after escaping from forced labor at a coalmine factory in Hokkaido during the war. The change of national origin in Shirato's work from Chinese to Korean probably responds to the "ambiguous" status of Korean residents in Japan during the 1950s.
5 It has since become known that this graduate student was Takemono Nobuhiro (a.k.a. Takita Osamu), a famous radical political activist who was arrested on the suspicion of murdering the Japanese self-defense official (Yomota 2004: 232). Takemoto appeared in Tsuchimoto Noriaki's documentary film about the Japanese New Left political activism *Prehistory of the Partisans* (*Paruchizan zenshi*, 1969).

25 Sampling Girls' Culture

An Analysis of *Shōjo* Manga Magazines

Jennifer Prough

These days the word "manga" conjures up a range of images, all of which include some notion of comic books or graphic novels from Japan. Images of dynamic black and white pages filled with characters with big eyes, spikey hair, and school uniforms, or *chibi* (small and chubby) characters come to mind. Manga are renowned for tackling weighty human concerns in long narratives, for comic-book-style stories that are not just for children. They have all but become a genre of global popular literature. But what is less well known outside of Japan is that almost all manga are first serialized in manga magazines; this follows the Japanese publishing convention of first printing texts in periodicals and then, if they sell well, as standalone books. In this chapter, I take a close look at *shōjo* manga within the context of *shōjo* manga magazines. Examining *shōjo* manga through the material object of a magazine shows how these visual narratives are shaped by their media form, as well as how the magazine context intertwines *shōjo* manga with broader trends in girls' culture.

Throughout this chapter, I use the term "to sample" as a framework because it works on three registers: (1) to give out a small amount of something for people to try; (2) to use a small group to represent a larger group; and (3) to use a small part of a recording or text as a part of another recording or text. *Shōjo* manga magazines perform all three tasks. They provide readers with small samples of serialized manga to see if they like them. They solicit readers' feedback and use a small group to represent the whole when making decisions about which manga to continue, and they include small amounts of consumer goods from girls' culture, like accessories and clothing, as prizes or presents for readers, enabling them to mix the world of manga into their daily lives. Thus my analysis focuses on the everyday uses of *shōjo* manga magazines, tracing their origin, their influence on the genre of *shōjo* manga, and the ways they link *shōjo* manga to the wider culture of girls' fashion and lifestyles.

My discussion of *shōjo* manga magazines concentrates on mainstream magazines: *Best Friends (Nakayoshi)*, *Ribbon (Ribon)*, *Girls' Friend (Shōjo furendo)*, *Special Edition Margaret (Bessatsu Margaret)*, *Cookie*, *Juliet*, and *Kiss*. These magazines are all published by prominent publishing houses Shūeisha and Kōdansha and target readers from elementary school through high school and into university. The specific examples in this chapter all come from the magazine *Cookie*. Established by Shūeisha in 2000, *Cookie* publishes *shōjo* manga titles for young women in their late teens and early twenties. I chose *Cookie* both because it has remained widely popular since its inception and it was one of the last *shōjo* manga magazines to be created. (New magazines have been rare after the economic downturn of the 1990s.) The *shōjo* manga editorial board at Shūeisha envisioned *Cookie* as a quintessential *shōjo* manga magazine for a new generation of girls who grew up reading *Ribbon*, the company's most read *shōjo* manga magazine. Thus *Cookie* serves as an example of a *shōjo* manga magazine in print that was conceived in the digital age yet preserves the sampling features of the magazines that preceded it.

Introducing *Shōjo* Manga Magazines

There are almost three hundred monthly, bi-monthly, and weekly manga magazines in Japan, primarily published by large publishing houses (Shuppan Nenpō 2013: 231). Given this scope, you can find manga magazines targeting nearly any demographic—boys and girls, young men and women, adult men and women. With thematic topics ranging from fantasy to economics, mahjong to motherhood, there are manga magazines for just about anything. As is clear even in this cursory list, gender remains a fundamental organizing principle. In fact, gender and age demographics have shaped the production of manga magazines from the start. The first children's magazines in which manga appeared in the early twentieth century were categorized as girls' (*shōjo*) magazines and boys' (*shōnen*) magazines. Still today, most manga magazines are produced within the girls' or boys' division of a publishing house, and, when sold in bookstores and convenience stores, they are shelved in girls' or boys', women's or men's, sections as well. This is one indication of the power of convention that shapes the creation of manga within the mainstream publishing industry in Japan. Of course, this organizing principle does not dictate who actually reads the manga magazines—cross-over readership is widely practiced and certainly not discouraged—but it does mean that, generally speaking, artists and editors have a particular demographic in mind as they craft stories for a specific magazine's readers. This is one of the subtle ways that the creation of manga narratives is shaped by their debuts in manga magazines.

Even though nearly all manga are first released in manga magazines, the publishing houses do not make money on the magazines. Rather, if a manga story is popular, it is recompiled into a book, and eventually a set of books, and licensed to anime and videogame companies, along with other media platforms (Prough 2011: 13). Thus publishing houses use manga magazines as a way to test out, or sample, which manga are popular enough to warrant further production and promotion. A typical manga magazine comprises twenty or so serialized manga. (Serialized manga refers to longer stories that are released piece by piece, often in thirty- to forty-page segments, each week or month, like television episodes.) These short manga are usually continued in the next magazine, and it is through this serialization of manga that editors determine which titles will be marketable in books and other crossover media. In between episodes, editors and artists converse about the content and characters, incorporating readers' feedback. Therefore, whether a manga ends after just a few episodes or continues for years does not depend solely on the artist's sense of how long the narrative arc should be but also on how popular the story is along the way. To be clear, we can often identify a link between creative talent and longer-running popular manga, but this is not necessarily what ensures the success and length of a manga. Here, too, we see the ways that manga stories are not simply featured in manga magazines for promotional purposes, but they are shaped by the process of production within the structure of manga magazines.

Moreover, interspersed between the manga titles in a *shōjo* manga magazine are a range of features that elicit readers' feedback on manga in order to determine the overall popularity. These features all draw readers outside of the realm of manga and connect them to wider girls' culture through fashion and accessory prizes, references to popular bands or celebrity idols, cooking and style pages, and the like. In particular, the few glossy, full-color pages at the beginning of each magazine sample girls' culture—juxtaposing and blending manga images and style with wider trends.

The dynamics of sampling within a *shōjo* manga magazine can be seen by examining the table of contents.[1] Flipping through the pages of a typical *shōjo* manga magazine, we see that most of the four-hundred pages are comprised of serialized manga stories. In serialized manga, the story remains unfinished, to be continued, in the next magazine. Typically, in the mix as well are short-story style manga in which the story starts and ends in that issue. This is the first way that *shōjo* manga magazines sample, by providing readers with nearly twenty episodes and short manga per issue, to read and determine which they want to purchase. In all, manga samples make up around 90 percent of the content of a typical *shōjo* manga magazine. The remaining thirty to forty pages include several standard non-manga features: for example, "*furoku*" (a list of presents you can order or win if you send in feedback), survey information, artist contest results, and an assortment of one- to two-page articles related to manga or manga artists. Of particular interest in this chapter, several of these non-manga features aim to encourage readers to buy the magazine and to submit their feedback on top manga titles and characters. One final thing that stands out while looking through a manga magazine is the lack of advertisements, although they have increased in the past few years. Most of the advertisements that do appear are for manga books, events related to the manga stories in the magazine, and other *shōjo* manga magazines published by the same publishing house. In sum, a close look at the contents of a typical *shōjo* manga magazine demonstrates the primacy of serialized manga stories for readers to sample, the presence of a select number of non-manga features that place manga in the wider context of girls' culture, and a lack of any content not related to *shōjo* manga.[2] Zooming back out of the pages of a magazine, in the next section I outline the ways that *shōjo* manga magazines developed over the course of the mid-twentieth century, highlighting the ways that manga magazines and the manga within them have evolved in relation to wider media trends.

Shōjo Manga Magazines in Context

In this brief history, I will demonstrate how *shōjo* manga magazines, and thus *shōjo* manga themselves, developed in response to changes in the media landscape across the late twentieth century. *Shōjo* manga magazines took on their current format in the late 1960s but grew out of a genre of children's general magazines dating back to the early twentieth century. Referred to as "general magazines" (*sōgō zasshi*), the earliest children's magazines like *Girls' Club* (*Shōjo kurabu*, 1923–1962) and *Boys' Club* (*Shōnen kurabu*, 1914–1962) were started in order to provide educational entertainment to children as mass media boomed in the 1920s (Prough 2011: 56). These magazines comprised a mixture of manga, short stories, serialized fiction, and articles about celebrities, as well as educational articles about current events and recent discoveries. Manga was just one part of this realm of entertainment for children.

As Japan began to recover from the strictures of austerity and censorship after World War II, there was a high demand for cheap entertainment, and publishers flocked to fill the need. *Girls' Club* and *Boys' Club* led the field, and new magazines like *Boys* (*Shōnen*), *Boys' King* (*Shōnen kingu*), *Boys' World* (*Shōnen sekai*), *Girls* (*Shōjo*), and *Girls' Book* (*Shōjo bukku*) followed suit. Yet in the late 1950s and early 1960s, the general children's magazines were not the only places where manga could be found; there were also manga books sold in candy shops and available for rent at the book rental stalls that could be found throughout streets of cities and towns (Takahashi and Yonezawa 1996: 35–86; Shimizu 1999: 85–89). Fueled with engaging stories by the likes of Tezuka Osamu, Ueda Toshiko, and Matsumoto Akira, manga grew in popularity, and the percentage of manga stories in the boys' and girls' magazines increased dramatically.

Throughout this period, as household income increased, so too did demand for consumer goods and among them magazines and books for all ages; children's general magazines grew in number, length, and vibrancy. In the early 1960s, these magazines underwent a visual renovation, moving to a larger size format, adding more pages, and including more color pages (Prough 2011: 35). Technological innovations, including a decrease in color printing costs, along with the advent of television, helped fuel this visual renovation. Perhaps the most famous example of the influence of visual media on the manga industry during this time is the work of Tezuka Osamu (1928–1989). His *Astro Boy* (*Tetsuwan Atomu*), serialized in *Boys* (*Shōnen*) magazine from 1952 to 1968, is heralded for having the pacing and flow of film.

Tezuka also wrote *shōjo* manga, including *Princess Knight* (*Ribon no kishi*), serialized in *Girls' Club* from 1953 to 1958, which was an immediate hit. The fast-paced action of these early Tezuka titles translated easily into the then new format of television anime.

By 1960, television was booming in Japan (Partner 1999: 162–166). This worried the magazine industry, prompting the development of weekly magazines to adopt the pace of television programs. Between 1959 and 1965, many children's general magazines moved from a monthly to weekly format, and more magazines were created (Maruyama 1999: 209). The weeklies dominated the children's magazine world throughout the 1960s, quickened the pace of magazine production, and required a significant increase in content. Because children's general magazines at this time included articles on celebrities, entertainment, and current events as well as manga, it would have been easy to increase the informational content; however, because manga had become such a critical feature, it remained a significant portion of magazine content. This demand heralded some of the early classics of *shōjo* manga by Takahashi Makoto, Mizuno Hideko, Watanabe Masako, and other artists. Many of these works are no longer widely known, in part because the practice of recompiling manga into collectible books was not yet widely practiced. Yet these artists' names are part of the manga pantheon, and their later works, such as Watanabe's *Glass Castle* (*Garasu no shiro*, from 1962) and Mizuno's *Honey Honey's Marvelous Adventure* (*Hanī Hanī no suteki no bōken*, 1968), were compiled into books and sold voraciously.

The late 1960s and early 1970s have been regarded as the golden age of manga, and it was in this critical period that an important development in publishing occurred: the invention of all-manga magazines. A prime example was *Weekly Shōnen Jump*, which debuted in 1968. Setting the trend for later manga magazines, it was filled almost exclusively with manga; no longer was manga interspersed with short stories or articles about celebrities. By the middle of the 1970s, there was a pantheon of all-manga magazines. Some existing general children's magazines, like *Best Friends* and *Ribbon*, switched to an all-manga format, while other new magazines like *Special Edition Girls' Comics* (*Bessatsu shōjo komikku*) and *Ciao*, were created.

With the increased volume of manga being created through the new genre of all-manga magazines, manga came of age. Through the convergence of an overall trend in the diversification of media and new demand for manga aimed at young adults, the current range of manga magazines targeting nearly every potential demographic developed. In the early 1980s, media industries began to move away from a model of having one mega hit or mega title that would appeal to all to thinking about titles through individual choice and hobby or interest related themes. This is sometimes referred to as "micro-masses," wherein increased demand in consumer culture leads to increased specialization in thematic topics or increased desire for market expansion (Ivy 1993; White 1995; Lukács 2010: 95–96). Thus manga magazines specializing in themes, like historical settings or mysteries, appeared. Perhaps the best known is the genre of "ladies comics" (*rediizu komikkusu*) through such magazines as *BE LOVE*, *Judy*, *Young You*, and *Office You*. This new genre of magazine featured manga that catered to young women working in offices, newlyweds, and new mothers. By this time, a generation of children had grown up reading manga and did not want to stop as they became adults, while the first generation of postwar artists were also anxious to explore this genre beyond the children's market. Spurred by wider media shifts towards diversification and internal dynamics of a still growing industry, manga magazines aimed at specific themes and at adult audiences proliferated into the plethora of magazines available today.[3]

By the turn of the twenty-first century, cellphones and the Internet posed a challenge to the manga industry, forcing it to respond as it did to the earlier threat of television. When I was conducting research for my book *Straight from the Heart: Gender, Intimacy, and the Cultural Protection of Shōjo Manga* (2011) from 2000 to 2002, the publishing houses were just establishing web divisions. At that time, each *shōjo* magazine had a website, which consisted of nothing more than a few images, the current issue's table of contents, and information about upcoming events. Although the web presence of manga magazines has greatly increased since then, their sites mostly mimic the content of their print magazines and are used for advertising rather than for encouraging interactivity between readers, artists, and publishers. Thus the features of *shōjo* magazines discussed in this chapter, which evolved as a part of the magazine business' attempts to encourage readers to buy their own copies of the magazines and send in feedback about what they would buy more of, have significantly changed in the digital age.

Shaping Manga, Sampling Stories

Returning to the pages of a typical *shōjo* manga magazine, in this section I focus on the ways that magazine production shapes manga, showing the culmination of the historical changes discussed above. When reading a manga book, even a multivolume set, we might imagine an artist crafting an engaging story, shaping characters we come to love or hate, setting the scene for those characters either somewhere foreign or on the familiar streets of Tokyo. This certainly happens in the creation of manga, but because of the structural system surrounding the production of manga magazines, writing manga stories is not quite this straightforward. Each magazine has an editorial team ranging from three to seven editors, depending on the frequency and stature of the magazine. Each editor is in charge of about twenty artists, some of whom have not yet published a manga but show promise and some who are currently publishing manga in the magazine, some rising stars and a veteran artist or two.[4] How frequently they meet and review a manuscript depends on what the artist is currently publishing, but editors and artists do meet and discuss drafts of manga in progress. In fact, especially for new artists with manga currently in production, the editor marks up the drafts and discusses necessary changes with them. Which is to say that the editorial process shapes both story and images. How hands-on this process is depends on how famous the artist is and on the personality of the editor. During my fieldwork, I sat in on several editor and artist conversations at both Shōgaku-kan and Shūeisha; some meetings were much like collaborative discussions with both parties adding to overall creation, and others were directed by an editor who gave directions about pacing, the spacing of word balloons, and, occasionally, character development. So *shōjo* manga stories are created by artists, but in dialogue with manga magazine editors.

It is not always obvious when reading a manga book that the "chapters" were originally serialized segments. In my conversations with editors, they highlighted the fact that there is a typical story arc for each thirty- to forty-page installment; when to put in comic relief or rising action and how to end while leaving something the reader will anticipate in the next episode is all part of the making of manga for magazines. As one young editor suggested:

> When working with new artists, I am the expert because I know the format and pacing of manga in a magazine. I can help new artists shape their stories. But with veteran artists, they are the experts, and I am just here to help them however they need it.[5]
>
> (Sōda 2001)

While this differs significantly depending on the editor and artist relationship and temperaments, the structured pacing shapes manga stories in production in ways that are not always visible in a manga book.

Another way that magazine production shapes *shōjo* manga stories is through the collection of readers' feedback. Here, editors and artists try to gauge what manga, and within a particular manga which characters, are popular. Each month readers are offered the chance to voice their opinions about which manga is their favorite and why, or who their favorite character is and why. This is the second way that *shōjo* manga magazines sample, by soliciting information to determine which serialized stories should continue. If a story does not prove popular enough, it will end even if the plot is not complete. Especially for new titles and new authors, this information is also used to shape storylines. In one of my meetings with an editor and artist, they explained that one of the side characters, a goofy guy who was originally meant for comic relief, was so popular among readers that the editor suggested giving him a larger role. "Today," she said, "He is the main male character" (Kodama 2002). Similarly, Deborah Shamoon (2007: 7–8), shares an anecdote from the famous manga artist Ikeda Riyoko's *The Rose of Versailles* (*Berusaiyu no bara*) demonstrating that readers' feedback was critical throughout the process of writing this now quintessential *shōjo* manga. In all of the incidents outlined here, we see the ways that the creation of manga in the context of manga magazines does more than merely feature the genre itself. Rather, the process of sampling manga stories in *shōjo* manga magazines in order to determine what will sell as books or across the media mix landscape shapes the stories themselves in significant ways.

Magazine Format, Non-Manga Features

I turn now to the non-manga features of *shōjo* manga magazines, demonstrating the ways that they relate to manga content, resemble fashion or lifestyle magazines, and connect manga magazines with the wider world of girls' culture. The first three to five pages of a *shōjo* manga magazine are glossy, full-color pages, often with one long foldout page, unlike the monochrome pages that fill most of the magazine. Surprisingly, this colorful gateway is only tangentially linked to manga; there are colorful images of a popular band, sometimes with fan art, or advertisements for an upcoming movie made from a manga title from the magazine. Moreover, these pages feature colorful glossy images of fashion goods and accessories that readers can send in for, called "Everyone's Service" (*Zennin saabisu*) or "Survey Prizes" (*Anketto kenshō*). In the case of "Everyone's Service," readers are encouraged to send in a small amount of money for postage in order to receive some of the accessories featured that month. Taking an example from the February 2006 issue of *Cookie*, three "courses" (A, B, and C), were offered, each featuring a set of stationery items adorned with images from the manga *Nana* by Yazawa Ai. The reader selects her first choice course and mails in the postcard included in the magazine, paying a small fee plus postage (Prough 2011: 67–69). As the name implies, everyone who submits a postcard for "Everyone's Service" by the deadline will get the item(s) they selected. This provides readers with a way to get lifestyle accessories featuring or in the style of their favorite manga, while requiring them to purchase a copy of the magazine.

The "Survey Prizes" are also commercial items that the reader can win, but this time there is a limited quantity. Typically, the publishing house has purchased or contracted for a limited quantity of higher end fashion or lifestyle accessory items like clothing, MP3 players, or bags. Readers who submit applications for "Survey Prizes" are selected at random. For example, a 2010 issue of *Cookie* offered 130 lucky readers the chance to win their choice of these thirteen styles of bags from "trendy to classic" (*Cookie* 2010: 7). Like "Everyone's Service," the application instructions and required postcard for the "Survey Prizes" are included near the back of the magazine. However, to be eligible for the "Survey Prizes," readers must answer six to ten questions about the manga from that month's magazine (Prough 2011: 69–72). Example questions include: list your top three manga in this issue; list any manga you do not like; rank the top five manga; list your favorite five characters from this magazine issue; and any other specific information the publishers might want to gather about possible prizes for the next issue or other trends. Thus fashion items or lifestyle accessories are the main currency for reader's feedback, which is used in part to hone *shōjo* manga stories.

These colorful gateways into *shōjo* manga magazines serve to connect the world of *shōjo* manga to girls' culture more broadly. By sampling trendy fashion and accessories, these magazines share an affinity with girls' fashion magazines. Yet after these glossy, full-color pages in the front of the magazine, the rest of the content is all manga. These stylish front pages that highlight consumer goods are related to manga in two main ways: (1) the goods have images of manga characters on them, or (2) the fashion items imitate the style of a particular manga character set of characters. "Everyone's Service" gives readers a chance to decorate their rooms and themselves with images of their favorite characters or logos from their favorite manga. In the abovementioned example from winter 2006, the file folders and calendars are emblazoned with either punk rock Nana or Cute Hachi (the two main characters from *Nana*), while the organizers have the logo and ask the reader to choose between the two character's styles—sleek and black or fluffy and white or pink—the aesthetic juxtaposition that drive story. Through these items, readers can express their preference for their favorite character. This brings the world of *shōjo* manga and its style directly into readers' everyday lives.

The fashion items frequently offered as "Survey Prizes" are a more complicated case. These do not carry images of or the logo for a manga or a magazine. They are typically bought directly from stores as giveaway goods. Typically, there are around thirty more expensive goods that a few lucky readers can win, and then a wider range (around one hundred) cheaper items that are given out. These items, advertised enticingly in the front color pages of a manga magazine, indirectly link *shōjo* manga stories to wider fashion trends. Within the pages of mainstream manga, characters are frequently depicted living trendy urban lifestyles, wearing the latest fashions for girls their age. These items make these links a bit clearer allowing a few lucky readers to acquire the fashions their manga characters love; in exchange, this sample provides magazines with important feedback. While the non-manga features highlighted here are ultimately a tiny portion of the manga magazines content, they sample manga images and fashion goods in ways that connect *shōjo* manga magazines to the wider world of girls' culture.

Conclusion: Sampling Girls' Culture

Examining *shōjo* manga from the perspective of its production in *shōjo* manga magazines demonstrates how manga stories are shaped by their debut in a manga magazine as well as how magazines sample girls' fashion trends to extend manga outside of their pages. Since their emergence in the late twentieth century, manga magazines have evolved a format designed to sample manga, try out storylines and characters, and maximize the sale of manga books. They include features to link *shōjo* manga to the wider world of girls' culture and to encourage girls to buy magazines and provide feedback, which, in turn, is used in conversations between editors and artists. Throughout this chapter, I have demonstrated the ways that *shōjo* manga magazines sample girls' consumer culture: first, manga are sampled through their juxtaposition in serialized manga magazines; second, a sample of readers' feedback is solicited through contests and requests in magazines; and finally, the non-manga features sample, or mix, wider consumer trends with manga styles within the context of the magazines.

In the end, the genre of *shōjo* manga cannot be reduced to its origins in a *shōjo* manga magazine, as the other chapters in *Introducing Japanese Popular Culture* attest. The stories are rich and engaging and get recompiled and retold across a wide range of media, from books to television to film and games. And yet, by looking at manga in situ, in the context of *shōjo* manga magazines, we get a more complex sense of how these stories are conceived and consumed.

Notes

1 The current table of contents for Shūeisha's *Cookie* and *Ribbon* can be found here: http://cookie.shueisha.co.jp/lineup/index.html; http://ribon.shueisha.co.jp/now/index.html.

2 *Shōnen* manga magazines also follow these parameters. In general, girls' magazines make wider use of the reader's pages and fashion item tie-ins than boys' magazines do, although this, too, varies according to the age of the target demographic.

3 It is important to note that the economic downturn that began in the early 1990s has affected the manga industry, albeit at bit later than other major economic sectors. By 1995 the Publishing Annals (*Shuppan Nenpō*) reported the first decline in overall manga magazine sales in decades (*Shuppan Nenpō* 1996). In general, there has been a slow but steady decline in manga magazine sales in the ensuing decades (*Shuppan Nenpō* 2013: 236–242, 2014: 225–237).

4 In the first decade of the twenty-first century, publishers have hired more employees on a contract basis, but, in general, the job of editor is an in-house, salaried position. When I was conducting my research, editor's explained that, when publishers advertise for new full-time recruits from the top universities each April, they typically hire between ten and fifteen new employees; one or two are assigned to the manga division. Customarily, editors, like many fulltime workers, are transferred to different departments or branches every five to seven years. Men still outnumber women in editorial positions. While the number of contract workers are not visible, the new full-time hires are lauded on the main publishing house websites after each hiring season. See for example, www.shueisha.co.jp/saiyo/new_staff/.

5 Pseudonyms have been used for all interviews at the request of the interviewees.

26 The Beautiful Men of the Inner Chamber

Gender-Bending, Boys' Love, and Other *Shōjo* Manga Tropes in *Ōoku*

Deborah Shamoon

In the manga series *Ōoku: The Inner Chambers* (2005–ongoing), Yoshinaga Fumi (b. 1971) presents an imagined history of Japan's Edo period (1603–1868) in which women rule the country, after a plague decimates the male population. The story follows the succession of female shōguns and the men of the inner chambers (*ōoku*), or harem. The gender-swapped premise of *Ōoku* allows Yoshinaga to explore not only Japanese history but also the conventions of the *shōjo* manga genre. Yoshinaga both celebrates and critiques the *bishōnen* (pretty boy) aesthetics of *shōjo* manga and the prevalence of homosexual romance. *Ōoku* plays with *shōjo* manga genre conventions, particularly the tendency to rely on cross-dressing, gender switching, and boys' love to avoid restrictive gender roles for girls. Rather than simply reversing genders, *Ōoku* ultimately transcends *shōjo* manga conventions to give a more nuanced critique of received gender roles for both males and females.

Shōjo Manga Genre Conventions

The genre of *shōjo* manga as it exists today was formed in the early 1970s, when young women artists known collectively as the Year 24 Group (*Nijū yonen gumi*, after the year of their birth, Shōwa 24 or 1949) took over the genre and instituted long-running, complex stories that focus on the inner lives of teenagers as they negotiate adolescent maturation. Even within fantasy, science fiction, or historical settings, the main point is depicting the often-stormy emotions of the main characters as they grow up.

The Year 24 Group expanded on existing aesthetics of illustration popular in girls' magazines to develop conventions for portraying emotions. Drawing characters with hugely exaggerated eyes dates back to the 1920s and is used to invite identification, identify the main character, and also to showcase the artist's individual style (Takahashi 2008: 122). Other conventions to convey emotion and to create visual interest where there is little physical action include emotive backgrounds of flowers, stars or clouds, and using an open or layered panel arrangement (Shamoon 2012: 116). There is also an emphasis on fashion and depicting the clothing of the main characters in loving detail (Takahashi 2008: 127).

This is not to say, however, that the stories in the *shōjo* manga genre are all trivial love stories about nothing more than fashion. One of the early classics of *shōjo* manga, *The Rose of Versailles* (*Berusaiyu no bara*, 1972–1973) by Ikeda Riyoko, uses the French Revolution setting to explore serious themes of social and gender equality. The main character, Oscar, is a cross-dressed woman who serves as a soldier in Marie Antoinette's Royal Guard and later takes a leadership role in the revolution. Girl readers loved Oscar for her cool sophistication and her assumption of masculine power without sacrificing her female identity (Shamoon 2012: 136). The most beloved aspect of the manga, however, is Oscar's romance with a fellow soldier, André. In many ways, André takes a more stereotypically feminine role as Oscar's subordinate and supporter, letting her literally wear the pants in their relationship (Shamoon 2012: 127). Themes of cross-dressing and gender-switching have remained common in *shōjo* manga as a way of creating more satisfyingly equal romantic relationships and getting around sexist structures.

Another key feature of *shōjo* manga initiated by the Year 24 Group is boys' love (*shōnen ai*, also called *yaoi* and abbreviated BL), or homosexual romance. The two pioneers of BL are Hagio Moto, with *The Heart of Thomas* (*Tōma no shinzō*, 1974), and Takemiya Keiko with *The Poem of the Wind and the Tree* (*Kaze to ki no uta*, 1976–1984), both set in boys' boarding schools. BL is sometimes surprising to those unfamiliar with *shōjo* manga—why would girls want to read about boys falling in love with each other, instead of with a girl? This attitude assumes that readers only identify with characters of the same gender as themselves. But Midori Matsui writes:

> It was apparent that the boys were the girls' displaced selves; despite the effeminate looks that belied their identities, however, the fictitious boys were endowed with reason, eloquence and aggressive desire for the other, compensating for the absence of logos and sexuality in the conventional portraits of girls.
>
> (Matsui 1993: 178)

In Hagio's and Takemiya's manga, the boys' feminine appearance invites girl readers to identify with them. Even when BL stories feature adult men as characters, often with one more stereotypically masculine and the other more feminine, it is a mistake to assume readers only identify with the feminine characters (Pagliassotti 2008: 71). Regardless, the *bishōnen*, the elegant, feminine boy, is the dominant ideal of male beauty in *shōjo* manga. Most of the male characters in *Ōoku* conform to this physical type, and the all-male inner chambers would seem to be an ideal setting for homosexual romance, although Yoshinaga takes the story in a different direction, as we shall see.

BL allows girls access to sexual fantasies detached from the dangers and stereotypes of heterosexual relationships. While sexual violence and rape do appear in BL, the fact that the characters are boys, not girls, provides a safe sense of distance, avoiding the threat of unplanned pregnancy. Not only can male characters more easily demonstrate sexual agency, but it is also easier for the characters to achieve more equality in their relationships. The appeal of homosexual romance to women is gradually gaining more acceptance in the United States, with the proliferation of fan fiction or "slash," which pairs up male characters from popular television shows, among other popular culture media. As Marni Stanley writes:

> Slash and *yaoi* interrupt the dominant narratives of manga, television, and even pornography by giving females a chance to play with boys and the male body in ways that male authors/artists have traditionally assumed to be their right to manipulate and play with the female body.
>
> (Stanley 2008: 107)

The fan discourse around BL emphasizes fantasy, or more specifically, indulgence in a fantasy world (McLelland 2006: 7). The first BL stories were set in turn of the century Europe, a fantastic and distant setting from the perspective of Japanese girls in the 1970s. As the genre has expanded, there is a spectrum from fantasy to more realistic stories. Fans of BL call themselves *fujoshi*, a pun on a term for an elegant lady, substituting a kanji meaning "rotten." These so-called rotten girls revel in their non-productive, self-indulgent fantasies, although they are often painfully aware that their interest is not widely accepted in Japanese society at large (Galbraith 2011: 211).

Over the years, *shōjo* manga has diversified to include a wider range of art styles and stories, although exaggerated eyes, graphic representation of emotion, and exploration of the inner psychology of the main characters remain dominant trends. As readers aged, an offshoot genre developed called "*josei* manga," for older readers, from late teens to twenties. *Josei* stories tend to have a more realistic setting and art style, and many feature heterosexual relationships and women characters with sexual and social agency. Regardless, BL remains popular with female readers. Yoshinaga draws on these conventions in *Ōoku*, particularly the aesthetic of male beauty, and the use of cross-dressing to explore power dynamics between genders. And although *Ōoku* does not prominently feature romance between male characters, the genre conventions of BL inform some key scenes, as we shall see in the next section.

Ōoku: The Inner Chambers

Ōoku has been serialized since 2005 in the bi-monthly manga magazine *Melody* and later compiled into collected volumes (Hakusensha, 2005–ongoing). The English translation is published by Viz under the title *Ōoku: The Inner Chambers* (2009–ongoing). Yoshinaga Fumi began her career writing *dōjinshi* (fan-produced manga based on commercial works) around André, the feminized love interest in *The Rose of Versailles*, for instance *André and I* (*Andore to watashi*, 1991). She made her professional debut in 1994, and her first breakout hit series was *Antique Bakery* (*Seiyō kottō yōgashiten*, Shinshokan 1999–2002), about the romantic entanglements of four men running a cake shop in contemporary Japan. She also published *dōjinshi* versions of her own story, in order to portray more explicit sex scenes than were possible in a mainstream publication. Even as a professional artist, she still retains strong ties to the self-publishing community that launched her career.

Ōoku was a major success for Yoshinaga, winning multiple prizes in Japan and the United States. Sections of the story were made into live-action films in 2010 and 2012, as well as a television series also in 2012. The English language translation has been rather controversial among fans, however, as it uses a modified version of Shakespearean English to reflect the historical setting. While the Japanese original also uses some pre-modern grammar and vocabulary, this kind of half-reconstructed classical language is more widely used in Japanese historical manga, television shows and movies, whereas English language historical dramas almost always use modern grammar. Online reviews reflect readers' discomfort with the unfamiliar language.[1]

Ōoku spans both the *shōjo* and *josei* manga genres. In manga publishing, genre labels are usually applied primarily based on the target demographic of the magazine in which a story is first serialized. By that definition, *Ōoku* is *shōjo* manga because it appears in the *shōjo* manga magazine *Melody*.[2] Because *josei* manga is aimed at late teens to young adults, stories can be more sexually explicit, more serious, and more complex. In terms of content, *Ōoku* is closer to *josei*, as Yoshinaga uses a sparse, realistic visual style and portrays a morally ambiguous storyline with adult (rather than teenage) characters. However, this chapter will discuss how it references the conventions of *shōjo* manga, particularly BL.

Ōoku is set during Japan's Edo period, which began when Tokugawa Ieyasu defeated his rival feudal lords (*daimyō*), ending hundreds of years of civil war. Ieyasu installed himself as shōgun, a military position technically below the emperor, but in fact wielding absolute political power, and inaugurated the Tokugawa clan as hereditary rulers. The alternate history of *Ōoku* begins around 1630, when an epidemic called the red-face pox (*akazura hōsō*) reduces the male population to one fourth of the female. Out of necessity, women begin to take on men's work, at first with some reluctance and confusion, but by the third generation, the women-run society seems normal, including women as shōgun and *daimyō*. As men remain vulnerable to the red-face pox, the few men who survive are considered weak and in need of protection.

There is no single main character in *Ōoku*. The series begins with the regime of the first female shōgun, Iemitsu (ruled 1623–1651), and continues through the entire Edo period. As in the real Edo period, the shōgunate closes the country, although in this case, from fear of invasion if it became known that the country was ruled by women. Yoshinaga uses the male names of the real shōguns and other major figures, and portrays many real historical incidents that would be familiar to a Japanese readership. She includes glimpses into the lives of peasants and merchants, as well as referencing real social trends and advances in technology, such as improvements in farming equipment, the rise of kabuki as popular entertainment, the formation of fire-fighting brigades, the rise of the merchant class, and shift from a rice-based to cash-based economy, as well as historical events including the Great Famine of Kan'ei (1642), the Great Fire of Meireki (1657), the incident of the Forty-Seven Rōnin (Ako Vendetta, 1703), and the eruption of Mount Fuji (1707). Volumes 8, 9, and 10 are set in the mid-1700s, as the shōgun Ieharu orders a select group of doctors and scholars of Dutch to search for a cure for the red-face pox, to restore the male population and guard against invasion. They discover a vaccine, similar to the real-life smallpox vaccine developed in Europe around this time. When Ieharu dies, a more conservative faction takes over the government and abolishes Dutch studies, but knowledge of the vaccine lives on. Ieharu leaves only a male heir, but as he was inoculated against the red-face pox, he is considered fit to rule, hence, the story continues in Volumes 11 and 12 with the ascension of a male shōgun, Ienari, and with the attempt to reinstate Dutch studies and vaccinate the male population.

In real life, the *ōoku* (inner chambers) was a closed section of Chiyoda Castle, housing the shōgun's wives, concubines, mothers, and daughters, as well as their many attendants. Unlike other Asian or Middle Eastern harems, it was ruled by women, not eunuchs, and the women were strictly confined within its walls, sworn to secrecy and forbidden contact with men (Seigle and Chance 2014: 24–26). The large number of wives and concubines was meant to ensure many heirs, although an even larger number of servants and administrators was needed, totaling around four hundred at its peak (Seigle and Chance 2014: 117). Seigle and Chance write that "secrecy and the active exclusion of outsiders lent the *ōoku* a special aura of mystique conducive to speculation and rumors, and at the same time its glamour and prestige invited commoners to imagine and fabricate life within its walls" (Seigle and Chance 2014: 8). Rumors included tales of sexually frustrated women turning to lesbianism and that it was the hidden seat of power in the shōgunate.

In Yoshinaga's manga, the inner chambers become the female shōgun's male harem, instituted to increase the likelihood of an heir through multiple partners. As in the real inner chambers, appointment at any rank is for life, and the men are not allowed to leave or communicate with their families. In many ways, it is an ideal *shōjo* manga setting: dozens of idle, beautiful boys and men at the height of fashion and prestige. Perhaps surprisingly, given Yoshinaga's previous publications, however, there are few stories of gay love in *Ōoku*. This may be in part due to Yoshinaga's commitment to historical accuracy (such relationships were technically forbidden in the inner chambers), but it is also an indication that this is not a self-indulgent fantasy romance but instead a more serious exploration of gender, as the following examples will discuss.

Iemitsu and Arikoto

Many BL tropes are apparent in the chapters dealing with the first female shō-gun Iemitsu and her concubine Arikoto. When the male shōgun Iemitsu dies of the red-face pox, Lady Kasuga, the head of the inner chambers, conceals his death from all but a few councilors and installs Iemitsu's young daughter in his stead under the same name, in order to preserve the Tokugawa lineage. In this transitional period, the female Iemitsu wears male clothing and hair-style but is painfully aware that she has no real power, as a mere figurehead secretly serving in her father's place. As a young girl, she is raped on the castle grounds by a low-ranking samurai who does not know who she is. As a result of the rape, she becomes pregnant, but the child dies in infancy. Unlike the later female shōguns, who dress as women and wield real power as a matter of course, Iemitsu is in many ways captive to the earlier patriarchal culture (Figure 26.1).

Arikoto is a concubine selected for her by Lady Kasuga, part of the process of converting the inner chambers from a female to a male harem. Iemitsu nicknames him O-Man, an indication that the character is loosely based on a real person of the same name, a Buddhist nun from Kyoto forced by the real Iemitsu to renounce her vows in order to join the inner chambers (Seigle and Chance 2014: 297). Arikoto is a typical *bishōnen* character: elegant, fashionable, beautiful, and gentle. Forced to grow out his tonsure, his long hair enhances his feminine appearance. Although coerced into joining the inner chambers against his will, as he gets to know Iemitsu and her sad past, he comes to genuinely care for her and views helping her as an extension of his Buddhist vows (2.226–227).

In a pivotal scene, Iemitsu attempts to humiliate three men of the inner chambers by forcing them to dress as women and dance for her (2.205). Iemitsu mocks their ridiculous appearance, just one instance of her cruelty, which is clearly a result of the trauma she has suffered. Arikoto suddenly appears, also dressed as a woman, but his effortless elegance and beauty put the others to shame, stopping Iemitsu's sadistic fun (2.223). Iemitsu first responds angrily, but Arikoto, now certain of his duty to treat her with compassion, remains calm and places his outer robe around her shoulders, saying, "It doth look so much more beautiful on you, my lord" (2.228). This kindness, combined with the acknowledgement of her femininity, at last cracks Iemitsu's composure and she weeps loudly, expressing for the first time her inner pain and her love for Arikoto.

In a sense, both Arikoto and Iemitsu retain traditionally gendered roles in this scene, with Arikoto serving as the stronger partner and Iemitsu turning to him for support. However, both are cross-dressed in this scene, which strongly recalls the romance between Oscar and André in *The Rose of Versailles*. Over the course of the third volume, Arikoto rises to become the head of the inner chambers, the *bishōnen* who sets the rules and style for generations of men to come. In other words, the standards of male beauty follow the

Figure 26.1 Arikoto (left) comforts Iemitsu (right) while both are cross-dressed.
Ōoku: The Inner Chambers, vol. 2, p. 228.
Source: Courtesy of Viz Media.

aesthetics of BL manga. While the relationships in *Ōoku*, like that between Arikoto and Iemitsu, are for the most part heterosexual, they can be read as re-introducing the female character to the homogender fantasy through cross-dressing.

The Ejima Affair

Even while celebrating the appeal of the *bishōnen*, Yoshinaga also offers some sly criticism of the ideals of male beauty in *shōjo* manga in her treatment of the Ejima affair. The real-life Ejima affair, which took place in 1714, was a major scandal in the history of the inner chambers. Ejima, a high-ranking lady in the inner chambers bureaucracy, conducted an affair with a kabuki actor, Ikushima Shingorō, culminating in a night of drunken revelry at a theater with a retinue of 130 (Seigle and Chance 2014: 176–177). For violating the inner chambers' curfew and engaging in immoral and profligate behavior, Ejima and Ikushima were exiled, and many others involved were also punished (Seigle and Chance 2014: 178). In the fictional version, Ejima, a man, is the advisor to the head of the inner chambers, and Ikushima, a woman, is a kabuki actor known for playing male roles. Contrary to many contemporary accounts which portray the real Ejima as degenerate, sex-crazed, and mad with power, Yoshinaga spends many chapters in volumes six and seven establishing the male Ejima as a model of rectitude and self-control, the victim of political rivalry rather than any personal failing (Figure 26.2).

Part of the reason for Ejima's chastity is his appearance—he is tall, hairy, and has large features. In other words, his body is extremely masculine, but in the female-dominated world of *Ōoku* that only values the *bishōnen*, he is considered freakishly ugly. The sight of Ejima's arm hair is so shocking to the child shōgun Ietsugu that she bursts into tears (7.23). He attempts to conform by shaving his heavy beard and body hair but is still mocked and reviled by the other characters. A flashback reveals that he entered service in the inner chambers because no woman would marry him (7.87). Most of the male characters in *Ōoku* conform to the *bishōnen* ideal, with delicate, feminine features, including long hair and exaggerated eyes. Yoshinaga draws Ejima with a hooked nose, protruding lips, and tiny eyes, encouraging the reader to also find him unattractive.

Although Ejima is introduced to Ikushima by rivals in the inner chambers who seek to corrupt and discredit him, the two share genuine affection. Ikushima assures Ejima that she finds his masculine appearance attractive. Criticizing the women who have scorned him, Ikushima reassures him, "They'd never seen a real man's body before they saw yours, I reckon. I daresay they had the mistaken belief that all men resemble the pale, smooth-skinned fops you see in *ukiyo-e* [woodblock prints]" (7.99). This line can be read as a criticism of the *bishōnen* ideal, an acknowledgment that the images women and girls enjoy in manga are mere fantasy and do not reflect real men's bodies. In other words, while the creation of female-directed sexual

Figure 26.2 The kabuki actor Ikushima Shingorō (top) dressed as a man onstage and Ejima (bottom). *Ōoku: The Inner Chambers*, vol. 7, p. 60.

Source: Courtesy of Viz Media.

fantasies have been empowering inasmuch as it provides women and girls with the opportunity to control the desiring gaze and not just be objects of a male gaze, the images of men that they produce are just as unrealistic and restrictive as are the images men create of women. By focusing so much on Ejima's pain, Yoshinaga shows the real social cost of these impossible fantasies, even the fantasies she herself has created.

A postscript on his storyline reveals that during the nearly thirty years of his exile, Ejima's fame grows; from his hut, he overhears women passing by commenting on his reputation: "I imagine he is most gallant, and most beauteous indeed!! Like someone who hath stepped straight out of an *ukiyo-e* picture!! How could he be otherwise, when he was the lover of Ikushima Shingorō?" (7.160, exclamation points in the original). This is the ironic happy ending granted his otherwise tragic story, to be remembered as conventionally attractive.

Ikushima receives comparatively little character development, but she also reflects a certain gender norm particular to *shōjo* manga. As a kabuki actor known for playing *aragoto*, or tough-guy roles, her appearance is similar to the *otokoyaku*, or player of male roles in the Takarazuka. (Takarazuka, founded in 1914, is a theater company in which girls play both male and female roles.) The *otokoyaku*, coolly masculine on stage but nevertheless clearly female, especially offstage, have long been the most popular with Takarazuka fans (Yamanashi 2012: 94). Like Oscar in *The Rose of Versailles*, they represent self-assured, powerful female characters who take on some masculine traits while remaining female. Ikushima's popularity with both male and female fans again reflects the values of *shōjo* manga, which Yoshinaga uses as the basis for this female-directed society.

Boys' Love in the Inner Chamber

Even more overt criticism of BL fantasies occurs in a brief episode in volume five, concerning the treatment of the male concubines by Tsunayoshi, the fifth shōgun. As in the case of the real-life Tokugawa Tsunayoshi, the female character is nicknamed the "dog shōgun" for her onerous laws protecting the rights and comforts of animals even above those of humans. Although Tsunayoshi's regime was long and relatively prosperous, it was also marked by capriciousness and cruelty. Writing on the real Tsunayoshi, Beatrice Bodart-Bailey remarks, "Tsunayoshi learned from an early age that rules applying to others did not necessarily apply to him" (34). In *Ōoku*, the female Tsunayoshi is pleasure-seeking and self-involved. Desperate to conceive another heir after the death of her only daughter, she increases the number of concubines and disguises her shame at having to sleep with them nightly by forcing them to perform for her amusement in increasingly debauched revelry. The men begin wearing red eye makeup as a kind of good-luck charm, which increases their *bishōnen* appearance (5.77). In one scene, while Tsunayoshi lies with two concubines at once, she orders them to have sex with each other for her amusement (5.125). As an earlier panel shows the two men sharing a knowing glance (5.123), readers might expect them to enthusiastically follow her instructions. After all, the intimate look is usually the beginning of a sex scene in BL erotica. Here, Tsunayoshi represents the usually absent female author/reader who commands/observes the fictional male characters. However, the scene subverts expectations of the BL genre—the men protest desperately (5.126–127), and one even threatens to kill himself rather than have sex with another man on her orders (5.129).

On one level, this scene illustrates Tsunayoshi's cruelty, ordering her subjects to perform for her with no thought to their feelings. On a metatextual level, the scene also forces readers to reconsider BL fantasies. If Tsunayoshi is like the BL author or reader, the men's negative reaction to her orders is a reminder of the limits of those fantasies. From Tsunayoshi's perspective, her order is not so outrageous; as she says, she is aware that there are homosexual couples within the inner chambers (5.126), and later chapters confirm that is true. But Yoshinaga never focuses on those relationships. Instead, we have this scene, where the male objects of the female sexual gaze resist their objectification.

But the scene goes further, revealing that Tsunayoshi herself feels objectified. As she says to the senior chamberlain who intervenes:

> Thou dost accuse me of humiliating those young men, when all I did was command them to lie with each other in front of me?! What is wrong with that?! I am so humiliated myself, every night! Each and every night, I fornicate with men while attendants lie awake behind a thin curtain, listening to every sound I make! Am I the ruler of this land, or a mere whore?!
>
> (5.134)

It is true that the shōgun was rarely granted privacy during sex (Seigle and Chance 2014: 139). The scene ends with this acknowledgment that sexual objectification cuts both ways, harming both the objectified and the objectifier. In the restrictive Tokugawa culture, regardless of which gender is in power, obsession with bloodline and heirs creates suffering on all sides.

Hiraga Gennai as *Yaoi* Artist

Another gesture towards *shōjo* manga tropes appears in the character of Hiraga Gennai. The real Hiraga Gennai (1728–1780) was a colorful character, trained in medicine and Dutch studies, known for his inventions (including an electrostatic generator) and for his satiric and pornographic writing and illustration. In *Ōoku*, Yoshinaga reimagines him as a free-spirited woman who assists in developing the vaccine for the red-face pox. The fictional Gennai, unlike most of the women in *Ōoku*, wears men's clothing and is occasionally mistaken for a man. Another measure of her gender-bending is her special status as one of very few women allowed regular access to the inner chambers. Even within the female-dominated society of *Ōoku*, her defiance of gender roles gives her more freedom, although she remains an outsider. Also unlike most of the characters in *Ōoku*, she engages in a long-term homosexual relationship. Like the real Gennai, she is well known for her racy illustrated fiction. Yoshinaga includes a portrait of Gennai in the overleaf of volume ten, showing her stretched out on the floor, working on a pornographic picture in the *ukiyo-e* style. Despite the Edo-era garb, with her foot in the air and her hair in a ponytail, she looks like a contemporary girl creating *yaoi*. The link between Edo period erotic prints and *yaoi* is an intriguing one—perhaps Yoshinaga is claiming a more exalted cultural tradition for sexually explicit manga, particularly *yaoi*, which has been so frequently reviled, its fans and creators stigmatized (Okabe and Ishida 2012: 207).

Conclusion

Although *Ōoku* depicts a world of female shōguns and switches the gender of many well-known historical figures, it is neither a mere gender swap nor does it suggest that the world ruled by women is in any way superior to actual, male-dominated history. To the contrary, Yoshinaga portrays most of the same excesses, abuses of power, and disasters that occurred in the real Edo period, many of which were caused or exacerbated by poor governance. The fictional female rulers are just as corrupt and petty as the actual male rulers. For example, Volume 10 ends with the senior counselors suppressing the new vaccine and executing the physician who developed it. His disciple, expelled from the inner chambers, is left to shout impotently outside the walls, "You women there, in Edo Castle! You've grabbed the reins of power now—are you satisfied?! For that's all you care about—your own status and authority!!" (10. 244). *Ōoku* is an exploration of the corrosive nature of absolute power and hereditary government, with social injustice and gender inequality perpetrated no matter who is in charge.

Although the manga does not depict a female-ruled utopia, the alternate world suggested by *Ōoku* offers a critique of popular assumptions about gender in Japan. Japanese culture is frequently depicted as intractably patriarchal and sexist, and the Edo period is seen as the pinnacle of the patriarchy, as well as a glorious past to which some nationalists and right-wingers aspire. By picturing an Edo period ruled by women but still reflecting every other familiar feature of that time, Yoshinaga suggests that gender roles are more fluid than we may assume. In particular, picturing the men in powerless, objectified positions disrupts the received narrative of Japanese culture and suggests a world where things could be different.

Finally, by playing with the genre expectations of *shōjo* manga and BL, Yoshinaga asks readers to reflect seriously on the limitations of those genres, even as her own narrative stretches the genre to encompass more serious, complex stories. While the BL genre has been a powerful means for girls to achieve agency in creating and consuming sexual fantasies, and Yoshinaga owes her popularity to BL, in *Ōoku* she reminds readers of the dangers of objectifying male bodies, even as she celebrates male beauty in her character designs. She also suggests that merely swapping genders (for instance, like the cross-dressed Oscar in *The Rose of Versailles* or boys who look like girls in BL manga) is not enough to correct the power imbalance between the sexes. While Year 24 Group wrote hopeful fantasies of idealized romance in the 1970s, in *Ōoku* Yoshinaga presents a more pessimistic view of persistent gender inequality.

Notes

1 "The greatest downside to this series is its English adaptation which, in an effort to create formal-sounding speech, utilizes an awkward, quasi-seventeenth-century style (referred to among critics as 'Fakespeare')" (Beasi 2010).
2 *Shōjo* magazine titles include *Ribon*, *Shōjo Friend*, *Margaret*, and *Shōjo Comic*. *Josei* magazine titles include *Be-Love*, *You*, and *Dessert*.

27 Cyborg Empiricism
The Ghost Is Not in the Shell

Thomas Lamarre

The cyborg is often said to challenge the subject-object and mind-matter oppositions associated with Cartesian dualism. Donna Haraway's 1985 "A Cyborg Manifesto" made the challenge explicit: "Late twentieth century machines have made thoroughly ambiguous the difference between natural and artificial ... and many other distinctions that apply to organisms and machines" (1991: 152). Haraway's cyborg implied a blurring of ontological distinctions between humans and machines, and this blurring of machine-human distinctions appeared to subvert received social distinctions and hierarchies related to nature and artifice, machine and human. Today, however, as Katherine Hayles (2006: 159–60) remarks: "the cyborg no longer offers the same heady brew of resistance and co-option. Quite simply, it is not *networked* enough." Computation and communication technologies seem to have outstripped the cyborg.

Yet the cyborg has persisted. Take, for instance, Shirow Masamune's cyborg manga, *Kōkaku kidōtai: The Ghost in the Shell*, which began serialization in 1989, not long after Haraway's essay.[1] It also proposes the cyborg as a techno-philosophical challenge to Cartesian dualism and has inspired a sprawling and still active media franchise comprising manga, animated films, animated television series, OVAs, novels, films, and videogames. The persistence of this cyborg series invites a closer look at Shirow's initial challenge to Cartesian dualism (and Haraway's).

I propose, however, a departure from the received tendency to deconstruct binary oppositions, to blur ontological distinctions. Building on Haraway's commitment to thinking the relation, I will consider Shirow's cyborgs from the angle of expanded empiricism, drawing on the radical empiricism of William James (1842–1910) and the non-dualism of Nishida Kitarō (1870–1945). These thinkers share with Haraway a commitment to posing questions of the self and subjectivity beyond the normative framework of dualism.

James went to the roots of empiricism, the tabula rasa. He radicalized this blank slate by stripping it of epistemological dualisms, that is, binary categories such as subject and object, or spirit and matter, form and matter. He established "a plane where nothing is pre-established, where no form of knowledge, no certainty—even virtual—has yet appeared, such that everything has the right to be constructed" (Lapoujade 1997: 18). He called this plane pure experience or immediate experience: "there is only one primal stuff or material in the world, a stuff of which everything is composed, and... we call that stuff of 'pure experience'" (James 2003: 2–3).

In his first, most widely read book, *Zen no kenkyū* (1911), translated as *An Inquiry into the Good* (1990), Nishida began with James's pure experience in order to stress the prior, virtual "unity" (*tōitsu*) of subject and object. For both Nishida and James, this unity or stuff does not belong to anyone, to a particular subject or object. It is no one's. Subsequently, Nishida claimed that pure experience was too subjective and formulated his philosophy of *basho* or "place," in which he also began to emphasize the *non* of non-dualism, on the "not-one" of experience (Nishida 2012). His philosophy turned to Buddhist-inspired forms of corporeal self-cultivation intended to undo the subjective self. James, in contrast, stressed the "more-than-one" of virtual unity, hence his commitment to pluralism, a pluriverse happening between and beyond universe and multiverse (Osaki 2015).

Building on these two ways of moving beyond dualism will allow me (a) to delineate the dominant tendency of Shirow's manga toward conflating personal and national sovereignty (the ghost is in the shell) and (b) to explore a minor tendency within the same manga toward a fusion of different dimensions without loss of difference—*the ghost is not in the shell*.

Ghost Emergent

Serialized between April 1989 and November 1990 and released in book format in Japanese (1991) and in English (1995), Shirow's *The Ghost in the Shell* consists of eleven story-chapters set between 2029 and 2030. Stories center on Section 9, a secret special ops unit led by Aramaki Daisuke, set up as an anti-terrorism squad under the Ministry of Internal Affairs but reconfigured by the end of the second chapter into an international hostage rescue unit reporting to the Prime Minister. Section 9 uses high-tech tactical armors, hence *kōkaku kidōtai* or "armored mobile troops." Characters range from humans with very minimal prosthetics and cyberization (such as Togusa), to humans with entirely prosthetic bodies and highly cyberized brains (such as Major Kusanagi Mokoto and Batō); gynoid robot operatives referred to as speakers; and spider-like intelligent mobile tanks called Fuchikoma.

The manga offers a diverse range of minds and bodies, variously combined. These "mind-beings" entail *differences in degree* rather than differences in nature. While the manga distinguishes between having a "ghost" (humans) and not having one (robots), new entities appear that undermine that distinction. Because the manga focuses on the degree of complexity in the material organization of functions, it defies a dualist opposition between human and nonhuman, offering an array of intelligent beings. It develops contrasts and gradations instead of shoring up dichotomies and oppositions. The seemingly endless gradations and permutations of mind-beings have made it a rich source for serialization. The series relies heavily on action and suspense, providing elaborate car chases, shoot-outs, battles, and conflicts, which are punctuated with espionage, concealed interventions, and secret societies. But plot is not the primary concern. Attention focuses more on degrees of technical complexity, on what might happen across gradations. Consequently, narrative beginnings and endings feel open to revision and further elaboration.

Its world has been augmented in animation, such as Oshii Mamoru's two animated films, *The Ghost in the Shell* (1995) and *The Ghost in the Shell: Innocence* (2004); Kamiyama Kenji's two animated television series, *The Ghost in the Shell: Stand Alone Complex* 1st Gig (2002–2003) and 2nd Gig (2004–2005) followed his television movie *The Ghost in the Shell: Stand Alone Complex: Solid State Society* (2006); and four animated prequel films under the general title *The Ghost in the Shell: Arise* (2013–2014). Shirow serialized more stories between 1991 and 1997, which were collected in two volumes, *Kōkaku kidōtai 2: Man-Machine Interface* (2001) and *Kōkaku kidōtai 1.5: Human-Error Processor* (2003), with the initial volume re-titled *Kōkaku kidōtai 1: The Ghost in the Shell*.

Chapters of the first volume present stand-alone stories, but a larger storyline emerges across Chapters 3, 9, 10, and 11, in which female cyborg Major Kusanagi Motoko encounters a new form of intelligence, accidentally generated through governmental experiments with AI, and now seeking a way to prolong his life beyond mere replication. (The manga presents it as male.) Because he hacks into human cyber-brains to control their actions, he is called the Puppet Master.

The opening pages of the manga explain cyberization: micromachines or nanites are used to graft circuitry into the brain, to provide direct connection between cyberbrains and between cyberbrains and computer networks. The image shows neurons swarming across a computer chip, forming an overgrown cluster. Chapter 5 of the manga, "Megatech Machine 02: The Making of a Cyborg," presents the state of the art in prosthetics, replacing all the organs of a human's body with artificial ones, except her brain and spinal cord (Shirō 1991: 99; Shirow 1995: 101). Cyberbrains thus retain some human neurons. But does the presence of human neurons make for a ghost, for genuinely human consciousness?

Shirow's response takes comic form. After a young female cyborg shows Motoko how cyborgs are constructed, the two chat in a café over sweets. Motoko muses, "Sometimes I wonder if I've already died, and what I think of as 'me' isn't really just an artificial personality comprised of a prosthetic body and a cyberbrain" (Shirō 1991: 104; Shirow 1995: 106). Her companion replies that they have gray matter, and people treat them just like humans. Motoko retorts that there is no way for them to see their own gray matter, to verify its presence. The question then is: how much human gray matter is needed to make for a cyborg, that is, a human with prosthetic replacements, rather than, say, a robot?

Motoko's concern is genuine, and yet, in the manga in general, because the distinction between human and machine entails difference in degree rather than nature, Motoko's insistence that neurons make for the human feels tenuous. Indeed, in the last panel, a multi-legged Fuchikoma pops up to say, if it were possible to make robots that close to humans, they'd be humans! A fine example of Shirow's astute use of manga conventions, this page (like many others) sets up a philosophical question, explores its implications, only to reverse its tone and deflate its aura of existential profundity (e.g., Shirō 1991: 94, 280). The two cyborgs laugh, and the final panel reinforces the gag-like timing. Instead of a scientific answer, Shirow evokes an intuitive sense of the situation.

His response recalls Nishida's notion of active intuition. Active intuition follows from Nishida's emphasis on place or *basho*, which might be construed as a groundless ground on which awareness emerges prior to subject-object distinctions. Active intuition entails a kind of reflexivity that implies both passive receptivity and productive or operative activity (Nishida 1987). As Nishida wrote in *The Awakening-to-Self Determination of Nothingness* (*Mu no jikaku teki gentei*, 1932):

> The determination of awakening-to-self (*jikaku*) must be an infinite process. Yet an infinite process does not necessarily allow the significance of awakening-to-self. There must be in awakening-to-self a dimension that goes beyond this process, which nonetheless encompasses it in it. Our self is not conceived as limit to such a process. To determine self, it is necessary for its *basho* (place or situation) to be directly self-determining.
> (Nishida 1965: 233–34)

On the one hand, the ground retreats: the number of human neurons in a cyberbrain is steadily diminishing. On the other hand, the ground encompasses: the presence of human neurons continues to determine what counts as the human. But there is something that goes beyond this process of neurons' retreating and encompassing: ghost. The ghost is not a property or attribute of a substrate. Nor is it a property of an organ. The manga presents memories in terms of recording and storage, that is, localized material traces, but the ghost is not in a location. The ghost arrives in a place (*basho*) that is determining yet disappearing—as giggles arise where the mind is in question.

Such a ghost goes hand-in-hand with technologization. Because there is not a cause-and-effect relationship between the material and immaterial (the number of neurons and the presence of a ghost), every material detail of a human body must be technologically reproduced. In this respect, Shirow's vision recalls that of Arthur Koestler who, in his 1967 book *The Ghost in the Machine*, rejects Cartesian dualism and presents mind as an emergent effect of the machine (1968: 211), imparting a pragmatic twist. Because the ghost is an emergent effect of the entire system in its every detail (machine), it is impossible to know where to cut corners. Every aspect of the original must be recreated to replicate the ghost. Structures and functions, such as bodily strength and sensory organs, can be enhanced in the process. Even the brain can be enhanced to interface with computers and other cyberbrains. The complexity of the brain and spinal cord makes them difficult to replicate, but that does not mean they will not someday be. The limit to prosthetics and cyberization is that of technological ability to replicate the material complexity of bodies. The encompassing and retreating *basho* is technologization, and the ghost, like active intuition, presents a moment of localized transcendence.

Tension thus arises between localized determinations (machine) and non-localized effects (ghost). Where Koestler emphasizes material determinations (machine-emergence), Nishida invites oscillation between two perspectives—the ghost is in the shell, the ghost is not in the shell. To remain true to the non-dualist stance, the relation between ghost and shell would have to adopt both stances at once, combining what Brian Massumi (2011) calls the pragmatic and the speculative.

Shirow's manga oscillates between these two perspectives, now lavishing attention on the pragmatic dimension of making cyborgs and regulating the production of new kinds of intelligence and existence; now stressing the speculative dimension through the surprise of new life forms. The art of Shirow's manga (and maybe of science fiction more generally) lies in how it composes, holds together, and works across these two dimensions, pragmatic and speculative. The task of criticism is to follow the unfolding complexity of this compositional art closely, to immerse itself in it.

Compositionally, Shirow's manga associates the pragmatic with the shell, treating it as a bounded entity or container, whose borders may be breached, threatened with dissolution, or otherwise overcome by speculative forces, which are depicted as ghosts not contained by or tied to a particular shell. The compositional logic gravitates toward the ghost *in* the shell, the ghost supported, contained, and protected within the shell. The same tendency may be observed in Nishida's notion of "encompassing" (Tremblay 2009: 127–134). While Nishida strives to distinguish encompassing from enclosing and enclosures, his conceptualization of places or fields tends toward a geometrical logic of the circle. Even if its center is nowhere and circumference everywhere, this circle introduces a bias toward thinking (and unthinking) the self on the basis of sovereign enclosures.

Sovereignty

The term *kōkaku* (carapace, exoskeleton, shell) invites insect- or spider-like designs: tactical armors for humans and cyborgs look like exoskeletons, and intelligent tanks such as Fuchikoma are partially modeled on jumping spiders. With such shells, the tool is not distinguished from the body (Parikka 2010: 28). Body parts become tool-like; armor-like bodies may act like weapons, and human limbs may sprout weapons, fingers may turn into highly articulated and extended tools for keyboard work, and cables may be plugged into the neck, at the base of the skull, transforming the brain into a console-like replay device. Maybe Motoko is a variation on the insect woman.

Despite these arthropod possibilities, the shell in Shirow's manga tends toward the logic of enclosure, and the ghost appears localized within the shell, protected by the armor-like carapace. Cyberized brains, too, have shells (*nōkaku*) and need barriers to protect them from hacking. The shell thus tends toward a conservative model of the self, situating it as a circumscribed entity surrounded by protective barriers that are constantly under attack and in danger of breach. As in Pheng Cheah's discussion of Sigmund Freud's model of the self, "the security of an *individual* psyche's interiority in its interaction with the external world and its management of internal excitations is the template for historical forms of sociality and political community" (2008: 194).

Take this scenario of communication between cyberized brains: to avoid radio communication, which can be detected and monitored, Motoko allows members of the team, all males, to dive into her brain (Shirō 1991: 13–14; Shirow 1995: 17–18). Not only do the men comment about noise in her brain (due to her period), pain in her hand, and a taste of tranquillizer, but they also dive too close to her ghost-line, despite her admonishments. At the bottom of the page appears an explanatory note: "Particularly severe are the crimes of wiz hackers who can break into the ghost (which also might be called the soul)" (Shirō 1991: 13; the passage does not appear in the English edition). The sequence envisions the relation between ghost and shell on the model of the sovereign self, with protective barriers not to be breached. The sequence presents transgression in highly gendered terms, as if a gang of loutish men were violating the female brain-body, which introduces a disturbing analogy between the autonomy of the ghost and female virginity or purity.

The nation-state and nationality are imagined in analogous terms, from the first page:

> In the near future, even as corporate networks stretch to the stars, and electrons and light course the globe, not all is informationalized (*jōhōka*), insofar as nation-states and peoples (*minzoku*) have not disappeared. On the edge of Asia lies a strange corporate conglomerate state, Japan.
>
> (Shirō 1991: 1; Shirow 1995: 5)

Section 9 works to protect the security of ghost and nation. It stops invaders whose attacks compromise the sovereignty of both. The sovereign self and the sovereign nation are conflated, rendered structurally identical. There appear free-ranging ghosts, hackers, globalization, informationalization, and new forms of life and intelligence that defy boundaries, but the goal of Motoko and Section 9 is sustain borders and prevent breaches. As they track down alleged cyber-criminals or terrorists, they speak disparagingly of corporations and the mass media, for these institutions, intentionally or due to irresponsibility, work to undermine the security of national boundaries.

Not surprisingly then, the manga praises self-reliance, personal responsibility, and rugged autonomy. Motoko reprimands the boy who asks if Section 9 has come to free them, "Do you just want to eat and contribute nothing, to be brainwashed by media trash? To sacrifice the nation's own future for your own selfishness? ... Create your own future" (Shirō 1991: 41; Shirow 1995: 45).

Subsequent entries into *The Ghost in the Shell* franchise prolong this dominant paradigm. Kamiyama's animations explore the problem of Japan's compromised sovereignty, Japan's political subordination to and economic dependency on the United States. The goal, sometimes explicit, sometimes implicit, is to bring Japan closer to uncompromised "full" national sovereignty. Yet the tone remains noirish, hard-boiled, as if cyborgs inhabited a fallen world in which the battle for full sovereignty is already lost but must be waged, if only to sustain a sense of honor, which takes the form of self-mastery. The aspirations of the cyborg and the nation are conjoined, fuelled by an impossible desire for transcendence, for full sovereignty via the best armature. For all the aura of technological progress and futurism, for all the emphasis on the eclectic quasi-renegade status of the cyborgs employed in Section 9, the outcome is social and political conservatism. This is hardly surprising: secret police, extralegal forces, black ops, and special ops do not generally lend themselves to radical democracy, socialism, or progressive politics.

Initially at least, this paradigm seems diametrically opposed to Haraway's efforts to push the cyborg toward subversive and transgressive ends. As Hayles (2006: 159) puts it, "Deeply connected to the military, bound to high technology for its very existence and a virtual icon for capitalism, the cyborg was contaminated to the core, making it exquisitely appropriate as a provocation." Yet Hayles concludes, cyborg contamination has today reached an impasse: on the one hand, it feels outdated technologically, and on the other hand, it focuses on the individual, but "the individual person—or for that matter, the individual cyborg—is no longer the appropriate unit of analysis, if indeed it ever was" (2006: 160).

If cyborg theory, like posthuman theory, reaches an impasse, it is not only due to individualism (see Chapter 8). The impasse comes of blurring ontological distinctions rather than sticking to the philosophy of relation, in which individuation rather than the individual would become the site of analysis (Combes 2012: 25–31). As Ian Hacking (1998) notes, Haraway's manifesto implies an initial distinction between humans and machines, or between organisms and mechanisms, which then becomes blurred and confused with historical appearance of the cyborg. This dualist separation of human and machine is conceptualized in juridical terms, in terms of a law of the sovereign subject, which is subverted.

Haraway and Shirow thus have something in common: an autonomously sovereign subject-body is undermined when permeated with heteronomous objects. Where Shirow's manga tends to deploy the cyborg as a mode of regulation that supplements national sovereignty at the historical moment of its corporate- and media-driven breakdown, Haraway's manifesto tries to mobilize the cyborg as a mode of transgression related to the postmodern breakdown of national sovereignty. The two stances—battling the dissolution of borders within techno-militarist regimes of perpetual regulation (Shirow), and blurring them to confront the subversive forces of capital on their own ground (Haraway)—are inverse images. Both posit the cyborg in terms of a politics of sovereignty (personal and national) and mechanisms of rupture and reinscription.

Yet both offer an alternative to the juridical model of sovereignty. In Shirow, it is the emergent, non-localizable ghost, and in Haraway, it is the commitment to thinking relationality. We thus return to radical empiricism. Restated via the feminist insight that "the personal is political, but the political should not be personal," this radical empirical stance declares, "the personal is political, the political impersonal" (Sharp 2011).

Mind Your World

When Section 9 infiltrates a welfare center secretly and illegally using orphans as a cheap labor, Motoko loses contact with Aramaki and must alone decide whether to advance. Her ghost urges her on: "It's whispering, do it!—my ghost" (Shirō 1991: 30; Shirow 1995: 34). Motoko is gauging the entire situation, but not consciously. Without knowing how she knows, she feels what to do, based on what's given by the whole situation, which could never be consciously assembled and evaluated, computationally—active intuition. While the intuition comes to her ("my ghost"), it belongs to the situation. This self is not distinct from its experiences. It does not stand back from what is happening. It does not command a privileged vantage to perceive reality as a whole. The ground of self is pure experience. This is where Nishida's *basho* loosens its encompassing hold, becoming a manifold plane.

What Motoko experiences is not within perception; it happens with and through perception. Ghost whispering is the non-localized relation running across shell, ghost, and world, and ghost is at once inside and outside the shell. The emergent ghost extends beyond the shell into a material-affective continuum. Motoko's ghost emerges from her exposure to it.

The ghost recalls a paradox of the mecha genre: material enclosure and psychic exposure do not stand in contradiction. They are two aspects of one event. Having a shell and a cyberized brain does not make for total protection or exhaustive knowledge. The cyborg cannot know everything nor act without risk. With its augmentations, the cyborg needs more feel for situations, more delicacy, not less. Feeling takes precedence over computation. This ghost of a feeling is not a side effect. It might be described as "extra-effect" (Massumi 2011: 20–21), and the cyborg subject as "superject" (Massumi 2011: 9).

This paradox helps to explain why cyborgs are so conservative in choice of body. Why do they hang onto human bodies? When your body is damaged, why opt to be refitted with an identical body? Why not take on an enormous mecha-spider body? In a spider body, however, you would no longer be you. This is not a matter of how others perceive you, a problem of recognition. This sense of self is related to how a body feels. How does a body feel moving through the world? The same applies to every enhancement and augmentation. Will it make you feel the world differently? Caution and conservatism follow from what initially seems to be a free-for-all (any-body-whatsoever for anyone-whosoever). After all, even if the shell does not produce the ghost in a causal fashion (the shell is a shared element of an occasion), every change in the shell ripples with ghostly consequences.

The lived abstraction of the cyborg becomes paradoxical in ethical terms. Upkeep of cyborg bodies is costly, and so cyborgs tend to side with the received conditions of capitalism: they fear losing the system that sustains them. Yet their servile dependence on the system generates a keen sensitivity vis-à-vis the system and its failures, which encourages an anti-authoritarian streak with a speculative turn, both particularly evident in Motoko.

In sum, the dominant paradigm of *The Ghost in the Shell* is that of securing the ghost within the shell, subordinating the speculative to the pragmatic, which culminates in a politics of suppressing or overcoming threats to personal and national sovereignty. But a counter tendency arises. This minor tendency does not simply stress the speculative power of the ghost over and above the shell. It strives for a fusion of different dimensions without loss of difference.

Such fusion is salient in the union (*yūgū*) of Motoko and the Puppet Master. Fusion at one level recalls heterosexual procreation and reproduction. At another level it is weird reproduction, for entities coded as male (Puppet Master) and female (Motoko) do not lose their identity through fusion. They inhabit a space of non-contradiction that allows both dimensions of the shared event, differentiation and integration, to proceed together. Their union implies a fusion of genders, too. Motoko awakens in a new body, apparently the best Batō could find for her, the body of a beautiful young man (which Batō saw as a woman's body). Apparently, one shell may have multiple ghosts, and multiple shells one ghost. Thus the manga pushes toward the creation of a new multitude, anticipating the release of the AI children of Motoko and the Puppet Master into the Net.

The final pages show how fusion happens compositionally. At the bottom of the penultimate page, a panel appears with the newly agglutinated being standing on a hill overlooking the city of skyscrapers. A speech bubble adds, "The Net is vast." The final page repeats the panel without the speech bubble and without additional panels. The panel is centered in the upper half of the page, solidly framed in rectilinear isolation. How does such a page present an event of creative fusion unfurling new multitudes?

Shirow's composition follows manga conventions for layouts. Pages usually deploy five to eight rectilinear panels, evenly spaced, and with variations in size and tone in keeping with the presentation of action, perception, and speech as well as overall balance of the page. To heighten drama Shirow enlarges panels instead of breaking or deforming them. When he breaks the panel, it is usually to enlarge a woman's body, a mecha, or a technological process, to combine expository attention to detail with illustrative brio. Shirow is famous for his covers and illustrations lavishing attention on cyberpunk women like Motoko lounging or posing like Vargas girls but in gleaming body-hugging fabrics or roped in techno-coils or cables reminiscent of SM, with augmented breasts, broad shoulders, and narrow hips.

The force of Shirow's style, then, does not lay in breaking panels. It lies in the articulation of relations within and between panels. An analogy arises between the panel and the body shell (*kōkaku*), and between the speech bubble and the brain shell (*nōkaku*). In this register, Shirow's preference for the integrity of panels is in keeping with the dominant tendency of the manga to insist on personal and national sovereignty. Yet a minor tendency also becomes evident. Instead of breaking panels or playing with free-form layouts, Shirow's manga attends to how each panel "feels" and "affects" the other panels on its page as well as pages preceding or following it. One panel can set the tone of a page, but only through a two-sided process in which each panel is affected by and affects the other panels. The process is at once relational (panel to panel) and qualitative (expressive tonality). Shirow sticks with conventions for panels and layouts, but to stress the mixing of action and communication, active communications, and communicative actions. The interesting moments then are not those when the panels break, but rather when panels present communication in the form of a brain dive or brain invasion. Dissolution of conventions happens within the panel, as dissolution of personal sovereignty occurs within the shell.

When the men dive into Motoko's brain, there appears, in the center of the page, a large panel, with blue tones evoking an oceanic dive, with lines of speech without bubbles, and characters arrayed in a fluid circle around the center (Shirō 1991: 14; Shirow 1995: 18). In this oceanic moment, orientation is not bilateral, but radial. Likewise, when brains are forcibly invaded, the panel presents a series of heads, turned at different angles to indicate different locations, with a jagged bolt of electricity connecting and zapping them (Shirō 1991: 37, 39; Shirow 1995: 41, 43). In such instances, one panel includes multiple dimensions, and because orientation is more radial than bilateral, action and communication cannot proceed in a linear, goal-oriented fashion. The manga thus forces a confrontation with the relationship between the inside and outside of panels. To what extent is the content inside the panel? Readers always feel the effect of one panel on others, effectively generating relations with and through panels. In such moments, the ghost is not in the shell, any more than the effect of manga is in the panel, or even in the page. These are moments enacting and anticipating the fusion that happens in the final chapter, in which data and images begin to swirl and bifurcate within panels, and Motoko's image takes up other images from different dimensions within its panels.

It makes sense then to end with a lone panel on a white page. The logic of Shirow's art is not one of all-connectedness, of an individual subject connected to others. It is a dissolution of the individual subject: the self dives to the level of pure experience, alone yet feeling and affecting the whole of its world, becoming one and multiple in a situation of non-contradiction. This is where cyborgs feel for others. If we are to contest and move beyond the dominant tendency toward personal and national sovereignty in *The Ghost in the Shell*, we must stick to these moments when the ghost (and the speculative) is not in the shell but in its world. We can then address the geopolitical dimensions of cyborg existence highlighted in the array of mind-beings in Shirow's manga: the personal and national are always political, but the political should not be limited, pragmatically or speculatively, to personal and national sovereignty, to questions about maintaining or dissolving borders of the subject. Shirow's cyborgs whisper that the political entails both a distribution of the sensible *and* of the non-sensible, across a multitude of mind-beings.

Note

1   The author's name is properly Romanized as Shirō, but he prefers to use Shirow in English translations.

PART IX
Popular Literature

28 Murakami Haruki's Transnational Avant-Pop Literature

Rebecca Suter

Introduction: The Murakami Phenomenon

Murakami Haruki is probably the best-known Japanese author of his generation. His 2010 novel *1Q84*, sixteen hundred pages and three volumes in the original Japanese, is exemplar of the success of his literature: the first printing sold out on the first day, and the first two volumes reached a million sales within a month. Translations in a variety of foreign languages, from Polish to Italian to English, began to appear shortly after the publication of the third volume and made equally impressive sales. The novel was one of the most complex and profound texts by Murakami; yet the literary value of the work itself does not seem enough to account for the cult status that the text and its author have reached among Japanese and international readers. The release of Murakami's following novel, *Colorless Tazaki Tsukuru and His Years of Pilgrimage* (*Shikisai o motanai Tazaki Tsukuru to, kare no junrei no toshi*, 2013, hereafter referred to as *Tazaki Tsukuru*), was announced weeks in advance, and sales were officially opened at midnight of April 12, 2013, with people lining up in the street outside bookstores all over Japan. In major stores, the event even included a countdown and an opening ceremony attended by the press and television networks. The book sold almost a million copies in the first six months (Oricon 2013a).

In Japan, Murakami has become a true pop icon: his readers call themselves "Harukista" (*Harukisuto*) and buy anything that he publishes, whether fiction or nonfiction, his original work or his translations of foreign authors. In April 2013, Japanese national television network NHK broadcast a reportage showing how many readers of *Tazaki Tsukuru* refused to use the dust jacket that normally hides the title of the book and instead preferred to flaunt their choice of reading, while others brought a copy of the novel along to blind dates as a way to break the ice.

Murakami's popularity in Japan would be best described as a form of fandom, an adoration that borders on obsession, of the kind normally reserved for popular culture icons such as singers and actors. In the United States, too, the author has gained an enthusiastic audience outside of the limited circle of readers of Japanese literature, arguably a rare feat for a Japanese author. While there are other contemporary writers that have gained a similarly broad readership outside Japan in more recent years, like Yoshimoto Banana or Ogawa Yōko, Murakami's popularity seems to be both broader and more enduring than any of those authors, as testified for example by the fact that three of his recent novels, *Kafka on the Shore*, *1Q84*, and *Colorless Tazaki Tsukuru* were listed in the *New York Times* 100 Notable Books for 2005, 2011, and 2014, respectively. One reason often mentioned by critics for Murakami's international fame is that the author is blessed with talented translators like Alfred Birnbaum, Philip Gabriel, and Jay Rubin, whose compelling style was influential in making Murakami approachable to the English-speaking audience. Yet this does not seem enough to fully account for the author's rise to literary stardom.[1] What are, then, the causes of the "Murakami phenomenon"?

In my book, *The Japanization of Modernity: Murakami Haruki Between Japan and the United States* (2008), I had sought an answer to this question in the author's creative appropriation of North American culture, comparable to the phenomenon that Iwabuchi Kōichi (2002) describes as the "Japanization" of Western culture in postwar popular media. My interpretation was that the appeal of Murakami was based on his ability to blend different cultural traditions, which satisfies his audience's taste for the exotic, and at the same time gives readers the opportunity to distance themselves from their own culture. Furthermore, I argued that thanks to his position on the boundary between "high" and "low" literature, Murakami breaks conventional distinctions between elite art and mass culture, thus appealing to an even broader range of different readers. The evolution of Murakami's career and the explosion of his international popularity in the new millennium all but confirmed this interpretation, and at the same time opened up new opportunities for critical reflection on the concepts of authorship, interculturality, and globalization. In this chapter, through an analysis of Murakami's narratives and their critical reception, as well as the development of a "Murakami franchise" that incorporates not only his fiction and nonfiction, but also his translations and secondary literature about him, I will show how this author subverts both the dichotomy between Japanese high literature and popular culture, and conventional views of the relationship between Japanese and foreign culture.

Pure Literature, Popular Culture, and Avant-Pop

From the beginning of his career, critics have often refused to consider Murakami's works as a legitimate part of so-called *junbungaku* (pure literature) because of their supposed superficiality and lack of social commitment. Arguably, Murakami's novels, particularly the ones that brought him to fame in the 1980s, radically diverged from the conventional model of *junbungaku*, which emphasizes direct engagement with politically sensitive topics and a high degree of intellectual sophistication. The fact that Murakami's works ostensibly lacked those elements, combined with the high sales of his novels, led critics to dismiss him as a purely commercial writer, unworthy of scholarly consideration. One of the harshest critics was Nobel Prize winner Ōe Kenzaburō, who in the 1990s famously described the fiction of Murakami as the ultimate expression of the decadence of contemporary Japanese literature:

> Lack of activity in the field of *junbungaku* can be substantiated objectively when we compare the volume of its publications with that of other types of literature, such as popular historical novels, science fiction, mysteries, and various nonfiction genres.... Amidst this trend, Haruki Murakami, a writer born after the war, is said to be attracting new readers to *junbungaku*. It is clear, however, that Murakami's target lies outside this sphere, and deliberately so. There is nothing that directly links Murakami with postwar literature of the 1946–1970 period. If I may be allowed a possibly hasty comment here, I believe that no revival of *junbungaku* will be possible unless ways are found to fill the wide gap that exists between him and pre-1970 writing.
>
> (Ōe 1995: 78–79)

As Ōe pointed out in the mid-1990s, Murakami's target audience did indeed lie outside, or rather beyond, the conventional audience of high literature, and deliberately so. At the same time, his stylistically experimental narratives and the psychological complexity of his characters made it difficult to simply categorize him as an author of *taishū bungaku* (popular fiction). As I will argue in this chapter, Murakami was neither attracting new readers to *junbungaku* nor steering old ones away from it, but rather attempting to produce a new kind of literature, that combines elements of both high art and pop culture. In this respect, I propose to read his literature as akin to what literary scholar Tatsumi Takayuki describes as Japanese "avant-pop" fiction (Tatsumi 2006).

The concept of avant-pop was coined in the early 1990s by writer and scholar Larry McCaffery and author Mark Amerika in order to challenge the idea, common in Euro-American literary criticism of the time, that the end of high modernism and the proliferation of postmodernist literature of the 1980s had resulted in the death of "serious literature." Questioning this view, Amerika and McCaffery advocated a different kind of literature, which could not be categorized as either modernist or postmodernist, and proposed to call this current "avant-pop" (Amerika 1993; McCaffery 1995). In the United States, avant-pop literature emerged in the 1990s as a reaction to the increasing separation between modernist high literature, which was meant to be politically committed and aesthetically sophisticated, and postmodernist mass culture, which was perceived and portrayed by intellectuals as bourgeois and banal. Avant-pop intended to overcome this binary distinction by recovering elements of both avant-garde art, which had been dismissed by postmodernists as elitist and out of touch with reality, and the kind of organic, wholesome popular culture that predated the emergence of mass culture, and could offer an instrument of resistance against the dominance of late-capitalist consumer society.

Avant-pop literature derived from early twentieth-century avant-garde the idea of using formal innovation as a means to shock readers out of complacency and was inspired by British pop art movements of the 1950s to attempt to recover a more meaningful role for popular culture, before and beyond its massification. Furthermore, it proposed to use popular culture as a way to reconnect to the sacred or supernatural dimension of daily life, lost in contemporary capitalist society but still alive in folk traditions. For this reason, much avant-pop literature belongs to the genre of science fiction, and this is where Tatsumi sees its closest connection to the Japanese literary world, as exemplified by the works of authors such as Shimada Masahiko or Numa Shōzō, that cannot be classified as either *junbungaku* or its mass-consumed counterpart, *taishū bungaku* (Tatsumi 2006: 31–34, 54–59).

While Murakami Haruki does not strictly speaking belong to this current, I see the category of avant-pop as a useful theoretical tool to explain this author's search for a different kind of social and political commitment in literature, one that does not deny the commercial/popular aspect of novels in contemporary society but still tries to offer an intellectual challenge to its readers. In particular, the quest for a connection, or reconnection, with the world of the supernatural, or what Matthew Strecher calls the "metaphysical realm" (Strecher 2014), has been a central theme in Murakami's fiction from the beginning of his career all the way to his most recent works.

One of the best examples of this use of a combination of high art, popular culture, and the supernatural in Murakami's fiction is arguably *1Q84*. The novel tells the story of a mathematics teacher and part-time writer, Tengo, and a professional murderer targeting men who committed acts of violence against women, Aomame, who in the year 1984 end up in a parallel reality, called by the author 1Q84. Like many of Murakami's works, the text is replete with references to popular culture, from jazz to fashion, as well as to works of high art, from classical music to canonical Japanese and Western literature.

More importantly, the novel addresses a number of politically sensitive aspects in Japanese contemporary history, such as the radicalization of some factions of the political left in the 1970s and their turn to violence and the rise of cult organizations in the 1980s, but does so in an indirect form, changing names and dates and referring to actual historical facts in a roundabout way. The novel's ultimate explanation for the dramatic events that affect the world of 1Q84 is a fantastical one, namely the existence of supernatural creatures called the Little People, that operate behind the scenes of Japanese politics by manipulating humans using them as "perceivers" and "receivers" of their messages. Too fantastical to belong to conventional high art, the novel is also too serious to be simply classified as entertainment (as testified by Murakami's repeated failure to win the Nobel Prize for Literature despite being one of the most favored candidates for several years in a row, including in 2012, 2013, and 2014). Indeed, its combination of pop and high art would be best described as avant-pop.

1Q84 is arguably one of the longest and most complex realizations of this approach to literature's function between entertainment and social commentary. The same vision of literature, however, also informed many of Murakami's earlier works. His first two novels, *Hear The Wind Sing* (*Kaze no uta o kike*, 1979) and *Pinball, 1973* (*1973 nen no pinbōru*, 1980) were criticized by Japanese intellectuals as apolitical because of their failure to discuss the so-called *zenkyōtō* (*Zengaku Kyōtō Kaigi*, All-university Joint Struggle League), the countercultural "collective battle" waged by the student movement against Japanese educational and political institutions in the 1960s. (For a summary of these criticisms, see Hasumi 1994; Karatani 1995). Interestingly, the novels do briefly mention the student movement, but they do so in an indirect and critical way, through casual conversations between the nameless narrator and his friend Nezumi (Rat). The latter in particular expresses his sense of alienation from the student movement and states that his disappointment with the failure of its "collective battle" largely contributed to making him feel disconnected from society at large (Murakami 1979: 117).

Two subsequent novels, *A Wild Sheep Chase* (*Hitsuji o meguru bōken*, 1982) and *Dance Dance Dance* (*Dansu dansu dansu*, 1988), follow the adventures of the same nameless protagonist after he leaves his hometown and loses touch with Nezumi. Here the narrator finally discovers a way of rebuilding a meaningful connection with the outside world, and in both instances, he is able to do so by entering a supernatural other world, described by the author as *achiragawa* (over there). In *A Wild Sheep Chase*, the narrator travels to Hokkaido in search of a ghostly sheep that possesses the mind of important political figures and uses them to manipulate the system, while in *Dance Dance Dance* he returns to the Dolphin Hotel in Sapporo, where he had stayed during the first trip, and he has some life-changing conversations with the Sheep Professor, who had helped him in his previous adventure and now lives on a phantom floor inside the hotel that only exists at certain times. In both cases, the narrator's experience with the supernatural is an opportunity for self-discovery through an exploration of his own unconscious. At the same time, the supernatural elements, particularly the ghostly sheep, are also used as a metaphor for the power dynamics of contemporary Japan, and have the effect of uncovering the dark side of the country's economic success and its apparently peaceful and equal society.

Similar dynamics are at play in *Hard-boiled Wonderland and the End of the World* (*Sekai no owari to hādo-boirudo wandārando*, 1985), that hints at the dangerous side of information society through a science fictional account of a futuristic Tokyo and the secret world underneath it. Similarly, *The Wind-Up Bird Chronicle* (*Nejimakidori kuronikuru*, 1995) addresses problematic episodes of Japanese history such as the so-called Nomonhan Incident, an aggressive incursion by Japanese troops into Mongolia in 1939, and more broadly Japan's occupation of Manchuria, but rather than discussing these events directly, the narrative frames them through the protagonist's metaphysical experience of travelling into *achiragawa* through a mysterious well in his neighborhood. Even some of Murakami's nonfiction works, such as *Underground* (*Andāguraundo*, 1997), a collection of interviews to the victims of the 1995 Tokyo subway sarin gas attack at the hands of the Aum Shinrikyō cult, refer to the existence of *achiragawa* in a metaphorical way, acknowledging the multi-layered nature of reality and insisting on the importance of including the non-rational dimension of experiences in our understanding of society.

Murakami's works are thus simultaneously very fantastical and very political: this is the author's peculiar brand of commitment in literature, which relies not on direct social commentary like conventional Japanese *junbungaku*, but on the use of popular fiction as a way of reconnecting with the supernatural and the subconscious. This simultaneous inward and outward movement is amplified by the strategies at play in Murakami's activity as a translator and cultural mediator.

Translator, Translated, and Transnational

From the beginning of his career, Murakami has also been enthusiastically translating works of North American literature; within Japan, his reputation as a translator is comparable to his popularity as a writer, and readers would often buy works by foreign authors simply because they have been translated by Murakami. A good example is Murakami's 2003 translation of J.D. Salinger's *The Catcher in the Rye* (*Kyatchā in za rai*), which attracted surprisingly high sales despite the fact that text was more than fifty years old and there already existed a popular and skillful translation by Nozaki Takashi. In the 2000s, Murakami also began to act as a cultural mediator in the opposite direction, presenting Japanese literature to the American public, for example, with his introductions to the English versions of works by renowned Japanese writers such as Akutagawa Ryūnosuke and Natsume Sōseki. These operations had the effect of further expanding the "Murakami franchise" to include a variety of texts and paratexts in both English and Japanese, blurring the boundaries between the role of author, translator, and critic.

That a novelist doubles as translator is not by any means a new phenomenon in Japan. Translated literature had played a crucial role in Japan ever since the Meiji period, and founding fathers of modern Japanese literature like Mori Ōgai and Natsume Sōseki were prolific translators. The 1950s also saw a new translation boom, this time mostly of North American fiction. Initially translations were mostly of mainstream white male authors from the 1920s and 1930s like Ernest Hemingway and John Steinbeck, possibly under the influence of the Allied Occupation institutions' determination to spread a positive image of the United States (Ara 2000: 4–5). In the 1960s and 1970s, the number of Japanese translations of American literature increased and their scope broadened, to include Jewish American (such as Saul Bellow, Philip Roth, Bernard Malamud, and Norman Mailer), African American, Native

American, and Asian American authors. The gender imbalance of translations of the 1950s was also redressed with the inclusion of authors like Joyce Carol Oates, Toni Morrison, Alice Walker, and Leslie Marson Silko.

In the 1980s, Murakami made his appearance onto the Japanese literary translation scene, together with Shibata Motoyuki, Professor Emeritus of American literature at Tokyo University. The two soon become the most established and influential translators of American literature in Japan, rendering into Japanese the works of Truman Capote, John Irving, and Paul Auster, among others. Miura Masashi noted that the translations of Murakami and Shibata significantly influenced not only the perception of American culture among the Japanese public, but also the style of an entire generation of young writers, such as Ono Masatsugu, Yanagi Hiroshi, and Satō Yūya, who grew up reading English language writers in the translation of Murakami and Shibata (Miura 2003: 16–20).

What does Murakami translate? In the 1980s and 1990s, he translated the complete works of Raymond Carver, and novels by Francis Scott Fitzgerald, Truman Capote, John Irving, Grace Paley, Paul Theroux, and Tim O' Brien. With the exception of Paley, they are all men; all white; and all from the East Coast with the notable exception of Carver. (The protagonists of their works also bear striking resemblances with Murakami's own characters, arguably another possible reason for his choice.) While they are critical of the "American dream" and write about the dark side of U.S. society, they are neither minority nor radical writers. This narrower and more conservative selection of authors might be interpreted as a regression from the expansion of Japanese translations of American literature of the 1970s in terms of race, class, and gender diversity. Interestingly, however, Japanese intellectuals did not criticize Murakami for the gender, class, or race bias of his choice of authors, but because of his alleged passive attitude towards foreign culture.

In this sense, some critics described Murakami as emblematic of a broader dangerous trend in publishing, which by devoting so much energy to translation risked driving readers away from Japanese fiction and in turn negatively affected the production of local literature (Miura 2003: 7–8). This was part of a broader discourse lamenting the "cultural trade imbalance" between Japan and the so-called West, within the context of the Japanese government's policy of *kokusaika* (internationalization), which saw the creation of a number of institutions devoted to the promotion of Japanese culture on the international level, such as the Japan Foundation and the Japan Society for the Promotion of Science.

The notion of *kokusaika* is an ambiguous one; as Marilyn Ivy (1995: 3) has pointed out, "instead of opening up Japan to the struggle of different nationalities and ethnicities," internationalization often meant the very opposite, "the thorough domestication of the foreign and the dissemination of Japanese culture throughout the world." In the 1980s and 1990s, Murakami, with his intense activity as a translator of foreign literature at the expense of the production of *junbungaku*, was seen as the antithesis of such policy and as a dangerous fallback into the "cultural trade imbalance" that had characterized the postwar years. Interestingly, as he began to acquire an audience outside of Japan, and particularly in the United States, Murakami went from being accused of passively importing American culture to becoming one of Japan's hottest export brands. However, he became an unusual kind of cultural ambassador; rather than contributing to the "dissemination of Japanese culture throughout the world," the internationalization of the Murakami franchise had the result of undermining conventional notions of national literature.

First of all, Murakami seems to have been able to escape the "exoticizing filter" through which Japanese literature is often perceived in the English-speaking world. This is partly attributable to the choices of his U.S. translators, Alfred Birnbaum, Jay Rubin, and Philip Gabriel, who often "domesticate" foreign elements in Murakami's fiction so that he does not sound "too Japanese" in translation. Thus, for example, Philip Gabriel notes how in *The Sputnik Sweetheart* he translated the "mont blanc" that a character is eating in a café as a generic "cake," in order to avoid the risk that people "think that she was eating an expensive fountain pen;" similarly, in the short story "Man-Eating Cats" he changed the "Royal Host" restaurant where the characters eat to a more widely known "Denny's" to increase readability (Gabriel, Rubin, and Fiskjeton 2001). Murakami himself commented on this aspect in *Night Conversations on Translation* (*Hon'yaku yawa*, 2000), where he notes how he enjoys reading the translated versions of his texts, as if they were entirely new novels (Murakami 2000: 16–18). However, when discussing his own translating practices, he declares that he strives to be as faithful as possible to the original:

> Even if they make a few changes to my work in the translation, as long as it's interesting I think it's good. But as for myself, as a translator I am quite faithful... I translate literally, word by word. Otherwise I don't see the point of translating. If you want to write it your way, then write your own novel.
>
> (Murakami 2000: 20)

On one hand, this could be interpreted as a sign of the power imbalance between Japanese and U.S. culture. As scholars of postcolonial translation have demonstrated, translators moving from a dominant-culture source text to a minority-culture audience tend to treat the source text with greater deference and translate it more literally, a mechanism that reasserts the hegemony of the source culture (Tymoczko 1999: 23–24). Murakami seems to fit this pattern: in his translations, he aims for faithful rendering, avoiding creative interventions and retaining as much as possible the original flavor of the American texts.

However, while Murakami makes himself invisible as a translator on the textual level, he is extremely visible on the paratextual one: his name is as prominent as that of the author on the book covers of his translations, and the books are often sold in the "Murakami corner" of stores rather than in the "foreign literature" section. One good example of such mechanism is the publication in rapid succession, beginning in 2004, of several re-translations of famous works that Murakami had always quoted as significant influences on his own writing, such as J.D. Salinger's *The Catcher in the Rye*, Francis Scott Fitzgerald's *The Great Gatsby*, Truman Capote's *Breakfast at Tiffany's*, and Raymond Chandler's *The Long Goodbye* and *Farewell, My Lovely*.

While we might be tempted to think that Murakami retranslated these works simply because he liked them personally and because he is famous enough that publishers let him do whatever he wants, I argue that these retranslations are more than a self-indulgent and commercial operation. Murakami's literature was highly influenced by these writers, and, as we have seen, he has been criticized for being a "passive receiver" of foreign culture for this reason. Having become a major exporter of Japanese literature overseas, Murakami now translates the authors that inspired him, and incorporates them into the "Murakami franchise." The works of Fitzgerald, Capote, and Chandler are marketed and received as part of a "Murakami world" that is composed of translations and re-translations, domestication and exoticization, which contributes to creating a mish-mash of cultures where notions of authenticity and authorship become blurred and ultimately irrelevant.

Such questioning of originality and authorship is commonly associated with Japanese popular culture, and specifically with the emergence of what Marc Steinberg describes as the "anime media mix" (see Chapter 23). According to Steinberg, one important effect of the media mix, the creative and industrial practice whereby characters and narratives travel between different media such as manga, anime, light novel, and videogame, results in a "fundamental reordering of the entirety of the work such that the primacy of the original is necessarily lost" (Steinberg 2012: 161). Through the complex interaction of literary influences and translations, Murakami extends a similar practice of displacement of the original to the realm of literature, challenging both the notion of a dichotomy between popular culture and high art, and the idea of national literature.

Conclusion: Switchboard Duty

Like the avant-pop literature analyzed by McCaffery and Tatsumi, Murakami's fiction recovers both elements of avant-garde art and a premodern vision of popular culture as a means of reconnecting with the supernatural. In addition, through his multiple positioning as author and translator, and his play with notions of authorship and adaptation, he challenges rigid notions of national literature, proposing a more complex form of transnational fiction. These two seemingly disparate operations have analogous effects, and work in conjunction with each other to produce new cultural forms. Both the supernatural and the foreign provide readers with a way to connect to their subconscious, and at the same time to connect to others.

As the Sheep Professor puts it in Birnbaum's (creative) translation of *Dance Dance Dance*: "Itallstartshere, itallendshere. Thisisyourplace. It'stheknot. It'stiedtoeverything…. Weconnectthings. That'swhatwedo. Likeaswitchboard, weconnectthings…. That'sourduty. Switchboardduty. Youseekforit, weconnect, yougotit. Getit?" (Murakami 1994: 83)

I see this "switchboard duty" as the main function of both the supernatural in the author's novels and short stories, and translations and paratexts in the Murakami franchise. I read this as emblematic of Murakami's specific brand of transnational avant-pop literature, which aims to break down conceptual and cultural boundaries and establish unusual connections, ultimately throwing into question the very idea of a unified and stable national culture and identity.

Note

1 Murakami's literature has become one of Japan's hottest exports in China and Taiwan, where the 2000s have seen the emergence of a whole related industry of merchandising and entertainment including theme cafés China (Hillenbrand 2009).

29 Thumb-Generation Literature

The Rise and Fall of Japanese Cellphone Novels[1]

Alisa Freedman

Especially around 2007 and 2008, the global press was filled of reports—incredulous, disparaging, mocking, bemused—of one of the latest "fads" from Japan: novels written, predominantly with thumbs, on cellphones and circulated on specialized websites. Reports focused on the *"keitai shōsetsu"* (cellphone novels) that took top ranks on Japan's bestseller book lists between 2004 and 2007 and were adapted into television dramas and feature films, among other media, and inspired sequels and spin-offs. Journalists (and slightly later, academics) speculated on the aesthetic and social significance of this new form of storytelling. While some questioned the literariness of these narratives and viewed them as fascinating but short-lived popular culture (e.g., Goodyear 2008; Onishi 2008), others praised them as epitomizing the creative and community-building potential of mobile communications (e.g., Hjorth 2014; Kim 2014). Whether intended or not, these global discussions furthered the association of Japan's national "brand" with innovative use of technologies and helped spread the idea of writing cellphone novels (although few of the Japanese bestsellers have been commercially translated outside of Asia).

Cellphone novels, the best-known examples of which were written by amateur authors younger than thirty-five, were perceived as heralding a change of the guard in the production of popular literature (e.g., Nagano 2010). The nickname "thumb tribe" (*oyayubizoku*) or "thumb generation" (*oyayubi sedai*), once signifying pachinko players, was applied as early as 2001 to youths adept at rapidly texting with their thumbs on their cellphones' ten-key pads. This generation relies less on their index fingers, the once dominant digit for dialing rotary phones and ringing doorbells, older modes of communication (Hills 2002). They have adapted easily to other thumb-controlled gadgets, such as hand-held game consoles. Thumb Tribe members, who arguably prefer texting to talking on phones, became accustomed to discussing their lives and seeking empathy through text messages, an idea that has influenced storytelling and enabled the rise of literary genres.

I argue that cellphone novels should be viewed as a generational phenomenon that changed popular literature—generation in terms of technological developments and age of authors—generally lasting from the increased use of

Japan's "3G" (third generation) phones in 2001 to the dominance of touch-screen "smartphones." The iPhone was first marketed in Japan in 2008 but did not become popular until 2011, in part because of the lack of features like preprogrammed emoticons found on Japanese cellphones. On one hand, the term "Galapagos Syndrome" (*garapagosu-ka*), denoting a strain of a global product with features only found locally, was coined in reference to Japanese 3G phones that were too advanced to be used elsewhere; this syndrome reflects both Japan's reputation for fashionable technology and anxiety about being an isolated "island nation" (Tabuchi 2009). On the other hand, Japanese cellphones have been on the vanguard of global trends, such as text messaging (Short Message Service, SMS) and emoji.

While overviewing the historical and social significance of cellphone novels and the discourses about them, I analyze how cellphone novels have reaffirmed, rather than undermined, the cultural significance of the print book in Japan and the dominance of the written word. Cellphone novels exemplified conventions of Japanese Internet use, including access patterns, visual languages, user identifications, and corporate tie-ins; they also represented increasing reliance on portable technologies. At the same time, they encouraged discussions about groups on the fringes of Japanese society, particularly delinquent girls, helping subcultures come to represent Japan in the global imagination. Cellphone novels were especially popular in Japan between 2005 and 2007, crucial years in the spread of the Internet (e.g., Facebook and YouTube went public around 2005) and the globalization of Japanese popular culture. Although the trend waned in popularity after around 2008, cellphone novels have had a lasting influence on how books and authors are defined. I contribute to the larger conversation about cellphone novels by focusing on their historicity and how they represent a pivotal time in the intersection of mobile technology, print media, and globalization of Japanese popular culture and by examining their literary narratives, aesthetics, genres, and publishing, as well as formats.

Keitai Culture and Language

"*Keitai denwa*" (portable phones), commonly referred to as "*keitai*," were developed and marketed in Finland (1971), United States (1973), and elsewhere before Japan's NTT (Nippon Telegraph and Telephone, established in 1952 and privatized in 1985) in 1979 launched the world's first fully automated commercial cellular network (called "1G" after digital "2G" service was established in 1991). NTT offered car phone service in 1979 and the "shoulder phone" (*shorudāhon*) that could be carried in a bag with a shoulder strap in 1985, reducing the size of this portable phone from seven pounds (three kilograms) to half a pound (220 grams) in 1991 (NTT DoCoMo 2014). NTT established DoCoMo—from "do communications over the mobile network" and a pun for "anywhere" (*dokomo*)—in 1992 and opened i-mode mobile Internet in 1999; competitor providers followed suit, and Japanese government regulations of digital media increased (e.g., the Basic Law on the Formation of an Advanced Information and Telecommunications Network Society, or IT Basic Law, [Kōdo jōhō tsushin nettowakku shakai keisei kihonhō, IT kihonhō] in 2000). In 2006, the Ministry of Information and Communications reported that more people in Japan accessed the Internet by cellphones than by computers (69.2 million compared to 66 million, with 48.6 million using both) (Williams 2006). Reasons included affordable cellphone packet plans, use of the Internet for leisure rather than work in a corporate system still reliant on paperwork, and the custom of browsing websites during spare time provided by long train commutes, the main mode of transportation in Japanese cities.

Such features as photo transmission (first provided by J-Phone, now part of Softbank, in 2000), ringtones, and preprogrammed emoticons added to the popularity of cellphones. The indispensability of cellphones to daily life has been evident through trends, such as personalization by adding decorative (*dekora*) touches, including straps with charms (*keitai sutorapu*), once one of Sanrio's most popular gift items as Christine Yano notes in her chapter. This can be read as part of a larger history of personalizing belongings, to make them instantly recognizable, express their individuality, and show affection for a community or culture. For example, "*netsuke*," miniature sculptures created around the seventeenth century, served as counterweights for *sagemono* pouches or small baskets hung from kimono sashes for carrying daily-use items.

SMS texts, 140–160 character messages, became popular in Japan as an inexpensive, private mode of communication in the late 1990s, predominant among female users of "pocket bells," stylish personal pagers and the then least expensive communication tool. (Pocket Bells were first introduced by NTT in 1968.) SMS altered customs of formal written communication, which has historically relied on set seasonal greetings and polite words to soothe social relationships. Abbreviations developed to save space and convey feelings but demanded communal knowledge to be understood. For example, SKY, for *Supā Kūki Yomanai*, meaning "super clueless," was popular SMS slang in 2007. Other slang extended common practices, such as reading numbers as sounds (e.g., "39" read "san-kyū" as "thank you" or as "mi-ku" to refer to the animated singer Hatsune Miku, analyzed in Chapter 12). Text languages, to which new words constantly have been added, can be viewed as an extension of the shared vocabularies that solidify social groups (see Chapter 10).

One of the first emoji—"picture characters" added to SMS to ensure the right emotional message is received and to share images without taking up much bandwidth—among mainstream users was a heart mark on the "Pocket Bell" pager in 1995. A set of colorful emoji was developed around 1999 by NTT designer Kurita Shigetaka to be preprogrammed into cellphones, starting with DoCoMo i-mode units; other providers adopted same characters with slightly different aesthetics. Japanese cellphone users also popularized "*kaomoji*," or "face characters," a form of ASCII artwork comprised of letters, punctuation marks, and other printable characters written on textboards like ASCII Net since the 1980s (see Danet 2001: 194–240). While American "smileys" :) are vertical, Japanese *kaomoji* are horizontal (^_^). (Earlier global antecedents to *kaomoji* and emoji include an 1862 newspaper transcript by Abraham Lincoln with a drawing of a laugh with a semi-colon and parentheses, which might have been a printer's typo, Lee 2009.) The yellow faces, holiday symbols, and other now iconic emoji, are part of Japanese "*kawaii*" (cute premised on seeming vulnerable) aesthetics, characterized by big heads, missing noses or mouths, and large eyes to show emotion. A standard set of emoji were incorporated into Unicode in 2010 and globalized in 2011 especially thanks to inclusion on iPhones, Windows phones, Facebook, and other platforms, while including images like the bowing man, receptionist woman, masked sick face, and foods like *dango* and *oden* that require knowledge of Japanese society to be understood.[2] Emoji demonstrates that popular culture trends need to have the right "cultural odor" (to borrow a term from Iwabuchi Kōichi 2002), the amount of a particular cultural context, in order to globalize. The model manifested by emoji is to be grounded in Japanese culture but understandable across nations. Along with cellphone slang, emoticons altered written communication, but, as I will now explain, competition among telecommunications providers and Internet sites helped transform literature.

Thumb-Generation Novels

In January 2002, NEC became one of the first corporations to promote reading novels on cellphones. For an inexpensive flat rate of one hundred yen per month, subscribers could receive installments from the "Shinchō Cellphone Library" (Shinchō keitai bunko), a limited digital collection of the Shinchō publishing company's paperback books. Advertisements promoted the service as a way to occupy time while waiting for and traveling on trains. One of the first available books was *Train Poster Stories* (*Nakazuri shōsetsu*), an anthology of uplifting tales by popular authors serialized on posters hung from the ceilings (*nakazuri*) of JR East commuter trains from September 1990 to September 1991 (Freedman 2010: 13–15).

The trend for new novels available for cellphone serialization began with *Deep Love: Ayu's Story* (*Deep Love—Ayu no monogatari*) written by a thirty-something man under the penname Yoshi. Yoshi, a former preparatory school teacher, was inspired in 2000 by the increasing use of i-Mode to open Zavn.net, a website for cellphone access, to publicize his original writings and photographs. To promote Zavn.net, Yoshi distributed cards with the URL in Shibuya. In May 2000, he began serializing *Deep Love*, the story of the decline of Ayu, a seventeen-year-old who engages in *enjo kōsai*, or compensating dating, an issue then debated in the mass media. After temporarily quitting, Ayu is forced back into prostitution to repay money she stole from an elderly woman to help her drug-addicted boyfriend Kenji. The woman had been saving for an operation to cure Yoshiyuki, a boy suffering from a heart condition. Before Ayu dies of AIDS, she sends her dog Pao to deliver a Christmas gift to Yoshiyuki, with whom she had become close. Reina, Ayu's friend, also forced into prostitution, was raped and gave birth to a daughter named Ayu, who is blinded from a fall.

Yoshi self-published *Deep Love* as a book for Zavn.net subscribers. As news of the story spread, Yoshi was offered contracts from mainstream publishers, which he declined because they proposed changes to the sexually explicit and violent content and to his casual, colloquial writing style. He worked with the smaller Starts Publishing (known for Oz-brand women's magazines) to reissue *Deep Love Complete Version: Ayu's Story* (*Deep Love kanzen han ~ Ayu no monogatari*) in 2002, followed by three sequels: *Deep Love: Host* (*Deep Love kanzen dai ni bu ~ Hosuto*), *Deep Love: Reina's Fate* (*Deep Love ~ Reina no unmei*), and *Deep Love Special Edition: Pao's Story* (*Deep Love tokubetsu han ~ Pao no monogatari*). These books are written horizontally, instead of vertically, and open from the left rather than from the right as had been the norm in Japan. Thus, by adopting the practice of reading SMS, they changed the appearance of the print page. They have larger font and wider margins than usual to recreate the experience of reading cellphone screens. *Deep Love* was adapted into five manga series from 2004 to 2006, a film (2004) for which Yoshi used Zavn.net to help cast, and two television series (2004 and 2005, TV Tokyo) that aired late night due to controversial content. *Deep Love* and later cellphone novels extended the concept of "media mix," or the release of one title in various platforms with adaptations timed to maintain popularity, which has been essential to the success of Japanese popular-culture franchises (see Chapter 23).

The best-known website for circulating cellphone novels has been Magic Island (Mahō no i-rando, "i" in "island" a pun for i-Mode, Figure 29.1), opened as a homepage provider in 1999, preceding the launch of Japan's local Amazon bookseller (Amazon.co.jp) by one year. Starting in 2000, Magic Island included a "book function" (BOOK *kinō*) enabling users to write stories in 1,000-character chapters, up to 500 pages, for free. In 2004, DoCoMo began offering unlimited domestic text messaging in their monthly packet plans, making cellphone-novel-writing affordable. The first Magic Island novel published as a print book was *What the Angels Gave Me* (*Tenshi ga kureta mono*, Starts Publishing, 2005) by Chaco, who became one of the most prolific cellphone novelists. The book, which sold more than one million copies (Emata 2007: 55), was published thanks in part to fans contacting presses with requests (Mahō no i-rando toshokan 2007: 38). Opening in March 2006, the compilation site Magic Island Library (Mahō no toshokan) allowed subscribers to browse, comment on, review, and rank novels. (Corporate and fan ranking of products, from books to horoscopes, is a popular marketing tool in Japan.) The establishment of such competitor websites as Wild Strawberries (Nō-ichigo) attest to the Japanese cultural notion that good ideas should be emulated. The primary publishers of cellphone novels have been Starts

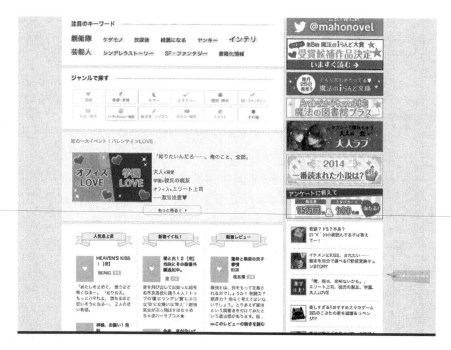

Figure 29.1 Magic Island (Mahō no i-rando) cellphone novel (*keitai shōsetsu*) website, February 2015.
Source: Author's screenshot.

Publishing and Goma Books (known for celebrity accounts). In 2007, Magic Island had between 4.8 and 5.2 million registered users, around 70 percent of whom were women, with a number of readers in upper primary school grades and junior high school (Emata 2007: 54–55; Mika 2006). Cellphone novels perhaps filled a gap in Japan for young-adult fiction, a growing genre in the United States, because of its attention to issues facing teenagers.

Many cellphone novelists are novice writers who do not aspire to literary careers. Almost all hide their identities behind one-word, cute-sounding, easy-to-remember names (e.g., Yoshi, Chaco, and Mei), combining the tradition of pennames in Japanese literature (especially common before World War II) with handle names on public Internet sites. The author of *Love Sky: Sad Love Story* (*Koizora: Setsunai koi monogatari*), ranked third in the 2006 bestseller list, shares a name with the protagonist, Mika, making this doomed romance between high-school students, one of whom is dying of cancer, seem premised on truth. The use of given names in Japanese society, where most people are called by their surnames, fosters a sense of intimacy.

Magic Island and similar websites offer a model of "joint creation" that extends the historical practice of reader comments in Japanese periodicals, such as in girls' comics (*shōjo* manga) magazines analyzed in Chapter 25.

Itō Yoshiaki, head of production at Magic Island, remarked that the readers and authors play a "game of catch"; authors toss chapters to readers, who then suggest changes and correct mistakes (Emata 2007: 55). Towa, winner of the first Japan Cellphone Novel Prize in 2006 (Nihon keitai shōsetsu taishō, established by Magic Island, Starts Publishing, and the Mainichi newspaper company) for *Clearness* (*Kurianesu*) thanked readers for lightening the mood of the story (Emata 2007: 55).

Professionally published book versions of cellphone novels dominated bestseller lists between 2005 and 2007, with film and television adaptations helping to increase sales. For example, *Threads of Destiny* (*Akai ito*) by Mei, the story of two junior-high-school students who were fated to fall in love and the troubles caused by friends and family, ranked second in 2007 (*Asahi Shinbun* 2007) and led to the sequel *Threads of Destiny ~ Fate* (*Akai ito ~ destiny*). In 2007, Starts Publishing published twenty cellphone novels, providing almost one-third of its income (Goodyear 2008); Goma Books and Magic Island together sold three million cellphone novels, beating sales of larger publishing companies (Lytle 2007). As Starts Publishing editor Matsushima Shigeru commented in a press interview, "[Readers] don't know when and which stories will disappear from cellphones and the Internet. They want to buy the books just because they want the things that have had an impact on their lives close at hand" (Emata 2007: 55). According to publishing conventions, books longer than 350 pages are divided into two volumes (upper and lower), each sold separately, with cover art and other design elements showing that they are a set. For example, the matching red and white covers of *Threads of Destiny* are perhaps a technique borrowed from Murakami Haruki's bestselling *Norwegian Wood* (*Noruwei no mori*, 1987), issued in red and green volumes to associate with color symbolism in the story and to encourage their use as Christmas presents.

The most popular cellphone novels cast underdog teenaged characters in the "pure love" (*jun'ai*) stories that had emerged as a distinct genre marketed to women and men, a convention of television dramas since the 1990s (see Chapter 5). In many instances, one or more of the characters falls in love for the first time, and the couple needs to overcome obstacles to be together; stories end or a character dies before love can be realized. A seminal pure love story but not a cellphone novel was Katayama Kyōichi's *Crying Out Love, In the Center of the World* (*Sekai no chūshin de, ai o sakebu*), which was adapted into a manga, film, and television series in 2004 and a Korean movie in 2005. Published by Shōgakukan in 2001, this tale of a boy in love with a girl dying of cancer became a bestseller in 2004, in part because of the efforts by a Shōgakukan salesperson to mobilize the book's fan base and the promotion by actress Shibasaki Kō, who appeared in the film version. In *Deep Love*, the protagonist Ayu seeks lost innocence and salvation through heterosexual romance with a boy dying of heart disease. Cellphone novels discuss issues rarely covered in other kinds of love stories, such as domestic abuse, rape, drug addiction, and suicide. In general, these books provide insight into the psychology of troubled youth but do not offer solutions to their hardships. As represented by *Deep Love*, many characters cannot overcome traumas that are often caused by their own bad decisions, and their stories end unhappily. The genre turns problems into issues of personal choice, thereby releasing the Japanese government, educational institutions, and public society from blame. They inspire tears but not activism.

Media theorists, including Hayamizu Kenrō (2008), have read cellphone novels as part of a popular culture interest in *"yankii."* Derived, but different from, American "Yankee," *yankii* is a subculture formed in the 1980s and 1990s largely of rebellious, even delinquent, male and female adolescents, who have their own fashions and notions of integrity and are more often associated with suburban and rural areas than cities. *Yankii* characters have populated other light fiction, such as Takemoto Novala's 2002 novel and 2004 film *Kamikaze Girls (Shimotsuma monotagari)*. The Akutagawa Prize, Japan's most prestigious literary award, has been given to more serious literature that encourages readers to consider causes and effects of youth subcultures, including Kanehara Hitomi's 2003 *Snakes and Earrings* (*Hebi ni piasu*) and Mobu Norio's 2004 *Introduction to Nursing* (*Kaigo nyūmon*). Cellphone novels advertise *yankii* characters, such as Aiko's *Yankii kare to nakimushi kanojo* (with the poorly translated English subtitle *Yankee Boyfriend and Crybaby She*, 2010).

Cellphone novels share literary techniques and visual qualities. Most often written in the first-person, they convey the sense of reading messages from friends. As Mei, author of *Threads of Destiny*, remarked in an interview with Goma Books, although it takes the average reader one to three minutes per page of a cellphone novel, it takes her hours of writing and revision to make pages seem that simple (Mahō no i-rando toshokan 2007: 9). Three kinds of dialogue dominate the stories, which are almost entirely devoid of narration: daily conversations, inner monologues, and words from the heart conveyed orally and through texts (Mahō no i-rando toshokan 2007: 160). In their guide for aspiring authors, Magic Island suggests using line spacing and paragraphing, along with square brackets and other punctuation, to create tempo and rhythm. They instruct that short sentences are easier to read on cellphones than long ones. Authors should consider sound, such as the ringing of phones and chimes of texts. Magic Island advises that authors write their novels on cellphones so that they can see how they will be read (Mahō no i-rando toshokan 2007: 160). In part due to screen limitations, cellphone novels are full of sentence fragments, which some critics have praised as emulating Japanese literary traditions of enmeshing poetry within prose to heighten emotions (e.g., Dooley 2008) but others have disparaged as poor writing (e.g., Onishi 2008). With the exception of stars (for emphasis and flair), heart marks (to show love), and musical notes (for ringing phones and arriving messages), most cellphone novels have few emoticons.

In other respects, cellphone novels perpetuate long-standing literary conventions, such as using awards to establish authorial careers and publishing stories in periodicals before releasing them as standalone books. The Japan

Cellphone Novel Prize parallels the Akutagawa Prize (and the companion Naoki Prize for popular fiction) given twice a year to up-and-coming authors for novellas appearing in magazines. While not making pretenses toward producing highbrow literature, Goma Books published versions of classics for which copyrights have expired in the style of cellphone novels, including Akutagawa Ryūnosuke's *Spider's Thread* (*Kumo no ito*). Nun and literary scholar Setouchi Jakucho (b. 1922) serialized the cellphone novel *Tomorrow's Rainbow* (*Ashita no niji*, 2008), inspired by the eleventh-century *Tale of Genji* (*Genji monogatari*) that she had previously translated (Okamura 2008). Jakucho took the penname "Purple" (Pāpuru), an allusion to Murasaki Shikibu, the *Tale of Genji*'s probable female author. (Murasaki means purple.)

Thanks to global media attention, the fad spread worldwide. For example, the first cellphone novel serialized in North America was *Secondhand Memories* (*Mukashi no omoide*) by Takatsu, a Japanese university student studying in Toronto, on Textnovel (founded in 2008) from 2009 to 2011 and featured in an English language textbook in Japan (Takatsu 2011). Yet by this time, the Japanese popularity for cellphone novels had waned, with the exception of the light high-school romance *Wolf Boy x Natural Girl* by a fifteen-year-old girl called "Bunny" (from a *Bambi* character) who began the story while in sixth grade and sold 110,000 copies in 2009 (Nagano 2010).

Keitai shōsetsu were an integral part of a larger mediascape, integrating technology and literature with subcultures and provide new modes of reader engagement. Concurrent with bestselling cellphone novels, stories written collectively on large Internet forums were published as books. Consumed by a different demographic and accessed primarily on computers, these Internet novels represent an alternative mode of collaborative writing. The most famous example is *Train Man* (*Densha otoko*), which became a bestselling book (October 2004), a film (June 2005), a television series (July–September 2005), a stage play (September 2005), four manga in *shōjo* and *seinen* styles (comics for girls and boys, respectively, 2005), and even an adult video (2005). An inspiring love story of an awkward twenty-two-year-old otaku (here, an avid fan of manga, anime, and games who frequents the Tokyo neighborhood of Akihabara) and a slightly older, fashionable working woman based on a supposedly real event, *Train Man* was created through anonymous posts on the expansive 2channel from March to May 2004 and reads like a dating guide to Tokyo. (Founded in 1999 by Nishimura Hiroyuki, 2channel has historically been Japan's most influential and expansive textboard.) The story centers on the couple and the online community who encouraged them. Along with text messages written in slang created on 2channel, subscribers posted ASCII artwork, both *kaomoji* and elaborate pictures; Shinchōsha company editor Gunji Yoko won the rights to publish the print book because she promised to maintain this format. For the print book, the collective author was given the name Nakano Hitori, a pun for "one among us." The real identity of Train Man remains unknown.

Key differences between cellphone and 2channel novels demonstrate the diversity of digital stories and their communities in this phase of Internet use. Cellphone novels epitomize the fast, easy qualities of mobile communication, while 2channel reflects a slower pace of web browsing. *Train Man* was heavily edited after the story was finished, while cellphone authors serialized chapters as they wrote them. The youth characters of cellphone novels have less access to power than Train Man, who had the leisure, finances, and support network to improve his life. Because of its older readership, empathetic characters, use of 2channel, and occurrence in years of national concern over falling marriage rates, *Train Man* inspired more discussion about changing gender norms, than cellphone novels did (Freedman 2009b).

The Legacy of Mobile Stories

Digital media has transformed Japanese literature by redefining authors, readers, characters, books, and enabling collaborative writing. Rather than rendering print media obsolete, cellphones and the Internet have created book formats and added new languages, thus exemplifying how the Japanese publishing industry has compensated for decreasing sales by increasing titles. There was a 0.4 percent rise in new books in 2007, a small but significant increase (Japan Book Publishers Association 2014). Related book types include the catchall "light novels" (*raito noberu*, a term coined earlier than *keitai shōsetsu*), various kinds of easy-to-read literature, often with ties to popular culture. At the same time, cellphone novels have furthered publishing conventions. For example, they borrow the Japanese custom of first serializing stories in magazines, newspapers, and other "disposable" subscription media, and then, if they are well received, publishing them as books. Awards and ranking are used to promote literary careers. They also demonstrate how surface attention to social issues can contribute to the dismissal of matters deserving more sustained consideration. As such, much popular fiction, while raising awareness of the need to solve problems facing contemporary Japan, tends to support the social status quo.

Arguably, cellphone novels heightened the value of the written word as a quality defining literature as an art form, for other digital modes of writing, such as emoticons, have failed to produce lasting literary styles. (Even books based on videogame narratives and Facebook posts, for example, are written mostly in words.) Although the *Oxford English Dictionary* chose the crying with joy emoji as the top "English word" of 2015 (Oxford University Press 2015), thus demonstrating the global popularity of emoticons, few original novels in any country have been written entirely in emoji. Emoji have been playfully used to render famous plots in new ways. For example, the OMG Shakespeare Series (with such titles as *Yolo Juliet*, co-written by Shakespeare and Brett Wright) and Fred Benson's crowd-sourced *Emoji Dick* translation of Melville's *Moby-Dick*, all available as print books, are based on fair-use stories well known enough to be understood without line-by-line reading.

The difficulties of writing and reading a story solely in emoji illuminate the parameters of the literary, while cellphone novels represent literature's diversification.

Developments in mobile technologies have made *keitai* writing obsolete. The first cellphone/e-book reader in Japan, Biblio (produced by Toshiba for KDDI [now AU] provider) that held around five thousand books (7GB) was released in in 2009. Unlike earlier Japanese e-book readers, Biblio had an online bookstore for users. Japanese sales of e-books available in cellphone formats rose from 283 million to 480 million between 2007 and 2010, many of which were manga titles (229 and 423 million in 2007 and 2011, respectively) (Japan Book Publishers Association 2014). Rakuten Kobo (Canadian subsidiary of the Japanese Rakuten e-commerce conglomerate) released the Kobo Touch e-book reader in Japan in July 2012, followed by Amazon's Kindle that October (four years later than in the United States), joining a handful of smaller e-book competitors. Starting with the iPhone, "smartphones" with larger screens and faster Internet access have offered more reading material. Goma Books filed for bankruptcy in September 2009, but cellphone websites offer imprint series, such as Keitai shōsetsu bunko (Wild Strawberry) and Mahō no i-rando bunko. While some English language cellphone novels sites like Quillpill no longer exist, the Textnovel website encourages subscribers to "get noticed" and make money writing cellphone novels (Textnovel n.d.).

Cellphone novels were a product of a short-lived but important moment when Japanese cellphones were on the vanguard of world technology, before falling behind other mobile devices. They bridged conventional patterns in the consumption of literature with storytelling techniques embraced by digital technologies. They included character types that represented problems facing a generation. Unintentionally and even ironically, cellphone novels—one the world's most portable, private, and disposable forms of literature—have demonstrated the continued desire for print books, cultural artifacts that permanently record stories and make it possible to repeatedly read them. They have assured the importance of the written word in the age of visual narratives.

Notes

1 A different version of this chapter was published in *Routledge Companion to Comparative Internet Histories*, edited by Mark McLelland and Gerald Goggin, 412–425 (Routledge 2017). Thank you to the editors for their helpful feedback and for allowing the republication. I am grateful to Kendall Heitzman and John Moore for their insights.

2 There is now a diverse array of emoticons, including the thousands of "stickers," large, animated original and famous characters available for free and purchase through the texting app LINE (starting in 2011). Also realizing the commercial potential of emoticons, global celebrities have sold apps with their own emoji, a trend begun with Kim Kardashian's *Kimoji* (2015).

PART X

Sites and Spectacles

30 *Hanabi*

The Cultural Significance of Fireworks in Japan

Damien Liu-Brennan

Introduction

In the Edo period (1603–1868), fireworks (*hanabi*) evolved from a simple amusement into a technologically advanced art form, distinctive culture, and potent symbol. The term "*hanabi*," comprised of the *kanji* characters for flower (*hana*) and fire (*bi*), not only denotes the physical entity of fireworks but also encapsulates their aesthetic and symbolic qualities. Fireworks festivals (*hanabi taikai*) are held all over Japan especially in the summer, forming a "*hanabi* season," and provide a reprieve from the formalities of everyday life, a communal celebratory space, and a chance for friendly competition. *Hanabi*'s other symbolic associations include the transience of life, nostalgia for lost times and youth, ephemeral beauty, and optimism for the future. These meanings were embraced in the years immediately following the March 11, 2011 triple disaster of earthquake, tsunami, and nuclear meltdown, exemplifying how popular culture can provide a sense of hope.

In this chapter, I argue that many of *hanabi*'s cultural nuances, communal uses, spatial associations, and symbolic meanings began in the Edo period and that *hanabi* demonstrates how this historical era still influences Japanese daily life and popular culture. I first survey the history of *hanabi*, outlining their evolution into a distinct culture and surveying key examples of the places, practices, and art forms that they inspired. Then I examine popular music and commercial film, two dominant mass-market media, to show how the meanings of *hanabi* in the Edo period have been extended in the twenty-first century. One of the outstanding aspects of *hanabi* is that their culture developed among the general populace and generally remained free for public viewing, unlike in Europe where viewing fireworks was often under the control of the aristocracy and associated elites. As I will show, this makes *hanabi* a quintessential form of and motif in popular culture, arising from the common people and symbolizing their hopes and values.

The History of *Hanabi*: Rise of a Distinct Summer Culture

Fireworks are a peaceful application of gunpowder. In Japan, an awareness of gunpowder, which was first developed in China in the ninth century, was documented as early as the thirteenth century; however, gunpowder weapons were not recognized until after 1543, when a Chinese merchant ship carrying Portuguese seafarers with European firearms made an emergency landing at Tanegashima, off the coast of what is now Kyushu. Firearms played a significant role in the various battles that led to the end of the Warring States era (Sengoku period, 1467–1603) and the unification of Japan under the Tokugawa Shōgunate. The shōgunate instituted numerous measures to prevent civil war and social unrest; for example, Japan was closed off to most foreign influences and Japanese people were prohibited from traveling abroad (*sakoku*, or "closed country" policy, starting around 1633). Regional lords (*daimyō*) were required to maintain residences in the capital city of Edo and to attend these residences in alternate years (*sankin kōtai*, starting in 1635). The general peace of the Edo period provided favorable conditions for the development of recreational fireworks, for there was a decreasing need for gunpowder weapons and an increasing demand for culture and entertainment, particularly in the rapidly developing city of Edo.

Although historical records indicate that basic *hanabi* were a leisurely summer pursuit in Edo during the early seventeenth century, it was not until 1733 that they were first used as a public display. This took place on the Sumida River in the neighborhood of Ryōgoku at the annual Ryōgoku Kawabiraki (river-opening festival), which celebrated the beginning of summer and the usage of the river for water activities, including "enjoying the cool of the evening" (*nōryō*). At this event, twenty *shikake hanabi* (fireworks attached to a frame that forms a design when set off) were lit as part of a *segaki* (Buddhist rite for the benefit of suffering spirits) to commemorate the numerous people who died of famine and cholera the previous year (Mutō 2000: 10). This marked the start of the historical association of Ryōgoku and *hanabi*. Thereafter, *hanabi* were used in this and other festivals to herald the beginning of summer.

A distinct *hanabi* culture evolved at Ryōgoku during the eighteenth and nineteenth centuries, adding to the resplendence of Edo. At the time, Ryōgoku was arguably the most popular *sakariba* (crowded entertainment quarter) in Edo, if not all of Japan, largely due to the fact that it was the only place in the capital city that *hanabi* were displayed.[1] Renowned author and inventor Hiraga Gennai (1728–1780) remarked of Ryōgoku in his satirical sermons *Rootless Weeds* (*Nenashigusa*, 1763), "One would marvel at these crowds and wonder if they had emptied the houses of all the provinces" (quoted in Hur 2000: 99).

At the *hirokōji* (open areas) on both sides of Ryōgoku Bridge and along the banks of the Sumida River, numerous *misemono goya* (exhibition booths) and *yatai* (temporary stalls), which were only permitted in the summer, provided a thriving atmosphere where crowds of men and women from different social classes could liberate themselves from the restrictions of the feudal order, escape the formalities and mundaneness of everyday life, and be entertained (Hur 2000: 92–93, 197). The Sumida River provided a supplementary entertainment space for viewing *hanabi* from several kinds of river craft, from the stately *yakatabune* (large-roofed pleasure boats) to the numerous *choki-bune* (small open boats). Drifting *hanabibune* (fireworks boats) displayed small *hanabi* for paying patrons who watched from other vessels or provided stages for larger displays that all visitors at Ryōgoku could enjoy.

The artistry of *hanabi* significantly improved chiefly through the efforts of two famous *hanabishi* (fireworks artisans or guilds), Kagiya and Tamaya, who were spurred on by the demands of enthusiastic revelers to see bigger, better, and more intricate *hanabi* spectacles at Ryōgoku. The competitions that arose between the two guilds, which peaked in the first half of the nineteenth century, attracted the general public, who came to Ryōgoku in ever increasing numbers. Accordingly, *hanabi* and the Ryōgoku *sakariba* evolved together and thrived off each other's success, supported by the patronage of the general public.

The city of Edo underwent socioeconomic changes as the economic power of the samurai class declined and that of the *chōnin* (townspeople) grew. Increasingly, *chōnin* were able to spend more on luxuries and leisurely pursuits. For example, merchant revelers were able to purchase *hanabi* for personal use or to sponsor Kagiya or Tamaya for private displays; while various groups, such as local boating agencies and teahouses, pooled their funds for grand displays, as was the case at the Ryōgoku Kawabiraki in 1733 (Sumidagawa Hanabi Taikai Jikko Iinkai 1983: 28). Because sponsorship brought recognition to benefactors, it was not uncommon for patrons to engage in personal competitions of pride, in which they purchased *hanabi* as a means to show off their wealth and status, continually upping the ante and often spending beyond their means (Mitamura 1975: 93–106).

Accordingly, *hanabi* at Ryōgoku became an increasingly popular theme in Edo period art and literature, particularly in the nineteenth century, which served to strengthen the spatial and metaphorical meanings associated with *hanabi* and to contribute to the culture developing around them. In particular, *hanabi* appeared in an overwhelming number of *ukiyo-e* (woodblock prints), an accessible mass-produced art form that typically depicted common people, places, and cultural trends, created by prominent artists, such as Utagawa Hiroshige (1897–1858) and Utagawa Toyoharu (1735–1814). *Ukiyo-e* showed the thriving summer atmosphere at Ryōgoku with revelers on rivercraft, crowds being entertained at the various *misemono goya* and *yatai* along the Sumida River, and *hanabi* bursting into bloom above the Ryōgoku Bridge.

Hanabi also appeared in popular literature at the time, especially in the many *meishō zue* (illustrated guides to scenic places), such as *Edo meishō zue* (*Illustrated Guide to Famous Sites of Edo*, 1834–1836) by Saitō Gesshin (1804–1878) and his family, which described similar scenes to those depicted in *ukiyo-e* and were usually accompanied by illustrations and poetic verses. In addition, Kitamura Nobuyo (1784–1856), described *hanabi* styles of his times in *Essays on Manners and Customs* (*Kiyū shoran*, 1830). Along with *Rootless Weeds* (1763) quoted above, Hiraga Gennai wrote about Edo's thriving *hanabi* culture in *The Modern Life of Shidōken* (*Fūryū shidōken den*, 1763). *Hanabi* became a standard seasonal word (*kigo*) for summer in *waka* (classical short poetry with many rules governing the inclusion of words and imagery). These and other literary works spread the fame of Ryōgoku and *hanabi* throughout Japan.

By the early nineteenth century, a number of regional areas began to emulate Edo's *hanabi* culture, as well as to develop their own styles and practices. Some localities incorporated *hanabi* into their existing summer religious festivals (*matsuri*), such as the Tenmangu Tenjin Festival in Osaka and the Gozu Tennō Festival in Kiyosu, Owari (now part of Aichi Prefecture). As in Edo, these festivals were abuzz with patrons attending restaurants, teahouses, *misemono goya*, and *yatai*. At festivals celebrated by rivers, patrons could also enjoy festivities on various kinds of boats, as they could in Edo. Some regions even became renowned for their own distinct styles of *hanabi*, such as *tezutsu hanabi* (hand-held bamboo cylinders woven with rope) from the Toyohashi region (now part of Aichi Prefecture) and the *ryūsei* (bamboo rockets) of Chichibu (now part of Saitama Prefecture). These regional practices also became the subject of art and literature, further increasing their fame. By the end of the Edo period, *hanabi* culture was evident throughout Japan.

Concurrently, *hanabi* took on additional aesthetic and symbolic connotations, including those that had been associated with flowers in Heian period (794–1185) poetry and other forms of classical art. *Hanabishi* developed fireworks that represented particular flowers or emulated other aspects of nature; hence, numerous botanical appellations were applied to *hanabi*, such as *kiku* (chrysanthemum), *botan* (peony), *yanagi* (willow), *chō* (butterflies), *tonbo* (dragonflies), and *chiri sakura* (falling cherry blossoms). Accordingly, viewers cultivated a sensibility toward *hanabi* that correlated with that of other seasonal observances, such as viewing cherry blossoms in the spring (*hanami*), the moon (*tsukimi*) and changing leaves (*momijigari*) in the autumn, and gazing at winter snow (*yukimi*). With each of these seasonal observances, a phase of life can be appreciated and contemplated (Shirane 2012). Together, they present a metaphor of life in its entirety: spring flowers are associated with birth, new growth, and youth; summer *hanabi* represent the peak of life's vitality; the full moon of autumn is symbolic of wisdom and completeness and autumn leaves, the withering and fading of old age; and, finally, winter snow alludes to the final passage leading to the desolation of death. *Hanabi*, however, have the power to encapsulate the sentiments of all the seasons at once, as was asserted in the preface of Rishō's *Book of Fireworks Secrets* (*Hanabi hidenshū*, 1817), the first book to be published on *hanabi* in Japan. Individual *hanabi* can therefore represent the ephemeral nature of life in its entirety.

This symbolic impact is exemplified in two Edo period practices still commonly today: first is the use of *senkō hanabi* (sparklers, literally: "incense stick fireworks") that mesmerizingly transition through a series of burning phases, each displaying characteristics representing a different stage of life, and thereby evoking a sense of nostalgia (Saitō 2005; Liu-Brennan and Bryce 2010).

Second is the launching of individual aerial *hanabi*. Launching large *hanabi* one by one allows each to be individually appreciated for its unique aesthetic, metaphoric, and sentimental qualities.

Although the Edo period was generally a time of strict government control over public events and culture, *hanabi* activity continued relatively unhindered, only temporarily affected by the Kansei Reforms (1790s) and the Tenpō Reforms (1840s), under which the shōgunate issued a number of edicts limiting expenditures and curbing entertainments in an attempt to restore what they perceived as declining economic and moral conditions. However, in the 1860s, the onset of civil unrest around Japan that culminated in the Meiji Restoration of 1868 led to a suspension of *hanabi* events from around 1863. Public displays of *hanabi* were permitted again in 1868, first resuming at the Ryōgoku Kawabiraki. After then, *hanabi* culture further expanded and diversified.

Woodblock prints depicting lively *hanabi* scenes were once again created in large numbers by a new generation of artists, including Toyohara Chikanobu (1838–1912) and Toyohara Kunichika (1835–1900). Scenes of Ryōgoku were similar to those of the Edo period but the depicted atmosphere, volume of people and boats, and the effects of the *hanabi* were exaggerated. Other *hanabi* events, such as displays at horseracing, carnivals, and diplomatic visits were also portrayed. *Hanabishi* developed more advanced styles of *hanabi* using new technologies acquired after the resumption of international trade in the Meiji period (1868–1912), including *hanabi* with better colors, "daytime *hanabi*" in which effigies explode from fireworks and float down on parachutes, and perfected large aerial *hanabi* that produce flawless round blooms, such as the previously mentioned chrysanthemums with trailing effects and peonies without trailing effects. Spherical chrysanthemum shells with multiple concentric cores were also perfected in the 1920s and are now commonly regarded as the representative fireworks of Japan (Figure 30.1).

Current Fireworks Practices: Retaining the Essence of Edo *Hanabi*

Hanabi usage was suspended during World War II but resumed shortly after. Over the subsequent decades, Japan's *hanabi* culture continued in a somewhat tentative and fluctuating manner, with various suspensions and resumptions due to government concerns over issues like traffic congestion and pollution. Since the late 1970s, however, there has been a significant resurgence of *hanabi* culture, largely in the interest of economic and community benefit. *Hanabi* are once again an important part of summer in Japan, with major festivals increasingly held during other times of year, including the Tsuchiura National Fireworks Competition (Tsuchiura Zenkoku Hanabi Kyōgi Taikai) in Ibaraki Prefecture held in autumn and the Chichibu Night Festival (Chichibu Yomatsuri) in Saitama Prefecture held in winter.

Figure 30.1 Shiniri kiku (chrysanthemum with a single core), Nagaoka (2008).
Source: Courtesy of the author.

In general, *hanabi taikai* maintain many attributes from the Edo period; for example, *hanabi* are still commonly launched one at a time, and traditional types of *hanabi* are still used. *Yatai* selling snacks, toys, local products, and other novelties are still part of the festival atmosphere. The funding structure that allows for both individual and communal contributions has been maintained, and the names of sponsors are displayed or announced over loudspeakers. It is also common for attendees at summer *hanabi taikai* to wear *yukata* (cotton kimono) or *jinbei* (men's two-piece cotton kimono) and for officials and the local fire departments to wear *happi* (workmen's coats). Iconic rivercraft are still present at current incarnations of the Sumida River Fireworks Festival (Sumidagawa Hanabi Taikai), as is the legacy of the competition between Kagiya and Tamaya, which is reflected by the use of two separate launching locations. Indeed, fireworks "competitions" have become a regular component of *hanabi* culture, and numerous annual contests are held around Japan where *hanabishi* can demonstrate their skills and innovative patterns, colors, and display formats. *Hanabi*'s symbolic associations discussed above have been perpetuated in the many festivals held for commemorative or dedicatory purposes. For example, the thriving "Light Up Nippon" program was established in 2011 to provide a series of *hanabi* displays in Northern Japan to commemorate the victims of the March 11 Triple Disaster, encourage local communities, and stand as a symbol of hope and optimism (Light Up Nippon). Similarly, all *hanabi taikai* in the summer of 2011 included commemorative displays dedicated to the victims of the disaster-stricken regions.

The most prominent example of commemorative *hanabi* in Japan is the Nagaoka Fireworks Festival (Nagaoka Matsuri Dai Hanabi Taikai), which originated in 1948 as a tribute to the victims of the firebombing of Nagaoka in 1945, in which 1,484 lives were claimed, and up to 80 percent of the city destroyed (Nagaoka Matsuri Kyōgikai 2006). Starting in 2005, specifically created, emotive "Phoenix" (*fenikkusu*) *hanabi* have also been added to this festival as a means to commemorate the devastating 2004 Chūetsu Earthquake in Niigata Prefecture. Another of the festival's crowd-pleasing features is the launching of the world's second largest individual firework, the *sanshakudama* (measuring approximately 90 cm [36 inches] in diameter and weighing up to 300 kg [660 pounds]) (Nagaoka Matsuri Kyōgikai 2006), which arose from a competitive rivalry to build the biggest *hanabi* with the nearby town of Katakai. Following the 2004 earthquake, there was some contention as to whether the expense of such *hanabi* as the *sanshakudama* could be justified. However, the *hanabishi* decided to proceed, believing that the *hanabi* would lift people's spirits and demonstrate that the town had recovered from the disaster (*The Japan Times* 2005).

The nearby Katakai Festival (Katakai Matsuri) won the rivalry, however, and launched the world's largest individual firework—the *yonshakudama* (measuring approximately 120 centimeters [48 inches] in diameter and weighing up to 420 kg [926 pounds]) (Izumiya 2007; Katakai Machi Enka Kyōkai 2015). Here, *hanabi* are dedicated to the *kami* (deity) of the local Asahara Shrine, with each *hanabi* having a special meaning for its sponsors. Essentially all *hanabi* at the Katakai Festival are selected and sponsored by individuals, families, or groups from the local communities to celebrate such milestones as birthdays and "coming of age" (turning twenty years old), to prevent against bad luck (like the *yakudoshi*, or "unlucky year"), and to offer prayers for the future. Dedications and sponsors' names are posted on signboards, printed in programs (*banzuke*), and announced over a loudspeaker.

In general, *hanabi taikai* are widely discussed in the mass media, attesting to their continued popularity and cultural significance. Each year as summer approaches, guidebooks, magazines, and websites spread the news of *hanabi taikai* held around Japan, giving access information, suggesting prime viewing positions, and estimating attendances, as well as describing *hanabi* styles, sizes, and numbers. Examples include the annual "mooks" (book-sized publications that have the glossy photographs and A4 paper size of magazines) issued by monthly magazines, such as *Pia Fireworks: Tokyo Metropolitan Edition* (*Hanabi pia—shutoken*) by the events magazine *Pia*. Without fail, numerous variety shows and documentaries about *hanabi* air on television, such as the documentary *The Mark of Beauty Viewing Manual: File 58 Fireworks* (*Bi no tsubo kanshō maniyuaru: File 58*, Katō Mitsuyoshi, dir. 2007).

In addition, *hanabi* are used in advertising campaigns as an icon of summer in a consumer economy that historically divides commodities, such as food, drinks, and fashions, according to the season. As summer approaches, numerous products incorporate *hanabi* designs on their packaging, and advertising posters on trains and in other public spaces, signs in shops, and television commercials abound with *hanabi* imagery. *Hanabi* motifs also adorn a variety of other goods, including jewelry, face towels, postage stamps, cellphone covers, and character goods. Essentially anything advertised in or even associated with summer is prone to being marketed with *hanabi*. It is virtually impossible to avoid exposure to *hanabi* during the summer, just as it is almost impossible not to hear them praised in music and film.

Hanabi in Popular Music and Film

With its expansion in the twentieth and twenty-first centuries, *hanabi* culture arguably has become as dominant as it was in the Edo period. The summer connotation of *hanabi* is apparent in music, film, and literature; where it not only marks the season but also evokes its sentiments and symbolic meanings, as it did as a *kigo* in Edo poetry. To illustrate, I will analyze key examples that have extended *hanabi*'s positive connotations; I have not found any popular culture that presents a negative image of *hanabi*.

Inclusion in lyrics by musicians spanning generations and genres further attests to how widely accepted their metaphorical meanings are. A prominent example of how *hanabi* is used to represent the bittersweet transient nature of summer is in the pop song "Goldfish Fireworks" (*Kingyō hanabi*, 2004) by female solo artist Ōtsuka Ai, a song of fleeting love and the hope it will not fade away. The song's accompanying promotional video (PV) reinforces this sentiment with the visual imagery of sparks of a *senkō hanabi*. An evocative short film by the same name (Sueda Takeshi, dir. 2004) based on the song and starring Ōtsuka, depicts an encounter at the end of summer between two longtime friends, who share a fleeting moment of reflecting on the past while gazing, mesmerized, at *senkō hanabi*. Hanabi's classical poeticism is evident in "Four Seasons" (Shunkashūtō, 2005) by Remioromen. The lyrics juxtapose the association of summer *hanabi* with the other seasonal markers of Edo-era art and literature (spring blooms, autumn leaves, and winter snow) to create a sense of nostalgia for each respective season and to collectively represent life in its entirety and the cyclical nature of things, whether intended or perceived. Another example, "Boyhood" (Shōnen jidai, 1990) by Inoue Yōsui, evokes the nostalgia for summer to show the poignancy of growing up. In the Okinawan-style cover version by Yanawaraba (2008), the summer sentiments are evoked even further by using drums to emulate the sound of *hanabi* exploding. Although there is no direct reference to *hanabi* in the lyrics, the song "Jupiter" (2003) by Hirahara Ayaka (sung to the tune of Jupiter from the orchestral movement *The Planets* by composer Gustav Holst) has become closely associated with *hanabi*, as it has been used to accompany the commemorative display of "Phoenix" *hanabi* at the Nagaoka Fireworks Festival each year since its inception in 2005.

Hanabi have had similar connotations when visualized in a variety of film genres. For example, the sentimental film *Fireworks from the Heart* (*Oniichan no hanabi*, Kunimoto Masahiro, dir. 2010), based on a true story, portrays the annual Katakai Festival and uses *hanabi* as a metaphor for hope, brevity of life, perseverance, resilience, and community. The story centers on Tarō, a social recluse (*hikikomori*) since his sister Hana, a high-school student, was diagnosed with leukemia. After returning home from a hospitalization, Hana encourages Tarō to join a local group of youths who are sponsoring a *hanabi* display at the Katakai Festival to celebrate their twentieth birthdays, the age of adulthood in Japan. Out of respect for his sister, Tarō obliges, but finds it difficult to fit in. After Hana's death, he quits the group and instead invests all of his efforts into creating special *hanabi* by himself, which are to be launched at the festival in memory of his sister. In an enlightening moment for both Tarō and the audience, the instructing *hanabishi* informs Tarō how important fireworks are to the people of the town and that they unite the people together in joy and ease their sorrows. The *hanabishi* then commends Tarō's achievements by declaring that he is one of them now. Tarō is then more readily accepted into the group, who are moved by his efforts, and he becomes less reclusive. After the display, Tarō learns that Hana had made him a framed image of a *hanabi* from flower petals to honor his achievements. The cleverly arranged visual compositions and thematic representation of *hanabi* effectively brings together and elevates the various metaphorical meanings, while at the same time teaching audiences about the historical Katakai Festival.

Almost as if to maintain the historic rivalry with the Katakai Festival, the film *Casting Blossoms into the Sky: The Story of Nagaoka Fireworks* (*Kono sora no hana: Nagaoka hanabi monogatari*, Ōbayashi Nobuhiko, dir. 2012) depicts the Nagaoka Fireworks Festival, familiarizing viewers with the history of this event and explaining why the city of Nagaoka readily accepted numerous families from the Tōhoku region who were dislocated by the March 11, 2011 Triple Disaster. The film perpetuates many of the metaphorical associations of *hanabi* that I have discussed and applies them to a community, rather than to individuals, while using visual images of *hanabi* to heighten sentimentality and encourage reflection. Aside from increasing the popularity of their respective *hanabi* festivals, these films promoted a general awareness of *hanabi* culture. To celebrate their releases, large displays of *hanabi* were dedicated to each film (Katakai in 2010 and Nagaoka in 2012), drawing even more attention to both the festivals and films.[2]

Use of *hanabi* in period films (*jidai geki*) further demonstrates the continuance of Edo period fireworks culture today. For example, *Sharaku* (Shinoda Masahiro, dir. 1995), set in the Edo period, tells the tragic story of an actor/artist and the publisher who produces his works. *Hanabi* culture around the Sumida River at Ryōgoku is featured. In one scene, as the protagonist reflects on his life and contemplates his future, *hanabi* burst slowly in the background, as if reflecting his thoughts and sentiments.

It is worth mentioning that television dramas and anime have also taught audiences about Edo period *hanabi* culture. A prime example is the 26-episode anime series *Oh! Edo Rocket* (*Ōedo roketto*, Mizushima Seiji, dir. 2007) that satirizes popular *hanabi* culture at the end of the Edo period and conveys *hanabi*'s associations of hope and optimism by telling the story of an alien trying to get help from the famous *hanabishi* Tamaya to build a rocket so she can return to the moon. Throughout the series, numerous historical aspects of Edo period *hanabi* culture are portrayed, simultaneously educating and entertaining the audience. *Oh! Edo Rocket* was based on a stage play that Nakashima Kazuki created for one of Japan's most popular theater groups Gekidan Shinkansen.

Conclusion

As these numerous songs, films, television programs, anime, and other popular media illustrate and large attendances at festivals attest, *hanabi* are still an integral part of summer in Japan, just as they were in the Edo period. The rivalries between artisans and localities inspired by *hanabi* have encouraged creativity and regional associations. The culture that has evolved around *hanabi* has provided a sense of escape from the formalities and restrictions of everyday life, has united communities, and has influenced the development of urban space. The many positive symbolic connotations of *hanabi* have helped alleviate senses of despair during times of natural and human-made disasters. *Hanabi* have extended classical symbolism of flowers and other aspects of nature and have become a common motif in popular art and literature. This has, in turn, added to the enjoyment of the visual spectacles of *hanabi*. *Hanabi* have not only made summer more enjoyable and memorable but have given it more historical resonance, emotional poignancy, and made it a time for reflection. It is not an overstatement to say that, to many people in Japan, *hanabi* represent summer itself.

Notes

1 There was a short period of *hanabi* activity on the Sumida River around the temporary island of Nakazu (not far from Ryōgoku), constructed in 1771 and dismantled in 1789.

2 To give another well-known cinematic example, the crime thriller *HANA-BI* (Kitano Takeshi, dir. 1997), the title of which reflects the volatile nature of the protagonist (as serene as a flower and as explosive as a firework), makes many direct and subtle references to *hanabi*. In one scene, a lit firework that had appeared to be a dud explodes unexpectedly, symbolizing the unpredictability of life and the votatility of the protagonist. As the effect it creates dissipates, a gorgeous woman is seen reminiscing, the *hanabi* thus reflecting both her sentiment and her beauty. It is also worth noting the role of *hanabi* in musical comedies and other genres featuring grand finales. For example, *Lady Maiko* (*Maiko wa lady*, Suo Masayuji, dir. 2014), the story of a rural girl who struggles as a *maiko* (geisha in training) in Kyoto, uses *hanabi* in the final dance number to augment the sense of celebration and to herald the character's achievements.

31 *Kamishibai*

The Fantasy Space of the Urban Street Corner

Sharalyn Orbaugh

From the late 1920s until the early 1970s, an entertainment medium called "*kamishibai*" (literally "paper theater") enjoyed enormous popularity in Japan. A form of street theater, *kamishibai* appealed particularly to children of the urban laboring classes, who could derive affordable entertainment from the daily visit of the *kamishibai no ojisan* (literally, "uncle *kamishibai*," the performer) to their neighborhoods with the latest installment of a serial narrative. At the sound of the performer's wooden clackers, children would gather from all directions. The performer would first sell them cheap candy, and then, while the children ate the sweets, would relate a set of three short narratives: a slapstick cartoon for the smallest children in the audience (ages three to eight), a melodrama for the older girls (eight to twelve), and an adventure story for the older boys (eight to twelve). Each narrative was illustrated with a series of hand-painted pictures, which were set in a small wooden stage fixed to the back of the performer's bicycle and pulled out one by one to reveal the next scene. In addition, the performer would add jokes, puns, songs, references to current popular culture, and sound effects, produced on drums, whistles, pots and pans—anything small and portable—to enhance the children's enjoyment. Although *kamishibai* began to die out in the 1960s and disappeared from the streets completely by the late 1970s, the sight of a *kamishibai* storycard (a cardboard card with a picture on one side and narrative or script on the other) or a bicycle-mounted stage, or the title of a popular serialized story, evokes instant nostalgia in many contemporary Japanese adults. Performances of traditional *kamishibai* at museums and cultural centers continue to attract enthusiastic crowds, as parents and grandparents attempt to convey their love of this vanished medium to today's children. As the media of popular culture have shifted over the years, new features are highlighted but other features are lost. When *kamishibai* disappeared from the urban street corner, the street corner itself changed, as we will see in the latter part of this chapter.

Kamishibai's significance did not disappear when it left the streets, however. It was a direct ancestor of today's globally popular manga and anime, and avant-garde Japanese artists from the 1960s, such as filmmaker Terayama Shūji and playwright Kara Jūrō, as well as contemporary film director Kitano

Takeshi, have explicitly claimed *kamishibai* as a direct influence on their art (Suzuki 2005: 46). *Kamishibai* is used today in nightclubs, at political demonstrations, and in a wide variety of edgy venues to communicate affectively rich and often politically charged messages to audiences of all ages.

Despite its humble origins as an entertainment medium for children, *kamishibai* contributed significantly to the construction of the social and national/imperial imaginaries in modernizing Japan in the 1930s and 1940s. This chapter will begin by explaining what *kamishibai* was, its vicissitudes as a medium and as a phenomenon, and how its fortunes were linked with various other developments of Japanese modernity—cultural, technological, economic, political, and architectural. Then it will address the ways that *kamishibai* produced significant social space, specifically the space of the "*machikado*" (street corner) in the 1930s, and the connections between this production of space and the social imaginary. It will elucidate the ways that the fantasy space produced by *kamishibai* was used during the war years to construct and maintain an *imperial social* imaginary capable of encompassing a range of classes, in both urban and rural areas, in Japan, on the battlefield, and in the colonies. And finally it will discuss the ways *kamishibai* remains influential today.

Types of *Kamishibai*

Kamishibai comes in two forms, the first of which is called "*gaitō kamishibai*," indicating *kamishibai* performed on street corners by professionals, who made their money through the candy that they sold to the children who gathered to see the plays. Street-corner *kamishibai* began in the late 1920s and remained popular through the mid-1960s, and even into the 1970s in some areas. The production and distribution of street-corner *kamishibai* was handled by production agents, known as "*kashimoto*" (literally, "lenders"), who commissioned stories and their hand-painted illustrations from professional artists, often employing a stable of in-house artists for this purpose. Each day the *kashimoto*'s writer would come up with the next segment of the serial narrative currently under production, and a set of about fifteen illustrations for the narrative would be sketched out by the lead artist. Then multiple copies of each set would be hand-painted, and the appropriate dialogue and "stage directions" written on the back of each card. The completed story card sets were then rented out to *kamishibai* performers, together with a bicycle equipped with a small stage and a storage area for holding the story cards and the candy the performers sold to make money. The *kashimoto*'s profit came from the rental fee they charged the performers for the story cards, candy, and equipment, and that of the performers from the volume of candy they sold to the children at a small mark-up.

In the 1930s and 1950s, some densely populated neighborhoods of large cities like Tokyo and Osaka were visited by as many as six different *kamishibai* performers each day (Kamichi 1997: 42). Children could distinguish the various performers by the varying sounds of the wooden clackers and report-edly were discriminating consumers (Kamichi 1997: 42). Since street-corner *kamishibai* was a commercial enterprise, its stories and pictures were designed solely to entertain. Storylines and pictorial styles were determined on the basis of whatever would best capture the imagination of the young clien-tele: gruesome monsters, evil stepmothers, and greedy, lecherous landlords were common fare. This was highly unusual in this time period. The 1920s and 1930s in Japan saw the construction of the concept of "childhood" as a distinct developmental phase, and the concomitant rise of both educational and entertainment media meant to appeal to this new demographic group. But most such media were created by adults with the aim of improving or teaching children; in contrast, *kamishibai* plays were nearly unique in having no pretense of providing educational content; whatever the children liked, they got more of. Moreover, children who watched *kamishibai* were using their own pocket money to make choices as consumers, a relatively new phenomenon.

The second type of *kamishibai* was called "*kyōiku*" (educational) *kamishibai*. These were plays intended for explicitly edifying purposes; they were me-chanically produced in large quantities, often sold in stores, and performed primarily by amateurs. Educational *kamishibai* emerged gradually in the 1930s, as an alternative to the very popular street-corner *kamishibai*, and played a significant role in wartime propaganda. After the war, educational *kamishibai* flourished in preschools and kindergartens, where it is still an important tool for early childhood education.

The Birth and Development of Street-Corner *Kamishibai*

Street-corner *kamishibai* is clearly an offspring of other performance forms popular in nineteenth- and early twentieth-century Japan, such as *utsushie* (projector slides painted on glass), *yose* (vaudeville hall storytelling), *rakugo* (comic storytelling), and *tachie* (puppet show), as well as much older per-formance genres such as *etoki* (using pictures to explain Buddhist scripture) (Orbaugh 2015: 43–44), but its particular characteristics grew out of a distinct historical moment characterized chiefly by intensive efforts at urban modern-ization as well as unemployment and poverty. Its exact origins are unknown, but what is certain is that by about 1928 there were a number of men in Tokyo touring the neighborhoods using pictures cut out of children's books to illustrate stories they narrated (Ishiyama 2008; Kamichi 1997; Yamamoto 2000). By 1930, this had developed into street-corner *kamishibai*, distributed through the *kashimoto* system.

It was in 1930 that the first original *kamishibai* serial was produced, *The Magical Palace* (*Mahō no goten*). That same year saw the debut of *Golden Bat* (*Ōgon Batto*) the most popular *kamishibai* serial ever created. The hero of *Golden Bat* always took the stage with the same triumphant fanfare by the narrator: "*Totsujo arawaretaru seigi no mikata Ōgon Batto*" (And now he suddenly appears:

the Golden Bat, a warrior for justice). The Golden Bat—who appeared to be a skeleton dressed in renaissance French clothing—did battle with all sorts of evil creatures, both human and monstrous, although his archenemy was an evildoer named Nazō. This narrative remained popular in *kamishibai* through the 1950s and into the 1960s and thereafter was made into a serialized manga story, an animated television series, and at least one film (Kata 1971: 29–30).

The phenomenal success of *kamishibai* was conditioned by the development of other popular culture media in the prewar period. Film technology, in the form of Edison's Kinetoscope, for example, was imported from the United States in 1896; by 1897 films were shown publicly in Japan accompanied by a "*katsudō benshi*" (film narrator). The first Japanese films were made in 1899, and the first Japanese film company, Nikkatsu, was started in 1912. By 1920, Shōchiku Studio had also been established, and film production standards in Japan were impressive (Yamamoto 2000: 17–18). In 1921 urban Japanese people listed the movies as their favorite form of entertainment (Yamamoto 2000: 21). Whether imported or domestic, these were, of course, silent films, so that the new profession of film narrator flourished throughout the 1920s. In 1929, however, Japan produced its first talkie, and the popularity of the silents gradually faded, leaving all the narrators out of work. Historians suggest that many of them turned for work to the newly emerging medium of *kamishibai* (Yamamoto 2000: 18, 26–27). The skill at performing dialogue that the film narrators brought to their storytelling performances may, in turn, have greatly influenced *kamishibai*'s quick rise in popularity. Similarly, *kamishibai* artists incorporated cinematic techniques, such as pans, wide shots, close-ups, and montage into their illustrations, enhancing the visual sophistication of their narratives.

The expansion of mass literacy and the concomitant rise in magazine and newspaper culture for the masses was also a factor that supported the growth of *kamishibai*. Newspapers and magazines had been around since the Meiji period, and in the 1920s there were already a number of established national newspapers: the *Osaka Mainichi*, *Osaka Asahi*, *Tokyo Asahi*, and *Tokyo Nichinichi*. But in the mid-1920s, new newspapers were established to appeal to the laboring classes, among whom literacy was at a new high of 92 percent (Yamamoto 2000: 15). Among these new newspapers was, for example, the *Tokyo Maiyū*, an evening paper that found popularity among the laborers, craftspeople, and shop owners of Tokyo's "*shitamachi*" (downtown, blue-collar) areas. The serialized novels featured in such newspapers brought serialized fiction into poorer households on a daily basis for the first time. Because these newspapers provided "*furigana*" syllabary glosses for all the "*kanji*" (Chinese characters), even children could enjoy the serialized fiction. In 1924, the *Tokyo Maiyū* also started a serialized comic: *The Travels of Dango Kushisuke* (*Dango Kushisuke man'yūki*), by Miyao Shige. By the late 1920s, Japanese children, even those of the poorer classes, had become accustomed to enjoying serialized narratives that came to their homes. *Kamishibai* catered to this new taste for serialized fiction but provided it in a form that was even more exciting and satisfying, given the vibrant colors of the illustrations and the antics of the performers.

Another venue for serialized fiction and manga aimed specifically at children were the magazines put out by the Kōdansha publishing company in the first three decades of the century: *Shōnen kurabu* (Boys' Club), launched in 1914; *Shōjo kurabu* (Girls' Club), in 1923; and *Yōnen kurabu* (Young Children's Club) for kindergartners, in 1926. However, these magazines were taken primarily by households of the middle and upper classes; children in the blue-collar areas of town may have occasionally seen such magazines but could not enjoy them on a regular basis (Yamamoto 2000: 17).

Histories of the new media that emerged in the 1920s give prominent place to radio because Japan adopted and supported this new technology more quickly than most other nations, after the Great Kantō earthquake of 1923 had revealed the need for a reliable information broadcasting network. Japan's first radio station, JOAK (later NHK), was launched in 1925 (Kasza 1988: 72). Eleven years later, in 1936, there were two million radio subscribers around the country—an impressive number, but, even at that time, there was little entertainment on the radio, particularly for children. A radio set in the 1930s cost just a little less than a month's wages for a laborer; consequently, radios were not common in the poorer areas of the cities (Sakuramoto and Konno 1985: 18). For this reason, despite later similarities in the two media, the emergence of radio seems to have had little influence on the popularity of street corner *kamishibai* in the prewar period. Significantly, however, educational *kamishibai* plays were used to enhance the popularity of radio in its early years, through shows titled "Kamishibai" that were included as part of NHK's ten-minute "*kodomo no jikan*" ("children's hour"), broadcast every day in the early evening (Orbaugh 2015: 46).

Finally, the rise of *kamishibai* was conditioned by economic factors, too: the recession that followed the 1923 earthquake in Japan and then the worldwide depression a few years later had left many Japanese men out of work by the end of the 1920s. To become a *kamishibai* performer required little in the way of equipment—and that little was in any case rented from the *kashimoto*—and no skills other than simple literacy and a willingness to try to entertain children. An untold number of the newly out-of-work men turned to *kamishibai* to try to make a living (Kamichi 1997: 28, 86–87; Sakuramoto and Konno 1985: 186).

All of the above factors contributed to the atmosphere that allowed *kamishibai* to flourish. And unlike most of the new media of the period—children's magazines, radio, and cinema—*kamishibai* flourished in nearly *all* the neighborhoods of the cities, the poor ones as much as, or more than, the middle-class and wealthy neighborhoods. *Kamishibai* was truly a mass-culture medium.[1] By 1933 there were 2,000 performers in Tokyo alone (Kamichi 1997: 34). And by 1937 there were some 30,000 street-corner *kamishibai* performers across Japan performing for an estimated one million children daily (Sakuramoto and Konno 1985: 186). After 1937, however, as the war in China escalated, increasing numbers of men, including *kamishibai* performers and artists, were conscripted into the military and for labor. During the war years, street corner *kamishibai* dwindled and disappeared, replaced by government-sponsored performances of educational *kamishibai*, discussed further below.

Almost as soon as the war ended, however, street corner *kamishibai* performers were back on the streets. For a demobilized soldier looking for work, this was an easy job to take up: it required no real training, just the ability to read the cards (or to memorize them as someone read them aloud) and the small rental fee for the equipment. Some immediate postwar *kashimoto* even provided housing, clothes, and food for their performers—a crucial bonus in those days of shortages and urban devastation (Kamichi 1997: 86). While the Allied Occupation government was puzzled by *kamishibai*—suspicious both of its role in wartime propaganda and its postwar links to Communist organizations—for the most part, SCAP allowed street-corner *kamishibai* to recover in peace in the late 1940s (Orbaugh 2012, 2015: 57–58).

The 1950s were the golden age of street-corner *kamishibai*, and it is notable that this was the case despite the rise in other popular media for children, such as entertainment radio and manga. In the postwar period radio sets were relatively affordable, and a broader spectrum of entertainment programming was broadcast, including serialized narratives. Rather than constituting dangerous competition for *kamishibai*, however, popular radio and manga heroes provided inspiration for *kamishibai* writers and performers, who created their own "spin-offs" of popular characters or storylines. In the early to mid-1950s, there were an estimated 50,000 *kamishibai* performers scattered through all the urban areas of Japan, performing for a daily audience of approximately five million children (Kamichi 1997: 87, Orbaugh 2015: 58).

By the mid-1960s, however, street corner *kamishibai* was rapidly disappearing. The advent of television into many households (television was sometimes called "*denki kamishibai*," "electric *kamishibai*," in its early years) at the time of the Tokyo Olympics in 1964 was certainly a factor, as well as the sudden boom in manga magazines targeting specific age-groups and genders (Kamichi 1997: 90). Economic prosperity and low unemployment may also have meant that fewer men were willing to consider itinerant *kamishibai* performer as a reasonable job prospect. Whatever the causes, this unique popular art form disappeared completely from the streets by the mid-1970s and now can only be experienced in museums.

Kamishibai and the Production of Urban Space

During the Meiji period, urban planners worked to remake Japan's capital Tokyo into a more "modern," European-style city, creating monuments, museums, public squares, and broad avenues, and trying to overlay a grid pattern onto the tangled alleyways where the laboring classes lived. After the wholesale destruction caused by the 1923 earthquake and subsequent fires, government planners and architects had virtually a blank slate in many areas of Tokyo upon which to impose their vision of the modern city. The reconstruction was officially completed in 1930, and other large cities in Japan began to follow Tokyo's example (Jinnai 1985). The year 1930 also marked the beginning of a decade of increasing nationalism and militarism in Japan, with the war in Manchuria beginning in 1931 and in China in 1937. The new city structures and the ways people were meant to use them were designed, among other things, to produce national subjects compliant with these ideological projects.

However, if we consider the phenomenon of *kamishibai* through the lens of social philosopher Michel de Certeau's conceptions of space, we find that hegemonically mandated and designed "place" was turned into "social space" through the embodied practices that constituted *kamishibai*'s material culture of production and consumption. Further, we find that the social space produced through the practices of *kamishibai* did not correspond to the government sanctioned social narrative of the 1930s.

From the point of view of the original consumers of the medium, the children, the particular social space constructed by *kamishibai* was the *machikado*, the street corner. In an evocative description, social historian Suzuki Tsunekatsu writes:

> *Kamishibai* was a theater that appeared suddenly on the street corner. By means of the interaction between the *kamishibai no ojisan* and the children who gathered, the familiar street corner transformed into a phantasmagoric theater beyond mundane reality. The *kamishibai* performer appeared and disappeared like a sudden breeze…. To be swept up in the 'transient whirlwind' created by the performer and to be immersed in fantasy was for children a time of delectable bliss.
>
> (Suzuki 2005: 7)

From extensive interviews with people who consumed *kamishibai* in its heyday, Suzuki identifies the medium's principal characteristics: (1) the special candy and fantasy atmosphere created on the street corner; (2) the appeal of the stories and the fact that they were completely indulgent of children's tastes; (3) the skill of the performers; (4) the special bond between the children, many of whom were from the lower classes, and the familiar *kamishibai* man, who was also far from wealthy; (5) the fact that the experience engaged multiple sensory faculties at once: taste, smell, hearing, sight, imagination, and often touch (as we see in photographs of children enjoying *kamishibai*, typically huddled close together and often carrying younger siblings (Orbaugh 2015); and (6) the fact that it was a group experience, one shared with friends and neighbors, of a live performance (Suzuki 2005: 47).

If, like most modern cities, 1930s Tokyo was designed as a "[place] built to organize and control the lives and movements of the 'city subjects' in the interests of the dominant" (Fiske 1992: 160), then the transient *machikado* street corner created by *kamishibai* is what de Certeau would call a "tactical" space, wherein the dispossessed use and manipulate "proper places" to create a space whose purposes differ from or are in opposition to hegemonic interests.

Educational *Kamishibai* and Propaganda

The magical, tactical, anti-hegemonic space of the *kamishibai* street corner did not go unnoticed or unchallenged, however. As soon as street-corner *kamishibai*'s popularity was established in the early 1930s, voices of concern and criticism were raised. Professional educators and parents' groups in particular, met to discuss the ills of the medium and published their conclusions in newspapers and magazines. One common complaint held that the stories featured in *kamishibai* were vulgar with no educational content (Ishiyama 2008: 47). The enormous popularity of stories about gruesome monsters or lewd behavior was particularly offensive to the critics, as it seemed to reflect the trend for the "erotic," "grotesque," and "nonsensical" (*ero, guro, nansensu*, buzzwords often used to characterize 1920s popular culture) that many adult entertainment venues featured at the time. Children gathering on street corners struck many observers as threatening, possibly leading to the formation of gangs (Ishiyama 2008: 47). In other words, several of the elements of *kamishibai* that might be considered oppositional to hegemonic discourse were seized upon as problematic by the normalizing impulses of cultural elites.

But some educators countered by writing about the instructive potential of the medium. In the mid-1930s the progressive Christian educator Imai Yone, for example, promoted the use of *kamishibai* in bringing wholesome messages to children of the urban poor (Suzuki 2005: 49). Similarly struck by *kamishibai*'s popularity among children of the lower classes, other educators thought that *kamishibai* could be a useful tool in extending education to impoverished rural areas, such as Tōhoku (Northeast Japan) (Kamichi 1997: 70–72). By 1938 an organization called the Nippon Kyōiku Kamishibai Kyōkai (National Association for Educational Kamishibai) had been established in Tokyo and had instituted a practice of making *kyōiku kamishibai* story cards with progressive messages available to urban social groups and rural teachers (Kamichi 1997: 77).

The most frequent theme of such stories was the kindness and sincerity of the laboring classes, especially in the countryside. The appeal of the stories was their almost naïve simplicity; however, the plays produced by the Nippon Kyōiku Kamishibai Kyōkai were notable for incorporating the results of research done by its members on effective storytelling techniques in the visual medium of film as well as influences from high-art movements such as primitivist woodblock prints and German expressionist woodcuts.

The play *The Quails* (*Uzura*), shown in Figure 31.1, is the most famous example of the Nippon Kyōiku Kamishibai Kyōkai's efforts to both support poor rural farmers and educate city dwellers about the kindness and sincerity of the laboring classes. Set in rural Tōhoku, beset by famine and terrible

Figure 31.1 Scene from *The Quails* (*Uzura*), produced by the Nippon Kyōiku Kamishibai Kyōkai, 1940. The young protagonist accompanies her father to town
to sell their crops.

poverty in the 1930s, it tells of a young girl from a farming family who accompanies her father to town to sell their crops. She makes a little money from the
things she sells, but rather than spending the profit on something for herself,
she buys some live quails to provide a nutritious meal for her sick mother.
When she gets the quails home, however, her mother, although touched by
the gesture, convinces her to set the birds free. (This play is notable for including two versions of the script, one in Tōhoku dialect for performance
there, and the other in standard Japanese for performance elsewhere.)

The success of *kamishibai* in 1930s progressive movements was hindered
when an influential educator named Kondō Ekio was arrested in the early
1940s for using *kamishibai* in his teaching; clearly the medium was a tool
for spreading Communism, according to the indictment. But the purported
connection between *kamishibai* and Communism was plainly no more than a
convenient pretext for harrassing and jailing progressives such as Kondō because government organizations were already actively requisitioning *kamishibai* narratives that promoted a pro-war agenda from the Nippon Kyōiku
Kamishibai Kyōkai (Kamichi 1997: 70).

In fact, as the war in China escalated, the government recognized the
potential in using such an effective popular medium for disseminating its own
messages. From this point of view, one of the central advantages of *kamishibai*

was its appeal to a broad range of classes, particularly the urban laborers and rural farmers, from whom so much cooperation was needed in support of the war effort. And it was not only on Japan's main islands that *kamishibai* was used for propaganda purposes. As Japanese settlers participated in the colonization of Korea, Taiwan, Manchuria, and China, street corner *kamishibai* and educational *kamishibai* had gone with them. As the war progressed, those areas, too, were the targets of explicitly propagandistic *kamishibai* plays, intended to rally the residents of Japan's colonies and occupied territories behind its war efforts.

One such play was *My Cute Granddaughter* (*Kawaii mago musume*, credited to the Nippon Kyōiku Kamishibai Kyōkai, 1942), which narrated the story of an elderly Korean man's trip to his son's home in the city to see his granddaughter for the first time since she was a baby (Figure 31.2). He discovers that the eight-year-old girl speaks Japanese almost exclusively, which disappoints him since he speaks no Japanese and sees no need to learn. But when he suddenly must get medical help when the girl is taken ill and the only doctors he can find are Japanese, he awakens to the necessity of learning the language. He goes home determined to study.

Government-sponsored *kamishibai* were mass produced and distributed through educational and government networks, and were sold in bookstores—a

Figure 31.2 Scene from *My Cute Granddaughter* (*Kawaii mago musume*), produced by the Nippon Kyōiku Kamishibai Kyōkai, 1942. An elderly Korean man travels to the city to see his Japanese-speaking granddaughter.

production and distribution process very different from street-corner *kamishibai*. The spaces of propaganda *kamishibai* performance were also different from those of street corner. During the war, propaganda *kamishibai* were performed primarily by amateurs: leaders in schools, farming villages, mines, and so on. Young women[2] who had been conscripted for war work were often recruited to visit these and other such sites—kindergartens, factories, "*tonarigumi*" (neighborhood association) meetings—to perform propaganda plays. This was one of the first instances when women performed *kamishibai*. One of the catchphrases of the government's *Kamishibai* section (part of the Nippon Shōkokumin Bunka Kyōkai [National Association for Young Citizens' Culture], established in 1940) was "*itsudemo, dokodemo, daredemo*" ([*kamishibai* can be performed] anytime, anywhere, and by anyone), promoting the medium's wonderful portability and flexibility (Orbaugh 2015: 95).

The original form of the medium, street corner *kamishibai*, was all about *performance*. The *kamishibai no ojisan* would add original songs; snippets from advertising jingles; sound effects; ad-libbed jokes, and so on, to make his performance fresh and entertaining. In contrast, propaganda *kamishibai* performers were instructed to read exactly the dialogue or explanation that was printed on each story panel; no deviations, jokes, or elaborations were allowed. Performers were not to smile or laugh as they worked and were cautioned not to try to make the audience laugh either. The amateur *kamishibai* performers were told to efface themselves and emphasize the story; to enhance this effect (as well as to make it easier to read what was on the cards), they were instructed to stand behind the stage, rather than next to it as the professionals did. The stage itself, no longer mounted on a bicycle, was shaped like a small suitcase, one side of which folded out to reveal the picture cards (Orbaugh 2015: 96–100).

Another significant difference between wartime and street-corner plays is that during the war more than 70 percent of the stories produced were aimed at an *adult* audience rather than, or in addition to, children (Kamichi 1997: 74). The plays mentioned above—*The Quails* and *My Cute Granddaughter*—are both examples for an adult or mixed-age audience.[3] The emphasis of much wartime propaganda in Japan, in all media, was on making young men into soldiers prepared to leave home with the explicit purpose of dying violently but beautifully for the sake of the Emperor and the nation, and making parents into patriots who were happy and proud to sacrifice their children to this cause (Orbaugh 2015: 220–225). Contrary to what one might expect, however, as the war went on, many *kamishibai* plays seemed to emphasize the *futility* of the war effort, but encouraged people on the homefront to struggle on anyway, because of their love for their family members off fighting on the front lines. Such plays were effective not because they raised hopes of victory but because they convinced viewers that everyone on the Japanese main islands and in the colonies was sacrificing and suffering all together and in the same ways so that to shirk one's duty was *mōshiwakenai* (unjustifiable, inexcusable) vis-à-vis one's compatriots.

If we think back to the salient media features of *kamishibai*, it is clear why it was such an effective vehicle for this sort of message. *Kamishibai* plays were performed, meaning that the storyteller's emotion could be conveyed to the audience in an unmediated manner. *Kamishibai* plays were simple and direct in tone, even though often based on sophisticated techniques for combining word and image for effective storytelling. This directness and simplicity resonated well with the rhetoric of "sincerity" that was fundamental to wartime ideology. Moreover, their simplicity and directness made *kamishibai* accessible to people of all classes, but particularly the laboring classes who had such important roles to play in the war effort. These same qualities helped *kamishibai* plays to communicate effectively with residents in Japan's occupied territories as well. And finally, unlike many other media, the consumption of *kamishibai* was always a group experience, shared with neighbors and family. Something of the magic of the evanescent *machikado* carried over from street-corner *kamishibai* into the grimmer propaganda version so that, even when the content of the plays was sad, the viewing experience was still valued as entertainment. The characteristics of *kamishibai* as a medium made it effective at linking suffering soldiers to those suffering on the homefront, linking cute young Chinese children on the continent to patriotic Japanese children at home, to create an imperial imaginary in which the laboring classes were central and heroic.

The Continuing Resonance of *Kamishibai*

From the 1950s, educational *kamishibai* has continued to flourish and remains a common tool in Japanese classrooms, particularly in preschools, kindergartens, and elementary schools. In fact, *kamishibai* is used as a medium for early education in many countries across the globe; the United States, France, Germany, and Canada, among many others. Moreover, many political activists and social action groups use *kamishibai* to deliver messages to audiences of all ages, although especially to children. There is a *kamishibai* performer at the Peace Park Museum in Hiroshima, whose plays talk about the experience of the atomic bombing. The descendants of Japan's hereditary outcast group, the former *burakumin*, as well as resident Koreans in Japan (*zainichi*), also use *kamishibai* in their work of educating society about the discrimination they still suffer. While the magical *kamishibai* street corner has disappeared, the medium continues to create new social spaces for new purposes.

Notes

1 The term "mass-culture" is used here as opposed to the more politically neutral "popular culture," as much early educational *kamishibai* was explicitly left-wing with the intent of awakening class consciousness. And while street-corner *kamishibai* was purely commercial, its practitioners—artists, scriptwriters, and performers—were often accused by the hyper-vigilant 1930s government of sneaking subversive messages into their plays.

2 There were very few female performers of street corner *kamishibai*, especially in the prewar period. When young women were recruited to perform propaganda *kamishibai*, therefore, it was the first time that appreciable numbers of women were involved in the performance side of the business, although many of the artists and scriptwriters in the *kashimoto* were female.

3 For many more examples of wartime plays for adults, see Orbaugh (2015), which includes summaries of forty-five plays and full translations of seven.

32 Shibuya

Reflective Identity in Transforming Urban Space[1]

Izumi Kuroishi

Socio-political transformations in Japan during Meiji, Taishō, and Shōwa periods influenced the growth of cities, including the conversion of the political system, advent of a citizen class, introduction and maturation of capitalism, change in the role of religion, and spread of European and American culture. Tokyo has been destroyed and rebuilt more than most other Japanese cities because of modernization efforts, war, and natural disasters; thus it amplifies contradictions and priorities in patterns of Japanese development (Freedman 2010: 17–18). While many European cities, such as Paris and London, have sustained their spatial foundation over the course of their historical development, as I will explain, Tokyo's growth, especially in the twentieth century, has been subordinated to the construction of the commuter infrastructure and the consumer economy (Figure 32.1).

Scholars of urban sociology, such as Yoshimi Shun'ya (2000) and Kitada Akihiro (2011), recognize the transformation of Tokyo's Shibuya district during the 1970s and 1980s as a symbolizing how the city has been designed as a place of consumption and how neighborhoods have been changed into media-oriented entertainment spaces. Yet much more than this can be learned about the historical and social background of Tokyo's spatial formation by examining the transformation of Shibuya in this period as a part of a larger process of the modernization of urban space and popular culture and by considering the marketing of Shibuya's retail space. Such analysis also reveals contradictions inherent in planning the diverse function of cities and how people use them. In this chapter, I draw from the business policies of both major department stores and the small local shops sustained in the backstreets and key theories of urban studies, especially those premised on fieldwork, to argue that understanding Shibuya's space is crucial to knowing the development of Tokyo's popular culture.

Shibuya from the Edo Period to the 1960s

Shibuya lies at the bottom of a valley. The train station is set at the focal point of six slopes, forming a hub where people of all classes mix and serving as a symbol of Tokyo's socioeconomic diversity. Aoyama Street marks

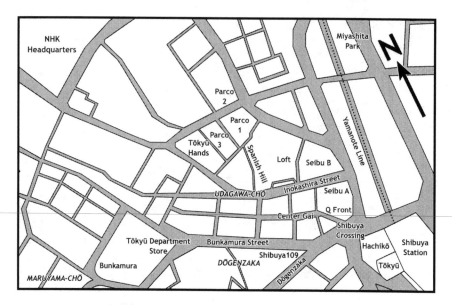

Figure 32.1 Map of Shibuya.
Source: Courtesy of John Moore.

the route of an important historical pilgrimage path to Mount Ōyama. The vast Aoyama Cemetery (Aoyama reien), Tokyo's only cemetery that includes foreigners, was laid out to the south in the Meiji period, while Omotesandō Street was created through the relocation of the area's temples and shrines when the Meiji Shrine (Meiji jingū, the Emperor's symbolic tomb) was built in 1920. Urban development here was frequently shaped by political factors. For example, a residential area known as Washington Heights, created for soldiers of the Allied Occupation forces (GHQ), took over the area of the headquarters of Japanese military beside the Meiji Shrine for almost twenty years (1946–1964) after World War II; its dismantling helped pave the way for commercial development and the influx of small stores. In 1964, the main venue for the Olympic Games, the event that represented Japan's recovery from the war, was built next to the site of Washington Heights. The headquarters for NHK (Nippon Hōso Kyōkai, Japanese public broadcasting, established in 1924), was moved there and gradually expanded through 1973. Subsequently, Ward Office Street (Kuyakusho-dori), running from Shibuya Station to NHK, was completed.

Economic factors also contributed to the formalization of different cultural areas around Shibuya Station, especially in Maruyama-chō and Udagawa-chō. Thanks to the extension of rail networks, Shibuya developed from the station, which was first opened in 1885 as a transfer stop along the Japan Railway (Nippon Tetsudō, Tokyo's first train route), connecting the developing suburbs to the city center. Subsequently, the Tamagawa Electric Railway (Tamagawa Denki Tetsudō, 1907), Tokyo City Railway (Tokyo Shigai Tetsudō, 1911), Tokyo-Yokohama Railway (Tōyoko, 1927), and Imperial City Electric Railway (Teito Shibuya, now Inokashira Line, 1933) all stopped at Shibuya. Currently, Shibuya Station is a hub for eight train and subway lines. The Tōkyū Electric Railway Corporation (Tōkyū Dentetsu Kabushiki-gaisha), which Shibusawa Eiichi (1840–1931) and his son formed in 1922 to help develop the nearby suburban residential area modeled on England's garden suburbs (Oshima 1996), absorbed the Tamagawa Electric Railway and Imperial City Railway. After taking control of Shibusawa's business, Gotō Keita (1882–1959) opened the Tōyoko Department Store (Tōyoko Hyakkaten, now Tōkyū Department Store) in 1934 and the Tōkyū Culture Hall (Tōkyū Bunka Kaikan) in 1954, forming a commercial and cultural area around Shibuya Station. The corporation also encouraged universities, such as Keiō University and Tōkyō Gakugei University, and high schools to develop campuses along stops of the Tōkyū Railway.

In addition, starting in the Edo period, the Maruyama-chō entertainment district developed along the old Ōyama Street (Ōyama kaidō) in Dōgenzaka, part of the abovementioned pilgrimage route. More than 420 geisha worked in that area before the Great Kantō Earthquake in 1923 (Shibuya Bunka Project). In the following years, Tsutsumi Yasujirō (1889–1964), the founder of the Seibu Railway Company (Seibu Tetsudō Kabushiki-gaisha) and father of businessman and author Tsutsumi Seiji (1927–2013), developed the small Hyakken-dana shopping street next Maruyama-chō by inviting 117 well-established stores to move there from Asakusa and Ginza, then mass culture and high culture shopping areas in Tokyo, respectively, that had been severely damaged in the earthquake and subsequent forty hours of fires (Maruyamachō-kai 2016). Hyakken-dana flourished with the development of railways, but after the reconstruction of Asakusa and Ginza, these stores returned to their original places. In the late 1920s and 1930s, Maruyama-chō and Hyakken-dana became popular entertainment districts. After World War II, many movie theaters opened in the area, and with the influence of the American culture emanating from Washington Heights, jazz cafés, bars, and nightclubs opened, creating a stylish, cosmopolitan cultural district.

Immediately after World War II, a black market opened in Udagawa-chō (Aoi 2013: 88–101). After the street vendors were evacuated by GHQ, local shop owners formed an association to create a shopping area in Shibuya Station's underground passageways in 1957. From the 1960s, international record shops and fashion stores selling American military surplus items appeared along the narrow passages and slopes in Udagawa-chō, just as they had in Hyakken-dana.

To summarize, three distinct types of commercial districts were established in Shibuya before the 1960s: (1) the area around Shibuya Station was the site of the Tōkyū Department Store and Culture Hall; (2) Maruyama-chō and Hyakken-dana were places of cafés, bars, and social entertainments; and

(3) Udagawa-chō was an area of small stylish international music and fashion shops. There were also residential areas along the slopes of Dōgenzaka and Miyamasuzaka. However, after entrepreneur Gotō Noboru (1916–1989) founded the main branch of the Tōkyū Department Store in 1967, nearby Maruyama-chō lost its appeal and, perhaps due to other societal pressures of the time, became an area of love hotels. Then critically, the Seibu Department Store was built in Udagawa-chō in 1969, marking the start of an enduring rivalry between the Tōkyū and Seibu companies. As I will explain next, this rivalry initiated another phase in Shibuya's consumer culture.

Tsutsumi Seiji's 1970s Urban Development Policies

The opening of the Parco store by the Seibu Distribution Company in 1973 was one of the most influential business strategies in Shibuya's growth. Parco (Italian for "park")—an aggregate of individual shops rather than a conventional department store where the same business occupies the entire building—changed the design and function of Japanese department stores. Ikebukuro Parco was opened and designed by Tsutsumi Seiji, founder of the Seibu Distribution Company and son of Tsutsumi Yasujirō, and planner Mishima Akira in 1969 and Shibuya Parco by Tsutumi and planner Masuda Tsūji in 1973 (Yui 1991: 246–357). (Ikebukuro is a Tokyo commercial district around another large terminal station.)

Tsutsumi believed that department stores should be social and cultural centers. From 1963 to 1964, he worked in Seibu Department Store's Los Angeles branch (opened in 1962) and learned business methods of American shopping malls. In 1966, he purchased the large Marubutsu Department Store (opened in 1954) that was part of the Ikebukuro Station building. Marubutsu was an acclaimed "terminal department store" (a department store that is part of a train station), which began as a mercery outside Kyoto Station in 1920. Tsutsumi was inspired by the business policies of the president of the Hankyu department stores, Shimizu Masashi (1901–1994), who in turn followed the ideas of Hankyu founder, Kobayashi Ichizō (1873–1957). Hankyu Umeda Station in Osaka, opened in 1929, was Japan's first terminal to include a department store as one of its floors; customers were encouraged to ride the Hankyu train line in order to go to the store. Kobayashi advocated a customer-oriented business philosophy and created a business model promoting suburban residential development by opening station department stores and cultural facilities, such as Tōhō cinemas and the Mainichi Broadcasting System, which started radio broadcasts from the Osaka Hankyu Department Store. Tsutsumi applied Kobayashi's methods, in addition to what he had learned in the United States, to develop a new suburban residential culture along the Seibu Railway from Ikebukuro Station.

The four central features of Mishima and Tsutsumi's Ikebukuro Parco meant to change consumer behavior and to fuse business with culture can be summarized as follows: first, in constructing its building, they maximized the potential of the long, irregular space alongside and attached to train stations. Inside the building, Mishima aggregated individual shops, creating town-square-like areas between them (Tsutsumi 1976; Ogawa 1982). This presented the whole store as a city and reproduced the atmosphere of streets inside. Second, to fuse the commercial and cultural, they designed open spaces including facilities (like art museums that displayed modern art not yet well known in Japan) and held music concerts. Mishima compared these open spaces to a town square, which he defined as a ritual place for cultural creation (Ogawa 1982). Third, because Mishima and Tsutsumi believed that the department store should express the spirit of the times, they employed up-and-coming designers as consultants. Their public relations department produced advertisements, newspapers, and posters using ultramodern graphic design influenced by American popular culture to associate Seibu with the values of the new generation. Artists included Yamaguchi Harumi, Tanaka Ikkō (1930–2002), Ishioka Eiko (1938–2012), and Fukuda Shigeo (1932–2009). Fourth, Tsutsumi and Mishima advocated that the department store could be an "integrated life industry" that would "build a new spiritual city in the suburbs" (Yui 1991: 384–385). They strove to convert consumers' lifestyles, spearhead business opportunities, and contribute to the localities in which their stores were built (Yui 1991: 384–385).

Inventions by Parco in the 1970s

The early 1970s was a time of large-scale department store construction in Shibuya, inspired largely by the rivalry between the Seibu and Tōkyū companies. After opening the Shibuya Seibu Department Store in 1968 in Udagawa-chō, the Seibu company opened three Parco buildings: Parco 1 (1973), Parco 2 (1975), and Parco 3 (1981). (Parco 2 was closed in 2011 and Parco 1 and 3 in 2016.) Seibu, to compete with Tōkyū (the company that was said to have invited them to Shibuya), found a way to connect the area near NHK with Shibuya Station. To help plan Parco 1 on Ward Office Street, Masuda conducted surveys of the fashions and consumer behaviors of the youths who gathered around Shibuya Station (Masuda 1984: 36–54, 168–181). He found that there were various districts with specific cultural atmospheres determined by their distance from the station; that youths preferred one-of-a-kind goods to those that are mass produced; and that people enjoyed leisurely wandering maze-like passages. Masuda and his employer Tsutsumi used these observations to develop the 600 meters between Parco and Shibuya Station. The two applied many methods Mishima developed earlier in Ikebukuro Parco.

They opened Seibu Theater (later renamed Parco Theater) at the top of Parco 1 in 1973 and built Parco 2 and Parco 3 to unify the surrounding area and demarcate it as a high-fashion shopping district. Masuda invented additional local characteristics and attractions. For example, the walls around the Parco buildings were professionally decorated with artwork inspired by American graffiti. Ward Office Street was renamed "Park Street" (Pāku sutorito). In addition, they designed cafés and pedestrian passages to give the sense that Parco is the main actor in the urban drama of the street.

Nakada Yasuo, owner of a local café, renamed the passage between Parco and Shibuya Station "Spanish Hill" (Supein-zaka) to give it a romantic atmosphere (Masuda 1984: 181). At Spanish Hill, shops and restaurants were constructed in a circulating course that provided pedestrians with a sense of discovery. These developments were also influenced by the small avant-garde underground theater, Jan Jan, that had existed in the area since 1969. Also, in 1969, Terayama Shuji (1935–1983), opened his Tenjō-sajiki Theater in Shibuya, which operated until his death. Parco thus found an innovative way to control and expand the theatrical culture developing in Shibuya since the 1950s.

Parco used other media to extend Shibuya's popular culture. For example, the Parco publishing company was established to launch the informational magazine *Surprise House* (*Bikkuri hausu*, 1974–1985) detailing the area's youth culture. Across was founded in 1977 as a research institution for the study of fashion and culture. It began fixed-point observations (mainly on fashion) from August 1980 and published the *Fashion Report* (*Ryūko-tsūshin*) magazine. (In fixed-point observation, urban observers stay on location and record the trends they see around them.) A television station in Parco was built in 1983, and a showroom was opened where people could interact with cars and other objects.

Thus by revitalizing the spatial and cultural characteristics of Shibuya's backstreets and small passages, Masuda unified consumer behavior and contemporary culture, dramatically changing urban space. He provided a common space for a variety of people, organized their interactions through media and advertising, and assimilated existing local cultures into a unified burgeoning urban culture available to diverse consumers.

Shibuya's Role in Japanese Urban Studies

Tsutsumi and Masuda's Shibuya developments were intrinsically linked to 1970s discussions in Japanese urban studies. In the 1960s, owing to the high growth of the postwar consumer economy, there was an increasing focus on the maintenance of people's living environments, and Japanese architects and urban planners eagerly learned from European and American designs and theories and from their peers, as is evident in the competition between the Seibu and Tōkyū companies. Matsuda and other planners were influenced by Kevin Lynch's *Image of the City* (1960), translated into Japanese by architect Kenzō Tange in 1968 (Kuroishi 2008). Lynch analyzed the mechanism through which pedestrians and residents experienced and imagined the urban landscape by focusing on five formal elements: paths, edges, districts, nodes, and landmarks.

Masuda also drew from Kon Wajirō (1888–1973), Japanese architectural scholar and designer of the 1920s. He was especially influenced by Kon's notion of complete enumeration research and fixed-point observation. Kon developed fieldwork surveys of the relationships between people, their possessions, and their living environments and pioneered studies of the significance of consumer culture in modernizing urban space with his artist friends and students. For example, Kon conducted the "Modernology" (Kōgengaku) survey in 1925, two years after the Great Kantō Earthquake. He investigated three main elements of people's lifestyles—behaviors, fashions and belongings, and houses—along with elements essential to urban space, such as signboards and the location of commercial establishments, to compare suburbs, slums, and commercial districts and to assess how the consumer economy impacted on the city and its residents (Kon 1972; Kawazoe 2004; Kuroishi 1998, 2000). He discussed how people recognize the urban space as theatrical and how their bodily rhythms and movements create urban space (Kon and Yoshida 1986; Kuroishi 2006, 2008). He explained the significance of social class and popular media, like advertising, in defining an area's characteristics. In his "Modernology" studies, small objects and everyday spaces bear the most important social and psychological meanings for people, and the structure of the urban space integrates people's social and bodily senses, habits, desires, and curiosities. In a sense, Kon described how the notion of urbanity of Tokyo was formalized through the interactions among the consumer economy, space, and people's senses, expressions, and activities. In his book *New Version of the Guide to Greater Tokyo* (*Shinpan dai-Tokyo annai*, 1929), he explains the formation of urban space as a place of consumption as well as the consumption of urban space. In other words, Kon created methods to survey how people and urban space interact and to make the space attractive to consumers.

The degree of penetration of consumer society and the impact of the media in the 1970s were, of course, very different from the 1920s, and Shibuya was not a major focus for Kon and his associates. In the 1960s and 1970s, to designers' groups, such as Konpeitō, Hinageshi, and Iryūhin Kenkyūjo, investigating the heterogeneous human factors in urban space, referred not only to the on-site methodology of Kon's surveys but also to his ideas about the multiple meanings of the urban phenomena as a counter theory to Kevin Lynch. As Masuda combined Lynch's structural approach and Kon's dynamic, consumer behavioral approach in designing the area in and around Parco, Shibuya became Japan's earliest experimentation of applying urban theories to commercial marketing projects.

Parco's Transformation in the 1980s

The Japanese critic Taki Kōji (1928–2011) argues that it is impossible to introduce the sense of urban space, the essential characteristic of which is heterogeneity, into a department store building because, no matter how many different stores are gathered together, the site will be viewed as one single facility (Taki 1976). According to this same logic, it is impossible to turn an urban space into a controlled shopping district. Masuda's works were commissioned by Parco and thereby emphasized the company's economic needs.

In his 1968 *The Right to a City* (*Le Droit à la Ville*), Henri Lefebvre discusses three kinds of urban planning by different social sectors:

> What is new, what is recent, is that [developers] are no longer selling housing or buildings, but *planning*.... The developers' project is presented as an opportunity and a place of privilege: the place of happiness in a daily life miraculously and marvellously transformed.... Parly II [a Paris commercial center opened in 1969] 'gives birth to a new art of living', a 'new lifestyle.' Daily life resembles a fairy tale.... Here is the image of the joy of living made real.
>
> (Lefebvre 1968: 30, translated for this chapter by Hester Higton)

Parco design can be summarized by Lefebvre's prediction about urban space produced entirely by the economic sector's methods of constructing the image of the joy of living. When Parco cleared the backstreets of Udagawa-chō in 1977, their work was generally viewed as making the city beautiful and enhancing its new charm. But their 1983 campaign, "Will you make the street your advertising medium?" (*Machi o senden baitai ni tsukaimasen ka*) was intended to "sell the city" (Masuda 1984: 129–165). While the former project was meant to bring more people to the backstreets, the latter project controled the streets' unique characteristics via Parco's spatial marketing strategy.

Although it continued to promote expensive goods and fashions, Parco's cultural influence declined during the bubble era of the 1980s. Tsutsumi believed that Shibuya had become "polluted" as a result of its seemingly uncontrollable youth culture; he believed that Seibu culture peaked between 1975 and 1982 (Tsujii and Ueno 2008: 108). With the expansion of Japanese economic activity, Seibu and Parco's business model of "New Urban Cultural Space," achieved through uniting the city with consumer space and through segmentation and media strategy, had reached its limits (Kitada 2011: 102–164).

For example, Kitada Akihiro explains how, in the bubble economy era, consumerism was established as an ideology by marketing that made excessive use of media and urban space, while the human aspects of urban space (which could not be explained rationally), with its various constituent parts and values, were turned into semantic elements in abstract contexts (Kitada 2011: 52–82). Hence, he argues that Parco's development of Shibuya by using excessive media and theatrical manipulation of space was the representative example of the "Disneyland-ization" of Tokyo, turning neighborhoods into theme parks. He found that there was a fashionable lifestyle called "Shibuya-kei" (Shibuya style) of visiting unique shops in the narrow streets in the Parco area until the 1980s, turning Shibuya into a mecca of popular fashions, but, after, young people avoided these shopping passages and paid no attention to their symbolic importance in Shibuya's identity.

Interactions Among Tōkyū, Parco, and Others After the 1980s

Shibuya's commercial and cultural zones continued to be shaped by the interactions between the Seibu and Tōkyū companies until the 1990s. The Tōkyū Group built a succession of stores in their area of Shibuya to compete with Seibu and Parco. The first was Tōkyū Hands (Tōkyū hanzu) in 1978, at first primarily a retailer of art-and-crafts products but later expanded to sell a range of creative household goods; in 1987, Seibu opened Loft in response. In 1979, the Tōkyū Group opened Shibuya109, comprised of speciality stores of youth fashions with a stage constructed in front to entice people away from Parco. In 1989, they opened the Bunkamura cultural center, which included a concert hall, theater, and art museum. At that time, they put forward the "synthetic life industry" project, covering every aspect of lifestyle (Mōri 1990).

Other groups changed the nature of the urban space Parco had created. Gangs of teenagers, imitating, among other things, the 1983 American movie *The Outsiders* (directed by Francis Ford Coppola and based on S. E. Hinton's 1967 novel) and influenced by American subcultures and hard rock, congregated on Center Gai (Central Street, that runs in front of the station and demarcates the Seibu and Tōkyū areas), creating a new street culture. The public harmony of Center Gai deteriorated, conveying the image of a "dirty region" that needed to be policed (Tsujii and Ueno 2008: 168). Subsequently, residents in peripheral residential areas, such as the wealthy neighborhood of Shōtō, organized *machizukuri undō* (a beautification campaign) supported by the ward government, and the district's Landscape Act (Keikan Jūrei) was enacted in 2000 to preserve Shibuya's public welfare by setting limits on the commercialization of urban space.

Although contradictions, such as the gentrification of Miyashita Park as a measure to remove the increasing homeless population of the area, soon became apparent at the end of the 1990s, movements by residents, such as the aforementioned *machizukuri undō*, have striven to re-evaluate the historical, geographical, and natural environment and its context through conducting fieldwork and thereby has articulated a local residential culture. Through this process, Parco's business model has been revised to focus on the mechanism for creating value in the everyday expression of urban life, which is based on their fieldwork surveys and research into the social space of Shibuya and Harajuku.

Shibuya in the Twenty-First Century

In the twenty-first century, Park Street has lost some of its cultural cache, especially after the closure of Parco 2 in 2011. A major reason was the change in the urban landscape and subsequent consumer and entertainment patterns initiated mainly by Tōkyū. In 2000, a huge television screen, Q's Eye, was built on the façade of the building Q Front by Tōkyū realtors to continually stream advertisements and entertaining short films. In the following six years, three more mega screens—109 Forum Vision, Glico Vision, and Super Riza Shibuya—were constructed around the scramble crossing in front of Shibuya station, the world's busiest pedestrian intersection. As the biggest two screens are owned by a Tōkyū related company, the massive media space in front of the station can be said to be controlled by Tōkyū. This sensorial exposure to media information increased Shibuya's sense of spectacle. The chaotic but unconsciously organized rhythm of pedestrians with these mega screens' bright, exciting images and sounds symbolized Shibuya's new sense of urban space and culture.

In addition, Tōkyū redeveloped the pedestrian space in front of Shibuya Station and then the entire area around it. The Tokyo Metro subway lines and Tōyoko railways have been connected underground at Shibuya Station, resulting in more development space above ground. Tōkyū also redeveloped the area next to the Tōkyū Culture Hall to construct the high-rise fashion and entertainment building Hikarie in 2012. In 2014, Tōkyū, along with Tokyo Metro and East Japan Railways (JR East), started a huge redevelopment project of the space vacated by the rerouting of the Tōyoko railway to construct three more high-rise buildings with offices, shops, and hotels. This reconstruction is so large that it is scheduled to continue until 2027. As part of this, in 2015 Tōkyū closed the historic Tōkyū Plaza, which had opened in 1965. Tōkyū started another redevelopment project in the Miyashita area, about 450 meters from the station, building skyscrapers with offices for new types of creative industries, shops, and housing.

While Tōkyū's efforts return the commercial center of Shibuya to the area around the station, in 2015, Seibu advanced a plan to redevelop the areas around Parco 1 and 3 by constructing high-rise buildings with offices, shops, and studios for young designers. They also proposed a reorganization of the pedestrians' networks on the slopes and passages to create circulatory movement in Shibuya.

As a response to these companies' aggressive projects, in 2010 the Shibuya Ward government proposed "Guidelines for Neighborhood Development around Shibuya Station" (Shibuya eki chūshin chiku machi-zukuri shishin), declaring the necessity of combining the concentration around the station and the circulation of pedestrians in the surrounding areas to create a comfortable and enjoyable city. But in 2013, Shibuya Ward published its "Revision of the Urban Development of the Fundamental Infrastructure of Shibuya Station Area" (Shibuya eki chūshin chiku kiban seibi toshikeikaku henkō no aramashi) to state that they are now aiming to reorganize urban space into a "safe, compact and multifunctional, international and comfortable area" by designating the station area as the center of Shibuya. The proposal image shows that Lynch's five elements discussed above are still used to create a highly functional and tightly organized entity. Notably, the rival urban designs of circulating around or centering on the station advanced by Seibu and Tōkyū, respectively, remain integral in Shibuya Ward's plans.

These discussions further reveal that the urban planning of Shibuya has been designed by prioritizing economic activities and has been greatly influenced by the rivalry between Seibu and Tōkyū. However, Shibuya Ward's 2013 plan also expresses the concern that the over-concentration of shopping and business districts at the station and the smooth connection of railways may make Shibuya a mere interchange and thus cause it to lose its significance. As the case of Shibuya has demonstrated, in the age of shrinking cities in Japan, it is not enough to simply sell a fashionable lifestyle; instead it is also necessary to elevate the quality of life of residents and cultivate the specific characteristics of cultural aspects to preserve the charm of the city.

In developing Parco, Tsutsumi initially tried to improve people's quality of life by introducing modern culture and high-quality consumer goods that went beyond a narrow focus on short-term profit. Masuda tried to realize Tsutsumi's idea by utilizing the spatial characteristics, as well as the counter-cultural elements, of the American culture and Japanese theater that previously existed in the area to create surrealistic yet intimate urban spaces and exaggerated their characteristics with media to create a popular culture of Shibuya-kei.

However, some people argue that Shibuya-kei lost its potency after the bubble economy era, subsequently affecting the cultural use of urban space. This process reveals that the preservation of a sense of authenticity and the rootedness to unique small, narrow places are necessary conditions for countercultures and subcultures to exist. The once thriving jazz music shops, cafés, bookstores, and fashion shops still remain in the narrow streets in Udagawa-chō and Maruyama-chō. From the end of the 1990s, *machi-zukuri* by local residents have become active all over Japan; these movements have acknowledged importance of fieldwork in finding ways to revitalize localities (Nitagai et al. 2008). The commercial areas I have described have been studied and preserved by residents and visitors' groups as the cultural heritage of Shibuya.

This chapter has examined the historical relationship between urban development, the consumer economy, and popular culture in Shibuya, the biggest changes in which were initiated by the rivalry between Parco and Tōkyū. The planners of these corporations used the heterogeneous and contradictory elements observed in fieldwork surveys of people's everyday lives to develop new business plans that shaped urban space. Diverse popular cultures have appeared in Shibuya, including those inspired by geisha, American jazz and fashions, suburban lifestyles, and theatrical counterculture. The synthetic cultures particular to Shibuya include Shibuya-kei, media designs, outsider culture, urban spectacles, concentrated consumer culture, and a heritage subculture. The dynamic shift in the different types of culture, space, and consumer economy in Shibuya reveals how each of these elements interact and invent new meanings through people's engagement with and experiences in this particular place. The transformation of Shibuya shows that the potential of a city lies is not only in its economy but also resides in the process of integrating people's commitment to finding new ways to shape their surroundings through their everyday lives.

Note

1 I would like to acknowledge the help of Izutsu Akio, who worked closely with Tsutsumi Seiji during the initial stages of establishing Shibuya Parco.

33 Akihabara

Promoting and Policing "Otaku" in "Cool Japan"

Patrick W. Galbraith

Introduction

Akihabara is an area located in Tokyo's Chiyoda Ward. Well known for stores selling home appliances, personal electronics, and computers, Akihabara was, for much of the second half of the twentieth century, called the "Electric Town" (*denkigai*). However, in the first decade of the new millennium, a competing image of Akihabara arose: the "Holy Land of Otaku" (*otaku no sei'chi*). Although a contested word, otaku means something like nerd, geek, or fan and is used in Japan to identify people who are deeply obsessive about something, most typically manga, anime, and computer/console games. Indeed, a walk down Chūō-dōri, the main street of Akihabara, reveals numerous advertisements for anime and game releases, almost all emblazoned with colorful, cartoony, cute girl characters. In an earlier period, the Electric Town stood as a beacon for those wanting to buy cutting-edge technology made in Japan. Today, the Holy Land of Otaku is a beacon for those wanting to buy character media and merchandise made in Japan. If Akihabara was once a symbol of the industrial output of "Japan, Inc.," it is now a symbol of the creative output of "Cool Japan." The idea of Cool Japan is tied to the increasing visibility of manga/anime fans in North America and Western Europe in the 2000s, as well as the subsequent public diplomacy strategy pursued by the Japanese government (Leheny 2006; Choo 2011). Accordingly, Akihabara has become something of a showcase of Cool Japan, and, in the process, the otaku gathering there have come under increasing scrutiny.

This chapter demonstrates how promoting otaku as part of Cool Japan coincided with policing "weird otaku" (*hen na otaku*) on the streets of Akihabara in the mid-2000s. In the story of Akihabara, we see conflicting perceptions of otaku as desirable and disruptive, normal and queer, part of Cool Japan and Weird Japan. Based on fieldwork conducted between 2004 and 2012, the chapter acknowledges at the outset that it is partial in both senses of the word: incomplete and committed to certain ends (Clifford 1986). In this chapter, I am consciously participating in the contest of meanings on the terrain of struggle that is popular culture (Hall 1998). My partiality comes from regular interactions and long-term relationships with people on the street, but I supplement this viewpoint with interviews with politicians and storeowners, participation in and observation of various events, and media analysis.

Redevelopment of Akihabara

In *Tokyo Concept 2000* (*Tōkyō kōsō 2000*), then Governor Ishihara Shintarō laid out a plan to make Akihabara a global base for the IT industry. The area was a natural choice, given its history as the Electric Town and subsequent association with computers and programming. The redevelopment of Akihabara, also known as the Crossfield Project, began in 2002 and included major players such as Kajima, NTT Urban Development, and Daibiru. The plan seemed to be succeeding; according to a March 2003 report by the Ministry of Land, Infrastructure and Transport, 742 software developers, Internet ventures, and data processing companies were located within a one-kilometer radius of Akihabara's central train station (Fujita and Hill 2005: 30). By 2005, the Akihabara Daibiru skyscraper was complete; the Akihabara UDX Building followed in 2006. On the other side of the station, in 2005, the Tsukuba Express rail line was completed, connecting Akihabara to a research hub and suburban communities in Ibaraki Prefecture. Right above the Tsukuba Express line terminal in Akihabara, Yodobashi Camera opened an eight-story mega store for convenient one-stop shopping.

The edge of Akihabara's so-called "redevelopment zone" (*saikaihatsu chi'iki*) falls right behind the stores lining Chūō-dōri, known for selling manga, anime, computer/console games, and related merchandise. Standing on Chūō-dōri in the old Electric Town, which was transformed into the Holy Land of Otaku by an influx of stores catering to manga/anime fans in the late 1990s (Morikawa 2012), one sees the new Electric Town looming behind. The architectural contrast is stunning: small and mid-sized stores occupying numerous odd-shaped buildings marked by advertisements featuring cute girl cartoon characters in the foreground and the glassy fronts of the Daibiru skyscraper and massive UDX Building in the background. Further away from the redevelopment zone, on the other side of Chūō-dōri, are smaller and more diverse stores in narrow alleys, basements, and backrooms, which are associated with niche obsessions.

"Revaluation" of Otaku

While used more casually today, the word otaku first appeared in 1983 as a label for manga/anime fans accused of being socially and sexually immature (Galbraith 2015). In the 1990s, media pundits discussed otaku in relation to horrendous crimes, such as Miyazaki Tsutomu's molestation and murder of girls between the ages of four and seven (Kinsella 1998) and doomsday cult Aum Shinrikyō's release of sarin gas on the Tokyo subway (Gardner 2008). Although the era of "otaku bashing" (*otaku basshingu*) is often overemphasized for dramatic effect, certainly the word otaku did not have a positive meaning in Japan. NHK (Nippon Hōsō Kyōkai; Japan Broadcasting Corporation), a semi-government organization, banned the word otaku from its broadcasts in the 1990s; 62 percent of Japanese respondents to a 1998 survey had a negative impression of otaku (Kikuchi 2008: 66). As late as the mid-2000s, qualitative interviews with Japanese university students who did not identify as otaku revealed shared negative assumptions about them (Kam 2013).

Concurrent to the redevelopment of Akihabara was the revaluation of otaku. Seno'o Ken'ichirō (2007), a major player in the Crossfield Project, argues that otaku contribute to Akihabara's status as a center for innovation. These thoughts are echoed by Kitabayashi Ken, who, in a report for the Nomura Research Institute, argues that otaku, due to active and creative participation in their obsessions, represent the "driving force for bringing about industrial innovation" (Kitabayashi 2004: 1). Kitabayashi suggests that otaku be "integrated" and their activities "used" to invigorate Japanese business (Kitabayashi 2004: 6–7). Significantly, Kitabayashi also points out otaku-driven innovation in the culture industries that produce globally competitive creative contents.

The revaluation of otaku as drivers of cultural innovation came at a time when many in Japan were looking to manga/anime as not only economic resources but also as potentially political ones. In 2002, American journalist Douglas McGray's article discussing Japan's decline as an industrial nation and rise as a source of "cool" culture made waves in Japanese policy circles (Leheny 2006: 219–222). The politicized celebration of anime is not as surprising because anime had performed exceptionally well in global markets since the late 1990s. Numbers released in 2004 showed that over 60 percent of the world's animation was Japanese in origin (JETRO 2005) and that Japanese "cultural exports" "increased 300 percent since 1992 [...] while exports as a whole increased only 20 percent" (KWR International 2004). The validity of these claims is less important than their consequences in the revaluation of otaku. If otaku drive the innovation of Japanese creative contents, then they also play a crucial role in driving contents that go global:

> Japan's success in the world animation, comics, and games software markets derives from fierce firm competition inside of Japan for the attention of a large, demanding and diverse range of consumers. [...] Animators test their products in Tokyo first before marketing them in Japan and overseas. And animators look to Tokyo's participatory antenna districts for new product ideas and strategies.
>
> (Fujita and Hill 2005: 57)

The most famous of these "participatory antenna districts" is Akihabara.

While one might question if otaku, for all of their potential impact on industrial and cultural innovation, are in any way "cool," anime is certainly seen as such by its fans. Consider that in 2003, Miyazaki Hayao's animated film *Spirited Away* (*Sen to Chihiro no kamikakushi*, 2001) won an Academy

Award; Murakami Takashi produced the animated short *Superflat Monogram* as a commercial for high-fashion brand Louis Vuitton; the techno-music duo Daft Punk released an anime music video called *Interstella 5555*; Quentin Tarantino included an anime sequence in his *Kill Bill: Volume 1*; and the Wachowskis produced *The Animatrix*, a series of anime shorts meant to flesh out the world established by their celebrated film *The Matrix* (1999), which was itself pitched as a live-action adaptation of anime. The success of anime overseas, which was understood abroad to be the spread of "otaku culture," fed into the discourse about Cool Japan.

Cool or otherwise, otaku became tied to Japan. For example, in 2004, Morikawa Ka'ichirō adapted his concept of Akihabara as an "otaku city"—first publicized as the book *Learning from Akihabara: The Birth of a Personapolis (Shuto no tanjō: Moeru toshi Akihabara*, 2003)—into an exhibition titled "OTAKU: persona=space=city," which opened at the Venice Biennale's Ninth International Architecture Exhibition. Sponsored by the Japan Foundation, "OTAKU" focused primarily on Morikawa's analysis of Akihabara but also explored the history of otaku in postwar Japan. Connections between otaku and Japan were made explicit by a sign over the entrance to the exhibition, which read "GIAPPONE/OTAKU" (translated into English, "JAPAN/OTAKU"). Although perhaps not Morikawa's intention, his exhibition resonated with and impacted the formation of discourse about a nationalized otaku celebrated overseas. As Morikawa's exhibition emphasizes, this important aspect of the revaluation of otaku often occurred as part of discussions about Akihabara, which intensified in the mid-2000s.

Indeed, in the mid-2000s, Asō Tarō made a name for himself as the Minister of Foreign Affairs by speaking about the global success of Japanese popular culture. Asō played up his manga readership and is rumored to have called himself an otaku. The truth of the rumor is less significant than the fact that Asō did not deny it, ostensibly because he was in an environment where it seemed somehow cool to be an otaku. During his career as Minister of Foreign Affairs (2005–2007), which overlaps with the redevelopment of Akihabara and revaluation of otaku, there can be little doubt that Asō saw otaku as political resources. In a well-reported and highly symbolic move, Asō, campaigning to become Prime Minister, held a rally in Akihabara on September 16, 2007. During his speech, Asō told the crowd, "Thanks to otaku, Japanese culture, subculture, is undoubtedly being transmitted to the world [...] Isn't this something that we should take more pride in?" (Tantei File News Watch 2007). The connection of (otaku) subculture to Japanese culture is striking, as is the positioning of otaku as a source of global success and national pride. Although he lost the election in 2007, Asō's association with otaku did not rule him out as a candidate, and, in fact, it seems to have made him more popular; he became Prime Minister in 2008. The overheated discourse about Cool Japan led to more and more attention being paid to otaku in Akihabara.

The Akihabara Boom

The so-called "Akihabara boom" (*Akiba būmu*) began with *Train Man* (*Densha otoko*), the story of an "Akihabara-style" (*Akiba-kei*) otaku who falls in love with a woman and is transformed by his relationship with her. In 2005, *Train Man* was adapted into a mainstream film and television drama, which cast an otaku as the leading man and heavily featured the Akihabara neighborhood. In stark contrast to the negative media image that took hold of the popular imagination in the 1990s, *Train Man* was a hit: the final episode of the drama, aired on Fuji Television, reached 25.5 percent of Japanese households (Freedman 2009b). *Train Man*'s story of "falling in love with otaku" reads like a parable of Japan's own evolving relationship with its outcast sons; the romance unfolds on the street in Akihabara. One of the immediate effects of *Train Man* was a massive influx of domestic tourism—Japanese coming to visit this "other Japan"—and media reporting on the Akihabara boom, which it helped create.

Increased media attention contributed to an intensification of what have been called "otaku performances." Since 1973, Akihabara customarily closed a section of Chūō-dōri, its main traffic artery, on Sundays to create a Pedestrian Paradise (*hokōsha tengoku*). As Akihabara transformed into the Holy Land of Otaku in the late 1990s and early 2000s (Morikawa 2012), there was a sense that manga/anime fans had taken over and extended the Pedestrian Paradise. The joyous atmosphere, familiar from anime conventions (Napier 2007), was not unlike a "festival" (*matsuri*). Otaku performances, which had existed in Akihabara since at least the late 1990s, spilled out onto the streets and were amplified by feedback loops from the growing number of people gathering in Akihabara, as well as by the increased media attention, in the mid-2000s. After *Train Man*, on the street in Akihabara, one could see amateur singing idols, costumed role-players, outrageous fans, cars and bikes decorated with anime characters, and more.

Akihabara's street culture and its connection to otaku was reported in Japan and overseas, contributing to the booming tourism. A Japan National Tourism Organization (JNTO) survey conducted in 2007 revealed that as many as 8.6 percent of foreign visitors to Japan set foot in Akihabara, 69 percent for the first time (JNTO 2008a). According to JNTO's calculations, Akihabara was the tenth most popular destination in Japan for foreigners—more popular than Tokyo Disneyland (JNTO 2008a). The NHK program *Cool Japan: Discovering Cool Japan, 2006-Present* (*COOL JAPAN ~ Hakkutsu! Kakko ii Nippon ~*), which introduces foreigners to various aspects of Japan and polls them on whether or not they think that these things are cool, conducted a survey of visitors to Akihabara for its August 30, 2007 episode, which revealed that five percent of all visitors to Akihabara were foreign tourists and 30 percent were Japanese tourists (NHK 2007).

The large number of Japanese tourists coming to Akihabara suggests widespread interest in otaku but not necessarily shared otaku interests, let alone any consensus that these otaku or their interests were perceived to be "cool." In fact, the connection between otaku and cool that COOL JAPAN was making through its foreign guests was not immediately apparent for many Japanese. Indeed, a Japan Travel Bureau's (JTB, Japan's largest travel agency) book titled *Cool Japan: Otaku Japan Guide* (*Cool Japan: Otaku Nippon gaido*, 2008), released in Japan in Japanese, seems to have been an effort to introduce this foreign idea to a domestic audience. The underscoring of the nation in JTB's book—appearing twice in the title, first as "Japan" in roman letters and then as "Nippon" in *katakana* (the Japanese syllabary used for foreign words) after it—and its association with otaku is striking. Thus "Cool Japan" before the colon becomes "Otaku Nippon" after it. However, the association of otaku with not only cool but also Japan proved to be more problematic on the street in Akihabara.

Tension on the Street in Akihabara

With all the interest in Akihabara, otaku on the street had the potential to become minor celebrities. In May 2005, for example, Fuji Television representatives handed out fliers requesting "real" otaku to act as extras during the filming of the *Train Man* television drama (Freedman 2009b). After the show had become a major hit, various television stations rushed crews out to film otaku in Akihabara. Film crews did not stop at the usual otaku-on-the-street interviews. One informant who was present for the filming of a year-end *Train Man* tie-in told me that the media was staging otaku contests. In retrospect, otaku contests—proving one's otaku-ness for the crowd and camera—foreshadowed the intensification of street performances that was to come.

One informant with whom I spent time on the street in Akihabara was an otaku performer regularly approached by the media. A tall, sinewy Japanese man with missing teeth, he did not immediately appear to be star material. What set this man apart, however, was his being an otaku, specifically a huge fan of anime. At the time, my informant was into the anime adaptation of *The Melancholy of Haruhi Suzumiya* (*Suzumiya Haruhi no yūutsu*, 2006), so much so that he went by the handle name (what he called his "Akiba name") of "Haruhi" and wore the main schoolgirl character's uniform. Stated another way, Haruhi was engaged in "cross-play," or cross-gendered costume play involving anime characters (in Japanese, *josō kosupure*). Haruhi referred to his relationship with media producers and camera crews as "work" (*oshigoto*), which he pursued to make a little money and gain recognition on the street.

While working with the mainstream media (and working the image of otaku and Akihabara), Haruhi's performances were not always welcome. In part, this had to do with the fact that Haruhi was not alone, and strange things happened when people gathered on the street to perform with him and watch. For example, many people in Akihabara who were fans of *The Melancholy of Haruhi Suzumiya* anime not only dressed as the main character but also performed the dance sequence shown during the ending credits of each episode. The dance accompanied the song "Sunny Sunny Happiness" (*Hare hare yukai*), which could be heard all over Akihabara and became something of an unofficial anthem of the street culture. Haruhi and some fifty costumed accomplices took over the Pedestrian Paradise to perform what they called the "Haruhi Dance" in summer 2007. While the performances drew complaints from local residents and businesses, who asked the police to be deployed to break it up (multiple times), videos of the Haruhi dance on Chūō-dōri in Akihabara circulated widely online and escalating otaku performances on the street. The meme-like spread of the Haruhi dance was not the only example of otaku performance in Akihabara. On any given Sunday, dozens of fan groups clustered around street idols and performed loud and wild cheerleading routines known as *otagei*, literally "the otaku art," but more liberally translated as the art of organized chaos.

With police being dispatched and performances disrupted, otaku were at times making outright political statements by gathering on the street. On June 30, 2007, I observed an estimated 500 men and women, many in costumes, as they took to the street in the Akihabara Liberation Demonstration (Akihabara kaihō demo). Organizers chanted slogans about keeping Akihabara for the otaku and stopping its redevelopment and use as a showcase for Cool Japan. These slogans, however, were the minority of voices, and the crowd following behind the organizers seemed to be more interested in participating in the festival. They marched and danced to the sound of "Sunny Sunny Happiness" coming from mobile speakers, sang along as an impromptu choir, and shouted, "Let me keep my Haruhi!" (As well as a more basic call and response: "Suzumiya!" "Haruhi!") Although at times seeming to devolve into noise, a message came through: we are otaku, and we are in Akihabara. The visibility of dozens of cross-playing men wearing the schoolgirl uniform of the Suzumiya Haruhi character was a statement, reinforced by the juxtaposition of these men with others wearing the costumes of Japanese student radicals of bygone days. On the street in Akihabara, which had become an important symbolic site for Cool Japan—recall Asō's campaign speech, delivered in September 2007, just a few months after the Akihabara Liberation Demonstration—one man carried a Japanese flag with the sign of anarchy spray-painted over the rising sun. The presence of this subversive symbol suggests that otaku performers were aware that they were somehow disrupting the nation, if not also the national agenda (Figure 33.1).

As complaints from local residents and business owners accumulated, the police became more aggressive in their attempts to control the street and started to engage in "public questioning" (*shokumu shitsumon*). While the media would stick a camera in an otaku's face and ask "What's in your bag?" to get a tantalizing peek into his or her private life, police asked the same question as part of supposedly random bag searches, which many of my informants saw as a form of harassment. Haruhi claimed that police would stop him regularly on the pretense of suspicion of shoplifting; they of course knew who he was, and found in his bag the Haruhi costume that they knew

Figure 33.1 The Akihabara Liberation Demonstration, June 30, 2007, showing a man
    dressed as Suzumiya Haruhi.
Source: Courtesy of Danny Choo.

would be there, which allowed them to ask follow-up questions about it.
They then pointedly reminded him that street performances are "forbidden"
(*kinshi*) in Akihabara. Street performances are not allowed in Chiyoda Ward,
where Akihabara is located along with the National Diet, Supreme Court
of Japan, Prime Minister's Official Residence, Nippon Budokan, Yasukuni
Shrine, and Imperial Palace. This conservative ordinance had been there all
along but had not been as aggressively enforced in Akihabara as in these other
places. Haruhi and other otaku performers had unintentionally violated the
ordinance. From this point on, police not only broke up street performances,
but also questioned those involved, followed suspected offenders in the area,
and issued citations.

  Promoting and policing otaku, the two sides to the Akihabara boom, were
thrown into stark relief by events during the Pedestrian Paradise in spring
2008. The first was the arrest of Sawamoto Asuka, a self-proclaimed "sexy
idol" who wore a short skirt, climbed railings at the side of the street, and
lifted her leg to appeal to "low-angle photographers." Although local residents and business owners complained about the indecency of Sawamoto's
performances, media reports proliferated, and her fans grew into a mob.
Some speculate that the media encouraged Sawamoto's performances (Akiba
Blog 2008a), but she was nevertheless arrested on April 25, 2008. After this,
programs such as *Information Live Miyane's Room* (*Jōhō raibu Miyane ya*), a talk

and variety program produced by Yomiuri Television—which had earlier interviewed Sawamoto on the street (Akiba Blog 2008a), no doubt titillating its viewers—now suggested that street performers in Akihabara were dressed too provocatively. Such performances, combined with other otaku performances and the swarms of camera crews they attracted, contributed to a general consensus that Akihabara had descended into a state of "lawlessness" (*muhō jōtai*) (Akiba Blog 2008b).

Despite public outcry over otaku street performances, otaku in an abstract form continued to be associated with Akihabara. For example, on May 4, 2008, just over a week after Sawamoto's arrest, the first installment of the Akihabara Otaku Festival (Akiba otaku matsuri), was held inside the highly controlled space of the UDX Building. Use of the word festival, which among otaku meant an event where things get a little crazy, seems to have been meant to tap into the energy of Akihabara. However, attendees were warned not to dance wildly or dress offensively; fliers explicitly banned male-to-female cross-play and "acts that are a nuisance to others." Recognizable otaku from the street, including Haruhi, were not allowed to join, where only a year before they had been the faces of Akihabara otaku festivals. The logic of the Akihabara Otaku Festival is domestication: otaku animals corralled and disciplined.

A month after Sawamoto's arrest, came the "Akihabara Incident" (Akihabara tōrima jiken), one of the worst mass slayings in postwar Japanese history. On June 8, 2008, Katō Tomohiro, a twenty-five-year-old dispatch worker (*haken*) stationed at a factory in Shizuoka Prefecture, rented a truck and came to Akihabara for the Pedestrian Paradise. Instead of joining the festivities, Katō ran down several people, jumped out of the cab, and rampaged across Chūō-dōri with a knife. By the time he was subdued, Katō had killed seven people and injured ten others. This proved to be the last straw. On June 12, 2008, the Chiyoda Ward Council decided to discontinue Akihabara's Pedestrian Paradise. What followed was a period of reflection and discussion about what needed to change if and when the Pedestrian Paradise was to open again. Part of what needed to change, it turns out, was otaku.

Managing Akihabara and Disciplining Otaku

In the wake of the closing of the Pedestrian Paradise, people began to question more openly the place of otaku in Akihabara and Cool Japan. A good example is Kobayashi Takaya, a member of the Chiyoda Ward Council. As a long-time resident of Akihabara—detailed in his book, *Akihabara Primitive Man* (*Akiba genjin*, 2006)—and publisher of *Akibatsū*, a free magazine promoting businesses in the area, Kobayashi presents himself as the representative of Akihabara and describes his political function as "managing" (*kanri*) the area (Personal interview 2009). While Kobayashi sees the value of otaku as enthusiastic consumers and potential innovators (along the lines of Kitabayashi 2004), in practice he is more ambivalent. In January 2008,

I heard Kobayashi speak at an event for entrepreneurs held in the Daibiru skyscraper in Akihabara's redevelopment zone. He adopted a long view of Akihabara, starting with its past as the Electric Town and moving to a bright future with the Crossfield Project. Seemingly missing from the narrative were otaku, more specifically the presence of manga/anime fans on the street. When asked what he thought about otaku performances, Kobayashi replied that this was just a minor episode in the history of Akihabara and seemed to suggest that otaku were not part of his vision of the future.

On April 21, 2009, with the Pedestrian Paradise still closed, I approached Kobayashi for a personal interview. Kobayashi confirmed that, while the Akihabara Incident had been the direct trigger for discontinuing the Pedestrian Paradise, the decision was based on a much deeper ambivalence about street performances. Kobayashi explained that his constituents, namely, local residents and business owners, were against street performances and the crowds they drew. Pointing to a tension between people who live in Akihabara and those who just visit for fun, Kobayashi argued that the problem with the Pedestrian Paradise specifically and Akihabara more generally is that "people coming to play turned it into a place of performance." To the key phrases "people coming to play" (*asobi ni kuru hito*) and "a place of performance" (*pafōmansu no basho*) Kobayashi added problematic "ways of using" (*tsukaikata*) the street. Put simply, some people were using the street in ways unauthorized by Chiyoda Ward and unpopular among local residents and business owners. Kobayashi told me that everyone around him was against reviving the Pedestrian Paradise if it meant the return of street performers.

That some of these performers could be described as "otaku" posed another problem for Kobayashi in his job of managing Akihabara. On the one hand, he saw that otaku contributed to the perception of Akihabara as a hot and happening place and that media and tourist interest invigorated the area. On the other hand, otaku were seen as out of control on the street, which disrupted the improved image of Akihabara and of otaku. Noting persistent negative stereotypes about otaku in Japan, Kobayashi drew a line dividing the newly improved image of otaku in Akihabara—predictably associated with *Train Man*—and what he called "weird otaku" (*hen na otaku*). For Kobayashi, Akihabara is ultimately a "showcase" (*shōkēsu*) but the showcase has no room for weird otaku—just as there was no room for Haruhi and his type of performance at the Akihabara Otaku Festival in the UDX Building, itself a kind of showcase of Cool Japan. If Kobayashi's political function is managing Akihabara, then he also must manage the weird otaku gathering there in order for his "city-making" (*machizukuri*) agenda to succeed.

Similarly, at the Area Open Mini Symposium in Akihabara (Chi'iki ōpun mini shinpojiumu in Akihabara), held on March 5, 2012 under the auspices of the Ministry of Economy, Trade, and Industry to assess its Cool Japan policy and the importance of Akihabara in it, Seno'o confided, "We struggled with that problem [of weird otaku]. There was actually quite a debate at the time [of the Crossfield Project] about Chūō-dōri being dotted with stores that you wouldn't want children to go into, and school trips kept their distance from Akihabara. They thought Akihabara was a scary place, or a weird city (*hen na machi*)" (METI 2012: 65). At the same event, Ono Kazushi, president of Onoden, founded in 1951 and now one of the oldest continually operating retailers of home electronics in Akihabara, argued that exposing tourists to an unfiltered Akihabara would leave them with the impression that Akihabara is a "weird city" (*hen na machi*), which he went on to warn could undermine Cool Japan (METI 2012: 64–65). "As a nation," Ono asked the audience dramatically, "what direction do you want to take Cool Japan by using Akihabara?" (METI 2012: 74). Note Ono's rhetoric here: as a nation (*kuni toshite*), it was time to think about how to use Akihabara (*Akihabara wo tsukatte*) more effectively. Akihabara as a showcase of Cool Japan was a matter of national concern, and Ono's message was clear: the place needs to be managed more effectively or Cool Japan might transform into Weird Japan.

Long before Seno'o and Ono's statements, Kobayashi and other stakeholders in Akihabara debated how to manage the revival of the Pedestrian Paradise and came to the conclusion that they needed increased surveillance of otaku performances and of the street. Otaku were already beginning to internalize the gaze, for example by asking one another to think about how their use of the street affected others and ruined the festival for everyone. In June 2009, Art Jeuness Akihabara, located on Chūō-dōri, hosted "AKIBA memory 2005–2007," an exhibition of black-and-white photographs of the Pedestrian Paradise in Akihabara, including many images of otaku performances. At the end of the exhibition, visitors were asked to complete a survey about the possible revival of the Pedestrian Paradise. When I visited the exhibition, I saw posted on the wall selected comments from visitor surveys, most of which asked for restraint and cooperation from all if and when the Pedestrian Paradise was revived. On January 26, 2010, Akihabara installed sixteen security cameras to monitor the street, with neighborhood associations investing in another thirty-four cameras (*The Japan Times* 2010). When the Pedestrian Paradise finally was reopened on January 23, 2011, it was a "trial" (*jikken-teki*) that was carefully monitored. Widely publicized new rules, which were just the old rules restated, included "no performances" (*pafōmansu kinshi*). Cooperation was ensured by the not-so-subtle presence of authority. Instead of costumed otaku performers, it was uniformed police and citizen volunteers who were most visible on the street. When a cross-player did appear in an anime costume, he was swarmed by media and escorted away by police (Figure 33.2).

Concluding Remarks: Weird Performances of Otaku in Akihabara

The media attention devoted to Akihabara and otaku in the mid- to late 2000s attracted tourists, but what they encountered there did not always meet their expectations. In 2007, Akihabara was the fifteenth most recommended

Figure 33.2 A "cross-player" is swarmed by reporters, volunteers, and police at the reopening of the Pedestrian Paradise, January 23, 2011.
Source: Courtesy of the author.

place for foreign visitors to Japan, but the eighth most disappointing (JNTO 2008b). Perhaps this is because of the cross-play and "weird otaku" performances, or perhaps it is because the history of Akihabara has made it a center for not all manga/anime fans but rather for a subculture of men attracted to cute girl characters that appear in media and material forms that might be associated with "Porno Japan" or "Weird Japan" (METI 2012: 64).

Or perhaps it is because otaku performances promoted as part of Akihabara and Cool Japan have been policed out of existence. For example, in the promotional pamphlet for JNTO's Visit Japan Year 2010 Winter Campaign, there is an entry titled "Pop Culture." Written in English, it reads in part, "Akihabara is where you will find all items related to animated cartoons and cartoon books, and is famous as the source of conveying *Otaku* [sic] culture to the world" (JNTO 2010: 7). The entry is illustrated with a photograph of a group of young Japanese men and women dressed in costumes on the street. Upon inspection, the photograph turns out to be otaku performing the Haruhi dance on Akihabara's Chūō-dōri during the Pedestrian Paradise; checked against archival footage, we can place this photographed performance in the summer of 2007.

In 2010, JNTO is using a photograph of an otaku street performance, an image from before the crackdown from police that made such performances impossible, to promote tourism to Akihabara. If Akihabara is, as JNTO suggests, a place for conveying otaku culture to the world, then what is being conveyed is completely out of sync with the street. In this way, caught between promotional discourse and police discipline, otaku performances are imagined as part of Cool Japan, but they are not actually allowed in Akihabara, Japan.[1]

Note

1 For another example of this dynamic, see Murakami Takashi and McG's *Akihabara Majokko Princess*, a video shot on location in Akihabara and shown at London's Tate Modern exhibition on *Pop Life: Art in a Material World* in October 2009. Playing up the fiction of Akihabara as an otaku wonderland without rules, the video prominently features street performances but was shot after the police crackdown effectively ended such performances.

34 Japan Lost and Found

Modern Ruins as Debris of the Economic Miracle

Tong Lam

Abandonment conjures ideas of desolation, disorder, and decline. Unsurprisingly, abandoned places seem to be an antithesis of Japan's ultramodern image. First-time visitors to Tokyo are often impressed by the extent of urbanism, state-of-the-art facilities, cleanliness, and highly organized everyday life. Historians of Japan, too, have argued that "sanitariness" and "purity" were some of the key concepts in understanding Japan's colonial and war efforts in the early twentieth century (Dower 1987; Henry 2014).

Despite Japan's clean, technologically savvy, and efficient image, the end of its high-speed economic growth, or the postwar "economic miracle," has actualized landscapes of devastation and unfulfilled promises unmentioned in tourist guidebooks. These include abandoned factories, mines, hotels, amusement parks, and other once thriving sites of production and consumption. Also, less known to the outside world is a burgeoning subculture in which these abandoned places have become popular destinations for ruins aficionados from all walks of life. Known as "*haikyo mania*" (ruin mania), "*haikyo hanchingu*" (ruin hunting), or simply "*haikyo*" (ruins), this activity of seeking out and documenting modern ruins started to gather momentum in the 1990s, often referred to as the "Lost Decade" (*ushinawareta jūnen*), when Japan's economic bubble burst. Today, major Japanese bookstores routinely stock *haikyo* books, which feature photographs and stories of desolate and forgotten places. There is no shortage of movies, videogames, and other media inspired by or staged in these abandoned sites. Additionally, there are many digital resources—designated websites, online forums, and even special apps—devoted to *haikyo*, creating an active community of ruin enthusiasts.

How do we make sense of this apparent contradiction between an orderly and efficient society on the one hand and the widespread existence of wastelands and abandoned places, as well as a growing interest in these modern ruins, on the other? This chapter uses two types of modern ruins—industrial and postindustrial—to reflect on the *haikyo* phenomena. I examine the social, technological, and historical conditions that have enabled the mass production and consumption of *haikyo* imagery, and suggest that, although modern Japanese ruins, especially when they appear in the form of dystopic fantasies, provide endless opportunities for entertainment, the physical ruins themselves are more than playgrounds. As the debris of history, these sites reveal the past dreams and ambitions buried beneath new social and economic conditions. The exploration of ruins has the potential to create critical awareness of Japan's neoliberal trends, in which job security and economic confidence have been washed away by privatization, globalization, and financialization (e.g., Allison 2013). More than being just a popular pastime, *haikyo* may also provide redemptive and liberating alternatives.

The "Ruins Boom"

Although *haikyo* only recently emerged as a form of popular culture, the dystopic imagination has long been an important part of Japanese art and culture, as evident in diverse examples ranging from 1920s nonsense (*nansensu*) literature (Freedman 2009a) to science fiction by authors such as Oshikawa Shunro (early 1900s), Mishima Yukio (1960s), and Satō Yūya (2000s). Arguably, imaginings of dystopia increased in the postwar period. Indeed, the connections between Japan's dystopic fascination and the country's experiences of wars and natural disasters have been noticed by many scholars, as exemplified by William Tsutsui's (2004; 2010) research on Godzilla (see Chapter 18). In the first film (*Gojira*, 1954), Godzilla, a prehistoric monster, was supposedly awakened by American nuclear testing in the Pacific, which triggered its signature radioactive fire or atomic breath. As Tsutsui explains, although Godzilla does not seem to have a consistent moral character and she (and later he) wavers between a destroyer and protector of Japan as the film series progresses, the atomic reference is an example of how the anxiety of the nuclear age entered into public consciousness. With Japan being the only nation to have experienced atomic cataclysm, Godzilla, as an allegory of nuclear technology running amok, tries to occupy a moral high ground, one that does not only indict the American nuclear policy but also atomic technology in general.

In fact, as long as Japan has been plagued by natural and human-made disasters, popular entertainment has been a way for the public to try to work out traumatic memories and a sense of vulnerability. Susan Napier (1993) has shown that annihilation fantasies appear in Japanese films, anime, and novels as a means to negotiate and reimagine the nation's precarious conditions. Likewise, in his study of Japan's dystopic imaginations, Tsutsui (2010) further highlights the recreational nature of these dark images, contending that the Japanese cities in these disastrous scenes are "plastic imagined landscapes" upon which such fantasies can be carried out. In other words, the audience does not confuse these virtual realities with their lived experiences. Tsutsui (2010: 123) therefore argues that these dystopic imaginations are not grim projections of Japan's fate but are instead an expression of the endurance of the nation. After all, one can argue that it is only through these imagined destructions that the spirit of rebirth prevails.

Artist Motoda Hisaharu's 2011 acclaimed and haunting "Neo Ruins" project is a good example of how real landscapes are being turned into annihilation fantasies. In a series of lithographs, Motoda creates not only dystopic visions of popular Japanese sites, such as the Kaminarimon Gate at the front of the Sensōji Temple in Asakusa and the ultra-hip Shibuya district but also of international landmarks and symbols, such as the Sydney Opera House and San Francisco's Golden Gate Bridge. Significantly, in the wake of the March 2011 earthquake, Motoda (2011: 88) increasingly acknowledged that his fictional ruins were not completely detached from reality. Similarly, I, too, argue that images of contemporary ruins in popular culture are more than just violent spectacles for mass consumption. Oftentimes, they also provide an opportunity for the audience to reflect on the conditions of their existence and the societal choices as a whole.

Indeed, more than Motoda's doomsday images, the distressed landscapes pursued by *haikyo* enthusiasts are far from empty fantasies. While these *haikyo* sites may have been forgotten in daily life, they are real. And as ruins of modernity, they are products of interconnected global processes. As such, modern ruins have not only been mushrooming in Japan but also in other advanced economies. From Manchester to Milan, globalization has led to the outsourcing of factory jobs to less-developed countries. Along with the disappearance of generally well-paid and secure industrial jobs is the appearance of abandoned factories and industrial wastelands. Major American "Rust Belt" cities like Detroit and Buffalo, for instance, have witnessed drastic economic and population decline in the past half-century, leaving behind abandoned buildings and vacant lands in their urban cores (Yablon 2009). In the case of Japan—although it, too, is transitioning from an industrial to a service-oriented postindustrial economy—the factors behind the surge of ruins were rather different. In the media headlines of the 1980s and 1990s, at least, the failure of Detroit was often blamed on the success of the Japanese automobile industry.[1] So, paradoxically, to a certain degree, it was Japan's earlier economic success that had exacerbated the problems of speculation and overdevelopment. When the inflated real estate and stock market began to crumble in the late 1980s, many businesses and industries vanished, creating a trail of economic ruins in cities and countryside alike.

The proliferation of the ruins of capitalism during Japan's economic downturn in the 1990s is sometimes referred to as the "*haikyo būmu*" (ruins boom) by ruin enthusiasts. The idea of "*būmu*," at one level, is an ironic reminder of the inverse relationship between economic growth and ruins. At another level, *būmu* connotes a cultural trend driven by various media forms. *Haikyo būmu*, therefore, does not only refer to the emergence of physical ruins but also to the rise of public interest in these abandoned places. Since the 1990s, a steady stream of ruins explorers have ventured into these abandoned properties to examine and visually document the traces of postwar Japan's rapid reconstruction and its subsequent carefree consumerism. As they enter these sites of play, nostalgia, and mourning, these ruin aficionados also share images and stories in social and traditional media, attracting an even larger contingency of armchair explorers who do not personally visit these offbeat places. Indeed, if modern ruins are a symptom of history, the global outbreak of nostalgic feelings for ruins too is a symptom that requires interrogation (Boym 2001).

Ruins as Playground

Just as modern ruins are not unique to Japan, the practice of visiting modern ruins is not a uniquely Japanese phenomenon. Commonly called "urban exploration" or "urbex," such activities have become increasingly noticeable in developed economies. Recently, urban exploration has even been featured in the mainstream media, including documentary films and reality television shows like the United States' Discovery Channel's *Urban Explorers* and Travel Channel's *Off Limits*. At the heart of this loosely connected global movement are young adults who infiltrate into abandoned places to document the untimely death of a recent past that is exotic and alien to them. Derelict factories, old hospitals, decommissioned military bases, and defunct power stations are among the prime examples of abandoned structures urban explorers frequent. The so-called exploration could mean discovering new sites as well as paying pilgrimage to already well-documented locations. In addition, while photography is generally an important part of the process, urban explorers like to emphasize the authentic experience of being there. But unlike "geocaching," which is a popular recreational activity of hunting for hidden objects by sharing GPS coordinates, many urban explorers are reluctant to share the specific locations of their finds.

Given its playful, nostalgic, and somewhat masculine nature, it is often believed that many participants in such activities, including those who appear in popular shows mentioned above, are white, young, urban, and middle-class males who are keen to find refuge from their daily boredom. But there are plenty of exceptions. Based on my personal observation, increasingly, women and middle-aged people are also actively involved in these activities, and this is equally the case in Japan. Meanwhile, although such activities sometimes subvert the notion of private propriety; as trespassing may be required, most of these adventurers are thrill-seekers rather than political activists. Regardless, urban explorers generally uphold a principle, epitomized in their popular motto: "take nothing but pictures, leave nothing but footprints" (Ninjialicious 2005: 26). Vandalism and theft are strongly discouraged. In fact, explorers regard vandalized sites as less desirable because these places have failed to convey a sense of "natural" decay.

Not all the urban explorers share their photographs and stories online, but those who do constitute an important component of the phenomenon. Undoubtedly, given the social, economic, and demographic backgrounds of these adventurers, many of them are "digital natives," namely people who grew up with the Internet. What makes urban exploration a kind of a movement is not only because of its shared principle but also the way in which information about abandoned sites is circulated. For example, digital cameras, photo streams, online forums, blogs, apps, and translation software are indispensable tools in the process. More often than not, digital photographs and video clips of ruins are the main attractions in these sharing platforms. In order to create a shock-and-awe effect, some urban explores like to manipulate the toning and saturation of their images of picturesque decay, creating kitsch and sensational visual effects that some critics have referred as "ruin porn" (Leary 2011).

Indeed, it is through the various platforms of social media that urban explorers from around the world are able to brag about their triumphal infiltrations and discoveries and forge communities, friendships, and competitions that transcend cultural and national boundaries. As a result of online sharing, even though numbers of urban explorers are relatively small, visual stories of modern ruins can reach a larger community of addicted armchair explorers. Thus, even if urban exploration is always place-specific and locally grounded, media technologies have made it a globally popular culture.

In spite of being a popular pastime for a selected demographic, the movement of urban exploration resonates with a range of cultural practices with diverse origins. In fact, there is a long history of appreciating the aesthetic and nostalgic value of ruins. For instance, around the turn of the early twentieth century, the sociologist Georg Simmel (1965 [1911]) already discussed how human fascination with ruins was unleashed by modernity. During that time, as Japan, too, was rapidly modernizing, ancient ruins equally became sites of nostalgia. The melancholic sentiments invoked by ancient castles, for example, were vividly captured in the popular song "The Moon over the Ruined Castle" (*Kōjō no tsuki*, composed in 1901).[2] In her well-known 1953 book *Pleasure of Ruins*, Rose Macaulay meditates on the strange charm of ruins, including many modern European ruins destroyed by World War II. Such tension between aesthetic pleasure and violence, progress and destruction, Macauley notes, is also expressed in the eighteenth-century concept of "ruin lust," which was a central preoccupation in European art and literature in the era of Romanticism (Macaulay 1953).

Aesthetics and nostalgia aside, there are also ruin explorers who increasingly use their documentation of urban blight to critique and make sense of globalization and its negative consequences (Lam 2013; Christopher 2014). Some explorers further theorize their ruin wanderings as being part of the right to the city that insists on gaining access to urban resources, transforming urban spaces, and forging social relationships (Garrett 2013). Others have referenced their adventure to "psychogeography," a political activism associated with the Situationist movement from the 1950s. Psychogeographers emphasize urban walking on unpredictable paths as a tactic for creating awareness about the surrounding urban landscapes. They believe that the emotional effect on the individual in a specific geographic setting can help to promote new cognition and reinvented everyday life (Debord 1977 [1967]; Richardson 2015). All in all, despite the fact that most urban explorers are not activists, consciously or unconsciously, many have intellectual claims and political agendas.

Figure 34.1 A female *haikyo* enthusiast exploring the iconic Hashima (Gunkanjima) ruin in Nagasaki Prefecture, 2011.
Source: Courtesy of the author.

Ruins of Production

As in the United States, where industrial decline has given rise to a cluster of shrinking cities along the Midwest and Northeastern states' "Rust Belt," Japan's economic stagnation and population decline have produced its own version of industrial ruins. Hidden behind the postcard images of cherry blossoms and high-speed rail are plenty of closed mines, outdated factories, and contaminated wastelands. Of these abandoned industrial sites, the deserted island-city Hashima, not unlike Detroit in the United States, stands out as the most iconic. After decades of neglect, the island has recently captivated a large domestic and global audience, drawing tourists and intruders alike. Located off the coast of Nagasaki Prefecture, Hashima is colloquially known as "Gunkanjima" (Battleship Island) due to its uncanny resemblance to the contours of a battleship. When the Mitsubishi shipping company commenced its industrial mining at the end of the nineteenth century, coal extracted from the seabed of the tiny island was used to power the company's growing fleet of steamships. But just like the Mitsubishi company itself, the island-city quickly became an integral component of Japan's colonial enterprise. By the time of the Asia-Pacific War (1931–1945), Hashima was part of the Japanese war machine with forced Korean and Chinese laborers responsible for some of the most dangerous underwater mining activities (Burke-Gaffney 1996).

After the war, Hashima continued to play an important role in Japan's rapid industrialization. As living conditions improved, the population expanded. By the late 1950s, there were more than five thousand people living in the 15-acre barren rock (Hirotoshi 2010). The dozens of concrete residential buildings built before and during this period would eventually become the backbone of the visually enthralling Gunkanjima ruinscape. In 2009, decades after its formal closure in 1974, the forgotten island slowly returned to the Japanese public consciousness as a spectacle when tour operators began offering ways to observe the derelict structures from a safe distance. Risk-taking urban explorers, meanwhile, started to infiltrate the island and roam undetected. Then, in 2012, the island suddenly created a global sensation, all thanks to *Skyfall* (Sam Mendes, dir., 2012), the James Bond film that refers to the island as the secret hideout of the movie's villain. Subsequently, in order to satisfy the public desire for imagery of the iconic site, even Google Street View has provided 360-degree panoramas of the abandoned city (Augment5 Inc. 2013).

The rise of Gunkanjima as Japan's ultimate industrial ruin is reinforced by the frequency in which the island has been used as a visual backdrop for popular entertainments. Take the 2003 *Battle Royale II: Requiem* (*Batoru rowaiaru tsū: rekuiemu*), for example, as Gunkanjima was the filming location for the relentless bloodbaths between teenagers, rebels, and government forces. In the 2005 videogame *Killer 7* (*Kirā sebun*), a first-person shooter that involves exploration and puzzle solving, it is the hiding place for a terrorist group. As the game progresses, the player eventually discovers the secret of this derelict but once thriving island. Another survival horror game *Forbidden Siren 2* (*Sairen tsū*, 2006) draws inspiration from the ruinscape of Gunkanjima, even though the island in the game takes on a different name. In fact, since the late 1990s, many action and adventure games, such as *Resident Evil* (*Baiohazādo*, 1996) and *Silent Hill* (*Sairento hiru*, 1999), have similarly employed a ruin theme in their stories and graphic designs.[3] In this respect, not unlike the imagined Tokyo destroyed by Godzilla over and over again, Gunkanjima, too, is a plastic landscape ready to host any catastrophic imagery.

Yet, whereas Gunkanjima functions as a futuristic dystopia for game players and moviegoers to act out fantasies of fighting villains or becoming superheroes, the real ruins of Hashima conjure a sense of nostalgia for Japan's postwar industrial glory and civic pride. In the 2002 documentary film *Hashima, Japan* by Carl Michael von Hausswolff and Thomas Nordanstad, the former Hashima resident Dotoku Sakamoto soberly walks through the ruins, from his childhood sweetheart's derelict home to an abandoned school, and recalls the human sacrifice that made progress possible. Dotoku is one of the most notable activists who seeks to preserve the legacy of Hashima. Among other things, he helped to propose nominating the island as part of the Meiji industrial sites for UNESCO World Heritage listing because of its vital importance in Japan's industrialization. Dotoku and his friends were hardly alone in their endeavor. In recent years, in addition to endorsements from the various levels of the Japanese government, there has also been a surge of academic interest in reconstructing the daily life of postwar Hashima when the island was still functional (Hirotoshi 2010). Moreover, the public fascination with the history of Hashima has resulted in a spontaneous outpouring of photographs, architectural drawings, and stories about hardship and human triumph that made postwar prosperity possible.

In a way, the celebration of Japan's economic success by conferring heritage status on Hashima and nearly two dozen other Meiji industrial sites can be seen as an attempt to incorporate private sentiments and collective memory into the official history of the state. Nonetheless, it remains uncertain whether all the counter-memories could be erased. During the nomination process, the controversial proposal encountered strong opposition from the government and activist groups of South Korea because the war crime of using forced laborers from Korea and China had not been properly acknowledged. Although the UNESCO heritage application was ultimately successful, Hashima's wartime history continues to haunt the triumphal narrative of the place. In Dotoku's reminiscence, there are no zombies but instead haunting ghosts of untimely deaths. Rather than outlaw villains, violent sea waves threaten people and buildings. And there are no fantasies to unfold, only the sorrows of devastation and unfulfillment. In other words, even if Dotoku's recollection does not constitute an outright indictment against the system, his nostalgic sentiments are nonetheless a subtle critique of the broken promises. "Perhaps none of these can ever be saved," Dotoku lamented helplessly, "but I would like people to know that there is at least one person, me, who feels something about this island" (Hausswolff and Nordanstad 2002).

Sentiments like Dotoku's are hitting a collective nerve not just because of the aesthetic pleasure associated with this iconic ruin. It is also because the closing of the island in 1974, shortly after the 1973 global oil crisis, came at the end of Japan's high-speed, two-digit economic growth. Hashima, in other words, has become a symbolic marker of the end of Japan's "miraculous" economy. Just as Hashima began to decay into a spectacular industrial ruin, the wealth and excess capital generated during the era of high-speed growth was brewing Japan's postindustrial economy for an asset price bubble that would ultimately result in a no less spectacular collapse of the real estate and stock markets a decade later. In sum, Hashima is a phantom of Japan's wartime history as well as its vanished postwar confidence. As such, the nostalgic stories and images of Hashima that have emerged in recent years are no doubt also narratives of failure, betrayal, and lost confidence.

Ruins of Consumption

If ramshackle mines and dilapidated factories are the scars of industrialization, then abandoned entertainment venues symbolize the consequences of Japan's bubble economy (1986–1991). The collapse of the asset price bubble in the late 1980s was a major factor that led to widespread business closures and

Figure 34.2 A derelict restaurant in an abandoned hotel in Hyōgo Prefecture, 2012.
Source: Courtesy of the author.

the loss of consumer confidence in what is subsequently known as the "Lost
Decade" of the 1990s. During this time, businesses dedicated to leisure and
consumption—themselves products of Japan's transition from an industrial
society to postindustrial one—were among those hardest hit. The staggering
real estate failure, coupled with a declining population, often meant that
there was little prospect for finding new investors for service-oriented establishments such as amusement parks, luxurious resorts, love hotels, and private
museums. Many of the large venues in the countryside, especially, were left
vacant and unattended.

Among the pioneers who set out to capture the dismal situation of Japan's
untimely economic collapse were writer Nakata Kaoru and photographer Nakasuji Jun. When Japan entered into a prolonged recession in the
1990s, Nakata and Nakasuji were in their twenties. Driven by their aesthetic
sensitivities and youthful, adventurous spirits, they ventured into derelict
properties to experience the eeriness of ruins firsthand. What had started
out as a hobby quickly evolved into a systematic, even epic, project that witnessed the consequences of the "economic tsunami" that had shaken Japan's
postwar confidence. As Japan entered the twenty-first century, due to the
continued recession, increasing income gaps and under-employment, as well
as exacerbating gaps between social classes (*kakusa shakai*), and other forms
of social and economic precarity, the "Lost Decade" became the "Lost Two
Decades" (*ushinawareta nijūnen*). Nakata and Nakasuji published their work on

the distressed landscape of post-bubble reality in a series of *Ruin Books* (*Haikyobon*) (Nakata and Nakasuji 2005, 2007, 2009, and 2012).

Among the hundreds of locations that Nakata and Nakasuji visited were desolate industrial facilities, schools, and hospitals; however, the sites that stand out most prominently in their adventures are abandoned entertainment venues, which, in many ways, were the quintessential examples of Japan's postindustrial economy. From eerie hot springs spas with no users to silent roller coasters with no riders, their collaborative work is an evocative testimony of Japan's ruins boom amid an untimely economic failure. More importantly, what appears in their images and commentaries is not just the physical decay of buildings and objects but also the moral decay associated with money, ambitions, desires, and hedonism. As a result, the appeal of their project, which commenced before the digital revolution in photography, does not rest on the manipulation of color saturation and toning done by amateurish ruin photographers today. Rather than aestheticizing decay, Nakasuji's photographs are intended to be straightforward documentation of an ongoing social and economic catastrophe, and his images are closer to news reportage than fine art. Their books are not printed on high-quality paper or in large formats like coffee-table books or art catalogues, and Nakata's writing is a combination of journalism and local history. In addition to simple dates, numbers, and names, he routinely tells the stories of how businesses were shuttered due to speculative and overambitious plans and comments on how communities and lives were shattered in the process. In this regard, their work is consistent with a genre of *haikyo* books commonly found in Japanese bookstores. Generally printed in a small format filled with factual information, these books (one of a few genres of ruin books) are marketed to a growing number of armchair explorers who seem less interested in the aestheticized spectacle of ruins than the haunting and precarious reality of post-bubble Japan.[4]

Ruins as Possibilities

Like Dotoku's sorrowful recollections of Hashima, the texts and images produced by Nakata and Nakasuji do not strongly indict the underlying political economy and neoliberal policies. Yet the stories they tell attest to the betrayal of postwar promises of security and growth (Allison 2013). Thus their works, and books like them, while being a part of the popular fascination with dystopic scenes, cannot simply be dismissed as "ruin porn" or mindless spectacle. Nostalgia aside, these plain documentations of Japan's precarious social and economic conditions render visible an urgent and agonizing situation, epitomized in the physical and emotional distress caused by social and economic ruination that are not routinely reported by the mainstream media.

Jordan Sand (2008) has noticed that the same economic collapse has inspired other professional Japanese artists, writers, and scholars to launch what is called the "Street Observation Science" (*rojō kansatsugaku*). Wandering the streets of Tokyo, these modern *flâneur*, or what Sand calls "streetscape ex-plorers," stroll, observe, and record the telltale signs of the collapsing econ-omy, such as suffering businesses, manholes, and fragments of demolished buildings.[5] Embedded in their nostalgic observations and photographic documentations is also a critique of the culture of consumption and specu-lation. Arguably, in the same vein, Nakata and Nakasuji's adventures, too, are a form of vernacular ethnography—one that caters to popular audience than to intellectuals—of Japan's unfulfilled promises and betrayed dreams. Rather than deploying sophisticated social theory, they came with cameras, curiosity, empathy, and a determination to witness the unfolding economic tsunami of their times. And they would soon be joined by many others who expose these off-track places thanks to the rise of digital technology and social media in the new millennium.

If by critiquing capitalist speculation, the street observationists of Tokyo offer "a new way to speculate on the past," as Sand puts it, then the nation-wide explorations by *haikyo* enthusiasts are historical speculations that could yield to new insights and alternatives (Sand 2008: 394). Indeed, a cursorily look at many of the Japanese books and websites dedicated to *haikyo* suggests that Nakata and Nakasuji's sentiments are not uncommon. As much as ruins function as the playground for *haikyo* adventurers, these sites are more than a virtual-reality. Buried in the spectacle of violence and destruction are for-gotten visions and dreams that were potentially liberating and enabling. The eerie scenes and decaying smells of modern ruins, therefore, demand us to pause and think, in addition to taking and posting photographs.

Haikyo practitioners, in this regard, do not consume ruin imagery passively. As aficionados, players, and critics of Japan's modern ruins, they actively inter-pret, share, and produce meanings for these historical remnants using popular media technologies. And dystopic visions are provocative precisely because they activate our innermost desires and fears. Furthermore, imageries from industrial and postindustrial ruins are arguably even more powerful because they bear a direct connection to history. In other words, unlike the Godzilla films or zombie-shooting videogames, there is no sequel or reset button in history. Thus, if the Japanese audience is fascinated by Nakata and Nakasu-ji's imagery of ruins or encouraged to empathize with Dotoku Sakamoto's sorrow, it is perhaps because they, too, are increasingly subjugated to the same precarious conditions generated by global capitalism and environmental hazards. In this sense, an image of ruin, even an aestheticized one, is more than a snapshot of an isolated event. It is a trapdoor to a lost world, a potential catalyst for reflection and action. And it is perhaps only through the aware-ness of the loss and unrealized possibilities that we find a new way forward.

Notes

1 Although globalization is a central part of the Detroit story, racism, misman-agement, and other factors inherent in American politics also contributed to the city's demise (Martelle 2014).

2 The music was composed by Taki Rentarō (1879–1903) and the lyrics written by poet Doi Bansui (1871–1952). Originally inspired by the ruins of Aoba Castle and Aizuwakamatsu Castle in Fukushima Prefecture, the song has been reinterpreted in various classical and jazz formats.

3 The island appears anonymously in music videos. For instance, the Japanese rock band B'z filmed the video for their 2009 single "My Lonely Town" on the island even though they made no specific reference to the geographical location.

4 A prime example of this genre is *Ruins of Japan* (*Nippon no Haikyo*, 2007), edited by Sakai Ryūji, which includes a long list of modern Japanese ruins. As a contrast, the popular *haikyo* website by the female Japanese urban explorer and videogame designer nicknamed Tomboy Urbex, provides haunting and spectacular images from Japan and elsewhere, and its theme is driven more by adventure than by journalism. This also speaks to differences in audience, marketing, and accessibility of print and digital media.

5 As Sand points out, Walter Benjamin (1999) has explained observations by the *flâneur*, the casual wanderer who observes street life from among the crowd, has provided an opportunity not just to understand what happened but to also see what might be redemptive (Sand 2008: 388). For the basic principles of "Street Observation Science," see Akasegawa, Fujimori, and Minami (1986).

PART XI
Fashion

35 Cute Fashion

The Social Strategies and Aesthetics of *Kawaii*

Toby Slade

What is *kawaii*, the Japanese version of cute or adorable? How did it become so ubiquitous? This chapter traces the beginnings of the modern manifestation of the aesthetic of *kawaii* to the early 1970s, a period following significant political and social unrest. While some aspects can be found earlier, especially its prevalence in manga and anime, this is when *kawaii* fully entered fashion and self-styling.

While in English the word "cute" derived from "acute" in the eighteenth century and originally meant clever and shrewd, in a self-seeking or superficial way, it lost its negative connotations to mean simply attractive in a pretty or endearing way. In Japanese, *kawaii* derived from the phrase, "*kawahayushi*," meaning a flushed face and implying embarrassment, and came to mean able to be loved, adorable, or cute (Maeda 2005). In both languages, the idea originated as something negative, either an ulterior motive or embarrassment, but became something positive without other connotations. Being *kawaii* now, like being cute, is an implicitly auspicious and good thing.

As I will demonstrate, while *kawaii* originally became popular in fashion and self-styling as a political statement of rebellion, it has developed its own self-sustaining logic. It gradually shed much of its rebellious role, becoming an aesthetic disconnected from its original purpose. As argued in our chapters on fashion, fashion often stands somewhere between high art and popular culture, claiming occasionally a central role in both. One thing that *kawaii* fashion does, however, is destabilize the distinctions of high and low by holding up a mirror to social and cultural structures that claim the space of maturity and seriousness by being deliberately neither. *Kawaii* is a central element of Japanese popular culture providing not just a contemporary look but also a set of behavioral norms and expectations.

To understand the evolution and function of *kawaii*, I first examine the scientific phenomenon on which *kawaii* is based and then track its adoption into illustrated popular cultures of manga and anime preceding its jump into fashion and other aspects of self-presentation and behavior. I establish an argument about the causes of *kawaii* by mapping its emergence onto key events in Japanese cultural history. While the timeline for establishing *kawaii* in this way—as an aesthetic—dating from just after and as a response to the failed student riots is not perfect and cultural causality is not the same as historical chronology, the argument that *kawaii* enters fashion for political reasons, as a subtle form of rebellion, is compelling. And it has parallels with changes in how youths worldwide saw and expressed themselves.

The Science of Cute

In 1949 the Austrian scientist, Konrad Lorenz, published *King Solomon's Ring* (English version 1969), in which he established a number of fundamental and now commonly known zoological concepts. The title referred to the Seal of Solomon, which supposedly gave the biblical king of Israel the power to talk with animals. Through this metaphor, Lorenz explores scientific concepts of animal intelligence and communication, such imprinting, a brief developmental period where animals, or humans, rapidly learn from copied stimuli. Lorenz also discussed how certain infantile features—a big head to body ratio, large round eyes, and awkward movements—trigger feelings of caring. This, he argued, was an instinctual behavior shared by humans. The features that he later called *"kindchenschema"* were facial and bodily traits that make creatures appear cute and activate in others the motivation to care for them (Lorenz 1969).

At its most basic, the science of cute is a biological imperative. It serves a clear adaptive function of impelling adult animals to take care of their young. Cuteness immediately incites nurturing instincts and, conversely, once the young are no longer cute, indicates an appropriate time when offspring are ready to care for themselves and should be moved on. What is interesting is that an animal does not necessarily have to be the same species to trigger these feelings in an adult. This is seen in instances of one animal placed in the litter of another and raised as an equal, something some species, such as brood parasites like cuckoos, have developed into an entire evolutionary strategy. This also explains, to some degree, human affection for their pets.

Further research has shown that animals, including humans, may have even evolved for greater cuteness as an evolutionary advantage. Barry Bogin (1997) has written that patterns of children's growth show an intentional increase in the duration of cuteness to trigger a corresponding increase in the period when resources and protection might be provided by older animals. There is longer allometry of human growth than in any other species, according to Bogin. Humans remain superficially infantile in appearance for a long time, as shown by the fact that the human brain reaches adult size when the body is only 40 percent grown.

The clarity of the science, however, is muddied by the addition of culture to the equation. Many behaviors and norms mimic natural processes. Historian Philippe Ariès is famous for the proposition that the concept of childhood is a development of the modern era (Ariès 1965). Ariès' thesis is that, in the Middle Ages, the nuclear family did not exist as the center of social organization, for children died too often to devote excessive resources to, were not protected from sexuality, and were not segregated in school systems but interacted with society as small adults. They had similar expectations as adults for work, play, and appearance; their clothes were simply smaller versions of adult clothing and not differentiated in any other way but size. Starting from the fifteenth century in France, childhood began to be seen as a separate stage of life. Children were kept separate from much of adult life, increasingly sent to school for longer periods, and protected from adult sexuality. In this way, cultural norms were mimetic of the evolutionary process, constructing social structures whereby children could remain cuter for longer. Bogin's evolutionary origins of human childhood, the uniquely evolved pre-reproductive stages of childhood and adolescence, are replicated in Ariès' cultural origins of human childhood.

The difficulty in determining exactly what cute is, however, lies in the overlap of an adaptive evolutionary strategy and a constructed social strategy. Cultural cuteness has become something more than a social strategy mimicking the biological function of impelling others to nurture. In Japan, it has more complex roles and meanings as a metaphor for rebellion against authority and as a symbol to contest patriarchal and hierarchical society by deliberately emphasizing the feminine and immature.

More Disney than Disney

Even before Lorenz had published his ideas, Walt Disney understood the unconscious appeal of things cute. Comics and animation, with their endless possibility for elasticity of form, provided the perfect place for the logic of cute to be exploited through drawn features. For example, progressively after his first appearance in *Steamboat Willie* (1928), Mickey Mouse evolved to become cuter. His head became proportionately larger, as did his eyes, his legs shorter and thicker, his face flatter, his nose smaller and more like a button than a snout, and he became generally more rounded. By the time of *Fantasia* (1940), he had developed many juvenile attributes, including the oversized wizard's gown he wears. Stephen Jay Gould (1980) argues that Mickey's cute changes parallel the cute changes that occurred in human evolution. Mickey evolved to be cuter for the same reason as juvenile humans: to inspire nurturing emotions (Gould 1980).

Tezuka Osamu, a pioneer of Japanese manga and anime, noticed the appeal of the large eyes and other cute elements of Disney's *Snow White* (1937) and *Bambi* (1942) and began to adopt, even exaggerate, these features in his own works like *Astro Boy* (*Tetsuwan Atomu*, 1952–1968). Tezuka, who was also responding to the trauma of the Second World War, drew his exaggerations of Disney with the conscious purpose of trying to erase the caricatures of evil, cunning Japanese with small eyes in American war propaganda (Gravett 2004: 26–28).

There are numerous theories about when the aesthetic of cute was incorporated into objects and texts in Japan. Several theories regard the

Edo period (1603–1868)—with its accelerated urbanization, pressure on living space to be smaller, and growth of wealth and accompanying material culture—to be the beginnings of a preference for things small and cute. Sugiyama Tomoyuki (2006) argues that this preference is exemplified in *netsuke*, miniature sculptures that became popular accessories in the seventeenth century. Others argue that, in Murasaki Shikibu's *Tale of Genji* (*Genji monogatari*, circa 1021), there are characters with pitiable qualities that could be described as cute (Shiokawa 1999: 93–125). These explanations are speculative and tend to assume that Japanese culture is an unbroken continuum stretching into the past and always in strict opposition to all that is foreign, rather than a nexus of information flows and occasional radical disjunctures.

Tezuka's adoption of a cute aesthetic is clear by his own admission; manga and animation provide clear starting points because of the exaggeration that drawn images allow. The popularity of manga and anime in Japan might also provide a possible line of causality for the popularity of *kawaii* in other areas, including fashion. Yet while the inclusion of cute features into popular culture is one thing, the desire to be cute oneself and to include it in one's own fashion and self-styling is another. It involves a change in young people's sense of self and in their attitudes towards adulthood and social hierarchies. In Japan, as in many places in the world, these social norms, often based on age and gender, were radically questioned in the late 1960s.

"Youthquake" and "Cutequake"

In 1960s London, *Vogue* editor-in-chief Diana Vreeland noted that fashion was changing in unprecedented ways. For the first time, a generation was not looking up to fashion leaders, such as the aristocracy, movie stars, or great designers but were instead looking down to the street. Teenagers, like The Beatles (1960–1970) and The Rolling Stones (formed in 1962) dominated the music scene, and this was changing fashion. Miniskirts, jumpsuits, loud colors, and skinny boyish models were all the rage. Vreeland (1965: 112) called this musical, cultural, and fashion movement "Youthquake," and the *Vogue* of her tenure promoted this spirited youth movement, booking models like Twiggy and Veruschka and featuring designers like Mary Quant and Betsey Johnson. The first post-World War II generation sought to not imitate older peoples' fashion styles but to define themselves against their parents' clothing. This was the first reversal in fashion where top-down (or trickledown) influence flows were replaced by street-up (or bubble-up) influence flows, with first designers, and then the upper classes, imitating the styles of the street. The postwar desire for participatory democracy and the potential of resistance, in the form of active protest and the symbolic form of clothing, was everywhere. It was, in large part, the result of knowing the horrors of war and nuclear terror, along with the rise of popular music and the revolutionary aspiration of 1960s social movements. Fashion trends and larger historical forces are not always intrinsically connected, but at key moments, such as this, they are tied tightly.

The 1964 Tokyo Olympics represented Japanese economic recovery from the war, but with wealth (although spread unequally) and reconstruction came various social tensions—for example between a younger generation keen to embrace the rebellious spirit and an older generation keen to protect the society they had sacrificed to rebuild. Student unrest at the end of the 1960s and beginning of the 1970s revolved in its specifics around the relationship between the university and the state (Takazawa 1996: 70–71) but can be viewed as a proxy for generational resistance to patriarchal, hierarchical social structure in general. In 1968, protest and resistance were generally seen, at least on Japanese university campuses, as an effective, and even cool, way to affect social change, challenge the acquiescence to the United States, replace hierarchical structures with more democratic ones, and resist the dominating logic of materialist, capitalist culture. The notion of struggle was central to the way student activism sought to redefine the character of Japan's democracy (McCormack 1971: 37–52). A distinguishing feature of the student agenda was an antipathy towards existing institutions and ideas governing Japanese society. There was a corresponding belief in individual and collective agency outside of existing institutions. Maturity, agency, active participation in democracy, and resisting authority were part of youth identity in this period.

Yet unable to effectively define itself and translate action into social change, the student movement collapsed by the early 1970s, as had similar movements in Paris in 1968. Partly, the symbolic space of the state over which groups were fighting was being abandoned as the logic of business and capital and the dreams of advertising and materialism replaced the nation as dominant in the public imagination. The government also decentralized the student movement by building rural campuses, such as Tsukuba University, moving potential protest out of Tokyo.

It is in this sense of the failure of action, the inevitability of social and economic structures, and surrender to materialism and popular culture that the modern form of the Japanese aesthetic of *kawaii* emerged. It emerged, however, not as an acquiescence to the sociocultural mainstream but as an ironic form of disassociation and resistance. The pleasure that derives from being and observing *kawaii* is not just the pleasure of desirability or of being deferred to or played up to in a normally gender-based power relationship but an ironic pleasure of knowing expression, similar to kitsch and camp, that undermines the seriousness of the dominant cultural values. *Kawaii* hides a political assertion of independence by pretending to be completely non-political. Self-styling and fashion use this perceived lack of political meaning to make potent political symbolism. Most ideological agendas seek to establish themselves as non-ideological and therefore true and natural (Žīžēk 1994). Both the patriarchal and hierarchical establishment of Japanese culture and undermining elements such as *kawaii* do just this.

The failure of the university riots to achieve reform was mirrored in another dramatic event played out on Japanese television. On November 25, 1970, author Mishima Yukio (b. 1925), went to the headquarters of Japan's Self-Defense Forces, tied up the commandant, and gave a speech to the assembled officers advocating a coup d'état to restore the Emperor to absolute power. When the officers mocked him and refused to take him seriously, Mishima committed ritual suicide (*seppuku*) with the help of his small group of followers. It is believed that Mishima did not think his coup d'état would succeed and instead was meant as a symbolic gesture of protest (Nathan 1974).

These events taken together, the student unrest on the left and the suicide of Mishima on the right, along with the left's increasing fragmentation and violence (evident by the 1972 Asama-Sansō Incident), can be seen as an end of violent action as political strategy; in addition, they perhaps can be seen as the high-water mark of resistance to capitalist material culture in Japan. Arguably, the symbolic concept of the nation state, over which both the political left and the right were fighting, was fading in importance as the logic of corporate Japan and its accompanying materialism fed by the dreams of advertising replaced it as the most important aspect of social organization.

This is the moment when *kawaii* becomes an increasingly important factor in Japanese fashion and culture. The emergence of *kawaii* in this period can be understood at first as a rebellious pleasure (although one not necessarily supported by Mishima or the student protestors) and the original *kawaii* fashion as an ironic mode of expression. Where Britain had a Youthquake, Japan was about to have a "Cutequake."

One of the first places this could be observed was in the handwriting of female secondary school students. In the early 1970s, teenaged girls began to use rounded handwriting with exaggerated circular letters (*maru-ji*), along with kitten letters (*koneko-ji*) and paedomorphic letters (*burikko-ji*) that included little drawings like hearts and smiles, part of a growing trend for "*gyaru moji*," or girl writing (see Chapter 10). Kazuma Yamane (1990) analyzes how *kawaii* handwriting began among students and became a spontaneous, underground trend, predating the technical means to produce round letters in manga. Sharon Kinsella (1995) has shown how graphological rebellion, which she has deemed the first form of *kawaii* culture, constituted an attempt by youth to establish their own language and express their own emotional needs outside the cultural establishment which placed the Japanese language as unassailable and highly serious. As this example shows, instead of conforming or openly rebelling, some youths acted in a cute way to undermine adult authority.

Thus *kawaii* undermines the seriousness demanded by the hierarchical nature of Japanese society and language. There is a rebellious pleasure in this, similar to the pleasure of kitsch: knowing something is in bad taste—or immature—but taking delight in the way it simply ignores the established rules of good taste or mature behavior. It is a reflexive pleasure of irony, knowing something would be socially construed as immature, but doing it anyway.

Fashion is a perfect target for this type of ironic rebellion. Fashion that could be interpreted as childish or innocent was taken up ironically by the no-longer-childish and no-longer-innocent. In these fashions, *kawaii* is not the absence of adulthood but an ironic comment on it and its undesirability. Starting with the popularity of the fashion brand Pink House, founded in 1973 by former-revolutionary students from Waseda University, various fashion designers used *kawaii* styling. Other brands formed around this period included Milk (1970 by Okawa Hitomi) that made frilly, layered, "Lolita-style clothes" (fashion that uses elements of English Victorian and Edwardian clothing to create a look that is romantic and nostalgic for a bygone form of femininity) and Shirley Temple (1974 by Yanagikawa Rei). The *kawaii* styles these brands sold were broadly popular, in both the more extreme styles of designers' boutiques and in their subtler influences on non-designer clothing. Their popularity can perhaps be attributed to consumers being predisposed to their rebellious and ironic undertones. Mainstream commercial interests also recognized the changing mood and accompanying aesthetic; Sanrio was one of the first and most famous to do so. Established in 1960 and originally a silk printing and then sandal making company, Sanrio shifted focus to design cute characters and merchandise after noticing that sales jumped whenever something cute was added to a sandal design (Belson and Bremner 2004). Sanrio launched the quintessentially cute character, Hello Kitty, in 1974 (see Chapter 3).

The essential difference between these examples and the *kawaii* aesthetic, such as that seen in Tezuka's 1950s manga, is that, by the 1970s, consumers and creators did not simply want to enjoy seeing *kawaii* things; instead they wanted to be *kawaii* themselves. *Kawaii* entered fashion and self-styling as a desirable look and state of being. As such, it is no longer reserved for a period of childhood but is adopted as an aesthetic disconnected from the original referent of childhood. In other words, *kawaii* transformed from a recognized look of childhood into an aesthetic that could be used socially and politically. While the British "Youthquake" was demanding that youths be considered independent and mature, the Japanese "Cutequake" ironically rejected maturity.

An Alternate Social Strategy

Kawaii has also been used by those being rebelled against. Brian McVeigh (2000) has argued that *kawaii* fashion, particularly in school uniforms and their deliberate alteration by their wearers, constitutes a form of resistance against the dominant ideology of uniformity: "[For] the powerful bureaucratizing forces of statism and corporate culture, *kawaii* represents a form of resistance associated with women, children, leisure and self-expression" (McVeigh 2000: 135–136). However, McVeigh also notes this resistance was quickly co-opted by the institutions it opposed, as evidenced by *kawaii* advertising campaigns and *kawaii* police mascots and logos. In addition, Kinsella

(2002) argues that school uniforms, particularly those for girls, constitute a key anti-symbol of rebellion and sexuality, and the fact that the iconic sailor uniforms come directly from Japanese imperial ambitions and military reforms makes their use as a *kawaii* symbol especially potent and political. (Yet this uniform can also be used to objectify and belittle.)

As an alternate social strategy, *kawaii* self-styling is a kind of refusal to cooperate with established social values but also to some extent with reality itself. It denies reality but is all the more powerful for doing so. Just as the aesthetic of cool ignores mainstream tastes, so, too, *kawaii* does not directly enter into or challenge mainstream cultural and aesthetic values but establishes its own values and aesthetics by ignoring them (Pountain and Robins 2000). It does not seek to be sexy, serious, or maturely beautiful but instead establishes the desirability of paedomorphism, the silly, and the adorably dysfunctional. It is a "demure rebellion" (Kinsella 1995) unlike more aggressive and sexually charged fashions of British youth rebellion; *kawaii* emphasizes immaturity and lack of agency, acting pre-sexual and vulnerable, even while being neither.

Both Pink House and Milk boutique in Harajuku have laid claim to the origins of *kawaii* in fashion (Kawamura 2012: 67–71). (Pink House launched its Lolita theme in 1979 and is now a purely Lolita themed brand.) With these brands, *kawaii* performs a political function of undermining current ideologies of gender and power. The later appearance of variations like gothic Lolita juxtapose the immaturity of romantic childhood with gothic symbols, creating the appealing contrast of life and death together in the same aesthetic. This fulfills the political and social needs of *kawaii*, being both desirable and somewhat helpless, while also rebellious, laughing at death, and challenging the seriousness of the mainstream.

With these brands as style leaders and following Sanrio's success, Valarie Steele (2010: 46) notes there was soon an explosion of *kawaii* clothes, white or pastel in color and with puffy sleeves and ribbons, and accessories, including white tights and frilly ankle socks. The fashion magazine *An An* proclaimed in 1975: "On dates we only want feeling, but our clothes are like old ladies! It is time to express who you really are" (quoted in Kinsella 1995: 229). The implication was that a true identity had been somehow repressed, and this real identity was the antithesis of conventional female fashion. The fashion magazine *CUTiE* was launched in 1986 with the subtitle "For Independent Girls," again implying that *kawaii* emancipated its adopter. *Kawaii* in *CUTiE* was portrayed as something daring and rebellious, and the magazine published many photographs of young people wearing their own fashions on streets and in clubs (Godoy 2007).

A Logic of Its Own: Social Utility and Aesthetics

There is a point where the social utility of any look declines and fashion starts to lose its original meanings and becomes less focused on its original purpose.

Part of this was the co-option of *kawaii* into commercial advertising and by the state, diluting the challenge it originally made against these structures. Another part is the inevitable logic of fashion itself, constantly reworking the past without regard for any particular political agenda, in a perpetual desire for novelty.

A prime example is "idols" (*aidoru*), young manufactured stars, made famous not because of exceptional talent or beauty but rather because they are cute and cheerful. Early examples include Yamaguchi Momoe (debut 1973), Pink Lady (debut 1976), and Onyanko Club (debut 1985). Television helped to create this new type of star, as the medium demanded simply a pleasant looking brightness that could always be switched on. Idols filled this role perfectly. And their principle currency was *kawaii*. They were required to make the audience want to take care of them, support, and nurture their careers rather than be in awe of their beauty or talents. Arguably, movie stardom was about always remaining a mystery, but, on television, idols became popular through over-supply and cheerful familiarity. Knowledge of the way this new appeal worked became an entire business model, seen most clearly in the example of AKB48 that Patrick Galbraith discusses in his chapter. This logic of *kawaii* marketing is one way in which the previously rebellious and empowering look of *kawaii* became incorporated into corporate management structures and manipulated for profit.

Thus through gradual institutionalization, *kawaii* has become aesthetized, its meaning expanding until it was broad enough to include everything. But perhaps the absence of meaning was part of *kawaii* all along. As Yuko Hasegawa points out, there is an element of *kawaii* that resists final definition and mature identity. Even Hello Kitty, as analyzed in Chapter 3, has no mouth making her expression deliberately incomplete and ambiguous. As Tom Looser explains in Chapter 38, Murakami Takashi (1999) in his *Superflat Manifesto* spoke of "the shallow emptiness of Japanese consumer culture" in a way both celebratory and critical. Sugiyama (2006) concurs with this expansion of meaning to the point of meaninglessness, arguing the current usage of *kawaii* is rooted in Japan's consensus valuing culture. The word "*kawaii*" is now spoken as a form of group bonding, and it has become so broad in meaning that no one can dispute it.

Searching for a reason for this expanding logic, Ozaki Tetsuya (2011) conflates otaku culture and *kawaii* as two sides of the same thing. He argues *kawaii* is a mechanism for relieving stress in a society with great social pressure to conform, and it acts as a means of escape from a system that does not make people happy (Ozaki 2011: 54). Ozaki's reasoning is that *kawaii* is a response to the collapse of the grand narrative as understood by Jean-François Lyotard (1998)—the end of a single story of identity. In the postmodern absence of a grand narrative to give life meaning—such as that of the nation, or an Emperor, God, or possible Marxist revolution—*kawaii* provides a simple piece of absurd happiness, nostalgic for a childhood moment when the lack of meaning in life was not understood.

The Future of *Kawaii* Fashion

In 2010 and 2011 three major fashion exhibitions claimed to be represent-ative of Japanese contemporary fashion; yet all were very different. *Future Beauty: 30 Years of Japanese Fashion* at the Barbican Gallery in London (2010) dismissed *kawaii* as not real fashion, reserving the term for designers like Rei Kawakubo, Yohji Yamamoto, and Issey Miyake. The agenda was to reaffirm fashion as high art by means of belittling *kawaii* fashion as "childishness, sim-plicity... vulgarity, exaggeration, artificiality, and ornament" (Fukai 2010: 13). There was a lionization of the gesture to restore dignity to older women, an oft stated goal of the all black creations of Yamamoto in particular, that implied *kawaii* was one way this dignity had been taken away. *Japan Fashion Now* at the Museum of the Fashion Institute of Technology in New York (2010) took a more ecumenical approach, interspersing designer fashion with such subcultural styles as Lolita and cosplay, with the agenda of democratiz-ing fashion. It was also more sociologically focused, contextualizing fashions by dividing the exhibition into Tokyo neighborhoods and including photos of the places where the fashion might be worn (Motoaki 2011: 20). As Hiroshi Narumi describes, the third exhibition, *Feel and Think: A New Era of Tokyo Fashion* at the Opera City Gallery in Tokyo (2011), sought to establish a new canon of Japanese designers after the great names of the 1970s and to remove clothing from the context of the body. All the designers featured or referenced the *kawaii* culture in which Tokyo is awash.

These three exhibits contested whether fashion was popular culture or high art. The element of *kawaii* seemed to be the very thing that was prevent-ing fashion from being considered art. Yet this seems to be a somewhat old-fashioned, modernist distinction; whereas one of the key elements of *kawaii* is that it laughs at attempts at high seriousness, it undermines the assumed authority of such a classification, and, in doing so, shows how it is a social construction which can be torn down like all others. In much the same way as Susan Sontag (2001 [1964]) defines "camp" as an artifice and frivolity that plays upon naïve middle-class pretentiousness, *kawaii* can also be seen in fash-ion as an ironic attitude which acts as an explicit defense of clearly marginal-ized forms: gay culture in the case of camp and youth, particularly female, but not exclusively, in the case of *kawaii*. Both aesthetics depend on the hypocrisy of the dominant culture and show how norms are socially constructed. And both are in the form of a big joke: acutely analyzing norms and presenting them humorously to confront society with its own preconceptions. In fashion, *kawaii* would also appear to be a postmodern aesthetic, rejecting modernism's abstraction, unity, subtlety, and fidelity to the body and pulling towards post-modern fashion's arbitrary shapes, figurative patterns, and disunity.

The use of *kawaii* is not simply an act of self-objectification and the abdica-tion of maturity but a more complicated gesture of challenging the hierarchy of seriousness which holds cultural establishments in high regard. *Kawaii* is a knowing absence of maturity, as it has to understand what the construct of maturity involves in order to renounce it. In this way, *kawaii* constitutes not just the lack of maturity but an ironic expression of maturity's undesirability. It knowingly uses silliness, play, and irony to establish an alternative to rigid, perhaps fossilized, mainstream culture and sociopolitical establishment which no longer seems to appeal to Japanese youth. *Kawaii* fashion continues to serve this rebellious function, although it now also constitutes the cultural mainstream and has proliferated in unintended forms and meanings. But this is part of the mechanics of fashion: clothing fashions always exceed their original instrumentality (Carter 2013), and *kawaii* fashions now assume a vast space in Japan's cultural imagination. Yet the pleasure to be found in *kawaii* fashion remains the same: a knowing, reflexive, pleasure of undermining and ignoring the seriousness of hierarchical Japanese maturity.

36 Made in Japan

A New Generation of Fashion Designers

Hiroshi Narumi

Introduction

Since the 1990s, Japanese fashion has experienced a dramatic upheaval as the globalization of fashion retail and production and the recession of Japanese economy have threatened its very existence. Fast fashion, cheaper Chinese production, and international (usually European) luxury brands have overwhelmed the domestic market; albeit targeting different consumer brackets, and the number of Japanese apparel companies and factories has significantly declined (Yamazaki 2011). For example, Tokyo's high-end Ginza neighborhood is lined with both expensive boutique shops of international luxury brands like the American Tiffany & Co. and the French Hermes, and large fast-fashion outlets like Sweden's H&M and Japan's own Uniqlo (short for "Unique Clothing"). With foreign brands dominating the high-end of the market and many consumers desiring the cheap but acceptable quality of fast fashion, Japanese mid-price clothing has become increasingly unpopular. The mid-range Japanese brands that used to fill department stores and shopping plazas have attracted fewer customers, and the department store itself, as a symbol of middle-class fashion aspiration, has experienced a decline.

In this chapter, I discuss Japanese fashion designers' creative, conceptual, and industrial responses to this existential threat. They have led to a redefinition of the concept of "Made in Japan" in the age of globalized fashion by basing their philosophies on Japanese culture and traditions, instead of following the latest trends from Paris, Milan, and New York, as fast fashion does with increasing speed and efficiency. For instance, the fashion brand matohu[1] developed a new type of clothing—*nagagi*. *Nagagi*, literally "long coat," is a flat form inspired by kimono patterns (see Figure 36.1). However, the fabric design has been modernized to suit T-shirts, jeans, and other common clothing. While matohu has offered a new series of *nagagi* each season, the shape has not changed. They hope the *nagagi* will be a timeless form that can be created in different fabrics and worn for years without going out of style.

Other designers share matohu's concept of "timelessness." Some fashion brands prefer to start from materials. For example, minä perhonen is known for its sophisticated fabrics and poetic textile designs. The designer Minagawa

Figure 36.1 Nagagi, a long coat from matohu's 2005 collection.
Source: Courtesy of matohu.

Akira has drawn almost every sketch and has discussed the processes of weaving, dying, printing, and embroidering with artisans. He aspires to create new "basics," clothes that can be worn on a daily basis. Although their clothes are expensive due to their craftsmanship, minä perhonen is supported by ardent customers. Another point I will make is that, while keeping a distance from the trends of the global fashion system and producing original clothes, some independent Japanese designers have sought an alternative way of making clothes by developing networks with customers. It is possible to say that they have rediscovered their own sense of "locality."

I have interviewed Japanese designers in Tokyo and Kyoto for several years. In addition, I helped curate the 2011 exhibition *Feel and Think: A New Era of Tokyo Fashion* (*Kanjiru fuku kangaeru fuku: Tokyo fasshon no genzaikei*), focusing on the works of ten fashion brands that stood out in the 2000s.[2] This exhibition focused on the emergence of a new generation after the long domination of three distinguished brands in the Japanese market and public imagination—Issey Miyake, Yohji Yamamoto, and Comme des Garçons (founded by Rei Kawakubo)—and showcased their new strategies and creative forms. This chapter extends that research and examines six brands considered to be the forerunners of a new generation of fashion designers in the 2000s: minä perhonen, mintdesigns, matohu, SOU·SOU, h.NAOTO, and keisuke kanda. minä perhonen, literally "my butterfly" in Finnish, was launched in 1995 by Minagawa Akira, who claims an affinity with Scandinavian culture and design. mintdesigns was founded by Katsui Hokuto and Yagi Nao in 2001 to create clothing that can be worn for a long time, regardless of the latest trends. matohu, with a double meaning of "to wear" and "to wait," was established in 2005 by a pair of designers, who trained at Comme des Garçons and Yohji Yamamoto, to show respect for the thoughtfulness of the design process. SOU·SOU, "yes, yes" in Japanese, was formed in 2002 by three designers who hoped to create a "new Japanese culture." Hirooka Naoto launched h.NAOTO in 2000 to remix various subcultural elements from punk and goth to Lolita, attracting Visual-kei musical performers who have been known to dress flamboyantly and to overturn gender binaries in fashion. Kanda Keisuke established his eponymous brand in 2005 and has offered *kawaii* (cute) styles for young women with whom he has established a network of support.

I will first survey the situation facing Japanese fashion in the early twenty-first century. Second, I will explore how these six brands have reinventing traditions and established networking with customers. Through this analysis, I will show how Japanese clothing designers have negotiated the tensions between the global and the local. Although these fashion brands are not necessarily popular among the general public in terms of sales, their creativity has been highly appreciated by journalists, buyers for shops, and fashion-conscious customers such that they occupy a large place in the Japanese fashion system via their influence. Whether ordinary consumers realize it or not, their clothing, and the images of clothing around them in popular culture, has been inspired by these brands.

Japanese Fashion in Transition

Especially since the 1990s, many international luxury brands, some under the ownership of the French LVMH conglomerate (Moët Hennessy–Louis Vuitton S.A., founded in 1987), have opened flagship stores in major Japanese cities. These boutiques are housed in eye-catching buildings by well-known architects, as exemplified by Louis Vuitton Omotesando, designed by Aoki Jun and opened in 2002. These luxury brands extended their market from Europe and the United States to Asia while making their products more appealing to Asian consumers via small cultural localizations. For instance, acknowledging their huge Japanese clientele, Louis Vuitton collaborated with Murakami Takashi to produce an original line of handbags in 2003 (see Chapter 38). This line netted over US$350 million for Louis Vuitton, and high-profile international celebrities like Madonna and Gwyneth Paltrow were seen proudly carrying the bags (Betts 2003).

Concurrently, inexpensive fast fashion became widely available to Japanese consumers. Uniqlo, the most successful Japanese fast-fashion brand, has a ubiquitous presence, with more than 800 stores found everywhere nationwide, from affluent fashion districts like Tokyo's Ginza to local train stations.[3] There are also around 140 stores in more than fourteen different countries, especially in Asia (Uniquely Positioned 2010). Uniqlo is especially remarkable in its innovation of pragmatic, high-tech materials, such as "heat-tech" (thermal undershirts) and synthetic fleece. Uniqlo offers clothing of the same design in a range of colors, has ties with Japanese and international designers and artists, and features global popular culture phenomena well known in Japan, from Moomins to Barbie. Furthermore, international fast-fashion brands, including H&M and Zara, have opened stores all over Japan as well as in other parts of Asia. This clothing has been called "real clothes" (*rearu kurōzu*) because of its affordability and wearability.

The fast-fashion business model reflects the current age of globalization in terms of production, distribution, and consumption. In order to reduce financial risk as well as production costs, these fashion labels outsource the production planning, raw material production, and manufacturing processes of their "real clothes" to cheap labor in China, Vietnam, and other East and Southeast Asian countries. Vertical integration of the different stages of clothing production also means that the time needed from design to retail can be as short as two weeks. The arrival of retail stock is designed so that there is always something new for customers to see, even if they visit the shop weekly. Many local Japanese manufacturers—dying and weaving factories, tailors, and even department stores—have not been able to compete with such overwhelming integration and resultant price competition and have gone bankrupt.

From the late 1990s, the international media started to notice Tokyo street subcultures, such as those intertwined with anime, manga, cosplay (costume play), and "decorative" (*decora*) popular culture. Especially to younger generations worldwide, Japanese fashion has become more about street fashion and less about high-profile designers such as Issey Miyake and Comme des Garçons (Keet 2007; Steele et al. 2010).

In this socioeconomic climate, the Japanese designers who were successful in the conspicuous consumption that characterized the 1980s bubble economy era have faced financial difficulties. In 2006, the Japanese Department of Commerce became the primary financial sponsor for Tokyo Fashion Week, which was then reorganized to become Japan Fashion Week Tokyo (JFW). Its declared goals included making Japanese designers better known to the rest of the world, as well as nurturing young Japanese talent (Mercedes-Benz Fashion Week Tokyo). However, few international buyers and journalists came to JFW; therefore, it failed to produce many business opportunities. In 2010, the Department of Commerce terminated its financial support for the event. Mercedes-Benz took over sponsorship starting from the spring/summer 2011 shows.[4] In contrast to the declining influence of JFW, a new fashion event aimed at teenaged girls, "Tokyo Girls Collection" (Tokyo Gāruzu Korekushon, sometimes abbreviated as TGC), was launched in 2005 and was open to the general public. Most participating brands have been apparel companies that follow the latest trends and provide inexpensive "real clothes" by adopting the process inspired by fast fashion. TGC has been widely welcomed by their target market, but fashion designers who value creative achievement over commercial success have lost potential customers and a showcase platform. In reaction, the brands discussed below have rejected the premise of cheap, rapidly changing fashion and, in the process, have redefined Japanese fashion and its role within popular culture.

Timeless Clothing and Textile Making: minä perhonen and mintdesigns

In the fashion climate of the early 2000s described above, the goals of opening boutiques in Japan or entering fashion shows in Paris, New York, or Milan became less obtainable for young designers. A significant number of designers staged collection shows in the late 1980s. While profitable for some, it was, at that time, seen as a necessary step in internationalizing a brand. Forgoing this dream of internationalization and responding to the threat of fast fashion, some designers have made long-lasting and innovative clothes using Japanese materials and have primarily targeted a Japanese market. minä perhonen and mintdesigns have exemplified this strategy by making their own original textiles covered with their own graphics in local factories.

In other words, these brands have emphasized the creative process of producing clothes. In the current fashion system, brands tend to buy materials from textile companies rather than making them themselves. Despite their limited financial resources, minä perhonen and mintdesigns have created original fabrics by dyeing, weaving, and making lace and embroidery in collaboration with local artisans. These designers claim that ready-made textiles make clothes seem ordinary; with original textiles, they can produce something special (Takagi et al. eds. 2012: 116).

While a design student, founder Minagawa Akira traveled to Scandinavia, where he felt a creative affinity with cultures and lifestyles. His brand aims to produce exceptional, enduring daily-use clothing (minä perhonen 2011: 12). From the start, Minagawa has collaborated with local Japanese manufacturers to create textiles based on his original graphic designs: hand-drawn sketches that are woven, dyed, or embroidered. In an interview, Minagawa claims that the historically close relationship between designers and craftspeople distinguishes Japanese fashions from those produced in North America, Europe, and Australia:

> I think the borders between Japan and the rest of the world do not exist anymore. Having said this, I know about Japanese artisans and their excellent manufacturing environment. In the West, designers use premanufactured fabrics for their work. In Japan, designers are in a position to order specific kinds of fabrics for their creations. This close relation with their clients is something unique to Japanese fabric manufacturers.
> (Takagi et al. eds. 2012: 96)

Minagawa thinks it important to make clothes with artisans in accord with local manufacturers to maintain originality and to support Japanese traditional industries. He stockpiles the textiles used in past collections and even reuses some in new designs, a practice rare for fashion brands. Minagawa explains his rationale:

> I would like to make soulful clothes that the wearer can cherish for many years, instead of changing every season under the unspoken rules of the fashion cycle. Because I have created the original designs for our textiles, I have re-used the same designs in various collections over an extended period of time. It is normal to treat a design as outdated after it is used for a season's collection. I would like to challenge this notion to see if any of my designs will look outdated.
>
> (Takagi et al. eds. 2012: 95)

After graduating from Central Saint Martins College of Art and Design in London, Katsui Hokuto and Yagi Nao established mintdesigns to create products that transcend short fashion cycles and become a long-term part of the wearer's life. They have manufactured their own original fabrics and printed patterns, characterized by colorful palettes, bold patterns, and simple yet distinctive shapes and forms. Their playful approach to design is reflected in their signature decorative motifs, such as a little girl holding a pair of scissors or original buttons made of paper. Yagi explains the importance of making original textiles:

> We didn't have to make our own fabrics. But an item of clothing will always look cheap if it's made of an inexpensive, mass-produced fabric. Even if the cutting of the garment is well done, it will still look like something we've seen somewhere else. It is wonderful to see a garment with the perfect harmony of great patternmaking, design, and graphics.
>
> (Takagi et al. eds. 2012: 113–116)

mintdesigns creates a variety of other goods, including bags, wallets, pencil cases, and chairs. Their philosophy is to design clothes as products. They have been inspired by Fukuzawa Naoto, the leading product designer for Muji, a Japanese brand known for its modern and timeless products.[5]

Thus by deliberately ignoring global trends, minä perhonen and mintdesigns have created their own styles from fabric to clothes. According to Yagi:

> In the apparel-making industry, it's usually very difficult to develop a new material from scratch unless you have a sufficient budget. But in our case, we carefully study how we can produce our own materials within the means at our disposal. We work closely with manufacturers and give them various suggestions so that they can produce our material in a small batch.
>
> (Takagi et al. eds. 2012: 113)

Some local factories are willing to work with young designers regardless of low profits. While many craftspeople at these factories are now quite old, designers hope to continue their traditions and make them alternatives to mainstream global fashions.

Reinventing Japanese Aesthetics: matohu and SOU·SOU

Some Japanese designers have tried to rediscover the aesthetic possibilities of kimono, a garment often viewed as premodern, outdated, and no longer everyday clothing. To them, wearing kimono liberates the body from Western-style clothing. However, it is difficult to combine kimono with other global fashions, as their constructions have derived from different cultures. Although there have been many fashions worldwide that have attempted to modernize kimono, most have been superficial mimicries lacking deep understanding of Japanese aesthetics. Two fashion brands, matohu and SOU·SOU, have attained this remarkable achievement by shedding new

Figure 36.2 Keii, the SOU·SOU men's line, 2015.
Source: Courtesy of SOU·SOU.

light on Japanese traditions. For example, Horihata Hiroyuki and Sekiguchi Makiko, the founders of matohu, have researched Japanese history. The double meaning of *"matohu"* reflects their desire to spend time fostering their own aesthetics thus requiring customers "to wait."

matohu's brand identity lies in reinventing Japanese aesthetics. In 2005, Horihata and Sekiguchi decided that the main theme of their collection of the next five years would be the "Beauty of Keichō." It is unusual for fashion brands to decide their themes this far in advance; instead they commonly decide seasonal themes according to current trends and the market. The matohu designers believed the Keichō period (1596–1615), when many classical arts like tea ceremony, ceramics, and painting developed, to be the golden age of Japanese culture. However, matohu did not transmit any nostalgia for the past or intend to emphasize Orientalist aesthetics for the Western market. Horihata explains their philosophy:

> Some people misunderstand our brand, thinking it is based on traditional Japanese decorative motifs. Our designs do not include any decorative motifs and patterns that you see on kimono. Instead, we want to create contemporary yet timeless pieces of clothing that can only be made by Japanese sensibility.
>
> (Takagi et al. eds. 2012: 85)

SOU·SOU (Figure 36.2), was jointly established in 2002 in Kyoto by fashion designer Wakabayashi Takeshi, textile designer Wakisaka Katsuji, and interior designer Tsujimura Hisanobu. Wakisaka worked in Finland and the United States for about two decades, and he received recognition abroad before returning to Japan. Together, they have made various goods, including clothing, shoes, textiles, and furniture and have had a tie-in with Uniqlo (starting in 2013). As Wakabayashi stated in a personal interview, the fast-fashion giant Uniqlo approached SOU·SOU to ask permission to use its existing textile designs for their products. Wakabayashi said that, although the tie-in products were mass-produced and made in China and thus against SOU·SOU's founding principles, he agreed because this was a valuable opportunity to get the attention of a large market. Uniqlo has often collaborated with promising designers and brands, including mintdesigns. Although such collaborations are usually limited in one season, the tie-in project has continued for years, demonstrating SOU·SOU's lasting presence in the mass market.

SOU·SOU's brand philosophy is to revive Japanese tradition within contemporary lifestyles (Wakabayashi 2013). Their clothes are characterized by a combination of modern-style textiles and the flat-form construction of traditional costumes. Their most popular product is *tabi* shoes. *Tabi* are traditional work shoes, with a separate big toe, used by such manual workers as carpenters and construction workers; they have also been worn in local festivals. SOU·SOU revived *tabi* as whimsical sneakers with contemporary textile patterns, as shown in Figure 36.2. SOU·SOU works with local factories and craftspeople who would have otherwise faced financial difficulties in the globalizing economy. They claim that their task is to protect these factories from bankruptcy.[6]

Both matohu and SOU·SOU have reassessed the aesthetics of historical Japanese clothing. Unlike designers in the previous generation, such as Mori Hanae in the 1960s and Yamamoto Kansai in the 1970s, they do not deliberately "orientalize" their culture in order to get attention from European and American journalists. Rather, as Horihata of matohu stated:

> We decided to create a brand that existed outside of the Western historical context but which was not an "avant-garde" philosophy. We wanted to pursue new forms of expression using non-Western apparel making techniques. We wanted to create clothes that would allow wearers to feel connected with the past while satisfying their desire for something contemporary and timeless.
>
> (Takagi et al. eds. 2012: 80)

Forming Affective Communities of Designers and Customers: h.NAOTO and keisuke kanda

Various Japanese youth subcultures, such as Lolita, cosplay, and Visual-kei, have been famous for their spectacular looks; shared clothing tastes unites their members. In other words, these groups' appearances are their identity as well as the symbol of their bonds. According to Kawamura Yuniya (2012), fashion brands have played a crucial role in the rise of the subcultures in Japan. This effort has been supported by business practices that help form emotional bonds among designers and their customers. h.NAOTO and keisuke kanda have forged affective networks with customers through activities related to their fashions. These relationships between the brands and their fans are so intense that they feel an intimate fellowship, which is different from a commercial relationship between brands and consumers.

Designer h.NAOTO's (real name Hirooka Naoto) hybridized subcultural style that combined Goth, Lolita, and punk and peaked in popularity in the early 2000s. His customers, mainly teenage girls, made pilgrimages to his boutiques, where parties, fashion shows, and concerts were held. As Hirooka explained, "In fact, girls don't have a lot of places where they can wear h.NAOTO, except when they go to Harajuku or to the concerts and special events. When girls from small towns outside of Tokyo come to our events, they change their clothes in the bathrooms of train station and slip into their h.NAOTO's outfits. They are so sincere, and that makes me happy" (Takagi et al. eds. 2012: 50).

h.NAOTO's rise to prominence coincided with the emergence of Visual-kei and Gothic Lolita subcultures. Immediately following its 2000 launch, the label caught the eye of such Visual-kei musicians as Luna Sea and L'arc en Ciel and their fans. The brand is credited with inventing the new style of "punk Gothic-Lolita." Since then, h.NAOTO has grown to encompass thirty different brands in response to the demands of its young clientele. Each of these "sub-brands" caters to a specific style inspired by looks like goth, cosplay, otaku, and anime, helping to unify members of a subculture through fashion.

Hirooka made the styles of various subcultures widely accessible to Japanese teenagers, crafting a decadently pop and kitsch universe. He commented, "First and foremost, my policy is to provide what my customers are looking for. As a designer, my job is not about transmitting or imposing my vision on the consumer. Rather, I would like to form a bond with my customers and exchange inspirations with them" (Takagi et al. eds. 2012: 50). This successful domestic brand has also gained popularity in the United States and Asia thanks to the export of manga, anime, and Lolita fashions. h.NAOTO took its first step toward global expansion by opening a store in San Francisco in October 2011, which closed in March 2013.

Designer Kanda Keisuke's eponymous brand (using lowercase k)[7] is famous for its "cute girl" style. His clothes have been inspired by Lolita fashion, high-school uniforms, and mini dresses, along with other styles popular among teenaged girls. He has often made his clothes by hand and claims that his clothes are love letters to his customers (Takagi et al. eds. 2012: 62). From the beginning, Kanda has traveled all over Japan for exhibits and pre-orders, while enjoying conversations with customers. The brand views building a network with its fans as central to its business model and brand philosophy.

In 2005, Kanda established the Candyrock Company. He started to make clothes during his college days at the prestigious Waseda University, and, even then, his unique business operation sets his label apart from his contemporaries. While keisuke kanda has expanded to produce factory-manufactured clothing, the designer continues to make customized and hand-sewn items. The number of his couture clients has grown to more than one thousand thanks to word-of-mouth marketing (Takagi et al. eds. 2012: 62).

Kanda thinks it more important to cultivate close ties to his customers in Japan than to succeed abroad. He confesses that his clothes depend on the taste of fans:

In my case, I do not have that kind of concern toward the West. I started engaging myself with fashion because I wanted to make a dress for the girl I liked…. I still do not know what *kawaii* stands for. One thing I do know for sure is that I love girls, and *kawaii* is a feeling that all girls tend to cherish… I am searching for this intangible quality. When I create women's clothes, I often ask girls for their opinions. 'Look, I don't really understand what I'm making. Do you think these are *kawaii*?' Actually, I am not interested in expressing my own aesthetics at all. All I'm doing is seeking approval from girls.

(Takagi et al. eds. 2012: 64–65)

h.NAOTO and keisuke kanda seem more concerned with their specific local contexts than with the norms of the global fashion system. Designers are often charismatic figures, telling their consumers what to wear and providing a top-down understanding of fashion. Yet both these brands are premised more on horizontal interpersonal relationships rather than on vertical hierarchies of power. Theirs could be a more useful strategy to attract customers than mass-produced, fast-fashion brands that garner no lasting loyalty.

Conclusion

The brands I discuss differ in terms of designs, goals, business scales, customers, and philosophies. However, the new wave of Japanese designers of the early 2000s has three main points in common: first, they have been inspired by various aspects of Japanese traditional and contemporary culture, including textiles, craftsmanship, aesthetics, kimono, and subcultures. Previous designers, for example, Mori Hanae and Yamamoto Kansai, also adopted Japanese traditional arts and decorative motives, but, arguably, they did so to attract Euro-American journalists and buyers. Born and raised in an era of economic prosperity, the new wave of designers neither feels nostalgia toward the past nor an inferiority complex toward the West for not having established their careers by garnering international attention. Instead, they have incorporated aspects of Japanese culture and tradition to stand out in the domestic market. (After the closure of h.NAOTO's San Francisco shop in 2013, SOU·SOU is currently the only one of the brands discussed to operate an overseas store.)

Second, designers in the 2000s are incongruous with the existing fashion system that constantly fabricates the latest trends and discards products every six months. On one hand, fashion concentrates on the present. On the other hand, the designers of minä perhonen and matohu claim to make timeless pieces. minä perhonen has reused textiles in their stock, and matohu has produced a regular long coat of the same shape every season. The designers of h.NAOTO and keisuke kanda have been inspired by their customers' particular desires. Neither has participated in Paris, New York, or Milan collections, and thus they do not use the means by which information about fashion has historically spread. It can be said that these designers more or less share an "anti-fashion ethos" in that they consider the significance of their clothes in terms of a longer timescale.

Third, they have sought their own ways to produce clothes. Many of the above designers have collaborated with Japanese artisans, who, in turn, have worked to realize what young creators want to make, thereby updating their artistic traditions. Apparel companies outsource their work abroad to cut production costs; however, these designers prefer to work with Japanese factories. While supporting the domestic economy, they have shown respect for craftsmanship and have helped its continuance. In addition, these brands have used strategies to form relationships directly with their customers, rather than merely resorting to commercial outlets to promote their work. As opposed to the conventional one-way relationship to consumers, they have held parties, exhibitions, and lectures to promote communication. Affective community may become a more important means for independent brands to establish their businesses.

As these six brands are diverse, it is impossible to label them under a single category. While some designers are concerned with traditional aesthetics, others are not. Some brands are reasonably priced so that teenagers can afford to buy them. Others are expensive enough to be only for sophisticated fashion-conscious adults. However, most brands are struggling to pursue creativity in the market dominated by cheap clothes and expensive bags with logos. It is not easy for independent creative designers to survive in such harsh commercial competition. They have not followed the paths of the likes of Miyake, Yamamoto, and Kawakubo, and instead have had to find reasonable profits in the shrinking economy of the domestic market. Their mobilization of the Japanese local resources, shaped by both artistic legacies and their current socioeconomic and creative context, has enabled them to develop specific identities and to have a lasting impact on the definition of Japanese fashion. It is these brands, their designs, and their ideas that will ultimately set the direction of popular fashion and its place in popular culture in Japan.

Notes

1 Many Japanese brand names use lowercase letters reflecting how Japanese language uses capital letters for emphasis in ways different from English.

2 The exhibition *Feel and Think: A New Era of Tokyo Fashion* was held at the Tokyo Opera City Art Gallery (October 18–December 25, 2011). It was then installed in the Kobe Fashion Museum (January 14–April 1, 2012), followed by the National Art School Gallery, Sydney, (June 20–August 17, 2013). This chapter derives from my research for the exhibition and the catalogue (see Takagi et al. 2012). I would like to thank the other curators: Takagi Yoko, Nishitani Mariko, and Hori Motoaki. I am also grateful to translators: Tamura Yuki, Tamura Maki, and Ishida Chihiro.

3 Uniqlo opened its first Unique Clothing Warehouse store in 1984 in Hiroshima, not Tokyo. The brand is now under the Japanese parent company Fast Retailing.

4 When Mercedes-Benz became the main sponsor, the title of Japan Fashion Week was changed to Mercedes-Benz Fashion Week Tokyo (MBFWT). The word Japan was removed.

5 Muji, or "Mujirushi ryōhin" ("No brand" or generic) was established in 1980 as part of Seiyu, one of Japan's biggest supermarket chains. Muji is a larger firm than the clothing designers discussed in this chapter and has made a wide range of mass-produced goods from stationery and clothing to furniture and prefabricated houses. Although its clothing line is popular, Muji is not thought of primarily as an apparel company.

6 According to my interview with Wakabayashi of SOU•SOU, the tie-in with Uniqlo does not apply to this case.

7 Like many other Japanese fashion designers, h.NAOTO and keisuke kanda follow the English style of writing first names before surnames. They use English letters as a means to express their imagined self-image.

37 Clean-Cut

Men's Fashion Magazines, Male Aesthetic Ideals, and Social Affinity in Japan

Masafumi Monden

Seemingly small changes in men's fashion magazines in Japan in 2012 provide insights into conceptions of masculinity. *Popeye* (launched 1976), underwent a makeover, going back to its original formula as "a magazine for city boys" (its tagline) and re-emphasizing its preference for European luxury brands, cultural content, and non-Asian models. Around the same time, *Men's non-no* (launched 1986), another quintessential men's fashion magazine, also went back to its basics, but the result was nearly the opposite: it increasingly encompassed casual, more down-to-earth aspects of young men's styles and expanded the presence of Japanese models.

What makes Japanese men's fashion magazines striking is their almost full focus on men's bodies and appearance. John Clammer (1997: 122) writes about the emphasis on fashion and appearance placed by these magazines. According to Clammer, such magazines are largely absent in Euro-American heterosexual men's culture. Valerie Steele (2000: 78) further highlights the particularity of Japanese men's fashion magazines, finding that, with the exception of certain European titles and regardless of their inclusion of fashion contents, Anglophone men's magazines such as *GQ* "could not really be considered fashion magazines." As Steele (2000: 78) argues, "the rhetoric on men's fashion (both within the magazines and in the wider Anglo-American culture) is based on an adamant denial that men are interested in fashion." Anglophone men's magazines are rarely referred to as fashion magazines due to "the importance of appearance and dress in definitions of femininity and the feminine gendering of fashion" (Rocamora 2009: 61). Therefore, magazines with fashion contents primarily targeted at men (and/or at unisex readerships) are instead called "lifestyle magazines."

Representations of "masculinity" in magazines targeted toward men reflect and shape cultural ideas of gender. Indeed, Paul Jobling (1999: 2) claims that much fashion photography and related media, "beckons us into a world of unbridled fantasies by placing fashion and the body in any number of discursive contexts." Such media has "either little or nothing to do with clothing, or else clothing itself seems to become an alibi for the representation of other contemporaneous issues and ideas." Fashion discourses, as produced through media texts like fashion magazines, moreover "are themselves shaped by, and dependent on, wider social forces and their relations with other fields" (Rocamora 2009: 58). Agnès Rocamora (2009: 58) argues that "statements about femininity in the field of fashion are not particular to this field but more generally inform discourses on women in today's society." Furthering Rocamura's argument, we can deduce that Japanese men's fashion magazines are a measure of the manifestation of Japanese conceptions of masculinity.

I outline the history of contemporary Japanese men's fashion magazines and explain how they correspond with various subtly nuanced styles. Then I examine how magazines use male models to create an affinity with their readers. These models can represent a slender, boyish, and *kawaii* male aesthetic, which, along with more muscular male ideals found in other sectors of Japanese culture, may be indicative of Japanese popular culture's elastic approach to the representations of masculinity. I then explore the amalgam of three desires men's fashion magazines evoke in readers in relation to men's fashionability: (1) to attract women's admiration, (2) to compete with and emulate other men, and (3) to simply indulge in their own pleasures. Because fashion media are constantly evolving, it is important to observe how these magazines respond to changing notions of masculinity and publishing.

A Brief History of Men's Fashion Magazines in Japan

Otokono fukushoku (meaning men's clothing but renamed as *Men's Club* in 1963) is considered to be one of the first Japanese men's fashion magazines. It was launched in 1954 by the publishing house, Fujingahō, as the first Japanese men's magazine for prêt-à-porter clothes. The magazine *Danshi senka* (*Men's Special Course*, 1950–1993) began earlier but was predominantly targeted at tailors (Ishizu 2010: 54–55). Featuring young athletes and actors like Akagi Keiichiro, as well as professional models like Ide Masakatsu, *Men's Club* at its beginning was particularly well known for its ties with the Japanese version of "Ivy-League" style, a fashion style inspired by students of American Ivy League universities in the 1950s and 1960s and Ishizu Kensuke's legendary brand VAN.

The current form of Japanese fashion magazines is said to have begun with the women's lifestyle magazine *An An* (launched in 1970). *An An*, along with its competitor *Non-no* (1971), both primarily consumed by women in their late teens and early twenties (Sakamoto 1999: 178), marked a shift from women's main conceptualization as housewives and mothers towards "consumers of fashion and luxury items" (Darling-Wolf 2006: 185). Its focus on consumption and visually-oriented contents have established various trends for men's magazines (Tanaka 2003: 224). A proliferation of men's fashion, starting around 1986, coincided with the launch of such men's fashion magazines as *Men's non-no* and *Fineboys*. Subsequently, Japan witnessed the rise and fall of many men's fashion magazines, including *Hot-Dog Press* (1979–2004), *Mr. High Fashion* (1980–2003), *smart* (1995–present), and *Street Jack* (1997–present). These titles, and the speed of their creation and demise, attest to Japanese men's interest in fashion and their financial capacity to indulge it starting from the mid-1980s.

Men's magazines offer several sartorial variations; there are a number of unofficial style categories, each with corresponding fashion magazines. This makes a multitude of modes of masculinity available (*Elastic* 2008). These styles include "*kireime*" (meaning neat and conservative, or fashion beginner) exemplified by *Fineboys*; "Casual-high fashion" (a mode stylistically similar to *kireime* but involving more expensive brand-name clothing and flamboyant coordinates) exemplified by *Men's non-no* and *Popeye*; and the luxury brands promoted by such magazines as *Vogue Hommes Japan* (2008–2012). In addition, there are magazines that showcase street fashions and subcultures, such as the monthly *Tune* (2004), a male equivalent to *FRUiTS* (1997) that largely features women. In all these magazines, fashion dominates over lifestyle content by more than 50 percent, and more than 70 percent in the case of *Popeye* (Monden 2012b: 300).

The types of models these magazines use reflect their attitudes toward men's fashion. For example, once preferring non-Asian and Eurasian models, *Men's non-no* has, as previously mentioned, gone back to its original ethnic aesthetic when the magazine photographed primarily Japanese models, such as Abe Hiroshi, Kazama Tōru, Tanihara Shōsuke, and Tanabe Sei'ichi. It is a Japanese magazine industry convention for a magazine to use the same models in every issue over long periods, establishing a particular look and trading off the popularity of models.[1] With their new model policies, both *Popeye* and *Men's non-no*'s makeovers seem to be successful. For one quick indication, *Popeye*, *Fineboys*, and *Men's non-no* ranked first, second, and third respectively in monthly men's fashion magazines ranking by *Honto* one of the largest online bookstores in Japan (*Honto rankingu*).

One might, however, wonder why some of these magazines, which are targeted mainly at Japanese men, feature non-Asian, let alone non-Japanese, models. Arguably, images of Euro-American culture presented in contemporary Japan, particularly those associated with the concepts of beauty and appearance, often blend with and reflect Japanese aesthetic preferences (Miller 2006: 149). Supporting this view, both non-Asian and Japanese models deployed in the Japanese magazines outline a popular mode of masculinity in contemporary Japan; namely, it values ideals of extreme slenderness and youthfulness. Furthermore, the presence of amateur models (*dokusha* models, literally "reader models") in magazines further endorses this mode of male image.

Amateur and Exclusive Models: Representing Male Aesthetic Ideals

Conventionally, amateur models are those whose main professions are other than fashion model; for example, many are students, shop assistants, and beauty stylists (Monden 2012a). Depending on magazines' editorial preferences, amateur models tend to differ from exclusive models in that their body shapes are closer to those of average Japanese men. For example, my data, largely compiled in 2010, 2011, and 2014, indicated that amateur models in *Choki Choki* generally have daintier bodies than models in *Men's non-no* (Monden 2012a, 2014: 54). The average ages of the models in both magazines are similar: twenty-three in *Choki Choki* and twenty-one in *Men's non-no*. But the average height of amateur models in *Choki Choki* is 173.2 cm (5 feet 8 inches) while that of *Men's non-no* models is 182.7 cm (6 feet). There is a gap of 10 cm (4 inches) between the tallest and shortest models in *Men's non-no*, but the gap is 15 cm (6 inches) in *Choki Choki*. This indicates that there are more physical variations in models in *Choki Choki* than models in *Men's non-no* whose body sizes are more uniform. This point is also applicable to *Fineboys*, whose former and current models like Matsuzaka Tori (183 cm [6 feet]), Nakajima Yuto (178 cm, [5 feet 10 inches]), and Hasegawa Jun (175 cm [5 feet 9 inches]) are taller than average Japanese men. But the magazine occasionally runs features like "A Style Selection Camp for Boys Under 170 cm (5 feet 7 inches) to Whom We Can't Lose" (Zettaini makerarenai, U-170 daihyō no fukuerabi gashuku!) (*Fineboys* 2011: 120–127), in which shorter amateur models, such as university student Kitamura Ryō (169 cm [5 feet 6.5 inches]), show style coordinates that can make them look taller. A 2012 survey conducted by the Japanese Ministry of Health, Labor, and Welfare (2014) indicates that the average height of Japanese men between the ages of nineteen and twenty-nine, the target demographic of these magazines, is 171.3 cm (5 feet 7.5 inches). This endorses Toby Slade's (2010: 549) argument that Japanese fashion magazines "rely on the notions of looks or categories with much more instructional text than their European counterparts," acknowledging magazines' readers who are much smaller than their exclusive models. Therefore, these magazines attempt to address realistic concerns in addition to promoting ideals.

The relative synchronicity between models and average men illuminates differences between Japanese and Anglo-European men's fashion cultures. Joanne Entwistle makes two points in relation to Euro-American high-fashion male models: first, "[t]he model's body, his look, is the product of nature, although his 'beauty' is most definitely cultural, produced as 'beautiful' by being chosen and valued within the fashion modeling world." Second, "[t]he lack of correspondence between the male fashion model's beauty and ideals of male beauty outside is evident" (Entwistle 2009: 200). Thus it can be deduced that the Euro-American fashion media in which these male models appear may not create a sense of congruency with their readers. Considering Entwistle's argument, the inclusion of models whose body sizes are closer to average Japanese men is significant because it demonstrates the magazines' sensitivity to social changes and trends and their desire to create a rapport between readers, models, and one preferred mode of masculinity in contemporary Japan.

Fabienne Darling-Wolf (2006: 189) has found that while *Non-no* constructs a visual and verbal discourse focusing on female friendship, its counterpart

Men's non-no shows models physically disconnected from one another, perhaps displaying prevalent notions of masculinity characterized by such traits as aggression, competitiveness, emotional ineptitude, and coldness (Itō 1993: 30–31; Nixon 1997: 296). While the magazine data I collected between 2007 and 2010 confirms Darling-Wolf's arguments, this has changed with the magazine's reinstatement of Japanese models. Now these men are more frequently presented in each other's company, smiling or chatting. Smiling male models are more prevalent in magazines like *Fineboys* that use amateur models. Such smiling men, which Susan Alexander (2003: 541) has termed "wholesome masculinity," provides an alternative to Susan Bordo's (2000: 129) idea of a binary mode of poses in which men are portrayed: "face-off," a hard and assertive masculine mode and "lean," an objectified, passive masculine mode.

"Wholesome masculinity" shows male models as unafraid of revealing their vulnerability (Alexander 2003: 541). This is important as male models are conventionally pictured in fashion media as having cold disdain in the "face-off" position. This manner accentuates a mode of masculinity that seems "powerful, armored emotionally impenetrable" (Bordo 2000: 186), hence portraying men as apathetic and machine-like (Attwood 2005: 88). If the "face-off" mode operates as armor for men, preventing them from revealing their vulnerability, representations of smiling boys in Japanese fashion magazines may indicate the increased acceptance of men who are sidestepping the contradictory interpellations from the hard/passive dichotomy that informs much societal discourse on what it means to be a man. It needs to be noted that fashion magazines do not mirror the society where they originated (Pollock 2003 [1988]: 8), but instead reflect the aims, biases, and ideologies of their creators/editors/transmitters and are intended to sell products. Nonetheless, these magazines reconstruct and convey notions of gender to their readers (Alexander 2003: 540). Men's fashion magazines also provide a view into how Japanese conceptions of youthful masculinity are manifested in popular culture. The increased embrace of "wholesome masculinity," combined with the slender, boyish bodies, contributes to the popularity of "*kawaii*," a certain kind of cute as a mode of male aesthetic sensitivity in mainstream Japanese fashion culture.

While the nature of *kawaii* is broad and difficult to specifically define (McVeigh 2000: 13; Miller 2011b: 24), it often includes qualities of seeming fragile, vulnerable, and youthful or infantile (Kinsella 1995: 229) and is applicable to both women and men, young and old (Koga 2009; Monden 2015; Nagaike 2012). *Kawaii* young men, as represented by such figures as Japanese boy group Arashi (see Chapter 14), are also called "*bishōnen*" (literally, "beautiful boys"; the members of Arashi have surpassed the age of thirty and thus technically are not *shōnen*—boys). On one hand, these beautiful young men with their clean-cut, wholesome, and almost childlike looks are theorized by some authors as embodying a female fantasy as non-threatening, idealized creatures that reflect "a subconscious female denial of the patriarchal, masculine male" because they are biologically male but yet to fully bloom into sexually mature manhood (Nagaike 2012: 104). On the other hand, Laura Miller (2006) has argued that women might be sexually attracted to the *kawaii* male aesthetic. In her anthropological studies, Merry White (1993) has found that, in Japanese culture, innocent appearance does not necessarily indicate sexual naivety.

The fact that the ideal male image flourishes in cultures targeted primarily at women, whether they are *shōjo* manga or idol boy bands, reinforces this hypothesis. Mark McLelland (2000: 277) argues that the ideal male image in men's popular culture, whether it is targeted at straight or gay men, tends to emphasize "the muscularity of the male figures." Such "hyper-masculine" muscularity of the male body is, until recent times, in stark contrast to the almost elf-like *bishōnen*, which otherwise might be preferred by many girls and women (McLelland 2000: 277; Miller 2006: 151). This parallel is, for example, evident when we see figures like Honda Keisuke (b. 1986), Japanese soccer player who appears half-naked in the 2014 Kirin Brewery Tanrei Nama (low malt beer) advertisement campaign with baseball player Tanaka Masahiro. Honda's direct, piercing gaze and hard "face-off" posture accentuate his muscles, and the context of the model as a star soccer player connotes his nude body as athletic rather than sensual. This image diverges from that of the male models, like Sakaguchi Kentarō (b. 1991), who are, as *Men's non-no* tell us, ostensibly appealing to heterosexual Japanese women (e.g., "Styles that got many likes by girls" [Joshi no iine wo atsumeta sutairu], *Fineboys* June 2015).

The presence of at least two different types of male physicality in Japanese popular culture (one muscular and the other slender) also signals elasticity in notions of male physical beauty. Yet the recent increase in beauty consciousness among Japanese men is at least partly reflective of women's "preferences" and their own desire to rebut an established, and perhaps more unattractive, mode of masculinity (Bardsley 2011: 133; Dasgupta 2000: 199; Miller 2006; Tanaka: 2003).

Such ostensibly appearance-conscious masculinity, particularly its close association with the "passive" position of being subjected to the gaze of on-lookers, both conventionally and unjustly defined as "feminine," can draw a set of criticisms. Indeed, young, beauty-conscious Japanese men and their fashionability have been negatively interpreted by older generations viewing them as representing "the loss of male power and martial virility" (Miller 2006: 126). For example, in a 2006 *Yomiuri* newspaper article, journalist Nagae Akira (2006: 23) laments that men endorsed by magazines like *Men's non-no* prioritize fashion over heterosexual romance and have contributed to the decline in Japan's birthrates. In 2005, then Prime Minister Koizumi Jun'ichirō declared low fertility rates to be a national problem, and because marriage is seen as a means to paternity, the reasons for Japan's late marriage rates (*bankon*) were also hotly debated (Freedman and Iwata-Weickgenannt 2011). In 2006, fashion-conscious young men were typified by the mass media, as "herbivores" (*sōshoku-kei*), men who do not show a strong interest in courting women. The term "herbivore men" was coined in 2006 by journalist Fukasawa Maki, and, in popular discourses, men and women have been divided into two groups, "herbivores" and "carnivores" (*nikushoku-kei*), based on their interest and initiative in love and marriage. Their apparent prioritization of their own personal interests over sexual romance and work-related ambition has similarly drawn criticism for being "feminized" (Nihei 2013: 66). Herbivore men have been contrasted to "carnivore women" (*nikushoku-kei onna*), who are believed to more aggressively pursue romance. Other terms have been coined, partly in jest, for men and women who fall in between these categories, such as "bacon-wrapped-asparagus man" (who seems carnivore on the outside but is herbivore on the inside) and "meat-rolled-in-cabbage man" (who seems herbivore on the outside but is carnivore on the inside). What is important to recognize is that images of masculinity in men's fashion magazines are more intricate than these negative and one-dimensional media reports; they negotiate images of media-hyped "feminized" males and more traditionally "manly" masculinity.

Male Fashionability and Readers' Three Desires

It is important to consider male consumers' agency in selecting their own fashion statements in light of the media context provided for them. In fact, the wearer's agency over fashion, especially if it involves mainstream or conservative styles, tends to be overlooked in studies that concern the body and appearance. This is particularly notable where fashion is analyzed from a sociocultural or gender perspective. Challenging this trend, Steele (1985: 143) argues that Victorian women, who were often considered to be victims of oppressive male objectification, "dressed not only for men or against other women, but also for themselves," and that "attractive dress gave its wearer considerable self-confidence, which contributed to an improved appearance" (Steele 1985: 142). I believe that this is still a fundamental aspect of dress and fashion and is equally applicable to men.

Japanese men's fashion magazines offer several, sometimes competing, reasons why men should care about fashion, or what I call an "amalgam of desires": (1) to attract others, (2) to compete or emulate, and (3) for one's own enjoyment. All three desires are represented in the March 2013 issue of *Fineboys*: a feature titled "Looking Fine Both In-and-Outside with the Tailored Jackets that Campus Beauty Queens Enthusiastically Support" (Daigaku misu ga gachi shijino teiraa jake de yanaigai ōkei) (*Fineboys* 2013a: 56–57) aims to attract admirers, while "A Pair of Black Pants is Both the Most Popular Item for Attracting Girls and for Guys to Wear" (Kuro pan wa joshi uke-do, danshi chakuyōritsu tomoni No.1) (*Fineboys* 2013c: 77–84) alludes to a dual desire, to appear attractive to young women and emulate and compete with men around the same age. Features like "Express Yourself Casually through Items with Colors and Patterns that You Select Seriously" (Gachi senshutsu no 'irogaramono' de sarige shuchou ittemiyo!) (*Fineboys* 2013b: 68–73) and "Respond to Temperature Change Perfectly with the Skills of Using a Shirt as the Foundation for a Layered Style" ('Shatsu' jiku no kasanegi waza de kion hen'ka ni kami taiou!) (*Fineboys* 2013d: 4–9), not only suggest that men dress to compete with each other but also to look good for their own practical and aesthetic purposes.

Ulrich Lehmann (2000: 9) wrote that fashion symbolizes "permanent novelty and constant, insatiable change." This is reflected in recent trends, one of which is the move to digital media. In April 2015, *Choki Choki* announced that it would end its monthly print run with its July issue. The editorial team then planned to focus on the magazine's online contents. Other magazines like *Popeye* and *Men's non-no* have used social media like Facebook and Instagram to strengthen ties with their readers. "Newer media do not necessarily supersede older media," writes Jay David Bolter and Richard Grusin, "because the process of reform and refashioning is mutual" (Bolter and Grusin 1999: 59; Rocamora 2012: 103). Men's fashion magazines continue to endure in the digital age.

In sum, the particularity of this group of Japanese men's fashion magazines lies in its focus on men's bodies and fashion. Their models, photographs, and articles promote a slender, boyish, and *kawaii* aesthetic, which, along with a more muscular male ideal found in other cultural sectors, elucidates elasticity of Japanese masculinity. An amalgam of three desires these magazines evoke in relation to men's fashionability calls into question persistent stereotypes about how men are assumed to engage with fashion. Because these magazines are sensitive to social changes and the desires of their readers, they can be seen as a barometer of changes in Japanese conceptions of masculinity.

Note

1 To give another example, *Fineboys* uses Japanese models chosen through auditions, along with "idol" celebrities from the Johnny &Associates talent agency. Popular actors Matsuzaka Tori and Daito Shunsuke started their careers as *Fineboys* models.

PART XII

Contemporary Art

38 Superflat Life

Tom Looser

Superflat art, as brought together under the galvanizing force of Murakami Takashi (b. 1962), is the best-known Japanese art movement of the 1990s and early 2000s. It has claims to Japanese cultural specificity; yet it is eminently tied to the aesthetics and economics of global art. It has invited controversy, with Murakami accused of merely appropriating the subcultural edginess of otaku culture, and the art described as superficial and designed simply to sell. Its impact, though, would seem to indicate something more. Murakami and his cohort argue for a redefinition of artistic practice, in which the divide between art and mass culture no longer makes sense and for an image form (a way of depicting the world) that comes out of modern and postmodern conditions but is defined by neither.

It is easy to see why Murakami's work invites criticism. His use of recurring imagery, such as the Mickey Mouse-like "DOB" character, the ubiquitous eyes, and the facile-looking multicolored flowers that blanket his work, or more generally, the factory-produced, high-gloss quality of much of his art, would seem to affiliate him with the shallower readings of Jeff Koons and Damien Hirst—again, as producing a pop art that, at best, ironically comments on our world of mass-produced commercialism, and, at worst, is nothing more than an expression of that very commercialism. In simple terms, Murakami's work seems to hover between an ironic critique and a clichéd embrace of mass culture.

At the same time, Murakami has appeared to take up direct social and political commentary in some of his work. A year before he wrote his more widely-known "Superflat Manifesto" (*Superflat Sengen*), Murakami wrote a "Tokyo Pop Manifesto" (*Haikei kimi wa ikiteiru: Tokyo pop-sengen* 1999: 58), in which he argued that "pop art" was an insufficient term for what had been going on in Japan; Japan, he wrote, had been forced into a postwar system that, under the cultural and military sway of America, left it in a child-like state.[1] But this child-like state, nonetheless, was accurately expressed in Japanese popular culture in a way that effectively served as a critique of Japan's immediate historical situation. For Murakami, "Tokyo pop" was therefore inherently more political than American pop art. Murakami then returned more fully to this approach in the last of his three Superflat shows, titled "Little Boy"—apparently a reference both to the atomic bomb dropped on Hiroshima and the social condition that characterized Japan in relation to the United States. Objects for the show (including toys) suggested engagement with immediate political problems that were otherwise repressed by official state policies.[2]

Both social critique and an embrace of popular culture are thus part of the Superflat idea, but these qualities are not what give it a claim to more radical difference or the status of being its own art movement; otherwise, it could be judged a failure. Instead, one might think of Superflat art's potency as coming from the way it takes the cultural conditions of its era and weaves them into a new way of seeing and understanding the world. This includes what might be thought of as the ecology of images prevalent in Japan by the 1990s, as well as the very market-driven context of global art within which Murakami developed his ideas. It is also technological; when Murakami (2000: 5) wrote in his "Superflat Manifesto" that superflatness is like a computer graphic in which "you merge a number of distinct layers into one," it still sounded like a new idea. While it is not an argument for a new avant-garde, it does hold its own vision of history: "it is an original concept that links the past with the present and the future" in its own way (2000: 5). Along with a vision of history, it suggests its own idea of concrete space: as Murakami put it, "the feeling I get [from Superflatness] is a sense of reality that is very nearly a physical sensation" (2000: 5). And while Murakami describes this as *Japanese* art and thinks that turning from American popular culture toward Japanese pop will provide a better route to critical awareness, he cites art historian Sawaragi Noi in saying that this is not a new, reversed nationalism. It is rather a critique of "the notion of 'human' that informs high art and nationalism [and] was invented in modern times to conceal the fact that humans themselves are a kind of 'monster'" (Murakami 2005b: 160). "This [Superflat] manifesto will replace the modern 'human manifesto' that made art into 'art'" (Murakami 2005b: 161).

As I will explore in this chapter, Murakami's Superflat art thus promises to transform how we think about culture, history, our own status as acting subjects, and even the idea of what it is to be human. The conditions for this change are found within the world of contemporary global, mass-produced, popular-cultural life, with the implication that global popular culture has within its own terms the potential to creatively evolve into new visions of life and other kinds of value. The question that nonetheless haunts Murakami's work is whether these Superflat promises are realized, or whether instead the Superflat ends up trapped within the terms of global popular culture and is only a newly enhanced flattening of history, politics, and self-creativity into the values of the marketplace alone.

Background: Japan's Postwar Image Ecology

It is possible and not entirely inaccurate to place Murakami's pop-inflected art within a much broader history of pop art, even within Japan. His ironic and even anarchic invocation of consumer marketing logic is reminiscent of the Japanese Dadaist MAVO movement of the 1920s. His use of mass-production technologies, his Hiropon factory studio founded in 1996 (legally incorporated as the Kaikai Kiki company in 2001), and his glossy aesthetics recall the more politically aloof pop art of Warhol and numerous other pop artists in Japan. The play of perspective and the proliferating images of eyes in the 1960s by pop artists like Tadanori Yokoo and Tanaami Keiichi are echoed in Murakami's own ever-multiplying eye imagery.

But Murakami's "Tokyo Pop Manifesto" makes clear that he does not consider the Japanese material to be equivalent to Western "pop art." And while some of his paintings appear to be similar to the abstract and surreal art that was attached to movements like Dadaism and MAVO, surrealism was meant as a means of uncovering and expressing the unconscious logic that helped structure modern life. Superflat art makes no such claim for an unconscious logic or for a modern subjectivity at all. The logic of Superflatness is different.

A simpler starting point might be the everyday forms of imagery in Japan of the 1980s and 1990s, when Murakami was starting out. The intertwining of art with popular culture and commercial life had come to typify life in Japan even before the 1990s, as discussed in Chapters 39 and 40. The setting for this is multifaceted. It includes the dense image saturation of urban everyday life that Japan was becoming known for, covering everything from multistory building surfaces, to omnipresent television screens, to endless magazines with imagery that was, at times, difficult to identify as specifically oriented towards either art, commerce, or design alone. The hyper-consumerism of this era also saw the full development of what Ōtsuka Eiji called the "media mix" (Ōtsuka 2001 [1989]), detailed in Chapter 23. The otaku subcultures emerged from within this hyper-consumerism, arguably in ways that developed a more interactive and even critical relation to consumption (see Chapter 33). Rather than simply following the dictates and fashions of the large culture industries, otaku seemed to offer the possibility that the very act of consumption might become creative—ultimately allowing them to reappropriate the role of producer for themselves, in a more artistic, self-creative world. This more idiosyncratic embrace of popular culture by the otaku gained added weight as Japan's bubble economy fell into a long recession in the 1990s (McGray 2002).

This is part of the general context within which Superflat art emerged. At its most open form, one might think of this as a consumer society characterized by an unusually interactive and creative relation between buying and selling, consumer and commodity, resulting in a generalized affective world of images and objects defined neither as art nor as commodity.

Of course, all this could still be viewed as simply a larger fantasy world, and part of what Sawaragi Noi described as Japan's postwar "ahistorical 'self-withdrawal'" (*jihei*) that led to the bubble economy as itself an "imaginary reality"—a frothy world insufficiently grounded in either a historical or economic reality that was bound to collapse (Murakami 2005b: 203). Murakami's

Superflat project is, arguably, trying to pull something more creative together out of the image world Japan had developed by the 1980s and 1990s.

The political references that he highlights in the *Little Boy* show really are only a small part of that project. To provide a clearer view of the values and possibilities within "Superflatness," I will draw on two significant variants of Superflatness in the work of others curated by Murakami and then return to Murakami himself.

Flatness versus Superflatness

Although Superflatness is not simply a matter either of formal or thematic flatness, the concept of a "flat" surface image is a good place to start. Flatness is a loaded term in contemporary art history. In particular, the understanding of space as Euclidean—with three-dimensional, perspectival depth—is generally thought of as definitive of the way in which the modern enlightenment subject understands the world. It anchors a stable, homogenous individual within a stable and homogenous space, and it is only depth that provides this clarity of relations; perspectival depth anchors the "real." Thus by emphasizing layered surfaces rather than homogenous spatial depth, Murakami is invoking some other means of putting together an image of the real.

One can think of Clement Greenberg's 1960 seminal essay on modernism, which argues that artistic modernity is defined by flatness and abstraction. For Greenberg, the preeminent medium of art within modernism is painting, and painting in its very nature is legitimately defined only by flat, two-dimensional surfaces. For Greenberg, this meant that painting, and modernist art, relinquished any claim to direct representation of the real; Greenberg in effect was reinforcing the idea of perspectival depth as the definition of the real. Superflatness, by contrast, has a greater claim to be presenting and creating an understanding of the real (art is not autonomous from the real), even while Superflat practices fit neither the classic depth model of modernism nor Greenberg's flatness. More radical reconfigurations of pictorial form are evident by Superflat artists.

The formal logic of Superflat layering of surfaces is best visible in works by Nara Yoshitomo (b. 1959). Nara was included in all three of the Superflat exhibits, and so is a central part of Murakami's mix, but he has at times held equal stature to Murakami and has his own style of Superflat.

Nara's might be thought of as a unique model of depth, with its own pictorial construction of history, culture, and identity. In one series, Nara plays with early modern *ukiyo-e* ("floating world pictures"). *Ukiyo-e* have long been thought of as "flat" pictures, without three dimensionality; the French impressionists embraced them as a primitive and premodern format that they could romantically imitate. Nara, though, carries it further, while returning *ukiyo-e* to their mass cultural roots[3] (these are in fact images of an early mass-cultural world more than an ancient primitivism), and drawing a new form out of them.

In Figure 38.1 (originally titled "Beauty Before the Mirror" by Kitagawa Utamaro (1790), Nara boils complicated relations between historical eras down to a matter of self-reflection and self-imaging. As in other prints in the series, Nara has taken an original Edo-era *ukiyo-e* print and created a palimpsest-like layering of different media, styles, authorship, and theme, all visible on a single surface. In this case, the observer still sees the original Edo-era woman gazing into a mirror, but Nara has painted one of his own characters into the mirror itself—it is her image that we see reflected and that we are gazing at. We thus relate to the Edo-era woman's identity only through the visibly different layer of Nara's image. Furthermore, while we are ourselves looking into the mirror—it should be our own reflection, too, (emphasized by Nara's over-painted phrase at the top, "Your Face Reflected!")—the woman's eyes are closed, thereby refusing any completed sense of reflected identity between her and the observer. Overall, it is a complex image of layers of identity and yet a refusal of identity between those layers. It is technically flat and resists any single perspectival observational position. Yet it does have depth and difference, history and identity, created through layering; it is a history and identity that works with layers of difference and resistance, rather than perspectival unity and consistency.[4]

Nara's *ukiyo-e* work thus is one way in which one can see a redefinition of "depth"—in his case, depth emerges out of the visible juxtaposition of layers of difference rather than a continuous organization viewed through a single "surface." Surface, therefore, has new weight as the site where identity and meaning emerge in the present (the meaning or identity of the original *ukiyo-e* can only be found in its juxtaposition with the contemporary over-painting on the surface—not in a single original past version alone); it is the opposite of a hermeneutics of a truth that lies fixed in the past.

Technologies of the Superflat

In Nara's case, the model of layering might be considered a formal play with modernism's depth, tied to the flat quality of mass cultural brand imaging. For Azuma Hiroki (b. 1971), another of Murakami's Superflat cohort, the forces pushing toward Superflatness are more clearly derived from the use of digital technologies, although still connected with mass cultural consumption.

In his talk for the first Superflat exhibition, Azuma, too, starts with the position that "European perspective is just an artificial institution" (2000: 8). Azuma is thinking less in terms of art, or pictorial form, and more generally about how we interact with the given world. Azuma has his own model of layered depth: in his view, we now tend to treat the world as consisting of a set of pre-constituted forms and ideas, along the lines of a computer database (the pre-given forms and ideas, however, seem to be derived from culture industries). We then take those elements—a figure from an anime series, for example—and play with them, both disassembling and reassembling them. In this early formulation of Azuma's database model, the result

Figure 38.1 Nara Yoshitomo, *Mirror* (In the Floating World), 1999.
Source: © Yoshitomo Nara.

is a "simulacra," a new form or identity that exists at the surface layer of life. This model apparently describes the way we treat all of life, with everything from history to culture working like a database of pre-constituted forms to be played with.

In Azuma's Superflat world there is therefore nothing truly created anew. Life and meaning are only built out of prefabricated elements that themselves no longer seem to embody or refer to more absolute truths, and there is no single accepted "true" narrative that tells us how the database elements should be formed into any particular identity. It is thus a model of subjectivity in which terms like culture, history, and self are only playfully put together. It is also a model in which there is no true production possible, only consumption of pre-constituted forms, and so, if there is any real creativity, it can only come out of consumption.

In these ways, Azuma gives us a Superflat subjectivity that is potentially more creative than the subject of Enlightenment modernity with its solid and determinative depth of a definitive original past. But the Superflat subject might also be shallower than the Enlightenment version. In Azuma's Superflat database, elements appear as little more than the equivalent of marketing images—a character that has no real story at all (other than something like the identity of a brand)—and life and subjectivity start to look like a play of pure, empty form. This is a far more postmodernist vision than Nara's, and Azuma's picture of life as empty form looks similar to critiques of Murakami's artistic vision.

Both Nara and Azuma help to provide a general sense of the ways in which the Superflat emerges out of a modern, mass-cultural everyday life while indicating a transformed relation to the world. One can see parallels to both Nara and Azuma in Murakami's approach, including a complicated reference to history and at least an implicit argument for an alternative to the classic structure of modern subjectivity. But Murakami's Superflat is unique.

Murakami's Superflat Image of Life

Perhaps even more than Nara and Azuma, Murakami's Superflat offers at least the possibility of a truly new, more creative image of history, culture, and subjectivity emerging from within the conditions mentioned above—including, on the one hand, a newly open image ecology, in which the distinctions between art, commercial design, and popular culture have become blurred, and, on the other hand, an environment in which these distinctions all threaten to collapse into the single order of commercial consumer capitalism and digital technology. Murakami's work, accordingly, continues to raise questions as to whether these are truly new images of life or whether they are ultimately just a new, more complete flattening into the single value system of global capital. So, if there is some emergent difference in Murakami's apparently flat and brand-like art modes, dependent as they are on recurring use of characters, in what way are they "Superflat?"

It is worth noting that Murakami sees his work as creating a real image of the world (and of himself), not just a fantasy or a fiction. In the *Super Flat* catalog (originally formulated as two words), commenting on his borrowing of everything from Edo-era screen painting to contemporary anime, he writes, "I would like to sketch 'Japan' in a 'super flat' style. Collecting the images in this book, I will fuse the images together ... I will call this work 'Japan'" (2000: 23). And in describing his creation of DOB as an intentional attempt to create a lasting "universal" character like Mickey Mouse, he nonetheless states that "over the years [DOB] has really become more of a self-portrait" (2003: 131–132).

Also, as noted above, his work is predicated on the idea of having real, identifiable origins, including those of culture and history. Murakami, at differing points, emphasizes the Edo era, the immediate postwar era, and the 1990s as historical grounds of his art, and stylistically he locates Edo-era screen painters, French Japonisme, and contemporary anime artists among others as primary influences.

But at the same time, Murakami works with universals—this, too, is part of his starting point and apparently what he takes to be the necessary starting point for creation within our world in general. The presumption, in part, seems to be that identity and difference can only now emerge out of a pre-given universal, as with his idea that DOB could be the basis for a self-portrait. The implication is that, even more than for Nara or Azuma, global capital and mass culture have inescapably become the only ground for identity and difference; the technologies that go with global culture, and the globality of culture itself, are part of this picture. Accordingly, while Murakami (2003: 130) says that his idea of beauty will always "stink of soy sauce," he has repeatedly noted that he had to go to Brooklyn first to develop his own, "Japanese" Superflat art.[5] And even at the basic level of artistic production—before one considers the more conceptual effects of Azuma's database—there is a technological basis to this universalizing starting point, as in the use of preprogrammed art software that Murakami always uses as a starting point. (He insists he would not have been able to create DOB without it.)

An image of the world thus apparently has to start at the level of the homogenous for Murakami; this is part of the flatness for him, and even a "true" origin like Edo-era Japanese art can only emerge in this flattened form,[6] as if first scanned through a standardizing software program or reduced to the shallowness of a brand. Still, like Nara's *ukiyo-e*, Murakami is able to layer these flattened sources into depth of meaning, and he is able to use his standardized figures like Azuma's database elements, not only to create new images but also to pull together different worlds into something new.

In his 2014–2015 Gagosian Gallery show (New York City), for example, Murakami used his skull figures as a starting point or ground, embossing them onto the canvas surfaces of all his paintings. On some paintings, Murakami painted pictures of skulls over the embossed skull canvases, and then graffitied the words "Death Hate I" in spray paint over the top. The skull-embossed canvases in another room serve as the base of huge murals over-painted with Buddhist and Taoist themes of death and destruction, and in another room are the surface for Murakami's flower faces, which themselves echo (among other things) the imperial chrysanthemum. Lastly, the skulls carry through to Murakami's DOB world and to paintings commenting on radiation in the show's final section; all of this is echoed in the construction of a temple within the gallery.

Thus the skulls carry the viewer and the works themselves across a range of materials, styles, and eras, and from a curator's personal thoughts ("I hate death"), to references to an eighteenth-century religious mural invoking Taoism by Soga Shōhaku (1730–1781), to imperial-style Japanese screens, and to Murakami's DOB self-portraiture amidst signs of religion and radiation, all framed by a Buddhist/Shinto temple gate that apparently was also meant to invoke the early Rashōmon city gate that once served as the entrance to Kyoto. This is a radical depth of history, meaning, and style, produced as layers of worlds, meanings, and values, and with the generic skull element acting as a "base" to carry the viewer from one value world to the next, in the same way that brand characters might carry a consumer from one commodity world to the next but now with truer diversity of value systems and without ever resolving these different layers and value systems into one.

Murakami's generic forms thus shape an identity that can only emerge out of, or exist as, this movement across layers of difference. Ultimately, Murakami's universal characters seem to hold the potential to become the figures of a creativity that expands beyond any stable creative subject—a kind of self that expands beyond the self. DOB, for example, may start with Murakami, but it then takes on its own life. As Murakami says, that character "begins walking by himself... The character is very strong" (Cruz et al. 1999: 17). It is as if Murakami could watch his own image develop and morph as it connects across different worlds. This is not just the irony of pop art.

At the same time, there is always the risk that Murakami's art resolves back into the universal image he takes as his starting point. This is true even for his ubiquitous eyes, which could be his most radical imaging mode. At times fully covering surfaces, without limit and without a face, the eyes might be taken as a boundless, polymorphic relation to the viewer, refusing any hierarchical fixing of symbolic systems or of "true" perspectival positions, and acting as wide open reflections of a self that is free of the strictures of race, culture, or place. But they might also add up to something much more totalizing. As Murakami put it, "when you start linking up [these eyes] one after another into infinity, at some point they break through," as if at some point all these perspectives will somehow add up to an overarching whole—faceless perhaps but a kind of subject position nonetheless; a new global subject that is flat and almost without identity or specific position at all, other than a totalitarian and even fascistic perspective.

Murakami's Superflat is neither classic modernism nor mere pop art. It suggests the possibility of newly envisioning a life that might emerge out of the global ecology of politics, economy, and technology that structure our everyday life. To the extent that Murakami is successful, he is returning to art the power to mediate the forces of the everyday and mold them into something new. Even if Murakami's Superflat view assumes universalized, flat, and almost archetypical layers of different worlds (from ancient Taoism to postwar toys)—as if that is all that our global mass culture and digital technologies can recognize—it nonetheless seems to insist that these are real worlds of difference, with different value systems, that can be layered and linked into ever new and open, multi-dimensional orders of perspective and life. This would be the positive reading of Superflat art. Imaging modes like DOB may help Murakami to both "untie the cords of art history" (Murakami 2003: 133), and to lay out before us the conditions for culture, history, and life to connect in new ways.

Yet Murakami's willingness to so fully embrace the contemporary conditions of artistic production—economic, technological, and thematic—also leave open the possibility that his art is nothing more than a more completed expression of these conditions as totalizing rather than an escape from them. If this is the case, then characters like DOB might be thought of as the movement and life (a vision underscored by Murakami's paintings of DOB as strands of DNA) of a newly totalizing global popular culture and of all of life now being flattened into that single value system, rather than a link with other ways of seeing identity and the world. This would be "super" flat life in an unhappier sense. In allowing for these two very different possible readings, Murakami presents us with the fundamental tensions of our era—this may be the real force of his work. Whether the Superflat is truly an opening of life from within consumer culture or just a flattening of things into a universal and even totalitarian brand, is part of the interest and "monstrosity"[7] that Murakami's work tells us is definitive of our time.

Notes

1 The "Superflat Manifesto" was published in both English and Japanese, as part of the Superflat catalog (Murakami 2000: 4–5). The earlier "Tokyo Pop Manifesto" was first published in Japanese only (1999: 58) and took a much more national, imperialist approach. In that earlier work, Murakami not only saw Japan as "infantilized by the West" but also saw "father America" receding from Japan (2005b: 152), and Japan therefore as a possible opening to a new kind of art theory. This idea of Tokyo Pop would then just a year later emerge into the more globally and bilingually framed Superflat.

2 Sawaragi Noi echoes these ideas in the same catalog, stating that while the Japanese pop cultural imaginary vacillates "between the desire to escape from historical self-withdrawal and to revert to it," the "creepy imagination" of this culture is nonetheless part of the reimagining of a history that has been otherwise repressed and therefore distorted (Sawaragi 2005: 204–205). It should not be surprising that Murakami also reproduces part of his "Tokyo Pop Manifesto" in the *Little Boy* catalog (Murakami 2005a: 152).

3 I use the term "mass culture" in the generic sense, referring to a world in which social relations are increasingly formed through the mediation of objects and ideas largely defined as commodities, rather than direct interpersonal relations like kinship or neighborhood proximity. *Ukiyo-e* served as this kind of mass-produced image, around which social communities might form. They also gained wide circulation, expanding even to aristocratic circles, and in this sense were part of a nascent popular culture.

4 In another work from the same series, Nara overlays the words "Cup Kid," and a bowl of noodles (referencing the Cup Noodle brand of instant ramen), onto an earlier *ukiyo-e*—reminding us that these flat images were, even in the Edo era, already part of an early mass culture.

5 Although Murakami started his career in a cosmopolitan, global context, he never gave up the claim to finding a "Japanese" style. As a student he worked in the conservative national style of Nihonga—the difference is that he seems to have taken the global as a starting point from which to find "Japanese" style rather than the other way around.

6 It is not surprising that the stylistic sources Murakami highlights all work with non-perspectival, flattened styles, and all were developed in relation to arts that were from outside Japan.

7 "[T]he Superflat project is our 'Monster Manifesto, and now more than ever, we must pride ourselves on our art, the work of monsters." (Murakami 2005a: 161).

39 Aida Makoto

Notes from an Apathetic Continent

Adrian Favell

Following the huge success of Murakami Takashi's (b. 1962) Superflat movement, Japanese contemporary art since 2000 has been mostly represented internationally by Murakami and artists associated with his style, such as Nara Yoshitomo (b. 1959) (see Chapter 38). The dominant fame of Superflat art poses an issue about the rival claims of Aida Makoto (b. 1965) who, in Japan, is often mentioned as the most representative artist to emerge during the 1990s. Edgy, erratic, and extraordinarily diverse in his production, Aida is often seen by even his most fervent admirers as an artist for domestic consumption only, too complex in his self-referential Japaneseness (Yamashita 2012). Yet his *oeuvre* deserves close attention, as it taps into live—often quite unpalatable—aspects of Japanese popular culture, articulating ambiguous commentary on attitudes, events, and politics well beyond Superflat's more commercial and exportable style.

Introducing Aida, this chapter explores his satirical use of images of young girls and trashy downtown salaryman culture ("salaryman," or "man who earns a salary," is the common Japanese term for "businessman"); his prolific art historical reference points and techniques; his sporadic but often nihilistic forays into politics, including the key theme of homelessness; and the resonance of his work after the earthquake, tsunami, and nuclear triple disaster of March 2011 (i.e., "post-3/11"). It also foregrounds the thorny question—self-consciously posed by Aida himself in numerous ironic works—of whether his *oeuvre* will ever gain the international recognition and sympathy he enjoys at home.

Edible Girls and Old Guys' Jokes

Questionably distasteful, highlights from the series *Edible Artificial Girls: Mi-Mi Chan* (*Shokuyō jinzō shōjo: Mi-Mi Chan*, 2001) are representative of Aida works. Aida is a conceptual artist working in a range of different media, which often display his remarkable powers of pastiche and satire. This series, begun in 1999, consists of a number of sketched drawings and illustrations, some of which were eventually made into plastic models and installations. In a traditional-style commercial note to accompany the works, which

Figure 39.1 From the series *Edible Artificial Girls: Mi-Mi Chan*.
Source: Courtesy of Mizuma Art Gallery.

mimics precisely the ingenuous tone of Japanese corporate marketing, Aida
explains how world food shortages necessitated the development of a range of
artificially cultivated miniature edible girls, who can be served in a range of
classical-style Japanese *izakaya* (pub food) dishes (Figure 39.1):

> Mi-Mi, who can be your good companion or kept in food storage, has
> taken a firm hold within our lifestyle in the role of a pet. With the great
> development of new flavors, we can now count on more than five thou-
> sand varieties of Mi-Mi. Mi-Mi provides most of the food on Earth...
> the bad habit of eating the meat of farm animals died out.... We are
> pleased to offer a good time from the hand skilled bio-confectioners
> handed down since our foundation.
>
> (Quoted in Aida 2007: 94)

A cheerful salaryman—who resembles the former Japanese Prime Minister
Mori Yoshiro (2000–2001)—is seen devouring one *oishiisō* (delicious looking) girl cooked in tempura; in another, a loving chef's hands squeeze out
bright orange roe from between a girl's legs. Sushi, *nabe* hot pot, and grilled
versions, of course, are all on the menu. Mi-Mi Chan is sweet and adorably "cute": we could imagine these images alongside the barrage of smiling
young and seductive female faces adorning free sales magazines or metro
advertisements in any major Japanese city. It is a grotesque, queasy, and distinctly pornographic satire served up by the "restaurant owner" Aida. On

one level, it is just another *oyaji* (old guy's) joke, familiar from many other male artists of Aida's generation. On another level—particularly in a society where women parliamentarians get laughed at and shouted down when they make speeches about supporting child care and working women[1]—Aida's work can be read as a brutal auto-diagnosis of gender relations and representations of exploitable "girls" as an abundant raw material in Japanese popular culture (Kinsella 2014).

Much of Aida's work plays along this borderline (Saitō 2008), defying prurient censorship while reveling in the resources provided by the everyday popular culture of Tokyo's *shitamachi* (downtown) working men's entertainment zones. This is not the "Cool Japan" cliché of Tokyo's fashion zones in Shibuya or Harajuku (see Chapter 32)—however weird and wonderful that may be—but the irretrievably "uncool" reality of backstreet male popular culture in downtown Ueno, rather than the otaku paradise of Akihabara, just up the road (see Chapter 33). Aida presents a much more realist, albeit sordid, vision of "real Tokyo," rather than the stylized fantasy "neo-Tokyo" sold to the world as J-Pop (Favell 2014a). Aida is thus a much better guide to the everyday culture of the metropolis than much of Japan's more commercial pop art. A good example of this is the *Monument for Nothing III* (2009), an enormous wall jigsaw bricolage in the shape of a traditional Japanese rake. It is, like many of Aida's works, a splurge of bile: full of images of cartoon girls, vomit-looking food, tacky billboard images, and drunken revelers. Aida presents his spin on this culture with a characteristically blank, nihilistic irony, laughing sheepishly, unshaven and hung over, with a can of Sapporo beer or a cigarette in hand.

Aida's frank exploitation of female bodies immediately opens him up to hostile critique. However routine these kinds of images are in Japan, such jokes are indefensible in any serious discussion about the place of women and could easily be read as symptomatic of much that is wrong with the society. But as art they demand an appreciation of how consistently Aida strikes a raw nerve in his representations, while always keeping his ultimate position elusive (Kinsella 2014). Some of Murakami's Superflat, particularly his promotion of cute "teenager"-style girls' artists, comes out of similar sources. But Murakami's games with girl culture, otaku weirdness, or nationalist politics always err on the palatable side. In order to make big international auction sales, Superflat consistently turned Japanese hardcore into Japanese kitsch. Aida's work, in contrast, is always over the line: raucous, ugly, and in your face, like the crows in Tokyo's Yoyogi Park at sundown (Tokyo struggles with an out-of-control crow population). And, unlike Murakami or Nara, who are "fun" but never really humorous in their work, Aida is uproariously funny—to those that see the (bitter, twisted) joke.

Global Parallels in Bad Taste

The most obvious international reference for Aida would be the mischievous Italian artist Maurizio Cattelan or the YBA (Young British Artists) bad boys, the Chapman Brothers. The 1990s Tokyo art scene, led by the young Murakami alongside others, was a direct parallel to the London art explosion led by Damian Hirst. Aida perhaps references a true, and quite authentic, Japanese national culture of which few viewers internationally want to be reminded.

Perhaps his greatest works, made in a rush of inspiration during and after the disastrous national "zero year" of 1995—in which a huge earthquake in Kobe was followed by the Aum Shinrikyō sarin gas attack on the Tokyo subway—are the *War Picture Returns* series (Sensōga Returns, 1995–1999). Executed on traditional Japanese sliding screens (*fusuma*), several of them display Aida's academic mastery of Nihonga: that is, Japanese painting in a "traditional" style and materials as was defined and institutionalized in the Meiji period. Others borrow the heavy style of wartime army paintings. Taken together, the series pokes an offensive needle in the eye of both Japanese nationalism and its triumphant foreign nemesis, American civilization (Mouri 2006). In one (*Beautiful Flag* [*Utsukushii hata*], 1995), appropriating typical fetishistic images but also referencing classical works, Aida restages Japanese and Korean schoolgirls standing in mock heroic poses with their respective flags against a war-torn backdrop; in another (*Gate Ball*, 1999), decrepit cartoonish representatives of East Asian economic cooperation play a game of croquet through temple gates with severed heads on a map of the region. In *A Picture of an Air Raid on New York City* (*Nyōyōku kuubaku no zu*, 1996), he imagines a Möbius strip of triumphant Mitsubishi Zeros bombing a burning American skyline, evoking both classical flying cranes and Edo era overviews of Kyoto (Yamashita 2014: 195). This last painting, Aida's most (in)famous, even earned him the reputation as a kind of millennial soothsayer: executed in 1996, then shown at the Whitney Museum in New York in 2003, in a provocative post-9/11 show about anti-Americanism. Aida has often been eerily prescient of world-shattering moments, although he stresses it is just a coincidence (Kondo 2011): he painted a sarin bottle in one of Ozawa Tsuyoshi's milk box Nasubi galleries in 1994, one year before the terrorist attack; his *Ash Color Mountains* (*Haiiro no yama*, 2009–2011), discussed below, looks sickeningly familiar after the television footage from Tōhoku (Northeast Japan) after the March 2011 disasters. Taken together, the *War Picture Returns* is as acute a psychoanalysis of Japan's Asian and Pacific psychosis as could be imagined. The series even gains strength from being didactic work, propped up like information posters on empty beer crates. Yet it is a dialogue with the Japanese nation, which has little or no resonance on a Western art market that expensively canonizes the Chapman Brothers' obsessions with Nazis or Maurizio Cattelan's sordid jokes about Hitler and the Pope.

Aida's difficulties internationally pose the question of whether any contemporary Japanese artist can pass into the Japanese pantheon of world-class artists without the affirmation of "*gaisen kōen*": the "triumphant return performance" after success and recognition abroad (Favell 2015). He had a negative and fruitless stay in New York in 2000, as he often discusses, unlike Murakami who made his name working in New York and Los Angeles. Instead, Aida has become, curiously, a kind of people's champion as the quintessential "national" artist back home. Much of his work plays on these ambiguities: of being Japanese, of loving and hating Japan, and of finding an authentic way of translating international and essentially alien art currents into Japanese form. In this, as well as in his ambiguous populist politics, Aida shows much of the influence of his youthful fascination with the writer Mishima Yukio (1925–1970), whose nationalist obsession with classical heritage, the painful modernization of Japan, and its subordination to the United States in the postwar period, gripped him as a teenager (Kataoka 2012: 35).

Academic and Historical References

Born in the northern prefecture of Niigata to a sociologist father and a science teacher mother, Aida had an apparently normal childhood. Geeky and shy of girls, he went to study oil painting at the Tokyo University of the Arts (Geidai) in the mid-1980s, graduating from his MFA in 1991 and part of a dynamic group of young artists centered on Murakami from the school (Favell 2014b). Acclaim in Tokyo followed soon after. As Aida's works eminently display, he is a master of historical reference: to classical works or traditional techniques and materials (often self-made, such as pigments, canvases, paper, or improvised trash), as well as to a range of internationally legible contemporary conceptual tricks. The hollowness or incompleteness of his mastery is often foregrounded: there is a slightly despairing sense in his bravura performance of old-fashioned skills—such as the piles of minutely etched human bodies that make up massive set piece paintings like *Blender* (2001)—even as he denies really being a painter. He publicly complains of being unable to finish his prolific ideas (Aida 2003).

Aida's technical skill and range is undisputed. One of his earliest works, *The Path through the Rice Fields* (*AZEMICHI*, 1991) is even used in Japanese art history textbooks. With photo-like precision, the young Aida painted the back of a schoolgirl's head, an image he conceived as a student idly looking at his girlfriend. Reimagined in a sailor-style school uniform, the parting in her bunched hair blends into a path through rice fields that recedes from the viewer into a sentimental (but crumbling) rural landscape. This was the work which convinced gallerist Mitsuma Sueo to sign him on the spot for his growing Mizuma Gallery; it had a similar effect for many in the Japanese art world (Yamashita 2014: 192), such is its pointed appropriation at once of Japanese art history, the iconography of national landscapes, and of contemporary subculture. The painting, another joke, is a self-referential and academic exercise quoting a famous Nihonga painting of a path through rice fields by Higashiyama Kaii (1908–1999), a famous postwar work that symbolized an alternative path for Japanese art free of the invasive influence of American power (Larking 2013). Aida's path similarly seeks a Japanese path through the false globalism of recent international art theory. That World

War II is still on his mind is quite typical of his generation, who grew up much too young to know the war, but alive to their parents' early memories. These 1960s children also grew up gorging on American popular culture and experienced the consumer craze of the 1980s as young adults, but they continue to share the ambiguous left-right nationalist resentments of older generations. Again, the mood is familiar in many artists of Aida's age: the same undertow can be found in Murakami's and occasionally Nara's work. It is, however, absent in the generations of artists who came of age after Japan's boom years ended in 1990.

Murakami and Aida respect each other but keep a distance. The one work of Aida's placed in Murakami's first international Superflat show in Los Angeles (2001) had the effect of distorting Aida's later reception internationally: his obviously otaku-style painting, *The Giant Member Fuji versus King Gidora* (*Kyodai Fuji tai'in VS Kingu Gidora*, 1993). This sensational, 20-square-meter manga image, executed in blown-up acetate and bright color acrylic, depicts in mock mythological style, an agonized Fuji (Japan?) being raped by a cartoon monster (the United States?). It is, obviously, a "neo-Japoniste" work: that is, a work like some of Murakami's, which references a classic work from the Edo period in the manner "Japoniste" modern European art incorporated traditional Japanese styles in the late nineteenth century. Underneath, as a template, is Hokusai's famous *shunga* (erotic woodblock prints made during the Edo era) of an octopus copulating with a fisherwoman. When unveiled by the influential curator/writer Nishihara Min at Ikeuchi Tsutomu's Roentgen Institute in early 1993, a phenomenal new raw talent was immediately recognized on the Tokyo scene (Favell 2012: 96; Nakazawa 2014: 88–89).

Unfortunately, squashed into Murakami's parade of young girl artists and commercial graphic art in Superflat, Aida was saddled with the label of being a manga or otaku artist (Aida 2012: 97). For sure, he has those references: almost automatic, it is said, among the clever nerdy otaku boys born in the 1960s, sat at home with their sci-fi toys and grubby manga (Sawaragi 2005). The media has occasionally suited him: for example, the stunning *dōjinshi* (homemade) manga *Mutant Hanako* (*Myūtanto Hanako*, 1997)—unknown in English but a cult to French manga specialists—which first existed in the form of three-hundred cheaply photocopied and stapled comic books sold at his gallery, then executed as part of the *War Picture Returns* series on hinged screens. In a full-length story, Aida retells the narrative of the Pacific War with the United States through a spectacularly pornographic and scatological tale of a Japanese schoolgirl, Hanako, given monstrous powers from her exposure to radiation during the atomic bombing of Hiroshima. Released as a superhero, she reverses history, after suffering the ignoble abuse of various American military figures, including General MacArthur, and the loss of her lover, a doomed Kamikaze pilot. This avatar of modern Japan saves the nation from defeat in the war through an outer-space science-fiction ending. Badly drawn, with much evidence of long feverish nights at work, it is another masterpiece of commentary on the psychosis of the nation. Later, in a half-baked attempt to translate the work abroad in San Francisco, Aida and his friends produced a comical, dubbed version with cheap stop-start animation and terrible accents. For Aida, it fulfilled a long-held desire to draw and publish an erotic manga, however unprofessionally executed: "Why am I so obsessed with erotic things? It is because I believe deeply that 'bad taste,' in its broadest definition, is one of manga's most fundamental sources of power" (Aida 2005: 24).

This work was a pivotal moment in Aida's career. His gallerist Mitsuma—who has always acted as a patient patron for an artist he is convinced is the greatest of his generation—showed the manga-covered screens to a new collector, Takahashi Ryutaro, a medical psychiatrist who thought it was a perfect piece for his office. Aida is the centerpiece of Takahashi's definitive collection of the 1990s and 2000s, meaning that his works have stayed in Japan and have been accessible to frequent and ever larger showings at home. Internationally, though, Aida has been less visible. After appearing at the second iteration of Superflat, *Coloriage* in Paris (2002), Aida was subsequently airbrushed to the margins of Murakami's post-1980s history of Japanese contemporary art in *Little Boy*, shown at Japan Society in New York in 2005 (Murakami 2005a). This hugely influential show and catalogue became the dominant reference point in defining the art of the 1990s from Japan internationally. Recently, this history has started to be challenged; for example, by curator David Elliott's (2011) revisionist *Bye Bye Kitty!!!* at the same venue, which heavily featured Aida.

Aida's steadily rising domestic recognition led eventually to a career-defining retrospective curated by Kataoka Mami at Tokyo's Mori Art Museum at the end of 2012 (Aida 2012). It also made Aida an odd kind of countercultural public hero for the anxious dark days after the 2011 Fukushima nuclear meltdown. Because of his incendiary reputation, many corporations would not touch the show with sponsorship, so Mitsuma resorted to crowdsourcing, making an Internet-based call for supporters large and small to underwrite the show. Large attendances at this sprawling, deliberately chaotic show further grew when, belatedly, a scandal blew up over the curtained-off room in which Kataoka had put Aida's most unpleasant works: the sickly-sweet paintings of smiling, amputated *bishōjo* (beautiful girls) of his notorious *DOG* series. Predictably, a certain portion of wider discussion about Aida focuses on his own fairly frank *lolicon* (Lolita complex) with young girls in his art, a motif to which Aida has continually returned. When asked about his own attitude to his often-shocking imagery, he says he has an effete—or "womanish," as he puts it—rather than macho, personality, and he often imagines himself as one of the *bishōjo* he is painting (Kinsella 2014: 166).

A further complication in assessing the misogyny that could easily be read into these paintings is the open collaboration he engages in with his wife Okada Hiroko (b. 1970). Also, a Mizuma Gallery artist, she directs the alternative puppet theater troupe, Gekidan ★Shiki, of which Aida is a central member, and herself practices an arguably feminist-style work with a similar black humor to Aida's, with installations and videos satirizing women's roles in Japan. Along with their computer prodigy teenage son, Torajiro, the Aida family as a whole courted further scandal at the Tokyo Museum of Contemporary Art (MOT) in July 2015. In a "family" group show—ostensibly aimed at children—Okada's satirical videos were paired, among other works, with a ridiculing video impersonation by Aida of Prime Minister Abe Shinzō (in office in 2006 and again from 2012) making a speech about Japanese "*sakoku*" (the historical national closure to the world experienced by Japan before the modern era), and a poster banner by their son denouncing the conformist stupidity of the Japanese education system. Once again, Aida was threatened with censorship and closure after a public complaint, although the show remained up (McKirby 2015).

Politics in an Apathetic Continent

The surprise success of Aida's Mori Art Museum show demonstrated that a wide Japanese audience was able to appreciate and understand some of what the artist was articulating without, for the most part, the kind of tabloid shock that would accompany this kind of show in Great Britain or the United States. For reasons surely to do with timing, Aida more than ever assumed the role of the beloved entertainer voicing sarcastic intellectual despair. While politicians have voiced a resurgent nationalism during the more belligerent rule of Prime Minister Abe, Aida's show reflected the black mood of a Tokyo living tensely in the unquantified mist of post-Fukushima radiation. In this, perhaps most effective were the near outsider art of the cheap and tacky *All Together Now* (*Minna to issho*, starting 2002) sketched posters, which randomly voice Aida's reactions to the absurdities of Japanese politics and morals. In one of the later ones, *Optical Illusion around 13th March 2011* (*2011 nen 3 gatsu 13 nichi atari no genshi*, 2011), he bitterly pictures a corporate fantasy in which robot men and dogs are set to work to quickly repair the exploded Fukushima reactor in a model of 1980s world-beating Japanese efficiency, of the kind supposedly epitomized by global technology leaders like Sony or Toyota. In a country ruled by bottled up self-censorship and byzantine modes of self-abnegation—for example, the stifling social norms referred to by so many young Japanese who escape to live and work abroad especially in the 1990s (Kelsky 2001; Sooudi 2014)—Aida voices without fear the back-stage home truths everyone knows and hears outside of formal hierarchies and institutions. Read this way, it is fleetingly possible to imagine him as the post-pop art voice of 1960s radical art reborn for a more cynical age. In another throwaway style series, *Posters* (1984), he brilliantly parodies the heavy-handed moral messages of public safety posters that elementary school children in Japan are sometimes forced to paint in class to reinforce good everyday collective behavior.

Yet Aida has never really stepped up to the plate politically: his vision has always been of an "apathetic continent," an anti-everything nihilism. It is an odd kind of politics, but perhaps appropriate for an advanced highly-developed nation in which democratic politics for many has become an alienating and distant spectator sport (Kingston 2012). On the other hand, Aida's influence has been highly visible in the now hugely successful art of a younger and more overtly political generation who have worked closely with him as teacher and mentor (Favell 2012). Once Aida's assistants, there is Chim↑Pom, whose post-3/11 interventions—supplementing graffiti onto the anti-nuclear work of Okamoto Tarō (1911–1996) in Shibuya Station and breaking into the Fukushima site to make new works—have been presented as a kind of anarchistic art, evoking the 1960s Situationist art movement in Paris (Worrall 2012); similarly, there is Endo Ichiro (b. 1979), who has become an emblematic figure in the post-3/11 period, touring around Japan in distinctive hand-painted yellow vans with the community message of hope *Mirai e!* (Go for Future!).

Aida's one obvious engagement has been on the issue of middle-aged male homelessness. These are his "brown" works, finding beauty out of cardboard and trash. There was the centerpiece of his contribution to the Yokohama Triennale in 2001: the mock Jackson Pollack rendering of a tramp's "naive art" using rotting tatami mats and found junk, (*Untitled 2001*, sometimes referred to in English as *Homeless on the Arakawa River*); and the laughably epic cardboard *Shinjuku Castle* (*Shinjuku-jō* 1995), an old samurai-style castle that was installed in an underpass in the shadow of the skyscrapers of the West Shinjuku financial and government district for the local homeless to live in. Aida's political wit has also been visible in video works: for example, a work that would be worthy of the best British television satire, *A Video of a Man*

Figure 39.2 A Video of a Man Calling Himself Bin Laden Staying in Japan, 2005.
Source: Courtesy of Mizuma Art Gallery.

Calling Himself Bin Laden Staying in Japan (Nihon ni senpukuchū no Bin Laden to nanoru otoko kara no bideo, 2005) (Figure 39.2). In this, set in the comfort of a rural *ryokan* (Japanese-style inn) with copious alcohol and *izakaya* dishes, Aida himself acts out Bin Laden, mellowing out and renouncing violence, while he muses about the world events he has influenced. The idea came to Aida after some friends told him that with a gray beard he was starting to look like the Al-Qaeda leader.

Laughter in Lost Translations

The point about Aida in many of the works discussed above is, in effect, the hardest thing to translate: the rambunctious, slapstick, spiteful, and sometimes plain silly humor found in nearly all his works, which takes its cue from Japanese stand-up variety shows or television comedy traditions, known as *owarai*. A case in point is another video work, unveiled at the large Shōwa 40-nen kai (The Group 1965) group show in Düsseldorf in 2011. The Group 1965 is a gang of Aida's close artist friends, including the social and relational conceptualist Ozawa Tsuyoshi, trashy pop-style photographer Matsukage Hiroyuki, manga artist Kinoshita Parco, electronics master Arima Sumihisa, and the sweet and nostalgic painter Oiwa Oscar. Their only unifying *raison d'être* is that they were *all* born in the (thereby self-evidently) momentous year, 1965, the fortieth year of the reign of the Showa Emperor. Together, with Aida, they celebrate the absurd side of Japanese popular culture, as well as a bitter nostalgia for its disappearing traditional urban landscapes: for example, of old *shokudo* (dining bars), *sentō* (bathing houses), and *kissaten* (coffee houses).

Aida's video for Düsseldorf, *Art and Philosophy #2 (Bijutsu to tetsugaku #2*, 2010), was one of his most trenchant commentaries, yet on the "lost in translation" problem that seems to doom him to cult status internationally. He has before made fun of this, such as his intransigent refusal to make translations of some his works, which he commented on at Yokohama in 2001 by hanging a Japanese-English dictionary next to the works for puzzled foreigners. In a closed room, on three simultaneous video screens, Aida performs, in costume, a live painting on glass by three stereotypical German, French, and English artists. As they paint, a typical "national" style work appears, while each of Aida's characters mouth philosophical and art theoretical statements in their native languages—each with a terrible Japanese accent. The German artist, intense and erratic, seems to be some kind of Anselm Kiefer figure, filling the screen with heavy and lumpy brown paint. The French artist, romantic and fey, dabs impressionistically at the screen, while smoking a Gauloise brand cigarette. The Anglo-American artist, meanwhile, starts out as an Oxbridge gentleman quoting Ludwig Wittgenstein and painting geometric abstractions. By the end, he has turned into an angry postmodern theorist, painting obscenities, reminiscent of Damien Hirst. The message here for young Japanese art students is how meaningless all these pretentious Western art theory references have become in this context. Perhaps a better association for Aida among the YBAs would be Tracey Emin: difficult, perverse, emotional, funny, and impenetrably British. Indeed, Aida even looks a little like her in his transvestite photographic work, *Self Portrait: A Girl of Sea Breezes* (*Shiokaze no shōjo*, 1989).

The reference in the video work, as in many others, is to Immanuel Kant: the eighteenth-century philosopher who laid out for all time the universal sources of beauty in human judgement in his *Critique on Aesthetic Judgement* (1790). Twentieth-century critical philosophy, from Sigmund Freud and Friedrich Nietzsche to Michel Foucault and Edward Said, was supposed to have made impossible this kind of belief in the transcendental sublime. Yet global curators marched all over the planet during the 1990s and 2000s, armed with clever postcolonial theories, while in practice assuming a facile universalism, in which they could recognize, select, and put value on works in every country, after just a few interviews with key art world figures (Stallabrass 2004). Thankfully, Aida has never been much understood by these curators; he has not been colonized. He is not so much a nationalist, as obdurately resistant to such globalist processing. He has always spoken of this as a kind of self-defeating mechanism: the last laugh of the "apathetic continent"; the "monument for nothing."

Murakami's Superflat movement, on the other hand, triumphed because it was the perfect vision of Japan to market during the heady years before the global financial crisis of 2008, in which "flat world" globalism seemed to be all triumphant (Friedman 2005). Superflat succeeded by reducing the Japanese nation to cartoon images and a simple digital code: easy to consume, like salmon sushi, for those looking for an imaginary "Cool Japan." But, as the gloss on Murakami's smiley flowers begins to pall, it is not surprising that the world has started looking for other visions of Japan, more in tune with a darker, more complex political and economic moment. The global era of the 1990s and 2000s is over; nations and their perverse, peculiar cultures and misunderstandings will just not go away. Aida paid little attention to the globalist fashions and ambitions that drove Superflat to success and so now stands as a much better guide to what happened in and to Japan since 1990. As the funniest man in Japanese art and a much-loved vaudevillian mainstay of the inner Tokyo art world, many artists, curators, and students in Japan have been ready to follow Aida, despite the frequent bad taste and sometime duff works that pepper his catalogues. For them, he has been the artist who best expresses their world, in all its beauty and joy, frustration and bile. Aida, meanwhile shows little sign of repenting or changing course: articulating the squeamish discomforts of the Japanese condition, with a shrug and a wry laugh, while blithely awaiting an international recognition which may or may not someday arrive.

Note

1 This refers to an incident at the Tokyo Metropolitan Assembly in June 2014 when a female politician was heckled during a speech urging more support for pregnant women. The incident was reported internationally as a new nadir in Japanese gender relations (Alter 2014).

40 Art from "What is Already There" on Islands in the Seto Inland Sea

James Jack

Embarking on a journey to an island in the Seto Inland Sea requires a change in pace. Departing from Tokyo on the bullet train (*shinkansen*) at 300 km per hour—passing the cities of Nagoya, Osaka, and Kyoto to the slow ferry at 25 km per hour—the scenery shifts from a forceful blur to a soft landscape dotted with islands. There is time to notice the small wooden boat floating in the harbor since only one ferry departs every few hours to the islands in the Seto Inland Sea. It is difficult to occupy time since most of the shops are closed at 11 a.m. This is far away from opulent boutiques in Tokyo's Roppongi district and endless stores on the back streets of Shibuya. Here, a shop with earth-toned clothing that appears to be from the 1980s. Next to it a dingy coffee shop—is it open or closed? This is where a global view of two islands in the Seto Inland Sea is born: a soft tidal harbor connecting maritime history with today's social landscape.

As an artist, I see the Seto Inland Sea in the first person. It is not a government statistic or an image in the popular media, but a friend coming to meet me as the ferry slowly approaches the dock. While zooming from the consumer culture landscape of Tokyo to the slow maritime life in the Seto Inland Sea, materials from the past have lives that continues beyond their original intentions. In his study of industrial ruins, Tim Edensor (2005: 830) finds modes of "social remembering" at work in marginalized spaces. The orderly commercial aims of the popular culture industry shift in the disorderly spaces of the islands in the Seto Inland Sea. I utilize "orderly" and "disorderly" to refer to a trend in art production to be organized within fixed exhibition spaces in highly-polished and professionally-marketed galleries with commercial aims in the making of the art itself, as objects or as gift-shop souvenirs, consumable and shaped by the structure and order that requires. Placing art on islands far from Tokyo, that cannot be consumed, only experienced, and incorporating elements of the past rather than just present-focused production and sales, disrupts the imposed commercialized order on art production and forms instead disorderly spaces for art. Here, I examine the social impact of two art sites where disorderly elements of the past are collaged with contemporary realities.

Figure 40.1 Ohtake Shinro, *Naoshima Bath "I ♥ YU,"* 2009.
Source: Photograph by Watanabe Osamu. Courtesy of Fukutake Foundation.

More specifically, I re-examine the orderly presentation of popular culture through alternative art projects that re-envision cultural trends occurring in Japan today. Contemporary artists often adopt anthropological approaches (Nakamura et al. 2013: 7), and I actively reflect on the perspective of participants in the production of artwork. I show that participants are more than just the producers or consumers, as the orderly aims of industries investing in popular culture might desire. Instead, they create an alternative vision of popular culture.

Just a few minutes' walk down a narrow alley from the main port of Miyanoura on the island of Naoshima is a vibrant bathhouse. This artwork *Naoshima Bath "I ♥ YU"*[1] (2009) (Figure 40.1) includes pillars painted in disparate patterns, plants hanging from countless verandas, rainbow stained glass, reassembled ship parts, gigantic palm trees, and much more. The construction of *Naoshima Bath* explodes onto the street, each material charged with a stunning presence yet impossible to isolate from the mix. Ohtake Shinro (b. 1955) is an artist who obsessively collects scraps, photos, lighters, and other objects from his travels which become part of his artworks. His artistic ventures include music, forming the noise band Puzzle Punks with the Boredoms' Yamantaka Eye during the 1990s (see Chapter 16). His collages fill one notebook after another and expand into room-size installations featured in exhibitions of his work across the globe. *Naoshima Bath* shares the collage aesthetic yet is different. It is a functional bathhouse in the community; a place where residents are employed and a space where people gather. With the closure of public bathhouses and schools across Japan, loss of community gathering spaces has become a recurring form of social remorse. This bathhouse engages with the community as part of a longer relationship begun decades earlier.

In the late 1980s, Fukutake Tetsuhiko, then head of the Benesse Corporation (leader in correspondence education and educational publishing), met Miyake Chikatsugu, then Mayor of Naoshima. Together they came up with the idea for a "Global Camping Site" as part of the tourist vision for the southern part of the island opening in 1989 (Kaida et al. 2012). After his untimely death, his son Fukutake Soichi developed the vision based on the idea that "economy is subordinate to culture" (Yamada 2013). In 1992, he built the Naoshima Contemporary Art Museum (now named Benesse House) to show his collection of contemporary art on the stunning oceanfront property above the campground. During the 1990s, the young Fukutake invited artists, curators, and architects to make new works in response to unique aspects of the island.

In 2004, the Kagawa Prefectural government proposed the idea of an art festival to Governor Manabe Takeki. A partnership between the Fukutake Foundation, Kagawa Prefecture, and curator Kitagawa Fram produced the first Setouchi International Art Festival (now Setouchi Triennale) in 2010. The Triennale was designed to be a large-scale showcase of internationally renowned artists to be compared with exhibitions of a similar scale, including Venice (established 1895) and São Paolo (1951). However, rather than emphasizing the participation of artists in national pavilions, the mission of Setouchi Treinnale is closer to Documenta (1955) in Germany for its focus on new works made in response to the place, its history, and its residents. It also cherishes cooperation with the local community utilizing methods that can be compared with the Busan Biennale (1981) in South Korea, where "learning councils" comprised of local residents work together with artists in the creation of their works. Based on a model from Kitagawa's Echigo-Tsumari Triennale (2000) in Niigata Prefecture, the volunteer organization Koebi-tai (Little Shrimp Squad) was established for the Setouchi Triennale to link artists, local residents, and supporters. This cooperative aspect has become one of the distinguishing factors of art activities in the Seto Inland Sea compared to the growing number of biennial/triennial exhibitions.

I expand on the orderly characterizations of popular culture in urban centers by drawing a more nuanced landscape that includes overlooked elements of the past. While working on the permanent artwork *Sunset House: The House as Language of Being* (commencing in 2010 and completed in 2013, hereafter referred to as *Sunset House*), (Figure 40.2) I have come to see disorderly aspects in the production of popular culture. Culture is not singular nor is it produced by one industry; instead, it includes multiple participants who are continually redrawing its shape. Historically, the Seto Inland Sea has provided raw materials for urban development while being

Figure 40.2 James Jack, *Sunset House: The House as Language of Being*, 2013.
Source: Courtesy of the Author.

the recipient of toxic industrial waste from commercial businesses from the Honshu mainland, byproducts of Japan's high-speed postwar growth. For example, stones from islands have been used in dams, roads, train tracks, and reclaimed land across Japan. Stones from Shōdoshima were used to lay the ground beneath Haneda's International Terminal (completed in 2010). These serve as an interesting counterpoint to the toxic automobile-industrial waste dumped on Teshima and nearby islands during the 1970s and 1980s. Today the islands are experiencing a new-found fame through art activities, contributing to a shift from urban centers of orderly culture production towards eclectic rural areas.

Unpopular Culture

What happens to out-of-date cars, houses with no residents, and schools that have been closed? Structures constructed for education, residence, and transportation are left in various states of disrepair. "Unpopular culture" refers to the culture of places, items, and ideas from the past that are no longer fascinating to the orderly trends of society today. The potential for aspects of unpopular culture to be transformed is expressed in artworks. For example, today public bathhouse culture is unpopular in Japan. I recall a visit I made to Tokyo's Tsuru no yu bathhouse on the last night before it closed and remember the lively community chatter that filled the changing room. The memory of a bathhouse which closed in one's own neighborhood across Japan may easily enter the mind of other visitors to *Naoshima Bath* as they re-experience unpopular culture in a lively form. These memories are further triggered by images of Japanese popular television stars of the 1950s and 1960s appearing on the walls and floors of the bathhouse. Scenes of female sea divers are painted on tiles in both the male and female sides of the bath, as well as appearing in a video erotically placed inside of a bench that bathers use while undressing.

According to one of the earliest curators of contemporary art in the islands, "Naoshima is a place that has a history and a culture that is now seen as old-fashioned" (Akimoto 2002: 220). In this context, a mixture of images from past decades stimulates new experiences. Ohtake fills surfaces of the bathhouse with an assemblage of colorful images, objects, and botanicals. Particularly vibrant are those sealed into the resin floor of the hot bath—vintage photographs, magazine pages of airbrushed women, along with book pages yellowed by time. An elephant replica upcycled (reusing discarded items to make a product of higher value than the original) from a closed *hihokan* (sex museum) in Hokkaido presides on top of the wall between the male and female bathing areas. This art accumulation overflows with disorderly remnants that might otherwise have been left behind. Ohtake intentionally turns his eye to those items being thrown away to make room for the latest trendy items consumed in popular culture. An observer of his work describes them as "intense travel scrapbooks crammed with discarded cultural artifacts—scavenged tickets, snapshots, tags, currency, newspapers, and other mass-produced printed matter shrugged off by popular culture" (Ohtake 1996: n.p.). His art activities in the Seto Inland Sea point towards a new twist on unpopular culture within the seemingly unsightly but increasingly rich fodder of the deep sea of the past.

Recent images of the Seto Inland Sea in the mass media have become visible on the global stage through artworks such as those by Ohtake.[2] Other artists, including Kusama Yayoi, James Turrell, Sugimoto Hiroshi, and Olafur Eliasson, also attract crowds. Just under one million visitors came to the first Setouchi Triennale (Benesse Holdings, Inc. 2010), with even more in 2013 when the Art Festival increased to three seasons (Hirano 2013). But there are easier places to see these artists' works: why travel to these quiet, inconvenient islands? Dilapidated houses, boarded-up hotels, and abandoned boats abound in the island landscape. Here it is easier to find closed schools than open ones. Population decline can be felt on all of Japan's islands: for example, on Shōdoshima, inhabitants are half of what they were in their postwar peak and on other islands only one-tenth of the postwar peak (Shōdoshima-chō 2010). Part of the success in the promotion of the Seto Inland Sea is thanks to global media images, which provide both an idyllic vision of the rural past and notions of the region as a trendy place with a bright future (Ellwood 2010; Williams 2011; Kaun 2015).

Framing this trend is Benesse Art Site Naoshima's idealistic goal:

> to present art in a way that makes visitors more aware of the fascinating qualities of the region and instills pride in the residents, encouraging them to think positively about the future and the possibilities of a more desirable way of life
>
> (Benesse Art Site Naoshima 2014: 2).

As one of the largest educational publishers in Japan, Benesse Holdings disseminates images of the artworks widely; yet the impact of Fukutake Foundation's art activities can also be found on a more intimate scale. Often it is difficult for individuals to appreciate the landscape closest to one's home for its banal familiarity. This was the sentiment of curator Mohri Yoshitsugu, who was born on the island of Shikoku, one of the main gateways to the Seto Inland Sea. However, through art activities, he began to see the "rhythm of each island and its landscape, not just as landscape but all that enters the senses … absolutely fascinating" (Mohri 2014). People are traveling to the islands for stays ranging from one day to one year or more, praising the nature, food, and people.

However, the increasing visibility of the region does not occur entirely *because of* art, but rather it occurs *together with* art. Models for cooperative artworks developed after the downfalls of public art in the 1980s (Lacy 1995), which too often saw society as an empty receptacle that could only view (read: consume) artworks. I focus here on the "cooperative approach," building upon the nuanced definitions of *kyōdō* (literally, "working together") studied in collaborative artworks produced in Niigata (Klein 2010). I refer to "cooperative" as the process in which participants are actively involved in multiple stages of the artwork.

In addition to the record number of visitors, people from urban centers are now moving to smaller islands. Many express the desire to become part of an alternative culture where participants are not satisfied with consuming television broadcasts, Internet releases, or magazine publications. They want to create their own collage of disorderly ideas actively striving for a more appealing future culture (Abe 2012). This ideal should not be seen from only one perspective. In playing with wasted, sidelined, decentralized, and forgotten aspects of Japanese culture, art activities in the Seto Inland Sea region are re-envisioning the unpopular to create new community gathering places.

A Meeting Place

Two doors down from where *Naoshima Bath* now stands, there was a general store where villagers used to gather—after work, waiting for the ferry, or just stopping to chat. In a story familiar to Japan's aging society, elderly proprietress Ms. Ochiai moved to the mainland so that her relatives could care for her, causing the store to close. For *THE STANDARD* (2001) exhibition, Ohtake revived the Ochiai General Store by adding posters, calendars, magazines, newspapers, bottles, red lights, and more to what was already there. A memorable jukebox with a playlist that included Bob Dylan, Ishikawa Seri, EMA and Leadbelly was played by visitors, bringing the electric guitar suspended from the ceiling to life. Ohtake's obsessive collection of memorabilia fit so well with the store that it was hard to tell where he had intervened. This spatial collage exemplifies Ohtake's (2005) philosophy of utilizing "*sude ni soko ni aru mono*" (that which is already there). Here, he reassembles popular

Figure 40.3 Ohtake Shinro, *Ochiai General Store*, 2001.
Source: Photograph by Fujisuka Mitsumasa. Courtesy of Benesse Holdings, Inc.

culture from past decades into a new form of art. Yet this was not Ohtake's first creative encounter with the islands.

Ohtake's creative work in the Seto Inland Sea began on Naoshima with *Shipyard Works* (1990), a boat frame half submerged into the earth related to the former shipyard where he established his studio in Uwajima on the other side of Shikoku. But it was through his work in the *Ochiai General Store* (2001) that he became truly immersed in the life of the community (Figure 40.3). This work included paintings of objects from Waikiki, Hong Kong, Egypt, and Jajouka as well as many items Ms. Ochiai had left in the store. The site became informally known as "Ochitake" store, combining "Ochi" from the owner's name and "take" from the artist's. Here Ohtake's approach of working with what is "already there" synchronizes with the views of artist Akimoto Yūji, who began working as a curator on the island of Naoshima in 1991. Akimoto went on to shape the direction of artworks with a sensitivity to the social history of Naoshima for over a decade, particularly evident in the Art House Project (opened 1997).

The cooperative production process utilized in many of the new artworks has been met with mixed reactions from the community. Naoshima resident Tanaka Takako explains, "It's not quite the peaceful and beautiful island that it used to be" (Benesse Art Site Naoshima 2014: 7). Yet there are few who doubt the need for change to the Seto Inland Sea region as it attempts to redefine itself after the environmental catastrophes of the 1980s and amidst current issues such as aging population. Toxic waste dumped on Teshima is being processed at a treatment facility on the north side of Naoshima that has operated as a smelting facility for a century. For the first *THE STAND-ARD* exhibition, sites at the facility included a clinic, barbershop, and ping-pong center, all used by past employees. Akimoto wants people to look at the island "from a different point of view and bring it to life" (Akimoto 2002: 220).

After the exhibition *NAOSHIMA STANDARD 2* (2006–2007) museums and art projects were also commissioned on nearby islands, such as Inujima and Teshima, drawing influence from the social history of each site; some artworks included significant community participation. Visitors traveled in surprising numbers to these once "inconvenient" islands by boat, bike, car, and on foot. Along their way through the countryside, they inevitably get lost. The rural countryside then becomes part of the playful journey from one artwork to another. In this way, both local and non-local visitors see beyond previous images of the region. In these newly created meeting places, past elements and stunning landscapes are discovered and rediscovered.

A House for Being

Art Setouchi is also a personal story. ("Art Setouchi" is the title for the year-round art activities, while the title "Setouchi Triennale" initiated in 2013 is used to refer to 2010 and 2016 as well.) As an artist, I have experienced these issues up close while working on *Sunset House*. When first encountering the raw mud walls of a half-century old shed on Shōdoshima, I felt they were full of stories. While listening to the elderly island residents, I learned the building had been a gathering space for stone quarry employees between 1930 and 1980, when the town prospered. Basalt stones from this now defunct quarry were laid underneath the tracks of the *shinkansen* that carried travelers from Tokyo to the Seto Inland Sea. Beginning with re-painting these deeply cracked mud walls with soil, I derived a way to paint open arc shapes into the interior with two shades of dust from local stones. I then began to envision ways for the stories of the community to be re-circulated in the site as a permanent artwork.

In the second year, I invited the community to insert their feelings into the tattered structure. While renovating the exterior walls, memories, dreams, and hopes were layered inside vernacular building materials. These words were only visible while the artwork was under construction, emphasizing the active process of remembering that occurs in the present. Afterwards, words inscribed within must be felt rather than seen. The disintegrating walls were empowered with words of hundreds of participants to stand once again as a gathering place. In the process of working with local materials and the community, links between social networks and material objects become visible. The language of participation is the responsibility of both artists and community, a process Tom Finkelpearl describes as "cooperative, participatory and coauthored" (2014). These links show new directions in overlooked aspects of Japanese culture from the past. Furthermore, they show contemporary Japanese culture is not only formed by popular images but also includes multiple stories occurring over time in diverse regions.

For example, granite stones have been integral to these islands' local economy and culture—in particular Shōdoshima, Teshima, and Inujima. In 1934, the same year the Seto Inland Sea was established as the first national park in Japan, a stone quarry opened in the town of Kōnoura on the southern tip of Shōdoshima. These two simultaneous events emphasize the duality of life in the islands, which, along with productivity and turbulence, come measures to help protect nature. The political and economic value of stones in the past is no longer relevant; now they have cultural value. Shōdoshima, once famous for supplying stones to build the original walls at Osaka Castle in the late sixteenth century, now invites tourists to come see Tofu Rock, Book Rock, and other natural sights. Amidst the façade of historic stones and the olive industry that also draws visitors, the less traveled north shore of Shōdoshima contains numerous granite quarries where mountains are carved into massive staircases. This is true on many islands: there is a light side that includes artworks and cafés along with a dark side that contains the spoils of industry.

I used two varieties of local stones to build the garden surrounding *Sunset House*: light granite stones from the northern tip of the island and dark basalt stones from the southern tip. Granite became the medium for each participant to write one fear, difficulty, or concern. Each stone was subsequently inverted so the text faced the earth, creating a stone garden imbibed with the challenges of the community. A garden once filled with burnt garbage and waste became an open space for new possibilities. To complete the garden, a meandering pathway was designed with crushed basalt stones, creating a contemplative pathway out of local materials.

Working in the Seto Inland Sea region, I see organizers, artists, and volunteers struggling, just like I do, with a confusing relationship to the local land. One of the tenets of Art Setouchi is a site-specific philosophy: artworks are made with an intimate relationship to the site where they are exhibited. Becoming more intimate with local culture is possible with enough time and motivation, but these efforts could be misdirected. Artworks can change people's minds and provide new views of what is already there. But what role can artists play in shifting societal trends? I have experienced shifts in the islands and residents while creating *Sunset House*. However, as an artist, I do not cause these shifts, rather I circulate existing tensions in words that temporarily appear then become an invisible part of the artwork. With the language of community participation, *Sunset House* is one way to reflect on the trend of cooperative culture production.

Can Art Change Society?

Not only in the Seto Inland Sea region but around Japan, art festivals are promoting alternative views of the countryside and its historical popular culture. Since 2000, curator Kitagawa Fram has attempted to rebrand images of rural Japan through radical art projects (Kitagawa 2005). Kitagawa established the Echigo-Tsumari Triennale in 2000 and directs the Setouchi Triennale (begun 2010), Ichihara × Art Mix (begun 2014, Chiba Prefecture), Japan Alps Art Festival (begun 2017, Nagano Prefecture), and Oku-Noto Triennale (begun 2017, Kanazawa Prefecture). This is based on a belief shared with Fukutake that culture should be prioritized above economics. In addition, Kitagawa firmly believes artists can serve as both motivators and mediators in local communities. However, urban centers remain a crucial base for these projects, as the flow of capital and media promotion still operates almost entirely in Tokyo. Nostalgia for rural Japan increases amidst the larger trend of people moving to cities for study, work, and employment.

One ambitious question posed by Art Base Momoshima, established in 2012 by artist Yanagi Yukinori as the successor to the Hiroshima Art Project (2006) and one of the more sustainable rural art projects in the Seto Inland Sea region, is relevant here: "What can art do for a better society?" (Yanagi 2014).

Art festival organizers' and benefactors' attempts to redirect cultural trends often have been met with success, but the effects of art making a better society are hard to quantify with data. Nonetheless, one figure from 2014 stands out: that year, the first school in Japan was officially re-opened on the island of Ogijima. With an average of forty schools closing in Japan every month (Ministry of Education, Culture, Sports, Science, and Technology 2014),[3] this example is rare but noteworthy. As an island with a population of just 184 residents (Takamatsu-shi sōmukyoku 2015) where art activities have been occurring since 2009, Ogijima could be seen as a qualitative shift in showing how art can change cultural perceptions of the countryside.

The Setouchi Triennale is most often highlighted with artist names and sponsors, but the thousands of volunteers and paid staff who sustain the festival embody its potential to change society. The aforementioned Koebi-tai started in 2009 to support daily activities of the festival. Members of this nonprofit group help prepare and maintain artworks as well as explain art sites during the festival. At my artwork, Koebi-tai volunteers included a broad range of people of all ages, including a city bus driver, a convenience store clerk, university students, and a train conductor. There were over 2,500 active members of Koebi-tai in 2010 and over 7,000 members in 2013, with an average age around thirty years (Koebi 2013; Setouchi 2010). The relationships fostered between local and non-local participants continue during the years in between each Triennale, as select artworks are kept open, musical events held, and local festivals flourish. These youthful members spark energy in the aging countryside and represent a reverse migration of young people away from urban areas.

The "cooperative dream" described by Kitagawa (2005) is realized by these volunteers, many of whom seek alternative lifestyles. Yasuda Chihiro, a young woman who moved to Naoshima from Tokyo just before the second festival began in 2013, explains, "In Tokyo I got money, but my heart wasn't fulfilled." While employed at a department store popular for its youth fashions, she felt, "I was killing myself [working so hard] … Other staff were having mental issues or health problems, so I felt like I should quit before that happened to me" (Yasuda 2014). On her first visit to Naoshima, she felt like she was taking a trip to Disneyland. Soon after, she quit her job, moved to the island, and found work just before the Triennale. For many visitors, including Yasuda, art is the first impetus to come to the Seto Inland Sea region, but the cooperative networks retain their interest. Linked with the vision of the festival, these networks support alternative methods for culture production outside of commercial activities centered in urban areas.

Conclusion

As I have discussed, art activities engaged with the social landscapes of the Seto Inland Sea region provide new perspectives on Japanese popular culture. Art's cultural and social value is prioritized over its economic value (Matsumoto et al. 2010) and will not necessarily save the countryside from economic hardship, population decline, joblessness, and aging. Yet art is providing options for people yearning for alternative lifestyles outside of commercial trends and fast-paced city life. Art activities in rural communities are not easily classifiable as high, low, or middlebrow culture; rather, they show disorderly components of popular culture. Art activities combining old-fashioned aspects of the past with new forms of "social remembering" have a lasting impact. Together organizers, artists, and participants diversify perspectives on the production of contemporary culture to include activities taking place outside of urban centers.

The dream of cooperatively producing culture among residents, artists, curators, and participants is being realized in Japan today. From the viewpoints I heard in the Seto Inland Sea region, commercialized popular culture arising in cities is leaving many people unfulfilled. Scholars have noted that local cultures in Asia are in danger of losing the interest of young people (Craig and King 2002), who are more attracted to the rapid influx of urban culture. Yet new perspectives on the past offer the potential to create new mixtures of old and new within this influx. I have looked outside urban borders of popular culture to find appeal in previously unpopular places. This search has led to rustic abandoned homes, cavernous school gymnasiums, and fallow farmlands, all fallen out of immediate use to society. Artistic views of these spaces ripe with potential contribute to culture formed in cooperative networks.

Stories, materials, and histories that already exist in the islands of the Seto Inland Sea are brought back into plain view through art activities. Here, new boundaries of disorderly popular culture stand in contrast to the orderly production of culture in urban centers. Cooperative art activities serve as stimuli for both visitors and residents to rediscover the value of culture in new places. Yet the sustainability of these cooperative activities after artists depart remains uncertain. This is where cooperative networks are truly engaged, as new-found life of art sites lie in the hands of supporters. The complex social landscape examined in the Seto Inland Sea region shows a depth beneath flat images of Japan often exported abroad (see Chapter 38). The hundreds of buildings being abandoned in the countryside might teach us more about the complexity of Japanese culture than the latest city skyscrapers, shopping malls, and sports venues. If culture is just to be thought of as something commercialized, consumable, and disposable, then this constant focus on the future is understandable. But culture is more than a marketing exercise; it can come not just from the expectation of a glossy future but from art created together with what is already there.

Notes

1 "I ♥ YU" puns the Japanese word for warm water (*yu*) with the English word "you"; therefore, the title means both "I love warm water" and "I love you."
2 Examples include articles in *Newsweek*, CNN, *The New York Times*, *Euro Times*, *Financial Times*, *Lonely Planet* guidebooks, and *The Japan Times*.
3 According to the Ministry of Education, Culture, Sports, Science, and Technology 482 schools closed in 2013 and 598 schools closed in 2012 across Japan, most of which were elementary schools (Ministry of Education, Culture, Sports, Science, and Technology 2014).

Glossary

3/11 Triple Disaster   Three disasters precipitated by a magnitude 9.0 Mw earthquake off the east coast of Japan on March 11, 2011. The earthquake is referred to as the Great Tōhoku Earthquake or Great East Japan Earthquake (Higashi Nihon daishinsai). It triggered a massive tsunami that reached heights of 40.5 m (133 feet) along the coast of Japan and traveled up to 10 km (6.2 miles) inland (USGS 2015; National Police Agency of Japan 2016). The tsunami produced three reactor meltdowns at the Fukushima Daiichi Nuclear Power Plant, causing large-scale evacuation and as yet unknown nuclear contamination of the surrounding area and food chain.

Anime   In Japan, refers to any kind of animation; however, outside of Japan, it denotes Japanese originated or heavily inspired products.

Aum Shinrikyō   Japanese doomsday cult responsible for the March 20, 1995 Tokyo subway sarin gas attack (Chikatetsu sarin jiken), which killed twelve people and injured more than a thousand. It remains Japan's most serious postwar act of terrorism.

Bishōnen   Literally, "beautiful boy." The most common aesthetic of male beauty in *shōjo* manga, featuring young men with slender bodies, long hair, and exaggerated eyes.

BL (Boys' Love)   Also called *shōnen ai* or *yaoi* (with different nuances among the terms), subgenre of *shōjo* manga and other manga or novels featuring love stories between two boys or men. Content ranges from chaste to explicit.

Bubble Era   Between roughly 1985 and 1990, a time of prosperity accompanied by greed and extravagance. The soaring stock market and rampant speculation in real estate built on cheap credit led to a rapid increase in the paper value of land assets. By 1990 the stock market and real estate bubble had burst, and Japan entered a deflationary spiral.

Būmu (boom)   Large-scale fad that explodes on the scene but does not last.

–chan, –san, –kun   In Japanese, suffixes are usually used after family or given names to indicate social position in relation to the speaker. Among the most common: *–san*, a semiformal title of respect between relative equals; *–kun*, used by superiors addressing juniors and usually, although

not always, for boys; *–chan*, an expression of endearment, for children, lovers, youthful women, and close friends.

Chibi   In manga, small, cute, rougher drawings of known characters.

Comiket (Comic Market, Komiketto, Comike)   Founded in 1975, biannual Tokyo comic market (August and December). Regularly attracting around half a million attendees (Comiket 2015), Comiket has become the largest public gathering in Japan and the world's largest independent comic fair. Comiket sells primarily *dōjinshi*.

Cool Japan   "Cool Japan" and "Gross National Cool" were originally part of an idea of Douglas McGray (2002) that Japan, although it had lost some of its status as an economic superpower since the collapse of the property bubble and the rise of China, had, however, emerged as a cultural superpower. McGray wrote that Japanese youth culture—including consumer electronics, fashion, and the phenomena of cuteness—consisted a form of "soft power." The idea of "soft power" is vague, sitting somewhere between national branding and the ability to influence foreign policy and project real power. Despite this, in 2010 the idea was formally integrated into Japanese government policy with the formation by the Ministry of Economy, Trade, and Industry of the Creative Industries Promotion Office with a budget for 2011 of 19 billion yen (US$170 million) (Mackay 2010).

Cosplay (*kosupure*)   Form of performance art, often at dedicated conventions or events, where participants wear elaborate costumes usually based on popular culture characters.

Decora   Fashion style of the late 1990s and early 2000s that emphasized decorating bags, garments, and personal technologies with cute accessories, often to excess. Clothing, usually layered, tended to favor pink or neon colors, but to be otherwise plain and comfortable.

Dōjinshi   Self-published, and often unlicensed, manga and other print media often featuring parodies or revisions of commercial popular culture products.

Dorama   Common term for Japanese fictional television serials. Also known as "idol dramas" (*aidoru dorama*, term coined by Taiwan Star TV), "pure-love dramas" (*junai dorama*), and "J-drama."

Emoji   "Picture characters" added to text messages to ensure the right emotional message is received. A set of colorful emoji was developed around 1999 by NTT (Nippon Telegraph and Telephone) designer Kurita Shigetaka to be preprogrammed into cellphones. A standard set of Unicode emoji, including the now iconic yellow faces, globalized after 2010 on iPhones, Facebook, and other platforms, while including images like the bowing man and masked sick face that require knowledge of Japanese society to be understood. Japanese cellphone users have also popularized "*kaomoji*," or "face characters," a form of ASCII artwork comprised of letters, punctuation marks, and other printable characters written on Internet textboards since the 1980s.

Enka Commercial music genre of mostly sentimental romantic ballads sung in a traditional pentatonic minor scale. The sound of scale itself, the songs' common themes—regret, lost love, and longing for home, as well as nonmaterial nationalism—give the genre a particularly nostalgic appeal (Yano 2002).

Freeter (furītā) Denoting people without fulltime employment, thought to be a mixture of the English "freelance" and the German "*arbeiter*," or laborer. The Japanese word for part-time job is "*arubaito*," from the same German root. The term is used for those who deliberately reject fulltime employment, those pursuing dreams outside standard careers, and those forced to seek casual employment because they could not find fulltime jobs.

Fujoshi Literally, "rotten girls." Dedicated fans of boys' love manga. Pun on a term for an elegant lady, substituting a kanji character meaning "rotten."

Galapagos Syndrome (*garapagosu-ka*) Term used to describe Japanese cellphones so technologically advanced they had little in common with devices in the rest of the world, similar to Darwin's animals on the Galapagos Islands that had evolved separately in isolation (Stewart 2010; Wakabayashi 2012).

Gekiga Literally, "dramatic picture." *Gekiga* loosely refers to a body of manga with long narratives and typically little or no comical effect, targeted at young adult male readers.

Great Kantō Earthquake Magnitude 7.9 Mw earthquake that struck the Kantō plain, on which Tokyo is situated, on September 1, 1923. The earthquake occurred at 11:58 a.m. when many people where cooking meals over fires, and, at the same time, a typhoon hit Tokyo Bay. As a result, firestorms broke out, causing the majority of the damage. Because of the widespread destruction, the earthquake was a catalyst for significant reconstruction and modernization (Weisenfeld 2012: 3).

Haikyo Literally meaning ruins, it has become the term for the exploration of human-made structures, often abandoned or derelict due to industrialization, depopulation, natural disasters, and other events or processes of loss. Although usually a hobby, *haikyo* is often approached with a scientific, archaeological, or historical rigor.

Hanabi Japanese word for fireworks and related festivals.

Harajuku Neighborhood in central Tokyo associated with youth culture and fashion.

Herbivore Man (*sōshoku-kei danshi*) Term, assuming heterosexuality, used to describe a man who is not assertive or interested in pursuing women romantically or sexually. Since the popularity of the term, other variants have appeared (in part in parody), such as *nikushoku-kei danshi*, (meat-eating man), for someone who seems sexually aggressive; *rōru-kyabetsu danshi,* (stuffed-cabbage man), for someone who appears on the outside to be sexually non-assertive but is actually aggressive underneath; and *asupara bakon danshi* (asparagus-wrapped-in-bacon man), for someone who seems interested in women but is actually not.

Hiragana One of Japanese's two phonetic alphabets, along with katakana, used for native words for which there is no kanji (Chinese character); for grammatical particles; verb and adjective inflections; in place of kanji for difficult or obscure words; and as an alternative to kanji for emphasis. Also used in pronunciation guides (*rubi*) sometimes printed above rare kanji.

Idol (*aidoru*) Manufactured star or group not necessarily with exceptional looks or talents but who are nonetheless attractive. Rather than being one thing in particular, idols perform multiple functions, from singing and dancing to modeling and acting.

Ikebukuro Commercial and entertainment neighborhood in northwestern Tokyo built around Ikebukuro Station, one of the world's busiest commuter hubs.

Izakaya Japanese style of casual drinking and eating establishment. Unlike in English or American pubs, customers sit and are served food along with drinks as a matter of course.

J-Horror Genre that emerged in the late 1990s, primarily based on popular horror tales or stories featuring contemporary characters facing random supernatural attacks, normally made in low budget with no stars.

J-Pop Coined by Japanese media in the 1990s as a blanket term for Japanese pop music, excluding *enka*. In addition to main J-pop genres that combine elements of various genres (e.g., rock, metal, hip-hop, and R&B), J-pop includes subgenres, such as anime music, idol pop (by boy bands and girl groups), and *chaku-uta* (digital ringtone music).

Japan Noise, Japanoise (*Japanoizu*) Mixes the words "Japanese" and "noise" to refer to the noise music scene in Japan. Noise music challenges the distinction between musical and non-musical sound in conventional music and is marked by a sense of musical freedom and punk-style rebellion. Most active in the 1980s and 1990s, it is still alive today,

***Josei* manga** Literally "comics for women," created particularly, but not exclusively, for readers in their late teens and early twenties. *Josei* manga are different to *shōjo* manga aimed at girls younger than twenty and "ladies' comics" (*redīsu komikkusu*) that tend to be more erotic.

K-Pop Emerged in the mid-2000s as a loosely defined term primarily used by international audiences outside of Korea. It can refer to Korean pop music in general, idol pop, or mainstream pop music since the early 2000s that combines elements of various genres, including hip-hop, R&B, and electronica.

Kabuki Japanese dance-drama known for elaborate make-up, energetic music, stylized movements, stories that glorify good and vanquish evil, rigorous training, the fact that all roles are played by men, and its attendant fan culture. Once popular among the Edo-period merchant class, kabuki rose in reputation to become a defining elite art form.

Kaijū Literally "strange beast," large destructive monsters. Featured in *kaijū eiga*, "strange beast movies," a subgenre of *tokusatsu* (special effects-based) entertainment.

Kamishibai Literally "paper theater," was a form of street theater using paper tableaux, mostly aimed at children of the urban laboring classes, popular from the late 1920s until the early 1970s.

Kanji Logographic characters used in the modern Japanese along with phonetic alphabets of hiragana, katakana, and sometimes *romanji*, or Latin script. Kanji are derived from Chinese characters and often have similar meanings but different phonetics and grammar.

Kashihon-ya Rental bookstore or lending library where a customer could borrow or read books for a small charge. *Kashihon-ya* was one of the places to access manga until the late 1960s, before manga magazines from Tokyo-centered publishers occupied the manga market.

Katakana One of two phonetic syllabify alphabets in the Japanese language. Katakana can be used for loan words integrated into Japanese, onomatopoeia, and technical terms and for rendering foreign words into Japanese or adding emphasis.

Kawaii Literally, adorable or cute, often premised on vulnerability. Denotes cuteness in the context of Japanese culture.

–*kei* Japanese suffix, literally meaning system, style, or subset, as in Shibuya-*kei* (Shibuya style) and *sōshoku-kei danshi* (herbivore men).

Keitai denwa Commonly shortened to *keitai*, literally, portable telephone, often of the flip-phone variety. Japan was an early adopter of mobile phone technology; some usage patterns, such as imputing Japanese characters and the desire for reading privacy while on crowded trains, led to features not adopted in other markets. Their ubiquity and particularities encouraged the development of a *keitai* culture, including *keitai shōsetsu*, or "cellphone novels." Since the development of the touch-screen "smartphone" (commonly called *sumaho*), many of these innovations and cultures have disappeared.

Keitai shōsetsu Literally, "cellphone novel," stories written on cellphones often by amateur authors and circulated through subscription websites. Some of the most popular have been published as print books and adapted into television dramas and other popular media. Especially influential between 2004 and 2007, the fad was made obsolete by touch-screen smartphones.

Kōhai Literally "junior." See *Senpai*.

Kyara, Kyarakutā Refers to a range of visualized fictional characters in the Japanese context. Often characterized by cute, simple, or unsophisticated designs, sometimes making their feelings or expressions ambiguous.

Lehman Shock (*rīman shokku*) Refers to the economic downturn caused by the collapse of Lehman Brothers on September 15, 2008 because of their overexposure to subprime mortgages in the United States. Because the Japanese branch of the firm, Lehman Brothers Japan, exerted much influence in the Japanese Bond Market, the collapse caused serious problems in Japanese credit markets and, consequently, the entire Japanese economy. Japanese often uses the term "*shokku*" (shock) for what English refers to as an economic "crisis."

Live houses In Japanese, *"raibu"* (live) refers to a concert, as in a "live" performance. Live houses are musical venues that prioritize the experience of hearing live bands, while also serving food and alcohol.

Lolita, Lolita fashion (*rorīta fasshon, lorīta fasshon*), lolicon, roricon In the context of Japan, Lolita refers to a fashion subculture that uses elements of English Victorian and Edwardian clothing to create a look that is romantic with a stylized nostalgia for a bygone form of femininity. There are a number of subsets each with their own fashion variants, including Gothic Lolita (*gosu rori*), Sweet Lolita (*ama rori*), and Classic Lolita. The word's etymology comes from Vladimir Nabokov's novel, *Lolita* and from the Japanese term *lolicon* (Lolita Complex), which refers to the sexualization of pre-pubescent girls in manga and anime, but many wearers of the fashion style reject any such sexualization.

Lost Decades (*ushinawareta jūnen*), Lost Generation (*ushinawareta sedai*) Japan's period of economic stagnation in the 1990s after the bursting of the Japanese stock market and real estate bubble. Although official unemployment rates were relatively low compared to the United States and Europe, the economy experienced years of deflation, and youth saw diminished job prospects. Companies reduced the hiring of regular workers in order to cut costs. As a result, many youths once graduating from high school or university could find only low-paying part-time or temporary jobs. This long deflationary era continued on past two decades, and thus can be better seen as "Lost Decades" There are those who believe that the Lost Decade is a myth, attributing Japan's economic underperformance to a declining population, as on a per-worker basis, between 1991 and 2012, Japan's output rose respectably (Fingleton 2013). Sometimes people who came of age during this period are called the "Lost Generation," adapting Ernest Hemmingway's phrase for those who came of age during World War I.

Magical girl (*mahō shōjo*) Girl, usually in her adolescence, who has the power to become a superhero, often with the help of an accouterment like a mirror or wand, and shown in an elaborate transformation scene. Also refers to the girl-centered fantasy genre of anime and manga featuring this character.

Manga, *Mangaka* Japanese term for comics, with *mangaka* specifying the artist who draws them. Outside of Japan, manga refers to comics produced in Japan or heavily influenced in style.

Matsuri* Japanese festivals, often seasonal and agricultural in origin. Some are centered on religious shrines or temples, although others like fireworks (*hanabi*) can be secular. *Matsuri* may involve food stalls, entertainments, and carnival atmospheres.

Mecha Humanoid robots or machines piloted by people and the science fiction genre that features them.

Media mix Popular and industry term used in Japan to denote a given franchise's serial extension across multiple media. Typically, a given property begins as a comic or novel, is adapted to a film or animation series, spawns soundtracks, toys or figurines, videogames, and production notes, along with newspaper articles, magazine features, and advertising—all of which form the media mix. The term media mix originates in marketing discourse of the 1960s, but in the 1980s it came to designate the anime and film franchising with which it is currently associated.

NHK Kōhaku uta gassen (Kōhaku, literally, "NHK Red and White Song Battle") Regarded as the most prestigious annual music show in Japan, it has been airing every New Year's Eve since 1951. Produced by Japan's national public broadcasting organization NHK (Nippon Hōso Kyōkai). The most popular musicians of the year are invited and divided into two competing teams—red team (women) and white team (men).

Nihonga Literally, Japanese-style paintings. Starting in the Meiji period (1868–1912) as interest in high culture from Europe and the United States grew, Japanese artists and artist schools were divided into two strands Yōga engaged with foreign art styles and techniques, while Nihonga used more traditional artistic conventions, techniques, and materials as a starting point.

Obento, Kyaraben Japanese lunchbox containing a number of foods in a compartmentalized box-shaped container. Lunchbox contents are sometimes styled into elaborate decorations made to look like characters or animals; these are known as *kyaraben* (character *bentō*).

Omotesandō Gently sloping, tree-lined avenue in southern Tokyo. It became known for architecture, as international and local fashion houses and other brands built impressive flagship shops there. The Harajuku end of the street is known as a center for youth culture, while the other end is known for upscale boutiques and restaurants.

Otaku Meaning something like nerd, fan, or anorak, otaku is used in Japan to identify people who are deeply obsessive about something, most typically manga, anime, and computer/console games. While used more casually today, the word otaku began in 1983 as a label for manga and anime fans accused of being socially and sexually immature.

Oyaji Literally meaning one's father, an old man, or one's boss, the term is used for any man considered no longer young. An "*oyaji* gag" (*oyaji gyagu*) is the type of joke that would be typically told by or appeal to an older man.

Pinku eiga Literally, "pink films," a Japanese genre of generally softcore pornography. Particularities of their production are more of a defining factor than stylistic elements: usually with a number of sex scenes, involving a narrative, and filmed with a low budget but on actual celluloid film (Richie 1987).

Purikura Clipped form of *purinto kurabu* (print club), a term used to describe both a booth where self-photographs can be taken and the product of those booths: small photo-stickers.

Rakugo Stylized Japanese form of comic storytelling, told by a single seated storyteller who, with only a Japanese fan or other small props, relays a complicated comic story involving a dialogue in which they voice a number of characters.

Rōnin   Historically referring to a samurai warrior with no master or lord. In contemporary times, *rōnin* has been used for a student who is no longer in high school but who has not yet been admitted to a university, often because they are taking an extra year to study on their own to gain a better university entrance grade. It can also refer to a salaryman who is between employers.

Salaryman (*sarariiman*)   Japanese male archetype of a white-collar worker whose income comes from a monthly salary and who is expected to be loyal to his company. Stereotypically associated customs of this employment arrangement, arguably more common in the 1990s than today, are that a company takes care of their members for life while the employees work long hours and socialize mainly within or on behalf of the company. Adherence to hierarchy, almost identical suits, commuting by train, and overwork are other associations. Once a title of prestige, it is now questioned on the grounds of its inherent sexism and demanding lifestyle and changes in Japanese employment that make lifetime employment more difficult.

Scanlations   Mixing of the words "scan" and "translation," the term is used mainly, but not exclusively, for Japanese manga that have been translated, and sometimes edited, by amateur fans and then made accessible on the Internet. This practice is problematic from the point of view of copyright law, among other issues.

***Seinen* manga**   Genre of manga marketed to adolescent males and men. *Seinen* manga includes more kanji (implying an older reading audience), diverse narratives, sexuality, and adult themes than *shōnen* manga (comics for boys).

Senpai   Senior or someone of higher age or rank in an organization, as opposed to *kōhai* (junior). This hierarchical distinction permeates Japanese customs and is found within many institutions and even among friends. The relationship implies reciprocal obligations, including the mentoring of juniors and the symbolic respect of seniors.

Shibuya   A ward of Tokyo and the urban hub surrounding Shibuya Train Station. It is one of the major centers for shopping, night life, and entertainment and is particularly known for youth fashion and popular culture. *Shibuya-kei* (Shibuya style) refers to a genre of music and fashion associated with the area.

Shinkansen   Literally, "new trunk line" and called "bullet train" in English, *shinkansen* can refer to the network of high speed trains in Japan or to one of the trains itself.

Shitamachi   Literally, "under city," historically refers to the physically and socioeconomically lower area of Tokyo surrounding the Sumida River. *Shitamachi* was used in juxtaposition to "Yamanote," a name that specified the place where upper classes generally lived. *Shitamachi* has the connotation of containing older-style industries and shops and working-class residential neighborhoods, somewhat equivalent to the idea of downtown.

Shōjo   Japanese word for girl. It is often used to refer to anything related to the culture of girls, such as *shōjo* manga, *shōjo* novels, and *shōjo* fashions.

Shōjo **manga**   Comics marketed generally toward teenage girls, which covers a range of genres, with its own set of visual tropes (e.g., large eyes to show emotion, flower symbolism, and differing sizes of frames on the page). Since the 1960s, *shōjo* manga has often been created by female artists and authors.

Shōnen   Literally meaning "a few years," the term is usually used to mean boy and boy culture, although in a legal sense it references youth without preference to gender. In popular culture, it is used to designate cultural products of interest primarily, but not exclusively, to boys.

Shōnen **manga**   Comics targeted at adolescent and pre-adolescent males. Some of the most famous examples have been serialized in the manga magazine *Weekly Shōnen Jump*.

Superflat   Self-proclaimed art movement by artist Takashi Murakami, influenced by Japanese popular culture and with the objective to question and celebrate its "shallow emptiness" (Murakami 2000).

Talent (*tarento*)   Japanese term for a star or personality, especially on television. Ironically, a television talent is not really required to have any, and is mainly expected to simply be jovial and easy to look at.

Tokugawa Shōgunate   Feudal military government from around 1600 to 1867, named for the clan in power. While there were still Emperors at this time, the real power lay with the Shōgun, and the Emperor was, at best, ceremonial.

Tokusatsu   Live-action fantasy shows featuring extravagant special effects. The most iconic are monster movie series (e.g., *Godzilla*). The term also applies to superhero *sentai* (team) shows (e.g., *Zyuranger*, which became the template for the U.S. *Mighty Morphin Power Rangers*), and to *henshin* (transformation) heroes (e.g., *Kikaider*).

Ukiyo-e   Literally "pictures of the floating world," the term refers to a method, style, and culture of woodblock printing that peaked in popularity in the late Edo period. Although technically intricate, they were printed in large numbers and easy to acquire, making them true popular culture. The literal meaning of the term refers not only to a hedonistic lifestyle that was often pictured but also to the Buddhist notion of the ephemerality of those same pleasures. *Ukiyo-e* influenced Impressionist, Post-Impressionist, and Art Nouveau and occupy a central place in the creation of modern art.

U.S.-Japan Security Treaty (Anpo)   Treaty of Mutual Cooperation and Security between the United States and Japan (Nihon-koku to Amerika-gasshūkoku to no aida no sōgo kyōryoku oyobi anzen hoshō jōyaku)—"Anpo jōyaku," or just shortened to "Anpo"—is the main military alliance between the two countries. First signed in 1952, it was significantly amended and re-signed in 1960. It is one of the longest alliances between two great powers.

V-Cinema   Feature films released directly onto video. The strategy and the term were coined by the Toei Video Company, which released its first straight-to-video title *Crime Hunter* (*Kuraimuhantā ikari no jūdan*, Okawa Toshimichi, dir.) in 1989. A number of today's notable Japanese filmmakers got their start shooting low-budget genre films for the video market, including Miike Takashi, Kurosawa Kiyoshi, and Aoyama Shinji.

Visual-kei   Music genre that emerged in Japan during the 1980s "band boom" period, influenced by "Glam Rock" (or "Glitter Rock") from the United States and United Kingdom. The term Visual-kei came from the concept of "visual shock" in the slogan of the band called X (also known as X Japan): "Psychedelic Violence/ Crime of Visual Shock." The genre plays up the visual element to complement the heavy metal and hard-rock music, as artists wear heavy makeup and outrageous costumes, blurring binary genders.

Yaoi   See BL (Boys' Love).

Yōga   Literally, Western-style paintings, see Nihonga.

Yuru kyara   Literally, "wobbly characters." *Kyara* is an abbreviated form of *kyarakutā*, from the English "character." The term denotes characters designed for public relations of local governing bodies, events, and goods, especially when in *kigurumi*, (full-body character suit) form. Those specifically created to promote a locality are called *gotōchi kyara* (local characters).

Zainichi   Literally meaning "Japanese resident," it potentially could refer to all nationalities of non-Japanese residing in Japan. However, the term mainly is used for Korean residents of Japan, and in particular those who are the legacy of the Japanese empire with colonialism in Korea from 1910 to 1945.

Bibliography

Abe Hiroshi. 2012. *Bokutachi wa shima de, mirai o miru koto ni shita* (We Chose to Envision the Future on an Island). Tokyo: Kirakusha.

Abel, Jonathan E. 2014. "Masked Justice: Allegories of the Superhero in Cold War Japan." *Japan Forum* 26: 187–208.

Across Henshushitu. 1989. *Gekkan Across* (Monthly Across). Tokyo: Parco Shuppan, June.

Administrator. *Miyazaki Hayao no Sekai in Ōsutoraria* (Hayao Miyazaki's World in Australia). Online at www.mixi.jp/view_community.pl?id=770838 [accessed May 27, 2015].

Agawa Hiroyuki. 2006. *Agawa Hiroyuki zenshū 17* (The Complete Works of Agawa Hiroyuki. Volume 17). Tokyo: Shinchōsha.

Aida Makoto. 1999. *Kodoku na wakusei* (Lonely Planet). Tokyo: Danvo Co.

———. 2003. *Mukiryoku tairiku* (Apathetic Continent). Tokyo: B.B.B., Inc.

———. 2005. *Mutant Hanako: un manga face à un monde asymétrique* (Mutant Hanako: A Manga for an Asymmetric World). Paris: Lézard Noir.

———. 2007. *Monument for Nothing*. Tokyo: Graphicsha.

———. 2012. *Tensai de gome nasai* (Sorry for Being a Genius)/*Monument for Nothing*. Tokyo: Mori Art Museum.

Aihara Hiroyuki. 2007. *Kyaraka suru Nippon* (Characterizing Japan). Tokyo: Kōdansha.

Aiko. 2010. *Yankii kare to nakimushi kanojo* (Yankee Boyfriend and Crybaby She). Tokyo: Starts Publishing.

Ainori. 1999–2009. Tokyo: Fuji Television.

Ainori 7: Mirai no chizu (Ainori 7: A Map to the Future). 2005. Tokyo: Gakken.

Ainori 9: My Love. 2007. Tokyo: Gakken.

Akasegawa Genpei, Fujimori Ternuobu, and Minami Shinbō, eds. 1986. *Rojō kansatsugaku nyūmon* (Introduction to Street Observation Science). Tokyo: Chikumo shobō.

Akiba Blog. 2008a. "Sawamoto Asuka-san masukomi (TV kyoku) shuzai de ketsudashi yarase?" (Was Sawamoto Asuka's Flashing Staged for the Mass Media [TV Stations] to Film?), April 21. Online at www.akibablog.net/archives/2008/04/ketu-080421.html [accessed August 17, 2015].

———. 2008b. "'Akihabara no hokoten ga muhō jōtai' masukomi (TV kyoku) darake" (Akihabara Pedestrian Paradise in a State of Lawlessness: Mass Media [TV Stations] Everywhere), April 14. Online at www.akibablog.net/archives/2008/04/akihabara-080414.html [accessed August 17, 2015].

Akimoto, Yūji. 2002. *The Standard*. Okayama: Naoshima Contemporary Art Museum.

———. 2005. *From House Project to Chichu Art Museum*. Lecture series at Tokyo University of the Arts. Online at www.nozawa.ddo.jp/mkp/2005/akimotogeidai20050714.MP3 [accessed October 15, 2015].

———. 2006. *Naoshima Standard 2*. Tokyo: Shinchōsa.

Aldrich, Daniel P. 2010. *Site Fights: Divisive Facilities and Civil Society in Japan and the West*. Ithaca, NY: Cornell University Press.

———. 2013. "Postcrisis Japanese Nuclear Policy: From Top-down Directives to Bottom-up Activism." In *Japan at Nature's Edge: The Environmental Context of a Global Power*, edited by Ian Jared Miller, Julia Adeney Thomas, and Brett L. Walker, 280–292. Honolulu, HI: University of Hawai'i Press.

Alexander, Susan M. 2003. "Stylish Hard Bodies: Branded Masculinity in *Men's Health* Magazine." *Sociological Perspectives* 46(4): 535–554.

Allen, Woody, director. 1966. *What's Up, Tiger Lily?* Los Angeles, CA: American International Pictures.

———, director. 1983. *Zelig*. Los Angeles, CA: Warner Bros.

Allison, Anne. 2004. "Cuteness as Japan's Millennial Product." In *Pikachu's Global Adventure: The Rise and Fall of Pokémon*, edited by Joseph Tobin, 34–49. Durham, NC: Duke University Press.

———. 2006. *Millennial Monsters: Japanese Toys and the Global Imagination*. Berkeley, CA: University of California Press.

———. 2013. *Precarious Japan*. Durham, NC: Duke University Press.

Alter, Charlotte. 2014. "Japanese Politician Sorry for Heckling Female Colleague." *Time*, June 23. Online at www.time.com/2911630/japan-politician-sorry-for-heckling-female-colleague/ [accessed December 15, 2015].

Amachi Shigeru. 2000. "Amachi Shigeru intabyū" (Amachi Shigeru Interview). In *Jigoku de yōi hai! Nakagawa Nobuo kaiki kyōfu eiga no gōka* (Shooting in Hell: The Fate of Nobuo Nakagawa's Horror Films), edited by Suzuki Kensuke, 23–26. Tokyo: Wise shuppan.

Amemiya Keita, director. 1995. *Jinzō ningen Hakaidā* (Mechanical Violator Hakaider). Tokyo: Toei Video.

Amerika, Mark. 1993. "Avant-Pop Manifesto: Thread Baring Itself in Ten Quick Posts." Online at www.altx.com/manifestos/avant.pop.manifesto.html [accessed February 5, 2015].

Amerika, Mark and Lance Olsen, eds. 1995. *In Memoriam to Postmodernism: Essays on the Avant-Pop*. San Diego, CA: San Diego State University Press.

Amino Testurō, director. 1994–1995. *Makurosu sebum* (Macross 7). Tokyo: Studio Nue.

Anahori Tadashi. 2014. "Strawberry Farmer Votes 4,600 for Rino Sashihara in AKB48 General Election—To No Avail." *Tokyo Kinky*, June 10. Online at www.tokyokinky.com/strawberry-farmer-votes-4600-for-rino-sashihara-in-akb48-general-election-to-no-avail/ [accessed July 26, 2015].

Anderson, Joseph L. and Donald Richie. 1983 [1959]. *The Japanese Film: Art and Industry* (Expanded Edition). Princeton, NJ: Princeton University Press.

Anime Anime. 2014. "Mahō no tenshi Kuriimii Mami Ōta Takako intabyū" (Magical Angel Creamy Mami Ōta Takako Interview). Online at www.animeanime.jp/article/2014/05/26/18822.html [accessed April 10, 2015].

Anime News Network. 2012. "Nico Nico Douga Renamed as Niconico in Service Upgrade." *Anime News Network*, April 26. Onlilne at www.animenewsnetwork.com/

news/2012-04-26/nico-nico-douga-renamed-as-niconico-in-service-upgrade [accessed January 26, 2016].

Anno Hideaki, director. 1995. *Shin seiki Evangelion* (Neon Genesis Evangelion). Tokyo: Tatsunoko Production, Gainax.

Anno Moyoco. 2004. *Hatarakiman.* (Woman Workaholic.) Volumes 1–4. Tokyo: Kōdansha.

Aoi Akihito. 2013. "Shibuya—yamiichi kara wakamonono machie" (Shibuya: From Black Market to a Town for Youth). In *Sakariba wa yamiichikara umareta* (Entertainment Districts Born from Black Markets), edited by Hatsuda Kanari and Hashimoto Kenji, 88–101. Tokyo: Soukyusha.

Aoyagi, Hiroshi. 2000. "Pop Idols and the Asian Identity." In *Japan Pop!: Inside the World of Japanese Popular Culture*, edited by Timothy J. Craig, 309–326. Armonk, NY: M.E. Sharpe.

———. 2005. *Islands of Eight Million Smiles: Idol Performance and Symbolic Production in Contemporary Japan.* Cambridge, MA: Harvard University Asia Center.

Aoyama Shinji, director. 1995. *Kyōkasho ni nai!* (Not in the Textbook!). Tokyo: Pink Pineapple.

———, director. 1996. *Waga mune ni kyōki ari* (A Cop, a Bitch, and a Killer). Tokyo: KSS.

———, director. 1997a. *Tsumetai chi* (An Obsession). Tokyo: Taki Corporation.

———, director. 1997b. *Wild Life.* Tokyo: Taki Corporation.

———, director. 1998. *Sheidī gurōbu* (Shady Grove). Tokyo: Bitter's End.

———, director. 1999. *Enbāmingu* (Embalming). Tokyo: Gaga Communications.

———. 2013. Interview by Tom Mes. Tokyo. May 6.

Ara Konomi. 2000. "Amerika bungaku" (American literature). In *Hon'yaku hyakunen: gaikoku bungaku to Nihon no kindai* (A Hundred Years of Translation: Foreign Literature and Japanese Modernity), edited by Hara Takuya and Nishinaga Yoshinari, 3–23. Tokyo: Taishukan shoten.

Arai, Andrea. 2003. "Killing Kids: Recession and Survival in Twenty-First-Century Japan." *Postcolonial Studies* 6: 367–379.

Ariès, Philippe. 1965. *Centuries of Childhood: A Social History of Family Life.* London: Vintage.

Artefact. 2013. "China AKB48 Otaku Votes $150,000 for Rino Sashihara." *Sankaku Complex*, June 8. Online at www.sankakucomplex.com/2013/06/08/china-akb48-otaku-votes-150000-for-rino-sashihara/ [accessed July 26, 2015].

Asahi Shinbun. 1970. "Uso no yōna honto no hanashi" (A True Story That Is Stranger Than Fiction). *Asahi Shinbun: Tokyo-ban*, March 14: 16.

———. 2004. "The Big Bang of Economic Recovery?" *Asahi.com*, November 17. Online at www.asahi.com/english/nation/TKY200411170151.html [accessed July 4, 2015].

———. 2007. "Futsū no wakamono ga keitai shōsetsu—besutoserā mo zokuzoku" (Average Young Adult Readers Turning to Cellphone Novels: The Bestsellers Continue). *Asahi.com*, February 11. Online at www.asahi.com/culture/news_culture/TKY200702100253.html [accessed December 29, 2015].

———. 2013. "AKB48 Becomes Bestselling Singles Female Artist ever in Japan." *Asahi.com*, May 28. Online at www.ajw.asahi.com/article/cool_japan/style/AJ201305280047 [accessed July 26, 2015].

Asai, Sumiko. 2008. "Firm Organisation and Marketing Strategy in the Japanese Music Industry." *Popular Music* 27(3): 473–485.

Ascheid, Antje. 1997. "Speaking Tongues: Voice Dubbing in the Cinema as Cultural Ventriloquism." *Velvet Light Trap* 40: 32–41.

Ashcraft, Brian and Shoko Ueda. 2010. *Japanese Schoolgirl Confidential: How Teenage Girls Made a Nation Cool*. Tokyo: Kodansha International.

Ashihara, Sunao. 1990. *Seishun den deke deke deke* (Jangling Strings of Youth). Tokyo: Kawade Bunko.

Atkins, E. Taylor. 2001. *Blue Nippon: Authenticating Jazz in Japan*. Durham, NC: Duke University Press.

Attwood, Feona. 2005. "'Tits and Ass and Porn and Fighting': Male Heterosexuality in Magazines for Men." *International Journal of Cultural Studies* 8(1): 83–100.

Augment5 Inc. 2013. *Gunkanjima: Google Maps Street View of Battleship Island*. Online at www.vimeo.com/69278864 [accessed August 20, 2017].

Azuma, Hiroki. 2000. "Superflat Japanese Postmodernity." Online at www.scribd.com/doc/99174676/Azuma-Hiroki-Superflat#scribd [accessed June 12, 2017].

———. 2001 *Dōbutsuka suru posutomodan* (Otaku: Database Animals). Tokyo: Kōdansha.

———. 2007. *Gēmuteki riarizumu no tanja: dōbutsuka suru posutomodan 2* (The Birth of Gameic Realism: The Animalizing Postmodern 2). Tokyo: Kōdansha.

Baccolini, Raffaella. 2004. "The Persistance of Hope in Dystopian Science Fiction." *Proceedings of the Modern Language Association* 119(3): 518–521.

Bardsley, Jan. 2011. "The Oyaji Gets a Makeover: Guides for Japanese Salarymen in the New Millennium." In *Manners and Mischief: Gender, Power, and Etiquette in Japan*, edited by Jan Bardsley and Laura Miller, 114–135. Berkeley, CA: University of California Press.

Barker, Valerie, and Hiroshi Ota. 2011. "Mixi Diary versus Facebook Photos: Social Networking Site Use among Japanese and Caucasian American Females." *Journal of Intercultural Communication Research* 40(1): 39–63.

Barks Global Media. 2011. "Dai 3 kai AKB48 senbatsu sōsenkyō: eigakan nama-chūkei, kokunai eigakan zen 97 sukurīn zenseki kanbai" (The Third AKB48 General Election for Select Members: Live Broadcast to Theaters, All Seats at 97 Domestic Screens Sold Out). Online at www.barks.jp/news/?id=1000070600 [accessed July 26, 2015].

Barthes, Roland. 1982 [1966]. *Empire of Signs*. Translated by Richard Howard. New York: Hill and Wang.

Baseel, Casey. 2014a. "AKB48 Fan Shows His Love the Only Way He Knows How: By Buying $300,000 Worth of CDs." *RocketNews24*, May 22. Online at www.en.rocketnews24.com/2014/05/22/akb48-fan-shows-his-love-the-only-way-he-knows-how-by-buying-300000-worth-of-cds/ [accessed July 26, 2015].

———. 2014b. "A Brief History of Japanese Girls' Rock." *RocketNews24*. Online at www.en.rocketnews24.com/2014/05/02/a-brief-history-of-japanese-girls-rock [accessed November 14, 2015].

Baudrillard, Jean. 1987. *The Evil Demon of Images*. Sydney: Power Institute Publications.

———. 1993. *The Transparency of Evil: Essays on Extreme Phenomena*. Translated by James Benedict. London: Verso.

———. 1994a. *Figures de l'altérité* (Figures of Otherness). Paris: Descartes & Cie.

———. 1994b. *Simulacra and Simulation*. Translated by Shelia Faria Glaser. Ann Arbor, MI: University of Michigan Press.

———. 1996. *The Perfect Crime*. Translated by Chris Turner. London: Verso.

———. 1997. *Ecran Total*. Paris: Galilée.

————. 2000. *The Vital Illusion*. Translated by Julia Witwer. New York: Columbia University Press.

Bauer, Ute Meta and Thomas D. Trummer. 2001. *AR: Artistic Research*. London: Koenig Press.

Bauman, Zygmunt. 2000. *Liquid Modernity*. Cambridge, MA: Polity Press.

BBC News. 2007. "Japan Birth Rate Shows Rare Rise." January 1. Online at www. news.bbc.co.uk/2/hi/asia-pacific/6222257.stm [accessed June 3, 2013].

Beasi, Melinda. 2010. "*Ōoku*, Volumes 1–3." *Manga Bookshelf*. July 22. Online at www.mangabookshelf.com/7734/ooku-vols-1-3/ [accessed February 15, 2015].

Beeton, Sue, Takayoshi Yamamura, and Philip Seaton. 2013. "The Mediatisation of Culture: Japanese Contents Tourism and Popular Culture." In *Mediating the Tourist Experience: From Brochures to Virtual Encounters*, edited by Joan Lester and C. Scarles, 139–154. Farnham: Ashgate.

Bekkiini. 2015. "Kore wa teiban no bokaroido meikyoku rankingu [Vocaloid] PV dōga" (This is a Standard Ranking of Famous Vocaloid Songs, with the Videos). Online at www.matome.naver.jp/odai/2135034939998395301 [accessed January 26, 2016].

Belson, Ken and Brian Bremner. 2004. *Hello Kitty: The Remarkable Story of Sanrio and the Billion Dollar Feline Phenomenon*. Hoboken, NJ: Wiley.

Benesse Art Site Naoshima. 2014. *Naoshima Note 12*. Naoshima: Benesse Art Site Naoshima.

Benesse Holdings, Inc. 2010. "Setouchi International Art Festival 2010 Report." Online at www.benesse-hd.co.jp/en/csr/feature/2010_3/index.html [accessed April 2, 2015].

Benjamin, Walter. 1999. *The Arcades Project*. Translated by Howard Eiland and Kevin McLaughlin. Cambridge, MA: Belknap Press.

Benkler, Yochai. 2006. *The Wealth of Networks: How Social Production Transforms Markets and Freedom*. New Haven, CT: Yale University Press.

Benson, Phil. 2013. "English and Identity in East Asian Popular Music." *Popular Music* 32(1): 23–33.

Bergstrom, Brian. 2014. "Avonlea as 'World': Japanese *Anne of Green Gables* Tourism as Embodied Fandom." *Japan Forum* 26(2): 224–245.

Berndt, Jaqueline. 2013. "The Intercultural Challenge of the 'Mangaesque': Reorienting Manga Studies after 3/11." In *Manga's Cultural Crossroads*, edited by Jaqueline Berndt and Bettina Kummerling-Meibauer, 65–84. New York: Routledge.

Betts, Kate. 2003. "Top Ten Everything 2003." *Time*, December 18. Online at www.content.time.com/time/specials/packages/article/0,28804,2001842_2001830_2002055, 00.html [accessed June 7, 2015].

Billboard Online. 1966. "Guitars and Drums Set Instruments Sales Pace." *Billboard Magazine*, July 16. Online at www.billboard.com/magazine-archive [accessed May 23, 2014].

Blangiardi, Rick. 2014. "Local Connection: Arashi." *Hawaii News Now*, October 8. Online at www.hawaiinewsnow.com/story/26741082/local-connection-arashi [accessed March 21, 2015].

Bodart-Bailey, Beatrice M. 2006. *The Dog Shōgun: The Personality and Policies of Tokugawa Tsunayoshi*. Honolulu, HI: University of Hawai'i Press.

Bogin, Barry. 1997. "Evolutionary Hypotheses for Human Childhood." *American Journal of Physical Anthropology* 104: 63–89.

Bogost, Ian. 2007. *Persuasive Games: The Expressive Power of Videogames*. Cambridge, MA: MIT Press.

"Bōkaru gurūpu no miryoku." (The Appeal of Vocal Groups). 1965. *Yomiuri Shinbun*, May 4: 6.

Bolter, Jay David and Richard Grusin. 1999. *Remediation: Understanding New Media*. Cambridge, MA: MIT Press.

Bordo, Susan. 2000. *The Male Body: A New Look at Men in Public and in Private*. New York: Farrar, Straus, and Giroux.

Borges, Jorge Luis. 2004. "Borges Night at the Movies." In *Subtitles: On the Foreignness of Film*, edited by Atom Egoyan and Ian Balfour, 112–120. Cambridge, MA: MIT Press.

Boston.com. 2013. "Japan's Most Popular Mascot Bear Kumamon Visits Boston." Novemer 13. *Boston.com*. Online at www.boston.com/uncategorized/noprimarytagmatch/2013/11/13/japans-most-popular-mascot-bear-kumamon-visits-boston [accessed June 17, 2017].

Bostrom, Nick and Anders Sandburg. 2009. "The Wisdom of Nature: An Evolutionary Heuristic for Human Enhancement." In *Human Enhancement*, edited by Julian Savulescu and Nick Bostrum, 375–416. Oxford: Oxford University Press.

Bourdage, Monica. 2010. "A Young Girl's Dream: Examining the Barriers Facing Female Electric Guitarists." *IASPM@Journal* 1(1): 1–16.

Bourdaghs, Michael K. 2012. *Sayonara Amerika, Sayonara Nippon: A Geopolitical Prehistory of J-Pop*. New York: Columbia University Press.

Boym, Svetlana. 2001. *The Future of Nostalgia*. New York: Basic Books.

Brasor, Philip. 2008a. "The Obsession Over Those Dumbed Down Cute Mascots." *The Japan Times*, August 3, 2008. Online at www.japantimes.co.jp/news/2008/08/03/national/media-national/the-obsession-over-those-dumbed-down-cute-mascots/#.VnHNk4SIJJo [accessed February 28, 2010].

———. 2008b. "The Ventures: Still Rocking After Fifty Years." *The Japan Times*, August 7. Online at www.japantimes.co.jp/culture/2008/08/07/music/the-ventures-still-rocking-after-50-years/#.VpNfdjaIK-Q [accessed December 20, 2015].

———. 2009. "The Noughties Played It Nice." *The Japan Times*, December 18. Online at www.japantimes.co.jp/culture/2009/12/18/music/the-noughties-played-it-nice/ [accessed March 2, 2015].

———. 2014. "Brush Up on Pop Idol Feuds Before the Exam." *The Japan Times*, May 10. Online at www.japantimes.co.jp/news/2014/05/10/national/media-national/brush-pop-idol-feuds-exam/#.U4p3gC8-Lx8 [accessed March 2, 2015].

Brophy, Philip. 1991. "The Animation of Sound." In *The Illusion of Life: Essays on Animation*, edited by Alan Cholodenko, 67–111. Sydney: Power Publications in association with the Australian Film Commission.

Bruns, Axel. 2008. *Blogs, Wikipedia, Second Life and Beyond: From Production to Produsage*. New York: Peter Lang.

Bukszpan, Daniel and Ronnie J. Dio. 2003. *The Encyclopedia of Heavy Metal*. New York: Sterling.

Burke-Gaffney, Brian. 1996. "Hashima: The Ghost Island." *Crossroads: A Journal of Nagasaki History and Culture* 4: 33–52.

Burton, Sarah. 2015. "Everything You Need to Know about Japan's Mascot Craze." *BuzzFeed*, May 11. Online at www.buzzfeed.com/sarahburton/everything-you-need-to-know-about-japans-mascot-craze#.jqM0QYBzm [accessed May 16, 2015].

Buteikkusha. 2013. *Kumamon handomeido BOOK* (Kumamon Handmade Book). Tokyo: Buteikkusha.

B'z Wiki. n.d. *B'z Wiki.* Online at www.bzwiki.o thelock.com [accessed May 14, 2014].

Calinescu, Matei. 1987. *Five Faces of Modernity: Modernism, Avant-garde, Decadence, Kitsch, Postmodernism.* Durham, NC: Duke University Press.

Canetti, Elias. 1985. *The Human Province.* London: Andre Deutsch.

Capote, Truman. 2008 [1958]. *Breakfast at Tiffany's.* Translated by Murakami Haruki. Tokyo: Shinchōsha.

Carlisle, Lonny. 1996. "Economic Development and the Evolution of Japanese Overseas Tourism, 1964–1994." *Tourism Recreation Research* 21(1): 11–18.

Carter, Michael. 2013. *Overdressed: Barthes, Darwin & The Clothes That Speak.* Sydney: Puncher and Wattmann Criticism.

Cawaii!. 2003a. "Sukina purikura kishu" (Print Club Machines We Like). *Cawaii!,* May, 148.

———. 2003b. "Fotojenikku teku oshiechaimasu" (Teaching You Photogenic Techniques). *Cawaii!,* May, 147.

———. 2003c. "Saikin purikura pōzi mihon-chō" (Sample Album of Recent Print Club Poses). *Cawaii!,* November, 41–145.

CBLDF (Comic Book Legal Defense Fund). n.d. "Customs." Online at www.cbldf. org/resources/customs/ [accessed February 2, 2015].

Chaco. 2005. *Tenshi ga kureta mono* (What the Angels Gave Me). Tokyo: Starts Publishing.

Chalfen, Richard and Mai Marui. 2001. "Print Club Photography in Japan: Framing Social Relationships." *Visual Sociology* 16(1): 55–77.

Chandler, Raymond. 2009 [1940]. *Farewell, My Lovely.* Translated by Murakami Haruki. Tokyo: Hayakawa shobō.

Chaney, Bryan. 2000. *More Than 'Sukiyaki' and Idols: Japanese Popular Music, 1945–1999.* Master's Thesis. University of Oregon.

Cheah, Pheng. 2008. "Crises of Money." *Positions* 16(1): 189–219.

Cholodenko, Alan. 1997. "'Objects in Mirror Are Closer Than They Appear': The Virtual Reality of *Jurassic Park* and Jean Baudrillard." In *Jean Baudrillard, Art, and Artefact,* edited by Nicholas Zurbrugg, 64–90. London: Sage Publications.

———. 2000a. "The Illusion of the Beginning: A Theory of Drawing and Animation." *Afterimage* 28(1): 9–12.

———. 2000b. "The Logic of Delirium, or the Fatal Strategies of Antonin Artaud and Jean Baudrillard." In *100 Years of Cruelty: Essays on Artaud,* edited by Edward Scheer. Sydney: Power Publications and Artspace.

———. 2007. *The Illusion of Life 2: More Essays on Animation.* Sydney: Power Institute.

Chong, Doryun. 2013. "Ohtake Shinro shiron" (Essay on Ohtake Shinro). *Bijutsu techō* 65(993): 72–80.

Choo, Danny, ed. 2009. *Otacool: Worldwide Otaku Rooms.* Tokyo: Kotobukiya.

Choo, Kukhee. 2011. "Nationalizing 'Cool': Japan's Global Promotion of the Content Industry." In *Popular Culture and the State in East and Southeast Asia,* edited by Nissim Otmazgin and Eyal Ben-Ari, 83–103. London: Routledge.

Christopher, Matthew. 2014. *Abandoned America: The Age of Consequences.* Versailles: Jonglez Publishing.

Chun, Jayson Makoto. 2007. *A Nation of a Hundred Million Idiots?: A Social History of Japanese Television, 1953–1973.* New York: Routledge.

Chung, Winnie and Steve McClure. 2000. "Sun Worshipping: Japan's Once-Reluctant Neighbors Now Devour J-Pop: Hong Kong." *Billboard,* August 19, 53 and 58.

Chute, Hillary L. and Marianne DeKoven. 2006. "Introduction: Graphic Narrative." *Modern Fiction Studies* 52(4): 767–782.

Clammer, John. 1997. *Contemporary Urban Japan: A Sociology of Consumption*. Oxford: Blackwell.

Clausewitz, Carl von. 1984 [1976]. *On War*. Translated and edited by Michael Howard and Peter Paret. Princeton, NJ: Princeton University Press.

———. 1989. *On War*. Translated and edited by Michael Eliot Howard and Peter Paret. Princeton, NJ: Princeton University Press.

Clements, Jonathan and Motoko Tamamuro. 2003. *The Dorama Encyclopedia: A Guide to Japanese TV Drama since 1953*. Berkeley, CA: Stone Bridge Press.

Clifford, James. 1986. "Introduction: Partial Truths." In *Writing Culture: The Poetics and Politics of Ethnography*, edited by James Clifford and George E. Marcus, 1–26. Berkeley, CA: University of California Press.

———. 1997. *Routes: Travel and Translation in the Late Twentieth Century*. Cambridge, MA: Harvard University Press.

Cohen, Jeffrey Jerome. 1996. "Monster Culture (Seven Theses)." In *Monster Theory*, edited by Jeffrey Jerome Cohen, 3–25. Minneapolis, MN: University of Minnesota Press.

Combes, Muriel. 2012. *Gilbert Simondon and the Philosophy of the Transindividual*. Cambridge, MA: MIT Press.

Comiket. 2015. "What Is Comic Market?" Online at www.comiket.co.jp/info-a/WhatIsEng201401.pdf [accessed March 16, 2016].

Condry, Ian. 2006. *Hip-Hop Japan: Rap and the Paths of Cultural Globalization*. Durham, NC: Duke University Press.

———. 2011. "Post-3/11 Japan and the Radical Recontextualization of Value: Music, Social Media, and End-Around Strategies for Cultural Action." *International Journal of Japanese Sociology* 20: 4–17.

———. 2013. *The Soul of Anime: Collaborative Creativity and Japan's Media Success Story*. Durham, NC: Duke University Press.

Consalvo, Mia. 2009. "Convergence and Globalization in the Japanese Videogame Industry." *Cinema Journal* 48(3): 135–141.

Constitution of Japan. 1947. Online at www.japan.kantei.go.jp/constitution_and_government_of_japan/constitution_e.html [accessed February 2, 2015].

Cookie. 2006. Tokyo: Shūeisha.

———. 2010. Tokyo: Shūeisha.

Cope, Julian. 2007 *Japrocksampler: How the Post-War Japanese Blew Their Minds on Rock 'N' Roll*. London: Bloomsbury.

Coppola, Francis Ford, director. 1983. *The Outsiders*. San Francisco, CA: Zoetrope Studios.

Corbin, David. 2014. "The Game That Saved Mixi, Japan's Facebook Rival, Is Coming to the US." *Tech in Asia*. Online at www.techinasia.com/mixi-monster-strike-america/ [accessed May 27, 2015].

Coren, Anna. 2012. "Talk Asia: Interview with Japanese Music Producer Yasushi Akimoto." *CNN*, January 13. Online at www.edition.cnn.com/TRANSCRIPTS/1201/13/ta.01.html [accessed July 26, 2015].

Corkill, Edan. 2012. "Disaster Looms Large for Artist 'Genius' Aida Makoto." *The Japan Times*, November 16. Online at www.japantimes.co.jp/culture/2012/11/16/arts/disaster-looms-large-for-artist-genius-makoto-aida/#.VmnNvFrVvlJ [accessed December 10, 2015].

Couldry, Nick and Henry Jenkins. 2014. "Participations: Dialogues on the Participatory Promise of Contemporary Culture and Politics." *International Journal of Communication* 8: 1107–1112.

Craig, Timothy J. and Richard King, eds. 2002. *Global Goes Local: Popular Culture in Asia*. Vancouver: University of British Columbia Press.

Crowther, Bosley. 1956a. "Horror Import; 'Godzilla,' a Japanese Film, Is at State." *New York Times*, April 28. Online at www.nytimes.com/movie/review?res=9A05E6DD1F3BE23ABC4051DFB266838D649EDE [accessed August 18, 2015].

———. 1956b. "Monsters Again: Old Creatures in New but Familiar Films Gadzooks! Invisible Monster." *New York Times*, May 6, 129.

Cruz, Amanda, Dana Friss-Hansen, and Miodori Matsui. 1999. *Takashi Murakami: The Meaning of the Nonsense of the Meaning*. New York: Harry N. Abrams.

Crypton Future Media, Inc. n.d.a. "For Creators." *piapro.net*. Online at www.piapro.net/en_for_creators.html [accessed August 27, 2015].

———. n.d.b. "Who Is Hatsune Miku?" Online at www.crypton.co.jp/miku_eng [accessed January 22, 2016].

Cubic You: Hikki's Unofficial Website. n.d. Online at www5.plala.or.jp/syn/disco/cubic_u.htm [accessed March 21, 2015].

Daily Sports. 2011. "Ōshima Yūko, seken no hihan o aete kuchi ni 'Tōhyō wa mina-san no ai'" (Despite Growing Public Criticism, Ōshima Yūko says, "Votes are love"). *Daily Sports*. June 9. Online at www.web.archive.org/web/20110728095426/http://headlines.yahoo.co.jp/hl?a=20110609-00000064-dal-ent [accessed August 21, 2015].

Danan, Martine. 1991. "Dubbing as an Expression of Nationalism." *Meta* XXXVI(4): 606–614.

Danet, Brenda. 2001. *Cyberpl@y: Communicating Online*. London: Bloomsbury.

Darling-Wolf, Fabienne. 2004. "SMAP, Sex, and Masculinity: Constructing the Perfect Female Fantasy in Japanese Popular Music." *Popular Music and Society* 27(3): 357–370.

———. 2006. "The Men and Women of *Non-no*: Gender, Race, and Hybridity in Two Japanese Magazines." *Cultural Studies in Media Communication* 23(3): 181–199.

Dasgupta, Romit. 2000. "Performing Masculinities? The 'Salaryman' at Work and Play." *Japanese Studies* 20(2): 189–200.

de Certeau, Michel. 1984. *The Practice of Everyday Life*. Translated by Steven Rendall. Berkeley, CA: University of California Press.

de Launey, Guy. 1995. "Not-So-Big in Japan: Western Pop Music in the Japanese Market." *Popular Music* 14(2): 203–225.

Debord, Guy. 1977 [1967]. *Society of Spectacle*. Translated by Fredy Perlman et al. Kalamazoo, MI: Black & Red.

Deleuze, Gilles. 1993. *The Fold: Leibniz and the Baroque*. Translated by Tom Conley. Minneapolis, MN: University of Minnesota Press.

———. 1994. *Difference and Repetition*. Translated by Paul Patton. New York: Columbia University Press.

Demont, Nate. 2014. "Guyatone History." Online at www.guyatoneus.com/history [accessed May 10, 2014].

Denes, Agnes. 1990. "The Dream." *Critical Inquiry* 16(4): 919–939.

Denison, Rayna. 2010. "Anime Tourism: Discursive Construction and Reception of the Studio Ghibli Art Museum." *Japan Forum* 22(3–4): 545–563.

Denshō. "Terminology and Glossary." *Densho: The Japanese American Legacy Project*. Online at www.densho.org/default.asp?path=/assets/sharedpages/glossary.asp?section=home [accessed March 23, 2015].

Dentsu Character Business Kenkyūkai. 1994. *Kyarakutā bijinesu: shitashimi to kyōkan no māketingu* (Character Business: Marketing of Intimacy and Sympathy). Tokyo: Dentsu.

DiNitto, Rachel. 2014. "Narrating the Cultural Trauma of 3/11: The Debris of Post-Fukushima Literature and Film." *Japan Forum* 26(3): 340–360.

Doherty, Thomas. 1988. *Teenagers and Teenpics: The Juvenilization of American Movies in the 1950s*. Boston, MA: Unwin Hyman.

Doležel, Lubomír. 2009. *Heterocosmica: Fiction and Possible Worlds*. Baltimore, MD: Johns Hopkins University Press.

Dooley, Ben. 2008. "Big in Japan: A Cellphone Novel for You, the Reader." *The Millions*, January 31. Online at www.themillions.com/2008/01/big-in-japan-cellphone-novel-for-you.html [accessed July 5, 2014].

Dower, John W. 1987. *War without Mercy: Race and Power in the Pacific War*. New York: Pantheon Books.

Dries, Josephine. 1995. *Dubbing and Subtitling*. Dortmund: European Institute for the Media.

Drieser, Theodore. 2010 [1925]. *An American Tragedy*. New York: Signet Classics.

Dutton, Fred. 2012. "*Tokyo Jungle*: The Story Behind 2012's Most Eccentric Action Game." *Playstation Blog*, September 26. Online at www.blog.eu.playstation. com/2012/09/26/tokyo-jungle-the-story-behind-2012s-most-eccentric-action-game/ [accessed May 1, 2014].

Dwango. 2015. "Enkaku" (Company History). Online at www.dwango.co.jp/corporate/history.html [accessed January 26, 2016].

Dyer, Richard. 1979. *Stars*. London: British Film Institute.

Edensor, Tim. 2005. "The Ghosts of Industrial Ruins: Ordering and Disordering Memory in Excessive Space." *Environment and Planning D: Society and Space* 23: 829–849.

egg. 2003. "E-girls no puri-chō show" (Display of *egg* Girls Print Club Notebooks). *egg*, November, 74–77.

Eisenbeis, Richard. 2012. "*Tokyo Jungle*: The *Kotaku* Review." *Kotaku*, September 3. Online at www.kotaku.com/5942860/tokyo-jungle-the-kotaku-review [accessed May 1, 2014].

Eisenstein, Sergei. 1988. *Eisenstein on Disney*. London: Methuen.

Elastic. 2008. "Categorization and Analysis of Men's Fashion Magazines." October 14. Online at www.taf5686.269g.net/article/13514077.html [accessed July 8, 2014].

Elliott, Carl. 2003. "Humanity 2.0." *Wilson's Quarterly* 27(4): 3–20.

Elliott, David. 2011. *Bye Bye Kitty!!! Heaven and Hell in Contemporary Japanese Art*. New Haven, CT: Yale University Press.

Ellsworth, Whitney, Robert J. Maxwell, and Bernard Luber, producers. 2006. *Adventures of Superman*. Los Angeles, CA: Warner Home Video.

Ellwood, Mark. 2010. "The Art of Splendid Isolation." *How to Spend It: Financial Times*. April 8.

Emata Takako. 2007. "Kētai hatsu shōsetuka ni naru" (Becoming a First-Time Cellphone Novelist). *AERA*, February 26: 54–55.

Emi Shuntarō. 2000. "Emi Shuntarō intabyū" (Emi Shuntarō Interview). In *Jigoku de yōi hai! Nakagawa Nobuo kaiki kyōfu eiga no gōka* (Shooting in Hell: The Fate of Nobuo Nakagawa's Horror Films), edited by Suzuki Kensuke, 37–40. Tokyo: Wise shuppan.

Emoji Dick. n.d. Online at www.emojidick.com [accessed December 31, 2015].

Endō Satoshi, director. 2007–2008. *Chiritotechin.* Tokyo: NHK.

Entwistle, Joanne. 2009 [2004]. "From Catwalk to Catalogue: Male Fashion Models, Masculinity, and Identity." In *The Men's Fashion Reader,* edited by Peter McNeil and Vicki Karaminas, 197–209. Oxford: Berg.

Fackler, Martin. 2014. "Japan Outlaws Possession of Child Pornography." *New York Times,* June 18. Online at www.nytimes.com/2014/06/19/world/asia/japan-bans-possession-of-child-pornography-after-years-of-pressure.html?_r=0 [accessed 14 January 2015].

Famitsū. 2012. "*Tokyo Jungle* direkutā Kataoka Shōhei shi & myūjikku purodūsā TaQ shi intabyū" (Interview with Tokyo Jungle Director Kataoka Shōhei and Music Producer TaQ). July 23. Online at www.famitsu.com/news/201207/23017783. html [accessed May 1, 2014].

Farber, Manny. 1998. *Negative Space: Manny Farber on the Movies.* New York: Da Capo Press.

Farley, Christopher John and Toko Sekiguchi. 2001. "Diva on Campus." *Time,* September 5: 58.

Favell, Adrian. 2012. *Before and after Superflat: A Short History of Japanese Contemporary Art 1990–2011.* Hong Kong: Blue Kingfisher/DAP.

———. 2013. "Aida Makoto: sekai wa naze Aida Makoto ni kanshin o mukenainoka?" (Aida Makoto: The World Won't Listen?). *Bijutsu techō* 65(977): 84–88.

———. 2014a. "Visions of Tokyo in Japanese Contemporary Art." *Impressions: Journal of the Japanese Art Society of America* 35: 69–83.

———. 2014b "Resources, Scale, and Recognition in Japanese Contemporary Art: 'Tokyo Pop' and the Struggle for a Page in Art History." *Review of Japanese Culture and Society* XXVIII: 135–153.

———. 2015. "Creative East-West Cosmopolitanism? The Changing Role of International Mobility for Young Japanese Contemporary Artists." In *Transnational Trajectories: Nation, Citizenship and Region in East Asia,* edited by Yasemin Soysal, 83–105. New York: Routledge.

Fawcett, Peter. 1996. "Translating Film." In *On Translating French Literature and Film,* edited by Geoffrey T. Harris, 65–88. Amsterdam: Rodopi.

Fineboys. n.d. *Fineboys Offical Homepage.* Online at www.hinode.co.jp/?page_id=77 [accessed May 29, 2015].

———. 2011. "Zettaini makerarenai, U-170 daihyō no fukuerabi gashuku!" (A Style Selection Camp for Boys under 170 cm [5 feet 7 inches] to Whom We Can't Lose). June: 120–127.

———. 2013a. "Daigaku misu ga gachi shijino teiraa jake de yanaigai ōkei" (Looking Fine Both In-and-Outside with the Tailored Jackets that Campus Beauty Queens Enthusiastically Support). March: 56–57.

———. 2013b. "Gachi senshutsu no 'irogaramono' de sarige shuchou ittemiyo!" (Express Yourself Casually through Items with Colors and Patterns that You Select Seriously). March: 68–73.

———. 2013c. "Kuro pan wa joshi uke-do, danshi chakuyōritsu tomoni No.1" (A Pair of Black Pants is Both the Most Popular Item for Attracting Girls and for Guys to Wear). March: 77–84.

———. 2013d. "'Shatsu' jiku no kasanegi waza de kion hen'ka ni kami taiou!" (Respond to Temperature Change Perfectly with the Skills of Using a Shirt as the Foundation for a Layered Style). March: 4–9.

————. 2015. "Joshi no iine o atsumeta sutairu" (Styles That Got Many Likes by Girls). June: 54–61.

Fingleton, Eamonn. 2013. "Now They Tell Us: The Story of Japan's 'Lost Decades' Was Just One Big Hoax." *Forbes*, August 11. Online at www.forbes.com/sites/ eamonnfingleton/2013/08/11/now-for-the-truth-the-story-of-japans-lost-decades- is-the-worlds-most-absurd-media-myth/#2809dd2a3fe4 [accessed April 6, 2017].

Finkelpearl, Tom. 2014. *What We Made: Conversations on Art and Social Cooperation.* Durham, NC: Duke University Press.

Fiske, John. 1992. "Cultural Studies and the Culture of Everyday Life." In *Cultural Studies*, edited by Lawrence Grossberg, Cary Nelson, and Paula Treichler, 154–173. New York: Routledge.

————. 2010. *The John Fiske Collection: Understanding Popular Culture*: Oxford: Routledge.

Fitzgerald, Francis Scott. 2006 [1925]. *The Great Gatsby.* Translated by Murakami Haruki. Tokyo: Chūōkōronsha.

The Flaming Lips. 2002. *Yoshimi Battles the Pink Robots.* Los Angeles, CA: Warner Bros.

Flash Exciting. 2005. "*Ainori* chōsaishin menbaa 14-nin maruhi shōtai zenbu barasu!!!" (The Private Lives of 14 of the Most Recent Members of *Ainori* Completely Exposed!). *Flash Exciting*, August 5: 16–22.

Fodor, István. 1976. *Film Dubbing.* Hamburg: Buske Verlag.

Ford, Sam and Henry Jenkins. 2009. "Managing Multiplicity in Superhero Comics: An Interview with Henry Jenkins." In *Third Person: Authoring and Exploring Vast Narratives*, edited by Pat Harrigan and Noah Wardrip-Fruin, 303–311. Cambridge, MA: MIT Press.

forsatan91 et al. 2014. 'Kumamon." *Know Your Meme.* Online at www.knowyourmeme. com/memes/kumamon [accessed May 14, 2014].

Foster, Jay. 2009. "The Lifestream, Mako, and Gaia." In *Final Fantasy and Philosophy: The Ultimate Walkthrough*, edited by Jason P. Blahuta and Michel S. Beaulieu, 47–60. Hoboken, NJ: Wiley.

Freedman, Alisa. 2009a. "Street Nonsense: Ryūtanji Yū and the Fascination for Interwar Tokyo Absurdity." *Japan Forum* 21(1): 11–33.

————. 2009b. "Train Man and the Gender Politics of Japanese 'Otaku' Culture: The Rise of New Media, Nerd Heroes and Consumer Communities." *Intersections* 20. Online at www.intersections.anu.edu.au/issue20/freedman.htm [accessed August 17, 2015].

————. 2010. *Tokyo in Transit: Japanese Culture on the Rails and Road.* Stanford, CA: Stanford University Press.

————. 2016. "*Death Note*, Student Crimes, and the Power of Universities in the Global Spread of Manga/." In *End of Cool Japan: Ethical, Legal, and Cultural Challenges to Japanese Popular Culture*, edited by Mark McLelland, 31–50. Oxford: Routledge.

Freedman, Alisa and Kristina Iwata-Weickgenannt. 2011. "'Count What You Have Now. Don't Count What You Don't Have': The Japanese Television Drama *Around 40* and the Politics of Women's Happiness." *Asian Studies Review* 35(3): 295–313.

Freedman, Alisa, Laura Miller, and Christine Yano, eds. 2013a. *Modern Girls on the Go: Gender, Mobility, and Labor in Japan.* Stanford, CA: Stanford University Press.

————. 2013b. "You Go Girl!: Cultural Meanings of Gender, Mobility, and Labor." In *Modern Girls on the Go: Gender, Mobility, and Labor in Japan*, edited by Alisa Freedman, Laura Miller, and Christine Yano, 1–17. Stanford, CA: Stanford University Press.

Freiberg, Freda. 1996. "*Akira* and the Postnuclear Sublime." In *Hibakusha Cinema: Hiroshima, Nagasaki and the Nuclear Image in Japanese Film*, edited by Mick Broderick, 91–101. London: Kegan Paul International.

Friedman, Thomas. 2005. *The World is Flat: A Brief History of the Twenty-First Century*. New York: Farrar, Straus, and Giroux.

Fujii Bonbon. 2013. *Kumamoto sapuraizu* (Kumamoto Surprise). Tokyo: Up-Front Works.

Fujita, Kuniko and Richard Child Hill. 2005. "Innovative Tokyo." World Bank Policy Research Working Paper. Social Science Research Network. Online at www.papers.ssrn.com/sol3/papers.cfm?abstract_id=660088 [accessed August 17, 2015].

Fukai, Akiko. 2010. "Future Beauty: 30 Years of Japanese Fashion." In *Future Beauty: 30 Years of Japanese Fashion*, edited by Fukai Akiko, Barbara Vinken, and Susannah Frankel, 13–26. London: Merrell Publishers.

Fukasaku Kenji and Fukasaku Kinji, directors. 2003. *Batoru rowaiaru tsū: rekuiemu* (Battle Royale II: Requiem). Tokyo: Toei.

———, directors. 1973–1976. *Jingi naki tatakai* (Battles without Honor and Humanity). Tokyo: Toei.

Fukue, Natsuko. 2009. "So You Wanna be a Johnny?" *The Japan Times*, April 14. Online at www.japantimes.co.jp/news/2009/04/14/reference/so-you-wanna-be-a-johnny/ [accessed March 2, 2015].

Fukuhara, Haruhiko. 1979. "Concerts Sparkle with Western Stars." *Rolling Stone*, May 26, 10–11.

Fukuyama, Francis. 2002. *Our Posthuman Future: Consequences of the Biotechnology Revolution*. New York: Farrar, Straus, and Giroux.

———. 2004. "Transhumanism." *Foreign Policy* 144: 42–43.

Funatoko, Sadao. 2008. *Gekkō Kamen* (Chapter Mammoth Kong). Tokyo: Victor Entertainment.

Furmanovsky, Michael. 2010. "Outselling the Beatles: Assessing the Influence and Legacy of the Ventures on Japanese Musicians and Popular Music in the 1960s." *Ryukoku University Intercultural Studies* 14: 52–64.

———. 2012. "The Father of Boy Bands." *Kansai Scene*. June 1. Online at www.kansaiscene.com/2012/06/the-father-of-boy-bands/ [accessed March 2, 2015].

Furuhashi Kenji. 1989. "C-kyū aidoru ni jinsei wo ageta seishokusha! Aidoru ga hito kara mono ni natta toki, mania ga umareta!" (The Clergymen Who Devote Their Lives to Third-Rate Idols: Maniacs Were Born When Idols Went from People to Objects). In *Otaku no hon* (Otaku Book), edited by Ishii Shinji, 24–39. Tokyo: JICC.

Futabasha. 2008. *Great Mechanics DX no. 7*. Tokyo: Futabasha.

Gabriel, Philip, Jay Rubin, and Gary Fiskjeton. 2001. "Translating Murakami: An Email Roundtable." Online at www.randomhouse.com/knopf/authors/murakami/complete.html [accessed February 5, 2015].

Galbraith, Patrick W. 2011. "*Fujoshi*: Fantasy Play and Transgressive Intimacy among 'Rotten Girls' in Contemporary Japan." *Signs* 37(1): 211–232.

———. 2014. *The Moe Manifesto*. Tokyo: Tuttle Publishing.

———. 2015. "'Otaku Research' and Anxiety about Failed Men." In *Debating Otaku in Contemporary Japan: Historical Perspectives and New Horizons*, edited by Patrick W. Galbraith, Thiam Huat Kam, and Björn-Ole Kamm, 21–34. London: Bloomsbury.

Galbraith, Patrick W. and Jason G. Karlin. 2012a. *Idols and Celebrity in Japanese Media Culture.* New York: Palgrave MacMillan.

———. 2012b. "Introduction: The Mirror of Idols and Celebrity." In *Idols and Celebrity in Japanese Media Culture,* edited by Patrick W. Galbraith and Jason G. Karlin, 1–32. New York: Palgrave MacMillan.

Galbraith IV, Stuart. 1998. *Monsters Are Attacking Tokyo!: The Incredible World of Japanese Fantasy Films.* Venice, CA: Feral House.

Gallagher, Mark. 2004. "What's So Funny about Iron Chef?." *Journal of Popular Film and Television* 31(4): 177–184.

GameFAQs. 2011. "What Do A.V.A.L.A.N.C.H.E. and S.O.L.D.I.E.R. Stand for Anyway?"

GameFAQs Forum. n.d. Online at www.gamefaqs.com/boards/197341-final-fantasy-vii/61289151 [accessed March 20, 2015].

Games^{tm} staff. 2014. "Game Changers: *Final Fantasy VII.*" *games^{tm}* 45: 142–145.

Gardner, Richard A. 2008. "Aum Shinrikyō and a Panic about Manga and Anime." In *Japanese Visual Culture: Explorations in the World of Manga and Anime,* edited by Mark W. MacWilliams, 200–218. Armonk, NY: M.E. Sharpe.

Garo. 1967. "Dokusha kōnā" (The Readers' Column). *Garo,* January: 144–245.

Garrett, Bradley. 2013. *Explore Everything: Place-Hacking the City.* London: Verso.

Gee, James Paul. 2003. *What Video Games Have to Teach Us about Learning and Literacy.* New York: Palgrave MacMillan.

Gerow, Aaron. 2010. "Kind Participation: Postmodern Consumption and Capital with Japan's Telop TV." In *Television, Japan, and Globalization,* edited by Mitsuhiro Yoshimoto, 117–150. Ann Arbor, MI: Center for Japanese Studies, University of Michigan.

Ghedin, Guido. 2013. "The Story of Mixi in Japan: The Rise, the Fall, and the Facebook Takeover." *Digital in the Round.* Online at www.digitalintheround.com/japan-mixi-facebook/ [accessed May 27, 2015].

Gibson, Ellie. 2012. "*Tokyo Jungle* Review: Dog Eat Dog Eat Monkey Eat Pig Eat Crocodile Etc." *Eurogamer,* September 25. Online at www.eurogamer.net/articles/2012-09-24-tokyo-jungle-review [accessed May 1, 2014].

Gillespie, Tarleton. 2010. "The Politics of 'Platform.'" *New Media and Society* 12(3): 347–364.

Gilroy, Paul. 1993. *The Black Atlantic.* Cambridge, MA: Harvard University Press.

Gioni, Massimiliano. 2013. "Ohtake Shinro: rongu intabyū" (Ohtake Shinro: Long Interview). *Bijutsu techō* 65(993): 18–33.

Glassman, Hank. 2012. *The Face of Jizō: Image and Cult in Medieval Japanese Buddhism.* Honolulu, HI: University of Hawai'i Press.

Glasspool, Lucy. 2014. "From Boys Next Door to Boys' Love: Gender Performance in Japanese Male Idol Media." In *Idols and Celebrity in Japanese Media,* edited by Patrick W Galbraith and Jason G. Karlin, 97–112. New York: Palgrave McMillan.

Glenday, Craig, ed. 2008. *Guinness: World Records 2009.* New York: Guinness World Records.

Godoy, Tiffany. 2007. *Style Deficit Disorder.* San Francisco, CA: Chronicle Books.

"Godzilla." 2004. *Entertainment Weekly,* May 6. Online at www.ew.com/article/2004/05/06/Godzilla [accessed August 18, 2015].

Goodyear, Dana. 2008. "I ♥ NOVELS: Young Women Develop a Genre for the Cellular Age." *The New Yorker,* December 2. Online at www.newyorker.com/reporting/2008/12/22/081222fa_fact_goodyear?currentPage=all [accessed July 5, 2014].

Gordon, Andrew. 1994. "The Disappearance of the Japanese Working Class Movement." Center for Labor Studies. University of Washington. Online at www.depts.washington.edu/pcls/documents/research/Gordon_Disappearance. pdf [accessed January 11, 2016].

Gottlieb, Nanette and Mark McLelland. 2003. *Japanese Cybercultures*. Oxford: Routledge.

Gould, Stephan Jay. 1980. "A Biological Homage to Mickey Mouse." In *The Panda's Thumb: More Reflections in Natural History*. New York: W.W. Norton & Company.

Gravett, Paul. 2004. *Manga: Sixty Years of Japanese Comics*. New York: Harper Design International.

Gray II, Richard J. and Betty Kaklamanidou. 2011. "Introduction." In *The 21*st *Century Superhero: Essays on Gender, Genre and Globalization in Film*, edited by Richard J. Gray II and Betty Kaklamanidou, 1–13. Jefferson, NC: McFarland.

Green, Joshua, and Henry Jenkins. 2011. "Spreadable Media: How Audiences Create Value and Meaning in a Networked Economy." In *The Handbook of Media Audiences*, edited by Virginia Nightingale, 109–127. Oxford: Wiley-Blackwell.

Greenberg, Clement. 1960. "Modernist Painting." In *Forum Lectures* (Voice of America). Washington, DC: Voice of America.

Greene, Tamsen. 2011. "Almost Famous: A Japanese Artist Bares All." *Modern Painters*. April: 40–42.

Gregersen, Andreas and Torben Grodal. 2009. "Embodiment and Interface." *The Video Game Theory Reader 2*, edited by Bernard Perron and Mark J. P. Wolf, 65–83. London: Routledge.

Grodal, Thorben. 2003. "Stories for Eye, Ear, and Muscles: Video Games, Media, and Embodied Experiences. In *The Video Game Theory Reader*, edited by Mark J. P. Wolf and Bernard Perron, 129–155. London: Routledge

Grossberg, Lawrence. 1992. "Is There a Fan in the House?: The Affective Sensibility of Fandom." In *The Adoring Audience: Fan Culture and Popular Media*, edited by Lisa A. Lewis, 50–65. London: Routledge.

Grunebaum, Dan. 2011. "Pantheon of Japanese Rock Gods." *Metropolis*, May 19. Online at www.metropolis.co.jp/arts/japan-beat/pantheon-of-japanese-rock-gods [accessed May 22, 2014].

Guinness World Record News. 2012. "Japanese Producer Johnny Kitagawa Produces the Most #1 Acts by an Individual." *guinnessworldrecords.com*. December 10. Online at www.guinnessworldrecords.com/news/2012/12/johnny-kitagawa-most-1-acts-producedby-an-individual-46316/ [accessed March 30, 2015].

Hacking, Ian. 1998. "Canguilhem Amid the Cyborgs." *Economy and Society* 27(2): 202–216.

Hagio Moto. 1996 [1974–1975]. *Tōma no shinzō* (The Heart of Thomas). Tokyo: Shōgakukan bunko.

Hahn, David. 2009. "Sin, Otherworldliness, and the Downside to Hope." In *Final Fantasy and Philosophy: The Ultimate Walkthrough*, edited by Jason P. Blahuta and Michel S. Beaulieu, 151–163. Hoboken, NJ: Wiley.

Hakuhōdō Research Center. 1985. *Taun wocchinngu—jidai no kūki o machi kara yomu* (Town Watching: Reading the Sense of the Times from Urban Space). Tokyo: PHP Kenkyūjo.

Hall, Stuart. 1998. "Notes on Deconstructing 'the Popular.'" In *Cultural Theory and Popular Culture: A Reader*, edited by John Storey, 442–453. Upper Saddle River, NJ: Prentice Hall.

Halterman, Del. 2009. *Walk—Don't Run: The Story of the Ventures*. Raleigh, NC: Lulu.Com.

Hamano Satoshi. 2012. *Maeda Atsuko wa Kirisuto wo koeta: Shūkyō toshite no AKB48* (Maeda Atsuko has Surpassed Jesus Christ: AKB48 as Religion). Tokyo: Chikuma shinsho.

———. 2015. "Shūkyō toshite no AKB48" (AKB48 as Religion). Invited lecture for the Kadokawa Summer Program Research Group. University of Tokyo, January 23.

Hamano, Shoko. 1998. *The Sound Symbolic System of Japanese*. Stanford, CA: CSLI Publications.

Han, Sam. 2011. *Web 2.0*. Oxford: Routledge.

Harada Nobuo. 1983. *Terebi dorama 30 nen* (Thirty Years of Japanese Television Dramas). Tokyo: Yomiuri shinbunsha.

Haraway, Donna. 1991. "A Cyborg Manifesto: Science, Technology, and Socialist-Feminism in the Late Twentieth Century." *Simians, Cyborgs and Women*, 149–182. New York: Routledge.

Harrison, Quentin. 2014. "Easy Breezy: Hikaru Utada's 'Exodus' Turns 10." *theqhblend*, September 8. Online at www.theqhblend.wordpress.com/2014/09/08/easy-breezy-hikaru-utadas-exodus-turns-10/comment-page-1/ [accessed April 4, 2017].

Harvey, David. 2013. *Rebel Cities: From the Right to the City to the Urban Revolution*. London: Verso.

Hasegawa, Kōichi. 2004. *Constructing Civil Society in Japan: Voices of Environmental Movements*. Melbourne: Trans Pacific Press.

Hasegawa, Yuko. 2002. "Post-identity *Kawaii*: Commerce, Gender, and Contemporary Japanese Art." In *Consuming Bodies: Sex and Contemporary Japanese Art*, edited by Fran Lloyd, 127–141. London: Reaktion Books.

Hasumi Shigehiko. 1994. *Shōsetsu kara tōku hanarete* (Distancing the Novel). Tokyo: Kawade shobō.

Hausswolff, Carl Michael von and Thomas Nordanstad, directors. 2002. *Hashima, Japan*. Online at www.nordanstad.com/portfolio/hashima/ [accessed January 15, 2015].

Hayles, Catherine. 2006. "Unfinished Work: From Cyborg to Cognisphere." *Theory, Culture, Society* 23(7–8): 159–166.

Hearn, Lafcadio. 1971 [1904]. *Kwaidan: Stories and Studies of Strange Things*. North Clarendon, VT: Tuttle.

Henry, Todd A. 2014. *Assimilating Seoul: Japanese Rule and the Politics of Public Space in Colonial Korea, 1910–1945*. Berkeley, CA: University of California Press.

Herron, Jerry. 2012. "The Forgetting Machine: Notes toward a History of Detroit." *Places*, January. Online at www.placesjournal.org/article/the-forgetting-machine-notes-toward-a-history-of-detroit/ [accessed December 20, 2014].

Hidaka, Tomoko. 2010. *Salaryman Masculinity: The Continuity of and Change in the Hegemonic Masculinity in Japan*. Leiden: Brill.

"Hikaru Utada." n.d. *Billboard.com*. Online at www.billboard.com/artist/303512/hikaru-utada/biography [accessed March 23, 2015].

Hill, Amelia. 2002. "Thumbs are the New Fingers for the GameBoy Generation." *The Guardian*, March 23. Online at www.theguardian.com/uk/2002/mar/24/mobilephones.games [accessed December 29, 2015].

Hillenbrand, Margaret. 2009. "Murakami Haruki in Greater China: Creative Responses and the Quest for Cosmopolitanism." *Journal of Asian Studies* 68(3): 715–747.

Hills, Matt. 2002. *Fan Cultures*. London: Routledge.

Hiraga Gennai. 1961 [1763]. *Fūrai Sanjin shū* (Hiraga Gennai Collection). In *Nihon koten bungaku taikei 55* (Anthology of Classical Japanese Literature: Volume 55), edited by Nakamura Yukihiko, 153–224. Tokyo: Iwanami shoten.

Hiraga, Masako. 1995. "'Blending' and Interpretation of Haiku: A Cognitive Approach." *Poetry Today* 20(3): 460–481.

Hirahara Ayaka. 2003. "Jupiter." Tokyo: Dream Music.

Hirano, Cathy. 2013. "Setouchi Triennale Recap." *Art City Takamatsu*. December 29. Online at www.art-takamatsu.com/mt/msearch.cgi?includeBlogs=3&tag=Art%20Setouchi&limit=20 [accessed March 20, 2015].

Hirano, Miki. n.d. "Landscapes from Those Scenes Are Found in Australia! To Travel the World of Miyazaki's Anime" (Ano bamen ni tōjō shita fūkei ga, Ōsutoraria ni atta! Miyazaki anime no sekai o tabi suru). Online at www.allabout.co.jp/gm/gc/78064/ [accessed May 31, 2015].

Hirano Shin, et al., directors. 2006. *Toppo kyasutā* (Top Anchor). Tokyo: Fuji Television.

Hirosue Yasushi. 2000. *Yotsuya kaidan* (Yotsuya Ghost Story). Tokyo: Kage shobō.

Hirotoshi Shibata. 2010. "'Kioku' no mujintō. Gunkanjima" (The Memory of an Abandoned Island: Gunkanjima). *Senshū daigaku shakai kagaku kenkyūjo geppō* (Senshu University Institute of Social Science Monthly Report). August–September: 59–75.

Hisaharu, Motoda. 2011. *Neo Ruins: Hisaharu Motoda Artworks, 2004–2011*. Tokyo: Editions Treville.

Hjorth, Larissa. 2014. "Stories of Mobile Women: Micro-Narratives and Mobile Novels in Japan." In *The Mobile Story: Narrative Practices with Locative Technologies*, edited by Jason Farman, 238–248. New York: Routledge.

Ho, Swee Lin. 2012. "Emotions, Desires, and Fantasies: What Idolizing Means for Yon-sama Fans in Japan." In *Idols and Celebrity in Japanese Media Culture*, edited by Patrick W. Galbraith and Jason G. Karlin, 166–181. New York: Palgrave MacMillan.

Holmberg, Ryan. 2010. *Garo Manga: The First Decade 1964–1973*. New York: Center for Book Arts.

Holston, Alicia. 2010. "A Librarian's Guide to the History of Graphic Novels." In *Graphic Novels and Comics in Libraries and Archives: Essays on Readers, Research, History, and Cataloguing*, edited by Robert G. Weiner, 9–16. Jefferson, NC: McFarland.

Honda Ishirō, director. 1954. *Gojira*. Tokyo: Tōhō.

———, director. 1955. *Gojira no gyakushū* (Gigantis, the Fire Monster). Tokyo: Tōhō Company.

———, director. 1959. *Gojira no gyakushū* (Godzilla Raids Again). Los Angeles: Warner Brothers and Tōhō.

———, director. 1963. *Kingu Kongu tai Gojira* (King Kong vs Godzilla). Tokyo: Tōhō and Universal International.

Honolulu Star Advertiser. 2004. "Billboard Hits: Hawai'i Top 10." *Honolulu Star Advertiser*. October 15. www.the.honoluluadvertiser.com/article/2004/Oct/15/en/en04a.html [accessed March 2, 2015].

Honto rankingu. n.d. *Honto Web*. Online at www.honto.jp/ranking/gr/bestseller_1101_1201_015_028007020000.html?dispTy=1&tbty=1&tpcl=4 [accessed May 24, 2015].

Horihata Hiroyuki and Sekiguchi Mariko. 2012. *Kotoba no fuku* (Clothes of Words). Tokyo: Kinmokusei.

Horikawa Hiromichi, director. 1961–1962. *Musume to watashi* (Daughter and Me). Tokyo: NHK.

Hoskinson, Jim and Laura Murphy, directors. 2015 "Paid Family Leave" *Last Week Tonight with John Oliver*. HBO. May 10.

Huang, Cheng-Wen and Arlene Archer. 2012. "Uncovering the Multimodal Literacy Practices in Reading Manga and the Implications for Pedagogy." In *New Media Literacies and Participatory Popular Culture across Borders*, edited by Bronwyn Williams and Amy Zenger, 44–60. Oxford: Routledge.

Huat, Chua Beng and Kōichi Iwabuchi. 2008. "Introduction." In *East Asian Pop Culture: Analysing the Korean Wave*, edited by Chua Beng Huat and Kōichi Iwabuchi, 1–12. Hong Kong: Hong Kong University Press.

Hur, Nam-Lin. 2000. *Prayer and Play in Late Tokugawa Japan: Asakusa Sensōji and Edo Society*. Cambridge, MA: Harvard University Asia Center.

Hutchinson, Rachael. 2014. "Teaching *Final Fantasy X:* Accounting for Nuclear Nostalgia." In *Between 'Cool' and 3/11: Implications for Teaching Japan Today*, edited by Mahua Batthacharya, 1–7. Conference Proceedings. Elizabethtown, PA: Elizabethtown College.

Ibuse Masuji. 1969. *Black Rain*. Translated by John Bester. Tokyo: Kodansha International.

Ichikura Haruo, director. 1989. *Sogeki* (The Shootist). Tokyo: Toei Video.

Iida, Yumiko. 2001. *Rethinking Identity in Modern Japan: Nationalism as Aesthetics*. London: Routledge.

Ikeda Riyoko. 2004 [1972–1973]. *Berusaiyu no bara* (The Rose of Versailles). Volumes 1–5. Tokyo: Shūeisha Bunkō.

Ikezoe Hiroshi and Tanigawa Tsutomu, directors. 2006. *Hanayome wa yakudoshi* (Fake Bride). Tokyo: TBS.

Imai, Nobuharu. 2010. "The Momentary and Placeless Community: Constructing a New Community with Regards to Otaku Culture." *Inter Faculty*. Online at www.journal.hass.tsukuba.ac.jp/interfaculty/article/viewFile/9/25 [accessed May 31, 2015].

Imamura Shōhei, director. 1989. *Kuroi ame* (Black Rain). Tokyo: Toei.

Infrastructures Lifetime-Extending Maintenance Research Center. *Gunkanjima 3D purojekuto* (Battleship Island: 3-D Project). 2014. Online at www.ilem.jp/research/gunkanjima/ [accessed June 19, 2015].

Inoue Yōsui. 1990. "Shōnen jidai" (Boyhood). Tokyo: For Life Music Entertainment.

Inside Scanlation. n.d. "First Generation: The classical Era." *Inside Scanlation.com*. Online at www.insidescanlation.com/history/history-1-1.html [accessed February 2, 2015].

Ippan Shadanhōjin Nihon Amyūzumentomashin Kyōkai. n.d. "Amyūzumentomashin no kiseki" (Amusement Machine Tracks). Online at www.jamma.or.jp/history/pdf/history_1990_03.pdf [accessed May 20, 2015].

Isada Masaya et al., directors. 2011. *Gou: Himetachi no Sengoku* (Gou: Princesses' Warring States Period). Tokyo: NHK.

Ishida Hidenori et al., directors. 2000. *Kamen Rider Kuuga* (Masked Rider Kūga). Tokyo: Toei Video.

Ishida Yōko. 1999. *TV dorama ōru fairu – 90s minhōhan* (Complete File on Television Dramas: 1990s Commercial Broadcast Volume). Tokyo: Asupekuto.

Ishiguro Noboru, director. 1982–1983. *Chōjikū yōsai Makurosu* (Super Dimension Fortress Macross). Tokyo: Studio Nue.

Ishikawa Tatsuzō. 1968. *Seishun no satetsu* (Bitterness of Youth). Tokyo: Shinchōsha.

Ishiyama Yukihiro. 2008. *Kamishibai no bunkashi: shiryō de yomitoku kamishibai no rekishi* (Cultural History of Kamishibai: Reading the History of Kamishibai through Documents). Tokyo: Hōbun shorin.

Ishizu Kensuke. 2010. *Itsumo zero kara no shuppatsu datta* (I Always Made My Start from Nothing). Tokyo: Nihon tosho centre.

Isomura Itsumichi, director. 1991. *Asatte Dance*. Tokyo: Daiei.

Itō Kimio. 1993. *'Otokorashisa' no yukue: dansei bunka no bunka shakaigaku* (The Path of Manliness: Cultural Sociology of Masculine Culture). Tokyo: Shinyōsha.

Ito, Mamoru. 2004. "The Representation of Femininity in Japanese Television Dramas of the 1990s." In *Feeling Asian Modernities: Transnational Consumption of Japanese TV Dramas*, edited by Kōichi Iwabuchi, 25–42. Hong Kong: Hong Kong University Press.

Itō, Masami. 2008. "Work-Life Balance Starts at Home." *The Japan Times*, January 9. Online at www.search.japantimes.co.jp/cgi-bin/nn20080109f2.html [accessed June 3, 2013].

Itoh, Hiroyuki. 2011. "Miku, Virtual Idol, as Media Platform: Transforming Media Creativity." Keynote address for "Miku@MIT," October 18. Cambridge, MA: Massachusetts Institute of Technology.

Ivy, Marilyn. 1993. "Formations of Mass Culture." In *Postwar Japan as History*, edited by Andrew Gordon, 239–258. Berkeley, CA: University of California Press.

———. 1995. *Discourses of the Vanishing: Modernity, Phantasm, Japan*. Chicago, IL: University of Chicago Press.

Iwabuchi, Kōichi. 1998. "Marketing 'Japan': Japanese Cultural Presence under a Global Gaze." *Japanese Studies* 18(2): 165–180.

———. 2002. *Recentering Globalization: Popular Culture and Japanese Transnationalism*. Durham, NC: Duke University Press.

———. 2004a. "How 'Japanese' Is Pokémon?" In *Pikachu's Global Adventure: The Rise and Fall of Pokémon*, edited by Joseph Tobin, 53–79. Durham, NC: Duke University Press.

———, ed. 2004b. *Feeling Asian Modernities: Transnational Consumption of Japanese TV Dramas*. Hong Kong: Hong Kong University Press.

———. 2004c. "Feeling Glocal: Japan in the Global Television Format Business." In *Television across Asia: TV Industries, Programme Formats, and Globalisation*, edited by J. A. Atkinson, Michael Keene, and Albert Moran, 21–35. London: Routledge.

———. 2010. "Undoing Inter-National Fandom in the Age of Brand Nationalism." *Mechademia* 5: 87–96.

Iwamoto Hitoshi, Kinoshita Takaō, and Hayashi Tōru, directors. 1998. *Oshigoto desu* (Women's Company). Tokyo: Fuji Television.

Izumiya Gensaku. 2007. *Hanabi no zukan* (Picture Book of Fireworks). Tokyo: Popurasha.

Jack, James. 2013. "Unearthing the Seto Inland Sea's Social Landscapes." *The Japan Times*, March 28. Online at www.japantimes.co.jp/culture/2013/03/28/arts/unearthing-the-seto-inland-seas-social-landscapes/ [accessed August 22, 2015].

Jacobs, Robert, ed. 2010. *Filling the Hole in the Nuclear Future*. New York: Lexington Books.

James, William. 2003. *Essays in Radical Empiricism*. Mineola, NY: Dover Publications.

Japan Book Publishers Association. 2014. *An Introduction to Publishing in Japan 2014–2015*. Online at www.jbpa.or.jp/en/pdf/pdf01.pdf [accessed December 29, 2015].

Japan Institute of Design Promotion. 2013. "Good Design Award of the Japan Chamber of Commerce and Industry." Online at www.g-mark.org/award/describe/40553 [accessed October 8, 2013].

The Japan Times. 2005. "Niigata Fireworks Company Plans Big Postquake Blast." *The Japan Times,* July 13. Online at www.japantimes.co.jp/news/2005/07/13/national/niigata-fireworks-companyplans-big-postquake-blast/#.VZhB1mCIKfQ [accessed July 4, 2015].

———. 2010. "Akihabara Gets Bank of Security Cameras." *The Japan Times,* January 27. Online at www.japantimes.co.jp/news/2010/01/27/national/akihabara-gets-bank-of-security-cameras/ [accessed August 17, 2015].

Japan Today. 2015. "Cross-Dressing Matsuko Deluxe: AKB Opening Tokyo Olympics 'Would Embarrass Japan'." *Japan Today,* January 29. Online at www.japantoday.com/category/entertainment/view/cross-dressing-talent-matsuko-deluxe-akb-opening-the-tokyo-olympics-would-embarrass-japan [accessed July 26, 2015].

Japanese American National Museum. n.d. *Hello! Exploring the Supercute World of Hello Kitty.* Online at www.janm.org/exhibits/hellokitty/ [accessed August 5, 2015].

Jenkins, Henry. 1992. *Textual Poachers: Television Fans and Participatory Culture.* New York: Routledge.

———. 2006. *Convergence Culture: Where Old and New Media Collide.* New York: New York University Press.

———. 2010. "Why Participatory Culture Is Not Web. 2.0." *Confessions of an Aca-Fan,* May 24. Online at www.henryjenkins.org/2010/05/why_participatory_culture_is_n.html [accessed August 28, 2015].

———. 2014. "The Reign of the 'Mothership': Transmedia's Past, Present, and Possible Futures." In *Wired TV,* edited by Denise Mann, 244–268. New Brunswick, NJ: Rutgers University Press.

Jenkins, Henry, Xiaochang Li, and Ana Domb Krauskopf. 2008. *If It Doesn't Spread, It's Dead: Creating Value in a Spreadable Marketplace.* Convergence Culture Consortium. Online at www.convergenceculture.org/research/Spreadability_doublesidedprint_final_063009.pdf [accessed December 26, 2015].

Jenkins, Henry et al. 2009. *Confronting the Challenges of Participatory Culture: Media Education for the 21st Century.* Cambridge, MA: MIT Press.

JETRO. 2005. "Japan Animation Industry Trends." *Japan Economic Monthly,* June. Online at www.jetro.go.jp/ext_images/en/reports/market/pdf/2005_35_r.pdf [accessed August 21, 2015].

Jhally, Sut. 1990. "Image-Based Culture: Advertising and Popular Culture" *The World and I,* Article #17591. Online at www.worldandlibrary.com [accessed May 29, 2014].

Jin (Shizen no Teki-P) and Shidu. 2015. *Kagerou Daze 1: In a Daze.* New York: Yen Press.

Jinnai Hidenobu. 1985. *Tokyo no kūkan jinruigaku* (The Spatial Anthropology of Tokyo). Toykyo: Chikuma shobō.

JNTO. n.d. "Enjoying a Shopping Spree in Akihabara." In *Japan: The Official Guide.* Online at www.jnto.go.jp/eng/indepth/exotic/animation/d01_akiha.html [accessed August 17, 2015].

———. 2008a. "JNTO hōnichi gaikyaku jittai chōsa 2006–2007: hōmonchi chōsa hen" (JNTO Survey of Foreign Visitors to Japan 2006–2007: Places Visited). Tokyo: International Tourism Center of Japan.

———. 2008b. "JNTO hōnichi gaikyaku jittai chōsa 2006–2007: Manzokudo chōsa hen" (JNTO Survey of Foreign Visitors to Japan 2006–2007: Level of Satisfaction). Tokyo: International Tourism Center of Japan.

————. 2010. *Official Guidebook: Visit Japan Year 2010 Winter Campaign.* Tokyo: JNTO.

Jobling, Paul. 1999. *Fashion Spreads: Word and Image in Fashion Photography since 1980.* Oxford: Berg.

Jolley, Nicholas. 2005. *Leibniz.* Oxford: Routledge.

Jones, Kent and Mitsuhiro Yoshimoto. 2003. Panel discussion on "The History of the Japanese Horror Films." *The Japan Society*, New York, December 1.

Jones, Mason. 1995–1998. *Ongaku Otaku.* San Francisco, CA: Fanzine.

JTB. 2008. *Cool Japan: Otaku Nippon gaido* (Cool Japan: Otaku Japan Guide). Tokyo: JTB Publishing.

Jung, Eun-Young. 2007. "Transnational Cultural Traffic in Northeast Asia: The 'Presence' of Japan in Korea's Popular Music Culture." Ph.D. dissertation. University of Pittsburgh.

Jung, Sun and Yukie Hirata. 2012. "Conflicting Desires: K-Pop Idol Girl Group Flows in Japan in the Era of Web 2.0." *Ejcjs* 12:2. Online at www.japanesestudies. org.uk/ejcjs/vol12/iss2/jung.html [accessed May 7, 2014].

Kagawa-ken tōkei jōhō dētabēsu (Kagawa Prefecture Statistical Information Database). 2010. Online at www.pref.kagawa.lg.jp/toukei/nenkan/file/02/20100200.xls [accessed September 1, 2015].

Kageyama, Yuri. 2006. "Cuteness a Hot-Selling Commodity in Japan." *The Washington Post*, June 14. Online at www.washingtonpost.com/wp-dyn/content/article/2006/06/14/AR2006061401122.html [accessed April 1, 2017].

Kaida, Naoko et al. 2012. "Study Trip Report: Naoshima and Teshima." Graduate School of Life and Environment Sciences, Tsukuba University. Online at www. envr.tsukuba.ac.jp/~jds/pdf/report_naoshima2012.pdf [accessed April 2, 2015].

Kaji Yūsuke. 2001. *Kōkoku no meisō: Kigyō kachi wo takameru kōkoku kurieitibu wo motomete* (The Meandering Course of Advertising: In Search of Creative Advertising that Will Increase Industry Value). Tokyo: Senden kaigi.

Kajiwara Ikki and Chiba Tetsuya. 2002. *Ashita no Jō* (Tomorrow's Joe). Tokyo: Kōdansha manga bunko.

Kam, Thiam Huat. 2013. "The Common Sense that Makes the 'Otaku:' Rules for Consuming Popular Culture in Contemporary Japan." *Japan Forum* 25(2): 151–173.

Kamichi Chizuko. 1997. *Kamishibai no rekishi* (The History of Kamishibai). Tokyo: Kyūzansha.

Kamiyama Kenji. 2002–2003. *The Ghost in the Shell: Stand Alone Complex 1ˢᵗ Gig.* Tokyo: Bandai.

————. 2004–2005. *The Ghost in the Shell: Stand Alone Complex 2ⁿᵈ Gig.* Tokyo: Bandai.

————. 2006. *The Ghost in the Shell: Stand Alone Complex: Solid State Society.* Tokyo: Bandai.

KAN. 2013. *Kumamon mon.* Tokyo: Up-Front Works.

Kanehara Hitomi. 2003. *Hebi ni piasu* (Snakes and Earrings). Tokyo: Shūeisha.

Kaneko Fuminori, director. 2010. *Ōoku.* Tokyo: Shōchiku.

————, director. 2012. *Ōoku—eien "Emonnosuke/Tsunayoshi" hen* (The Inner Chamber: Forever. "Emonnosuke/Tsunayoshi" Chapters). Tokyo: Shōchiku.

Kaneko Fuminori et al., directors. 1998. *Ōoku—tanjō "Arikoto/Iemitsu hen"* (The Inner Chambers: Beginning. "Arikoto/Iemitsu Chapters"). Tokyo: TBS.

Kant, Immanuel. 1987. *Critique of Judgement.* Translated by Werner S. Pluhar. Foreword by Mary Greggor. Indianapolis, IN: Hackett Press.

Karatani Kōjin. 1995. "Murakami Haruki no 'fūkei'" (The 'Landscape' of Murakami Haruki). *Shūen o megutte* (Apropos of the End). Tokyo: Kōdansha.

Karlin, Jason G. 2012. "Through a Looking Glass Darkly: Television Advertising, Idols, and the Making of Fan Audiences." In *Idols and Celebrity in Japanese Media Culture*, edited by Patrick W. Galbraith and Jason G. Karlin, 72–93. New York: Palgrave MacMillan.

Karnas, Stephen. 2014. "Japanese Social Networking: Can Mixi Survive Line, Facebook, Twitter, Instagram, Etc.?" *Akihabara News*. Online at www.akihabaranews.com/2014/12/27/article-en/japanese-social-networking-can-mixi-survive-line-facebook-twitter-instagram [accessed May 27, 2015].

Kashiwara Tatsuro. 2013. *Takeda awā kūsō tokusatsu sirīzu: Urutora kyū kara sebun made* (Takeda Hour Fantasy Tokusatsu Series: From Ultra Q to Ultraseven). In *Tokusatsu Nippon* (Tokusatsu Japan), 86–88. Tokyo: Takarajimasha.

Kasza, Gregory J. 1988. *The State and the Mass Media in Japan, 1918–1945*. Berkeley, CA: University of California Press.

Kata Kōji. 1971. *Kamishibai no Shōwa-shi* (The History of Kamishibai in the Showa Period). Tokyo: Tachikaze shobō.

Katakai Machi Enka Kyōkai. 2015. *Echigo Katakai Matsuri: Asahara Jinja shūki taisai hōnō hanabi banzuke Heisei 27 nendō* (Echigo Katakai Festival: Asahara Shrine Autumn Grand Festival Dedication Fireworks Program 2015). Niigata: Katakai Machi Enka Kyōkai.

Kataoka, Kuniyoshi. 2002. "Emotion, Textual Awareness, and Graphemic Indexicality." In *Culture, Interaction, and Language*, edited by Kuniyoshi Kataoka and Sachiko Ide, 214–242. Tokyo: Hitsuzi shobō.

Kataoka, Mami et.al. 2012. "Japan, the Chaotic, and Aida Makoto." In *Tensai de gome nasai* (Sorry for Being a Genius)/*Monument for Nothing*, Aida Makoto. 33–46. Tokyo: Mori Art Museum.

Kataoka, Shōhei, director. 2012. *Tokyo Jungle*. Tokyo: Sony Computer Entertainment.

Katayama Kyōichi. 2001. *Sekai no chūshin de, ai o sakebu* (Crying Out Love, In the Center of the World). Tokyo: Shōgakukan.

Katō Mitsuyoshi, director. 2007. *Bi no tsubo – kanshō maniyuaru: file 58—hanabi* (The Mark of Beauty—Viewing Manual: File 58—Fireworks). Tokyo: NHK.

Katsuno, Hirofumi. 2006. "Kikaida for Life: Cult Fandom in a Japanese Live-Action TV Show in Hawai'i." In *In Godzilla's Footsteps: Japanese Pop Culture Icons of the Global Stage*, edited by William M. Tsutsui and Michiko Ito, 167–180. New York: Palgrave Macmillan.

Katsura Chiho. 2000. "Kaidanken Gisai: Nakagawa Nobuo." In *Jigoku de yōi hai! Nakagawa Nobuo kaiki kyōfu eiga no gōka* (Shooting in Hell: The Fate of Nobuo Nakagawa's Horror Films). Edited by Suzuki Kensuke, 66–67. Tokyo: Wise shuppan.

Kaufman, Matthew. 1993–1998. *Exile Osaka*. Osaka: Fanzine.

Kaun, Katharina. 2015. "Art, Nature, and Tradition in Perfect Balance in the Seto Inland Sea." *euronews.com*. January 29. Online at www.euronews.com/2015/01/29/art-nature-and-tradition-in-perfect-balance-in-the-seto-inland-sea/ [accessed April 4, 2015].

Kawabata, Shigeru. 1991. "The Japanese Record Industry." *Popular Music* 10(3): 327–345.

Kawaguchi Jun. 2008. *77 Boa Drum*. DVD. Commons.

———. 2010. *77 Boa Drum*. DVD. Thrill Jockey.

Kawaguchi, Morinosuke. 2007. *Geeky-Girl Innovation: A Japanese Subculturalist's Guide to Technology and Design*, Berkeley, CA: Stone Bridge Press.

Kawahara Kazue. 1998. *Kodomokan no kindai*: Akai tori *to 'dōshin' no risō* (Children's Modernity: *Akai tori* and the Ideal of Childish Innocence). Tokyo: Chūōkōronsha.

Kawamori Shōji, director. 1995. *Makurosu purasu* (Macross Plus). Tokyo: Bandai Visual, et.al.

———. 2013. *Bijon kurieetā no shiten* (Perspective of a Vision Creator). Tokyo: Kinema Junpōsha.

Kawamura, Yuniya, 2012. *Fashioning Japanese Subcultures*. London: Bloomsbury.

Kawazoe Noboru. 2004. *Kon Wajirō: sono kogengaku* (Wajiro Kon and His Modernology). Tokyo: Chikuma shobō.

Kayama Rika. 2001. *87% no Nihonjin ga kyarakutā wo sukina riyū* (Why 87 Percent of Japanese Like Characters). Tokyo: Gakushū Kenkyusha.

Kazuhaya, K., and R. Hosokawa. 2004. "What's This Year—Music." Online at www. interq.or.jp/www1/kunioki/year/music/rc_ms99.shtml [accessed March 21, 2015].

Keet, Philomena. 2007. *The Tokyo Look Book*. Tokyo: Kodansha International.

Kelsky, Karen. 2001. *Women on the Verge: Japanese Women, Western Dreams*. Durham, NC: Duke University Press.

Kelty, Christopher. 2013. "From Participation to Power." In *The Participatory Cultures Handbook*, edited by Aaron Delwiche and Jennifer Jacobs Henderson, 22–32. New York: Routledge.

Kikuchi Satoru. 2008. "'Otaku' sutereotaipu no hensen to Akihabara burando" (The Akihabara Brand and Changes in the "Otaku" Stereotype). *Chi'iki burando kenkyū* (Research on Place Branding) 4: 47–78.

Kim, Kyoung-Hwa Yonnie. 2014. "Genealogy of Mobile Creativity: A Media Archeological Approach to Literary Practice in Japan." In *The Routledge Companion to Mobile Media*, edited by Gerard Goggin and Larissa Hjorth, 216–224. New York: Routledge.

Kimura Takafumi, Katsuta Natsuko, and Ohara Taku, directors. 2012. *Umechan sensei* (Dr. Ume-Chan). Tokyo: NHK.

Kinema Junpōsha. 1993. *Kinejun eiga bideo iyābukku 1993* (Film and Video Yearbook 1993). Tokyo: Kinema Junpōsha.

Kingston, Jeff. 2012. *Contemporary Japan: History, Politics and Social Change Since the 1980s*. Oxford: Wiley-Blackwell.

Kinoshita Mayumi et al., 2014. "Kumamon no tsukurikata/How to make 'Kumamon'." In *Chi'iki burando no tsukurikata/How to make a Local brand*, edited by Toshihiro Takahashi, 2–19. Tokyo: Ei Shuppan sha.

Kinsella, Sharon. 1995. "Cuties in Japan." In *Women, Media, and Consumption in Japan*, edited by Lisa Skov and Brian Moeran, 220–254. Honolulu, HI: University of Hawai'i Press.

———. 1998. "Japanese Subculture in the 1990s: *Otaku* and the Amateur *Manga* Movement." *Journal of Japanese Studies* 24(2): 289–316.

———. 2000. *Adult Manga: Culture and Power in Contemporary Japanese Society*. Honolulu, HI: University of Hawai'i Press.

———. 2002. "What's Behind the Fetishism of Japanese School Uniforms?" *Fashion Theory* 6(2): 215–237.

———. 2014. *Schoolgirls, Money and Rebellion in Japan*. London: Routledge.

Kinsui Satoshi. 2003. *Vuācharu Nihongo: yakuwarigo no nazo* (Virtual Japanese: The Riddle of Role Language). Tokyo: Iwanami shoten.

Kiridōshi Risaku. 1993. *Kaijū tsukai to shōnen: Urutoraman no sakka tachi* (Kaijū Tamer and the Boy: Scriptwriters of Ultraman Series). Tokyo: Takarajimasha.

Kitabayashi, Ken. 2004. "The *Otaku* Group from a Business Perspective: Revaluation of Enthusiastic Consumers." Tokyo: Nomura Research Institute. Online at www. nri.co.jp/english/opinion/papers/2004/pdf/np200484.pdf [accessed August 17, 2015].

Kitada Akihiro. 2011. *Kokoku toshi Tokyo sono tanjō to shi* (Birth and Death of Tokyo, Advertising City). Tokyo: Chikuma gakugei bunko.

Kitagawa Fram. 2005. *Kibō no bijutsu kyōdō no yume Kitagawa Fram no 40 nen: 1965–2004* (Fortieth Year of Dreams of Kitagawa Fram's Cooperative and Hopeful Art: 1965–2004). Tokyo: Kadokawa gakugei shuppan.

———. 2014a. *Bijutsu wa chiiki wo hiraku: daichi no geijutsusai 10 no shisō* (Echigo Tsumari Art Trienniale Concept Guidebook). Tokyo: Gendai kikaku shitsu.

———. 2015. *Art Place Japan: The Echigo-Tsumari Triennale and the Vision to Reconnect Art and Nature*. New York: Princeton Architectural Press.

Kitagawa Masahiro. 2013. *Yamaguchi Momoe → AKB48: A·I ·DO·RU ron* (From Yamaguchi Momoe to AKB48: On the I-D-O-L). Tokyo: Takarajimasha shinsho.

Kitahara Yasuo, ed. 2006. *Minna de kokugo jiten—kore mo, Nihongo* (Dictionary of Japanese for Everyone—This, Too, is Japanese). Tokyo: Taishukan.

Kitamura Hidetoshi, Nagano Yasutada, and Hatakeyama Toyohiko. 2004. *Jinzō ningen Kikaidā* (Android Kikaider). Tokyo: Toei Video.

Kitamura Nobuyo. 2004 [1830]. *Kiyū shoran* (Essays on Manners and Customs). Volume 3. Tokyo: Iwanami shoten.

Kitano Takeshi, director. 1997. *Hana-bi* (Fireworks). Tokyo: Bandai, TV Tokyo, Tokyo FM, and Office Kitano.

Kitazumi, Takashi. 2006. "Low Birthrate Threatens Japan's future: Support, Job Flexibility May Prompt Couples to Have More Children." *The Japan Times*, November 9. Online at www.search.japantimes.co.jp/cgi-bin/nb20061109d1.html [accessed June 3, 2013].

Klein, Christina. 2003. *Cold War Orientalism: Asia in the Middlebrow Imagination, 1945–1961*. Berkeley: University of California Press.

———. "Collaboration between Local and Non-Local Actors in the Echigo Tsumari Art Triennial." *Contemporary Japan* 22(1/2): 153–178.

Klein, Jeff. 2004. "Extreme Dubbing Challenge." *New York Times*, April 25. www.nytimes.com/2004/04/25/arts/television-extreme-dubbing-challenge.html [accessed August 18, 2015].

Klepek, Patrick. 2012. "The Humans Are Dead, Long Live the Beast." *Giant Bomb*, October 31. Online at www.giantbomb.com/articles/the-humans-are-dead-long-live-the-beast/1100-4433/ [accessed May 1, 2014].

Knight, Tara. n.d. *Mikumentary*. Online at www.taraknight.net [accessed August 27, 2015].

Kobayashi Takaya. 2006. *Akiba genjin* (Akihabara Primitive Man). Tokyo: Yell Books.

Kobayashi Yoshinori et al., directors. 2006. *Anfea* (Unfair). Tokyo: Fuji Television.

Kobayashi Yoshinori et al. 2012. *AKB48 hakunetsu ronsō* (AKB48 Heated Debate). Tokyo: Gentōsha.

Kodama, Kaori. 2002. Interview by Jennifer Prough. May 2002. Tokyo.

Koebi. 2013. "Tokutei hieiri katsudō hōjin setouchi koebi nettwāku jigyō hōkoku" (Specified Nonprofit Corporation Koebi Network Program Report). Online at: www.koebi.jp/themes/main/pdf/pdf_houkoku_h25.pdf [accessed September 3, 2015].

Koestler, Arthur. 1968. *The Ghost in the Machine*. New York: Macmillan.

Koga Reiko. 2009. *Kawaii no teikoku: mōdo to media to onnanoko tachi* (The Empire of *Kawaii*: Mode, Media, and Girls). Tokyo: Seidosha.

Kojève, Alexandre. 1980 [1969]. "In Place of an Introduction." In *Introduction to the Reading of Hegel: Lectures on the Phenomenology of Spirit*, edited by Allan Bloom, 3–30. Ithaca, NY: Cornell University Press.

Kojima, Gōseki and Koike Kazuo. 2000. *Lone Wolf and Cub*. Volume 1. Portland, OR: Dark Horse Comics.

Komatsu Kazuo, ed. 2001. *Yūrei* (Ghost). Tokyo: Kawade shobō shinsha.

Kon Wajirō. 1972. *Kogengaku* (Modernology). In *Kon Wajirōshū* (Collected Works of Kon Wajirō). Volume 1. Tokyo: Domesu shuppan.

———. 2001 [1929]. *Shinpan dai-Tokyo annai* (New Version of the Guide to Greater Tokyo). Tokyo: Chikuma gakugei bunko.

Kon Wajirō and Yoshida Kenkichi. 1986 [1931]. *Kogengaku saishu* (Modernology Collection). Tokyo: Gakuyo shobō.

Kondo Aki. 2003. *Rirakkuma 4kuma manga* (Rirakkuma's Four-Bear Manga). Tokyo: Shufu to seikatsu sha.

Kondo Hidenori. 2011. "Interview with Aida Makoto." *Tokyo Source* 65, July 29. Online at www.tokyo-source.com/interview.php?ts=65 [accessed July 6, 2015].

Kondo, Junko. 2012. *Revitalization of a Community: Site-Specific Art and Art Festivals: A Case of Art Site Naoshima*. Master's Thesis. University of Jyvaskyla. Online at www. urn.fi/URN:NBN:fi:jyu-201205301764 [accessed February 3, 2014].

Kondo Kensuke. 2006. *Hyakunen aisareru kyarakutā no tsukurikata* (How to Make Characters Lovable for 100 Years). Tokyo: Goma bukkusu.

Kono, Tommy. 2013. "Kyary Pamyu Pamyu Shares Her Take on Minegishi Minami's Apology and Japanese Idol Culture." *AKB48 Wrap Up*, February 15. Online at www.akb48wrapup.com/2013/02/kyary-pamyupamyu-shares-her-take-on-minegishi-minamis-apology-and-japanese-idol-culture-in-french-tv-show/ [accessed July 26, 2015].

Kosuga Hiroshi. 2007. *Geinō o biggu bijinesu ni kaeta otoko Johnny Kitagawa no senryaku to senjutsu.* (The Man Who Changed Entertainment into Big Business: Johnny Kitagawa's Strategies and Tactics). Tokyo: Kōdansha.

Koyama, A. C. 2007. "History of Greco Guitars." Online at www.music-trade. co.jp/GrecoHistory1.html [accessed April 17, 2014].

Kubo, Yuka. 2013. "Bijin no kijun o kaeru kamoshirenai, Shinderera tekunorojii ga omoshiroi" (Standards for Beauty Might Change: The Interesting Cinderella Technology). *Tokyo University of Technology Topics*, February 8. Online at www.teu. ac.jp/info/lab/project/media/dep.html?id=62 [accessed May 23, 2015].

Kubota, Kenji. 2004. *Lonely Planet*. Mito, Ibaraki: Art Tower Mito.

Kudō Eiichi, director. 1998. *Andō gumi gaiden gunrō no keifu* (A Tale of Scarfaces). Tokyo: Tōei Video.

"*Kuime* (Over Your Dead Body) Press Note." 2014. Tokyo: Kuime Seisaku iinkai and Tōei.

Kuki, Shūzō. 2011. *Reflections of Japanese Taste: The Structure of Iki*. Translated by John Clark. Sydney: Power Publications.

Kumamoto Brand Office. 2015. Personal Communication, April 20.

Kumamoto Ken. 2012. *Kumamoto Ken Eigyō buchō Kumamon da mon! ~ Marugoto Kumamon BOOK* (It's Kumamon, Kumamoto Prefecture Business Department Head!: All about Kumamon Book). Tokyo: Takeshobo.

Kumar, Matthew. 2013. "GDC 2013: Crispy's Failed Pitches and Why SCEA Didn't Want to Publish *Tokyo Jungle*." *Edge*, March 30. Online at www.edge-online. com/news/gdc-2013-crispys-failed-pitches-and-why-scea-didnt-want-to-publish-tokyo-jungle/ [accessed May 1, 2014].

Kumashiro Tatasumi, director. 1974. *Seishun no satetsu* (Bitterness of Youth). Tokyo: Tōhō.

Kunimoto Masahiro, director. 2010. *Oniichan no hanabi* (Fireworks From the Heart). Japan: Go! Cinema.

Kuroishi, Izumi. 1998. *Toward an Architecture as a Container of Everyday Life: Works of Kon Wajirō*. Ph.D. Dissertation. University of Pennsylvania.

———. 2000. *Kenchiku gai no shiko: Kon Wajirō ron* (External Ideas of Architecture: Ideas and Works of Kon Wajirō). Tokyo: Domesu.

———. 2006. "Phenomenological Urban Studies and the Redevelopment of Shibuya." Conference paper. Association for Asian Studies Conference Japan.

———. 2008. "Kogengaku no toshi, toshi no Kogengaku" (Urban Space of Modernology and Modernology for Urbanism). *Bijutsu Forum* (Art Forum) 21: 101–106.

Kurokawa Shin. 1965. "*Meyasubako 7: Aru yatsu no uta*" (A Guy's Poem). *Garo*, September: 116–117.

Kurosawa Akira, director. 1955. *Ikimono no kiroku* (I Live in Fear). Tokyo: Tōhō.

Kurosawa Kiyoshi, director. 1989. *Suīto hōmu* (Sweet Home). Tokyo: Tōhō.

———, director. 1995–1996. Katte ni shiyagare!! (Suit Yourself or Shoot Yourself). Tokyo: KSS.

———, director. 1997. *Kyua* (Cure). Tokyo: Daiei.

———. 2013. Interview by Tom Mes. Tokyo. October 31 and December 9.

Kurosawa Susumu, 2007. *Nihon rokku Ki GS hen Konpurito: Psychedelia in Japan 1966–1969*. Tokyo: Shinko Music.

Kurosawa Yasuharu. 2000. "Kurosawa Yasuharu intabyū" (Kurosawa Yasuharu Interview). In *Jigoku de yōi hai! Nakagawa Nobuo kaiki kyōfu eiga no gōka* (Shooting in Hell: The Fate of Nobuo Nakagawa's Horror Films), edited by Suzuki Kensuke, 32–36. Tokyo: Wise shuppan.

Kushner, Barak. 2006. "*Gojira* as Japan's First Postwar Media Event." In *In Godzilla's Footsteps: Japanese Pop Culture Icons on the Global Stage*, edited by William M. Tsutsui and Michiko Ito, 41–50. New York: Palgrave Macmillan.

KWR International. 2004. "Japan Regains its Position as a Global Cultural and Trend Leader." *KWR International*, February 14. Online at www.kwrintl.com/press/2004/jet-3-27-04.html [accessed August 21, 2015].

La Trecchia, Patrizia. 1998. "Dubbing: An Italian Case Study." *Perspectives: Studies in Translatology* 6(1): 113–124.

Lacy, Suzanne, ed. 1995. *Mapping the Terrain: New Genre Public Art*. Seattle, WA: Bay Press.

LaFleur, William R. 1986. *The Karma of Words: Buddhism and the Literary Arts in Medieval Japan*. Berkeley, CA: University of California Press.

Lam, Tong. 2013. *Abandoned Futures: A Journal to the Posthuman World*. Darlington: Carpet Bombing Culture.

Lamarre, Thomas. 2009. *The Anime Machine: A Media Theory of Animation*. Minneapolis, MN: University of Minnesota Press.

Lamerichs, Nicolle. 2014. "Embodied Fantasy: The Affective Space of Anime Conventions." In *The Ashgate Research Companion to Fan Cultures*, edited by Linda Duits, Koos Zwaan, and Stijn Reijnders, 263–274. Farnham: Ashgate.

Landers, Peter. 2015. "'Pear Fairy' Funassyi Shakes Up Japanese Character World." *The Wall Street Journal*, March 5. Online at www.blogs.wsj.com/japanrealtime/2015/03/05/pear-fairy-funassyi-shakes-up-japanese-character-world/ [accessed on December 16, 2015].

Lapoujade, David. 1997. *William James, Empiricisme et pragmatisme*. Paris: Presses Universitaires de France.

Larking, Matthew. 2013. "Nihonga beside Itself: Contemporary Japanese Art's Engagement with the Position and Meaning of a Modern Painting Tradition." *Literature and Aesthetics* 23(2): 24–37.

Leary, John Patrick. 2011. "Detroitism." *Guernica*. January 15. Online at www.guernicamag.com/leary_1_15_11/ [accessed January 15, 2015].

Lebra, Takie. 1976. *Japanese Patterns of Behavior*. Honolulu, HI: University of Hawai'i Press.

Lee, Hye-Kyung. 2009. "Between Fan Culture and Copyright Infringement: Manga Scanlation." *Media Culture and Society* 31(6): 1011–1022.

Lee, Jennifer 8. 2009. "Is That an Emoticon in 1862?" *New York Times*, January 19. Online at www.cityroom.blogs.nytimes.com/2009/01/19/hfo-emoticon/?_r=0 [accessed October 18, 2015].

Lee Pak, Gloria. 2006. "On the Mimetic Faculty: A Critical Study of the 1984 Ppongtchak Debate and Post-Colonial Mimesis." In *Korean Pop Music: Riding the Wave*, edited by Keith Howard, 62–71. Kent: Global Oriental.

Lefebvre, Henri. 1968. *Le Droit à la Ville (The Right to the City)*. Paris: Anthropos.

Leheny, David. 2006. "A Narrow Place to Cross Swords: 'Soft Power' and the Politics of Japanese Popular Culture in East Asia." In *Beyond Japan: The Dynamics of East Asian Regionalism*, edited by Peter J. Katzenstein and Takashi Shiraishi, 211–236. Ithaca, NY: Cornell University Press.

Lehmann, Ulrich. 2000. *Tigersprung: Fashion in Modernity*. Cambridge, MA: MIT Press.

Leibniz, Gottfried Wilhelm. 2010. *Theodicy*. New York: Cosimo Classics.

Leibniz, Gottfried Wilhelm and Nicholas Rescher. 1991. *G.W. Leibniz's Monadology: An Edition for Students*. Pittsburgh, PA: University of Pittsburgh Press.

Lent, John A. 1989. "Japanese Comics." *Handbook of Japanese Popular Culture*, edited by Richard Gid Powers, Hidetoshi Katō, and Bruce Stronach, 221–242. New York: Greenwood Press.

Leplan. 2010. "Japanese No. 1 Social Netwok Reaches 20 Million Users." *Buzzon*. Online at www.buzzom.com/2010/04/japanese-no-1-social-network-reaches-20-million-users/ [accessed May 27, 2015].

Leslie, John. 1996. *The End of the World: The Science and Ethics of Human Extinction*. New York: Routledge.

Lewis, David. 1986. *On the Plurality of Worlds*. Oxford: Blackwell Publishing.

Light Up Nippon. 2011–2015. *Light Up Nippon*. Online at www.lightupnippon.jp [accessed February 3, 2013].

Lim, Tai Wei. 2013. "Spirited Away: Conceptualizing a Film-Based Case Study through Comparative Narratives of Japanese Ecological and Environmental Discourses." *Animation* 8: 149–162.

Liu, Marian. 2010. "Japanese Superstar Utada Hikaru Finds Her Way in the U.S." *Seattle Times*, January 16. Online at www.seattletimes.com/entertainment/japanese-superstar-utada-hikaru-finds-her-way-in-the-us/ [accessed December 17, 2015].

Liu-Brennan, Damien and Mio Bryce. 2010. "Japanese Fireworks (Hanabi): The Ephemeral Nature and Symbolism." *International Journal of the Arts in Society* 4: 189–202.

Livedoor. 2014. "Kumamon no kai kaigai de wa 'satan to tesaki'? Funasshii inbōsatsu mo (Kumamon Mystery: Is He 'Satan's helper' Overseas? Also, Funashii Conspiracy Theory). *Livedoor.com*. Online at www.news.livedoor.com/article/detail/8865789/ [accessed May 26, 2014].

Longfellow, Brenda. 2004. "The Great Dance: Translating the Foreign in Ethnographic Film." In *Subtitles: On the Foreignness of Film*, edited by Atom Egoyan and Ian Balfour, 337–353. Cambridge, MA: MIT Press.

Lorenz, Konrad. 1969. *King Solomon's Ring*. Translated by Marjorie Kerr Wilson. London: Methuen.

———. 1971. *Studies in Animal and Human Behavior*. Cambridge, MA: Harvard University Press.

Lukács, Gabriella. 2010. *Scripted Affects, Branded Selves: Television, Subjectivity and Capitalism in 1990s Japan*. Durham, NC: Duke University Press.

———. 2013. "Dreamwork: Cell Phone Novelists, Labor, and Politics in Contemporary Japan," *Cultural Anthropology* 28(1): 44–64.

Lund, Sara. 2007. "From Sara Lund (Drummer 67)." *77 Boadrum*, September 9. Online at www.viva-radio.com/77Boadrum/words.php [accessed April 19. 2015].

Lynch, Kevin. 1960. *The Image of the City*. Cambridge, MA: MIT Press.

Lyotard, Jean-François. 1998. *The Postmodern Explained to Children: Correspondence, 1982–1985*. Translated by Thomas Pefanis. London: Turnaround Books.

Lytle, J. Mark. 2007. "Mobile Novels Outsell Paper Books in Japan." *TechRadar*, August 9. Online at www.techradar.com/us/news/phone-and-communications/mobile-phones/mobile-novels-outsell-paper-books-in-japan-154848 [accessed July 8, 2014].

Macaulay, Rose. 1953. *Pleasure of Ruins*. New York: Walker and Company.

MacDonald, Heidi. 2013. "How Graphic Novels Became the Hottest Section in the Library." *Publishers Weekly*, May 3. Online at www.publishersweekly.com/pw/by-topic/industry-news/libraries/article/57093-how-graphic-novels-became-the-hottest-section-in-the-library.html [accessed February 2, 2015].

MacDougall, David. 1998. *Transcultural Cinema*. Princeton, NJ: Princeton University Press.

Mackay, Mairi. 2010. "Can Japan Profit From Its National 'Cool'?." *CNN*, November 19. Online at www.edition.cnn.com/2010/WORLD/asiapcf/11/19/japan.cool.money/ [accessed March 17, 2016].

Maeda Tomiyoshi. 2005. *Nihon gogen daijiten*. (Dictionary of Japanese Entomology). Tokyo: Shōgakkan.

Maerkle, Andrew. 2009. "Dipping into Modern Art at Naoshima's Bathhouse." *The Japan Times*, August 28. Online at www.japantimes.co.jp/culture/2009/08/28/arts/dipping-into-modern-art-at-naoshimas-bathhouse/#.VdiB5HjwGfQ [accessed August 22, 2015].

Mahō no i-rando toshokan, ed. 2007. *Kono keitai shōsetu ga sugoi* (These Cellphone Novels Are Awesome). Tokyo: Goma bukkusu.

Mann, Denise. 2014. *Wired TV*. New Brunswick, NJ: Rutgers University Press.

Marchi, Dave. 2015. Personal Communication with Christine R. Yano. November 15.

Marotti, William. 2013. *Money, Trains, and Guillotines: Art and Revolution in 1960s Japan*. Durham, NC: Duke University Press.

Martelle, Scott. 2014. *Detroit: A Biography*. Chicago, IL: Chicago Review Press.

Martin, Daniel. 2009. "Japan's Blair Witch: Restraint, Maturity, and Generic Canons in the British Critical Reception of *Ring*." *Cinema Journal* 48(3): 35–51.

Maruyama Akira. 1999. *Tokiwasō jitsuroku* (The Real Story of Tokiwasō). Tokyo: Shōgakukan bunkō.

Maruyama, Keiji and Shuhei Hosokawa. 2006. "Yearning for Eleki: On Ventures Tribute Bands in Japan." In *Access All Eras: Tribute Bands and Global Pop Culture: Tribute Bands*, edited by Shane Homan, 151–165. New York: Open University Press.

Maruyamachō-kai. 2016. Maruyamacho.net. Online at www.maruyamacho.net/ [accessed January 27, 2016].

Marx, W. David. 2012. "The *Jimusho* System: Understanding the Production Logic of the Japanese Entertainment Industry." In *Idols and Celebrity in Japanese Media*, edited by Patrick W. Galbraith and Jason G. Karlin, 35–55. New York: Palgrave McMillan.

Massumi, Brian. 2011. *Semblance and Event: Activist Philosophy and the Occurrent Arts*. Cambridge, MA: MIT Press.

Masuda Tsuji. 1984. *Parco no Senden senryaku* (Parco's Marketing Strategy). Tokyo: Parco shuppan.

Matrai, Titanilla. 2014. "Nihon eiga ni okeru yōkai—*Yotsuya kaidan* o megutte" (Phantoms in Japanese Film: The Case of *Yotsuya kaidan*). *Kokusai Nihongaku: Hōsei daigaku kokusai Nihongaku kenkyūsho kenkyū seika hōkokushu* (International Japanese Studies: Hōsei University Bulletin of International Japanese Studies) XI: 85–97.

Matsue, Jennifer. 2009. *Making Music in Japan's Underground: The Tokyo Hardcore Scene*. New York: Routledge.

Matsui, Midori. 1993. "Little Girls Were Little Boys: Displaced Femininity in the Representation of Homosexuality in Japanese Girls' Comics." In *Feminism and the Politics of Difference*, edited by Sneja Gunew and Anna Yeatman, 177–196. St Leonards, NSW: Allen and Unwin.

Matsui, Takeshi. 2009. "The Diffusion of Foreign Cultural Products: The Case Analysis of Japanese Comics (Manga) Market in the U.S." Unpublished Manuscript. Princeton University. Online at www.sfu.ca/cmns/courses/2011/488/1-Readings/ Matsui_Manga_Paper_CACPS.pdf [accessed January 21, 2015].

Matsui Tsuneo and Tanaka Akio, directors. 1966–1967. *Ohanahan*. Tokyo: NHK.

Matsumoto, Akako, Hideaki Sasajima, and Motohiro Koizumi. 2010. "How Can and Should We Evaluate Art Projects? Case Study on Setouchi International Art Festival 2010." Japan Association for Cultural Economics. Online at www.jace. gr.jp/ACEI2012/usb_program/pdf/6.7.1.pdf [accessed February 20, 2014].

Matsumoto Guitars. 2014. "Fujigen kaisōki (erekigitā saisen hajimari)" (The Creation of Fujigen [The Start of the Electric Guitar]). *Garakuta gitā hakubutsukan* (Guitars of the World). Online at www.geocities.jp/guitarofworld/MatsumotoGuitars5. html [accessed May 10, 2014].

Matsumoto Yaeko et al. 1999. *That's terebi dorama 90's*. Tokyo: Daiyamondosha.

Mayumi, Kozo, Barry D. Solomon, and Jason Chang. 2005. "The Ecological and Consumption Themes of the Films of Hayao Miyazaki." *Ecological Economics* 54(1): 1–7.

McCaffery, Larry. 1995. *After Yesterday's Crash: The Avant-Pop Anthology*. London: Penguin.

McClure, Steve. 2000a. "J-Pop Gains in Reluctant Markets." *Billboard*, January 15: 49.

———. 2000b. "Japanese Pop Sweeps Across Asia." *Billboard*, January 8: 42, 86.

McCormack, Gavan. 1971. "The Student Left in Japan." *New Left Review*, I(65): 37–53.

McCurry, Justin. 2015. 'Character Assassination as Japan's Mascot Ranks Are Trimmed." *The Guardian*, April 9. Online at www.theguardian.com/world/2015/apr/09/character-assassination-japan-mascot-ranks-finance-ministry [accessed January 31, 2017].

McGray, Douglas. 2002. "Japan's Gross National Cool." *Foreign Policy*, May and June: 44–54.

McKee, Alan, ed. 2006. *Beautiful Things in Popular Culture*. Oxford: Wiley-Blackwell.

McKirby, Andrew. 2015. "Artist Aida Defiant Over Latest Work." *The Japan Times*, July 28. Online at www.japantimes.co.jp/news/2015/07/28/national/artist-aida-defiant-latest-work/#.VmuKYoSIJJo [accessed December 15, 2015].

McKirdy, Euan. 2014. "Japanese Cuteness Overload Could Result in Mascot Cull." *CNN*, May 12. Online at www.edition.cnn.com/2014/05/12/world/asia/osaka-mascot-cull/ [accessed June 17, 2017].

McLelland, Mark. 2000. "No Climax, No Point, No Meaning? Japanese Women's Boy-Love Sites on the Internet." *Journal of Communication Inquiry* 24(3): 274–291.

———. 2006. "Why are Japanese Girls' Comics Full of Boys Bonking?." *Refractory: A Journal of Entertainment Media*, December 4. Online at www.refractory.unimelb.edu.au/2006/12/04/why-are-japanese-girls%E2%80%99-comics-full-of-boys-bonking1-mark-mclelland/ [accessed May 30, 2014].

———. 2011. "Thought Policing or Protection of Youth? Debate in Japan over the 'Non-Existent Youth' Bill." *International Journal of Comic Art* 13(1): 348–367.

———. 2012. "Australia's Child-Abuse Materials Legislation, Internet Regulation, and the Juridification of the Imagination." *International Journal of Cultural Studies* 15(5): 467–483.

———. 2016. "Introduction: Negotiating Cool Japan in Research and Teaching." In *End of Cool Japan: Ethical, Legal, and Cultural Challenges to Japanese Popular Culture*, edited by Mark McLelland, 1–30. Oxford: Routledge.

McCloud, Scott. 1994. *Understanding Comics: The Invisible Art*. New York: Harper Perennial.

McDonnell, Evelyn. 2013. *Queens of Noise: The Real Story of the Runaways*. Cambridge, MA: Da Capo Press.

McLuhan, Marshall. 1964. *Understanding Media*. New York: Mentor.

McVeigh, Brian. J. 2000. *Wearing Ideology: State, Schooling, and Self-Presentation in Japan*. Oxford: Berg.

Mei. 2007a. *Akai ito* (Threads of Destiny). Volumes 1 and 2. Tokyo: Goma Books.

———. 2007b. *Akai ito ~ Destiny* (Threads of Destiny: Destiny). Vols. 1 and 2. Tokyo: Goma Books.

Men's non-no. n.d. *Men's non-no Web*. Online at www.mensnonno.jp/ [accessed May 29, 2015].

Mendes, Sam, director. 2012. *Skyfall*. Beverly Hill, CA: Metro-Goldwyn-Mayer and Columbia Pictures.

Mercedes-Benz Fashion Week Tokyo. n.d. *Mercedes-Benz Fashion Week Tokyo*. Online at www.tokyo-mbfashionweek.com [accessed August 16, 2015].

Mes, Tom. 2006. "Yoshinori Chiba." Online at www.midnighteye.com/interviews/yoshinori-chiba/ [accessed May 5, 2013].

Mes, Tom and Jasper Sharp. 2004. *The Midnight Eye Guide to New Japanese Film*. Berkeley, CA: Stone Bridge Press.

METI (Ministry of Economy, Trade and Industry). 2010. "Cool Japan/Creative Industries Policy" Online at www.meti.go.jp/english/policy/mono_info_service/creative_industries/creative_industries.html [accessed January 27, 2015].

———. 2012. "Dai 3 kai chi'iki ōpun mini shinpojiumu in Akihabara paneru disukasshon gijiroku" (Minutes of Panel Discussion at the 3rd Area Open Mini Symposium in Akihabara). Online at www.meti.go.jp/policy/mono_info_service/mono/creative/ref2_fy23_creative_OMS_records.pdf [accessed August 17, 2015].

Miike, Takashi, director. 1991a. *Ledī hantā koroshi no pure*ryūdo (Lady Hunter). Tokyo: Shochiku Home Video.

———, director. 1991b. *Toppū minipato tai* (Eyecatch Junction). Tokyo: Japan Home Video.

———, director. 1995. *Shinjuku kuroshakai* (Shinjuku Triad Society). Tokyo: Daiei.

———, director. 1996. *Gokudō sengokushi fudō* (Fudoh: The New Generation). Tokyo: Gaga Communications.

Mika. 2006. *Koizora ～ Setsunai koi monogatari* (Love Sky: A Sad Love Story). Vols. 1 and 2. Tokyo: Starts Publishing.

Mikami Shinji. 1996–2015. *Baiohazādo* (Resident Evil). Tokyo: Capcon. PlayStation.

Miles, Maria and Vandana Shiva. 1993. *Ecofeminism*. Halifax, Nova Scotia: Fernwood Publishing.

Millard, André. 2004. "Introduction: American Icon." In *The Electric Guitar: A History of an American Icon*, edited by André Millard, 1–16. Baltimore, MD: Johns Hopkins University Press.

Miller, Laura. 2003. "Graffiti Photos: Expressive Art in Japanese Girls' Culture." *Harvard Asia Quarterly* 7(3): 31–42.

———. 2005. "Bad Girl Photography." In *Bad Girls of Japan*, edited by Laura Miller and Jan Bardsley, 127–141. New York: Palgrave Macmillian.

———. 2006. *Beauty up: Exploring Contemporary Japanese Body Aesthetics*. Berkeley, CA: University of California Press.

———. 2011a. "Subversive Script and Novel Graphs in Japanese Girls' Culture." *Language & Communication* 31(1): 16–26.

———. 2011b. "Cute Masquerade and the Pimping of Japan." *International Journal of Japanese Sociology* 20(1): 18–29.

minä perhonen. 2011. *minä perhonen?*. Tokyo: BNN.

Minagawa Akira. 2003. *minä wo kite tabi ni deyou* (Let's Go to Trip with minä). Tokyo: Dai X Shuppan.

Ministry of Education, Culture, Sports, Science, and Technology. 2014. *Statistical Handbook of Japan*. Online at www.mext.go.jp/b_menu/houdou/26/11/1353354.htm [accessed April 12, 2015].

Ministry of Health, Labor, and Welfare. 2014. "Kōsei tōkei yōran heisei 26 nendo, dai 2 hen: hoken" (Health and Welfare Statistics in Japan, 2014. Chapter 2: Health). Online at www.mhlw.go.jp/toukei/youran/indexyk_2_1.html [accessed October 15, 2015].

Minori shobō 1983. *Gekkan Out*. January. Tokyo: Minori shobō.

Miranda, Carolina A. 2014. "Hello Kitty is Not a Cat, Plus More Reveals Before Her L.A. Tour." *Los Angeles Times*, August 24. Online at www.latimes.com/entertainment/arts/miranda/la-et-cam-hello-kitty-in-los-angeles-not-a-cat-20140826-column.html#page=1 [accessed June 27, 2015].

Mita Munesuke. 1996. *Gendai Nihon no kankaku to shisō* (The Thought and Sensibility of Contemporary Japan). Tokyo: Kōdansha.

Mitamura Engyo. 1975. *Mitamura Engyo zenshū* (Complete Mitamura Engyo). Tokyo: Chuō kōronsha.

Mitsui, Tōru. 1997. "Interactions of Imported and Indigenous Musics in Japan: A Historical Overview of the Music Industry." In *Whose Master's Voice?: The Development of Popular Music in Thirteen Cultures*, edited by Alison J. Ewbank and Fouli T. Papageorgiou, 152–174. Westport, CT: Greenwood Publishing Group.

Mitsumoto Tadanobu, Yoshioka Sho, and Katsuki Mirai, eds. 2014. *Tōei V shinema taizen* (Tōei V-Cinema Encyclopedia). Tokyo: Futabasha.

Mitsuno Michio et al., directors. 2009. *BOSS 1*. Tokyo: Fuji Television.

—— et al., directors. 2011. *BOSS 2*. Tokyo: Fuji Television.

Miura Jun. 2004. *Yuru kyara daizukan* (Big Encyclopedia of Local Characters). Tokyo: Fusōsha.

Miura, Masashi. 2003. *Murakami Haruki to Shibata Motoyuki no mō hitotsu no Amerika* (Murakami Haruki and Shibata Motoyuki's other America). Tokyo: Shinshokan.

Miyadai, Shinji. 2011. "Transformation of Semantics in the History of Japanese Subcultures Since 1992." Translated by Shion Kono. In *Mechademia 6: User Enhanced*, edited by Frenchy Lunning, 231–258. Minneapolis, MN: Univeristy of Minnesota Press.

Miyagawa Ichirō. 2000. "Miyagawa Ichirō intabyū" (Miyagawa Ichirō Interview). In *Jigoku de yōi hai! Nakagawa Nobuo kaiki kyōfu eiga no gōka* (Shooting in Hell: The Fate of Nobuo Nakagawa's Horror Films), edited by Suzuki Kensuke, 44–47. Tokyo: Wise shuppan.

Miyake Yoshishige et al., directors. 2007. *Kekkon dekinai otoko* (The Man Who Cannot Marry). Tokyo: Fuji Television.

Miyamoto, Ken'ichi. 2013. "Japanese Environmental Policy: Lessons from Experience and Remaining Problems." Translated by Jeffrey E. Hanes. In *Japan at Nature's Edge: The Environmental Context of a Global Power*, edited by Ian Jared Miller, Julia Adeney Thomas, and Brett L. Walker, 222–251. Honolulu, HI: University of Hawai'i Press.

Miyamoto, Musashi. 1982. *A Book of Five Rings*. Translated by Victor Harris. Woodstock, NY: The Overlook Press.

Miyao, Daisuke. 2013. *The Aesthetics of Shadow: Lighting and Japanese Cinema*. Durham, NC: Duke University Press.

Miyazaki, Hayao, director. 1984. *Kaze no tani no Naushika* (*Nausicaä of the Valley of the Wind*). Japan: Toei.

——, director. 1988. *Tonari no Totoro* (My Neighbor Totoro). Tokyo: Studio Ghibli.

——, director. 1989. *Majo no takkyūbin* (Kiki's Delivery Service). Tokyo: Studio Ghibli.

——, director. 1997. *Mononoke hime* (Princess Mononoke). Tokyo: Studio Ghibli.

——, director. 2001. *Sen to Chihiro no kamikakushi* (Spirited Away). Tokyo: Studio Ghibli.

——, director. 2004. *Hauru no Ugoku Shiro* (Howl's Moving Castle). Tokyo: Studio Ghibli.

Miyoshi, Masao. 1991. *Off Center: Power and Culture Relations between Japan and the United States*. Cambridge, MA: Harvard University Press.

Mizoguchi Kenji, director. 1952. *Saikaku ichidai onna* (Life of Oharu). Tokyo: Shin-Tōhō.

Mizuki, Shigeru. 2012. *NonNonBa*. Montreal, QC: Drawn & Quarterly.

——. 2013. *Kitarō*. Montreal, QC: Drawn & Quarterly.

Mizukoshi, Shin, Yoshitaka Mouri, and Osamu Sakura, eds. 2014. *5 Designing Media Ecology: The Politics of Creativity* 2.

Mizushima, Seiji, director. 2007. *Ōedo roketto* (Oh! Edo Rocket). Japan: Madhouse.

Mobu Norio. 2004. *Kaigo nyūmon* (Introduction to Nursing). Tokyo: Bungei shunjū.

Mohri, Yoshitsugu. 2014. Interview by James Jack at Shionoe Museum, Takamatsu, March 9.

Moles, Abraham A. 1986. *Psychologie du Kitsch*. Translated by Manzawa Masami. Tokyo: Hōsei University Press.

Monden, Masafumi. 2012a. "Japanese Men's Fashion Magazines." In *Berg Encyclopaedia of World Dress and Fashion*, edited by Joanne B. Eicher. Online at www.dx.doi. org/10.2752/BEWDF/EDch6511 [accessed September 5, 2015].

———. 2012b. "The Importance of Looking Pleasant: Reading Japanese Men's Fashion Magazines." *Fashion Theory* 16(3): 297–316.

———. 2014. *Japanese Fashion Cultures: Dress and Gender in Contemporary Japan*. London: Bloomsbury.

Mōri Akihide. 1990. *Tōkyū no bunka senryaku sogo-seikatsu jōhō sangyo e no yabo* (Tōkyū's Cultural Strategy: Ambition toward a Synthetic Life Information Industry). Tokyo: Softbank Business.

Mōri Jinpachi. 2011. *Shirato Sanpei-den: Kamui den no shinjitsu* (The Legend of Shirato Sanpei: Truth about The Legend of Kamui). Tokyo: Shōgakkan.

Mōri, Yoshitaka. 2009 "J-Pop: From the Ideology of Creativity to DIY Music Culture." *Inter Asia Cultural Studies* 10(4): 474–488.

Moriarty, Colin. 2012. "*Tokyo Jungle* Review." *IGN*, September 13. Online at www. ign.com/articles/2012/09/13/tokyo-jungle-review [accessed May 1, 2014].

Morikawa Ka'ichirō. 2003. *Shuto no tanjō: moeru toshi Akihabara* (Learning from Akihabara: The Birth of a Personapolis). Tokyo: Gentōsha.

———. 2012. "Otaku and the City: The Rebirth of Akihabara." In *Fandom Unbound: Otaku Culture in a Connected World*, edited by Mizuko Ito, Daisuke Okabe, and Izumi Tsuji, 133–157. New Haven, CT: Yale University Press.

Morimi, Tomihiko. 2004. *Yojōhan shinwa taikei* (The Mythical System of the 4.5-Tatami-Mat Room). Tokyo: Ōta shuppan.

Morimoto, Mariko and Susan Chang. 2009. "Western and Asian Models in Japanese Fashion Magazine Ads: The Relationship with Brand Origins and International versus Domestic Magazines." *Journal of International Consumer Marketing* 21(3): 173–187.

Morita, Mutsumi. 2011. "No Stopping the AKB48 Juggernaut." *Daily Yomiuri Online*, June 24. Online at www.yomiuri.co.jp/dy/features/arts/T110622002086. htm [accessed July 26, 2015].

Morse, Anne Nishimura and Anne Havinga. 2015. *In the Wake: Japanese Photographers Respond to 3/11*. Boston, MA: Museum of Fine Arts.

Morse, Terry and Honda Ishirō, directors. 1956. *Godzilla, King of the Monsters!* Embassy Pictures, TransWorld Releasing Corporation, and Tōhō.

Motion Picture Producers Association of Japan, Inc. "Statistics of Film Industry in Japan." Online at www.eiren.org/statistics_e/index.html [accessed September 16, 2014].

Motoaki, Hori. 2011. "Exhibition Contemporary Fashion—A New Collaboration between Architecture and Fashion." In *Feel and Think: A New Era of Tokyo Fashion*, edited by Hori Motoaki, 20–23. Munich: Prestel.

Mouri, Yoshitaka. 2006. "Subcultural Unconsciousness in Japan: The War and Japanese Contemporary Artists." In *Popular Culture, Globalization and Japan*, edited by Matthew Allen and Rumi Satanato, 174–191. New York: Routledge.

————. 2014. "Freedom of Expression and Rise of Preventive Power." In *5 Designing Media Ecology: The Politics of Creativity* 2: 22–37.

Murakami Haruki. 1979. *Kaze no uta o kike.* Tokyo: Kōdansha. Translated by Alfred Birnbaum under the title *Hear the Wind Sing* (Tokyo: Kodansha English Library, 1987).

————. 1980. *1973-nen no pinbōru.* Tokyo: Kōdansha. Translated by Alfred Birnbaum under the title *Pinball, 1973* (Tokyo: Kodansha English Library, 1985).

————. 1982. *Hitsuji o meguru bōken.* Tokyo: Kōdansha. Translated by Alfred Birnbaum under the title *A Wild Sheep Chase* (New York: Kodansha International, 1989).

————. 1985. *Sekai no owari to hādo-boirudo wandārando.* Tokyo: Shinchōsha. Translated by Alfred Birnbaum under the title *Hard-Boiled Wonderland and the End of the World* (New York: Kodansha International, 1991).

————. 1988. *Dansu dansu dansu.* Tokyo: Kōdansha. Translated by Alfred Birnbaum under the title *Dance Dance Dance* (New York: Kodansha International, 1994).

————. 1991. *Noruwei no mori* (Norwegian Wood). Tokyo: Kōdansha.

————. 1995. *Nejimakidori kuronikuru.* Tokyo: Shinchōsha. Translated by Jay Rubin under the title *The Wind-Up Bird Chronicle* (New York: Knopf, 1997).

————. 1997. *Andāguraundo.* Tokyo: Kōdansha. Translated by Alfred Birnbaum and Philip Gabriel under the title *Underground* (London: Harvil Press, 2000).

————. 2009–2010. *1Q84.* Tokyo: Shinchōsha. Translated by Jay Rubin and Philip Gabriel (New York: Knopf, 2011).

————. 2013. "Come costruire una pila di gattini addormentati… cercando di non svegliarli: Rebecca Suter intervista Murakami Haruki" (How to Build a Pile of Sleeping Kittens… Trying Not to Wake Them Up: Rebecca Suter Interviews Murakami Haruki). In *JapanPOP: Parole, Immagini, Suoni dal Giappone Contemporaneo* (JapanPOP: Words, Images, and Sounds from Contemporary Japan), edited by Gianluca Coci, 43–60. Rome: Aracne Editrice.

Murakami Haruki and Shibata Motoyuki. 2000. *Hon'yaku yawa* (Night Conversations on Translation). Tokyo: Bungei shunjū.

Murakami Takashi. 1999. "Haikei kimi wa ikiteiru: Tokyo pop-sengen" (Hello, You Are Alive: Tokyo Pop Manifesto). *Kōkoku hihyō* (Advertising Criticism), April: 58–60.

————. 2000. *Supa furatto = super flat.* Tokyo: Madora Shuppan.

————. 2003. *Summon Monsters? Open the Door? Heal? Or Die?* Tokyo: Kaikai Kiki.

————, ed. 2005a. *Little Boy: The Art of Japan's Exploding Sub Cultures.* New Haven, CT: Yale University Press.

————. 2005b. *Geijutsu kigyo ron* (The Art Entrepreneurship Theory). Tokyo: Gentosha.

Murakami Takashi and McG, directors. 2009. *Akihabara Majokko Princess.* London: Tate Modern.

Musamura Yasuzō and Kunihara Toshiaki, directors. 1983. *Stewardess monogatari* (Stewardess Story). Tokyo: TBS.

Museo d'Arte Ghibli. 2015. "Welcome" *Ghibli Museum, Mitaka.* Online at www.ghibli-museum.jp/en/welcome/ [accessed May 31, 2015].

Mushi Production. 2008. *Tetsuwan Atomu.* DVD Box 1. Tokyo: Nippon Columbia Co., Ltd.

Mutō Teruhiko. 2000. *Nihon no hanabi no ayumi* (History of Fireworks in Japan). Tokyo: Rīburu.

Nagae Akira. 2006. "Iroke ha fuyou? *MEN'S NON-NO*" (No Sexiness Sought? *Men's non-no*). *Yomiuri Shinbun*, June 5, 23.

Nagai Gō. 1968–1972. *Harenchi Gakuen* (School of Shame). Tokyo: Shūeisha.

Nagaike, Kazumi. 2012. "Johnny's Idols as Icons: Female Desires to Fantasize and Consume Male Idol Images." In *Idols and Celebrity in Japanese Media*, edited by Patrick W. Galbraith and Jason G. Karlin. 97–112. New York: Palgrave McMillan.

Nagano, Yuriko. 2010. "For Japan's Cellphone Novelists, Proof of Success is in the Print." *Los Angeles Times*, February 9. Online at www.articles.latimes.com/2010/feb/09/world/la-fg-japan-phone-novel9-2010feb09 [accessed July 9, 2014].

Nagaoka Matsuri Kyōgikai. 2006. *Wishing for Peace: the Nagaoka Grand Fireworks— Nagaoka ōhanabi inori*. Tokyo: Nagaoka Matsuri Kyōgikai Bungei Shunjū.

Nagaoka Yoshiyuki. 2010. *Manga wa naze kiseisareru no ka: yūgai o meguru hanseiki no kōbō* (Why Has Manga Been Censored?: A Half-Century History of the Battles over the Harmfulness). Tokyo: Heibonsha.

Nagasaki Shunichi, director. 1982. *Yamiutsu shinzō* (Heart, Beating in the Dark). Tokyo: Cinema Hauto.

———, director. 1989. *Yūwakusha* (The Enchantment). Tokyo: Cinema Hauto.

———, director. 1991. *Yoru no sutorenjā kyōfu* (Stranger). Tokyo: Toei Video.

———. 2013. Personal communication with Tom Mes. September 15 and November 13.

Nagayama Kōzō, director. 1991. *Tokyo rabu sutōrī* (Tokyo Love Story). Tokyo: Fuji Television.

———. 1997. *Rabu jenerēshon* (Love Generation). Tokyo: Fuji Television.

Nagayama Kōzō, Suzuki Masayuki, and Usui Hirotsugu, directors. 1996. *Rongu bakēshon* (Long Vacation). Tokyo: Fuji Television.

Nagumo Seiichi and Sakuma Noriko, directors. 2007. *Hatarakiman* (Woman Workaholic). Tokyo: Nippon Television.

Nak, Thenarry. 2012. "The Nak of It: Topping the Charts" (A Look at the Japanese Sales Charts). *idolminded.com*. Online at www.idolminded.com/2012/11/the-nak-of-it-topping-the-charts-a-look-at-the-japanese-sales-charts/ [accessed March 9, 2015].

Nakagawa Nobuo. 1969. "*Tōkaidō Yotsuya kaidan* enshutsu zakki" (Essay on My Direction of *Tōkaidō Yotsuya Ghost Story*). In *Kinema junpō zokan: kyōfu to kaiki* (Kinema Junpo Supplement: Horror and Fear), August 20: 81–94.

———. 1987. "Obake eiga sonota: watashi no kirokueiga ron" (On Ghost Films and More My Documentary Film Theory). In *Eiga kantoku Nakagawa Nobuo* (Film Director Nobuo Nakagawa), edited by Takizawa Hajime and Yamane Sadao, 106–107. Tokyo: Libroport.

Nakagawa Osamu. 1996. *Giso suru Nippon: kokyō shisetsu no Disneylandization* (Faking Japan: Disneylandization of Public Facilities). Tokyo: Shokokusha.

Nakamura, Fuyubi, Morgan Perkins, and Olivier Krischer, eds. 2013. *Asia through Art and Anthropology: Cultural Translation Across Borders*. London: Bloomsbury.

Nakane Takuya, and Shōtarō Tsuji, directors. 2007. *Ishi-chan no dōbutsu oukoku dajare kikō. Minami no rakuen Tasumania 1000km Jyūtan* (Ishi-chan's Comic Travelogue of the Animal Kingdom: Journeying 1000 km to the Southern Paradise of Tasmania). Tokyo: TV Asahi.

Nakano Hitori. 2004. *Densha otoko* (Train Man). Tokyo: Shinchōsha.

Nakano Masaaki. 2000. *Tokyo Nobody: Nakano Masaaki no shashinshū* (Tokyo Nobody: The Photography of Nakano Masaaki). Tokyo: Little More.

Nakata Hideo, director. 1998. *Ringu* (Ring). Tokyo: Tōhō.

———, director. 2002. *Honogurai mizu no soko kara* (Dark Water). Tokyo: Tōhō.

Nakata Kaora and Nakasuji Jun. 2005. *Haikyobon* (Ruin Book). 2007. Tokyo: Taiyō Tosho.

———. 2007. *Haikyobon 2* (Ruin Book 2). Tokyo: Taiyō Tosho.

———. 2009. *Haikyobon 3* (Ruin Book 3). Tokyo: Mirion Shuppan.

———. 2012. *Haikyobon 4* (Ruin Book 4). Tokyo: Mirion Shuppan.

Nakazawa, Hideki. 2014. *Art History: Japan 1945–2014.* Second edition. Tokyo: Aloalo.

Nakazawa, Keiji, Art Spiegelman, and Project Gen. 2004. *Barefoot Gen: A Cartoon Story of Hiroshima.* San Francisco, CA: Last Gasp Publishers.

Naoshima chō tōkei jōhō (Naoshima Town Statistical Information). 2015. Online at www.town.naoshima.lg.jp/government/files/02_jinkosetai.xls [accessed April 12, 2015].

Naoshima Meeting V: Art, Region, Locality: Between Macro and Micro Perspectives. 2000. Tokyo: Benesse Corporation.

Napier, Susan. J. 1993. "Panic Sites: The Japanese Imagination of Disaster from *Godzilla* to *Akira.*" *The Journal of Japanese Studies* 19(2): 327–351.

———. 2005. *Anime from* Akira *to* Howl's Moving Castle: *Experiencing Contemporary Japanese Animation.* New York: Palgrave Macmillan.

———. 2007. *From Impressionism to Anime: Japan as Fantasy and Fan Cult in the Mind of the West.* New York: Palgrave Macmillan.

Nathan, John. 1974. *Mishima: A Biography.* Boston, MA: Little, Brown and Company.

National Police Agency of Japan. 2016. "Damage Situation and Police Countermeasures Associated with the 2011 Tohoku District—Off the Pacific Ocean Earthquake." March 10. Online at www.npa.go.jp/archive/keibi/biki/higaijokyo_e.pdf [accessed March 16, 2016].

Natsume Fusanosuke and Takekuma Kentarō. 1995. *Manga no yomi kata* (How to Read Manga). Tokyo: Takarajimasha.

Natsume Fusanosuke and Osamu Takeuchi. 2009. *Mangagaku nyūmon* (Introduction to Manga Studies). Kyoto: Mineruba shobō.

Negri, Antonio. 1999. "Value and Affect." *boundary 2* 26(2): 77–88.

Newitz, Annalee. 2000. "What Makes Things Cheesy?: Satire, Multinationalism, and B-Movies." *Social Text* 18(2): 59–82.

Newman, James. 2013. *Videogames.* Second edition. London: Routledge.

NHK. 2007. *COOL JAPAN ~ Hakkutsu! Kakko ii Nippon ~ Akihabara* (Cool Japan: Discovering Cool Japan—Akihabara). August 30.

NHK Archives. n.d. *NHK Meisakusen minogashi natsukashi: kaigai shuzai bangumi Afurika tairiku o yuku* (NHK Lost Masterpieces: The Overseas Reporting Program African Journey). Online at www.cgi2.nhk.or.jp/archives/tv60bin/detail/index.cgi?das_id=D0009010016_00000 [accessed August 13, 2015].

NHK Online. n.d. *Sekai fureai machiaruki: yoku aru shitsumon* (*Walk the town, encounter the world* FAQs). Online at www6.nhk.or.jp/sekaimachi/faq/index.html [accessed August 13, 2015].

Nichi Nichi Shinbun. 2014. "Roshia hyōshiki ni 'Kumamon'!?" (Kumamon on a Russian sign!?) *Nichi Nichi Shinbun,* May 14, 45.

Nihei, Chikako. 2013. "Resistance and Negotiation: 'Herbivorous Men' and Murakami Haruki's Gender and Political Ambiguity." *Asian Studies Review* 37(1): 62–79.

Nihon Keizai Shinbun. 2013. "Betsuyaku Minoru *Yotsuya kaidan* o gendaifū ni kaisaku" (Betsuyaku Minoru Adapted *Yotsuya Ghost Story* in the Contemporary Interpretation). *Nihon keizai shinbun*, June 20, 40.

Nimiya Kazuko. 2006. *Kyarakutā baka ichidai* (Life of a Character Freak). Tokyo: Basilico.

Ninjialicious. 2005. *Access All Areas: A User's Guide to the Art of Urban Exploration*. Toronto, ON: Coach House Books.

Nishida Kitarō. 1965. *Mu no jikaku teki gentei* (The Awakening to Self-Determination of Nothingness). *Nishida Kitarō zenshū* (Collected works of Nishida Kitarō). Volume 6. Tokyo: Iwanami shoten.

———. 1987. *Intuition and Reflection in Self-Consciousness*. Translated by Valdo H. Viglielmo, Takeuchi Toshinori, and Joseph S. O'Leary. Albany, NY: State University of New York Press.

———. 1990. *An Inquiry into the Good*. Translated by Masao Abe and Christopher Ives. New Haven, CT: Yale University Press.

———. 2012. *Place and Dialectic: Two Essays*. Translated by John W. M. Krummel and Shigenori Nagatomo. Oxford: Oxford University Press.

Nishitani, Keiji. 1999. "Emptiness and Sameness." Translated by Michele Marra. In *Modern Japanese Aesthetics: A Reader*, edited by Michele Marra, 179–180. Honolulu, HI: University of Hawai'i Press.

Niskanen, Eija. 2007. "Untouched Nature, Mediated Animals in Japanese Anime." *Wider Screen*. Online at www.widerscreen.fi/2007-1/untouched-nature-mediated-animals-in-japanese-anime [accessed May 31, 2015].

———. 2010. "Riding Through Air and Water—The Relationship Between Character, Background, Fantasy, and Realism in Hayao Miyazaki's Films." In *Imaginary Japan: Japanese Fantasy in Contemporary Popular Culture*, edited by Eija Niskanen, 16–19. Turku, Finland: International Institute for Popular Culture. Online at www.iipc.utu.fi/imaginaryjapan/ [accessed May 31, 2015].

Nitagai Kamon et al. 2008. *Machizukuri no hyakkajiten* (Encyclopedia of the Township Movement). Tokyo: Maruzen.

Nitobe, Inazo. 1969. *Bushido: The Soul of Japan*. Rutland, VT: Charles E. Tuttle Company.

Nittono, Hiroshi et al. 2012. "The Power of Kawaii: Viewing Cute Images Promotes a Careful Behaviour and Narrows Attentional Focus." *PLoS ONE* 7(9). Online at www.journals.plos.org/plosone/article?id=10.1371/journal.pone.0046362 [accessed August 17, 2017].

Nixon, Sean. 1997. "Exhibiting Masculinity." In *Representation: Culture Representation and Signifying Practices*, edited by Stuart Hall, 293–323. London: Sage Publications.

Noda Minoru, ed. 2000. *Fainaru fantajii VII kaitai shinsho za kompuriito – kaiteiban* (*Final Fantasy VII*, the Complete Dissection: Revised Edition). Tokyo: Studio BentStuff/ Enterbrain.

Noda Yusuke et al., directors. 2014–2015. *Massan*. Tokyo: NHK.

Noppe, Nele. 2010. "*Dōjinshi* Research as a Site of Opportunity for Manga Studies." In *Comics Worlds and the World of Comics: Towards Scholarship on a Global Scale*, edited by Jaqueline Berndt, 115–132. Kyoto: International Manga Research Center, Kyoto Seika University.

Noriega, Chon. 1996. "Godzilla and the Japanese Nightmare: When *Them!* is U.S." In *Hibakusha Cinema: Hiroshima, Nagasaki and the Nuclear Image in Japanese Film*, edited by Mick Broderick, 54–74. London: Kegan Paul International.

Nornes, Abé Mark. 1999. "For an Abusive Subtitling." *Film Quarterly* 52(3): 17–34.

Norris, Craig. 2009. "Manga, Anime and Visual Art Culture." In *The Cambridge Companion to Modern Japanese Culture*, edited by Yoshio Sugimoto, 236–260. Cambridge: Cambridge University Press.

———. 2013. "A Japanese Media Pilgrimage to a Tasmanian Bakery." *Transformative Works and Cultures*. Online at www.journal.transformativeworks.org/index.php/twc/article/view/470/403 [accessed May 31, 2015].

Nosu, Kiyoshi and Mai Tanaka. 2013. "Factors That Contribute to Japanese University Students' Evaluations of the Attractiveness of Characters." *IEEJ Transactions on Electrical and Electronic Engineering* 8(5): 535–537.

Novak, David. 2013. *Japanoise: Music at the Edge of Circulation*. Durham, NC: Duke University Press.

NTT DoCoMo. 2014. "NTT DoCoMo History Square." Online at www.history-s.nttdocomo.co.jp/index.html [accessed January 15, 2016].

Nunokawa Yūji 2013. *Kuriimii Mami wa naze sutekki de henshin suru no ka?* (Why does Creamy Mami Transform with a Stick?). Tokyo: Nikkei BP-sha.

Nyeberg, Amy Kiste. 2010. "How Librarians Learned to Love the Graphic Novel." In *Graphic Novels and Comics in Libraries and Archives: Essays on Readers, Research, History, and Cataloguing*, edited by Robert G. Weiner, 26–40. Jefferson, NC: McFarland.

Ōbayashi Nobuhiko, director. 2012. *Kono sora no hana: Nagaoka hanabi monogatari* (Casting Blossoms into the Sky: The Story of Nagaoka Fireworks). Japan: PSC and TM Entertainment.

Occhi, Debra J. 1999. "Sounds of the Heart and Mind: Mimetics of Emotional States in Japanese." In *Languages of Sentiment: Pragmatic and Conceptual Approaches to Cultural Constructions of Emotional Substrates*, edited by Gary B. Palmer and Debra J. Occhi, 151–170. Amsterdam: John Benjamins.

———. 2009. "Tiny Buds Whispering: Ideologies of Flowers in Contemporary Japanese." *Social Semiotics* 19(2): 213–229.

———. 2010. "Consuming Kyara 'Characters': Anthropomorphization and Marketing in Contemporary Japan." *Comparative Culture* 15: 77–86.

———. 2012. "Wobbly Aesthetics, Performance, and Message: Comparing Japanese *Kyara* with their Anthropomorphic Forebears." *Asian Ethnology* 71(1): 109–132.

———. 2014a. "Yuru Kyara, Humanity, and the Uncanny Instability of Borders in the Construction of Japanese Identities and Aesthetics." *Japan Studies: The Frontier* 7(1) 1–11.

———. 2014b. "Sloppy Selfhood: Metaphor, Embodiment, Animism, and Anthropomorphization in Japanese Language and Culture." In *Language, Culture and Cognition in the 21st Century: Intersection of Cognitive Linguistics and Linguistic Anthropology*, edited by Masataka Yamaguchi, Ben Blount, and Dennis Tay, 124–144. New York: Palgrave Macmillan.

Ōe, Kenzaburō. 1995. *Japan, the Ambiguous and Myself: The Nobel Prize Speech and Other Lectures*. New York: Kodansha International.

Oedekerk, Steve, director. 2002. *Kung Pow! Enter the Fist*. Century City, CA: 20th Century Fox.

Ogawa Michiaki. 1982. *Seibu no creative waku: fushigi daisuki* (Seibu's Creative Works by Seibu: Love for Curiosity). Tokyo: Ribroport.

Ogawa Yoshimasa. 2000. "Hanabi, matawa kanashisa no kesshō: *Tōkaidō Yotsuya kaidan* shōron" (Fireworks or Crystallization of Misfortunes: An Essay on *Tōkaidō*

Yotsuya Ghost Story). In *Jigoku de yōi hai! Nakagawa Nobuo kaiki kyōfu eiga no gōka* (Shooting in Hell: The Fate of Nobuo Nakagawa's Horror Films), edited by Suzuki Kensuke, 72–73. Tokyo: Wise shuppan.

Ogura Hisao and Takamaru Masataka, directors. 1998. *Nuusu no onna* (Newswoman). Tokyo: Fuji Television.

Ohnuki-Tierney, Emiko. 1990. "The Monkey as Self in Japanese Culture." In *Culture through Time: Anthropological Approaches*, edited by Emiko Ohnuki-Tierney, 128–153. Stanford, CA: Stanford University Press.

Ohtake, Shinro. 1996. *Atlanta 1945+50*. Atlanta, GA: Nexus Press.

———. 2005. *Sude ni soko ni aru mono* (That Which is Already There). Tokyo: Chikuma shobō.

———. 2010. *Naoshima sentō* I♥湯 (Naoshima Bath: I♥YU). Tokyo: Seigensha.

Ōji Masashi. 2012. *"Tokyo Jungle* wa seimei no sanka: Crispy's Kataoka Shōhei shi x shashinka Nakano Masaaki shi ga kataru *Tokyo Jungle, Tokyo Nobody* no tanjō hitsuwa to kyōtsūkō" (*Tokyo Jungle* as a Paean to Life: Kataoka Shōhei of Crispy's and Photographer Nakano Masaaki Discuss the Secret Origins and Connections Between *Tokyo Jungle* and *Tokyo Nobody*). *4Gamer,* June 11. Online at www.4gamer. net/games/119/G011923/20120607099/ [accessed May 1, 2014].

Oka-Doerge, Cosima. 2015. Personal communication with Ian Condry, July 17.

Okabe, Daisuke and Ishida, Kimi. 2012. "Making Fujoshi Identity Visible and Invisible." In *Fandom Unbound: Otaku Culture in a Connected World*, edited by Mizuki Ito, Daisuke Okabe, and Izumi Tsuji, 207–224. New Haven, CT: Yale University Press.

Okajima Shinshi and Okada Yasuhiro. 2011. *Gurūpu aidoru shinka ron: "Aidoru sengoku jidai" ga yattekkita!* (On the Evolution of Group Idols: "The Idol Warring States Period" is Upon Us!). Tokyo: Mainichi komyunikēshonzu.

Okamura, Naoto. 2008. "Author Nun Finds New Outlet in Cellphone Fiction." Reuters.com, September 26. Online at www.www.reuters.com/articlePrint?articleId= USTRE48P12I20080926 [accessed July 5, 2014].

Okawa Toshimichi, director. 1989a. *Kuraimuhantā ikari no jūdan* (Crime Hunter). Tokyo: Toei Video.

———, director. 1989b. *Kuraimuhantā 2 uragiri no jūdan* (Crime Hunter 2). Tokyo: Toei Video.

Okura Wakaba. 2013. "Guankanjima o sutorītobyū de arui te miyo u" (Walking on Gunkanjima with Google Street View). Online at www.googlejapan.blogspot. jp/2013/06/blog-post_28.html [accessed June 20, 2015].

O'Neill, Gerard K. 2000. *The High Frontier: Human Colonies in Space: 3rd Edition*. Burlington, ON: Apogee Books.

Onishi, Norimitsu. 2004. "What's Korean for 'Real Man'? Ask a Japanese Woman." *New York Times*, December 23. Online at www.nytimes.com/2004/12/23/world/asia/ whats-korean-for-real-man-ask-a-japanese-woman.html?_r=0 [accessed October 13, 2015].

———. 2005. "Ugly Images of Asian Rivals Become Best Sellers in Japan." *New York Times*, November 19. Online at www.nytimes.com/2005/11/19/world/asia/ ugly-images-of-asian-rivals-become-best-sellers-in-japan.html [accessed October 13, 2015].

———. 2008. "Thumbs Race as Japan's Bestsellers Go Cellular." *New York Times*, January 20. Online at www.nytimes.com/2008/01/20/world/asia/20japan.html [accessed July 5, 2014].

Ono, Philbert. 1996. "Hiromix." Online at www.photoguide.jp/txt/HIROMIX [accessed May 20, 2015].

Onoe Kikunosuke. 2013. "Onoe Kukunosuke-san 'Yosuya kaidan' obon ni hatsuyaku de idomu" (Mr. Kikunosuke Onoe Challenges *Yotsuya Ghost Story*). *Nihon keizai shinbun*, June 24, 14.

Orbaugh, Sharalyn. 2012. "How the Pendulum Swings: Kamishibai and Censorship Under the Allied Occupation." In *Censorship, Media, and Literary Culture in Japan: From Edo to Postwar*, edited by Tomi Suzuki, et al., 161–171. Tokyo: Shin'yōsha.

———. 2015. *Propaganda Performed: Kamishibai in Japan's Fifteen-Year War*. Leiden: Brill.

Oricon. 2009. "Nenkan CD shinguru rankingu 2009 nendo" (Yearly CD Single Ranking 2009). Online at www.oricon.co.jp/rank/js/y/2009/ [accessed July 26, 2015].

———. 2010. "Nenkan CD shinguru rankingu 2010 nendo" (Yearly CD Single Ranking 2010). Online at www.oricon.co.jp/rank/js/y/2010/ [accessed July 26, 2015].

———. 2011. "Nenkan CD shinguru rankingu 2011 nendo" (Yearly CD Single Ranking 2011). Online at www.oricon.co.jp/rank/js/y/2011/ [accessed July 26, 2015].

———. 2012. "Nenkan CD shinguru rankingu 2012 nendo" (Yearly CD Single Ranking 2012). Online at www.oricon.co.jp/rank/js/y/2012/ [accessed July 26, 2015].

———. 2013a. "Murakami Haruki-shi ga 4nen buri sōgō ichii nidō shui kakutoku rekishihatsu" (Murakami Haruki Becomes the First Author in History to Rank First Overall on the Bestseller Twice after Four Years). www.oricon.co.jp/news/2031454/ [accessed February 5, 2015].

———. 2013b. "Oricon 2013 nenkan: ongaku and eizo ranking daihappyo" (Oricon 2013: Grand Announcement of Music and Video rankings). *Oricon Ranking*. Online at www.oricon.co.jp/music/special/2013/musicrank1215/index.html [accessed March 2, 2015].

Oricon Style. 2004. "SMAP 'Sekai ni hitotsu dake no hana,' shinguru uriage rekidai 9-i ni" (SMAP's "The One and Only Flower in the World" Becomes the 9th Ranking Single in Music History). Oricon Style. August 3. Online at www.oricon.co.jp/news/ranking/5139/ [accessed June 3, 2013].

Orwell, George. 1949. *1984*. New York: Signet Classic.

Osaki, Harumi. 2015. "Pure Experience in Question: William James in the Philosophy of Kitarō Nishida and Alfred North Whitehead." *Philosophy East and West* 65(4): 1234–1252.

Osaki, Tomohiro. 2013. "Nationalism Rearing Ugly Head with Greater Frequency: Rightwingers Think Nothing of Making Public Death Threats." *The Japan Times*, May 29. Online at www.japantimes.co.jp/news/2013/05/23/national/nationalism-rearing-ugly-head-with-greater-frequency/#.UdOkVlOoWR0 [accessed July 8, 2013].

Ōsawa Jō. 2008. "Shin-Tōhō no obake eiga to *Tōkaidō Yotsuya kaidan*: janru no fukkatusu to kakushin" (Shin-Tōhō's Ghost Films and *Tōkaidō Yotsuya Ghost Story*: Revival and Innovation of the Genre). In *Kaiki to gensō e no kairo: kaidan kara J-horā e* (Circuit for Horror and Illusion: From Ghost Stories to J-Horror), edited by Uchiyama Kazuki, 67–99. Tokyo: Shinwasha.

Ōsawa Masachi. 1996. *Kyoko no jidai no hate* (The End of the Era of Fiction). Tokyo: Chikuma shobō.

Oshii Mamoru, director. 1983. *Dallos*. Tokyo: Bandai, Yomiuri, and Studio Pierrot.

————, director. 1995. *The Ghost in the Shell*. New York: Polygram Video.

————, director. 2004. *The Ghost in the Shell: Innocence*. Universal City, CA: DreamWorks Home Entertainment.

Oshima, Ken. 1996. "Denenchōfu: Building Garden City in Japan." *Journal of the Society of Architectural Historians* 55(2): 140–151.

Ōshima Nagisa, director. 2004. *Ninja bugei-chō* (Band of Ninja). Tokyo: Ponīkyanion.

Ōta, Tōru. 2004. "Producing (Post-) Trendy Japanese TV Dramas." Translated by Nasu Madori. In *Feeling Asian Modernities: Transnational Consumption of Japanese TV Dramas*, edited by Kōichi Iwabuchi, 69–86. Hong Kong: Hong Kong University Press.

Ōtani Yoshio. 2012. *Janiken: Janiizu bunkaron* (Johnny's Studies). Tokyo: Shinano.

Ōtomo Katsuhiro, director. 1988. *Akira*. Tokyo: Tōhō.

Ōtsuka Ai. 2004. "Kingyō hanabi" (Goldfish Fireworks). Avex Trax.

Ōtsuka Eiji. 1996. *'Kanojotachi' no rengō sekigun: sabukaruchā to sengo minshushugi* (The United Red Army of "Those Women": Subculture and Postwar Democracy). Tokyo: Kadokawa shoten.

————. 2001 [1989]. *Teihon Monogatari shōhiron* (A Theory of Narrative Consumption: Standard Edition). Tokyo: Kadokawa.

————. 2010. "World and Variation: The Reproduction and Consumption of Narrative." Translated by Marc Steinberg. In *Mechademia 5: Fanthropologies*, edited by Frenchy Lunning, 99–116. Minneapolis, MN: University of Minnesota Press.

Ōtsuka Eiji and Hashimoto Eiji. 2012. *Manga wa ikani shite eiga ni narō to shita ka: eiga teki shuhō no kenkyū* (How Manga Becomes Film: A Study on Cinematic Techniques). Tokyo: NTT shuppan.

Ōtsuka Eiji and Tajima Sho-u. 1989. *Mōryō senki Madara* (Mōryō War Record Madara). Volume 1. Tokyo: Kadokawa.

————. 2007. *MPD Psycho*. Volume 1. Milwaukie, OR: Dark Horse Comics.

Oxford University Press. 2015. "Oxford Dictionaries Word of the Year 2015 Is…" *Oxford Dictionaries*. Online at www.blog.oxforddictionaries.com/2015/11/word-of-the-year-2015-emoji/ [accessed December 31, 2015].

Ozaki, Tetsuya. 2011. "Japanese Contemporary Art in the Heisei Era." Translated by Kaori Ihara and Joe Earle. In *Bye Bye Kitty*, 48–65. New York: Japan Society.

Pagliassotti, Dru. 2008. "Better Than Romance? Japanese BL Manga and the Subgenre of Male/Male Romantic Fiction." In *Boys' Love Manga: Essays on the Sexual Ambiguity and Cross-Cultural Fandom of the Genre*, edited by Antonia Levi et al., 59–83. Jefferson, NC: McFarland.

————. 2009. "GloBLisation and Hybridisation: Publishers' Strategies for Bringing Boys' Love to the United States." *Intersections* 20. Online at www.intersections.anu.edu.au/issue20/pagliassotti.htm [accessed January 21, 2015].

Painter, Andrew A. 1996. "Japanese Daytime Television, Popular Culture, and Ideology." In *Contemporary Japan and Popular Culture*, edited by John Treat, 197–234. Honolulu, HI: University of Hawai'i Press.

Pāpuru. 2008. *Ashita no niji* (Tomorrow's Rainbow). Tokyo: Mainichi Shinbunsha.

Parikka, Jussi. 2010. *Insect Media: An Archaeology of Animals and Technology*. Minneapolis, MN: University of Minnesota Press.

Pariser, Eli. 2011. *The Filter Bubble: What the Internet is Hiding from You*. New York: Penguin Press.

Park, Si-soo. 2014. "Anti-Hallyu Voices Growing in Japan." *Korea Times*, February 21. Online at www.koreatimes.co.kr/www/news/culture/2014/02/386_152045.html [accessed February 15, 2014].

Partner, Simon. 1999. *Assembled in Japan: Electrical Goods and Making of the Japanese Consumer*. New York: Columbia University.

Patten, Fred. 2004. *Watching Anime, Reading Manga: 25 Years of Essays and Reviews*. Berkeley, CA: Stone Bridge Press.

Patterson, Randy. 2012. "Tak Matsumoto." *Boomer City*. Online at www. boomerocity.com/index.php/reviews-interviews/interviews/125-tak-matsumoto [accessed May 10, 2014].

Penal Code. 1907. Online at www.cas.go.jp/jp/seisaku/hourei/data/PC.pdf [accessed July 3, 2015].

Perone, James E. 2008. *Mods, Rockers, and the Music of the British Invasion*. Santa Barbara, CA: Praeger Publishers.

Petersen, Robert S. 2009. "The Acoustics of Manga." In *A Comics Studies Reader*, edited by Jeet Heer and Kent Worcester, 163–171. Jackson, MS: University Press of Mississippi.

Pia. 2014. *Hanabi Pia—shutoken 2014* (Pia Fireworks: Tokyo Metropolitan Edition, 2014). Tokyo: Pia.

Piel, L. Halliday. 2010. "Loyal Dogs and Meiji Boys: The Controversy over Japan's First Children's Story, Koganemaru (1891)." *Children's Literature* 38: 207–222.

Pieterse, Jan Nederveen. 1995. "Globalization as Hybridization." In *Global Modernities*, edited by Mike Featherstone, Scott Lash, and Roland Robertson, 45–69. London: Sage Publications.

Piette, Alain. 1998. "Translation Onscreen." In *Teaching Translation and Interpretation 4*, edited by Eva Huang, 189–195. Amsterdam: John Benjamins.

Pollock, Griselda. 2003 [1988]. *Vision and Difference*. London: Routledge.

Poole, Robert Michael. 2012. "Johnny's World." *Newsweek*, December 2. Online at www.eres.library.manoa.hawaii.edu/login?url=http://search.ebscohost.com/login.aspx?direct=true&db=f5h&AN=84575000&site=ehost-live [accessed May 17, 2014].

Popeye. n.d. *Popeye Official Website*. Online at www.magazineworld.jp/popeye/ [accessed May 29, 2015].

Popteen. 2004. "Purikura kisshu: Chō tettei hikaku" (Types of Print Club: A Super Complete Comparison). *Popteen*, June, 196–201.

———. 2008. "PopGirls no Hikaru Meiku purikira taiketsu" (PopGirls Makeup Print Club Sparkle Showdown). *Popteen*, February, 156–157.

Postman, Neil. 1970. "The Reformed English Curriculum." In *High School 1980: The Shape of the Future in American Secondary Education*, edited by A.C. Eurich. Quoted in "What is Media Ecology?" Online at www.media-ecology.org/media_ecology/index.html [accessed January 26, 2016].

Pountain, Dick and David Robins. 2000. *Cool Rules: Anatomy of an Attitude*. London: Reaktion Books.

Power, Natsu Onoda. 2009. *God of Comics: Osamu Tezuka and the Creation of Post-World War II Manga*. Jackson, MS: University Press of Mississippi.

Prough, Jennifer S. 2011. *Straight from the Heart: Gender, Intimacy, and the Cultural Production of Shōjo Manga*. Honolulu, HI: University of Hawai'i Press.

Pukumuku. 2013. *Kantan! Wakariyasui! Kyarakutā dezain* (Simple! Easy to Understand! Character Design). Tokyo: Genkousha Mook.

Puri Kenkyūbu (Print Club Research Department). Online at www.fumi23.com/puri/rankingofmachines [accessed May 20, 2015].

Purikura Kōjō Iinkai. 1996. *Purinto Kurabu sūpā tsukainaoshi chō-toru, haru* (Notebook for Super Mastery of Print Club—Taking and Pasting). Tokyo: Takeshobō.

Pustz, Matthew. 1999. *Comic Book Culture: Fanboys and True Believers.* Jackson, MS: University of Mississippi Press.

Rabuberi. 2006. "Daisuki purikura e no michi" (On the Way to Our Favorite Print Club). *Rabuberi,* June, 102–103.

Raku Job. 2008. "Nyūsu: Akiba otaku matsuri no goannai" (News: Introducing the Akihabara Otaku Festival), May 2. Online at www.raku-job.jp/blog/2008/05/akiba.html [accessed August 17, 2015].

Rayns, Tony. 1998. "Mochizuki Rokuro: A Supreme Pragmatist." *Catalogue 27th International Film Festival Rotterdam,* 230–235. Rotterdam: IFFR.

———. 2000. "This Gun for Hire." *Sight and Sound.* May: 30–32.

Reid, George M., director. 1966. *Beloved Invaders: The Golden Era of the Ventures.* Vancouver, BC: Interfilm Production.

Remioromen. 2005. "Shunkashūtō" (Four Seasons). Speedstar Records.

Retro Gamer Staff. 2011. "The Making of *Final Fantasy VII.*" *Retro Gamer* 96: 25–33.

RIAJ (Recording Industry Association of Japan). 2012. *Statistics and Trends.* Tokyo: Recording Industry Association of Japan. Online at www.riaj.or.jp/e/issue/pdf/RIAJ2012E.pdf [accessed July 26, 2015].

———. 2014. *RIAJ Yearbook 2014.* Tokyo: Recording Industry Association of Japan. Online at www.riaj.or.jp/e/issue/pdf/RIAJ2014E.pdf [accessed March 11, 2015].

Rich, B. Ruby. 2004. "To Read or Not to Read: Subtitles, Trailers, and Monolingualism." In *Subtitles: On the Foreignness of Film,* edited by Atom Egoyan and Ian Balfour, 153–169. Cambridge, MA: MIT Press.

Richardson, Tina, ed. 2015. *Walking Inside Out: Contemporary British Psychogeography.* London: Rowman & Littlefield.

Richie, Donald. 1987 [1972]. "The Japanese Eroduction." *A Lateral View: Essays on Culture and Style in Contemporary Japan,* 156–169. Berkeley, CA: Stone Bridge Press.

———. 2001. *A Hundred Years of Japanese Film.* Tokyo: Kodansha International.

———. 2003. *The Image Factory: Fads and Fashion in Japan.* London: Reaktion Books.

Ridgely, Steven C. 2010. *Japanese Counterculture the Antiestablishment Art of Terayama Shūji.* Minneapolis, MN: University of Minnesota Press.

Rishō. 1817. *Hanabi hiden shū* (The Book of Fireworks Secrets). Osaka: Osaka shorin kōchiya.

Rocamora, Agnès. 2009. *Fashioning the City: Paris, Fashion, and the Media.* London: I. B. Tauris.

———. 2012. "Hypertextuality and Remediation in the Fashion Media: The Case of Fashion Blogs." *Journalism Practice* 6(1): 92–106.

Rocket News. 2011a. "200 mai ijō no AKB48 no CD wo gomisuteba de hakken! Koko made sarete ninki wo eru koto wo membā wa dō omou ka?" (Over 200 Copies of AKB48's CD Discovered in the Garbage! What do the Members Think about Taking Things This Far for Popularity?). Online at www.rocketnews24.com/2011/05/30/200%E6%9E%9A%E4%BB%A5%E4%B8%8A%E3%81%AEakb48%E3%81%AEcd%E3%82%92%E3%82%B4%E3%83%9F%E6%8D%A8%E3%81%A6%E5%A0%B4%E3%81%A7%E7%99%BA%E8%A6%8B-%E4%BA%BA%E6%B0%97%E3%81%A8%E6%9B%B2%E8%81%9E%E3%81%84/ [accessed July 26, 2015].

———. 2011b. "Nai nai Okamura ga AKB48 sōsenkyō wo mondaishi 'zo tto shiteiru no boku dake?' 'osawari wa akushukai dake desho" (Nai Nai Okamura Problematizes the AKB48 General Elections: "Am I the Only One Appalled by This?" "You Only Get to Touch Them at Handshake Events!") Online at www.rocketnews24.com/2011/06/12/%E3%83%8A%E3%82%A4%E3%83%8A%E3%

82%A4%E5%B2%A1%E6%9D%91%E3%81%8Cakb48%E7%B7%8F%E9%81%B8
%E6%8C%99%E3%82%92%E5%95%8F%E9%A1%8C%E8%A6%96%E3%80%8C
%E3%82%BE%E3%83%83%E3%81%A8%E3%81%97%E3%81%A6%E3%81%84/
[accessed July 21, 2015].

Rose, Mike. 2012. *"Tokyo Jungle* Studio Not Afraid to Be Japanese." *Gamasutra: The Art and Business of Making Games*, October 30. Online at www.gamasutra. com/view/news/179952/Tokyo_Jungle_studio_not_afraid_to_be_Japanese.php [accessed May 1, 2014].

Ross, Andrew. 1989. *No Respect: Intellectuals and Popular Culture*. New York: Routledge.

RPGAMER. 1998. *Final Fantasy VII – Complete Script*. Online at www.rpgamer. com/games/ff/ff7/ff7cscript.html [accessed 13 June 2014].

Ruh, Brian. 2004. *Stray Dog of Anime: The Films of Mamoru Oshii*. New York: Palgrave Macmillan.

———. 2009. "Early Japanese Animation in the United States: Changing Tetsuwan Atomu to Astro Boy." In *The Japanification of Children's Popular Culture: From Godzilla to Miyazaki*, edited by Mark I. West, 209–226. London: Rowman & Littlefield.

Rupp, Katherine. 2003. *Gift-Giving in Japan: Cash, Connections, Cosmologies*. Stanford, CA: Stanford University Press.

Russell, Gabrielle. 2008. "Pedophiles in Wonderland: Censoring the Sinful in Cyberspace." *The Journal of Criminal Law and Criminology* 98(4): 1467–1500.

Russell, Mark James. 2012. "The Gangnam Phenom." *Foreign Policy*, September 27. Online at www.foreignpolicy.com/2012/09/27/the-gangnam-phenom/ [accessed March 21, 2015].

Ryan, Marie-Laure. 1992. *Possible Worlds, Artificial Intelligence, and Narrative Theory*. Bloomington, IN: Indiana University Press.

Ryfle, Steve. 1998. *Japan's Favorite Mon-Star: The Unauthorized Biography of "The Big G."* Toronto, ON: ECW Press.

Sabin, Roger. 1993. *Adult Comics: An Introduction*. London: Routledge.

Saenz, Aaron. 2011. "Japan's Virtual Pop Star Hatsune Miku Rocks Los Angeles!" *Singularity Hub*. July 7. Online at www.singularityhub.com/2011/07/07/japans-virtual-popstar-hatsune-miku-rocks-los-angeles/ [accessed August 28, 2015].

Sahlfeld, Miriam. 2010. "The Protection of Minors and Its Effect on Cultural Diversity: An Example of Content Reglation in Digital Game Environments." In *Governance of Digital Game Environments and Cultural Diversity*, edited by Christopher Beat Graber and Mira Burri-Nenova, 202–236. Cheltenham: Edward Elgar.

Said, Edward. 1979 [1978]. *Orientalism*. New York: Vintage Books.

Saimon Fumi. 1990. *Tokyo rabu sutōrī* (Tokyo Love Story). Volumes 1–4. Tokyo: Shogakukan.

Saitō Gesshin. 1996 [1834–1836]. *Edo meishō zue* (Guide to Famous Sites of Edo). In *Shintei Edo Meishō zue* (Guide to Famous Sites of Edo: Revised Edition). Volume 1, edited by Saitō Yukio et al., 126–127. Tokyo: Chikuma shobō.

Saitō Kimiko. 2005. "Senko Hanabi." *Proceedings of the Eighth International Symposium on Fireworks*. Shiga, Japan. April 18–22: 317–322.

Saitō, Sayuri. 2003. "Print Club Creator Changes Focus to Future." *Daily Yomiuri Online*. Online at www.yomiuri.co.jp/intview/0204dy27.htm [accessed May 20, 2003].

Saitō Tamaki. 2008. *Artist wa kyōkai sen jyo de odoru* (Artists are Dancing on the Border Line). Tokyo: Misuzu Shobō.

———. 2011a. *Beautiful Fighting Girl.* Edited and translated by J. Keith Vincent and Dawn Lawson. Minneapolis, MN: University of Minnesota Press.

———. 2011b. *Kyarakutā seishin bunseki* (Character Psychoanalysis). Tokyo: Chikuma.

———. 2011c. "Ikōtaishō no tezawari (Touch of the Transitional Object)." *Geijutsu Shinchō*, 62(9): 88–95.

Sakaguchi, Hironobu, director. 2001. *Final Fantasy: The Spirits Within.* Tokyo: Square Pictures.

Sakai Masayoshi. 2014. *Aidoru kokufu ron: Seiko, Akina no jidai kara AKB, Momokuro jidai made tōku* (A Theory of Idol National Wealth: Explained from the Time of Matsuda Seiko and Nakamori Akina to that of AKB48 and Momorio Clover Z). Tokyo: Tōyō keizai shinpōsha.

Sakai, Naoki. 2008. *Translation and Subjectivity: On "Japan" and Cultural Nationalism.* Minneapolis, MN: University of Minnesota Press.

Sakai, Ryūji. 2007. *Nippon no Haikyo* (Ruins of Japan). Nagoya: Indivijon.

Sakamoto, Kazue. 1999. "Reading Japanese Women's Magazines: The Construction of New Identities in the 1970s and 1980s." *Media, Culture, & Society* 21(2): 173–193.

Sakuramoto Tomio and Konno Toshihiko. 1985. *Kamishibai to sensō: jūgo no kodomotachi* (Kamishibai and the War: Children on the Home Front). Tokyo: Marujusha.

Salinger, J. D. 2003 [1951]. *Kyatchā in za rai* (Catcher in the Rye). Translated by Murakami Haruki. Tokyo: Hakushuisha.

Sand, Jordan. 2008. "Street Observation Science and the Tokyo Economic Bubble." In *The Spaces of the Modern City: Imaginaries, Politics, and Everyday Life*, edited by Gyan Prakash and Kevin M. Kruse, 373–400. Princeton, NJ: Princeton University Press.

Sano Motohiko, director. 2008. *Atsuhime* (Princess Atsu). Tokyo: NHK.

Sanrio. n.d.a. "Hello Kitty Con 2014." Online at www.sanrio.com/hellokittycon/ [accessed August 5, 2015].

———. n.d.b. "Home of Hello Kitty." Online at www.sanrio.com/sanrio50 [accessed April 2, 2010].

———. n.d.c. "Small Gift Big Smile." Online at www.sanrio.com/about-sanrio/ [accessed August 30, 2015].

———. 2009a. *The Hello Kitty 35th Anniversary Book.* Tokyo: Sanrio.

———. 2009b. *Hello Kitty Memories.* Tokyo: Sanrio.

———. 2009c. *Three Apples: An Exhibition Celebrating 35 Years of Hello Kitty.* Torrance, CA: Sanrio.

Sasaki, Maana. 2013. "Gender Ambiguity and Liberation of Female Sexual Desire in Fantasy Spaces of Shōjo Manga and the Shōjo Subculture." *CTSJ: Journal of Undergraduate Research* 3(1): 4.

Sata, Masanori and Hirahara Hideo, eds. 1991. *A History of Japanese Television Drama.* Tokyo: Japan Association of Broadcasting Art.

Satō, Dai. 2014. "Dai Satō Panel Discussion, Moderated, and Translated by Ian Condry." Anime Boston, March 22. Hynes Convention Center, Boston, MA.

Satō Kenji. 1992. *Gojira to Yamato to bokura no minshushugi* (Godzilla, Yamato, and the Democracy of Our Generation). Tokyo: Bugei Shunjū.

Sawaragi, Noi. 2005. "On the Battlefield of 'Superflat': Subculture and Art in Postwar Japan." In *Little Boy: The Arts of Japan's Exploding Subculture*, edited by Murakami Takashi, 187–207. New Haven, CT: Yale University Press.

Sayawaka. 2013. *AKB shōhō towa nani datta no ka?* (What was AKB Business?). Tokyo: Taiyō tosho.

Scandal Band Wiki. n.d. Online at www.scandal-japan.wikia.com/wiki/SCANDAL_Japanese_Band_Wiki [accessed January 10, 2016].

Schattschneider, Ellen. 2003. *Immortal Wishes: Labor and Transcendence on a Japanese Sacred Mountain*. Durham, NC: Duke University Press.

———. 2009. "The Work of Sacrifice in the Age of Mechanical Reproduction: Bride Dolls and Ritual Appropriation at Yasukuni Shrine." In *The Culture of Japanese Fascism*, edited by Allan Tansman, 296–317. Durham, NC: Duke University Press.

Schilling, Mark. 1997. *The Encyclopedia of Japanese Pop Culture*. New York: Weatherhill.

———. 2007. *No Borders, No Limits: Nikkatsu Action Cinema*. Godalming: FAB Press.

Schodt, Frederik L. 1983. *Manga! Manga! The World of Japanese Comics*. Tokyo: Kodansha International.

———. 1988. *Inside The Robot Kingdom: Japan, Mechatronics, and the Coming Robotopia*. Tokyo: Kodansha International.

———. 1994. *America and the Four Japans: Friend, Foe, Model, Mirror*. Berkeley, CA: Stone Bridge Press.

———. 1996. *Dreamland Japan: Writings on Modern Manga*. Berkeley, CA: Stone Bridge Press.

———. 2007. *The Astroboy Essays*. Berkeley, CA: Stonebridge Press.

———. 2013. "The View from North America: Manga as Late Twentieth-Century Japonisme?" In *Manga's Cultural Crossroads*, edited by Jaqueline Berndt and Bettina Kummerling-Meibauer, 19–26. New York: Routledge.

Scholz, Trebor. 2013. "Introduction: Why Does Digital Labor Matter Now?" In *Digital Labor: The Internet as Playground and Factory*, edited by Trebor Scholz, 1–16. New York: Routledge.

Schwartz, Rob. 2013. "King of the Hits." *Billboard* 125(4): 35–36.

Seabrook, John. 2012. "Factory Girls: Cultural Technology and the Making of K-Pop." *The New Yorker*, October 8. Online at www.newyorker.com/magazine/2012/10/08/factory-girls-2 [accessed February 3, 2015].

Seaton, Philip and Takayoshi Yamamura. 2015. "Japanese Popular Culture and Contents Tourism–Introduction." *Japan Forum* 27(1): 1–11.

Seidensticker, Edward G. 1983. *Low City, High City*. New York: Knopf.

Seigle, Cecilia Segawa and Linda H. Chance. 2014. *Ōoku, the Secret World of the Shogun's Women*. Amherst, NY: Cambria Press.

Sekai fureai machiaruki (Walk the Town, Encounter the World). 2005–present. Tokyo: NHK.

Seno'o Ken'ichirō. 2007. *Akiba wo purodūsu: saikaihatsu purojekuto 5 nenkan no kiseki* (Producing Akihabara: The Miracle of the Five-Year Redevelopment Project). Tokyo: Ascii shinsho.

Setouchi kokusai geijutsu jikko iiinkai. 2010. (Setouchi International Art Festival Executive Committee). Art Setouchi 2010: Sōkatsu hōkoku (Art Setouchi 2010 General Report). Online at www.setouchi-artfest.jp/images/uploads/news/report_20101220.pdf [accessed April 12, 2015].

Setouchi kokusai geijutsusai 2013 (Setouchi Triennale 2013). 2014. Tokyo: Bijutsu shupppansha.

Shakespeare, William and Brett Wright. 2015. *Yolo Juliet*. New York: Random House.

Shamoon, Deborah. 2007. "Revolutionary Romance: *The Rose of Versailles* and the Transformation of Shojo Manga." In *Mechademia 2: Networks of Desire*, edited by Frenchy Lunning, 3–17. Minneapolis, MN: University of Minnesota Press.

———. 2011. "Films on Paper: Cinematic Narrative in Gekiga." In *Mangatopia: Essays on Manga and Anime in the Modern World*, edited by Timothy Perper, and Martha Cornog, 21–36. Santa Barbara, CA: Libraries Unlimited.

———. 2012. *Passionate Friendship: The Aesthetics of Girls' Culture in Japan*. Honolulu, HI: University of Hawai'i Press.

Shapiro, Jerome F. 2002. *Atomic Bomb Cinema*. London: Routledge.

Sharp, Hasana. 2011. *Spinoza and the Politics of Renaturalization*. Chicago, IL: University of Chicago.

Sharp, Jasper. 2008. *Behind the Pink Curtain: The Complete History of Japanese Sex Cinema*. Godalming: FAB Press.

Shiba, Tomonori. 2014. *Hatsune Miku wa naze sekai o kaeta no ka?* (Why did Hatsune Miku Change the World?). Tokyo: Ōta Shuppan.

Shibuya Bunka Project. n.d. "Key Person: Suzuya Kiriko." Online at www.shibuy abunka.com/keyperson.php?id=15 [accessed January 26, 2016].

Shibuya-ku. 2010. "Shibuya eki chūshin chiku machi-zukuri shishin" (Guidelines for Neighborhood Development around Shibuya Station). Online at www.city. shibuya.tokyo.jp/kurashi/machi/pdf/shibuya_shishin7_1.pdf [accessed October 12, 2015].

———. 2013. "Shibuya eki chūshin chiku kiban seibi toshikeikaku henkō no aramashi" (Revision of the Urban Development of the Fundamental Infrastructure of Shibuya Station Area). Online at www.city.shibuya.tokyo.jp/kurashi/machi/ kiban_seibi_aramashi2013.html [accessed October 13, 2015].

Shimizu Isao. 1999. *Zusetsu manga no rekishi* (An Illustrated History of Manga). Tokyo: Kawade Shobō.

Shimizu Kazuhiko, director. 1997. *Aguri*. Tokyo: NHK.

Shimizu, Michiko. 2009. "Changes in the Image of Hello Kitty as seen in Ichigo Shinbun." *The Bulletin of Kansai University of International Studies* 10: 101–116.

Shimoda, Atsuyuki. 2014. Interview by Tom Mes. Tokyo. March 17.

Shimokawa Kōshi. 2009. *Seifūzokushi nenpyō 1945–1989* (An Almanac of Sexual History, 1945–1989). Tokyo: Kawade shobō.

Shimotsuki Takanaka and Shida Takemi. 2003. *Tetsuwan Atomu kompuriito bukku* (Astro Boy: Complete Book). Tokyo: Media Factory.

Shimoyama Ten, director. 2014. *Kikaidā reboot* (Kikaider Reboot). Tokyo: Kadokawa.

Shimura Miyoko. 1998. "Saikō *Shinshaku Yotsuya kaidan*" (Reexamination of *New Interpretation of Yotsuya Ghost Story*). *Eigagaku* 12: 77–87.

Shinbō, Akiyuki, and Yase Yūki, directors. 2014. *Mekakushiti akutāzu* (Mekakucity Actors). Tokyo: Shaft.

Shinoda Masahiro, director. 1995. *Sharaku*. Tokyo: Shochiku-Fuji.

Shiokawa, Kanako. 1999. "Cute but Deadly: Women and Violence in Japanese Comics." In *Themes in Asian Cartooning: Cute, Cheap, Mad, and Sexy*, edited by John A. Lent, 93–126. Bowling Green, OH: Bowling Green State University Popular Press.

Shirane, Haruo. 2012. *Japan and the Culture of the Four Seasons: Nature, Literature, and the Arts*. New York: Columbia University Press.

Shirato Sanpei. 2005. *Kamui-den zenshū* (The Legend of Kamui: Complete Works). Tokyo: Shōgakkan.

————. 2009a. *Kieyuku shōjo* (The Vanishing Girl). Tokyo: Shōgakkan Kurieitibu.

————. 2009b. *Ninja bugei-chō: Kagemaru-den* (Scroll of Ninja Martial Arts: The Legend of Kagemaru). Tokyo: Shōgakkan kurieitivu.

————. 2011. *Karasu no ko* (The Crow Child). Tokyo: Shōgakkan Kurieitibu.

Shirō Masamune. 1991. *Kōkaku kidōtai: The Ghost in the Shell*. Tokyo: Kōdansha.

————. 2001. *Kōkaku kidōtai 2: Man-Machine Interface*. Tokyo: Kōdansha.

————. 2003. *Kōkaku kidōtai 1.5: Human-Error Processor*. Tokyo: Kōdansha.

————. 2005. *Ghost in the Shell 2 = Kōkaku kidōtai 2: Man-Machine Interface*. Translated by Frederik L. Schodt and Toren Smith. Milwaukie, OR: Dark Horse Comics.

Shirow, Masmune. 1995. *The Ghost in the Shell*. Translated Frederic L. Schodt and Toren Smith. Milwaukie, OR: Dark Horse Comics.

Shochat, Ella and Robert Stam. 1985. "The Cinema after Babel: Language, Difference, Power." *Screen* 26(3–4): 35–58.

Shōdoshima-chō (Shōdoshima Town). 2010. Online at www.town.shodoshima.lg.jp/oshirase/tyoutyou-semi/PDF/fukushi-iryo.pdf [accessed September 3, 2015].

Shōwa 40 nen kai. 2008. *Shōwa 40 nen kai no Tokyo annai* (Tokyo Guidebook Compiled by the Shōwa 40 nen kai). Tokyo: Akio Nakagawa Publishers.

Shuppan Nenpō, ed. 2012. *Shuppan shihyō nenpō: 2012-nenban* (Annual Indices of Publishing: 2012 Edition). Tokyo: Zenkoku Shuppan Kyōkai.

————, ed. 2013. *Shuppan shihyō nenpō: 2013-nenban* (Annual Indices of Publishing: 2013 Edition). Tokyo: Zenkoku Shuppan Kyōkai.

Simmel, Georg. 1965 [1911]. "The Ruin." In *Essays on Sociology, Philosophy, and Aesthetics*, edited by Kurt H. Wolff, 259–266. New York: Harper and Row.

Sims, Calvin. 2000. "In Japan, Tarnishing a Star Maker." *New York Times*, January 30. Online at www.nytimes.com/2000/01/30/world/in-japan-tarnishing-a-star-maker.html [accessed March 2, 2015].

Slade, Toby. 2009. *Japanese Fashion: A Cultural History*. Oxford: Berg.

————. 2010. "The Contemporary Japanese Consumer." In *The Fashion History Reader: Global Perspectives*, edited by Giorgio Riello and Peter McNeil, 546–549. Oxford: Routledge.

Smith, Michelle J. and Elizabeth Parsons. 2012. "Animating Child Activism: Environmentalism and Class Politics in Ghibli's *Princess Mononoke* (1997) and Fox's *Fern Gully* (1992)." *Continuum* 26(1): 25–37.

Sōda, Naoko. 2001. Interview with the Author. April 2001. Tokyo.

Sontag, Susan. 2001 [1964]. "Notes on 'Camp.'" In *Against Interpretation and Other Essays*, New York: Picador.

————. 2001 [1965]. "The Imagination of Disaster." In *Against Interpretation and Other Essays*. New York: Picador.

Sooudi, Olga. 2014. *Japanese New York: Migrant Artists and Self-Reinvention on the World Stage*. Honolulu, HI: Hawai'i University Press.

Sophie. 2012. "Worry for the Right Reasons: K-Pop and Kohaku." *Seoulbeats*, December 10. Online at www.seoulbeats.com/2012/12/worry-for-the-right-reasons-k-pop-and-kohaku/ [accessed July 5, 2013].

SOU·SOU. 2015. "SOU·SOU X Uniqlo." Online at www.sousou.co.jp/other/uniqlo/ [accessed June 7, 2015].

Southan, Rhys. 2012. "Les U. Knight on the Voluntary Human Extinction Movement." *Let Them Eat Meat*, March 29. Online at www.letthemeatmeat.com/post/19882645501/les-u-knight-on-the-voluntary-human-extinction [accessed May 1, 2014].

Spiegelman, Art. 1986. *Maus: A Survivor's Tale*. New York: Pantheon Books.

Square. 1991. *Final Fantasy IV*. Tokyo: Square. SNES.

———. 1994. *Final Fantasy VI*. Tokyo: Square. SNES.

———. 1997. *Final Fantasy VII*. Tokyo: Sony Computer Entertainment. PlayStation.

———. 2001. *Final Fantasy X*. Tokyo: Squaresoft. PlayStation 2.

Square Enix. 2003. *Final Fantasy X-2*. Tokyo: Square. PlayStation 2.

———. 2006. *Dirge of Cerberus: Final Fantasy VII*. Tokyo: Square Enix. PlayStation 2.

———. 2008. *Dissidia Final Fantasy*. Tokyo: Square Enix. PlayStation Portable.

———. 2010. *Final Fantasy XIV*. Tokyo: Square Enix. Microsoft Windows. Online.

———. 2011. *Final Fantasy XIII-2*. Tokyo: Square Enix. PlayStation 3.

Square/Square Enix. 2003. *Final Fantasy XI*. Tokyo: Sony Computer Entertainment. PlayStation 3. Online.

Stage48. 2009. "AKB48 13th Single Senbatsu Sousenkyo 'Kamisama ni Chikatte, Gachi Desu'" Online at www.stage48.net/wiki/index.php/AKB48_13th_Single_Senbatsu_Sousenkyo_%22Kamisama_ni_Chikatte_Gachi_Desu%22 [accessed July 26, 2015].

———. 2010. "AKB48 17th Single Senbatsu Sousenkyo 'Kaasan ni Chikatte, Gachi Desu'" Online at www.stage48.net/wiki/index.php/AKB48_17th_Single_Senbatsu_Sousenkyo_%22Kaasan_ni_Chikatte,_Gachi_Desu%22 [accessed July 26, 2015].

———. 2011. "AKB48 22nd Single Senbatsu Sousenkyo 'Kotoshi mo Gachi Desu'" Online at www.stage48.net/wiki/index.php/AKB48_22nd_Single_Senbatsu_Sousenkyo_%22Kotoshi_mo_Gachi_Desu%22 [accessed July 26, 2015].

———. 2013. "AKB48 32nd Single Senbatsu Sousenkyo ~ Yume wa Hitori ja Mirarenai" Online at www.stage48.net/wiki/index.php/AKB48_32nd_Single_Senbatsu_Sousenkyo_%22Yume_wa_Hitori_ja_Mirarenai%22 [accessed July 26, 2015].

Stallabrass, Julian. 2004. *Art Incorporated*. Oxford: Oxford University Press.

Stanley, Marni. 2008. "101 Uses for Boys: Communing with the Reader in Yaoi and Slash." In *Boys' Love Manga: Essays on the Sexual Ambiguity and Cross-Cultural Fandom of the Genre*, edited by Antonia Levi, Mark McHarry, and Dru Pagliassotti, 99–109. Jefferson, NC: McFarland.

Steele, Valerie. 1985. *Fashion and Eroticism: Ideals of Feminine Beauty from the Victorian Era to the Jazz Age*. Oxford: Oxford University Press.

———. 1988. *Paris Fashion: A Cultural History*. Oxford: Oxford University Press.

———. 2000. "Fashioning Men." In *Material Man: Masculinity Sexuality Style*, edited by Giannino Malossi, 78–83. New York: Harry N. Abrams.

———. 2010. "Is Japan Still the Future?" In *Japan Fashion Now*, edited by Valerie Steele et al., 96–97. New Haven, CT: Yale University Press.

Steele, Valerie et al. 2010. *Japan Fashion Now*. New Haven, CT: Yale University Press.

Steinberg, Marc. 2012. *Anime's Media Mix: Franchising Toys and Characters in Japan*. Minneapolis, MN: University of Minnesota Press.

Sterling, Marvin Dale. 2010. *Babylon East: Performing Dancehall, Roots Reggae, and Rastafari in Japan*. Durham, NC: Duke University Press.

Stevens, Carolyn S. 2005. "I Quit My Job for a Funeral: The Mourning and Empowering of a Japanese Rock Star." In *The Making of Saints: Contesting Sacred Ground*, edited by James F. Hopgood et al. 143–151. Tuscaloosa, AL: University of Alabama Press.

————. 2009. *Japanese Popular Music: Culture, Authenticity and Power*. New York: Routledge.

————. 2014. "Cute but Relaxed: Ten Years of Rilakkuma in Precarious Japan." *M/C Journal* 17(2). Online at www.journal.mediaculture.org.au/index.php/mcjournal/article/view/783 [accessed May 30, 2014].

Stevens, George, director. 1951. *Place in the Sun*. Los Angeles, CA: Paramount Pictures.

Stewart, Devin. 2010. "Slowing Japan's Galapagos Syndrome." *Huffington Post*, June 12. Online at www.huffingtonpost.com/devin-stewart/slowing-japans-galapagos_b_557446.html [accessed March 21, 2015].

Strauss, Neil. 1998. "The Pop Life: End of a Life, End of an Era." *New York Times*, June 18. Online at www.nytimes.com/1998/06/18/arts/the-pop-life-end-of-a-life-end-of-an-era.html [accessed January 11, 2016].

Strecher, Matthew. 2014. *The Forbidden Worlds of Murakami Haruki*. Minneapolis, MN: Minnesota University Press.

Strub, Whitney. 2010. *Perversion for Profit: The Politics of Pornography and the Rise of the New Right*. New York: Columbia University Press.

Studio Ghibli. 2002. *Itsumo no Ghibli nisshi* (Studio Ghibli Diary). Online at www.ghibli.jp/15diary/000102.html [accessed May 31, 2015].

————. 2005–2015. "Sakuhin no butai wa doko desu ka?" (Where Are Our Films Set?). *Studio Ghibli*. Online at www.ghibli.jp/40qa/000026.html [accessed May 31, 2015].

————. 2009. *Ghibli no fūkei: Miyazaki sakuhin ga kaita Nihon/Miyazaki sakuhin to deau Europa no tabi* (Ghibli's Scenery: Japan Depicted in Miyazaki Hayao's Works/European Travel Encountered through Miyazaki Hayao's Works). Tokyo: Studio Ghibli.

Sturken, Marita 1997. *Tangled Memories: The Vietnam War, the AIDS Epidemic, and the Politics of Remembering*. Berkeley, CA: University of California Press.

Suda Goichi. 2005, director. *Kirā Sebun* (Killer 7). Osaka: Capcon. PlayStation 2.

Sueda Takeshi, director. 2004. "Kingyo hanabi" (Goldfish Fireworks). Tokyo: Avex Group.

Sugiyama Tomoyuki. 2006. *Kūru Japan: sekai ga kaita garu Nihon* (Cool Japan: The Japan That the World Wants to Buy). Tokyo: Shōdensha.

Sumidagawa Hanabi Taikai Jikko Iinkai. 1983. *Hanabi shitamachi Sumidagawa: Ryōgoku no hanabi 250-shūnen kinenshi* (Shitamachi Sumida River Fireworks: Ryōgoku Fireworks 250th Anniversary Commemorative Publication). Tokyo: JICC Sumidagawa hanabi taikai jikko iinkai.

Suo Masayuji, director. 2014. *Maiko wa redī* (Lady Maiko). Tōhō.

Suter, Rebecca. 2008. *The Japanization of Modernity: Murakami Haruki between Japan and the United States*. Cambridge, MA: Harvard East Asia Series.

Suzuki Kōji. 2000. "Suzuki Koji Lecture on *Ringu*." The Japan Society, New York, April 1.

Suzuki Masayuki, director. 1998, 2000, 2002, and 2013. *Shomuni*. Series 1–4. Tokyo: Fuji Television.

Suzuki Tsunekatsu. 2005. *Media toshite no kamishibai* (*Kamishibai* as a Medium). Tokyo: Kyūzansha.

Szarkowska, Agnieszka. 2005. "The Power of Film Translation." *Translation Journal* 9(2) Online at www.bokorlang.com/journal/32film.htm [accessed December 17, 2015].

Tabuchi, Hiroko. 2009. "Why Japan's Cellphones Haven't Gone Global." *New York Times*, July 19. Online at www.nytimes.com/2009/07/20/technology/20cell.html?_r=0 [accessed July 8, 2014].

Takagi, Yoko et al., eds. 2012. *Feel and Think: A New Era of Tokyo Fashion*. Munich: Prestel.

Takahashi, Mizuki. 2008. "Opening the Closed World of Shōjo Manga." In *Japanese Visual Culture*, edited by Mark W. MacWilliams, 114–136. Armonk, NY: M.E. Sharpe.

Takahashi, Toshie. 2010. "MySpace or Mixi? Japanese Engagement with SNS (Social Networking Sites) in the Global Age." *New Media & Society* 12(3): 453–475.

Takahashi Yōji and Yoshihiro Yonezawa, eds. 1996. *Shōnen manga no sekai II, kodomo no Shōwashi, Shōwa 35–64 nen* (The World of Boys' Manga, Part II: Shōwa Children's History, Shōwa 35–64). *Bessatsu Taiyō* (*Taiyō* Supplemental Volumes). Tokyo: Heibonsha.

Takamatsu-shi sōmukyoku (Takamatsu City General Affairs Bureau). 2015. Online at www.city.takamatsu.kagawa.jp/file/17564_L25_270401.pdf [accessed April 12, 2015].

Takatsu. 2011. "Secondhand Memories Now Complete." *Espresso Love Blog*. March 9. Online at www.takatsu.wordpress.com/2011/03/09/secondhand-memories-now-complete [accessed July 10, 2014].

Takazawa Koji. 1996. *Rekishi to shite no shinsayoku* (The New Left as History). Tokyo: Shinsensha.

Takemiya Keiko. 1993 [1976–1984]. *Kaze to ki no uta* (The Poem of the Wind and the Tree). Volumes 1–8. Tokyo: Chūō Kōronsha.

Takemoto Kōichi et al., directors. 2002. *Himitsu sentai gorenjā* (Secret Squadron Five Rangers). Tokyo: Tōei Video.

Takemoto, Novala. 2008. *Kamikaze Girls*. Translated by Masumi Washington. San Francisco, CA: Viz Media.

Takemura Mitsuhige. 1999. *Utada Hikaru no tsukurikata* (How to Create Utada Hikaru). Tokyo: Takarajima.

Takeyama, Akiko. 2005. "Commodified Romance in a Tokyo Host Club." In *Genders, Transgenders, and Sexualities in Japan*, edited by Mark McLelland and Romit Dasgupta, 200–215. London: Routledge.

———. 2010. "Intimacy for Sale: Masculinity, Entrepreneurship, and Commodity Self in Japan's Neoliberal Situation." *Japanese Studies* 30(2): 231–246.

Taki Koji. 1976 "Departo toiu kūkan" (The Space of a Department Store). In *Town 9: Koen ga aru, bijutsukan ga aru, kok owa machi desu* (If There Are a Park and Art Museum, Then It's a Town), edited by Tsutsumi Seiji, 7–8. Tokyo: Seibu Hyakkaten Bunka jigyobu.

Tanabe Yumiko. 2013. *Undōkai ni! Tenuki jitan no kyara onigiri* (For Sports Meets! Quick and Easy Character Rice Balls). Online at www.cookpad.com/recipe/2236914 [accessed May 16, 2013].

Tanaka Hidetomi. 2010. *AKB48 no keizaigaku* (The Economics of AKB48). Tokyo: Asahi shinbun shuppan.

Tanaka, Keiko. 2003. "The Language of Japanese Men's Magazines: Young Men Who Don't Want to Get Hurt." In *Masculinity and Men's Lifestyle Magazines*, edited by B. Benwell, 222–242. Oxford: Blackwell Publishing.

Tanaka Kenji, director. 2011–2012. *Kānēshon* (Carnation). Tokyo: NHK.

Tanaka, Tomoaki. 2013. "The Market Strategy of Yamaha Electric Guitar—The Relation between Market and Marketing on a LM Instrument." *Journal of Tokyo Keizai University* 278: 67–91.

Tange Kenzo and Tomita Reiko. 1968. *Toshi no imeji*. Translation of Kevin Lynch, *The Image of the City*. Tokyo: Iwanami shoten.

Tanigawa, Nagaru and Ito Noizi. 2009. *The Melancholy of Haruhi Suzumiya*. New York: Little, Brown and Company.

Tanioka, Masaki. 1999. *V shinema damashi nisenbon no doshaburi wo itsukushimi* (V-Cinema Soul: Affection for a Downpour of Two-Thousand Films). Tokyo: Yotsuya Round.

———. 2005. *V shinema keppūroku* (Record of V-Cinema Bloodshed). Tokyo: Kawade Shobō Shinsha.

Tanizaki Jun'ichirō. 1977 [1933]. *In Praise of Shadows*. Translated by Thomas J. Harper and Edward G. Seidensticker. Stony Creek, CT: Leete's Island Books.

Tantei File News Watch. 2007. "Jimin sōsenkyō Akiba de Asō shi '2ch ni odoroita'" (Ahead of Liberal Democratic Party General Election, Asō Tarō is "surprised by 2channel"), September 17. Online at www.ftp.tanteifile.com/newswatch/2007/09/17_01/index.html [accessed August 21, 2015].

Tasaki Ryūta et al., directors. 2002–2003. *Kamen Raidā Ryūki* (Masked Rider Ryūki). Tokyo: Tōei Video.

Tatsumi, Takayuki. 2006. *Full Metal Apache: Transactions between Cyberpunk Japan and Avant-Pop America*. Durham, NC: Duke University Press.

Tatsumi, Yoshihiro. 2005. *The Push Man and Other Stories*. Translated by Yūji Oniki. Montreal, QC: Drawn & Quarterly.

———. 2006. *Abandon the Old in Tokyo*. Translated by Yūji Oniki. Montreal, QC: Drawn & Quarterly.

———. 2008. *Good-Bye*. Translated by Yūji Oniki. Montreal, QC: Drawn & Quarterly.

———. 2009. *A Drifting Life (Gekiga hyōryū)*. Translated by Taro Nettleton. Montreal, QC: Drawn & Quarterly.

———. 2010a. *Black Blizzard*. Transated by Akemi Wegmüller. Montreal, QC: Drawn & Quarterly.

———. 2010b. *Gekigagurashi* (Gekiga Life). Tokyo: Honno zasshisha.

Tavares, José Pedro, Rui Gil, and Licinio Roque. 2005. "Player as Author: Conjecturing Online Game Creation Modalities and Infrastructure." *Proceedings of DiGRA 2005 Conference: Changing Views—Worlds in Play*. Volume 3. Online at www.digra.org/wp-content/uploads/digital-library/06278.49263.pdf [accessed March 20, 2015].

Terranova, Tiziana. 2004. *Network Culture: Politics for the Information Age*. London: Pluto Press.

Textnovel. n.d. *Textnovel*. Online at www.textnovel.com/home.php [accessed December 31, 2015].

Tezuka Osamu. 1999. *Tezuka Osamu: Boku wa mangaka* (Tezuka Osamu: I Am a Comics Artist). Tokyo: Nihon tosho sentā.

———. 2008. *Astro Boy: Volumes 1 and 2*. Translated by Frederick Schodt. Milwaukie, OR: Dark Horse Comics.

———. 2010. *Ayako*. New York: Vertical.

———. 2011. *The Book of Human Insects*. New York: Vertical.

Toby, Ronald. 1984. *State and Diplomacy in Early Modern Japan*. Princeton, NJ: Princeton University Press.

Togashi Shin, director. 1983–1984. *Oshin*. Tokyo: NHK.

Toku, Masami. 1997. "Spatial Treatment in Children's Drawings: Why Do Japanese Children Draw in Particular Ways?" *Marilyn Zurmuehlen Working Papers in Art Education* 14: 165–184.

———. 2007. "*Shōjo* Manga! Girls' Comics! A Mirror of Girls' Dreams." *Mechademia 2: Networks of Desire*, edited by Frenchy Lunning, 19–32. Minneapolis, MN: University of Minnesota Press.

Tokuma shoten. 2009. *Animage Original*. Volume 3. Tokyo: Tokuma shoten.

Tokyo Hive. 2012. "AKB48 Achieves a Guinness World Record for Their 90 CMs for 'Wonda Coffee.'" *Tokyo Hive*, March 6. Online at www.tokyohive.com/article/2012/03/akb48-achieves-a-guinness-world-record-for-their-90-cms-for-wonda-coffee [accessed July 26, 2015].

———. 2013a. "AKB48's Latest Single is the Best Selling Single for a Female Group." *Tokyo Hive*, June 7. Online at www.tokyohive.com/article/2013/06/akb48s-latest-single-is-the-best-selling-single-for-a-female-group [accessed July 26, 2015].

———. 2013b. "AKB48's Latest Single 'Heart Ereki' Sells Over a Million Copies in One Day." *Tokyo Hive*, October 30. Online at www.tokyohive.com/article/2013/10/akb48s-latest-single-heart-ereki-sold-over-a-million-copies-in-one-day [accessed July 26, 2015].

———. 2013c. "AKB48 Score Their 16th Million-Selling Single." *Tokyo Hive*, December 16. Online at www.tokyohive.com/article/2013/12/akb48-score-their-16th-million-selling-single [accessed July 26, 2015].

Tokyo News Mook. 1994. *Terebi dorama zen shi: 1953–1994 tīvui gaido* (Complete History of Japanese Television Drama: TV Guide for 1953-1994). Tokyo: Tōkyō nyūsu tsūshinsha.

Tomboy Urbex. n.d. *Tomboy Urbex*. Online at www.tomboy-urbex.com/ [accessed November 14, 2015].

Tomine, Adrian. 2005. "Introduction." In *The Push Man and Other Stories*, by Tatsumi Yoshihiro. n.p. Montreal, QC: Drawn & Quarterly.

Tomino Yoshiyuki, director. 1979–1980. *Kidō senshi Gandamu* (Mobile Suit Gundam). Tokyo: Sunrise.

toshiokun77. 2013. *Sekai e habataku yuru kyara Kumamon* (Kumamon: The *Yuru Kyara* That Travels the World). Online at www.youtube.com/watch?v=K0wz7qLZ5aw [accessed May 24, 2014].

Towa. 2007. *Kurianesu* (Clearness). Tokyo: Starts Publishing.

Toyama Keiichiro, director. 1999. *Sairento hiru* (Silent Hill). Tokyo: Konami. PlayStation.

———, director. 2006. *Sairen tsū* (Forbidden Siren 2). Tokyo: Sony. PlayStation 2.

Toyohara Ken'ichi, Sano Isamu, and Yamashita Akio. 1960. *Afurika tairiku o yuku* (Journeys Around the African Continent). Tokyo: Futami shobō.

Treat, John Whittier. 1995. *Writing Ground Zero: Japanese Literature and the Atomic Bomb*. Chicago, IL: University of Chicago Press.

Tremblay, Jacynthe. 2009. "The Potential of Nishida's 'Encompassing' Language'." *Essays in Japanese Philosophy* 4: 127–134.

Tsuburaya Eiji et al., directors. 2009. *Urutoraman* (Ultraman). Tokyo: Tsuburaya Productions.

Tsuburaya Hajime et al., directors. 2009. *Urutorasebun* (Ultraseven). Volume 7. Tokyo: Tsuburaya Productions.

Tsuchimoto Noriaki, director. 1969. *Paruchizan zenshi* (Prehistory of the Partisans). Tokyo: Ogawa Productions.

Tsujii Takashi and Ueno Chizuko. 2008. *Post shōhi shakai no yukue* (The Direction of Post-Consumer Society). Tokyo: Bunshun shinsho.

Tsukada Masaki et al., directors. 2003. *Kamen Raidā sutorongā* (Masked Rider Stronger). Tokyo: Toei Video.

Tsurumi Shunsuke. 1973. *Manga no sengo shisō* (Postwar Theory in Manga). Tokyo: Bungei shunjū.

Tsuruta Norio, director. 1991. *Honto ni atta kowai hanashi* (Scary True Stories). Tokyo: Japan Home Video.

Tsuruya Namboku. 1959. *Tōkaikō Yotsuya kaidan (Tōkaidō Yotsuya Ghost Story)*. Revised edition by Kawatake Shigetoshi. Tokyo: Iwanami shoten.

Tsutsui, William M. 2004. *Godzilla on My Mind: Fifty Years of the King of Monsters*. New York: Palgrave Macmillan.

———. 2006. "Introduction." In *In Godzilla's Footsteps: Japanese Pop Culture Icons on the Global Stage*, edited by William M. Tsutsui and Michiko Ito, 9–19. New York: Palgrave Macmillan.

———. 2010. "Oh No, There Goes Tokyo: Recreational Apocalypse and the City in Postwar Japanese Popular Culture." In *Noir Urbanisms: Dystopic Images of the Modern City*, edited by Gyan Prakash, 104–126. Princeton, NJ: Princeton University Press.

———. 2014. "For Godzilla and Country: How a Japanese Monster Became an American Icon." *Foreign Affairs* (May 23) Online at www.foreignaffairs.com/articles/141472/william-m-tsutsui/for-godzilla-and-country [accessed July 19, 2015].

Tsutsumi Seiji, ed. 1976. *Town 9: Koen ga aru, bijutsukan ga aru, kok owa machi desu* (If There Are a Park and Art Museum, Then It's a Town). Tokyo: Seibu Hyakkaten Bunka jigyobu.

Tucker, Guy Mariner. 1996. *Age of the Gods: A History of the Japanese Fantasy Film*. New York: Daikaiju Publishing.

Tymoczko, Maria. 1999. "Post-Colonial Writing and Literary Translation." In *Post-Colonial Translation: Theory and Practice*, edited by Susan Bassnett and Harish Trivedi, 19–40. London: Routledge.

Udagawa, Yukihiro. 2005. "Wheels and Bridges, The Intensity of Poetic Symbolization: Rediscovering the Work of Nakagawa Nobuo." In *Tokyo FILMeX 2005 Official Catalog*, edited by the Tokyo FILMeX Organizing Committee, 36–37. Tokyo: Tokyo FILMeX Organizing Committee.

Ueda Hisashi, Kan Satoshi, and Otsuka Tōru, directors. 2009. *Ohitorisama* (Party of One). Tokyo: TBS.

Uji Masaki, director. 1958–1963. *Basu dōri ura* (Off the Bus Route). Tokyo: NHK.

"Uniquely Positioned." 2010. *The Economist*, June 24. Online at www.economist.com/node/16436304 [accessed June 7, 2015].

Uno Tsunehiro. 2011. *Ritoru pīpuru no jidai* (The Age of Little People). Tokyo: Gentosha.

U.S. Geological Survey (USGS). 2015. "Magnitude 9.0—Near the Coast of Honshu, Japan." *USGS: Science for a Changing World*. March 23. Online at www.earthquake.usgs.gov/earthquakes/eqinthenews/2011/usc0001xgp/usc0001xgp.php [accessed March 16, 2016].

Usui, Kazuo. 2014. *Marketing and Consumption in Modern Japan*. London, Routledge.

Usuta Kyōsuke 2014. "Yuru kyara densetsu Kumamon jyanai ka monogatari" (A Story of the Legendary *Yuru Kyara* Kumamon…Isn't It?) *Weekly Shōnen Jump*, April 22: 221–231.

Utada, Hikaru. 2009. *Easy Breezy*. 2009. Youtube music video Island Def Jam Music Group. Online at www.youtube.com/watch?v=RpqTJySA5Sc [accessed March 23, 2015].

———. 2010. "First Important Announcement in a While." *Hikki Texts.* August 10. Online at www.hikki.blogspot.com/search?updated-max=2010-09-16T20:25:00 %2B10:00&max-results=10&start=10&by-date=false [accessed October 11, 2015].

Utsumi, Hirofumi. 2012. "Nuclear Power Plants in 'The Only A-bombed Country': Images of Nuclear Power and the Nation's Changing Self-Portrait in Postwar Japan." In *The Nuclear Age in Popular Media: A Transnational History, 1945–1965,* edited by Dick van Lente, 175–201. New York: Palgrave Macmillan.

Various. 2014. "Kumamon Memes." Online at www.memecenter.com/ search?query=kumamon [accessed May 14, 2014].

Vicendeau, Ginette. 1988. "Hollywood Babel." *Screen* 29(2): 24–39.

Vreeland, Diana. 1965. "Youthquake" *Vogue,* January 1: 112.

"X-Japan." n.d. *Uncyclopedia.* Online at www.uncyclopedia.wikia.com/ wiki/X_Japan [accessed June 3, 2014].

Wachowski, Lana, and Andy Wachowski, directors. 1999. *The Matrix.* Los Angeles, CA: Warner Bros.

Wakabayashi, Daisuke. 2012. "Japan's 'Galapagos' Mobile Dilemma." *The Wall Street Journal,* August 16. Online at www.blogs.wsj.com/digits/2012/08/16/japans-galapagos-mobile-dilemma/ [accessed March 2, 2015].

Wakabayashi Takeshi. 2013. *Dentō no tsuzuki wo dezain suru* (Designing the Next Tradition). Kyoto: Gakugei Shuppansha.

Wakamatsu Setsuro and Hirano Shin, directors. 2000. *Yamato nadeshiko* (Perfect Woman). Tokyo: Fuji Television.

Wakasugi Katsuko. 2000. "Wakasugi Katsuko intabyū" (Wakasugi Katsuko Interview). In *Jigoku de yōi hai! Nakagawa Nobuo kaiki kyōfu eiga no gōka* (Shooting in Hell: The Fate of Nobuo Nakagawa's Horror Films), edited by Suzuki Kensuke, 27–31. Tokyo: Wise shuppan.

Waksman, Steve. 1999. *Instruments of Desire: The Electric Guitar and the Shaping of Musical Experience.* Cambridge, MA: Harvard University Press.

Washburn, Dennis. 2009. "Imagined History, Fading Memory: Mastering Narrative in *Final Fantasy X.*" In *Mechademia 4: War/Time,* edited by Frenchy Lunning, 149–162. Minneapolis, MN: University of Minnesota Press.

Watanabe Michiaki. 2000. "Watanabe Michiaki intabyū" (Watanabe Michiaki Interview). In *Jigoku de yōi hai! Nakagawa Nobuo kaiki kyōfu eiga no gōka* (Shooting in Hell: The Fate of Nobuo Nakagawa's Horror Films), edited by Suzuki Kensuke, 48–53. Tokyo: Wise shuppan.

Watanabe Yoshio, director. 2007. *Dondo hare* (Perfect Blue Sky). Tokyo: NHK.

Watson, Dave. *Sore Diamonds.* Online at www.eyevocal.ottawa-anime.org/ boredoms/boreside.htm [accessed July 19, 2015].

Web Anime Style. 2006. "Shinario Eedaba sōsakujutsu dai-59-kai: Minkii Momo enchō saikai arekore" (Scenario "Eedaba" Creativity, number 59: All about Minky Momo's Restart and Extension). Online at www.style.fm/as/05_column/shudo59. shtml [accessed April 10, 2015].

Weisenfeld, Gennifer. 2012. *Imaging Disaster: Tokyo and the Visual Culture of Japan's Great Earthquake of 1923.* Berkeley, CA: University of California Press.

Weisman, Alan. 2007. *The World without Us.* New York: Picador.

Wertham, Fredric. 1954. *Seduction of the Innocent: The Influence of Comic Books on Today's Youth.* New York: Rinehart & Company.

White, Merry. 1993. *Material Child.* Berkeley, CA: University of California.

———. 1995. "The Marketing of Adolescence in Japan: Buying and Dreaming." In *Women, Media and Consumption in Japan*, edited by Lisa Skov and Brian Moeran. 255–273. Honolulu, HI: University of Hawai'i Press.

Whitman-Linsen, Candace. 1992. *Through the Dubbing Glass: The Synchronization of American Motion Pictures into German, French, and Spanish.* New York: Peter Lang.

Wikipedia. 2015. "AKB48 Theater." Online at www.ja.wikipedia.org/wiki/ AKB48%E5%8A%87%E5%A0%B4 [accessed July 26, 2015].

Williams, Ingrid K. 2011. "Japanese Island as Unlikely Arts Installation." *New York Times*, August 26. Online at www.nytimes.com/2011/08/28/travel/naoshima-japan-an-unlikely-island-as-art-attraction.html?_r=0 [accessed August 1, 2015].

Williams, Martyn. 2006. "More Mobile Internet Users than Wired in Japan." *Infoworld*, July 5. Online at www.infoworld.com/d/networking/more-mobile-internet-users-wired-in-japan-259 [accessed July 7, 2014].

Williams, Walter Jon. 2009. "In What Universe?" In *Third Person: Authoring and Exploring Vast Narratives*, edited by Pat Harrigan and Noah Wardrip-Fruin, 25–32. Cambridge, MA: MIT Press.

Williamson, Kate T., Jennifer Butefish, and Maria Soares. 2004. *Hello Kitty Everywhere!* New York: Harry N. Abrams.

Willis, Christopher. 2008. "Evolutionary Theory and the Future of Humanity." In *Global Catastrophic Risks*, edited by Nick Bostrum and Milan M. Ćirković, 48–72. Oxford: Oxford University Press.

Witt, Stephen. 2015. *How Music Got Free: The End of an Industry, the Turn of the Century, and the Patient Zero of Piracy.* New York: Viking.

Wood, Christopher R. 2009. "Human, All Too Human: Cloud's Existential Quest for Authenticity." In *Final Fantasy and Philosophy: The Ultimate Walkthrough*, edited by Jason P. Blahuta and Michel S. Beaulieu, 167–184. Hoboken, NJ: Wiley.

World Photo Press. 2009. *Figure Oh.* Issue 134. Tokyo: World Photo Press.

Worrall, Julian. 2009. "Bathing in Timeless Memories." *The Japan Times*, August 28. Online at www.japantimes.co.jp/culture/2009/08/28/arts/bathing-in-timeless-memories/#.VdiCu3jwGfQ [accessed August 22, 2015].

———. 2012. "Chim Pom's Spatial Tactics: An Art of Public Space." In *Chim⇧Pom: Super-Rat*, edited by Abe Kenichi, 218–224. Tokyo: Parco.

Wright, Lucy. 2004. "Wonderment and Awe: The Way of the Kami." *Refractory: A Journal of Entertainment Media* 5. Online at www.refractory.unimelb.edu. au/2004/02/03/wonderment-and-awe-the-way-of-the-kami-lucy-wright/ [accessed May 31, 2015].

———. 2005. "Forest Spirits, Giant Insects, and World Trees: The Nature Vision of Hayao Miyazaki." *Journal of Religion and Popular Culture* 10(1): n.p.

WWD.Com. 2015. "Menzu-shi *Choki Choki* ga kyūkan" (Men's Magazine Choki Choki Will Be Discontinued)." *WWD.Com*, April 22, Online at www.wwdjapan. com/business/2015/04/22/00016222.html [accessed May 29, 2015].

Yablon, Nick. 2009. *Untimely Ruins: An Archaeology of American Urban Modernity, 1819–1919.* Chicago, IL: University of Chicago Press.

Yabumae Tomoko. 2007. *Ohtake Shinro zenkei: retrospective 1955–2006.* (Ohtake Shinro Panorama: Retrospective 1955–2006). Tokyo: Grambooks.

Yagi, Kentarō. 2010. "Art on Water: Art that Revitalizes Insular Communities Facing Depopulation and Economic Decline." *Nakhara: Dynamic City: Land, Water, and Culture* 6: 119–130.

Yamada, Mio. 2013. "Architecture and Art of a Setouchi Summer." *The Japan Times,* July 29. Online at www.japantimes.co.jp/life/2013/07/29/style/architecture-and-art-of-a-setouchi-summer/#.VdiC_3jwGfQ [accessed August 22, 2015].

Yamada Tōru. 2000. *Kyarakutā bijinesu: kawaii no umidasu kyodai shijou* (Character Business: Huge Market Created by Kawaii). Tokyo: PHP Kenkyujo.

Yamaguchi, Masao, 1991. "The Poetics of Exhibition in Japanese Culture." In *Exhibiting Cultures: The Poetics and Politics of Museum Display,* edited by Ivan Karp and Steven D. Lavine, 57–67. Washington, DC: Smithsonian Institution Press.

Yamamoto Kajirō. 2015. *Hawai Mare oki kaisen* (The War at Sea from Hawai'i to Malay). Tokyo: Tōhō.

Yamamoto Taketoshi. 2000. *Kamishibai: machikado no media* (Kamishibai: Medium of the Street Corner). Tokyo: Yoshikawa kōbunkan.

Yamamura, Takayoshi. 2009. "Anime Pilgrimage and Local Tourism Promotion: An Experience of Washimiya Town, the Sacred Place for Anime 'Lucky Star' Fans." *Hokkaido daigaku bunka jigen manejimento ronshū* (Hokkaido University Collection of Scholarly and Academic Papers). *Web-Journal of Tourism and Cultural Studies* 14: 1–9.

Yamanashi, Makiko. 2012. *A History of the Takarazuka Revue since 1914: Modernity, Girls' Culture, Japan Pop.* Boston, MA: Global Oriental.

Yamane Kazuma. 1990. *Gyaru no kōzō* (Structure of the Girl). Tokyo: Sekaibunkasha.

Yamane Sadao. 1993. *Eiga wa doko e iku ka? Nihon eiga jihyō '89-'92* (Where is Film Going? Contemporary Criticism of Japanese Films, '89–'92). Tokyo: Chikuma shobō.

Yamano, Sharin. 2005. *Manga Kenkanryu / Hating the Korean Wave.* Tokyo: Shinyusha.

Yamashita, Yūji. 2012. "Aida Makoto, Pretend Villain—Premeditated Quotations from Japanese Art History." *Tensai de gome nasai* (Sorry for Being a Genius)/ *Monument for Nothing,* 191–196. Tokyo: Mori Art Museum.

Yamataka Eye. 2007. *Boadrum 77.* Live performance program notes. July 7.

Yamazaki Mitsuhiro. 2010. *Zōhoban gendai apareru sangyō no tenkai* (The Development of the Contemporary Apparel Industry). Second edition. Tokyo: Senken Shinbunsha.

Yanagi Yukinori. 2014. *Art Base Momoshima kaikan kinen ten* (Art Base Opening Memorial Exhibition). Hiroshima: Hiroshima Art Project.

Yanawaraba. 2008. "Shōnen jidai" (Boyhood). Tokyo: Papaya Records Japan.

Yano, Christine R. 2002. *Tears of Longing: Nostalgia and the Nation in Japanese Popular Song.* Cambridge, MA: Harvard University Asia Center.

———. 2004a. "Letters from the Heart: Negotiating Fan-Star Relationships in Japanese Popular Music." In *Fanning the Flames: Fans and Consumer Culture in Contemporary Japan,* edited by William W. Kelly, 41–58. Albany, NY: State University of New York Press.

———. 2004b. "Raising the Ante of Desire: Foreign Female Singers in a Japanese Pop Music World." In *Refashioning Pop Music in Asia: Cosmopolitan Flows, Political Tempos and Aesthetic Industries,* edited by Allen Chun, Ned Rossiter, and Brian Shoesmith, 159–172. London: Routledge.

———. 2013a. "'Flying Geisha': Japanese Stewardesses with Pan American World Airways." In *Modern Girls on the Go: Gender, Mobility, and Labor in Japan,* edited by Alisa Freedman, Laura Miller, and Christine R. Yano, 85–106. Stanford, CA: Stanford University Press.

———. 2013b. *Pink Globalization: Hello Kitty's Trek across the Pacific.* Durham, NC: Duke University Press.

Yasuda, Chihiro. 2014. Interview by James Jack at Café Konnichi-wa, Naoshima, March 7.

Yoda, Tomiko, and H. D. Harootunian, eds. 2006. *Japan after Japan: Social and Cultural Life from the Recessionary 1990s to the Present*. Durham, NC: Duke University Press.

Yokoyama Yasuko. 2008. "*Yotsuya kaidan* eiga no Oiwa tachi: kabuki to wakare betsuno onna e" (Oiwa in *Yotsuya Ghost Story* Films: From Kabuki to Different Women). In *Kaiki to gensō e no kairo: kaidan kara J-horā e* (Circuit for Horror and Illusion: From Ghost Stories to J-Horror), edited by Uchiyama Kazuki, 145–170. Tokyo: Shinwasha.

Yomiuri Shinbun. 1965. "Bōkaru gurūpu no miyroku" (The Appeal of Vocal Groups). *Yomiuri Shinbun*, May 4.

———. 1996a. "Purikura kao-shashin shiiru ga dai hitto" (Print Club—Face Photo Seals a Big Hit). *Yomiuri Shinbun*, June 4, 28.

———. 1996b. "Hassō mugendai, kenkyū kaihatsu no genba kara" (Infinite Conceptualization from the Research and Development Scene). *Yomiuri Shinbun*, December 26, 9.

———. 1996c. "Joshi chūkōsei ni daininki Purinto Kurabu" (Print Club a Huge Hit among Female Junior High and High-School Students). *Yomiuri Shinbun*, June 17, 17.

———. 1997. "Kamera wa joshikōsei no hitsujuhin" (The Camera Is a Necessity for High-School Girls). *Yomiuri Shinbun*, July 15, 13.

———. 2012a. "Media senryaku to sutōrī sei de keizai kōka o takameru 'Kumamon'" (Kumamon: Boosting Economic Effect through Media Strategy and Backstory). April 4. Online at www.adv.yomiuri.co.jp/ojo/tokusyu/20120405/201204toku4.html [accessed January 10, 2016].

———. 2012b. "Posuto AKB wa dō suru? Aidoru sengoku jidai no yukue" (What Will Happen Post AKB48? Traces of the Idol Warring States Period). October 9. Online at www.ameblo.jp/zatsu-you/entry-11376466431.html [accessed August 21, 2015].

Yomota Inuhiko. 1999. *Manga genron* (Essays on Manga). Tokyo: Chikuma gakugei bunko.

———. 2004. *Shirato Sanpei-ron* (Essays on Shirato Sanpei). Tokyo: Sakuhinsha.

———. 2006. *Kawaii-ron* (Theory of Cute). Tokyo: Chikuma shobō.

Yonezawa Yoshihiro. 1980. *Sengo shōjo manga shi* (History of Postwar *Shōjo* Manga). Tokyo: Shinpyōsha.

Yōsensha. 2011. *Bessatsu otona anime: mahō shōjo magajin* (Otona Anime Extra: Magical Girl Magazine). Tokyo: Yōshensha.

Yoshi. 2002. *Deep Love kanzen han ~ Ayu no monogatari* (Deep Love Complete Edition: Ayu's Story). Tokyo: Starts Publishing.

———. 2003a. *Deep Love kanzen dai ni bu ~ Hosuto* (Deep Love Complete Edition Part 2: Host). Tokyo: Starts Publishing.

———. 2003b. *Deep Love ~ Reina no unmei* (Deep Love: Rena's Fate). Tokyo: Starts Publishing.

———. 2003c. *Deep Love tokubetsu han: Pao no monogatari* (Deep Love Special Edition: Pao's Story). Tokyo: Starts Publishing.

Yoshi and Yoshii Yū. 2004. *Deep Love ~ Ayu no monogatari* (Deep Love: Ayu's Story). Tokyo: Kōdansha.

Yoshida Akio, Katō Hirotake, and Kitagawa Masakazu, directors. 1992. *Tokyo erebētā gāru* (Tokyo Elevator Girl). Tokyo: TBS.

Yoshida, George. 1997. *Reminiscing in Swingtime: Japanese Americans in American Popular Music 1925–1960*. San Francisco, CA: National Japanese American Historical Society.

Yoshida Ken, director. 2008. *Araundo 40 ~ chūmon no ooi onnatachi* (Around 40: Demanding Women). Tokyo: TBS.

Yoshikawa Yuichi. 1995. *Hansen heiwa no shisō to undo—Komentaru sengo 50 nen* (Antiwar and Peace: Ideology and Campaigns: Commentary of the Fifty-Year Postwar). Tokyo: Shakai hyoronsha.

Yoshimi Shun'ya. 2000. *Toshi no doramatsurugi: Tokyo sakariba no shakaishi* (Dramaturgy of the City: Social History of the Entertainment Areas of Tokyo). Tokyo: Kobundo.

———. 2003. "'America' as Desire and Violence: Americanization in Postwar Japan and Asia during the Cold War." *Inter-Asia Cultural Studies* 4: 433–450.

———. 2009. *Posuto sengo shakai* (Post-Postwar Society). Tokyo: Iwanami shoten.

Yoshimoto, Banana, et.al. 1991. *Nakazuri shōsetsu* (Train Novel Posters). Tokyo: Shinchōsha.

Yoshinaga, Fumi. 1991. *Andore to watashi* (André and I). Self-published.

———. 1999–2002. *Seiyō kottō yōgashiten* (Antique Bakery). Volumes 1–4. Tokyo: Shinshokan.

———. 2005–2013. *Ōoku*. Volumes 1–12. Tokyo: Hakusensha.

———. 2009–2014. *Ōoku: The Inner Chambers*. Volumes 1–9. Translated by Akemi Wegmüller. San Francisco, CA: Viz Signature.

Yuasa, Masaaki, director. 2004. *Maindo gēmu* (Mind Game). Tokyo: Studio 4°C.

———, director. 2010. *Yojōhan shinwa taikei* (The Tatami Galaxy). Tokyo: Madhouse.

Yui Tsunehiko. 1991. *Sezon no rekishi* (History of Saison). Tokyo: Ribroport.

Yuyama Kunihiko, director. 1982–1983. *Mahō no purinsesu Minkī Momo* (*Fairy Princess Minky Momo*). Tokyo: Asahi Productions.

Zahlten, Alexander. 2007. *The Role of Genre in Film from Japan: Transformations 1960s-2000s*. Ph.D. Dissertation. Johannes Gutenberg University.

Zahlten, Alex and Kimihiko Kimata. 2005. "Norio Tsuruta." *Midnight Eye*. Online at www.midnighteye.com/interviews/norio-tsuruta/ [accessed August 7, 2013].

Zenor, Jason. 2014. "Sins of the Flesh? Obscenity Law in the Era of Virtual Reality." *Communications Law and Policy* 19(4): 563–589.

Žižek, Slavoj. 1994. "The Spectre of Ideology" In *Mapping Ideology*, London: Verso.

Index

Locators containing 'n' refer to notes, those in *italics* refer to figures.